DAVID BOWIE | STARMAN

ALSO BY PAUL TRYNKA

Iggy Pop: Open Up and Bleed
Denim (with Graham Marsh)
Portrait of the Blues

DAVID BOWIE | STARMAN

BY

PAUL TRYNKA

Little, Brown and Company

New York | Boston | London

Little, Brown and Company
Hachette Book Group
237 Park Avenue, New York, NY 10017
www.hachettebookgroup.com

First Edition: July 2011

Little, Brown and Company is a division of Hachette Book Group, Inc.
The Little, Brown name and logo are trademarks of Hachette Book Group, Inc.

The publisher is not responsible for websites (or their content) that are not owned by the publisher.

Library of Congress Cataloging-in-Publication Data
Trynka, Paul.
    David Bowie : starman / Paul Trynka. — 1st ed.
       p. cm.
    Includes bibliographical references.
    ISBN 978-0-316-03225-4
    1. Bowie, David.   2. Rock musicians — England — Biography.   I. Title.
    ML420.B754T79 2011
    782.42166092 — dc22
       [B]   2010048727

10 9 8 7 6 5 4 3 2 1

RRD-C

Printed in the United States of America

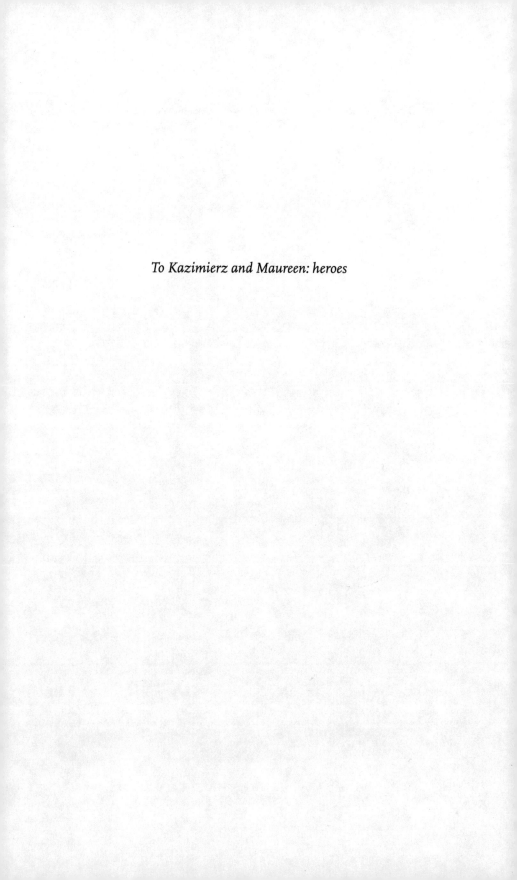

To Kazimierz and Maureen: heroes

Contents

PART 2

WHERE THINGS ARE HOLLOW

PROLOGUE

Genius Steals

Thursday evening, seven o'clock; decadence is about to arrive in five million living rooms. Neatly suited dads are leaning back in the comfiest chairs, mums in their aprons are clearing away the dishes, and the kids, still in school shirts and trousers, are clustered around TVs for their most sacred weekly ritual.

The members of the tiny studio audience, milling around in tank tops and dresses, clap politely as he strums out two minor chords on his blue twelve-string guitar. The camera cuts from his hands to his face, catching the barest hint of a smirk, like a child hoping to get away with something naughty. But then as his friends Trevor, Woody, and Mick Ronson clatter into action with a rollicking drumroll and throaty guitar, the camera pulls back and David Bowie meets its gaze unflinchingly. His look is lascivious, amused; as an audience of excited teens and outraged parents struggle to take in the quilted multicolored jumpsuit, the luxuriant carrottop hairdo, the spiky teeth, and those sparkling, mascaraed come-to-bed eyes, he sings us through an arresting succession of images: radios, aliens, "get-it-on rock 'n' roll." The audience is still grappling with this bizarre spectacle as a staccato guitar rings out a Morse code warning and then, all too suddenly, we're into the chorus.

From the disturbingly new, we shift to the reassuringly familiar; as he croons out "There's a starman," his voice leaps up an octave. It's an ancient Tin Pan Alley songwriter's trick, signaling a release, a climax, and as we hear of the friendly alien waiting in the sky, the audience suddenly recognizes a tune, and a message, lifted openly, outrageously, from "Over the Rainbow," Judy Garland's escapist, Technicolor wartime anthem. It's simple, sing-along, comforting territory and lasts just four bars before David Bowie makes his bid for immortality, less than sixty seconds after his face appeared on *Top of the Pops*, the BBC's family-friendly music program. He lifts his slim, elegant hand to the side of his face as the platinum-haired Mick Ronson joins him at the microphone — then casually, elegantly, he places his arm around the guitarist's neck and pulls him lovingly toward him. There's the same octave leap as he sings "starman" again — this time, it doesn't suggest escaping the bounds of Earth; it symbolizes escaping the bounds of sexuality.

The fifteen-million-strong audience struggles to absorb this exotic, pansexual creature; in countless households, the kids are entranced in their thousands as parents sneer, shout, or walk out of the room. But even as the kids wonder how to react, there's another stylistic swerve; with the words "let the children boogie," David Bowie and the Spiders break into an unashamed T. Rex boogie rhythm. For thousands of teenagers, there was no hesitation; those ninety seconds on a sunny early evening in September 1972 would change the course of their lives. Up to this point, pop music had been mainly about belonging, about identification with their peers. This music, carefully choreographed in a dank basement under a South London escort agency, was a spectacle of not-belonging. For scattered isolated kids around the UK, and soon on the American East Coast, and then on the West Coast, this was their day. The day of the outsider.

IN the weeks that followed, it became obvious that these three minutes had put a rocket under the career of a man all too recently tagged as a one-hit wonder. Most people who knew him were delighted, but there were hints of suspicion. "Hip Vera Lynn," one cynical friend called it in a pointed reference to "The White Cliffs of Dover," the huge wartime hit that had also ripped off Judy Garland's best-known song; this was too knowing. A few weeks later, to emphasize the point, David started singing "somewhere over the rainbow" over the "Starman" chorus — as if to prove Pablo Picasso's maxim that "talent borrows, genius steals."

And steal he had — with a clear-eyed effrontery as shocking as the lifted melodies. The way he collaged several old tunes into a new song was a musical tradition as old as the hills, one still maintained by David's old-school showbiz friends, like Lionel Bart, the *Oliver!* writer and musical kleptomaniac. Yet showing the joins brazenly, like the elevator shafts of the Pompidou Centre or the stock photos appropriated by Andy Warhol, was a new trick, a postmodernism that was just as unsettling as the postsexualism Bowie had shown off with that arm lovingly curled over Mick Ronson's shoulder. Rock and roll was a visceral medium, born out of the joy and anguish sculpted into the first electric blues in the turmoil of postwar America. Was it now just an art game? Was the carrot-haired Ziggy, potent symbol of otherness, just an intellectual pose?

When David Bowie made his mark so elegantly, so extravagantly, that night on *Top of the Pops* in a thrilling performance that set the seventies as a decade distinct from the sixties, every one of those contradictions was obvious — in fact, they added a delicious tension. In the following months and years — as he dumped the band that had shaped his music; when his much-touted influence Iggy Pop, the man who'd inspired Ziggy, dismissed him as a "fuckin' carrot-top" who had exploited and then sabotaged him; when David himself publicly moaned that his gay persona had damaged his career in the United States — those contradictions became more obvious still.

So was David Bowie truly an outsider, or was he a showbiz pro exploiting outsiders, like a psychic vampire? Was he really a starman, or was it all cheap music-hall tinsel and glitter? Was he gay, or was it all a mask? There was evidence aplenty for both. And that evidence accumulated as his career continued, as fans witnessed, wide-mouthed, momentous shows like his wired, fractured appearance on *Dick Cavett* and his twitchy but charming camaraderie on *Soul Train*. How much of this bizarre behavior was a performance, a carefully choreographed sequence?

In the subsequent years, David Bowie, and those around him, would struggle to answer this question. He'd emerged from a showbiz tradition propelled by youthful ambition, his main talent that of "repositioning the brand," as one friend put it; that calculation, that "executive ability," as Iggy Pop described it, marked him as the very antithesis of instinctive rock-and-roll heroes like Elvis Presley. Yet the actions that signaled the death of rock and roll announced a rebirth too. Maybe this wasn't rock and roll like Elvis had made rock and roll, but it led the way to where rock and roll would go. Successors like Prince and Madonna, Bono and Lady Gaga—each seized on "repositioning the brand" as a set-piece example of how to avoid artistic culs-de-sac like the one that had imprisoned Elvis. For Bowie himself, though, each brand renewal, each metamorphosis, would come at a cost.

Inevitably, as David Bowie's career moved ever onward, generations of fans wondered what lay behind those masks. Over the years, some accounts have represented him as a flint-hearted rip-off merchant; others have portrayed him as a natural-born genius with some minor character flaws. Yet as the hundreds of friends, lovers, and fellow musicians who speak within the following pages attest, the truth is far more intriguing.

The truth is, David Bowie, behind the glitter and showmanship, didn't just change himself on the outside; he changed himself on the inside as well. Since Dr. Faustus sold his soul, since Robert Johnson found himself at the crossroads, artists and musicians have struggled to transcend the talents they were born with. David Bowie, a youth with ambition and more charm than talent, seemed to achieve that magical alchemy: he transformed himself, and his destiny.

DAVID BOWIE | STARMAN

PART I

I Hope I Make It on My Own

CHAPTER 1

When I'm Five

Everything seemed gray. We wore short gray flannel trousers of a thick and rough material, gray socks, and gray shirts. The roads were gray, the prefabs were gray, and there were still quite a few bomb sites around in 1956 — these also seemed to be made of gray rubble.

— Peter Prickett

IT WAS A COLD, wet November in 1991, like the cold, wet Novembers of his childhood, when David Bowie asked his driver to take the scenic route to the Brixton Academy. The smoke-filled tour bus pulled slowly through Stansfield Road, just a few hundred yards from the venue, paused briefly outside a large, anonymous three-story Victorian house, and then moved on.

Bowie had been chatty, open, almost surprisingly vulnerable in the past twelve weeks, but he remained silent for a few minutes as he gazed out the window. Then he turned around, and guitarist Eric Schermerhorn, sitting next to him, could see tears trickling down his employer's cheeks. "It's a miracle," David Bowie murmured. He was unashamed of his vulnerability. "I probably should have been an accountant. I don't know how this all happened."

For Schermerhorn, who'd witnessed Bowie's showmanship and poise close up, the mental image of David Robert Jones inspecting a company spreadsheet was ludicrous. And the doubt David had expressed to Schermerhorn a few days before—that he didn't even know if he could sing—was even more bizarre; Schermerhorn had seen the man's almost mystical ability to hold a show together and dominate a crowd. Over the forthcoming months, Schermerhorn would learn from Bowie's friends and from his own observations about the man's organization, his "executive abilities," his talent for working the system. Yet here he was, surveying the scene of his childhood, convinced this was some kind of accident. The idea was ridiculous. Hadn't someone so eminently glamorous always been fated to be a star?

DAVID Bowie has described himself as a "Brixton boy" more than once. Although his stay there was brief, it's an apt term. Brixton in January of 1947 was a unique location, the cultural focus of South London, blessed with its own racy glamour, battered but unbowed by the Luftwaffe and Hitler's terror weapons, whose destruction was visible wherever you walked.

It was natural that David's father, Haywood Stenton Jones, should gravitate toward Brixton, for its vaudeville traditions matched his own fantasies. Born in Doncaster on November 21, 1912, and brought up in the picturesque Yorkshire brewery town of Tadcaster, he had a tough childhood: His own father had died in the First World War, and his mother soon afterward. Raised by the local council and by an aunt, Haywood Jones came into an inheritance from the family footwear business when he was eighteen. "So he bought a theatre troupe. What a wise idea!" David recounted years later. The enterprise lost Haywood much of his fortune, and he invested what was left in a London West End nightclub that catered to boxers and other exotic characters; during this short-lived venture, he also acquired a wife, pianist Hilda Sullivan. When the nightclub burned up most of his remaining cash, Haywood developed a stomach ulcer. The idea of working for a children's charity came to him in a dream; it was both an escape route from his own troubles and a way of helping kids who'd suffered fractured childhoods like his own. In September of 1935 he started work at Dr. Barnardo's at Stepney Causeway, an imposing, Gothic-style complex of buildings in the heart of London's East End that had provided a refuge for homeless children since the 1870s.

When the Second World War broke out, Haywood was among the first to enlist; he served with the Royal Fusiliers, who fought in France, North Africa, and Europe. When he returned to a battered but victorious London in October of 1945, Haywood rejoined Barnardo's as general superintendent to the chief of staff. Like many marriages during the war, Haywood's didn't last; it was doubtless damaged by his affair with a nurse, which produced a child, Annette, born in 1941.

Haywood met Peggy Burns, a waitress at the Ritz Cinema, on a visit to a Barnardo's children's home at Tunbridge Wells soon after he returned, and he married Peggy when his divorce from Hilda came through, eight months after the birth of his second child. David Robert Jones was born at the family's new home at 40 Stansfield Road, Brixton, on January 8, 1947.

In that immediate postwar period, Brixton was cold, damp, soot blackened, scarred by bomb damage, but still bustling. Its prewar raciness and music-hall glamour were only enhanced by its recent history, and in 1947, Brixton looked especially—to use one of David's favorite words—dystopian. This part of South London had been judged expendable in the Second World War: Churchill's spymasters had manipulated press reports of where Hitler's futuristic V-1 flying bombs were landing, ensuring that the vengeance weapons fell short and hit South London rather than the wealthy West End. More than forty of the pioneering cruise missiles smashed into Brixton and Lambeth—entire streets both behind and in front of the Joneses' house were flattened. Most of the rubble had been cleared away by 1947, but the area retained its foreboding gap-toothed look for decades.

David's first winter was grim. Britain in late 1947 was grim. The Second World War had invigorated American capitalism but had left Britain tired—and near broke. There were no streetlights; there was no coal; gas supplies were low, and ration cards were still needed to buy linen, fuel, "economy" suits, eggs, and the scraggy bits of Argentinean beef that were available only intermittently. Christopher Isherwood, the writer who would one day advise David to move to Berlin, visited London that year and was shocked by its shabbiness. "London is a dying city," one Londoner said, counseling him not to return.

For parents, life was hard. Yet for the children who scampered around this urban wilderness, it was a wonderland: the empty, bomb-damaged houses were playgrounds and museums, full of intriguing treasures abandoned by long-vanished tenants.

In later years, many of Peggy Burns's friends would notice her contempt for the left-wing Labour Party, yet given what life was like that winter, her attitude was understandable. The British had been exhausted by the war, but peace had brought no improvement in living standards. In Brixton it was impossible to find soap; the local Woolworth's was lit by candles; constant scouring of the local shops was required to find terry toweling for nappies; and at the end of February the Labour government introduced power rationing, with homes limited to five hours of electricity a day. During that same time, Haywood Jones and all of the Barnardo's organization wrestled with the problem of thousands of children displaced by the war.

David loved his father — to this day he wears a gold cross Haywood gave him when he was in his teens — but in 2002, when asked about his relationship with his mother, he quoted Philip Larkin's famously bleak "This Be the Verse," the poem that starts "They fuck you up, your mum and dad." The occasion was an informal live chat with interviewer Michael Parkinson; the line drew laughter, as had many of David's quips, but as David went on to quote the remaining lines about misery deepening like a coastal shelf, the titters gave way to uncomfortable silence.

The madness of Peggy Burns's family would one day become part of the Bowie legend, but as far as the young David Jones was concerned, it was coldness, a simple lack of emotion, that characterized his relationship with his mum. Peggy's sister Pat said of their mother, Margaret Mary Burns, née Heaton, that "she was a cold woman. There was not a lot of love around," and Peggy seems to have inherited that coldness. Yet according to family lore, in her youth Peggy was good with children, working as a nanny before falling in love with the handsome Jack Isaac Rosenberg, son of a wealthy Jewish furrier. Rosenberg promised to marry Peggy but disappeared before the birth of their son, David's half brother, Terence Guy Adair Burns, on November 5, 1937.

There were darker shadows in Peggy's past too. In 1986 David's aunt Pat—"the frightful aunt," as he later termed her—detailed the troubled history of the Burns family. Peggy's siblings included three sisters—Nora, Una, and Vivienne—who, according to Pat, suffered from varying degrees of mental instability, what one writer termed the Burns "family affliction." This history later inspired the theory that David Jones was forced to construct alter egos to distance himself from the madness within. Ken Pitt, David's manager, knew David, Peggy, and Pat as well as anyone and describes this theory as "unconvincing." Although David would later gleefully celebrate his family, announcing "most of them are nutty—in, just out of, or going into an institution," most people considered Haywood friendly and sincere and found Peggy talkative with many traces of her former vivaciousness once you got to know her.

Peggy's second child, Myra Ann, the result of another wartime romance, was born in August of 1941. The child was given up for adoption, but by the time Peggy met Haywood, she was ready to settle down to a conventional life, agreeing to marry the Yorkshireman on the condition he'd accept Terence as his son. Hence, for the first nine years of his life, David had an elder brother to snuggle up to, and when Terry left home in 1956 to join the air force, he remained the object of David's hero worship. The messy, confused nature of the Jones household was hardly unusual—illegitimate births had soared in wartime Britain (some historians blame a shortage of rubber and a subsequent fall in condom production). David's troubled relationship with his mother echoed those of contemporaries such as John Lennon and Eric Clapton, both of whom were raised in households that today would have a social worker knocking on the door.

As David grew into a toddler, austerity kept its tight grip, but glimmers of hope started to appear in 1953, a year treasured by many kids because it marked an end to sweets rationing as well as the advent of television. Haywood Jones was one of thousands who bought new sets so their families could watch the coronation of the glamorous young Queen Elizabeth. Just a few weeks later, the six-year-old David sneaked downstairs for another TV landmark: *The Quatermass Experiment,* the pioneering BBC science fiction series that had all of Britain glued to the screen. This "tremendous series" would leave its mark on David, who remembers how he'd watch each Saturday night "from behind the sofa when my parents had thought I had gone to bed. After each episode I would tip-toe back to my bedroom rigid with fear, so powerful did the action seem." The program sparked a lifelong fascination with science fiction and—by way of its theme tune, the dark, sinister "Mars, the Bringer of War" from Holst's *The Planets*—the emotional effects of music.

Brixton was the perfect breeding ground for a future Ziggy Stardust: Waterloo, the mecca of music-hall artists for a century or more, was just down the road, while Brixton's own Empress Theatre hosted Tony Hancock, Laurel and Hardy, and countless other variety stars. "Show-business people were scattered all the way from Kennington to Streatham," says David's near neighbor photographer Val Wilmer; many locals still talked of Charlie Chaplin, who had grown up just north of Brixton. Sharon Osbourne, five years younger than David, lived on the other side of Brixton Road with her father, Don Arden, a failed nightclub singer and comedian, and she remembers being surrounded by "all the vaudeville artists." Kids could look out and see comedians chatting in the corner shop or a racy character in a cheap suit and hat on his way to or from a show carrying a case that might contain a ventriloquist's dummy, a banjo, or a set of knives for his knife-throwing act.

David's home at 40 Stansfield Road was a typical roomy, three-story Victorian house shared, during most of their eight years in Brixton, with two other families. In later years, with conventional rock-star spin, David Bowie described his Brixton youth as if it were a walk on the wild side, with gangs roaming the streets. The local kids did indeed wander around the area freely, but their prey was butterflies, tadpoles, and other urban wildlife. "It was unbelievable," says David's neighbor and schoolmate Sue Larner, "there were these huge spaces from the bomb sites, and ruined houses, which seemed like mountains to us, covered in buddleia: they were our playgrounds." Derelict buildings at the bottom of Stansfield Road were sinister, yet fragrant—kids scampered around the sweet-smelling blooms with butterfly nets, for there were more butterflies around then than before or since, while the many pools and ponds in South London's abandoned bomb sites were packed with tadpoles and newts. Rats also meandered casually through the abandoned buildings, and local kids still remember the sound of mice scurrying around the drafty, uncarpeted Victorian houses; at night, the children clutched hot water bottles for warmth and comfort.

In those early years, the tiny Jones family kept themselves to themselves. Most local kids played out on the street, but David generally remained with his mum, and Haywood spent his days at Stepney. In 1951, David started at the Stockwell Infants School, three minutes' walk away on Stockwell Road, one of Brixton's main streets. He remembers wetting his pants on the first day; happily, friendly milk lady Bertha Douglas kept a supply of clean knickers for such common emergencies. The school's lofty Victorian building looked severe and had a characteristic aroma of disinfectant and rubber shoes, but the staff was mostly loving and kind: "It was a sweet, friendly school, small and cozy," remembers schoolmate Suzanne Liritis. "The teachers used to tell us things like 'You're special, Jesus loves you,'" says her friend Susan Larner.

Behind the Victorian primness, things were racier than they seemed. The headmistress, Miss Douglas, was tall and thin with severe scraped-back gray hair. This formidable woman lived with Miss Justin, who taught in the junior school. Only later did Sue and her friends conclude "they were obviously a sweet lesbian couple." If any parents suspected a relationship, they were unconcerned, for as Larner points out, "Lots of women had lost their beaus in the war." They took the conventional British attitude: exotic sexuality was fine, as long as it was kept behind closed doors. Just don't do it in the street and frighten the horses, as the saying went.

Most of the families around Stansfield Road were large, and kids in the neighborhood were almost invariably accompanied by their brothers and sisters. Maybe that's the reason that few of them remember David. Appropriately enough, one of the only children who did notice him, Sue Larner, now a sculptor, happened to register the nice-looking, well-scrubbed boy's skill at art: "None of us had much to do with boys, but I do remember showing him a few tricks on the drawing board—and he showed me even more. He showed me how to draw a woman's bonnet, with the neck, without having to draw a face first. He was good."

On weekends, or after school, the five-year-old David's universe was bounded by the bomb sites on Chantrey Road and the far side of Stockwell Road, where all kids played; turning left on Stockwell Road, he'd immediately reach the school playground; turning right, he'd reach two sweetshops, the nearest overseen by a kindly gay gentleman. Farther down Stockwell Road was the Astoria; later a famed rock venue—the Academy—whose attractions would include David Bowie, in the fifties it was still a thriving local cinema, with morning matinees featuring cowboy movies, Zorro, and Laurel and Hardy. On the way to the cinema there was a bookshop that spilled out onto the pavement, filled with comics and kids' books. There was a large dairy, with horse-drawn carts, but the main feature that dominated Stockwell Road was Pride and Clarke's, a celebrated motorbike and car showroom that sprawled across a row of maroon-painted buildings, later immortalized in Antonioni's *Blow-Up*. This was where David, the future car geek, could ogle BSAs, Rileys, and other legendary British bikes and cars.

There was another intrinsic part of Brixton's appeal: the sound of calypso and the smell of curried goat, brought by the new generations of Caribbean immigrants arriving in the area. But these were things David would have gotten only a whiff of, for in 1954, Haywood Jones and family packed up and moved to suburbia.

The beloved poet laureate John Betjeman described the sub-urbs as the home of "a new kind of citizen," and as proof of its futurism, David's new hometown, Bromley, was the birthplace of H. G. Wells. From the fifties onward, the suburbs were an object of both horror and aspiration—the upper classes despised the neat, mock-Tudor houses, while the middle classes flocked to the neatly manicured streets. Today, like many English market towns, Bromley is bland and overrun by chain stores—Wells's birthplace is now a Primark clothing outlet. But in the fifties it was a place in flux, a short train ride from London but friendly and small scale: "It was actually quite charming," says David's boyhood friend Geoff MacCormack, "even soulful."

The move to Bromley marked Haywood's promotion from board secretary to public relations officer. Haywood's colleagues regarded him as "unassuming but cheerful—good company." His new home was a small but neat Edwardian terraced house in Plaistow Grove, a cul-de-sac near the railway line; although unthinkably cramped by American standards, it was all their own, perfectly in keeping with the family's modestly respectable status.

Parts of Bromley were middle-class enclaves, 1930s fake-Tudor houses with leaded windows to proclaim their superior status, but poverty was never far away. Children and their parents were encouraged to save six cents a week in the Burnt Ash Boot Club to help them buy adequate footwear, and there were plenty of Dick-ensian sights. A rag-and-bone man walked the streets uttering the "Any old iron" cry familiar from Victorian times. Several roads still had gas lighting, and in most parts of Bromley there was hardly a car to be seen parked at the curb. United Dairies, which had a yard behind the Burnt Ash School, still used horses to deliver milk, left on everybody's doorstep each morning. Even in the 1950s, electricity supplies were erratic; radios and record play-ers were usually plugged into the light sockets in the ceilings, while electric clocks often slowed down in the afternoon, the time of heavy demand, then sped up again at night. Few people owned phones—the Joneses were an exception.

David joined Burnt Ash School a couple of years after most of the other kids and didn't particularly stand out during the first few terms. But with his fine, perhaps slightly feminine features, he was a good-looking boy—a fact his female classmates noticed later. Within a year or so David was part of a small gang of school-mates. This included Dudley Chapman and John Barrance, boys who lived nearby and were invited to David's eighth birthday party. Even at this age, many kids noted the cramped interior of the Joneses' modest two-up, two-down house. Eight-year-old John Barrance thought the family seemed restrained, quiet—"They were perfectly pleasant, but I think they had a 'don't touch this, don't touch that' attitude." David's friend Max Batten shared more easygoing good times with him, enjoying lollipops and chatting with Mrs. Jones; one memorable afternoon, he and David sneaked upstairs at Plaistow Grove, unwrapped Haywood's service revolver, and played with it furtively before carefully replacing it in the drawer where it had been concealed.

Though few of his contemporaries considered David's child-hood anything out of the ordinary, in later years, it would be por-trayed as dysfunctional—mostly by David himself, who, in the mid-1970s, when he was in his most flamboyantly deranged phase, loved to proclaim "everyone finds empathy in a nutty fam-ily." Peggy in particular was singled out as the perfect example of repression and eccentricity, but the most damning recollection of others is that she was a snob; in general, only the middle-class kids were treated to cups of tea at Plaistow Grove, and David seemed to learn which of his friends could be ushered in the front door and which ones should wait at the garden gate. In fairness, it's possible Peggy simply preferred boys who, like David, were trained to say "please" and "thank you." Well-brought-up York-shire lad John Hutchinson, who enjoyed sitting in the back room with its cozy fireplace and photos on the mantelpiece, maintains that "she was nice," remembering how in future years she would knit outfits for his young son, Christian. Some of the tensions between Peggy and David were simply due, says Hutchinson, to the generational shift that would soon grip the country, the advent of the teenager, and the fact that, as he puts it, "It became cool to put down your parents." In future years, Peggy's sister Pat bore witness to other tensions within the family. When the family first moved to Bromley, Terry apparently stayed behind in Brixton, which was thought to be more convenient for his job as a clerk in Southwark. Later he joined David, Peggy, and Haywood at Plaistow Grove, but his stay there was brief, and he left for National Service in 1955. Not one of David's friends remember seeing Terry at the Joneses' house. If parents "fuck you up," as Philip Larkin put it, Terry undoubtedly suffered more than his brother.

Peggy's friend Aubrey Goodchild maintains that David's mum was "good company. Forthright, though. And conservative in her politics." And many kids shared the same frustrations as David. Compared to America, with its comics and consumer booms, Britain was staid, and its kids felt suffocated. "We were shabby," says Bromley schoolgirl Dorothy Bass. "Everything seemed gray," remembers another contemporary, Peter Prickett. "We wore short gray flannel trousers of a thick and rough material, gray socks, and gray shirts. The roads were gray, the prefabs were gray, and there were still quite a few bomb sites around in 1956 — these also seemed to be made of gray rubble." Life was predictable, defined by rituals. Some of the routines were oddly comforting, like the distributing of tiny glass bottles of free milk at school every morning at eleven, the playing of the national anthem on BBC radio and TV before they closed down for the night, and David's volunteer school routine, putting up the climbing ropes in the playground each morning.

For its time, Burnt Ash was a modern school. It emphasized the arts, particularly in the form of music and movement classes, during which the pupils were encouraged to express themselves and dance around in their underwear (no one owned any gym clothes). In other respects it followed 1950s norms: a strict uniform policy, formal assemblies with hymns, and the cane for misbehaving boys.

Headmaster George Lloyd was, as one pupil puts it, "interesting." Slightly portly and jolly, he gave classes in music and reading, individually tutoring his pupils. He was "gentle," affectionate with the children, and often sat alongside the boys as they read, putting his arm around favored pupils. There were a few boys for whom he seemed to have real affection, "and one of them," says a schoolmate, "was David. He definitely did like David."

At ten or eleven, David had fine, almost elfin features; his hair was cut in bangs, he was average in height, and slightly skinny. But there was an energy and enthusiasm about him that entranced George Lloyd and others, the beginnings of his knack for charming people. As early as his teens, he had developed a talent for using charm "as a weapon," says a later confidant, writer Charles Shaar Murray. "Even if you'd fallen out, when you met David again you'd be convinced within five minutes that he had barely been able to function in the years he hadn't seen you. I know, for a time, I developed a kind of platonic man-love for him."

It was this charm, this ability to be whoever his companion wanted him to be, that would be the making of David Bowie; it's what brought him his breaks, opportunities his ever-active mind worked out how to exploit. In these early days, that charm was not deployed so intensely—or so ruthlessly. Still, "he was just, somehow, one of the kids you noticed," says schoolmate Jan Powling, "bright, quite funny, with oodles of personality." He was invariably neatly dressed—more so than his classmates. "Always well scrubbed, with clean fingernails," says Powling, "in short, the kind of boy that if you were his mum, you would have been really proud of him."

Well-scrubbed, polite, every suburban mother's dream son, the ten-year-old David Jones also stuck to middle-class convention by enrolling in the local Scout pack and the Church of England choir. "We were slung in," says fellow Cub Scout Geoff MacCormack, "because that's what parents did with kids then. We didn't kick up a fuss; we just got on with it." Like Keith Richards, one of the unlikeliest champions of Robert Baden-Powell's Scout movement, these kids lapped up the outdoor adventures. The weekly pack meetings and services became a crucial part of David's world; it was there that he met MacCormack and George Underwood, who would prove the most enduring friends of his life.

Together, the three donned cassocks, surplices, and ruffles for church services, as well as for the frequent weddings that would become David Bowie's first paying gigs as a singer: "Not only were you paid five shillings — a princely sum in those days," says Mac-Cormack, "but if the ceremony took place in the week, you got a day off school."

George Underwood's family lived on the other side of Bromley, so he was enrolled at a different primary school. Tall for his age, good-looking, with an easy, relaxed, but passionate air about him, he would become the closest friend of David's youth. Their relationship would go through some rocky patches but would be a formative one in both of their lives. For the glue that held their friendship together was rock and roll.

For most members of David and George's generation there was a "eureka" moment, the instant when rock and roll exploded into each one's consciousness, an escape route from the gray world. For both boys, that moment hit in 1955. Toward the end of that year, *Blackboard Jungle* caused a sensation in the UK, generating widespread outrage as politicians denounced its baleful influence. Around that same time, Haywood arrived home from Stepney Causeway with a bagful of singles that he'd been given. That night, David played each of the records, by Fats Domino, Chuck Berry, and Frankie Lymon and the Teenagers. "Then," he says, "I hit gold: 'Tutti Frutti' by Little Richard — my heart nearly burst with excitement. I'd never heard anything even resembling this. It filled the room with energy and color and outrageous defiance. I had heard God." More than anyone else, Little Richard would be his career-long role model: "I always wanted to be Little Richard — he was my idol."

Born Richard Penniman, the most controversial, genre-busting early rock and roller would be a potent touchstone. Many of David's contemporaries, such as the Stones' Keith Richards, would cite Muddy Waters and Chuck Berry as their heroes — they represented authentic blues forged deep in the Mississippi Delta. Little Richard was a city boy; he had made his name in New Orleans, studying outrageous performers like Guitar Slim and

Esquerita, hanging out in a campy, cross-dressing scene where fur-coated queens competed to deliver the best impressions of Dinah Washington and Sarah Vaughan. His records were a far cry from Muddy's deep, soulful songs of yearning and sexual bravado; they were mini-explosions of sound, cranked up using the city's best session men, designed to pack the maximum thrills possible into the two minutes and thirty seconds allowed by the South's jukebox operators. Richard Penniman didn't rely on his innate musicianship and thrilling voice only; he packaged his music in outrageous showmanship and brightly colored suits in an act honed by his presence at literally hundreds of competitive cutting concerts across the South at which the best R & B performers vied for supremacy. Later still, he would come out as gay; eventually, he would find God; much later, David Bowie's wife would buy one of Richard's suits for her husband. Over all those years, David Jones would treasure the first Little Richard records he bought on Bromley High Street.

Elvis Presley would be another idol—all the more so when David discovered he shared a birthday with the ultimate white rock-and-roll icon—but Little Richard would remain the touchstone of David's musical identity.

Fatefully, Little Richard became the first American rock and roller to be beamed into the homes of British television viewers. On February 16, 1957, the BBC unveiled its momentous *Six-Five Special*, a TV show aimed at teenagers. It included segments of classical music, dance competitions, and a short extract from the movie *Don't Knock the Rock*, with Richard performing "Tutti Frutti." Over the next few weeks, the program would feature more Little Richard, British rockers Tommy Steele and Adam Faith, plus, tellingly, Lonnie Donegan.

Like many British teenagers, David Jones and George Underwood idolized Little Richard but copied Lonnie Donegan. Today, Donegan's music is comparatively neglected, but the influence of his DIY ethos lives on in British music from the Beatles to the Sex Pistols. Donegan's take on American performers like Leadbelly was gloriously naive—his music was made on the simplest of instruments, and his technical deficiencies were part of his charm. It might take a schoolboy years of work to sound like Little Richard or Chuck Berry, but that same schoolboy could attempt Lonnie's brand of folksy music—skiffle, as it's called—after just a few afternoons of practice. Donegan's homegrown skiffle signaled the end of the UK's outdated dance culture and inspired a generation of British rock and rollers, among them the eleven-year-old Jones and Underwood. For all the kids raised in postwar austerity, this was a moment they'd anticipated for years: "We'd waited and waited for something fabulous to happen," says George Underwood. "And it *did* happen. That was the catalyst. And from then on, music was the one thing we talked about constantly."

At Burnt Ash, there were several kids who'd become known as rock-and-roll fans—one of them, Ian Carfrae, later of the New Vaudeville Band, was admonished by the headmaster for bringing "Rock Around the Clock" into 1955's Christmastime gramophone-listening sessions. But while David became the best-known fan, George Underwood got his rock-and-roll act together before everyone else. He'd already bought a huge Hofner acoustic guitar and formed a duo with a family friend when he met David—who had a ukulele and a burning desire to be in a band. In the summer of 1958, roughly a year after they met, the two traveled down to the eighteenth Cub Scouts summer camp on the Isle of Wight. "We put a washboard bass in the back of the van, and David's ukulele, and between us we managed to conjure up a couple of songs around the campfire. And that was our first public performance. Neither of us had any claim to virtuosity—but we wanted to sing."

THAT tentative first show, with David strumming and George singing, was not the only rite of passage that year. The previous autumn David had taken his eleven-plus, the crucial exam that would determine his future school. The Burnt Ash pupils were well prepared under the gimlet eye of David's respected and feared teacher Mrs. Baldry, and David and most of his friends passed.

The rigid pecking order of schools in the area started with Beck-enham and Bromley Grammar at the top, followed by Bromley Technical School—which opened in 1959 and was aimed at future commercial artists and engineers—with Quernmore Sec-ondary Modern languishing in the rear. Later in life, David would advise one of his closest friends, "Do the contrary action," and he himself first did that at the age of eleven. Though David's results were good enough for the grammar school, against all convention he opted for Bromley Tech, and he talked his parents into support-ing his decision.

Some of the inspiration for this precociously unconventional move undoubtedly came from George Underwood, who was also heading for Bromley Tech. The Tech's links with the nearby Brom-ley College of Art meant he would join a wider community of art-school kids, students who would ultimately come to define postwar Britain. Contemporaries and near neighbors the Stones' Keith Richards and the Pretty Things' Dick Taylor—"the war babies," as Richards would describe them—were already embarked on the same course. The notion that a generation of kids could make a living through art was novel, born of the radical rework-ing of the British educational system in 1944; the art-college sys-tem provided the foundation of Britain's future influence on art, advertising, publishing, movies, and fashion. As countless ex-pupils point out, art college taught them that they didn't have to work in an office or a factory—they could make a living with "ideas." This freedom was all the more powerful for being combined with an unrelenting postwar work ethic: "We understood then," says David's friend Dorothy Bass, "that after your two years at art col-lege, you would have to pay your dues."

Bromley Tech had moved to a new site alongside Bromley School of Art just one year before, and with its airy concrete-and-glass building it seemed modern and forward-looking. Yet its aca-demic structure aped the English public school system, with pupils organized into houses and some teachers dressed in gowns and mortarboards for formal assemblies (to which Catholic and Jewish students were not invited). Every morning, David and his

friends sang Victorian-era hymns like "Onward, Christian Soldiers" and murmured "amen" in response to prayers for the royal
family and other pillars of the establishment.

For all the formality of Bromley Tech, the quality of teaching
was variable—except in the art department. This was housed in a
custom-designed building with north-facing windows to give better natural light for painting. Owen Frampton, the head of the
department, was undoubtedly the school's best-liked teacher. He
was enthusiastic—David describes him as "an excellent art
teacher and an inspiration"—but no pushover. Owen, or Ossy,
had a superb eye for art, and he could unerringly spot mischief,
says John Edmonds. Edmonds once threw a snowball at a teacher
unobserved, or so he'd thought until he was pulled out of class by
the beady-eyed head of art who'd seen the incident. "I did gain a
respect both for his eyesight, and his skills with the skipper,"
he recalls ruefully.

Frampton was a man of eclectic background and tastes—he
had served in the Guards in wartime, designed wallpaper for the
Sanderson company, could explain in inspiring terms both classical and modern art (David would mention him as the source of
his interest in the painter Egon Schiele), and played guitar. So did
his son Peter, who enrolled at Bromley Tech in 1961. Peter, David,
and George soon became well known around the school. George
and David found a spot in the stairwell that had a natural echo.
"My big hero was Buddy Holly—although David wasn't a big fan,
we used to do Buddy Holly numbers," says George. "David was a
great harmonizer, so we used to work on a lot of that material
together, by the stairs." Peter would sit on the school steps with a
guitar showing kids how to play Shadows and Ventures riffs, and
he started calling himself Paul Raven.

David paid rapt attention during Owen's art classes. He
sketched with charcoals and hung out in the art department,
but year by year his interest in other subjects declined to the point
that, in year three, his school report described him as "a pleasant
idler." At fourteen, he had succumbed to the obsessions that
would define the years to come: music and girls. He would feed

both these addictions after school in a quintessentially suburban location on Bromley High Street: Medhurst's department store, a huge Victorian building that sold furniture and other household goods and also boasted one of South London's best gramophone departments.

Housed in a long narrow corridor, the gramophone section was overseen by a discreetly gay couple named Charles and Jim. Although they stocked the customary chart hits and sheet music, the partners were also aficionados of modern jazz music and specialized in American imports. David turned up most afternoons after school to check out new releases at their listening booth. His interest in music had become an obsession, and in those years he would buy singles and albums by Elvis Presley and Little Richard, as well as by UK artists, like Joe Brown. As time went on, his tastes became more and more eclectic, and, encouraged by Terry, his record collection expanded to include jazz releases by Charlie Parker and Charles Mingus. Soon he gained the status of a regular; Jim, the younger of the two partners, would let him have records at a discount, as would Jane Green, the assistant. Soon, David explains, she "took a liking to me. Whenever I would pop in, which was most afternoons after school, she'd let me play records in the 'sound booth' to my heart's content till they closed at five thirty. Jane would often join me and we would smooch big-time to the sounds of Ray Charles or Eddie Cochran. This was very exciting as I was thirteen or fourteen, and she would be a womanly seventeen at that time. My first older woman."

The Medhurst's gramophone booth became a prime hangout for many Bromley teenagers seeking glamour on Bromley High Street. In this small world in the early sixties, the arrival of an Indian curry house was an event of seismic importance, as was the opening of two Wimpy coffee bars shortly afterward, one in North Bromley and one in South Bromley. The teenagers would hang out in the library gardens south of the market square, trying to look cool in their mostly shabby clothes—the girls wore black pullovers from Marks and Spencer, the nearest they could get to a Parisian Beat look, while David took trips to town in search of

"Italian trousers." These rebels with a cause included David, George Underwood, and Geoff MacCormack; there was also a merchant seaman named Richard Dendy who brought back obscure records from New York, plus Dorothy Bass, who went out briefly with George, their relationship mainly inspired by their shared love of music.

George was charming, good-looking, remembers Dorothy, well known around Bromley, "but not pushy, not 'look-at-me.' Neither was David... really," she continues, "but he was really driven. David shows the difference between someone who's good—and someone who devotes their life to what they believe in."

Nearly all the recollections of Bromley Tech pupils seem to feature George and David as a pair; of the two, George was better known, better remembered. He was ebullient, lovable, more expansive. David was cool; people noticed his clothes or his hair or his possessions, but not so much his personality. In his later days, when David's first band became known around school, he was kind to younger kids, but several of his contemporaries share the impression of Len Routledge, who remembers, "I think I envied him, or resented him, as kids do. Because he had a better lifestyle than us, and a father who'd bring him things some of us could never expect: a full American football kit, the saxophone, etc. I genuinely admired what he achieved... but the comfortable circumstances of his life contrasted sharply with me, and many of the other boys."

Most of the Bromley kids remember David getting a saxophone and brandishing it around Bromley Tech. He'd wanted a baritone sax, but he had to settle for a Grafton alto, a cheaper but nonetheless glamorous cream-colored plastic art deco concoction that Haywood bought him around 1960. For a short time, David managed to cadge some lessons from baritone player Ronnie Ross, a man who'd performed with Ted Heath and other big bands and who lived nearby. Although the musical value of the eight or so lessons from Ronnie was negligible, their name-dropping value was incalculable and probably helped David score a Saturday-morning job at Furlong's, the record and instrument store in

South Bromley. This little music shop, run by a pipe-smoking, trumpet-playing trad jazz fan, was a mecca in Bromley's tiny musical landscape; its notice board provided a hotline for news of local bands' formation and dissolution, and David's role, of turning customers on to "new sounds," helped fuel his credibility in the music community and—just as crucially—with local girls.

Even though peers like George Underwood overshadowed David as musicians, David's confidence got him noticed. The most celebrated example of this was when the tech pupils took what was for almost all of them their first foray outside England, a school trip to Spain over the Easter holidays in 1960. Many families couldn't afford the trip; David was one of the first, and the youngest, to sign up. The small troop took the ferry to Dieppe, then a bus all the way to Spain. There they saw a bullfight, goggled at Franco's armed militia, and moaned about the spicy foreign food. Most of the tech students exchanged smiles or played soccer with the Spanish kids; Jones spent much of the day with the local talent, "off chatting to the girls," classmate Richard Comben remembers. David's prowess was commemorated in the school magazine's reference to "Don Jones, the lover, last seen pursued by 13 senoritas."

David describes his behavior once he discovered girls as "terrible," a quintessential slick operator, but as far as Bromley's girls were concerned, he was anything but, says Jan Powling. "He was nice, charming—not at all any kind of show-off." She knew David from Burnt Ash Junior, and around their third year at secondary, David asked her out on a date. As was traditional, he phoned Mr. Powling to get his permission a day or two before the outing, which at some point became a double date. Hence four teenagers took the 94 bus to the Bromley Odeon cinema: David's moral support was Nick, a Bromley Tech acquaintance, while Jan was accompanied by Deirdre Jackson, her friend from Burnt Ash Secondary. It was unfortunate, reflects Jan, that Deirdre was one of the most popular girls in her year, with a blond bob and trendy clothes; at the end of the evening, David departed arm in arm with Deirdre, while Jan had been paired off with Nicholas. "But

I don't blame David," she adds generously, "she was one of the prettiest girls we knew."

Not everyone was as forgiving of David's slick behavior. One example of David's duplicity would become famous in Bromley Tech folklore and subsequently in rock-and-roll history, for it would leave David marked, an outward sign of what was later taken to be his alien nature.

George Underwood was involved in the celebrated fracas— which is all the more ironic, as Underwood is the most likable and mild-mannered of characters. The cause was an act of outright skullduggery by George's friend in the spring of 1962, when both of them were fifteen; George had arranged a date with a Bromley schoolgirl, Carol Goldsmith, but David told him she had changed her mind and decided not to turn up. Soon George discovered that David, who fancied Carol, had lied; Carol had waited in vain for George for an hour or so before going home, distraught that she'd been stood up. David's plan was to swoop on the abandoned girl, but when Underwood discovered the dastardly scheme, there was an altercation. Underwood, enraged, impulsively punched his friend in the eye, and by some mishap scratched his eyeball. "It was just unfortunate. I *didn't* have a compass or a battery or various things I was meant to have—I didn't even wear a ring, although something must have caught. I just don't know how it managed to hurt his eye badly...I didn't mean it to be like that at all."

The damage was serious; David was taken to the hospital, and his schoolmates were told he was in danger of losing the sight in his left eye. Underwood, mortified, heard that Haywood and Peggy Jones were considering charging him with assault. David was in the hospital for several weeks, and George eventually plucked up enough courage to go see Haywood. "I wanted to tell him it wasn't intentional at all, I didn't want to maim him, for God's sake!"

David's eye injury resulted in the paralysis of the muscles that contract the pupil, leaving the pupil permanently dilated and giving that eye the appearance of being a different color than his other eye; additionally, his depth perception was shot. "It left me with a wonky sense of perspective," David explained later. "When I'm driving, for instance, cars don't come toward, me, they just get bigger." It was weeks before David returned to Bromley Tech, and at least a month before he talked to George. The rift meant that David missed out on a momentous event, the arrival of rock and roll at Bromley Tech, in April of 1962. Owen Frampton was one of the key figures in the event, overseeing the lights and the sound system. His son's band, the Little Ravens, played the first half, sandwiched between a magician and a dance duo; George and the Dragons came on after the intermission, a louder, more raucous show than Frampton Junior's band: "Very avant-garde for the time," says Pete Goodchild, who was in the audience.

Underwood wonders to this day how the band would have sounded if his friend had appeared on the stage with him. By the summer term, their friendship was repaired, although Underwood suffered pangs of guilt for years afterward — "I was always looking at him thinking, Oh God, I did that." Eventually, David would thank George for the notorious eye injury — "he told me it gave him a kind of mystique" — although for decades George would get irritated when David said he had no idea why his friend had punched him. "He gave the impression he doesn't know why I did it. And he should have known."

Underwood's disappointment that his best friend missed the George and the Dragons' Easter show was as short-lived as the band. George went on to play in the Hillsiders and Spitfires over this period, and soon after Easter teamed up with the Kon-Rads, a rather old-fashioned dance-based band formed a few months earlier by drummer Dave Crook and guitarist Neville Wills.

Once George was in, he invited David along too, asking him to join the band on saxophone but with the proviso "I'm the singer — but you can do a couple of numbers." David brought his Grafton down to rehearsals. "He looked a bit like Joe Brown at the time, so we said you can do 'A Picture of You' and 'A Night at Daddy G's.'"

David Bowie's first public performance took place just a few weeks later, on June 12, 1962, at the Bromley Tech PTA school fete. This was the tech's biggest summertime event to date — the PTA bought a new sound system for the show, and four thousand parents and locals attended. No one got to hear David's Joe Brown impression that afternoon; the Kon-Rads' set consisted strictly of instrumentals.

David, his hair arranged in a blond pompadour, his cream-colored sax slung over his shoulder, stood next to George Underwood, who picked out Shadows' riffs on his Hofner guitar. David looked "cool, well dressed," according to schoolmate Nick Brookes. It was a pretty impressive debut, but there was a clear consensus among most of the audience about who would go on to stardom: David's taller, better-looking, more popular friend. "It was George was the singer, who did a great Elvis impression," says Bromley Tech pupil Roger Bevan, who remembers, like many other pupils, Underwood's dark, glossy hair and Elvis sneer. "Everyone reckoned he was going to be big."

CHAPTER 2

"Numero Uno, Mate!"

I was ambitious ... but not like he was ambitious.

—George Underwood

N LATE 1962, reputations were fast being made in southeast London as a new wave of rock-and-roll young bucks set out to kill off England's staid, suffocating music scene. Kent schoolboys Mick Jagger and Keith Richards were bonding over Chess record sleeves and renewing their friendship at Alexis Korner shows, and the future Pretty Things were emerging from the same Kent scene; there were similar setups in West London, Surrey, and Newcastle as dozens of musicians, from Eric Clapton to Eric Burdon, Paul Jones to Keith Relf, embarked on a fast lane to fame.

So what was an underage kid with a sax to do? David Jones, just a couple of years younger than most of those figures, was marooned, destined to miss the wave that everyone else was catching. While Clapton was becoming God, David was merely a cool kid in class; well liked, noted for his skinny trousers and blond hair, cheerful and indulgent with younger students, who'd follow him around the playground asking about music or baseball. The damaged eye added a dangerous, disconcerting glamour to his otherwise conventional pretty-boy looks, but as far as native talent went, David seemed like a supporting act to his friend George Underwood—taller, more relaxed, more masculine, the center of attention at Bromley Tech.

Most of the kids who saw the Kon-Rads remember few details of the first shows, but that wasn't the point; they were out there, living the new DIY ethos. Today, their Conway Twitty and Joe Brown covers would sound gauche and naive, but to their peers at the time, they were sweeping away England's suffocating conformity, its self-satisfied dance bands and crooners.

Yet before their career ever got going, it turned out that the Kon-Rads were not unified fighters for the cause. In late 1962, when drummer Dave Crook left their always fluid lineup, a putsch in the ranks saw George Underwood booted out. To this day, the central characters dispute what happened in their schoolboy band. As far as George Underwood is concerned, the new drummer was the villain of the story: "He just didn't like me for some reason. He was trying to get me out of the band and got one of his friends, not to beat me up, but to give me some kind of warning. It was really intimidating, I was almost crying—it was horrible." George, for all his talent, was simply too nice—"a gentleman," he explains; he didn't protest. He even lent them his guitar amp, since "without it, they were fucked." It was an early lesson in the ruthlessness of the music industry for Underwood—albeit not one he'd take to heart.

At first, David was unconcerned by his friend's departure. He was fascinated by new drummer David Hadfield, who seemed like a pro already compared with the rest of the Kon-Rads. Hadfield had grown up in Cheshunt, Hertfordshire, where he'd teamed up with Harry Webb, later famous as Britain's homegrown rock and roller Cliff Richard, at secondary school. Hadfield had hyped his Cliff credentials in a drummer-seeks-work ad placed in Furlong's music shop, and David, along with guitarist Neville Wills, was intrigued; they questioned the drummer closely over coffee at the Bromley Wimpy. Rhythm guitarist Alan Dodds joined them for a rehearsal in Neville's living room a few days later, and they all agreed that Hadfield was in. Hadfield would become David's closest musical confidant for nearly a year; together, they'd hustle for shows, paint backdrops, and update their set list.

Over the following weeks, Hadfield discovered that the blond-haired sax player who looked younger than his fifteen years was by far the most ambitious band member: "He was very, very boyish, blond, and didn't look his age at all. But he carried himself well — and he just wanted to be part of show business. You could feel it."

Hadfield was ambitious too, although he's adamant that he played no part in the ousting of George Underwood and didn't know that the Kon-Rads had even played in public. David would become his main confidant, but David was also, as far as the other Kon-Rads were concerned, a pain; he wasn't practical, they told each other, he didn't understand the way the music business worked. The Kon-Rads were the first musicians to encounter David Bowie's restlessness, his urge to keep pushing relentlessly forward. In the main, they resisted his pressure, and the results would be a key part of the sax player's musical education, for the Kon-Rads were, in David's terms, a failure. They hit the London scene at a time when it was throwing out the most amazing breaks — and they blew every one of them.

Over the end of 1962 and the beginning of 1963, Jones and Hadfield spent every minute avoiding their day jobs. David was supposedly studying for his O levels, and Hadfield had recently found a job as an invoice clerk in Borough, but the band rehearsed so often and intensively at Bromley's St. Mary's Church hall that they were hounded out after complaints about the noise; they were forced to move to a damp prefab building down the street. Soon the Kon-Rads were playing most weekends in small halls and pubs around southeast London, including in Bromley, Beckenham, Orpington, and Blackheath.

Over their yearlong existence, the Kon-Rads changed lineups continuously, adding bassist Rocky Shahan and, later, a singer, Roger Ferris; Hadfield brought in girlfriend Stella Patton and her sister Christine as backup vocalists. During that year, the two Davids spent nearly all their spare time working together; the younger David was good company, energetic, enthusiastic, and practiced incessantly on the saxophone (meanwhile, his school-work languished). Jones became a good sax player, mastering a raunchy King Curtis–style tone on the Conn tenor to which he'd recently switched, and there was something about the way he stood onstage, relaxed, the sax hanging at his side, that was effort-lessly cool. But his fellow Kon-Rads were unimpressed by many of David's ideas for updating their outfits and their set list: "When you've got seven people in the band you can't change things over-night," says Hadfield. "Our attitude was, if we go out on a limb we're going to lose all our local bookings—and lose what popu-larity we have."

But there was a bigger world out there than local bookings, a world populated by people such as Joe Meek, the pioneering gay producer who had scored a huge hit that summer with his space-rock song "Telstar." Meek had recorded some of the UK's most radical early rock-and-roll hits in a self-built studio crammed into a tiny flat above a leather-goods store on Holloway Road. He was an obsessive; he recorded day after day without a break, audition-ing hundreds of bands and lavishing each session with sonic adornments, and within a few weeks of Hadfield's joining the Kon-Rads, the band made their way up to Meek's flat for an audi-tion session. The producer was already known for becoming obsessed with some of the young musicians in his studio, often hassling young, blond lookers, but for the Kon-Rads session he was uncommunicative and surly, unimpressed by their best shot, a sappy version of "Mockingbird." The insipid, undistinguished ditty, sung by Roger Ferris, was later consigned to one of Meek's notorious tea chests full of abandoned material. David was the only band member who chatted with the producer for more than a couple of minutes, quizzing him about his productions. But their conversation was cut short when David was called to help carry the band's gear down to their old *Evening News* delivery van wait-ing outside. Meek never called them back, and in their postmor-tem the band members acknowledged the possibility they weren't "original enough." Still, David's suggestion that they try to write their own songs was ignored by Hadfield and Neville Wells, who insisted that their live audience preferred familiar cover songs. (Perhaps the session was not a total loss, though, for it's possible the concept of "Telstar," a quirky, otherworldly novelty song based on a celebrated space shot, lodged in young David Jones's mind.)

A second failure was harder to stomach, for this time it involved one of David's friends and rivals. After submitting a demo recording to the Rediffusion TV company, the Kon-Rads won a place on *Ready Steady Win!*, the talent-contest spin-off of the show *Ready Steady Go!* There was snickering from the audience and judges during the heat as the Kon-Rads, in matching suits, set up their lavish backdrop, drum riser, and lights before launching into an impeccably played set of covers. The winning band, the Trubeats, played their own songs and gave a stripped-down performance highlighting their blond, good-looking teenage guitarist, Peter Frampton, now a student at Bromley Grammar School, who won over boys and girls alike. The Kon-Rads' performance was mocked in a press report that declared "the band has nothing original to offer."

It was David, the youngest member, still at school, who was always the first to rebound from such setbacks: "He kept pushing," says Hadfield. "He wanted to write more things, change how we dressed, [saying], 'We've got to go out on a limb.'" The older musicians tried to persuade David he was being impractical. They were convinced he was addicted to gimmicks, an impression reinforced when he announced that he was assuming a new name, "David Jay." David persisted in his schemes, persuading Neville to write music to go with his lyrics for several songs, including "I Never Dreamed." The composition—with dark lyrics inspired by newspaper reports of a train crash, and a peppy tune reminiscent of the Tremeloes' music—made its way into their set, alongside their predictable lineup of Chris Montez, Shadows, and Beatles numbers, as well as the raunchier sax-based songs that David pushed for. And at the same time as he tried to influence their sets, David started to make an impression live: "He looked good, he had a way of standing with his sax slung round his neck—it was very manly, if that's the right word. He was getting noticed more, guys and girls seemed to like him."

Two possible breaks had ended in failure; then, in the summer of 1963, it looked like the third time might be the charm. Bob Knight, a Bromley entrepreneur, managed to interest his friend Eric Easton in the band. Easton was the comanager of the Rolling Stones, who were on the brink of the big time; the Kon-Rads started hanging out in his office on Oxford Street. They were introduced to Brian Epstein, and finally, via Easton, they scored their big break: a trial session for Decca, the Stones' label, on August 30.

Determined not to repeat their previous mistakes, the band members showcased their own material, including "I Never Dreamed." But their first formal studio session, complete with engineers in white coats, was a disaster; Hadfield was "a nervous wreck," the rhythm tracks were a mess, and the results weren't even deemed worthy of a playback. By the time Decca confirmed it wasn't interested in the band, David had already announced he was leaving.

There was little explanation of why: "There was no arguing with him. He simply said he wanted to do his own thing," says Hadfield, who is convinced that the young sax player was "not a band kind of person" and had simply deserted the band following the setback. Years later, David explained his defection was inspired by very different reasons: "I wanted to do a version of [Marvin Gaye's] 'Can I Get a Witness'—and they didn't. That was why I left the Kon-Rads." George Underwood, David's coconspirator, backs up his version: "We were determined to do music we enjoyed playing—not copying what was in the Top Ten."

David had coaxed Underwood to make some guest appearances with the Kon-Rads earlier that summer, and the two had spent months sharing their musical obsessions as they planned their own band. By now David was spending all of his free time rehearsing and hanging out at Vic Furlong's, Medhurst's, Bromley's two Wimpy bars, and George's house, his voracious appetite for music bordering on the obsessive. The two enjoyed a glorious summer, despite the fact that David's O-level results arrived and it turned out he'd failed every one but art. He seemed blithely unconcerned; his mother was dismissive of his musical ambitions, but Haywood seemed, as far as friends could tell, indulgent of David's fantasies. Nonetheless, David finally caved in to the pressure to get a "proper" job, and Owen Frampton used his connections with the commercial-arts sector to find him a position as a runner and pasteup artist at the New Bond Street office of Nevin D. Hirst, a small Yorkshire-based ad agency.

The sole nine-to-five job of David Jones's life would in the future enable him to pronounce on the world of design, marketing, and manipulation as a self-styled expert; in later years he'd chat about how the advertising industry had been the prime force, alongside rock and roll, in shaping the latter half of the twentieth century—the fact he'd worked "as an illustrator in advertising" became a key component of his self-image. Yet as he admits, his involvement with the industry was brief: "I loathed [it]. I had romantic visions of artists' garrets—though I didn't fancy starving. Their main product was Ayds slimming biscuits, and I also remember lots of felt-tip drawings and pasteups of bloody raincoats. And in the evening I dodged from one dodgy rock band to another."

Although his commitment to the job was faint, David was lucky to have a hip boss, Ian, an indulgent, Chelsea-booted, crop-haired blues fan who sent David on errands to the celebrated Dobell's Jazz Record Shop, ten minutes' walk away, on Charing Cross Road. This was the mother lode of hip blues, the place Eric Clapton shopped for obscure imports that he then replicated, astounding audiences, who figured that Eric had invented the riffs he'd actually lifted from Albert King and Buddy Guy. David embarked on a similar search for source material; Ian suggested he pick up John Lee Hooker's *Country Blues* album, and David spotted Bob Dylan's debut on the racks too. "Within weeks George and I had changed the name of our little R&B outfit to 'The Hooker Brothers,' and included both Hooker's 'Tupelo' and Dylan's 'House of the Rising Sun' in our set."

The pair were so carried away with enthusiasm that they started playing shows as a trio with drummer Viv Andrews before they'd even gotten a proper band together. Billed as the Hooker Brothers, or sometimes as David's Red and Blues (a druggie reference to the mods' favorite barbiturate pills), they guested between sets at the Bromel Club in the Bromley Court Hotel. Today, as Underwood admits, the notion of two kids from Bromley reinventing themselves as Mississippi bluesmen seems ludicrous — "but it was something we needed to get out of our system!" David's first compliment from an "experienced" musician came from those early shows, when the Hooker Brothers shared a bill with jazzman Mike Cotton at the Bromel Club. It was a brief performance, sandwiched between the two halves of the Mike Cotton Sound's trad jazz–influenced set. "Well done," the venerable twenty-six-year-old congratulated the wannabe bluesmen after their set, "you must be very brave."

Brave they seemed in the autumn of 1963 when they played several brief shows at the Bromel. Yet by December, when the Rolling Stones cracked the Top 20 with "I Wanna Be Your Man," a tiny nucleus of British musicians was about to refashion British rock and roll. Two bands emerged in the Stones' wake—the Yardbirds, who'd taken over the Stones' Crawdaddy residence, and the Pretty Things, whose Dick Taylor had played with Keith Richards in an early version of the Stones. By December, the Pretties were known around the Bromley scene, thanks to Dorothy Bass, David's schoolmate (and, briefly, George's girlfriend), who owned a car and was therefore recruited as the Pretties' roadie.

With the sense that they were about to catch a wave, David and George stepped up their efforts to form a full band; it was David who spotted a classified ad in *Melody Maker* from a Fulham outfit seeking a singer. That trio—guitarist Roger Bluck, bassist Dave Howard, and drummer Robert Allen—were, in truth, more in tune with the spirit of Chet Atkins than Muddy Waters, but Jones and Underwood both joined and worked on "roughen[ing] them up." Their set was based on songs that countless Brit blues boomers would cover: Elmore James's "Early One Morning" and

Howlin' Wolf's "Spoonful" and "Howlin' for My Baby." The band's name came from another blues classic, Slim Harpo's "[I'm a] King Bee."

For the King Bees' tiny audience—perhaps a couple of dozen local kids—the group was a torchbearer for a new music: "This was a completely different animal from Sonny Boy Williamson's blues," says Dorothy Bass. "That was where it came from—this was where it was going. People like us were taking something old, forgotten, and used it to create a new sound, something that spoke to us."

Bass was probably the King Bees' closest follower, hanging out with them at Wimpy bars, coffee shops, parties, and gigs. She knew David well; he was likable, cheerful, enthusiastic, but almost bland and boring in his single-mindedness: "All he wanted to do was practice, and listen to tapes or records that he'd got hold of. That was his life. Everybody regarded themselves as an expert in music—but he really was. What made him different was he would pass a party, or anything, up if there was something he needed to do for his music. For the other kids, that was inconceivable."

For David, the lesson of the Kon-Rads ran deep: he was convinced that finding new, hip music before the competition did was the key to success. His view of how this could be achieved was simplistic. When he and George discovered Bob Dylan's debut album at Dobell's, David remembers how "we added drums to 'House of the Rising Sun,' thinking we'd made some kind of musical breakthrough. We were gutted when the Animals released the song to stupendous reaction." The Animals, of course, had learned their trade playing night after night at Newcastle's Club A'Gogo; David would never pay his dues in such a yeoman fashion. For a start, although he, rather than George, had taken on the role of lead singer, he was reticent as a front man. When Dorothy Bass was roped in to drive the Pretty Things to their shows in southeast London, David would often come up and chat to singer Phil May and the band's founder, Dick Taylor, who says, "We did like him. Skinny little blond fella. Though I don't think I ever saw him sing."

As a singer, skinny and likable was about it: "He was very self-contained," says Bass, who saw most of the King Bees' shows. "I didn't think he reached out to the audience very much; maybe he was concentrating on what he was singing. He didn't actually seem sexy to me. George was gorgeous...I wouldn't say I dismissed David; he was blond, he was okay, but I didn't see him as a sex symbol. There was no interacting or giving anything to the audience. Not that that bothered us. They were people onstage, our age, and that's all that mattered."

Onstage, David hadn't mastered the swagger of contemporaries like Mick Jagger and Phil May. Offstage, though, he was a natural—a hustler. He was aided by his father, who by then had worked in PR for nearly a decade, and David had an innate understanding of the fact that a hustler loves another hustler. For this reason, the letter that helped him secure the release of his debut single became better known than the single itself.

History would have it that David Bowie grew up estranged from his parents. Peggy certainly became irritated by his musical ambitions, given that David was firmly attached to the family purse strings for years; at the time, youths were expected to graduate from school and then hold down steady jobs for decades, so her intolerance would have been shared by most parents. Haywood's reaction was more complex: he was conventional, but indulgent. He and David were more alike than many realized— calm, often kind in a distinctively low-key way, but both with a nervous fizziness, the most obvious sign of which was Haywood's chain-smoking (which David soon imitated, to the extent of using the same brand, Player's Weights). There was the conventional generation gap between father and son—one familiar to many of David's friends, several of whom had absent or dead fathers—yet Haywood's youthful obsession with the entertainment world had not been entirely extinguished. Hence it was Haywood and David who, in January of 1964, came up with a "concocted" sales pitch for David's new band. Shameless, "over the top," according to George Underwood, Haywood and David's joint concoction would kick off David's career.

Around Christmas 1963, David noticed several news stories

devoted to John Bloom, an aggressive entrepreneur who'd blazed a famously fiery trail through Britain's cozy old-fashioned household-appliance industry, starting with washing machines, then moving on to dishwashers and refrigerators. He seemed to have a financial golden touch, and father and son typed a letter suggesting he put his golden touch to work in the most up-and-coming industry of all, pop music. "If you can sell my group the way you sell washing machines," David suggested, "you'll be on to a winner."

Before sending the letter, David showed it to George—who protested. "His dad helped him concoct the letter—and it *was* concocted in that it said things like that famous quote 'Brian Epstein's got the Beatles and you should have us.'" Undeterred, David assured him, "Don't worry. It will be all right." His instincts were on the money. Bloom, amused by the youngster's chutzpah, passed the letter on to Les Conn, a friend from the Jewish scene in Stamford Hill. Within a couple of days, a telegram arrived at David's house instructing him to call Conn's Temple Bar number.

It was a lucky happenstance. Invariably described as a small-time manager, Les Conn was in fact neither small time nor a manager. His connections were impeccable and included Beatles publisher Dick James, movie star Doris Day, and emerging music moguls Mickie Most and Shel Talmy; he played vital roles in advancing the careers of the Shadows, Clodagh Rodgers, and the Bachelors. However, to describe him as a manager would be to imply some degree of organization or the ability to oversee a career, qualities that were noticeable by their absence in this charming, supremely scattered man.

Bob Solly, who also met Les that spring, remembers the aspiring mogul proclaiming, "Conn's the name, con's the game!" before showing off his credentials in the form of a suitcase full of parking tickets he was hoping to evade. A short, slightly pudgy bundle of energy, he'd shoot out rapid-fire yarns and schemes in a cheeky, vaguely posh voice, often punctuated by sudden pauses as he searched for the vital document or press cutting he'd been brandishing just a few seconds earlier.

Conn epitomized the charming amateurism of the British music scene in 1964. He had set up Melcher Music UK for Doris Day before being recruited by Beatles publisher Dick James as a song plugger. He was a moderately successful publisher, a dreadful songwriter—and a genius at spotting talent, for over the next few months he would take up both the future David Bowie and the future Marc Bolan, giving both of them their first career breaks.

Bloom had asked Conn to check out the King Bees to see to whether it was worth booking them, cheaply of course, for his upcoming wedding-anniversary party, on February 12, 1964. Conn remembers the King Bees playing in his flat. "They were a nice bunch," he remembers. "It wasn't commercial music they played, it was underground, really. But David had charisma, George too." And that was enough to get them the gig.

Their debut, though, was a disaster. Some of the King Bees' blues evangelism started to desert them when they turned up at the Jack Club for the party in jeans and suede Robin Hood boots and noticed disapproving looks from the moneyed crowd, which included Sir Isaac Wolfson and Lord Thomson of Fleet. The King Bees were asked to follow the Naturals, a well-scrubbed Beatles cover band with a pristine back line of Vox amplifiers, which the King Bees plugged into as they launched into their opening song, "Got My Mojo Workin'." Unfortunately, David's mojo didn't work with Bloom, who sidled over to Conn and yelled, "Get them off! They're ruining my party." The King Bees shuffled from the stage, making way for the highlight of the evening, a duet between rocker Adam Faith and armed forces sweetheart Vera Lynn. "David did cry when I told him to leave the stage," says Conn, "but I said to him, Don't worry, one person was impressed—and that was me."

Conn would become David Bowie's first champion in the music business, and a few weeks later he pulled up in his Jaguar outside Plaistow Grove for a meeting with David's parents, who needed to cosign their seventeen-year-old son's management contract. Peggy, Conn noted, was the chattier of the two; Haywood was "friendly—but very serious, a civil-servant type." Both parents were surprised, and impressed, that just a few months into his career, David had signed with the self-styled mogul who had connections to the Beatles. Conn assured them it would take him little time to conjure up a record deal and that David was on the brink of the big time.

David, however, showed no surprise at all; he boasted a bright-eyed teenage confidence and reacted to every break as if it were his by right. Years later, he'd claim that much of this apparent confidence was bravado and that he suffered from low self-esteem. Some of this seems to be fashionable therapy-speak, for in real life—chatting up girls, greeting a roomful of strangers, and walking into a recording studio—he had confidence that was unshakable. In later years he'd learn to be more subtle, offsetting this confidence with a charming, flirtatious bashfulness, but the seventeen-year-old David Jones seemed almost ruthless in his self-promotion. Enthusiastic, receptive, with an often brilliant sense of deadpan humor, he was also, say observers like Les Conn, "brash." "He was sure he was going to be big. But the charm came later as he got more success."

David's attitude was exactly like that of another aspiring singer Conn met later that year at Denmark Street's La Gioconda coffee bar: Mark Feld, who at this point had yet to metamorphose into Marc Bolan. The two were, says Conn, "very similar. They totally believed in themselves, both of them. It was me that brought the two of them together, and they both had exactly the same attitude, which was, We are going to make it." The two would practice their far-fetched stories on each other, both becoming masters of bullshit, as David fondly recalls. "Marc was very much the mod, and I was sort of neo-beat-hippy... So there's me and this mod. And he goes, 'Where d'you get those shoes, man? Where d'you get your shirt?' We immediately started talking about clothes and sewing machines. 'Oh I'm gonna be a singer and I'm gonna be so big you're not gonna believe it, man.' 'Oh, right! Well I'll probably write a musical for you one day then, cos I'm gonna be the greatest writer ever.'" The pair shared a talent for rabid self-promotion and an unabashed flirtatiousness with both men and women. David's confidence was always tempered by his interest in people and how they ticked; Marc was far more abrasive. Over the next decade, their careers became intertwined; friends, like the DJ and scenester Jeff Dexter, described them as "like brothers." Each took pride in, and was sometimes tortured by jealousy of, the other's achievements. At the outset, their relationship revolved around trading grandiose fantasies in La Gioconda over cups of coffee cadged from Les Conn.

Over the summer, Conn used his contacts to arrange David's band's first West End gigs, including one at the Roundhouse. When it came to sorting out publishing and record deals, he stayed close to home. Dick James Music looked after the publishing, while Conn used his freelance A and R role at Decca to schedule a session at the company's studios in Broadhurst Gardens, West Hampstead. For the record's A-side, the band members were presented with an acetate of a song by Paul Revere and the Raiders, "Louie, Louie Go Home"—published, naturally, by Dick James Music. "We were simply given the single and told to learn it," says Underwood, adding that in the hurried production process the band "soon started to feel like cogs in a machine." The musicians were left to arrange their own B-side, for which David and George reworked the traditional folk song "Little Liza Jane," modifying the lyrics and adding a guitar line borrowed from Howlin' Wolf's "Smokestack Lightning": "It took around fifteen minutes, sitting in my mum's kitchen," says Underwood. "The big influence was Huey 'Piano' Smith's version."

The recording was brisk, the standard three-hour session. Underwood was nervous; David was unflappable. "You'd better get used to this!" he told the others, and when it came time for him to do the singing, with the rest of the band adding backup vocals, there was not a hint of nerves: "He was very confident. Certain he was going to make it," says Conn.

Yet it became obvious he wasn't going to make it with this record.

There have been few recording debuts as undistinguished as

that of David Bowie. Both sides of the single plodded along in drearily conventional beat-boom fashion. On "Liza Jane," the wonderful energy and sprightliness of Huey Smith's famous song was bowdlerized; where Huey's song was simple, the King Bees' version was trite. David's voice was horribly generic, a John Lennon wannabe with a phony London accent. The single sounded like exactly what it was: a rushed attempt to cash in on the emerging blues boom without any of the zest or attitude of the Stones or the Animals. Conn had to call in all his favors to get Decca to even release the single, which came out on their revived Vocalion label — "Peter Stevens, who was in charge of releases, didn't rate it at all," says Conn, who nonetheless got to work exploiting all his contacts for radio and jukebox play and overseeing a press release extolling the "action-packed disc which features the direct no-holds-barred Davie Jones vocal delivery!"

Conn's press release didn't mention the other King Bees. It also revealed that the single had been flipped to make "Liza Jane" the A-side; another surprise for the band was the writing credit on "Liza Jane," which was assigned to Les Conn. Conn remained adamant that he had written the song, pointing out that "if I had done that to David, why would he have continued to work with me?" Yet his recollections of the writing were vague; for instance, his suggestion that the song title "maybe came from a girl David was going out with." Although today David says he can't remember anything about how the song was written, Underwood's story of how "Liza Jane" was cooked up in his mum's kitchen from a Huey Smith recipe is the one that rings true. But as George explains, "We didn't want to rock the boat, and figured if Les wanted a piece of the action, he could have it." Ironically, Conn's manipulation of the songwriting credits prevented Dick James Music, which famously owned the Beatles' songs, from securing an option on the future David Bowie's material too.

JUNE of 1964 was the high point of the King Bees' brief existence. David and George spent most of it hanging out in Bromley, talking music and sipping coffees or being bought drinks at

Henekey's wine bar on High Street, while the rest of the King Bees remained in Fulham. There was a show at Justin Hall in West Wickham on June 5 to mark the record's official release date, and there were parties throughout the week. Then on Friday, June 19, David Jones returned with his band to the Rediffusion studio—the scene of his humiliation with the Kon-Rads—to celebrate the sweet victory of his TV debut, on *Ready Steady Go!* They devoured the experience like the teenagers they were, overawed by the Crickets—who woke up briefly from a jetlag-inspired sleep to acknowledge George's excited remarks that he'd witnessed their 1958 show at the Elephant and Castle's Trocadero cinema—*Sirch.*—and by John Lee Hooker, who was in a nearby dressing room to record another Rediffusion show. "I've seen him close up!" David breathlessly informed George, "go and look at those hands, those fingers!" The King Bees' performance passed in a flurry of excitement—and then passed into oblivion.

During the next few days, David and George basked in their temporary fame, wearing new mohair suits and playing more shows. But George and David sat in the South Bromley Wimpy bar scouring that week's *Melody Maker,* and it became obvious that "Liza Jane" was not going to trouble the charts.

For George Underwood, the release of "Liza Jane" was "an achievement in itself." But for David—who had been singing for less than a year, whose voice was mediocre, and who had yet to write a song on his own—this wasn't good enough. There had been some talk about David or George joining another band even before the single was released, yet George was shocked by the way his old school friend simply announced one day in July: "I've decided to break the band up—and I've found another band."

The guitarist was devastated. "At the time it was something like, You bastard! Are you just gonna leave us in the lurch?" Only later did he realize that David had been sounding out how committed he was for some months. "I was ambitious in my head—but not like he was ambitious. He'd decided to throw everything into it." In later years, he'd read about other ambitious types, such as Neil Young, recognizing the same brutality with which they dropped approaches or bands that didn't work and realizing that it made sense: "What's the point of sticking with it if it's not working?"

For George, being in a band was a passion, one to be shared with his friends. Discovering that David had an entirely different agenda was a shock. Just as striking was how unapologetic George's bandmate was—indeed, there was a kind of purity about his attitude; David's selfishness was cheerful, instinctive, almost childlike in its lack of malevolence. George was one of the first, but not the last, to hear what would become a guiding philosophy: "Numero uno, mate!"

CHAPTER 3

Thinking about Me

There'd be six girls at the front, and half a dozen of us queens at unable to read *the back... hanging on his every move.* Pop Music Time

—Simon White

L
ONDON 1964 HAS BEEN immortalized in popular history as swinging, racy, its joyous heart beating to the throb of Jaguar engines and pill-popping mod anthems, buzzing with the illicit thrills of cheap sex and gangster cool. In reality, this glorious state of affairs was confined to the tiniest group of insiders. David Jones was one of them. That fateful year, David Jones sashayed confidently into the epicenter of swinging London, hanging out with the scene's hippest stars, participating in the shag-tastic promiscuity, convincing many he had more right to be there than they had. Within a year, he had become a leading face in the scene, distinguished in every respect except one—his music.

The nerve with which the seventeen-year-old engineered his next career move illustrated perfectly how he worked. On July 19, 1964, he walked into the smoke-filled living room of a suburban semi in Coxheath and confused its occupants, a Kent six-piece called the Manish Boys, who'd been expecting to see a different David Jones, a black American singing GI who they hoped would give their horn-heavy blues vital grit and credibility. They were surprised when, accompanied by the fast-talking Les Conn, a blond, skinny, suede-booted youth entered through the sliding glass doors. They were even more surprised about half an hour later to find they'd hired him as their singer.

The Manish Boys worked more closely with David than any outfit right up to the Spiders from Mars. It was with them that he first attracted notice as a singer; it was likewise with them that he discovered the cornucopia of sexual options available in a country eagerly unshackling itself from the prurience and dreariness of the fifties. Together they crafted a horn-driven, versatile R & B based on one of David's musical obsessions at the time, Sounds Incorporated, and together they made David's first decent record. Their achievements were all the more surprising considering that their first meeting was so sketchy.

After their disappointment at the realization that the "skinny white kid" was from Bromley, the Manish Boys had only the briefest conversation with him. Les insisted on playing them the King Bees' single, which was, after the buildup he gave it, "disappointing. But David wasn't," says keyboardist Bob Solly. "He was a good lively personality, an obvious showman. And he looked good." The band's leaders, Solly and sax player Paul Rodriguez, ultimately decided to recruit their new singer because they liked his clothing and — hilariously — appreciated his punctuality. As Solly points out, "His appearance struck us more than anything. And the fact he was reliable. Ninety percent of people who join bands should be working in a cupboard somewhere on their own — because they have no idea about working with other people. From that first meeting, David was absolutely spot-on punctual — like he was working in a theater. And theater people, however bizarre they are, tend to be very, very punctual."

For all his love of anarchic rock and rollers, David Jones was an old-fashioned trouper with a sense of style and a sense of timing. The new kid fitted right in with the Manish Boys, for they too were troupers. They were mostly, like David, only children, "hence more pushy," says Solly, "because we only had ourselves to think about," filled with a childlike obsession with music, which for all of them represented an escape from the austerity of their upbringing.

The band revolved round Solly and Rodriguez, both three years older than David. John Watson played bass and sang. Guitarist Johnny Flux joined the band two weeks before David and was another natural-born hustler; he had previously sold newspaper advertising space (and went on to create kids' TV robot Metal Mickey). Woolf Byrne, on baritone sax, drove and maintained the band's rickety Bedford van, while drummer Mick Whitehead had been persuaded to walk out of his job as an apprentice barber to join the band.

During that first meeting, the band members were impressed by David's statement that he was writing his own numbers, although they spotted that his only song, "Don't Try to Stop Me," was a straight lift from Marvin Gaye. David was up-front about suggesting new material, most notably from James Brown's *Live at the Apollo;* the Manish Boys' set soon included material by Ray Charles ("What'd I Say"), Solomon Burke ("Stupidity"), and even Conway Twitty ("Make Me Know You're Mine"), and in August they hit the road with their new singer.

A couple of the Manish Boys, including Woolf Byrne, had been unimpressed by the new recruit. Yet during that autumn's shows around England's south, playing to audiences ranging from a couple of dozen to a couple of hundred, Woolf began observing something curious: "I had thought that Johnny's voice was better—deeper and growlier. Then we realized, very soon, that when John sang the kids kept on dancing and behaving the way they did before. When David sang a number they stopped to look."

Byrne observed how bit by bit, Davy started using the microphone, getting close up to it when singing in a soft, Dylanesque drawl, and pulling back for a James Brown–style squeal. He sang with an English accent rather than a fake American drawl. As they racked up more shows, the band members noticed that Jones's delivery became more powerful—occasionally he was so carried away by the music that he smashed the maracas he used on "Bo Diddley" into the mike stand. Eventually, Bob Solly got into the habit of bringing a small knife with him to pry the mara- cas' little ball bearings from the keys of his Vox Continental organ. "Then I realized he had changed us completely," says Woolf. "We used to simply stand onstage and play; that changed, then the music we played was different, then our dress became different as well." "It was simple enough, what he did," says Paul Rodriguez. "He simply knew how to grab a microphone and perform."

Those first months with the Manish Boys were confused, care- free, rarely boring. The band shared one another's clothes, sleep- ing on friends' floors while mooching off their parents for food, shelter, and cash. Over this summer, David redesigned his life. He quit his job at Nevin D. Hirst and seemed to base his new image on the Beat novels he was reading. He was the most nomadic of the group; the others might stay away from home for a day, but he would bum around with friends for a week. This fit in with his often-voiced love of Dylan, Jack Kerouac, and *On Being Negro in America,* one of many books he picked up in paperback at Bromley South Station. During their gigs, their practice sessions at Charlie Chester's Casino or in a warren of rooms and brothels on Windmill Street, and their socializing at the Regency Club—a hangout for the Kray twins—the Manish Boys developed an intense, jokey bond, like soldiers in a grueling campaign. Their intimacy extended to the girls who, that autumn of 1964, were omnipresent, their names and phone numbers written in pink lipstick all over the band's green Bedford van. At the end of a show, while his friends packed away amplifiers and equipment, David was out on the dance floor, chatting up his female audience—"getting in there first," as the lingo went.

In many respects, the Manish Boys' lives were identical to those of other teenagers in the first half of the twentieth century: they had few clothes; they walked for miles to see their friends, many of whom didn't own a phone; they chatted with their mums for hours over endless cups of tea, waited ages for buses, ate egg and chips in cheap "caffs." But in the most crucial respect, their lifestyles were transformed: along with music, sex became the driving force of their existence. There was a winning charm and jokiness about David's approach, but in his bandmates' opinion he became obsessive in his pursuit of women. Solly cites one time when David tried to interest him in Sue, a blonde he was attempting to cast off. "I tell you, Bob," David assured him earnestly, "she's clean as a whistle!" They were open about their sexual escapades, such as the episode when David and Johnny simultaneously shagged two sisters, alongside each other, in their Gillingham B and B, but David's friends accused him of being completely out of control at times. On their way home one foggy evening, the band members spotted a woman hitchhiking, pulled over, and let her in the van, where David sat next to her, chatting intensely. A short distance down the road, Woolf, who was at the wheel, suddenly shouted, "Eeeuurgh, what's that smell?" Realizing the woman was a vagrant, he pulled over and mercilessly insisted their passenger get out. David's annoyance, the others speculated, had nothing to do with sympathy for the homeless woman. "Would he have?" they asked one another, before responding in chorus, "Yes, he would!"

After uniting David with the Manish Boys, Les Conn declined to take his managerial cut of the band's intermittent live earnings, but he still hustled on its behalf. At the end of September he secured an audition with Mickie Most, who, in the wake of the Animals' "House of the Rising Sun," was probably the biggest independent producer in London. The band set up at one of their regular haunts, Charlie Chester's Casino on Archer Street, and then ran through a couple of numbers. As was his habit, Most made his decision on the spot and asked, "Do you want to record for me, boys?" In unison, they shouted, "Yes!"

THERE was another meeting with Mickie Most to talk through their material, on the evening before the recording session. At Regent Sound the next day, October 6, the band ran through their three songs, overseen by Decca's Mike Smith. On "Hello, Stranger," "Duke of Earl," and "Love Is Strange," David's singing was flawless—but on every take of "Love Is Strange," John Watson's and Johnny Flux's vocals were ragged and out of sync. As Smith played back the song, pointing out the problem, tension mounted—and the singers got more nervous. Except, that is, for David; he was "totally cool and calm," Solly remembers, easing the tension with deadpan jokes, not for a moment betraying any concern as they struggled for a decent take. Their three hours ran out; their big break had turned to dust. "Don't worry," David assured the others, his confidence apparently undented. "We'll get it next time."

This was the most potent sign that the band's youngest member was "mature beyond his years," as Woolf remembers. He could astutely work out the politics of a meeting well before his friends. The most notable example was when the Manish Boys auditioned at London Palladium in January of 1965, hoping for a residency at Hamburg's legendary Star Club.

The set had gone well, and Bob Solly looked on as the Star Club's promoter called David over. The two exchanged a few words and smiles before David returned to the stage.

"What did he say?" Solly asked eagerly.

"Oh, he asked me, 'Which way do you swing, Davy, boys or girls?'" David told him.

"So what did you say?"

"Oh, I told him, 'Boys,' of course!"

The story illustrated his growing talent as a hustler—and it came as no surprise when they heard the audition was a success, and they'd be booked into the Star Club over the summer. The same skills came to the fore when Woolf and Davy were nursing coffees in La Gioconda, the hip wood-paneled coffee bar in Denmark Street that was a favorite musicians' hangout, and a BBC researcher approached them to ask if their long hair had ever caused them problems. Both of them fancied a TV appearance and five-guinea fee, but it was David who came up with the idea of a League for the Protection of Animal Filament, a support group for oppressed longhairs that existed entirely in his own imagination.

That chance meeting with the researcher led to a ninety-second interview on *Tonight* with Cliff Michelmore, broadcast on November 12, 1964, that was destined to be one of David's great

TV appearances; he does such a consummate, humorous job of selling nothing. The league that this cool-as-a-cucumber youth was promoting was a convenient fiction, but everyone was in on the joke, and any prejudice the viewer might have felt at such an unashamed self-publicist was dispelled by Davy's mock complaints: "We're all fairly tolerant, but for the last two years we've had comments like 'Darlin'' and 'Can I carry your handbag' thrown at us. And it has to stop!"

The Manish Boys' other singer, John Watson, was three years older than David, with a better voice, more experience, and more education — but he was effectively invisible by comparison with his upstart colleague. Although in future years, manager Ken Pitt schooled David Bowie in how to deal with the media, this short snippet, now a YouTube classic, shows Pitt was working with a natural. Whereas Davy Jones's debut as a singer had been forgettable at best, his debut as a self-publicist was unimpeachable.

The TV slot convinced the band they were headed for the big time, a conviction reinforced when Les Conn negotiated a deal with the Arthur Howes Agency, Britain's leading promoter of package tours, for a string of dates headlined by Gene Pitney alongside Gerry and the Pacemakers, the Kinks, and Marianne Faithfull, opening on December 1. It was a cheerily intimate affair; the artists shared the same bus, which picked them all up one by one across London as they started the tour. Pitney was avuncular and good-humored, the troupe's alpha male — which, sadly, sabotaged David's attempts to chat with Marianne Faithfull, who sat alongside Gene throughout the tour, immune to David's charms. So were the Kinks, who were "hoity-toity," says Manish Boy Bob Solly, and rarely mingled. David was unoffended and promptly introduced a cover of "You Really Got Me" into the Manish Boys' set.

The tour was a perfect opportunity to try out a new number, "I Pity the Fool," picked out as the band's debut single by Shel Talmy, an American producer who shared an office building with Howes. A onetime child prodigy who'd appeared on NBC's *Quiz Kids* program, Talmy had "bullshitted" his way into the UK by claiming to have produced the Beach Boys then backed up his bullshit by producing a string of super-compressed high-energy hits for the Who and the Kinks. Shel was intrigued by the band and their singer: "Les Conn told me I should listen to this guy—and Les was right, he always had a great ear for talent."

"I Pity the Fool" was perfect for the Manish Boys' dense, horn-heavy sound—although copying the grizzled vocal on the original acetate, by Memphis bluesman Bobby Bland, was an intimidating task for a Bromley teenager. The afternoon before the session, the pressure was ratcheted up on guitarist Johnny Flux too when the band bumped into Jimmy Page—fast emerging as London's leading session guitarist—at the 2i's Coffee Bar, and Page mentioned he was playing guitar on the session and would be bringing his brand-new fuzz box with him.

For all their bullishness, the Manish Boys were nervous during the session, which took place at London's IBC studio on January 15, 1965. "But David was *certainly* not intimidated," says Talmy. "That was what I liked about him." In fact, David's singing was transformed, completely different from his forgettable debut. Confident, impassioned, with perfect microphone technique, he was a man who, like Shel Talmy, bullshitted his way into a job—and then delivered.

Clunky, naive, and all the better for it, the song became an unsung classic of British blues, a fact spotted right away by Jimmy Page. "Good session," he complimented the band as he packed away his Fender Telecaster, "but I don't think it's a hit." He softened the blow by donating a riff he'd played while warming up, telling David he was welcome to use it in one of his own songs (it turned up years later as "The Supermen"). David was already telling people about his work as a songwriter, although on the evidence of "Take My Tip," the B-side of the single, he didn't have much of a future; set to a clunky, clichéd chord sequence, distinguished only by intricate lyrics, the song was a mediocre pastiche of Georgie Fame, one of the band's current obsessions.

The run-up to the release of "I Pity the Fool," on March 5, was filled with more live dates and more plotting by the irrepressible

Les Conn, who hyped the single with his usual brio, once more stoking up the "furor" over long hair that had kicked off in November. Conn had persuaded an old friend, BBC producer Barry Langford, to feature the Manish Boys on the show *Gadzooks!* but publicly floated the fiction that the BBC had refused to allow the band into the studio until the singer cut his flowing blond locks. "I had big placards made, Let's Be Fair to Long Hair," remembers Les Conn gleefully, "and we said we'd parade around the BBC building until they relented!" The artificial controversy—which was a shameless imitation of similar media shenanigans arranged for the Pretty Things and the Rolling Stones—helped David win press in the *London Evening Standard*, the *Daily Mail*, the *Daily Telegraph*, and the *Daily Mirror*.

Despite the trumped-up controversy, the record disappeared into oblivion. The Manish Boys had hoped that "I Pity the Fool" would catapult them into the big time; instead, their live dates began to dry up, and the Star Club dates fell through, leaving a huge gap in their schedule. There were arguments about billing; Davy, who invariably had the shows around Bromley advertised as "Davy Jones and the Manish Boys," expected the single to be released under the same banner. Solly maintains it was a shortage of cash, rather than arguments about the name, that dealt the deathblow; the band's van, their most vital asset, broke down, and Woolf had already left when the band's split was finally announced in the *Kent Messenger* in April. "We were dragging it out," says Solly, "but we'd all had enough."

The slow death of the Manish Boys was made more painful for David by the runaway success of his friend George Underwood. Les Conn had continued hustling for George, whom he considered "just as talented as David. And really, he was a much nicer guy, he didn't have that 'I'm the cat's whiskers' [mentality]." Les had taken both George and David to see Mickie Most, and it turned out that Mickie "simply liked George better." Most treated Underwood almost like a son, driving him around town in his Rolls-Royce, advising him on life, money, and the music business before deciding he needed a more glamorous name. Underwood was therefore given the nom de rock of Calvin James, after Mickie's son Calvin, and was treated like a star every time he dropped into the RAK office. David did not take his friend's success well. Every time they bumped into each other on Bromley High Street, George felt David looking at him "like daggers."

The last few Manish Boys shows were riotous; at Cromer on March 13, Davy and Johnny Flux, who'd started camping it up together more and more after their Gillingham escapade, were banned from the venue. Their final show was at Bletchley on April 24; the band returned to Maidstone on their own, since David disappeared with a fan who was hosting a party in town. There were no formal good-byes; the next time Solly and Rodriguez saw David was in Shel Talmy's office building, where he was obviously planning something new.

It turned out David had an exit strategy in place. And this time, there would be no doubt about whose name would get top billing.

THE Lower Third had formed in 1964 in Margate, a bustling Regency resort on the edge of Kent, a lively holiday destination with its tea dances and donkey rides and old-fashioned traditional sideshows complete with headless lady. After propping up the bills at a bunch of local shows, guitarist Denis Taylor, drummer Les Mighall, and bassist Graham Rivens decided it was time to turn professional. Leaving pianist Terry Boulton and guitarist Robin Wyatt behind, they decided to head for the bright lights; they packed supplies of food and toilet paper in their converted ambulance and they rented a flat in Pimlico, in central London.

The three had been hanging out around Denmark Street for only a week or so when they had their first sight of the young David Jones in La Gioconda. "Blimey, I thought," says Denis Taylor, "there goes Keith Relf of the Yardbirds!" The band had put out word they needed a singer and arranged auditions at La Discotheque on Wardour Street, a regular haunt where they'd played as a five-piece: "But the funny thing was, he came along with an alto sax, so we thought he was a saxophonist."

David had brought moral support in the form of singer Stevie

Marriott, whom David had first met at a Manish Boys rehearsal earlier that year. A jam session followed, based around a funky version of Little Richard's "Rip It Up." "Stevie was great," remembers Taylor, "probably a better singer than David."

Then, puzzlingly, Stevie left and David took the microphone, sounding "exactly like Keith Relf" on the Yardbirds' "I Wish You Would." Soon he'd convinced the Lower Third of his impeccable connections: "He told us a few tricks of the trade—I got the impression that Shel had taught him a lot. And he looked amazing. So we decided to get him in."

The meeting took place just as the Manish Boys were falling apart, depressed at their failure. There was no hint of this in David's demeanor—in fact, his confidence had increased. In both the King Bees and the Manish Boys, Davy Jones had shared the singing and the leadership of the band. With the Lower Third, the eighteen-year-old took creative control, pushing Taylor, who was three years older, to learn new songs as well as assist with David's own compositions. A cornerstone of their live set was a cranked-up version of the Yardbirds' take on "I Wish You Would"; David aped Keith Relf's vocal style—he'd started playing the harmonica too, for an even better carbon copy. Other obvious influences were the Kinks, whose "All Day and All of the Night" was also pressed into service, and the Who. In his first few months with the Lower Third, David saw both groups several times and pressured Taylor to adopt a similar bombastic guitar sound: "That was a learning curve, that was." Taylor shudders today at the thought of it.

True to form, David penned a press release within a few weeks of joining the band, detailing how the new group, Davie Jones and the Lower Third, featured "TEA-CUP on lead, DEATH on bass and LES on drums." The one-page document was the first evidence of the new spelling of his name; it reminded its readers of "the legendary Banned Hair tale" and promised another appearance on *Gadzooks!* plus a new single, "Born of the Night," "destined to rush up the charts." (The song was a demo, cobbled together at a friend's rehearsal space.)

Now that he'd taken over leadership of a band, David seemed

liberated; there was an irrepressible energy about the way he'd throw himself into a project. Just eight or ten weeks after securing his first songwriting credit with "Take My Tip," Davie was describing himself as a songwriter, dropping in at Shel's studio to demo material and submitting songs to other performers (he'd had his first song covered, thanks to Leslie Conn, who'd arranged a Kenny Miller recording of "Take My Tip" in February). Most of those early songs were dreadful, but he kept submitting them; stylistically they veered from Dylan imitations to Gene Pitney knockoffs. Talmy noticed David "sounded like lots of different people at different times," and that much of the material was "not great" — still, there was something about David that he liked; as many people were, he was attracted to David's "energy," the way he kept coming up with ideas. Whereas George Underwood would get depressed by setbacks, David seemed untouched by them; the fleeting taste of success he'd enjoyed so far simply fed his appetite for more. Today, he points out how such setbacks "never, ever" made him feel pessimistic, "because I still liked the process. I liked writing and recording — it was a lot of fun for a kid. I might have had moments of, 'God, I don't think anything is ever going to happen for me.' But I would bounce up pretty fast."

As David spent more time in the West End around Denmark Street, he started to hang out at the FD&H publishing house and record shop on Charing Cross Road, strumming on guitars or chatting with shop manager Wayne Bardell; the two became friends. Bardell had accompanied David to the first Manish Boys recording date, and, like the Manish Boys, he noticed David was "very confident, without being arrogant — this was not a person who got stressed." He watched David progress from being a part of the band with the Manish Boys to being the leader of the Lower Third. Then one day, David came in, sat down behind the counter, and made a "very curious" remark. "It was, you know, 'Wayne? When I'm famous I'm not gonna speak to anybody — not even the band.' It was a strange thing to say — it stuck in my head." Only then did he reflect how David was always "friendly. But I suppose he was never really giving much away."

A few weeks after David teamed up with the Lower Third, drummer Les Mighall went back to Margate for the weekend and never returned. David located new drummer Phil Lancaster, who helped complete the band's transformation to a cranked-up, super-violent style heavily influenced by the Who, a sound honed during the band's busy summer spent gigging in Margate and other southeast resorts.

It was a blissful period for the band and Davie, working on songs and hanging out together in their London flat, at Plaistow Grove, or in Margate. Davie seemed a natural band member, up for a laugh, knowing when to joke around and when to snap into focus. And on the side, he and Denis worked on commercials for Youthquake Clothing and Puritan, both cooked up and recorded in their Who-influenced style at R. G. Jones studio in Wimbledon, where David made most of his demos through 1966.

In retrospect, it's slightly bizarre that Talmy, who'd helped define the sound of the Who and the Kinks, should have produced an unashamed pastiche of his own work in the form of "You've Got a Habit of Leaving," David's next single. The song spliced the two-chord trick of "My Generation" with the languid melody of "Tired of Waiting for You." Worse still, David had abandoned the vocal distinctiveness he was reaching for on "I Pity the Fool." Only in the final seconds does the single take off, as Denis Taylor smashes into a heavy rolling three-chord sequence and the rest of the band freaks out. But those final moments too are a rip-off, copied almost note for note from the Who's "Anyway, Anyhow, Anywhere."

The single, according to legend, featured Les Conn's singing on its flip side the Herman's Hermits pastiche "Baby Loves That Way." In fact, Conn says he didn't attend the session — nor did the single benefit from his consummate schmoozing skills, and it promptly disappeared without a trace. By this point, Les was disenchanted with the music business; he'd subsidized Davie and Mark Feld for months, his only payback the time the two of them painted his office "in a shitty green color. And it didn't look very good." Les had also helped Mark score a singles deal with Decca for "The Wizard" that November. It met with as little success as David's efforts: "I was going broke looking after them. And I was getting very depressed with the music business—so I had to say good-bye."

With by now familiar resourcefulness, David had a replacement in mind, another regular at La Gioconda named Ralph Horton. Horton became a crucial figure over the next year. There was never any doubt about his commitment—"He would have done anything to further David's career," says John Hutchinson, who worked with him, "so he could have made a good manager." Yet Horton's time with David was dominated by troubles with money and disputes with David's musicians, who, like Denis Taylor, "didn't like Ralph from the start." Bassist Graham Rivens is even more vehement: "I hated him. It wasn't just the fact he was a fuckin' poofta—I hated everything about him."

Ralph Horton was in his late twenties, but the slightly pudgy, invariably stressed-out manager seemed older, despite the rock-and-roll affectation of black leather gloves in combination with dark suit, dark shirt, and black-framed Buddy Holly specs. Horton had grown up in Handsworth, just outside Birmingham, where his family ran a butcher shop. By 1964, he'd built up the Ralph John Agency with John Singer, booking local acts, including the Tuxedos and Denny Laine, who was then with the Diplomats. When Denny Laine and the Moody Blues moved to London, Horton came with them, and in 1965 he was working as a booking agent at the Kings Agency at 7 Denmark Street, next door to La Gioconda.

Horton appeared on the scene just as David's progress hit another road bump; EMI was pressuring Shel Talmy, who had enough on his plate with the Kinks and the Who, to terminate David's singles deal. "David was good, but not great," says the producer. "He was going to get better but wasn't in the same league as Pete Townshend and Ray Davies. And EMI simply felt the market wasn't buying it." The split was amicable. David seemed unconcerned, for Horton assured him he could drum up another deal. Even so, the aspiring manager did sense his own limitations, for on September 15, Horton called a well-known publicist named Ken Pitt to discuss involving him in David's management. Pitt explained he was too busy to take on another client; he also suggested that Davie Jones's name was a problem. Pitt already knew of the David Jones who went on to join the Monkees as well as the South London war poet and painter of the same name.

Horton would not give up on Pitt and continued to call him. He also took seriously Pitt's reservations about David's name. It turned out David had an alternative in mind. He had already tried on different names for size, including his David Jay nom de saxophone, and during his Kon-Rads period, he had seen the movie *The Alamo* and become obsessed with the character played by Richard Widmark: Jim Bowie. "He called himself Bowie at least once in the dressing room," says Kon-Rads drummer David Hadfield, "and started dressing in this tasseled leather jacket." The day after their first telephone conversation, Horton wrote to Pitt telling him his protégé would henceforth be known as David Bowie. All those involved were enthusiastic about the new name, although it would, of course, generate arguments about its pronunciation in playgrounds and high school classrooms for the next decade. David always pronounced the name to rhyme with *Snowy*, Tintin's faithful terrier, but his northern colleagues, like Mick Ronson, pronounced the *Bow* part to rhyme with *plow*.

The new name epitomized David's fantasies of glamour and stardom and also helped consign his earlier, failed single to history. Mark Feld, who recorded his debut single at Decca studio two, followed his example. By the time "The Wizard" was released, on November 19, 1965, Mark Feld had christened himself Marc Bolan and concocted, with Les Conn's encouragement, an engagingly ludicrous press release about a wizard-inspired trip to Paris. Friends and rivals, David and Marc kept close tabs on each other's progress.

Throughout that summer and autumn, Horton put his contacts to good use, booking repeat appearances for David at the Marquee and the 100 Club, a run of shows in Bournemouth, where the band was already building a following, and on the Isle of Wight. The shows saw the band at its peak. "Brilliant," says

Taylor. "They were really good," says John Hutchinson, "a proper band." David and the Lower Third shared bills with the Pretty Things, Gene Vincent, and the Who (whose Pete Townshend asked David and the band, "Shit, was that one of my songs you just played?"). The Lower Third often drew a better response than the guest stars and built up a rapport with most of them, sailing out on the Isle of Wight ferry every week, sharing a tiny trailer, and hanging out on the beach. Horton's contacts with the Marquee helped score them a string of shows on Saturday mornings at the club, playing live in support of guest artists like the Kinks and Stevie Wonder, who would lip-synch to their own records that were then broadcast on Radio London, complete with audience applause. The optimistic mood brightened further with a trip to Paris in November for dates at the Club Drouot.

Between shows, David worked on songs, often with the whole band crammed into his bedroom at Plaistow Grove. Today, David voices the insecurities that he would never admit back then. "I didn't know how to write a song — I wasn't particularly good at it. I had no natural talents whatsoever...and the only way I could learn was to see how other people did it. I wasn't one of those people who came dancing out of the womb like Marc — I was stumbling around," he says. But he was persistent, struggling to build a basic musical vocabulary, humming lines and tunes that Denis Taylor had to interpret, varying the chords until he and David found one that they liked. It was slow work, like feeling their way through a maze in the dark. David "wanted the music done straightaway — but he was very patient, too," says Taylor, "and this would go on for days." On "You've Got a Habit of Leaving," David had simply told Denis to move his hand up and down the fret board. Now they added new tricks, ninths, sevenths, and minor chords, which brought a complexity to David's material: "Some of it was morbid. Quite miserable." During these extended writing sessions through the end of 1965, David worked on "The London Boys," a vignette of pill-popping boys dressed in their finery that was obviously influenced by the wistful feel of some of Ray Davies's songs, such as "See My Friends."

A little clunky in places—which only added to its charm—"The London Boys" was an anthem for a new generation of kids, an obvious ancestor of Bowie epics like "Lady Stardust" and "All the Young Dudes": a celebration of otherness, right down to the clothing, the hint of homoeroticism, and the evocation of Judy Garland in its "too late now, 'cos you're on the run" climax. Its combination of world-weariness and naïveté embodies the persona that David would inhabit for a decade or more: a man-child—a strangely calm and mature youth, and a waiflike, childishly earnest adult. In future years, David Bowie's androgyny would be widely—and justifiably—celebrated, but this man-child aura was an important part of his personal, often devastating charm.

"The London Boys" was a harbinger of another typical Bowie technique—hitching a ride on a youth movement while simultaneously distancing himself from it. In the mod scene, as in others, David was a latecomer, trailing behind pioneers like Marc Bolan, who'd made his mark back in September of 1962 via a seven-page feature in *Town* magazine shot by celebrated war photographer Don McCullin. Late he may have been, but David was instantly accepted by mod pioneers like Jeff Dexter, the DJ and leading face who'd been comparing lapels and partings with Marc Bolan for years: "I checked out David at the Bromel Club in 1964; he was sharp." Marc's and David's obsession with clothes cemented their relationship; together, they ventured down Carnaby Street looking for reject garments in the bins outside the stores.

More significant, for just a few weeks, David joined forces with the band that would become the leading light of the mod movement. In the days following his Lower Third audition, David had continued hanging out with Steve Marriott at La Gioconda, and when Marriott teamed up with the future Small Faces, David sat in on their rehearsals and helped them haul their gear around. For the first couple of shows he guested on vocals. "He was great," says drummer Kenney Jones. "He was absolutely one of us. A wonderful mod, with a great hairdo, a great personality, and a great look—really cared about his image." Over this period, David became a "fifth Small Face." Yet he would never mention this intriguing collaboration with the Small Faces, which foundered thanks to the problem that had plagued most of his efforts, namely, his shameless imitation of others' styles. "We were not into protest songs," says Jones, "and David was. In the end, we decided he was too Dylanish."

The band's rejection was presumably a crushing blow, for David never mentioned it to any of his confidants. To this day, says Jones, who of course went on to play with both the Faces and the Who, "I still think about David, personally, and hang on to those memories of our misspent youth." Although David never publicized his involvement with the Small Faces, he remained respectful of Stevie Marriott, who, propelled by his glorious voice and his songwriting partnership with bassist Ronnie Lane, achieved the fame for which David yearned.

Despite such setbacks, Bowie's brief career as a mod was crucial, for the youth movement established all the essential principles with which he outraged Britain in 1972. In most respects, glam was modernism pushed to the max, and it's no coincidence that the founding troika of glam—Bowie, Bolan, and Bryan Ferry—were all definitive mods (the only difference in philosophy was that the mod ideal was exclusive, aimed only at peers, whereas glam was designed to be publicized—knowingly pimped, with an ironic giggle). In 1964, the notion of preening peacock males who bonded with fellow males over a side vent or suit lining, oblivious to the scorn of outsiders, was outrageous—and powerful, in the monochrome period when simply wearing a pink shirt was a provocative statement. There were no famous role models you could point to to deflect the scorn of the un-hip; apart from your peers, you were on your own. Hence mod was the domain of the unashamed narcissist, and David Bowie and Marc Bolan became two of the most committed narcissists in London.

THERE was an obvious gay frisson about mod—and indeed "The London Boys." The city's mod and gay crowds shared the same clubs and many values; Le Duce on D'Arblay Street was nominally gay, whereas the Scene, nearby in Ham Yard, was nominally mod, but you could pose or dance to ska in either one. Plenty of mod boys experimented with their sexuality, as well as their clothing, around Soho in 1964 and 1965—it was no surprise to anyone that David was one of them.

Mike Berry was one of many kids who'd somehow fallen into a dream job, working for the publishers Sparta Music. History has not recorded how this man signed David to his first significant publishing deal, but Mike met him via their mutual music-shop friend Wayne Bardell and used to drop in on David when he was earning odd pennies at Southern Music over the winter, packing up manuscripts to send out to arrangers. They went out for a drink, "and I fell in love with the boy, in more ways than one."

For Berry, as for David, this was an electrifying period: "Life seemed black and white until 1964. Then it suddenly burst into color." As was true for many of this generation, Berry's rebellion against monochrome, straitlaced values included his sex life too: "They were incredible times," he says. "I knew I was bisexual, I had a girlfriend and fancied other people—then we all suddenly thought, Nobody cares! Anything goes!"

David and Mike's friendship had a sexual element: Mike had investigated the contents of David's trousers, but such fumblings were brief, for, he says, "Mostly, we'd talk about things. At the time he was semi-straight, and semi-gay; we talked mainly about music, or politics, what was happening with the Cuban crisis— none of us were sure we'd be alive the next year. Or we'd talk about, Do we fancy him or her, who's had who, and of course nobody knew who was telling the truth."

David was cool, playful, funny, "and there was something waiflike about him. And of course those eyes struck you straight- away, they were unforgettable." David's slim, almost elfin good looks helped him pass easily in and out of the gay-oriented scene— he flaunted his campiness, but it was nonetheless all a bit of a laugh; in fact, the campiness helped him attract more girls. In the main, he was voraciously heterosexual. Occasionally he'd go on dates with Dana Gillespie, a sixteen-year-old ex–public school girl with unforgettable cleavage whom he'd met in the Manish Boys' final days; sometimes Dana would bring along her friend Sarah Troupe for a double date. David had also been briefly involved with Annie Howes, his agent's daughter, but it seemed to his friends that he "had a girl in every port," as Denis Taylor puts it. "Wherever we were, some bird would pop up."

Still, in mid-1960s Soho, a certain rough-trade appeal was great for the career. This definitely applied to Marc Bolan, who, according to onetime manager Simon Napier-Bell, had "no great hang-ups" about whom to sleep with. By late 1965, David was beginning to build up his own following in the West End's gay-management clique, particularly around the Marquee Club, where, says employee Simon White, "There'd be six girls at the front, and half a dozen of us queens at the back, with Ralph [Horton] hanging on his every move."

Many of Ralph Horton's connections revolved around the Marquee and Radio London; both places had a strong gay contingent, all of whom loved speculating about David's relationship with Horton. In a characteristically sleazy and entertaining anecdote, Simon Napier-Bell claimed on his Web site in 2006 that Horton had offered him David's sexual favors to sweeten a comanagement deal. David's confidant Mike Berry insists the story is "ridiculous. It would never have happened in a million years. David was always in control of what he wanted."

Painted by history as a cynical exploiter, Ralph Horton—who died in 2009—was in fact "a nice, gentle person who was completely out of his depth," says Terry King, who gave Horton his first London job and later fired him. Rather than exploiting David, Horton was simply besotted with him and reveled in displaying his handsome client at clubs around town. Horton's obsession, however, meant that the first months of 1966 were dominated by backbiting and dubious financial dealings, for his jealousy of friends of his charge inspired a seemingly irrational campaign to separate David from his closest confidants, especially the Lower Third.

It seemed to Denis Taylor, Bowie's main musical foil in the group, that Horton's influence was negative right from the start:

"We had good laughs together when we were a group. David was great fun, one of the lads. And we had hard times too, the van breaking down, but he didn't mind—he mucked in." After Horton took over, David started to spend less time in the band's converted ambulance in favor of a cushier, more upholstered existence: "And so he got himself a nice lazy little job of pissing off with Ralph in his Jaguar Mark X," says Taylor. "It was very disappointing."

Worse still was the air of sleaziness around Horton's financial affairs, typified by a deal he made in November of 1965 with a London businessman, Ray Cook, to borrow £1,500, a sum worth roughly £30,000, or $50,000, in today's currency. A vague contract promised return of the money once David was earning over £100, about $150, a week. David played his part in charming Cook into the deal, and Ken Pitt, who as Bowie's next manager had to unravel these financial tangles, is not alone in believing Cook was taken for a ride: "I felt sorry for him. It was not a good situation."

Horton's one coup was to secure a new recording contract through Tony Hatch, whom he'd originally met by way of Denny Laine. The house producer for the Pye label, Hatch became one of the best-known music moguls in the UK, the Simon Cowell of the seventies, due to his role on the *New Faces* talent show. He thought Horton was pleasant enough, "but I recognized he wasn't 'top echelon'—he was still in the junior league. And I suspected if David had a hit, there would be a new manager along soon."

Hatch was impressed by David, though—primarily because he wrote his own songs. Pye was a strange agglomeration, spliced together from the Polygon and Nixa labels. Hatch had joined it as a part-time producer, setting up A and R meetings in the afternoon so he could fulfill his national service as arranger for the Coldstream Guards military band (another Pye act) in the mornings. His workload was immense, so the fact that he didn't have to find material for David was crucial: "The one thing that struck me is he had a lot of songs—different songs." Hatch went to see the Lower Third at the Marquee to check out the material. "I remember 'The London Boys'—there were a lot of songs about his background. There was one about the Hackney Marshes [a rough-and-ready park in East London], which is probably in some archive somewhere." (Sadly, David's other Pye material seems to have disappeared.)

With Hatch's numerous distractions, it took some time to tie up a recording contract; the publishing stayed close to home, for Mike Berry signed him to Sparta. The deal brought in a small advance, and together with the money from Raymond Cook, the cash flow enabled high living and lavish drinking parties at Horton's Warwick Square flat. David acquired a guitar during this high-living period, and although his playing was at best rudimentary, he worked up songs like "It's Lovely to Talk to You" and "Maid of Bond Street." In the autumn the Lower Third demoed "The London Boys," which they considered a standout song, but Hatch and Pye turned it down at their weekly sales meeting. According to Hatch, the main reason was not the downbeat subject matter or the references to pill popping but that "it takes too long to get going. It would never make a single."

Its replacement was far more concise, with a simple three-chord chorus once again lifted shamelessly from "Anyway, Anyhow, Anywhere." But while "Can't Help Thinking about Me" thieves exactly the same three-chord trick as "You've Got a Habit of Leaving," it makes far better use of it, with that punchy chorus allied with a subtle verse whose minor-key chords perfectly match the foreboding lines of a "question time that says I brought dishonor."

The verse alone was a huge leap forward in David's work, but it was combined with another sophisticated technique, a bridging section that raises the excitement level ("it's too late now") before we reach the release of the chorus. This was a song as story, one musical vignette giving way to another, a technique that became a cornerstone of David Bowie's great songs.

The lyrics too are subtle, with hints of a crime that blackened the family name and a chorus that slightly subverts expectations, for according to pop convention, the protagonist should have been thinking about a "you," not a "me." In many cases it's simplistic to assume David is the subject of his own lyrics, but here, the accusation of blackening the family name echoes some of Peggy's complaints. She'd been hospitable to the Manish Boys—nice, well-spoken, middle-class lads—but she'd lost patience with David's ambitions and demonstrated a sneering suspicion of his mates from Margate: "She didn't like us at all," says Denis Taylor ruefully. "I remember her telling me, 'You're leading my boy astray—he was never like this before.'"

It is appropriate that David Bowie's first grown-up song should be about leaving home. It also shows a dividing line between fantasy and reality: Peggy's irritation is understandable, for her son had given up his job in advertising two years earlier, was still firmly attached to the family's purse strings, and seemed destined to stay attached to them.

Hatch realized the song's virtues instantly—"It was a standout"—and played piano for the session at Pye's Marble Arch studios on December 10. Although Hatch had reservations about the performance—Graham Rivens's bass part speeds up noticeably halfway through—the Lower Third clatter along with élan, driven by a neat twelve-string acoustic and superb singing. The David Bowie we know and love croons darkly before losing all restraint in the impossibly thrilling run-up to the chorus. The single betrays some influences—notably Pete Townshend's "The Kids Are Alright," as well as that chorus chord sequence—but transcends them thanks to its innate drama as the singer, song, and band carry the listener along in their headlong rush.

The single was released on January 14, 1966, a week after David turned nineteen; Ralph Horton had borrowed more money from Raymond Cook for a launch party and to help buy the single onto the charts. There was a party that evening at the Gaiety Bar in Strathearn Place to celebrate the release; the band walked through nearby Hyde Park to get there, while David took a ride in Ralph's Jaguar. All the musicians dressed up and mingled with the Pye staff and celebrities; the most famous was Freddie Lennon, John Lennon's incorrigible absentee father, who was enjoying a brief flurry of notoriety. "It was a really weird party," says Taylor. "Freddie Lennon, this peculiar old geezer, a bit inebriated, wandering around saying, 'Do you know who I am?'"

David was effervescent that night, friendly with the Lower Third—"like we were a proper band"—meeting and greeting the minor industry figures, mouthing to his band *This is it!* Rail-thin, his hair in a mod bouffant, he loved being at the center of the hub-bub, taking off to charm one huddle of guests after another, flirting with the Pye secretaries, and adopting an obliging, likely-lad persona with the company's suited execs. He was young, he had made his first great single, and he had no doubt that, finally, this *was* it.

CHAPTER 4

Laughing Gnome

*I had a minor obsession about David — I just thought he was the
most talented, magical person . . . I think I would have signed him
even if he didn't have such obvious talent.*

—Hugh Mendl

FOR A TINY GAGGLE OF FANS around Denmark Street, David
Bowie was a star. At home in Plaistow Grove, he was anything but. Although he disappeared often to Ralph Horton's basement apartment at 79 Warwick Square, he still relied on
Haywood and Peggy for handouts. Haywood sometimes intimidated David's fellow musicians, but they discovered that behind
his straitlaced exterior, he was surprisingly well informed about
David's career—and supportive. With Peggy it was a different
matter; by the end of 1965, her patience had run out. David's band
used to joke about how they were forced to wait outside David's
house in their converted ambulance while he chatted to his mum,
but David seemed unconcerned and never mentioned a word of
any family hassle.

After the huge buildup for "Can't Help Thinking about Me,"
its chart performance was underwhelming; it missed the UK's
main chart, the *Record Retailer* Top 40. Although Radio London
pushed the single heavily and placed it at number 25, it was

probably Raymond Cook's money that helped grease the song's path to number 34 on the *Melody Maker* chart. Tony Hatch remembers even this modest success was enough to make David "very excited," and the producer was mildly encouraged: "I did see David as a long-term artist. And I knew we had a lot more material to play with."

Yet a slightly dodgy Top 40 placing did not help generate live shows, the only reliable means of raising cash, and while Ralph Horton was not good at wheeling and dealing for money—"too wimpish," according to flatmate Kenny Bell—he was good at spending it. It was Bell who'd first sublet a room to Horton in the Warwick Square flat, previously home to the Moody Blues, and over the end of 1965 and beginning of 1966, he saw Horton spending "like a big shot. Cars, booze, you name it. I don't know how much money Ralph got from Raymond Cook, but he certainly fancied himself as a big spender."

Much of Horton's spending was designed to impress David, who was learning, says Bell, "to dominate Ralph. Really, Ralph was a bit of a wuss, and I think David ended up controlling him."

Unable to restrain either his own spending or his protégé, Ralph decided to pick on people he could control, namely, the Lower Third. Even before "Can't Help Thinking about Me" was released, Horton had been planning the removal of Denis Taylor: "He decided to pick on one of us to bring us to heel—and he didn't like me," says Taylor. "He wanted to get rid of me and the other two could stay."

The band started to suspect Horton of trying to drive a wedge between the three of them and David when Horton took David home in his Jag after another run of Paris Drouot shows, leaving the Lower Third to struggle back in their old ambulance. During a layoff for the band in January, their income dwindled to nothing. As a short run of shows approached, Taylor asked when they could expect to be paid. "That's when Ralph made his big mistake," says Taylor. "He told us we were not getting any money, as it was all going into advertising."

Although Horton's hostility was focused mainly on Taylor, the manager's confrontational attitude succeeded in uniting all of the Lower Third. Following a show in Stevenage on January 28, the band asked for their share of the take. Horton informed them there was none. "He told us it had gone on expenses," says Rivens. "Like running his Mark X Jag, I guess."

After a Marquee show the next morning, the Lower Third was booked at the Bromel Club, David's home venue. The band met Ralph at the club; Taylor told Ralph it was no pay, no play. This time, Horton told Taylor, "You are *definitely* sacked!" at which point Phil Lancaster weighed in: "If he goes, we go!" To break the standoff, Taylor informed the manager, "You can have half an hour to think about it. When we come back, tell us what you want to do."

After each band member downed a half-pint of lager in a nearby pub, the Lower Third returned. "We were convinced he was going to pay us," says Rivens, "but he wouldn't. So we simply packed up our gear and walked." Taylor went up to David and asked if he'd stick up for them and prevent the walkout. David responded by bursting into tears. "He didn't want us to go. But he'd probably been listening to Ralph, all the things he'd made up." By this point the club was packed with Bromley art-school students and various friends and fans of David, and the Lower Third band members were convinced that David or Ralph would relent and run after them. Neither did.

"We thought within a few days [David] would come running back," says Graham Rivens. "But of course he couldn't do that, because Mr. Horton was pulling the strings." After a couple of days waiting for David's call, the Lower Third carried on without him for a few shows, then split up and joined other bands.

The departure of the Lower Third marked a triumph for Ralph Horton; it would also be symbolic in David's career. His peers and rivals, like Jagger, Lennon, and indeed Steve Marriott—whose third single with the Small Faces, "Sha La La La Lee," had soared to number 3 on the charts while David's single languished at the bottom—were all committed to their own bands, building up a grassroots following, show after grueling show. This was an English rock-and-roll convention that David ignored; his vision was more old-fashioned, akin to the tinselly showbiz of the fifties, when managers nurtured their protégés like mother hens. There was something unmistakably square about David's loyalty to "numero uno" and rejection of the gang mentality of rock and roll. And in the short run, his career would suffer.

Ralph Horton reveled in the job of finding a compliant backup band for his charge, placing an advertisement for replacement musicians in *Melody Maker* that same week. Bassist Derek Fearnley was among the first to turn up at Warwick Square. Thirty seconds after he walked into the basement apartment, he decided he wouldn't take the job: "I just felt this strange, gay atmosphere—it made me feel very uncomfortable."

Ushered in by Horton, Derek saw a skinny, campy young man reclining on a bed. Confused, Derek tried to assess the situation as David started detailing how he wrote all his own material. Then David produced a cigarette pack—"Literally, a piece of card from a fag packet, with some chords written on the back"—and the bassist found himself intrigued. David picked up his twelve-string and strummed through some chords, humming along. After eight or so bars, Fearnley was transfixed: This was not the predictable R & B most London musicians were churning out. "Then by the time we got maybe halfway through I thought, I don't care what's going on here—I want to work with this guy."

Guitarist John Hutchinson went through a similar process; he heard from Jack Barry at the Marquee that there was a singer looking for a new band, turned up for an audition at the club on Saturday, and jammed along with David on a Bo Diddley riff. Hutchinson—Hutch—and David soon established a natural musicians' rapport, a bond of which Ralph Horton was, says Hutch, jealous. Horton wanted a pliable band of nonentities who wouldn't challenge his own relationship with Bowie. And for that reason, says Hutch, "[This band was] more meek. We did it and we acted like a backing band."

Drummer John Eager joined up at the same time as Fearnley, and Hutch suggested a keyboard player, Derek "Chow" Boyes, whom he knew from the Yorkshire club circuit. Radio London DJ

Earl Richmond, who introduced their sets at the Marquee, named them the Buzz, and within a couple of days they were filling in for the Lower Third at a string of live dates and, on March 4, on *Ready Steady Go!*, lip-synching to "Can't Help Thinking about Me." Steve Marriott was on the same show with the Small Faces, jumping around and joshing with David as the cameras rolled. It was good-natured fun, but it demonstrated how David was falling behind the Small Faces' singer, who "had a lot more exposure, success, confidence, and natural character [than David]. That's the one thing I remember from that show," says Hutch.

A few weeks later, the effects of the Lower Third's departure became more obvious when the Buzz turned up at Pye's Marble Arch studios to record a follow-up to "Can't Help Thinking about Me." There were no tempo changes or cranked-up guitars on "Do Anything You Say"; it was neat and well played, but the Spector-ish gloss and Motown-style on-beat drums couldn't mask a horrible blandness. The thrill had gone—David sounded like a bad Tom Jones imitator.

Released to capitalize on a near hit, "Do Anything You Say" stalled; David's career seemed to do the same. And although David had built up a small following at the Marquee, when he and the band ventured outside of London for a short tour in April, their set left audiences confused, according to Derek "Dek" Fearnley. The tour included dates in Scotland, where "to be honest, the kids didn't really get it." Realizing the audience wanted some familiar songs, David introduced covers of "Knock on Wood" and Tim Hardin's "If I Were a Carpenter." The Buzz as a group was "competent, but not dynamic," according to Hutch. "I never thought it was that strong musically." Without the foil of the Lower Third, David's music was confused, to the extent that his period with the Buzz would be airbrushed out of history—most notably by himself. Much later he would claim that "for a number of years I worked with rhythm and blues bands—my participation in them formed my own black ties." It's understandable that he'd forgotten his most forgettable music.

Many fans and friends of the time remembered David's work

with the Lower Third—few of them mentioned the Buzz. The band worked up a funkier, more jazzy style than their predecessors had but were milder and tamer in both music and mentality. Sacking the Lower Third might have suited Ralph Horton, but it seemed an act of self-sabotage. David appeared unconcerned. As the Buzz observed, he liked hanging out with a band, sharing his obsessions and flights of fancy, but he was fundamentally a loner; his fantasy was to live a "nomad" lifestyle. This was the main attraction of Horton's flat, for by then David was open about the claustrophobia of living with his mother and father. Claustrophobia also led to the rapid turnover of people with whom he worked; the moment they started making demands or seeing themselves as permanent fixtures, David started seeing them as part of the dullness and convention that oppressed him. As Dek Fearnley, the man closest to David in 1966, observed, even at the time, "He wanted to get away from home. And he wanted to get away from being in a band in exactly the same way, if that makes sense."

David's "dreaminess," his escapism, was his most powerful and charming character trait. He knew how to make a boring situation, like waiting for a bus or train, entertaining: "He was on a higher plane, really," says Fearnley. "He wouldn't be talking about the weather or the latest Who single; he was simply off in his own world." This man-child blend of escapism and hard-nosed careerism was intriguing; there were constant flights of fantasy and obsessions that his friends were drawn into. In essence, this seemed to be a mind-control technique, used to blot out the everyday details of life in Bromley. In a different person, such escapism and daydreaming would have been the marks of an ineffectual Walter Mitty character—but David labored to turn his fantasies into reality, spending long hours working on arrangements and planning the next steps in his career.

In fact, with the failure of "Do Anything You Say," it seemed that David didn't have a career, but that hardly impaired his ability to move on. This time around, it wouldn't be the band that was ditched in order to break the deadlock but the man who had, just a few months earlier, seen off the Lower Third. According to

Kenny Bell, Ralph Horton was aware he was becoming surplus to requirements: "He came to the end of any money he had to spend on David and realized David would probably be off. So the best thing he could do was score a deal with somebody else and at least retain something." Desperate to secure help—and, just as important, money—Horton reapproached Ken Pitt.

A crucial character in David Bowie's history, Ken Pitt is also one of the most complex—and misunderstood. Generally seen as a traditional, old-school figure, a campy showbiz manager in the tradition of Brian Epstein, Ken Pitt is in reality far more complicated and intriguing.

Born and raised in Southall, Middlesex, Pitt studied art at the School of Photo-Engraving and Lithography on Fleet Street and worked briefly for two London print companies before joining the army in March of 1941. He worked in signals, landed at Gold Beach on D-day, and was among the first Allied troops to arrive at Belsen; he served briefly in Palestine before returning to the family home in Southall, where he debuted in the music business as an MC for a local dance band. Pitt soon established himself as a key PR figure in the UK's nascent record industry, and by 1956 he was representing Stan Kenton, Billy Eckstine, Billy Daniels, and Liberace. In 1966, Pitt had a thriving business operating in both management and PR; his major acts including David Anthony's Moods and Manfred Mann. At the beginning of the year, he had turned down a plea from Mike Prustin to comanage the recently renamed Marc Bolan. But when Ralph Horton came to see Pitt in his office on April 5, insisting that Pitt "had the keys to the doors that are being slammed in our face at the moment," Pitt was interested enough to turn up for a show at the Marquee on April 17 without ever having heard any of David Bowie's music.

WINSTON Churchill, hailed by many as the ultimate Great Briton, once explained how he'd brought America to Britain's aid in the Second World War: "No lover ever studied every whim of his mistress as I did those of President Roosevelt." David Bowie, self-styled Great Briton, showed a similar mastery of political realities. He knew his performance on April 17 would be one of the most important in his life—and he delivered. As Pitt says, "If you went to see David Bowie and David Bowie knew you were coming, he would put on a show for you. Which he did for me. And yes, I was greatly impressed. With everything. Everything."

The band, Pitt says, was forgettable, playing vaguely mod music. David himself was another matter. Pitt had worked with Sinatra and Bob Dylan and could recognize charisma. David had it. Although Pitt retained few details of the songs David and the Buzz played, he remembered David's beige sweater, which had buttons down one shoulder: "It looked like something your mother had made, but I noticed it fitted him very well. It was... different."

The band ran through the set; none of the numbers particularly registered with Pitt until the last song. At which point, says Pitt, the lights went down, a single spot shone on David, and he launched into an impassioned rendition of "You'll Never Walk Alone"—a classic show-business tune that Ken knew from Judy Garland's version. Pitt was transfixed: "I had simply never seen anything like that before."

After the show, David came up to greet Pitt and Horton, and the three of them went back to Ralph's flat, where they chatted for a very long time. Pitt noticed that when he raised a subject that was new to David, the young singer became animated. "He had this habit of sitting on one leg and then rocking backwards and forwards in a chair when he got excited. I noticed after I discussed something he would have this look, and his eyes were bright. That impressed me very very much."

Taking command of the situation, this man-child, who seemed as eager to learn as he was to take control, turned to Ralph and said, "Let's do a deal with Ken."

There is an intriguing footnote to David Bowie's acquisition of the manager who steered his career over the next four years. Ken Pitt ascribes his conversion to David Bowie as the result of David's performance of a Judy Garland song. But Bowie's music director and bassist Dek Fearnley, who arranged most of the material, is adamant that for that performance, the Buzz closed the show with Tony Newley's "What Kind of Fool Am I." The discrepancy perfectly illustrated David Bowie's ability to be whatever the object of his attention wanted him to be.

IN later years, Bowie fans and writers would make much of the subtext of that night's conversation, which saw Ralph Horton hand over control to Ken Pitt; in some imaginations the undercurrents of that evening were comparable to Joe Orton's *Entertaining Mr. Sloane,* the play that immortalized London's gay culture. But the participants were more complex than the clichés we've inherited. Ken Pitt, a fan of Judy Garland, a devotee of Oscar Wilde, and a supporter of the emerging Campaign for Homosexual Equality, was also a married man who often mentioned his romances with Hollywood glamour girls.

Tall and gangly, rather refined and formal-looking, Pitt could expound with equal enthusiasm on the virtues of both Keats and the Velvet Underground in his clipped, measured tones and was a master of the elegantly phrased, slightly waspish letters that were an essential management tool in London's old-school music industry. Pitt "doesn't believe" in applying labels to sexuality—"People always have to say now. It was better when people didn't have to say." His vagueness is consistent with that of other rock managers, such as Andrew Loog Oldham, who was straight but loved camping it up to seem more like Brian Epstein and Kit Lambert, the gay managerial archetypes in the swinging London of 1966.

In other respects, Pitt was anything but vague. From the outset, he injected some professionalism into David's business affairs—he paid the bills that started to cascade into his office. Pitt's trademark acerbity shows in his comment that Ralph's management of David's affairs, notably his using David's income to pay his own bills, "was not the usual way of doing things." Over subsequent months, Pitt paid for outstanding phone bills, new shirts, and endless running costs for the band van, all marks of his devotion to David's cause.

Pitt's enthusiasm was in stark contrast to the situation at Pye;

in June, Tony Hatch started producing "I Dig Everything," then, dissatisfied with the Buzz's performance, he replaced them all with session musicians. The resulting single, with its cheesy, chirrupy organ and Austin Powers–style grooviness, bore more of Hatch's production trademarks than any of his previous Bowie sides had, and the result, says Hatch himself, was "that it didn't work at all. We were getting further away from what we had with the Lower Third single, rough as it was."

Although it was obvious that "I Dig Everything" was destined for oblivion, David was unconcerned. "He knew those songs weren't that good, it's just what was needed at the time," says John Hutchinson, who sensed that Bowie was ready to move on. Hutch, meanwhile, was pessimistic about the Buzz's future and confided to David that he planned to get married and find a conventional job. David found the notion of getting married bizarre, and the night before the wedding, he tried to talk Hutch out of it: "We were in Dunstable, he'd found these two girls, and he wanted me to go off with him and the girls instead." David was supposed to turn up for the wedding but unsurprisingly was absent the next day. Hutch left in search of married bliss and a regular income in Yorkshire and was replaced by Billy Gray.

Despite the attractions of the female fans who turned up at his shows, David was fast becoming disenchanted with live perfor-mances, live audiences, and, seemingly, rock and roll in general. By the autumn of 1966, the British beat boom was subsiding. With the Beatles retiring from live shows and the presence of Frank Sinatra and Tom Jones in the Top 10 alongside the Kinks and the Small Faces, the charts were—from a modern perspective—charmingly diverse and kitschy, with none of today's predictable rock conformity.

David's own mental state reflected the era, for there was kitsch and charm in the way he spent his afternoons at Dek Fearnley's brother's house in Sussex, observing the family coming and going, playing with Fearnley's nieces and nephews. He was relaxed, soaking up what was a carefree environment by comparison with his own straitlaced, claustrophobic family home. The silly, or comic, moments were what struck him most—including the time when the shamefaced Fearnley admitted he'd subtracted seven years from his age when he joined the Buzz and was in fact twenty-seven. "You're joking?" asked David, incredulous at the thought that he was hanging out with such an ancient codger, an uncle no less, who hadn't settled down yet. Three months later, when David started to run through a new song named "Uncle Arthur"—about a thirty-two-year-old who "still reads comics, follows Batman"—Dek realized he had been immortalized.

Alan Mair, whose group the Beatstalkers was managed by Ken Pitt, also spent many afternoons with David, being shown his songs and, later, hanging out in the office. He sometimes brought his three-year-old son, Frankie, with him, and David and Frankie built up such a rapport that a couple of times Mair left the toddler in David's care. Like Uncle Dek, Frankie and his toy soldiers were captured in song, "The Little Bombardier"—though the situation was altered, made into a story where "Little Frankie Mair" is an adult figure who enjoys hanging out with kids and subsequently attracts suspicion. The song, a playtime waltz, perfectly illustrates David's mind-set of cheeky humor, childlike wonder, and adult cynicism. This wasn't Bowie's only babysitting job, for in quiet times he looked after Lucy, the daughter of Tom Parker, a friend from Kent who played piano with the New Animals. "Kids just trust and gravitate towards some people," says Mair. "David is one of them."

Mair knew both Pitt and Bowie well and saw the manager's influence on Bowie close up. In later years, Pitt's detractors would contend that he wanted to turn Bowie into an all-round entertainer. In fact, Bowie had joined Pitt as a singer in a rock band; soon he would change into a songwriter with a unique worldview. In that respect, Pitt's influence was the making of him. "His intentions were right; he was saying, Put makeup on, dress flamboyantly—be gregarious!" says Mair. Pitt's role was not so much to educate David as to give him license to see himself as an artist—and at the same time encourage him to write more, pushing his songs to other artists.

Pitt knew that David was going nowhere with Pye, where Hatch was being pressured by managing director Louis Benjamin to drop David's contract, and Pitt already had a new record company in mind. Early in October he funded a recording session with the Buzz, once more at R. G. Jones in Wimbledon, where David produced a second version of "The London Boys," plus new songs "Rubber Band" and "Please Mr. Gravedigger." Together, these quirky, observational songs represented a radical turnaround from David's Pye material, and Pitt was confident that they would help him score a record deal. "What I wanted was an album that would act like a CV," says Pitt. "I had not come across another nineteen-year-old who wrote songs like that. I went to Decca determined to get an album deal—although that was theoretically impossible, because they didn't make albums except if you'd had a hit."

Pitt made his approach to Decca via Tony Hall, the company's promotions manager. Hall had become the key figure in the establishment of the label's "hip" Deram imprint. He was taken with Bowie's songs—"they sounded like Anthony Newley Two"—and passed Pitt along to Hugh Mendl, who was transfixed.

Mendl was one of the most senior executives in the British music industry; in fact, he had literally invented a huge section of it through his discovery of Lonnie Donegan and Tommy Steele, and he launched many significant careers throughout the sixties, often while battling Decca's innate conservatism. He rated the nineteen-year-old singer with a string of failed singles behind him as one of the most inspirational talents he had ever worked with: "I had a minor obsession about David—I just thought he was the most talented, magical person." Mendl was well aware of the resemblance between Bowie's voice and that of Anthony Newley, another Mendl signing, but was untroubled by it: "The [resemblance] was purely vocal. They were entirely different. Tony was an actor. David was...David Bowie." He says, "I think I would have signed him even if he didn't have such obvious musical talent. But he did have talent. He was bursting with creativity."

An effusive but rather patrician character, Mendl had been

expected to join the diplomatic service after graduating from Oxford—but despite the skepticism of his grandfather Sir Sigismund Mendl, then chairman of Decca, he worked his way up through the family company. Better educated and more worldly than Tony Hatch, the man who had signed David to Pye, Mendl's near obsession with David is recognizable as the same heterosexual crush that writer Charles Shaar Murray remembers David Bowie exploiting so potently in the seventies. David's discovery of this power was as significant a breakthrough as his improving skills at songwriting. David Bowie had grasped a fundamental truth: before you can *be* a genius, you have to *seem* like a genius.

Mendl's fascination with Bowie inspired him to release Bowie's self-produced R. G. Jones track as his single debut; in-house producer Mike Vernon would oversee the album. Vernon had his own impressive track record, championing acts like Eric Clapton and Fleetwood Mac, and he too was impressed with the young singer's intellect: "There was talk of a lot of things, concepts and poetry that went right over my head," he remembers, leaving the impression he wasn't totally convinced by David's young-genius persona. But there was no denying Bowie's creativity, for with the prospect of an outlet for the songs and pictures that were flowing through his head, music was pouring out of him.

During the autumn of 1966, David wrote frenetically; in one early list of contenders for his debut album, he and Pitt itemized more than thirty songs, including "Over the Wall" and now-forgotten compositions such as "Say Goodbye to Mr. Mind" and "Lincoln House." His ambition extended to abandoning traditional instrumentation in favor of a more orchestral approach, influenced by both Brian Wilson's groundbreaking *Pet Sounds,* released that summer, and the fact that he no longer had his own backup band. Guitarist Billy Gray left in November, and the others were "let go" a week later. Ralph Horton, still acting as a kind of comanager, wrote to Pitt, who had left for a trip to America and then Australia, and explained that they had decided to give up live shows and that David "hates ballrooms and the kids." Poignantly, Dek, Chow, and John "Ego" Eager offered to stay on without pay after the last show, in Shrewsbury on December 2, and also to help out with his album, inspiring another flood of tears from David.

Bowie approached this critical rite of passage with the sense of calm and organization that had so impressed the Manish Boys, and with two characteristics that would come to define his career: a willingness to take creative risks and a genius for delegation. He had assured Mendl and Vernon that he would oversee all the arrangements for the album—a task usually looked after by a specialist. Then he told bassist Dek Fearnley that the two of them would do this crucial job together.

Fearnley's sole qualification was childhood piano lessons; he was intimidated by the prospect, but David confidently steered him well beyond his comfort zone. Aided by a dog-eared edition of Freda Dinn's *Observer's Book of Music,* a guide to the principal orchestral instruments, they attacked their task. "It was bloody hard work," says Fearnley. "I knew how to read the staves and that a bar had four crotchets; David had never seen or written a note, so I was the one qualified to write stuff out."

The two worked for hours at Dek's brother Gerald's piano, David humming, Dek scribbling. The arrangement for "Rubber Band" was their first experiment with this method. The quirky, Heath Robinson feel enhanced the song's off-kilter charm, but as work on the album proper started at Decca's studio 2 in Hampstead on November 14, 1966, the pressure was ratcheted up. "We didn't have enough time," says Dek, "and it got embarrassing handing over these scribbles to these musicians from the London Philharmonic!" By Christmas, the two were behind schedule, and Fearnley was left to arrange a couple of songs on his own, including "The Laughing Gnome," and explain the charts to the musicians while David oversaw proceedings from the control room.

Mike Vernon remembers being handed a pile of papers and helping to assemble each song "like a jigsaw puzzle," but he and engineer Gus Dudgeon enjoyed the challenge of recording comedy voices and miking up the gravel that would be used in recording "Please Mr. Gravedigger." Most of the musicians were supportive, transposing parts written in the wrong key, although one "absolute bastard" clarinetist simply handed his manuscript back to Fearnley, said, "There are five notes in this bar. There should be four," and refused to play.

Just before Christmas, Neil Slaven, who oversaw the artwork for many of Decca's album sleeves, dropped in on the session. Mike introduced him briefly. David chatted with Slaven— "Hello, Mike's told me all about you!"—interrogating the blues fan about his record collection, seemingly fascinated by his expertise on obscure Chess records. A slightly bizarre, slim, undeniably impressive young man with floppy, collar-length hair and a schoolboyish, fey, "theatrical" air, Bowie seemed a world apart from the rock and blues musicians Slaven and Vernon normally hung out with. And then Slaven watched from the control room, dumbstruck, as Vernon rolled the tapes and this intense but campy apparition shuffled around Decca's studio 2 crunching scattered pebbles and stones that he had shaken over the studio floor, apparently to make some kind of background track for a spoken-word piece.

When Slaven heard a rough mix of the epic that Vernon and Bowie were crafting, he was even more disconcerted: a monologue delivered in a theatrical, nasal cockney voice that sounded as if the speaker had a bad cold, accompanied by found sounds like the crunching of gravel and the rustle of driving rain. The subject was apparently a Lambeth gravedigger, "a little old man with a shovel in his hand." Although Slaven heard this "song" just once or twice, it stuck with him, and he never got the strange spectacle he had witnessed out of his head. What was most striking was the way this studio neophyte delivered this extravagant confection without a trace of embarrassment. It should have been ludicrous, but despite himself, Slaven was impressed: "I thought, Here is someone who really is an individual talent—someone who truly follows his own ideas."

The track in question, "Please Mr. Gravedigger," was, by most objective standards, dreadful. Its description of "Mary Ann, [who] was ten, full of life" obviously refers to ten-year-old Lesley Ann Downey, who was tortured and murdered by the notorious Moors murderers, Ian Brady and Myra Hindley. The song was tasteless and exploitative — but it also illustrated how the nineteen-year-old David Bowie had learned to use the recording studio itself as an instrument, a lesson that was at the heart of his future career. Today, it ranks as both a bad-taste period piece and an example of artistic courage.

THE drawn-out sessions — complete with French horns and English whimsy, just like the Beatles' sessions for *Sgt. Pepper,* which was recorded around the same time — resumed after the Christmas break; "The Laughing Gnome" was finished in January of 1967, and the final three tracks, including a rerecorded "Rubber Band," were wrapped up in February.

Predictably, most of the personnel involved remembered the session for "The Laughing Gnome" — which was released as a single on April 14 — as one of their favorites. Vernon forgot his doubts and dived in, suggesting more variable-speed effects, and engineer Gus Dudgeon "totally went crazy," says Vernon, coming up with gnome puns and chirpy voices.

In future years, "The Laughing Gnome" would be the early Bowie song singled out for ridicule. Yet as long as one is happy to abandon all notions of taste, the song is brilliantly crafted, from Dek Fearnley's opening oboe melody through to the breakdown after the chorus as David intones "said the laughing gnome." One of the rare songs on the album where the execution matches the ambition, "The Laughing Gnome" is infectious — like a skin ailment — and charmingly reminiscent of those summer afternoons David spent playing with little Frankie Mair. In the admittedly narrow niche of pseudopsychedelic cockney music-hall children's songs, it reigns supreme.

When Vernon wrapped up the sessions, on February 25, the producer felt a profound sense of achievement merely to have realized Bowie's kitchen-sink epic. But the satisfaction didn't extend to optimism about the album's prospects: "If I'm honest, I really thought it didn't have any chance of commercial success — whatsoever."

The end of the album also marked the official end of David's

relationship with Ralph Horton, for on January 19, David's comanager retired from the music business, later joining the RAC. Haywood Jones was left to deal with the letters from Raymond Cook
that arrived at Plaistow Grove, plaintively asking about Horton's
whereabouts in the hope of getting paid back for his "loan."

David, meanwhile, was buoyed with the enthusiasm of Deram's
executives, most of whom thought "The Laughing Gnome" and
"Love You Till Tuesday" were surefire hits. But even as the biggest
artistic achievement of his life approached its release, David
was — in what would become characteristic fashion — preparing
to move on.

The inspiration arrived via a white-label acetate that Ken Pitt
had acquired on his trip to New York. As an art enthusiast, Pitt
had engineered a visit to Andy Warhol's Factory on East Forty-
seventh Street. Initially unaware of Warhol's involvement in the
music scene, Pitt had nonetheless briefly met Lou Reed and was
given an acetate of the Velvet Underground's as-yet-unreleased
debut album. After a promotional trip to Australia with another
management charge, Christian St. Peters, Pitt returned to London and eventually handed over the acetate to David. The album
is still a treasured possession and a source of pride that "not only
was I to cover [a] Velvets' song before anyone else in the world, I
actually did it before the album came out. Now that's the essence
of mod."

In forthcoming years, David Bowie would become the world's
best-known champion of the Velvets, but in 1967, his attempts to
assimilate its narco-deadpan thuggery resulted in some of his
most ludicrous music.

Part of the inspiration came in the form of the Riot Squad, a
London five-piece led by Bob Flag that over various lineups had
worked with Larry Page and Joe Meek. Bob Flag, its feisty, eccentric sax player, had bumped into Bowie during a Buzz show at the
Marquee the previous August and renewed his acquaintance over
coffees at La Gioconda, mentioning his band was holding auditions for a singer. Bowie volunteered, partly for a laugh, partly to
help them out, and partly so he could experiment with some new

material—for, although Dek was still on the scene, keyboardist Chow had bailed out halfway through the Deram sessions.

The new band worked through material at the Swan pub in Leytonstone on March 15 and 16, readying David for the Riot Squad's support slot with Cream in Basildon on March 17. Seven shows later, David enlisted the band's help for an after-hours Decca session with Gus Dudgeon to record his cover version of the Velvets' "Waiting for the Man" plus David's own "Little Toy Soldier."

"Waiting for the Man" would become a touchstone of David's career, and this early version was effective, stripped down and funky, with taut sax and harmonica embellishing the stomping on-beat drums and a rangy bass riff—all neatly underpinning David's carbon-copy Lou Reed drawl. However, it was David's own—using that term loosely—"Little Toy Soldier" that was truly arresting (or maybe just criminal). A juxtaposition of cockney music hall and the Marquis de Sade, the song is the aural equivalent of a P. T. Barnum sideshow monstrosity, a monkey's body stitched to a fish's tail. David's hearty main melody introducing Little Sadie sounds like cheery English rocker Tommy Steele; then, eight bars in, he drops in an entire musical section—"taste the whip, and bleed for me"—lifted wholesale from the Velvets' "Venus in Furs." This theft, it must be pointed out, took place before Warhol made the technique of "appropriation" respectable.

Recorded too late for inclusion on the Deram album, the two songs would become a high point of the Riot Squad's live set. For "Little Toy Soldier," David, in psychedelic makeup, his hair combed back, brandished a whip and lashed Bob Flag, who wore whiteface and a bowler hat, like one of *Clockwork Orange*'s droogs, plus protective padding. The shows were anarchic, hilarious—like those of contemporary Bonzo Dog Doo-Dah Band, whom Flag later joined—and reminiscent of Marc Bolan's chaotic shows with the hippie outfit John's Children. Unsurprisingly, the audience was confused. "But David was always a laugh. He liked us because we'd do anything," says Flag. The same could be said of David, who occasionally would reach over and fondle Flag's hair; the audience was left unaware this was a shared joke about the wig the thirty-six-year-old sax player wore to disguise his advanced years.

THE Riot Squad provided backup for David at his Tiles show to mark the release of "Laughing Gnome" on April 13, but David otherwise remained an anonymous member of the band for their performances, right through the end of May. Although in later years he often mentioned how early he'd picked up on the Velvet Underground, for his own career he stuck to the mainstream in search of a breakthrough. Certainly, there was no connection between the Riot Squad's lovably cranky recordings and the smug, show-business gloss of "Love You Till Tuesday," which was rere-corded with an orchestra directed by Ivor Raymonde, best known for "I Only Want to Be with You."

With its gelatinous strings and trite, complacent lyrics, "Love You Till Tuesday" was a naked statement of David's yearning for a hit and had none of the charming eccentricity of his Deram album, which was released on June 1, the same day as the Beatles' rather more successful *Sgt. Pepper's Lonely Hearts Club Band*. By the time he completed the album, David had jettisoned no fewer than five bands in his drive for mainstream success. The failure of "Love You Till Tuesday" demonstrated that ruthlessness and ambition alone were not enough.

Yet as just a few people at the time noticed, ambition was not the only thing that drove David Bowie. For during that early sum-mer of 1967, much of it spent lovingly teaching the Riot Squad his songs line by line and playing them Frank Zappa records up in his bedroom at Plaistow Grove, his friends grew to appreciate another compulsion: an intoxicating, childlike obsession with music that had deepened and crystallized in the years since he had pored over album sleeves at Medhurst's in Bromley. At heart earnest and obsessive, David Bowie was a simple fan boy, his fan-like compulsion sometimes battling, sometimes complementing his ruthlessness. Only with failure would the fan-boy part of him be allowed to surface. Failure, it turned out, would be the making of David Bowie.

CHAPTER 5

I Wish Something Would Happen

It was a bit like going into the Warhol Factory—if you wanted to hang out you had to learn heavy manners. And David came in, learning moves. He was clearly absorbing a lot—mutating.

—Mick Farren

THE SUDDEN INACTIVITY following the polite but restrained reception for David's Deram debut was a shock. His teenage masterwork had disappeared into oblivion; he had stalled, and 1968 would be a year that David Bowie would sit around Ken Pitt's flat in Manchester Road, his legs tucked under him in trademark fashion, sighing, "I wish something would happen."

Despite its negligible sales, the album did win some prominent supporters. *Melody Maker's* Chris Welch had been turned on to the album by the Nice. Penny Valentine, of *Disc,* was even more influential: a lucid, widely feted, but unpretentious critic, she had an unerring ear for both talent and a hit. She supported David faithfully over the next five years, celebrating his talent without, for the moment, predicting success. "She did love him," says Chris Welch, "but she did mention how he wouldn't stop ringing her up."

Haywood Jones was in regular contact with Ken Pitt. As ever, he was politely grateful for Pitt's efforts on behalf of his son, but David's nocturnal songwriting activities were adding to the stress in Plaistow Grove—for Terry, David's half brother, had reappeared on the scene. After his national service in the Royal Air Force, Terry had lived intermittently with Peggy's sister Pat; around this time, he became reconciled with his stepfather, Haywood, and the long-absent prodigal son moved into the tiny, overcrowded house. The eventual solution to the overcrowding was for David to move in with Ken. Bizarrely, this relocation to his manager's flat in Manchester Street was the first time the twenty-year-old had officially left home. Now the aspiring nomad had to rely on handouts from Ken rather than Haywood.

Although David had long overstayed his welcome at his parents' cramped two-up, two-down, it wasn't just Peggy's disapproval that he was trying to evade. After Terry arrived back in Bromley, David started sharing some of his musical obsessions with him. Terry had turned him on to many musicians, from Eric Dolphy to John Coltrane, and, hoping to reciprocate, David had taken his half brother to see Cream at the Bromel Club in February of 1967. It was Terry's first encounter with high-volume rock and roll, and the experience was disastrous. According to David, "About halfway through he started feeling very, very bad. I had to take him out of the club because it was really starting to affect him—he was swaying... He'd never heard anything so loud."

As they emerged from the doorway onto Bromley Hill, Terry collapsed on the pavement: "He said the ground was opening up—and there was fire and stuff pouring out the pavement, and I could almost see it for him, because he was explaining it so articulately." Terry had suffered a schizophrenic episode; he told David he regularly had such visions. This revelation was overwhelming, disturbing, but David did not share his reaction with anyone; his response, initially at least, was to try to banish thoughts of it. As far as most people were concerned, David was an only child. That was certainly how he behaved.

Once Haywood had installed David in Manchester Street, cramming David's books and records into his tiny Fiat 500, David settled himself in the neat, comfortable bachelor pad. Many of his afternoons were spent wandering around Fitzrovia and the other quiet, elegant Georgian streets around Manchester Square. Often he'd return from his magpie trips with childish enthusiasm, presenting Pitt with his new discoveries: a Victorian children's book he'd bought from Pollock's Toy Museum, brass bells from some swinging clothes shop, or simply chestnuts, flowers, and leaves that he'd come across in the street. At other times, David could be found shuffling through the bookshelves on either side of the living-room fireplace, pulling out works like Saint-Exupéry's *Le Petit Prince*, various first editions of Oscar Wilde and Aubrey Beardsley—who was a distant relation of Pitt—and collections of typographer Eric Gill and German expressionist Egon Schiele. Pitt enjoyed his role as mentor, and in Pygmalionesque manner, he took David to cultural hot spots and to the local Italian place, Restaurant Anticapri. It's possible that Pitt exaggerates his education of the nineteen-year-old, whom he describes as "not a cultured person" in those early days, but there's no doubt David was soaking up influences.

David enjoyed those months closeted with Ken, including the erotic undercurrent of his host's sexual orientation. On several occasions he frolicked around the flat naked; Pitt noticed his "long, weighty penis" and concedes that "David was a tease." On one occasion Pitt emerged from the bathroom naked and David, laughing, mimed measuring Pitt's penis, putting on an awed expression. The incident was recounted by one writer to illustrate the sexual frisson between them, but Pitt rejects that interpretation: "It was simply funny. Any sexual undertone was in their minds, not ours." To this day, Pitt, who knows better than anyone how David used his sexuality to win people over, professes himself ignorant of his charge's true sexual orientation: "Is David gay? I honestly don't know."

Bowie's arrival at the flat confirmed his status as Pitt's main client, and the manager constantly fired off letters looking for press, songwriting, and acting opportunities. Deram had gone quiet after the release of *David Bowie*—Tony Hall, one of David's supporters, had left, while Mendl and his friend Dick Rowe, both responsible for the label, were beset with political problems. The main focus of David's commercial activities started to center around his publishers, Essex Music.

David had been introduced to Essex by Tony Hall, an old friend of the company's celebrated proprietor David Platz. Ralph Horton had signed David to Essex during Pitt's trip to the United States, much to Pitt's chagrin, for he had been chasing a much bigger advance. But this alliance would prove vital over the next couple of years, placing Bowie within a sprawling musical nexus that included production companies overseen by Denny Cordell and later Gus Dudgeon, plus publishing clients that included Anthony Newley, Lionel Bart, Lonnie Donegan, the Moody Blues, and, from the spring of 1967, Marc Bolan. This ensured Marc and David continued to tread similar career paths, though these diverged when it came to songwriting, for Marc kept his songs to himself while David was evangelical about pushing his material and getting it heard.

The motivation was social as well as professional. For David, sharing his songs was how he related to people. In the later days of the Riot Squad he happily spent hours teaching his songs to Croke Prebble, who replaced him as singer. The same applied to his involvement with the Beatstalkers, then Scotland's leading live band, a tight-knit posse of Glaswegians who would have intimidated many outsiders. But not David. "He had incredible confidence," says bassist Alan Mair. "No matter where you were, he would pick up a guitar and sing full blast. Most people would be cagey, even Freddie Mercury was quite humble or quiet [in a similar situation], but David would flabbergast me."

David gave the Beatstalkers his song "Silver Tree Top School for Boys," a neat, "Waterloo Sunset"–style story of a dope-addled boys' school. More significant, "Over the Wall We Go" was recorded by a Robert Stigwood protégé named Oscar, later famous as sitcom actor Paul Nicholas. A playground ditty based on "Pop Goes the Weasel," "Over the Wall" failed to trouble the charts but nonetheless found an audience. "I played it all the time at Middle

Earth in the Roundhouse," says DJ Jeff Dexter. "It was a perfect record to play against the Pigs, man, a psychedelic comedy record—and it had this *fer-lum fer-lum fer-lum* beat that idiot dancers love." The single also became a late-night Radio London favorite, a campy psychedelic classic loved by those who'd grown up on Billy Cotton and the Goons and could cackle along in dope-enhanced hilarity.

None of these modest successes helped to sell David's own recordings, though, and Ken Pitt remembers his frustration at a logjam of material, recorded at Plaistow Grove and on an open-reel recorder at Manchester Street, that seemed destined never to be released. One evening Bowie vented his frustration, says Pitt, by telling him, "I'm going to write some Top Ten rubbish," then proceeded to write a song that was neither. "Let Me Sleep Beside You" would be his first collaboration with Tony Visconti, the producer with whom he's most associated; the finest song Bowie had written to that point, it also became the cause of his biggest artistic setback.

Tony Visconti had arrived in London in April of 1967 at the invitation of Denny Cordell, who'd worked with him briefly in New York. Cordell was overextended; Visconti had production experience and—crucially—turned out to be a brilliant arranger. Within weeks he was teamed with Denny Laine and Procol Harum, while his addition of a woodwind quartet to the Move's "Flowers in the Rain" helped propel it to number 2 on the charts. Visconti had already brought Marc Bolan's new project Tyrannosaurus Rex to Essex when David Platz played him an album by another Essex writer, David Bowie.

Visconti was intrigued, mostly by the album's diversity. "It was like a demo, trying everything: Look, I can do this, and I can do that too!" He was introduced to David in a tiny room at Dumbarton House, Essex Music's Oxford Street headquarters; the two built a rapport straightaway, both of them fast talking and obsessive with almost encyclopedic musical tastes. The producer listened to a number of David's demos and picked out "Let Me Sleep Beside You" as much for its folk-rock style as for its content.

Taking control of the project, Visconti located the musicians and wrote out every note of the music—"I had to, as we only had three hours for the session"—and produced the recording at Advision. The result was David's most coherent, concise song since "Can't Help Thinking about Me." Its lyrics—"I will show you dreams where the winner never wins"—were vaguely Dylanish; its "dededu-dum dededum" vocalizing Bolan-ish. His voice sounded mature and free of affectation, and in the middle eight, his double-track vocals are a foretaste of *Ziggy Stardust*'s rock-and-roll yell.

A gorgeous track, it was rejected by Decca's regular Monday singles-selection panel. The decision marked the beginning of a minor crisis for David (and a major crisis for Deram, as Denny Cordell and Platz switched allegiance to EMI over this same period). David had so far endured his career setbacks with a characteristic calm, but during these months he started to voice his pain. Steve Chapman was in charge of Essex Music's demo studio, where he helped David record songs and cut acetates of the "amazingly creative" demos David crafted at Manchester Street. The studio was tiny, and they spent long hours in conversation; the seventeen-year-old Chapman looked up to the worldly, intelligent singer: "He had this amazing palette of ideas, Tibetan philosophy, mystical concepts." But late in 1967, shortly before Chapman left to join a band named Junior's Eyes, he noticed "David sounded quite depressed. He told me, 'I'm thinking of chucking it in. Really, I'd like to become a Buddhist monk.'"

Those frustrating afternoons, often spent hanging around with no prospect of recording, eventually put paid to the youthful arrogance that Leslie Conn remembered. Ken Pitt persevered, sending a copy of the album to Mickie Most to drum up interest—Most didn't reply—and fruitlessly chasing acting and commercials jobs. By the spring of 1968, the crisis of confidence had extended to Bowie's manager, according to Alan Mair, who after quitting the Beatstalkers had been given the use of a spare office by Ken Pitt: "I think Ken Pitt had reached the stage where he didn't know what to do with him. One day he said to me, 'Do you want to be David's personal manager?' I wasn't interested—but I think Ken had reached the point where he was pulling his hair out." The situation deteriorated further in March, when Deram rejected "In the Heat of the Morning" and "London Bye Ta-Ta." It was particularly painful for Hugh Mendl. "It was so hard," he reflects sadly; "he was a wonderful person—but at that time it was me against fate."

In the Bowie story, the Deram staff have generally been cast as villains, but "In the Heat of the Morning," despite its elegant Visconti string arrangement, was undistinguished, its style essentially that of the Deram album minus the cockney vocal. And in the end, it was Bowie and Pitt's decision to walk. "David came in and said, 'I don't think anything's happening for me as a singer,'" says Mendl. "He told me, 'I'm going to go and do dancing—so could I please be released?'"

Mendl had long, tortuous conversations with his friend Dick Rowe, who was in similar straits with Cat Stevens; he'd left Deram that spring after a bout of tuberculosis. Distressed that the label was falling apart, Mendl agreed to let David go, "but I had the feeling I was being a bit conned." At the time he thought that the move was perhaps a piece of grandstanding by Bowie and that he had some masterwork up his sleeve. Mendl couldn't have been more wrong.

DAVID'S claim that he was planning a new career as a dancer was, for the moment, true.

The move seemed bizarre at the time; in retrospect, it marked the transition from a conventional career progression to a series of inspired leaps into the unknown. In 1968, with only a couple of decent songs to his name, the twenty-one-year-old David Bowie did not have many of the hallmarks of a great artist. The one that he undoubtedly did have was courage.

This fascinating digression started when a secretary in Ken Pitt's office sent a copy of the Deram album to actor and dancer Lindsay Kemp. Kemp was "absolutely enchanted by the songs—and by the voice. It was reminiscent of my other favorite singers, like Anthony Newley and Jacques Brel; a husky, smoky voice that was plaintive, damaged. And I was able to identify with that."

The performer started using "When I Live My Dream" to open his show at the Little Theatre Club off St. Martins Lane; David took Kemp up on his invitation to come see a performance and was "very flattered," says Kemp. "And the show fascinated him, with me as Pierrot. And we met afterwards and it was love at first sight." After the show, David followed Lindsay to his flat in Bateman Street, Soho; there, he beheld a British version of the New York underworld depicted by the Velvet Underground. "My flat was filled with strippers, hookers, pimps, and druggies," remembers Kemp fondly. Kemp had assumed, given the wide-eyed quality of the Deram album, that Bowie would be "as innocent as a child," but he was proven wrong: "He looked around, then he sat down—and was completely at home."

The story of Kemp's life is theatrical, picaresque, and rather heroic. He was born in Birkenhead, and his sailor father was lost at sea when Kemp was two. Kemp's mother encouraged him to dress up and paint his face, and then, worried he'd taken to it too well, sent him to naval college, where he read ballet books and learned to survive by "enchanting the boys," dancing covered in red paint and toilet paper. After art college in Bradford, where he was friends with David Hockney, he trained with, and then was thrown out by, the Ballet Rambert. Aided by the bald, muscular, and partially blind collaborator Jack Birkett—the Incredible Orlando—he developed an unconventional hybrid of drag, mime, and song and dance, and he became one of London's most respected dance teachers, working out of his studio on Floral Street.

Mick Farren, future underground scenester and member of the Deviants, painted backdrops for Kemp along with fellow ex–St. Martins students. He liked Kemp, but along with many friends, he found Kemp's scene intimidating: "It was a bit like going into the Warhol Factory—if you wanted to hang out you had to learn heavy manners. And David came in, learning moves. He was clearly absorbing a lot—mutating."

Kemp in person is engaging and sweet rather than intimidating. With his natural ebullience, he revels in recounting extraordinary yarns that vary with the telling, as he readily admits. Kemp fell in love with David the first afternoon they met; the dancer spent his time discussing his passions, which included "the the- ater, the music hall, silent movies, the Oriental and ritualistic the- ater, Kabuki, Jean Genet, the Theater of the Absurd." Their interests hardly overlapped; it was David's "great sense of humor" that sealed their relationship, and they often traded imperson- ations of music-hall stars and movie icons like Laurel and Hardy.

Kemp says it was a love affair as well as a working relationship that commenced that day. On their first "date" David took Lindsay to the Tibetan Society, and soon David suggested a title for a new work, "Pierrot in Turquoise," on which they would collaborate: "Turquoise is the Buddhist symbol for everlastingness. And of course I wore turquoise costumes, as a nineteenth-century-inspired clown."

As plans developed for the Pierrot show, David attended dance classes at Floral Street. In those days, said Kemp, "He wasn't a very good mover, but he was equipped with the essential thing: a desire to move. And I taught him to exteriorize, to reveal his soul. And he had all this inside him, anyway."

Sadly, no complete record exists of the show that Kemp and director Craig Van Roque crafted based on the ancient tale of Pier- rot and Harlequin but with a modern, anarchic slant. The press reviews at the time suggest that the performance was less than the sum of its parts but that the parts were beguiling. Bowie played Cloud, who, in addition to singing, observed and com- mented on events in Brechtian fashion. He contributed "Colum- bine," one of the finest songs of his folk-rock period, simple and elegant; "Threepenny Pierrot," a variant of "London Bye Ta-Ta"; and, in the early version, "Maids of Mayfair" — "A real craftsman's song," says Kemp's musical collaborator Gordon Rose, who would later take over as musical director at the Palladium. "I can still remember it—it had a theme, a chord sequence, and a good hook."

The plot revolves around Pierrot's unrequited love for Colum- bine, who is seduced by Jack Birkett's Harlequin. The most mem- orable scene is "Aimez-Vous Bach," which depicts Pierrot's despair: The lovelorn character cuts open his belly, throws out his heart, and dances away using his entrails as a jump rope while pianist Michael Garrett improvises around Bach's French Suites. Often Kemp extended the scene well beyond its normal duration, basking in the attention.

The tiny troupe hustled gigs around the country, sending out letters that Kemp and Garrett dictated while the partially sighted Birkett bashed away at a typewriter; Oxford Playhouse on December 28, 1967, was the first, followed by three nights at Whitehaven's Rosehill Theatre, a jewel-like folly built in a converted barn on the grounds of an eighteenth-century house owned by arts patron Miki Sekers.

Sekers was a Hungarian immigrant who'd founded a celebrated textile company; the company made parachutes as well as the silk for Princess Margaret's wedding dress. The textile magnate donated the silk that Russian designer Natasha Korniloff used to craft the show's brightly hued costumes. Korniloff was the only member of the troupe with a driver's license; barely tall enough to see over the wheel, she was charged with coaxing the overloaded van, packed with the troupe members and their costumes, from Oxford up to Cumbria for the run of shows.

According to Lindsay Kemp, Rosehill was the scene of a bizarre love triangle that played out in the farmhouse that the troupe took over. Nestled in a drafty four-poster bed that he says he had been sharing with Bowie, waiting for his lover's return, Kemp heard "noises through the wall." Venturing into the cold night, he discovered Bowie curled up with Natasha. "I was traumatized," says Kemp. "Totally destroyed."

Kemp does admit that his subsequent well-publicized suicide attempt was "theatrical"—an attempt to slash his wrists produced only surface wounds. "Some of those stories *are* exaggerated. And I've given several versions." One of those stories has his blood drenching his costume in that night's performance, ensuring rapturous applause from the crowd. Pianist Michael Garrett remembers that at one point during the evening, Kemp sat on the edge of the stage holding the audience rapt with a long soliloquy inspired by his star-crossed love affair.

Kemp and Korniloff were united in both their anger at their two-timing lover and their grief. "We cried on each other's shoulders," says Kemp. The treacherous Cloud was then forced to sleep on a chaise longue in the hall for the next two nights ("the poor sod"). Despite such backstage shenanigans, says Michael Garrett— who was also besotted with Natasha—the attitude, in sterling showbiz fashion, was that the show must go on: "Lindsay was *always* having affairs with a member of the cast, and there were *always* arguments and fights. David was actually a gentleman. In any case, we would always go onstage sozzled—which helped."

After the short run of dates finished, the cast dispersed, although David continued to drop in on Lindsay at the dance center. Time, the great healer, did its work, and eventually the dancer's bruised heart "began to recover," at least enough so that he could work with David for more performances in March.

ALTHOUGH he'd largely kept his distance from psychedelia in 1967, David was content to drift along in its slipstream in 1968. He immersed himself in the underground scene, hanging out with characters like Jeff Dexter and Lesley Duncan—the striking, dark-haired songwriter and backup vocalist who later sang on Pink Floyd's *Dark Side of the Moon*—at Lindsay's top-floor flat on Redington Road, which offered a breathtaking, panoramic view of Hampstead Heath. For a few weeks they had regular Thursday-night flying-saucer meditation sessions during which, says Dexter, "We hoped the flying saucers would come and take us away."

In these late-night consciousness-expanding sessions, David would take any spliffs handed around, but he wasn't a committed dope smoker; photographer Ray Stevenson noticed his tendency to "hold the joint for a bit—and then pass it on." According to the Lower Third, he'd boasted that he was first turned on to grass by Donovan and had encountered "amazing visions"—but his drug of choice remained filtered cigarettes, at least a pack a day. During the heyday of acid David rarely, if ever, turned on—at least not with the aid of LSD. Jeff Dexter points out that he'd assumed everyone present at the evening saucer sweeps was into psychedelics "but I discovered many years later lots of people who I thought were psychedelicized with me weren't."

The sessions at Redington Road incorporated meditation based on Tibetan Buddhism, and the participants, including David, had the idea that "we could all communicate with other worlds," says Dexter. Ken Pitt suggests that David's practice of Buddhism mainly involved burning a couple of joss sticks, yet David studied Buddhism with dedication, visiting Tibet House to meet the Lama Chime Rinpoche. His fascination with Tibet inspired the stately "Silly Boy Blue," which, although obviously influenced by "Walk on By," boasted one of the most beautiful melodies of his Deram album. While David was never a full-blown devotee, his Buddhist credentials, says Jeff Dexter, were convincing: "When I first went to Samye Ling, the monastery up in Scotland, he'd already made an impression with the head monk, Chogyam Trungpa Rinpoche. And he signed the book before me—so he already had more than a couple of joss sticks." Another friend, Ray Stevenson, remembers David's real anger at China's treatment of Tibetan monks: "He told me all about Chime, and the atrocities that were inflicted—I remember that anger, it stayed with me."

Some of David's interest in Buddhism, it turned out, was stimulated by a new figure in his life: Hermione Farthingale. Lindsay Kemp had recommended the classy, sweet red-haired dancer, along with David and a couple of others, for walk-on roles in "The Pistol Shot," part of the BBC drama series *Theatre 625;* the episode was recorded in January and broadcast on May 20, 1968. Bowie and Hermione had minor roles dancing a minuet together in period costume, which was enough to spark a relationship, much to Kemp's chagrin—"because I still had hopes. Although Hermione was a wonderful girl, I must admit."

David's relationship with Hermione would mark what his friends saw as a transformation in his outlook; he was relaxed, almost playful. Hermione was upper class—her father was a solicitor in Edenbridge—relatively conservative, quiet, and "sensitive," says her flatmate Vernon Dewhurst. "She was a lovely girl, quite intense, and quite serious, compared to David." They made a sweet couple—Hermione the more self-consciously intellectual, David the joker. He didn't strike anyone as particularly bookish or highbrow—generally, he was simply a laugh, had a good sense of humor, was always joking.

In August of 1968, the pair set up housekeeping together at 22 Clareville Grove, just off the Old Brompton Road, an elegant street in South Kensington filled with upmarket shops and clubs. The refined but cozy three-story Georgian house belonged to boutique owner Breege Collins. Her boyfriend, Tom, was a literary Henry Miller type; photographer Vernon Dewhurst rented a back room along with his girlfriend, model and future Bond Girl Zara Hussein; another couple had conventional office jobs; and David and Hermione rented the first floor. The place "always smelled nice," according to Ray Stevenson; "you could tell it was mostly girls lived there." Hermione's sense of style was evident in the Lloyd Loom chair, a vase of dried grasses in the cast-iron fireplace, lace on the bed's headboard, and burlap cushions on the floor.

For nearly six months in this cozy little setting, David seemed uncharacteristically at ease, content. His songs of that spring— "In the Heat of the Morning," "London Bye Ta-Ta," "Karma Man"—were generally elegant, like his surroundings. By sheer hard work and ambition, he had begun making himself into a craftsman. David continued to experiment with new songs, although it was obvious he was lagging behind Marc Bolan, who had finally lodged himself in the public consciousness with the Visconti-produced "Debora," which reached number 34 that May. Bolan kept it basic, rock and roll with some clever wordplay and a Donovan yodel. He had achieved something vital; his music was memorable and distinctive. Four years into David's recording career, it seemed doubtful that he would ever manage this feat. Although living with Hermione had rubbed off much of his competitive aggression, Marc's success still rankled: "Oh yeah! Boley struck it big, and we were all green with envy... It was terrible; we fell out for about six months. He got all sniffy about us who were down in the basement. But we got over that."

For all his pangs of jealousy, David could be happy for his ex-mod mate: "They were like brothers," says Ray Stevenson. "It was a good rivalry," says Jeff Dexter, "young blokes' rivalry." The two were remarkably similar: fey and boyish, confident and flirtatious — and exceptionally talkative. David could expound on a wider variety of subjects than Marc, says Stevenson, who points out that Marc's favorite topic was probably himself. David often talked Marc up to his friends, and when Bolan was preparing his debut album, Bowie suggested that George Underwood, who'd turned to art to make a living, design the sleeve. When the album was a hit, Bowie seemed pleased; it marked a calmer, less competitive side of his character, inspired primarily by Hermione.

Bolan talked up David to his friends, telling them he'd given David an instrument he'd been toying with, the Stylophone, a toy keyboard played with a stylus that featured two buzzy synthesizer waveforms and a groovy faux-mahogany case (Visconti remembers that the quirky plastic gadget was actually a gift from Ken Pitt). But there was jealousy there too; according to Tony Visconti, when David supported Tyrannosaurus Rex at a Middle Earth show on May 19, Bolan insisted Bowie should not sing; instead, David improvised "Yet-San and the Eagle," a mime based on China's invasion of Tibet and set to a tape of "Little Boy Blue." The performance, as MC Jeff Dexter observes, took "a lot of front" and was lapped up by the audience, bar a couple of noisy Maoists.

By the autumn of 1968, Ken Pitt was gradually being excluded from Clareville Grove's cozy little world; his task, it seemed, was fielding letters from Haywood Jones, who was wondering if his son would ever make a living wage from his music. Pitt and Jones had discussed whether the cabaret scene might represent the solution for David's lack of money. The suggestion, says Pitt, came from Haywood and was agreed to by David. Pitt helped Bowie rehearse a routine that included performing some of his own songs to a taped background, intersong patter, and — in a poignantly ludicrous detail — props in the form of four cutout Beatles. The idea was stillborn — one agent who witnessed a run-through told Pitt, "It's a great act, but where can I book it? It's too good."

For Bowie and Visconti, the abortive move into cabaret came to epitomize Pitt's out-of-touch, old-school attitude—and the increasing backbiting between the Pitt and Visconti camps anticipated many such battles in David's career. In the absence of any clear direction from David himself, Pitt continued investigating openings for acting jobs while also hoping to advance Bowie's musical career with a promotional film based on some of his recent material, including "Let Me Sleep Beside You." In the meantime, David paid the bills by working at Legastat, a photocopy shop near London's High Court frequented by lawyers and barristers.

With the cabaret idea abandoned, David turned his attention once more to the underground movement; after placing an ad in its house journal, the *International Times,* he recruited Tony Hill—previously guitarist with the Misunderstood—to team up with him and Hermione. Named Turquoise, the "multimedia trio" performed their first show at the Roundhouse on September 14; for their second show, they renamed themselves Feathers. Hill was unimpressed by the trio and left after three shows to form his own band, High Tide.

Fortunately the indefatigable Hutch, David's companion from the Buzz, had left his job in Canada and returned to London. With a new taste for folk music, a day job as draftsman for a refrigeration company at Hornsey (which meant he didn't need paying), and his down-to-earth Yorkshire demeanor, Hutch was a better fit for the band than Hill, and he found David more congenial than in the old days: "He was happy and relaxed, which I'd never really seen in the Buzz—probably down to Ralph, whose trousers and everything else were too tight. David had come out of that and was happy with Hermione."

The music too was more spontaneous, worked out in the top floor at Clareville Grove, Hutch on his Harmony six-string acoustic, David on his Gibson twelve-string. David was still searching out music, absorbing Hutch's recent influences, like Leonard Cohen and Joni Mitchell, and turning Hutch on to a new obsession of his, Jacques Brel.

Bowie had first heard Brel's songs when he was hanging

around Lesley Duncan's flat, having become besotted with her; they briefly enjoyed what David describes as an "on again, off again" relationship. Lesley had previously had a fling with Scott Walker and had the distressing habit of playing Scott's songs whenever David was around at Redington Road. Initially offended, Bowie became intrigued by the Jacques Brel songs that Walker was singing; once his jealousy subsided, he became a fan of Scott Walker, but more crucially he became obsessed with Brel. When *Jacques Brel Is Alive and Well and Living in Paris*—Eric Blau and Mort Shuman's Greenwich Village show based on Brel's songs—came to London later in 1968, David was in the audience. Hutch spent many evenings at Clareville Grove working out the chords for "Port of Amsterdam" and "Next," which they incorporated into their repertoire.

The new trio played their first "multimedia" show together at Hampstead's Country Club on November 17; one wonders if, as he floated across the stage during the band's naive, almost child-like performance, David recalled his music and movement classes from Burnt Ash. David and Hermione's mini-ballet was danced to a spoken-word piece played on a cassette recorder. David performed a solo mime, "The Mask," with a similar taped backing, while Hutch, persuaded he had to do a spoken-word piece, settled on "At Lunchtime" by Liverpool poet Roger McGough because "at least he was a northerner."

For all the so-called experimentation of London's underground scene, most audiences were confused or unmoved by the Feathers' performances. Their recordings show why. In October, Visconti managed to wangle a session at Trident, funded by Essex, to record "Ching-a-Ling." A piece of childlike whimsy with lyrics about azure clouds and crystal girls, it seemed an unsuccessful attempt to ape Marc Bolan. The best that can be said about this lightweight ditty is that it anticipated the summer jug-band feel of future hits like the Mixture's "The Pushbike Song." Perhaps the song's blandness can be explained with the theory that domestic harmony doesn't usually inspire great works of art. If that was the case, a solution to the problem was imminent.

* * *

WITH its low ceilings and creaking floorboards, Clareville Grove was not conducive to privacy, and toward the end of 1968, flatmate Vernon Dewhurst heard two kinds of sounds emanating from David and Hermione's room. One was more frequent arguments between the two. The other was David working out a new song. He showed it to Hutch after a couple of days, by which time he'd already thought of overlaying its claustrophobic chords with the sinister, comic buzz of his Stylophone and had completed most of the lyrics, which opened with the words "Ground Control to Major Tom." "He was immensely proud of it," says Dewhurst, one of the first people to hear the new song, "but I remember laughing about the Stylophone."

"Space Oddity" was born fully formed, and although it has been said that Hutch wrote the opening chord sequence, he points out that he merely changed some chord shapes to add to the song's ethereal, disjointed feel. The song's distinctive harmonic structure was defined by David's limited, unconventional guitar style, while its lyrics were tightly plotted. In fact, the piece was not organized like a song, with verses, choruses, and a middle eight; it was more like a work of drama. David describes the song as arriving almost instantaneously, inspired by his trip to see Stanley Kubrick's *2001: A Space Odyssey*. "I went stoned out of my mind to see the movie and it really freaked me out, especially the trip passage." For the first time, a song had arrived without conscious effort or as an attempt to mimic others—the first song that derived from David's unconscious, rather than his ambition.

Hutch learned the song and worked out a harmony vocal, and two points struck him, as they strike today's listener: the simplicity of the melody and the complexity of the structure. The main melody, accentuated by the Stylophone, is made up of two notes a semitone apart; the most claustrophobic melody possible, the perfect metaphor for the narrator's isolation. Meanwhile, the song's structure is arranged exactly as a script, with the simplest of chords anchoring the basic opening dialogue, and the melody and chords becoming more expansive as the story unfolds—and

Major Tom steps into the void. As Hutch observes, "Most musicians make songs with a structure that has been used before—his songs have a structure he dreams up for himself."

While it's the words that have drawn most attention on this song, it's the harmonic structure that renders it extraordinary. Each chord change manipulates the mood—as Ground Control tells the major he's made the grade, the chord swerves from the opening line's minor to a cheerily optimistic major, a psychological judder that tells us of the disconnect between Ground Control and the astronaut. It's a consummate piece of songwriting, the first evidence that Bowie might indeed be the genius he'd said he was two years earlier.

An extra surreal frisson has been added by the intriguing suggestion, made by writer Nicholas Pegg and others, that the hero's name was inspired by Tom Major, a failed trapeze artist from Brixton whose unlikely career became celebrated when his son, John Major, became the British prime minister in 1990. Sadly, the intriguing possibility that a poster for Tom Major's circus act had lodged itself in the young David Jones's memory is impossibly remote, for two decades before David's birth, Tom Major had retired from showbiz in order to make garden gnomes (and may therefore have influenced a far less classic Bowie song).

The "Space Oddity" sense of numbness and alienation has inspired speculation that its genesis involved heroin—rumors encouraged by David in the mid-seventies when he was playing up his image as a long-term druggie. Those close to him at the time—including Ray Stevenson, whose brother Nils would later succumb to heroin addiction—dismiss the idea. "I don't think David and Hermione were even into smoking dope," says Hutch. "They were into white wine. There was a side of the scene with a lot of sitting in basements and getting wasted, but not those two." Even David's own account of watching Kubrick's *2001* stoned on grass doesn't tally with the recollections of people like Tony Visconti, who remembers him coughing and spluttering when inhaling a joint. Instead, the bleakness of the song seems to have been inspired by his arguments with Hermione—rows noticed by those around them, people who had been genuinely affected by the feeling of bliss that, along with the smell of joss sticks, permeated the elegant Georgian hallways of Clareville Grove. That bliss, unique in David's life so far, would not reoccur for many years. Its loss marked his rise to the star status he'd craved for so long.

According to Ken Pitt, David's new song surfaced after he asked David to write a "special piece of new material" for a promotional film he'd been planning in the hope of getting David exposure on German or British TV. Shot on Hampstead Heath and at Clarence Film Studio on Deptford Creek, the film featured nine segments, including the trio performing "Ching-a-Ling," an overdubbed "Sell Me a Coat," and a lip-synched "Let Me Sleep Beside You." The most historically significant section included a studio version of "Space Oddity," with David contributing a kooky solo on the ocarina. The footage is marvelously campy, all the more so for the wig David had to sport because he'd gotten a haircut for a tiny TV role in *The Virgin Soldiers*. Bowie puts his dance training to use, simulating weightlessness before succumbing to the embraces of a pair of space nymphettes.

Without a doubt, the most bizarre curio of the promo film was David's mime of "The Mask," for which he wears Elizabethan-style white tights that flatter his pert buttocks and well-packed codpiece ("'The Mask' was always Ken Pitt's favorite," observes Hutch tartly). To his own voiceover, he mimes the tale of a boy who finds a mask in a junk shop, puts it on, and discovers it holds the secret of fame; at the climax, as the hero performs at the Palladium, the mask strangles him.

The short, hilarious film was both gauche and prescient; even as David Bowie attempts to court fame in an almost variety-style performance, he anticipates its corrosive effects. That ambivalence would be reflected in the months that followed as he finally achieved the fame for which he'd hungered. As the film showed, few other artists were as conscious of the duality of fame as David Bowie. Fewer still, after the fame from that first hit had ebbed away, would find themselves even more addicted.

CHAPTER 6

Check Ignition

David was adored on all sides... He has to be in that situation,
otherwise you don't get ahead. You could call it manipulation, but
what the hell.

—Calvin Lee

A s 1968 turned to 1969, hippie unity was splintering
forever. Idealism and whimsy were shouldered aside by a
wave of denim-clad, blues-riffin' musos preaching a gos-
pel of authenticity. Bands like Led Zeppelin and Free exploded
onto the scene, and the elfin, languid 1969 David Bowie was just
as out of sync with the new dress-down era as he'd been in his
previous Anthony Newley mode. During that disastrous period
he'd been powered forward by a brash, luminous confidence and
some artful, unfocused songs. This time around, that youthful
confidence was battered. But he had one crucial factor in his favor:
a copper-bottomed classic song, "Space Oddity." It was his ace in
the hole, and he played it with a new subtlety.

Over these months, acquaintances noticed traits that would
become characteristic of the twenty-something David Bowie: the
way he'd earnestly quiz people to find out how they ticked; how he'd
search out allies and file them in his mental Rolodex for future use
without mentioning them to his current friends. Often, he seemed

strangely passive, leaving decisions to others, content to bury his still-bruised ego. As one friend, musician and *International Times* writer Mick Farren, puts it, "You got the feeling he didn't want to show his cards—because he didn't have many to begin with."

Those who fell out with David in later years often described his behavior from this period on as cold and manipulative; in reality, although unusually secretive, he was easygoing, following the flow, simply taking advantage of random opportunities. One such chance came when he was visiting Barrie Jackson, an old Bromley friend who'd moved down the street to Foxgrove Road in Beckenham. Hearing music drifting from the top flat, Mary Finnigan, a tenant of the Foxgrove Road building who was sunbathing in the garden, called out, "Who's playing?"

After a few moments, David came downstairs to share the sunshine and, says Finnigan, the tincture of cannabis she was enjoying. A week or so later, in April of 1969, David moved in with Mary and her two children at 24 Foxgrove Road. His friends had only just noticed the absence of Hermione, who David told them had left for New York. They missed David's elegant, red-haired companion but were impressed by how quickly he'd lined up a replacement. "We were very jealous," says David's friend Ray Stevenson. "He never had to pay any rent."

Mary Finnigan had an impeccably middle-class background, but after a brush with the law, a conviction for drug possession— ultimately overturned—and a consequent brief stretch in the Holloway prison in 1967, she had taken up the hippie cause as a writer for the *International Times*. She and David soon became lovers, and she took on the singer as her new cause. She helped organize a regular folk club at the Three Tuns on Beckenham High Street, and by its fourth week, on Sunday, May 25, the venture was titled the Beckenham Arts Lab and had started drawing in street musicians, puppeteers, poets, and other artists. Working with the eclectic group of volunteers, David immersed himself in mime and the visual arts as well as music. The group became his main focus of activity after his partnership with Hutch came to an end. After long days in the office, the Yorkshireman spent many intense evenings working on material with David. In April, when a hoped-for deal with Atlantic failed to materialize, Hutch returned to the north in search of a decent salary to support his wife and young son. David appeared unconcerned, but later Hutch heard he'd been telling his friends, "Hutch thought we were never going to make it." It seemed, Hutch thought, that "David simply had no grasp of the concept of having a family to feed."

With Hutch's departure, David got more involved in Arts Lab meetings. The group boasted two formidable administrators in the form of Finnigan and Nita Bowes (later an adviser to Tony Blair and daughter-in-law to the celebrated aristocrat and politician Tony Benn); they pursued government grants and talked of setting up a countrywide network of arts organizations. The pair dominated the group's debates; David was more soft-spoken but earnest and thoughtful, as happy talking about puppeteers and street theater as about music. According to Keith Christmas, who along with David was one of the group's main musical draws, the audience's motivations were not as highfalutin as the organizers': "It was a terrific gig from day one. Because the pub looked quite normal from the front, but at the back was a large room and conservatory, with its own entrance. So people could get down there and get off their faces in the warm evenings."

Throughout the Arts Lab period, David's talk was peppered with fashionable underground sentiments, yet a few people close to him at the time wondered how profound his conversion to the cause was. Alan Mair is one of several who were "not a hundred percent sure about the hippie-trippie thing. I thought his mind was somewhere else." But David's hippie collectivism and talk of being off his face did at least signal his independence from Ken Pitt, who viewed such behavior with abhorrence. Keith Christmas, later a leading light of the folk revival spearheaded by Fairport Convention and others, was certain that Bowie was a fellow traveler, although not necessarily for cynical reasons: "He recognized there were groovy people—and he liked groovy interesting people. And he knew that most of the big talent was making acoustic music, so he wasn't slow to have a go."

For David Bowie, the hippie movement represented a seam of inspiration to be mined rather than a guiding philosophy. Even while he was taking his foot off the career accelerator, at heart he remained a traditional entertainer. "Space Oddity," a highlight of his Three Tuns set, embodied this contradiction. It would be the perfect sixties anthem, with its trendy sci-fi theme and rejection of materialism. Yet friends like Tony Visconti believed it was a gimmick song, just like Joe Meek's "Telstar," and to get it released David would have to indulge in plenty of old-school music-biz networking.

Fortunately, David had fallen in with one of London's finest networkers back in June of 1967 at a party in New Bond Street. Calvin Mark Lee was a doctor of pharmacology who in 1963 had won a grant to pursue postgraduate research under the internationally renowned Arnold Beckett. Lee's criteria for meeting people were that they be "beautiful, creative, and intelligent," and since few scientists could check all three boxes, Lee's new project became Swinging London. Soon the thirty-three-year-old's social circle included Lionel Bart, Dandy Fashions' John Crittle, Stan Owsley, Mike Nesmith, and Jimi Hendrix. The influential, wayward folksinger Anne Briggs was briefly his girlfriend, and a wall of photos, many of naked subjects, in his Kings Road flat diarized his eclectic social and sexual acquaintances. If that were not enough to mark his exotic status, Calvin Lee wore on his forehead a glittery plastic disk—a diffraction grating that shimmered in the light like a hologram and proclaimed his star-child credentials, as it would for Ziggy Stardust a few years later.

Lee had met David at a reception at Chappell Music three weeks after the release of his Deram album, back in 1967. From early 1969, when Lee was given an expense account by Mercury Records and a role as head of promotions for the label, he became an integral part of David's social scene—which was now fiendishly complicated, for as Lee explains, "David was adored on all sides. You have Ken, you have me, you have Hermione. So there were certain amounts of jealousy." The two, says Lee, shared a sexual relationship that was remarkable partly for its brevity. He remembers David's incessant, crippling headaches, which he believes were "brought on by all these various tensions." Today, he accepts that David's flirtation with him was partly driven by ambition. "He has to be in that situation, otherwise you don't get ahead. You could call it manipulation, but what the hell."

Still, Calvin understood David's music, and he was one of the first to hear "Space Oddity." He considered it "otherworldly," in every sense, and set about on a mission "to clandestinely push David Bowie."

Lee had an ally at Mercury named Simon Hayes who had come to the label's attention as manager of the Fool, the London design collective and band that Mercury had signed on the bizarre theory that the group had painted John Lennon's Rolls-Royce and so were the next best thing to having the Beatles. Hayes negotiated the band's deal with Mercury before being offered the job of head of international A and R by the company's cofounder Irving Green in January of 1969. Hayes and Lee knew each other from the London fashion and art scene, and according to Hayes, "Lee was really on the case with 'Space Oddity,' a total convert. He wanted to sign David—and I said, 'Fantastic idea.'" David Bowie would be his first major signing.

The process, however, was fraught with complications, thanks to the labyrinthine corporate and internal politics of the Mercury Philips empire, an organization described by Philips manager Olav Wyper as "a disaster." The UK arm, Philips, was a joint venture between Mercury USA and the Dutch electronics conglomerate; the American company retained its own London office, overseen by Lou Reizner.

Reizner had his own musical ambitions; his best-known achievements would be overseeing the sound track for *Tommy* and the disastrous *All This and World War II*, which set Beatles' covers to black-and-white wartime cine footage. He also fancied himself a singer and saw Bowie as a rival, which meant Calvin Lee had to work surreptitiously to advance his friend's career.

Reizner's dislike of Bowie would soon be intensified by another figure in the web of relationships that surrounded the singer, a girlfriend of the Mercury exec who was also involved with Calvin Lee and who, in January of 1969, had declared her fascination with David Bowie after accompanying Reizner and Lee to a Feathers show at the Roundhouse. Her name was Angela Barnett.

As Mark Pritchett, a long-term friend of David Bowie, puts it: "Angela Barnett was a complicated character at the time—let alone now." Pritchett's description is as apt as anyone's. Angela Barnett, an American citizen who arrived in London in the summer of 1966 to study at secretarial college and then at Kingston Polytechnic, later claimed she had been a key figure in securing David Bowie's next record deal. In fact, the key figures in the signing, notably Simon Hayes, remember Angie's involvement in this early stage as peripheral—but she would become a prime mover in almost every aspect of his career for the next four years.

In 1975, David Bowie would tell writer Cameron Crowe that he met his future wife "because we were both fucking the same guy." The guy was Calvin Lee, and Bowie's boasts about his bisexuality would become a pivotal element in his public persona. Angie was the cocreator of this persona, yet her contribution to David's career went much further. From the moment she appeared on the scene, following her first "date" with Bowie, on May 30, 1969, Angela Barnett electrified everyone around her. As Ray Stevenson puts it, "She was a bit of spunk. She was American. The English sit around whining; Americans get out there and do things."

The couple met over a Chinese meal with Calvin Lee on his expense account, after which the trio carried on partying at the Speakeasy, where the group King Crimson was playing one of its first London shows. As they sat, talking and flirting, Angie thought the Mercury promotions man was trying to serve her up as a kind of sexual delicacy for the singer he'd helped sign. The two looked quite similar, with their clear skin and almost elfin features; Angie dominated the conversation, as was her habit, while David's remarks were mostly amused or dry. That night, David returned with Angie to her tiny flat above a travel agent's in Paddington.

Soon after the relationship began, Angie and David played out a scene that would come to typify their time together. She knew full well he was "like an alley cat" but one morning she nonetheless succumbed to a bout of jealousy—or theatricality—when he told her that he was going out: She threw herself down the stairs. Without batting an eye, David stepped over her on his way to the door and politely took his leave.

For the time being, Ken Pitt remained blissfully unaware of Angela Barnett's existence, and he exchanged letters with Simon Hayes during April and May of 1969 as the Mercury A and R department put together a deal. With Hayes largely absent in New York and Chicago, David Platz and Essex Music took charge of the recording session for the song that had won over Hayes and Lee. Earlier in the year, Ken Pitt had sent a demo of "Space Oddity" to George Martin, hoping the Beatles' producer would agree to oversee a Bowie recording. After chasing him for several weeks, Pitt eventually found out from Martin's secretary that he was unimpressed. There was a more surprising knockdown to come— from the man who'd produced all of David's recent material, Tony Visconti.

Today, the stripped-down bleakness of "Space Oddity" gives it a certain purity. Yet that purity belies its origins, for most of those concerned in releasing it considered it a good song but distinguished mainly by the marketing opportunity it represented: its association with the Apollo moon landing scheduled for late that July. It was a good gimmick. According to Simon Hayes, the notion that the single would tie in with that July's moon shot was what drove the signing: "Everybody was always looking for a hook—that was it."

Even though Tony Visconti threw himself into planning the album that would follow "Space Oddity," he disliked the song itself: "I didn't like the idea of capitalizing on the man on the moon," he says today. "I thought it was a cheap shot." He was a "principled hippie," and Visconti's celebrated distaste for the song made sense at the time, though today he concedes, "I've grown to like it a bit." Meanwhile, having rejected the song, he helped ensure its eventual success by suggesting several of the key figures in its recording—a role he would adopt for many subsequent David Bowie works, even those that did not bear his name.

The imminent Apollo launch meant that contractual negotiations, and the session, needed tying up quickly. Gus Dudgeon, who had recently joined the Essex empire, worked in the office next to Visconti's; Visconti called him up and suggested he take over the song. Dudgeon, who knew David well through their work on the Deram album, thought Bowie's demo of the song was "unbelievable. I couldn't believe my luck. I had to phone Tony just to make sure he wanted me to do it. He claimed there was a lot of better stuff on the album, at which stage Bowie and I sat down and planned the record—every detail of it."

The session was tightly budgeted and choreographed: Dudgeon sketched out a plan, adorned with squiggles denoting a Stylophone or Mellotron part; Visconti suggested guitarist Mick Wayne and keyboard player Rick Wakeman, then still at music college. String arranger Paul Buckmaster was another Essex contact. Only the members of the rhythm section were experienced hands—drummer Terry Cox had played with Alexis Korner and Pentangle, and bassist Herbie Flowers had been working sessions since he'd been talent-spotted by Paul McCartney in 1967.

The recording session for "Space Oddity," on June 20, 1969, was one of those rare occasions when everyone involved sensed the historic importance. According to Gus, "When we hit that studio we knew exactly what we wanted—no other sound would do," although there were happy accidents that changed the final result. Guitarist Mick Wayne thought he'd finished an early take and was about to retune a bass string on his Gibson ES-335, but Dudgeon liked the effect of the warped note swamped with reverb and told him to repeat the sound on the next take. Rick Wakeman, who played the Mellotron, found "it was one of half a dozen occasions where it made the hair stand up on your neck and you know you're involved in something special. 'Space Oddity' was the first time it ever happened to me." Terry Cox remembers the consensus that a breakthrough was finally imminent: "That excitement definitely did transmit itself to me too."

The sense of event was heightened by the presence of Calvin Lee, who was waiting to hurry the tape off for mastering: "I remember him coming in and whipping it off to the factory straightaway," says Dudgeon. "That's how things were on that day."

Less than three weeks after the session, the single was pressed and released to an enthusiastic critical reception. One of the most welcome reviews came from Penny Valentine, a writer at *Disc*, who was not only respected but had a nose for a hit; she pronounced that the record was "going to knock everyone senseless."

Outside the perfection of that single session, though, confusion reigned. Mercury in America was sufficiently confident of the single's prospects to green-light work on an album, which started on July 20. Yet Philips in the UK was disorganized; managing director Leslie Gould had been given notice that he was being replaced, which meant it was Essex, David's publishers, who took control of the sessions. Planning was nonetheless sketchy; according to Visconti, the album was mapped out at a meeting of himself, Bowie, and David Platz: "As David's previous album was all over the place musically, the master plan was to keep him on course with one style." Visconti envisaged a folk-rock sound based around David's twelve-string guitar and suggested using Mick Wayne's band, Junior's Eyes, whom he'd recently produced; they were likable, younger, and less expensive than the usual session musicians, just "a bunch of blokes he could hang out with," says guitarist Tim Renwick. The band—which Renwick and drummer John Cambridge had joined only recently—knew little about David, "only the 'Laughing Gnome,' so we didn't know what to expect."

For his Deram album, David had been confident in overseeing the music; this time around, much of that confidence seemed to have been knocked out of him. During their introductory chat, the band found him "kind of nervous and unsure of himself," says Renwick. "He was a bit of an unlikely solo artist—a lot of solo artists are very pushy and egocentric [but] he wasn't like that at all." David was strikingly vague about what he wanted: "There was very little direction," says Renwick. "It was odd that there wasn't a figure saying, 'That worked—that didn't work.'"

John Cambridge would be David Bowie's drummer for the next nine months—crucial months in the singer's musical development. This was a time when David, according to legend, was an "ice man," battling inner demons, using and discarding musicians like guitar picks. In contrast, Cambridge found David energetic, jokey, "but not pushy." Instead, he was content to be led, most notably by his new girlfriend, who became a permanent fixture that summer.

Visconti too, while enthusiastic, was reluctant to take control: "I was not a very good producer yet and I hadn't started to engineer. I had only made the first Tyrannosaurus Rex album and the Junior's Eyes album." His inexperience was noticed by the band, who liked him but thought, says Renwick, he was "sort of overpolite." Hence, the album was not orchestrated—it was improvised, cooked up on the spot, which gave it a delicious tension. For even as Bowie was turning his back on hippie values, he was relying on people like Mick Wayne—who was talented, disorganized, and "very druggy"—to give shape to his vision.

The sessions, at Trident Studios, in a little Soho alleyway, were drawn out over the summer and early autumn. A session would be booked with no indication of what songs would be recorded, and the day's work would start with David sitting on a high stool with his twelve-string, saying, "I've got this one." After playing through the song a couple of times he'd smile at the band and ask them, "Shall we have a go?" For his acoustic numbers, assisted by Keith Christmas, the process was even more basic. And thus David Bowie's second album was pieced together.

The rather chaotic recording—which Visconti describes as "personal and warm in many ways but often ragged"—would make this album unique in David Bowie's catalog. His intricately worked words were set against a loose, hobo backdrop where, as on "Unwashed and Somewhat Slightly Dazed," the results were obviously influenced by Dylan's first electric sessions. Other obvious touchstones include Tim Hardin, whose crystalline descending chord sequences are echoed in both "Cygnet Committee" and "Wide-Eyed Boy from Freecloud"—and Simon and Garfunkel,

snatches of whose "Mrs. Robinson" pop up in "Letter to Hermione." The overall effect mirrors the David Bowie that everyone
from that time remembers: intense but passive, intriguing but
introverted.

The lack of direction afflicting David was entirely explained by
his personal life, for as Visconti explains, "Calvin Lee was besotted with David—and his hidden agenda was to have him as a boyfriend. But Angie Bowie, who arrived on the scene during the
recording of the album, squashed all possibility of that." The business backdrop was even more chaotic: Calvin Lee was operating
in a semiofficial capacity, mailing promo copies of the single after
hours and offering encouragement at many of the sessions, which
were often interrupted by "a nerdy American character, Robin
McBride, from Mercury," says Visconti. "[He] turned up on our
doorstep and we were told that we were all answerable to him. I
despised him."

During the weeks after the single's release, the machinations
around its creator became more complex. Before the sessions,
David had told Visconti that Ken Pitt was too old school: "After the
record," he stated, "I'll be dropping him." Pitt, meanwhile, pushed
the single by sending polite letters to BBC Radio, *Top of the Pops*,
and other outlets, augmenting his efforts with an attempt at chart-
rigging in a deal with a character named Tony Martin, who
offered to massage the single onto the *Record Retailer* chart for a
hundred pounds. Pitt acceded, handing over more than a hundred and forty pounds in total, but the single languished outside
the Top 40. To this day, Pitt remains slightly shamefaced about
the episode—yet according to other figures in the industry, Pitt's
distaste for getting down and dirty was a crucial failing. "Ken was
too gentlemanly," says Olav Wyper, later general manager of Philips. "He thought the way to make this a hit was to put money in
somebody's pocket. Which wasn't enough."

The American release was even more confused. Simon Hayes
had received an early pressing of "Space Oddity" and played it at
Mercury's Wednesday sales conference in Chicago. "Everyone
had been excited about the record. But when they heard it they all

said: This is a sad story about a guy lost in space. And we're gonna release it when there's a space shot happening—and there's a real possibility we could lose a man in space?"

With Mercury presidents Irving Green and Irwin Steinberg fast losing their nerve, there was a rush edit, says Hayes, which censored most of the references to Major Tom's fate (it must have made for a very short record). The single was eventually released in a modified U.S. version "with absolutely no promotion behind it," according to Hayes, "and it died a slow death, as these things do."

Blissfully oblivious of all the corporate machinations, David was genuinely excited as the date of the moon shot approached, July 20. He, Angie, and Ray Stevenson stayed up for the TV coverage. Stevenson found it disappointing: "It was dull, black-and-white fuzzy footage of people walking slowly," but he observed that "David was very excited." David later described his state as "over the moon! And they used [the single] as part of the background track—I couldn't believe they were doing that. Did they know what the song was about?"

According to Stevenson, the most memorable part of the evening was when Angie went out for a walk and returned saying that "suddenly she's seen them—little green men, and all this nonsense." Ray was impressed by Angie, but it was at this point that he started to have doubts. If David was skeptical, he concealed it. "He humored her, and asked all the questions that a charming person would."

Amid the mess of people competing for David's attention—"vampires and predators," as Ken Pitt terms them—Pitt especially suspected Angie's influence, seeing her presence behind disturbing aspects of David's behavior, including an attempt in June to negotiate an advance with publisher David Platz behind Pitt's back. Partly to reestablish his preeminence, Pitt organized a trip to a pair of song festivals in Malta and Pistoia, Italy, at the end of July. Bowie would sing "When I Live My Dream," judged sufficiently middle of the road for such events, against a background tape, but the main purpose of the trip, says Pitt, was merely the prospect of "a little fun and sun." Angie dropped in for the Italian leg of the trip—savoring Pitt's suspicious reaction—following which David and Ken returned to London, in David's case directly to a show at the Three Tuns. It was only when David arrived in Beckenham that he received a message that his father was ill. He seemed to sense the situation was serious: "Someone else can host tonight," he yelled at his fellow volunteers. "Just get me home."

Ray Stevenson was enlisted to drive David to Plaistow Grove, where it was obvious that Haywood's condition was grave; he'd been suffering lung complaints for some years, probably linked to his heavy cigarette habit, and had now succumbed to pneumonia. Sitting down at the kitchen table with Peggy for countless cups of tea, Ray found David's mum was relatively composed while David was "panicky. It was obvious he really loved his dad."

David spent most of the next two days at Plaistow Grove. On August 5, 1969, he called Pitt to tell him his father had died. Pitt joined him at the house, where he sorted through Haywood Jones's papers. They had been left in perfect order: "He was always wonderful," says Pitt. "I wish he could have witnessed David's success."

John Cambridge, the Junior's Eyes drummer, was becoming closer to David as the sessions continued; he speculates that his broad Yorkshire accent and dry humor reminded David of Haywood. A few days after his father's death, David told John that his phone had rung several times at five thirty: "I'd pick it up and there was no one there," he told John. "I just knew it was my dad seeing if I was all right."

Poignantly, the most significant live show of David Bowie's life to date came on August 16, just five days after Haywood's funeral. The Beckenham Free Festival had been planned for several months and included every member of Bowie's social circle, with the notable exception of Ken Pitt. Mark Pritchett, who was reading his poetry at the festival, met David early in the morning, and he was buoyant, fired up by the beautiful weather and the feverish activity. Short of microphones, they drove round to Mark's house in Haywood Jones's tiny Fiat 500 to borrow some. "Good grief!" David laughed as they pulled up on Southend Road. "I've just taken the lease on the place opposite—we'll be moving in in three weeks. Come and see us!"

The afternoon was frenzied for all involved; even those who, like photographer and blues musician Dave Bebbington, thought David's new girlfriend was too pushy were impressed by the way Angie "made things happen," selling burgers from a stall to raise cash. Every member of the Arts Lab was busy with some assignment at the Beckenham Recreation Grounds, whether it was the sound system, moving gear, puppet shows, or impromptu street theater events. The festival was endearingly amateurish—John Peel, who was scheduled to emcee, was replaced by a medical student from Blackheath named Tim Goffe, and local bands playing blues and Chuck Berry numbers dominated the bill, which included Keith Christmas, Bridget St. John, and the Strawbs.

As David's afternoon performance approached, however, the mood turned sour; it was "a combination of stage fright and thinking about his dad," says Pritchett. Dave Bebbington, who photographed David's solo set from onstage, remembers, "There was little chat in between the songs; you could tell he was thinking, I have to be a trouper, I'm going to play my set and go home."

For Mary Finnigan, the day had started stressfully with a missing van and amps; it got worse that afternoon, when she remembers David calling her and Lee "materialistic assholes" as they totaled up the day's takings. "I don't remember him being unpleasant," says Bebbington, "just detached. He wanted to go home." David was absent from the celebratory curry at an Indian restaurant on Beckenham High Street that night; there were complaints from some, says Bebbington, that "David [was] being really shitty." Bizarrely, no one seemed to link his mood to his having buried his father five days earlier. The bickering, and the fact that Mary had been supplanted by Angie as David's lover and muse, signaled the end of David's close involvement with the Arts Lab, which had become for David a place where "everybody wanted a piece of him," says Bebbington.

When David came to commemorate that sunny but emotionally clouded Bromley afternoon a few days later in the recording studio, he was in a sweeter mood. Charmingly homely, with a tiny Woolworth's reed organ carefully miked up by Visconti, "Memory of a Free Festival" would be, along with "Cygnet Committee," a highlight of David Bowie's second album. Whereas "Cygnet Committee" was complex, having evolved out of an earlier song, "Lover to the Dawn," its lyrics a densely argued dissection of hippie values, this song was simple, poignant, and evoked the ambivalence that had enveloped David that year. When he sang "Oh, to capture just one drop of all the ecstasy that swept that afternoon," the melody swept upward with yearning for a hippie nirvana that others thought they had attained but that he knew he hadn't. A jewel of a song, it ended in the glitzy tinsel of a chorus borrowed from "Hey Jude," a comedown perhaps, but as Tony Visconti points out, "In the shadow of the Beatles it was hard to have an original idea in those days."

"Memory of a Free Festival," one of the last songs to be recorded, would close David's Philips album, which bizarrely featured the same eponymous title as its Deram predecessor. It was an appropriate farewell, bidding good-bye to the hippie culture— and, in several instances, people—that had nurtured Bowie for the past nine months. Mary Finnigan and Calvin Lee, who left Mercury later that year, were two more people from whom David moved on as he and Angie settled into Haddon Hall, the building he'd pointed out to Pritchett.

Given the confused welter of emotions that surrounded his father's death—grief, sympathy for his mother as well as irritation at the constant arguments with her—it's hard to decipher David Bowie's feelings about the modest success of his purported breakthrough single, for in the wake of the moon landings, "Space Oddity" slipped into the UK charts at number 48 on September 6, 1969—before dropping, seemingly, into oblivion.

For most of the Philips staff, that, apparently, was that. But they were not reckoning on Olav Wyper, the company's newly appointed general manager, young, dynamic, and handsome, with a GI Joe jutting jaw that signaled his can-do attitude. Before joining Philips, Wyper had discussed the job with his secretary

Sue Baxter, whom he planned to bring with him from CBS. Enthusiastic about the move, she remarked, "That company has been a disaster for two years—but at least by the time we arrive they will have a hit on their hands." Intrigued, he'd gone out and bought "Space Oddity." "Sue told me it was a sensational record, and she was right," he says.

On his first day in the Stannard Place office, Wyper was surprised to notice that the sales, promotion, and marketing staff were sitting around with no new releases to work on, "so I asked, Well, what happened to that Bowie record? Oh, we tried, but it didn't go anywhere." With nothing else for them to promote, Wyper set the entire staff to work on "Space Oddity": "This never happened before or since," says Wyper. "It was purely because we had this three-week window with no major releases."

In the last week of September, "Space Oddity" jumped up the charts to number 25, rising steadily to peak at number 5 in a fourteen-week chart run.

When David's album was released, on November 4, he was up in Scotland for a short series of shows backed by Junior's Eyes. That band was at its peak; an October 20 BBC session, with its superb version of "Let Me Sleep Beside You," easily surpasses the band's work on David's album and offers a tantalizing glimpse of how that earlier material could have sounded had it been worked up live first. But they were "odd gigs," says guitarist Tim Renwick, "a couple were quite rough—on one there was a cage up front in case the audience got out of control." David was nervous, slightly out of place amid the hard-bitten, hardworking band members, most of whom were heavy dope smokers, especially Mick Wayne and his wife, Charlotte, who were "eyes on the wall, very stoned, always." There were lighter moments—Junior's Eyes singer Graham Kelly remembers Bowie challenging him to a race after a few drinks in a vegetarian restaurant, whereupon they grabbed their friends and sped through the frozen Edinburgh streets, Bowie on the hood of his car, Kelly on the hood of the band's Transit.

After the success of the single, David's second album shuffled out in a rather halfhearted manner. By this point, Calvin Lee's relationship with Mercury was troubled, much to Ken Pitt's glee, and Olav Wyper, who'd championed "Space Oddity," was "completely underwhelmed" by the album: "I think David had too much control of the album, and didn't defer enough to Visconti." Visconti, meanwhile, is "not particularly proud" of the work: "I don't think David had settled on who he was as yet." David, tellingly, says of this period, "I was looking for myself," which provides some explanation for his behavior—"weak, almost," as one friend puts it, mentioning his reliance on people like Angie and, before her, Mary Finnigan to deal with his disagreements with Ken Pitt and others.

Today, *David Bowie* is unique in its creator's catalog, thanks to its endearing lack of artifice. Yet even at the time it was obvious it didn't have the acuity and intensity of albums by folk rockers such as Tim Hardin and Simon and Garfunkel. While the *Observer*'s Tony Palmer famously rhapsodized over David's "quite devastatingly beautiful" looks, the reviews mostly commented on the thoughtful lyrics and suggested that Bowie was a follower rather than a pioneer. Bowie's own pronouncements to *Music Now* writer Kate Simpson betrayed his awareness that he lacked a convincing, coherent worldview, shown by his praise of celebrated right-wing politician Enoch Powell for at least standing up for a cause: "whether it's good or bad is not the point."

More worryingly, Simpson's feature mentions her friends' perception that David was a "one-hit wonder," a dread phrase that would crop up with monotonous regularity over the next few years. Obviously intelligent, he nonetheless lacked the talent of a John Lennon for encapsulating an agenda in a song or a sentence. Six years after he'd formed the King Bees, David had scored his first hit single, yet the underwhelming impact of his album seemed to rob him of all momentum. To many, he simply seemed all over the place.

Yet, for a few key people, David's live shows, notably his showcase at the South Bank Purcell Room on November 20, demonstrated not a lack of focus but bravery. BBC producer Jeff Griffin was about to stake his reputation on an innovative series of concert broadcasts the following spring, opening with Led Zeppelin. When he saw Bowie at the Purcell Room, Griffin was "blown away. I'd read about him working with Lindsay Kemp, but it wasn't until I saw him there that I realized there was far more to him than the average rock star...he was doing brave things, singing Jacques Brel songs. He was one of those rare performers who just had that extra dimension to him, something that's hard to describe."

Fascinated by the fact that Bowie had moved on so dexterously from his "twee, but fun" Deram debut, Griffin penciled in a Bowie show for the spring. By which time, David would have moved on again.

CHAPTER 7

All the Madmen

*It sounded a bit of a mess... [but] in the center of all this chaos,
mayhem, and noise, David was extremely relaxed.*

—Mark Pritchett

I T WAS THEIR GRACELAND, the ostentatious, rambling, and
slightly decaying headquarters where David and Angela Bowie
enjoyed marital bliss, interior decoration, and sexual frolics.
Innocent teenage American girls would one day walk in and
fondly imagine themselves imprisoned in some reimagined Victorian melodrama; cynical journalists would enter its imposing
hallway and be overawed by the Bowie mystique. It was a location
where the musical and fashion values of an entire decade would
be realigned.

Angie had spotted Haddon Hall, at 240 Southend Road in
Beckenham, back in the summer of 1969; Beckenham was just
down the road from Bromley, a relatively green and leafy suburb
celebrated mainly as the home of children's-book author Enid Bly-
ton. Angie and David agreed to move into flat 7 early in September, and they established themselves there at the end of the
month. The building was the epitome of crumbling magnifi-
cence, an opulent high Victorian house that even at the time

struck resident John Cambridge as reminiscent of Elvis's grandiose Memphis home.

The building, which boasted a magnificent entrance hall, was
divided into flats; David and Angie's flat was on the ground floor,
but they also had the use of the staircase, which led visitors up to a
small half landing dominated by a magnificent Gothic stained-
glass window; from there the staircase divided, ascending to a gallery at the next level that gave on to a set of sealed-up doorways,
later commandeered as sleeping space. Tony Visconti and his girlfriend, Liz, moved into Haddon Hall in December, taking the
back bedroom on the ground floor and sharing a huge living
room, complete with lavish open fireplace, with David and Angie;
soon Tony persuaded Mr. Hoys, the owner of the house, to let him
build a rehearsal space in the basement.

Royalties from the "Space Oddity" single—which by January
had sold 138,656 copies in the UK—trickled in slowly, but the
single's success pushed up the fee for David's live bookings to a
magnificent hundred pounds or more. Flush for the first time in
his life, David took to spending money like a duck to water. After
passing his driving test and returning his father's Fiat to Peggy,
he bought a Rover 100, complete with luxurious leather seats and
walnut dashboard, and he and Angie became familiar figures at
the antique shops on Old Kent and Tower Bridge roads, acquiring
art deco lamps, William Morris screens, and mahogany chests of
drawers.

The establishment of their own palace at Haddon Hall marked
the crowning of Angie as queen to Bowie's king. It was an impressively fast rise to power, but even for her most recent acquaintances, it was no surprise. Born in Cyprus in 1950 to an American
mining-engineer father and a mother of Polish extraction, educated at a British-run boarding school in Montreux, Switzerland,
Mary Angela Barnett was self-sufficient, energetic, and irresist-
ibly loud; she reveled in telling listeners of her scandalous expul-
sion from the Connecticut College for Women for a lesbian affair,
and to most Brits in the era before affordable transatlantic travel,
she seemed ravishingly cosmopolitan.

Brought up in sophisticated international surroundings, she was nonetheless as at home scrubbing Haddon Hall's wooden floorboards to erase the smell of cat pee as she was distinguishing a genuine art nouveau light fixture from a reproduction. But from the spring of 1970 onward, as John Cambridge puts it, "You met Angie before you met David." Their union would always be as public as it was personal, like the celebrity liaisons brokered by Hollywood PR representatives eager to maximize their column inches. Cambridge was one of those people who found Angie irritating—"too domineering and shouting"—and saw firsthand how Angie forced David into decisions he didn't want to make, notably firing Ken Pitt.

The first public statement of their love affair was "The Prettiest Star," the only new song David wrote over the winter of 1969 (absence made his heart grow fonder, for Angie disappeared to see her parents in November, partly to flee Peggy's phone calls accusing her of "living in sin"). Languid, uncharacteristically simple, it would be almost unique in Bowie's canon, a conventional love song, its lyrics speculating on their future fame as a professional couple: "you and I will rise up all the way."

As an anthem to Angie, it was appropriate that "The Prettiest Star" also marked the passing of Ken Pitt's influence. Ken Pitt dropped in at Trident for the session—an event that was becoming comparatively rare. It was around one in the morning on January 8—David's twenty-third birthday—and as Pitt wandered around the control room he exchanged only a few words with Bowie and Tony Visconti, who were chatting to Godfrey McLean and Delisle Harper, drummer and bassist from Gass, a funky Santana-ish band that Visconti recruited for the recording. Photographer David Bebbington watched Pitt tell no one in particular that he'd just dropped in to see another of his clients, Billy Eckstine, at the Talk of the Town club. Bebbington started to feel embarrassed at how Ken was being cold-shouldered. Pitt proudly mentioned that he'd been working with Eckstine for twenty years, and Bebbington briefly admired Pitt's loyalty before wondering what Eckstine—once a cutting-edge bandleader, now a mannered middle-of-the-road crooner—had in common with Bowie. When Pitt left the studio a few minutes later, no one but Bebbington seemed to register he'd gone.

A second visitor was more welcome. At Tony Visconti's suggestion, Marc Bolan, accompanied by his wife, June, dropped in to play lead guitar on "The Prettiest Star," and while mutual friends at the time remember Marc being brotherly to David, on this, their only official joint recording, their rivalry soured the atmosphere: "He came in and it was daggers," remembers Visconti. "Everyone's having a good time, then Marc comes in and the atmosphere chilled up."

Visconti had spent a good few days vibing up Marc, who was enthusiastic about showing off his newly acquired electric guitar skills and had carefully prepared his guitar melody. David too was upbeat, complimenting Marc effusively, when June Bolan suddenly broke into a tantrum, bitching that "the only good thing about this record is Marc's guitar." Marc hurriedly packed up his Fender Strat, and the pair left without another word.

The squabble highlighted the tension that would always exist in the relationship between David Bowie and Marc Bolan. Marc enjoyed talking up David, but although he'd predicted "Space Oddity" would be a hit, Marc seemed irritated to be proven right. This was a clear illustration of how the teenage "arrogance" that Leslie Conn remembered came from different causes. David was generally happy when his friends did well; not Marc. What was confidence in Bowie equated to bravado in Bolan—a distinction for which June Bolan had an explanation, which she shared with Ray Stevenson: "She had this theory: It was because Marc had a small dick and David had a monster. A lot of their personalities come from this: David can charm the girl and know that through to the conclusion of this encounter he's not going to disappoint. Marc couldn't."

David made a good show of seeming unconcerned by Marc's petulance—he was cheerful on the drive back to Beckenham in his Rover in the small hours of the morning, buying a huge Chinese takeout meal on the way and spreading it over the walnut dashboard.

Calm David might have been in the face of such troubles, but often his music suffered from the confused mess of personalities surrounding him, for he, more than most people, relied on others. That night's show at the Speakeasy typified the confusion. Tim Renwick—now David's preferred guitarist ahead of Mick Wayne—was booked at the last minute but found David's passivity and lack of direction irritating: "It wasn't like 'Right, here we go.' It was more like 'What's next?' and then nothing." John Cambridge wasn't even told there was a show; he'd turned up for a drink at the Speak along with Junior's Eyes' Roger the roadie only to be asked at the last moment, "Do you have your drums?" Fortunately, he kept them in the trunk of his Mini Minor. The last-minute request marked his debut as Bowie's official drummer.

SOON after the Speakeasy show Cambridge moved into Haddon Hall too and came to enjoy the eccentric domesticity. In later years, Haddon Hall would become celebrated for its sexual excesses. Yet the atmosphere was more Bloomsbury set than Haight-Ashbury: Angie made an excellent hostess, greeting visitors effusively, proffering tea and cookies. At other times there were schoolboy jokes—David and John Cambridge chasing each other around with water pistols or exchanging deadpan Yorkshire banter. Cambridge's humor was celebrated, sometimes witty and so dry it often took the listener several seconds to register the joke. ("Maybe I overdid it," he reflects today. "Angie didn't always appreciate all me jokes.")

The deliciously fin de siècle ambience at Haddon Hall became even more pronounced when Angie found a housekeeper in the Edwardian shape of Donna Pritchett—who lived across the road and whose son, Mark, a pupil at Dulwich College, had been drawn into the Arts Lab set. Donna ruled the kitchen, cooking up a Sunday roast in an emergency and dispensing endless cups of tea. She would generally brook no nonsense, chiding David if he burned the furniture with a cigarette; David and Angie were adept at charming her, sending her greeting cards and little messages written on the backs of ten-shilling notes. ("David was cute like that," observes Mark.)

In fact, David proved remarkably chipper over the period, far more resilient in the face of the poor sales of the Philips album than he had been about his Deram debut—the influx of money from the "Space Oddity" single helped, of course. But there was a more traumatic source of disquiet in his personal life, one that he'd voiced publicly in the later days of the Arts Lab. During one of their getting-to-know-you meetings, as everyone sat arranged in a circle of stack-up chairs, David announced, "I have a brother in Cane Hill."

Most of those present were unaware David had a brother; nearly everyone was aware of Cane Hill. Built in 1882, the asylum was a huge Gothic complex intended to provide a sympathetic, modern environment for the "incurably insane," with extensive grounds and outdoor pavilions from which the inmates could enjoy views of London. Nevertheless, the building, on a commanding hill in Coulsdon, ten miles southeast of Beckenham, was regarded as a terrifying place. It was famous locally as the insane asylum that had housed Charlie Chaplin's mother, who had been confined to a padded cell and hosed down with freezing water, a primitive antecedent of electroshock therapy. The establishment was more enlightened in the 1960s, but there was a justifiable fear for inmates and their relatives that once they walked through its imposing gates, they would never return. As Hannah Chaplin told her son when he visited her, "Don't lose your way—they might keep you here."

After his national service in the Royal Air Force and his move into Plaistow Grove, Terry had enjoyed a brief period of domestic harmony, although it was overshadowed by illness; it was during this period that David had taken Terry to see Cream in Bromley and witnessed the effects of what was later diagnosed as schizophrenia. For a time, while he stayed with his mother and stepfather, Terry's condition was stable, but in the wake of Haywood's death, Terry deteriorated. Peggy—who was in the process of moving to a flat on Albemarle Road in Beckenham—was unable to cope with her son, precipitating his move to Cane Hill. According to friends, Peggy found the prospect of visiting Terry at the hospital too traumatic to endure; instead, her sister Pat went with her husband, Tony Antoniou.

Around 1969 and 1970, when David first had a home of his own, he provided shelter for his half brother, and at various times Terry was seen around Haddon Hall on release from Cane Hill. He met many of David's closest friends in the process; he was friendly, sometimes chatty—especially about soccer—sometimes confused. But in the long term, David proved as unable to cope with Terry's illness as his mother had been.

Those who saw David and Terry together were never in doubt that "Terry adored his brother"; as Mark Pritchett remembers, "He was a lovely chap." David obviously loved and respected Terry, citing him again and again as the source of many of his key musical and literary interests. But the principal emotion that Terry inspired in his half brother was, says Pritchett, "guilt."

In the opinion of David's aunt Pat, who in the 1980s publicly chastised David for his lack of attention to Terry, that guilt was justified—in her view, David simply turned his back on his half brother. In fairness, there was probably little he could have done. Ray Stevenson, who spent much time around Haddon Hall as Terry's mental health deteriorated, points out, "I've known some schizophrenics and there is not much you can do to help—they are how they are and it's horrible. You have to just not think about it. So I'd never slag him off for putting Terry in a...mental box."

Bowie's fear of the madness in his family would become a common theme—it's the stuff of classic drama and has been a prism through which many have chosen to analyze his career. Throughout this period, David was notably calm, controlled; he couldn't have seemed more sane. Yet, as anyone who has been emotionally close to someone suffering from schizophrenia or paranoia knows, "madness" is contagious; the descriptions of a schizophrenic's visions can be more affecting, and seem more convincing, than genuine, banal experiences. When he wrote songs, David empathized with his half brother; in everyday life,

David felt helpless. Terry's plight was an issue that David dealt with in song, rather than in reality, with the result that, says Mark Pritchett, "David built up a lot of guilt about him. And I think the darker songs are actually tributes to him."

With "The Prettiest Star" as yet unreleased, few performances to occupy him, grief for his dad, troubles with Ken, and the traumas of Terry and Peggy, it was hardly surprising that Bowie spent much of January cocooned at Haddon Hall. To make matters worse, his band, Junior's Eyes, was falling apart. Mick Wayne's increasing ingestion of drugs caused most of those around him to agree with singer Graham Kelly, who says, "I loved the guy—but working with him was a nightmare." By the end of January 1970, every member of the band knew the group would split; the only question, as singer Kelly remembers, was "Which way would people jump—and who would go with Bowie?" With the BBC In Concert session scheduled for February 5, David needed to move quickly.

Tim Renwick was the obvious front-runner. But John Cambridge, the first official recruit to David's outfit, had another prospect in mind, a ferociously talented guitarist who'd played in his previous band, the Rats. "I'd been pestering [David and Tony] to death, so finally I go down to Hull to find Mick Ronson. I knew where he worked; I arrive and he's creosoting this training ground. I'm telling him I've got in with this band in London, David Bowie, it's really good, and it needs a guitarist. And he's going, 'Oh, I don't know, I got in with a band in Sweden and was ripped off and I'm not about to do that again.' So I'm thinking, I just pestered them two to let me come down here—and now I've got to pester him to go up there!"

Cambridge's persuasion worked; Ronson turned up for the band's show at the Marquee on February 3. The guitarist commented enthusiastically after the show, as was his way. But "even if it was shite, Mick would still say it was good," Cambridge explains. The drummer introduced Bowie to Ronson at the venue, but David was distracted; only when they all returned to Haddon Hall and Ronson picked up an acoustic and started to play did

Bowie register his presence. At that moment, as Tony Visconti describes it, "Everything was starting to click into place."

MICK Ronson's career had interlaced with Bowie's over the previous five or six years by way of fellow Yorkshiremen like John Hutchinson, who had shared the bill with the Rats at venues across the northeast. Ronson was born and raised in Hull, once a prosperous and confident Victorian city but by the late sixties in the grip of a long-term industrial decline. Mick Ronson was a unique musician, cutthroat in terms of his musical ambition but remarkably laid back when it came to advancing his own career.

Local musician Keith Herd witnessed one of Ronson's first tentative shows with his band the Crestas and bumped into the guitarist regularly in the local music shop, Cornell's. In 1967, after Herd set up a tiny recording studio in his living room, Mick turned up with his new band, the Rats, "and I couldn't believe how he'd come on." Playing a Fender Telecaster, Ronson had mastered "heavy guitar—using the amplifier and volume to get incredible sustain. It was the first time I'd ever heard it done."

The four-minute-long piece that the Rats constructed, "The Rise and Fall of Bernie Gripplestone," was a Who-influenced mini opera, distinguished solely by Ronson's howling guitar. Although it had shades of Hendrix, Townshend, and Mick's principal guitar idol, Jeff Beck, Ronson's playing was already unique: concise, tough rhythm guitar one moment, wildly fluid lead the next. It was made all the more thrilling by Ronson's talent for bending a note to scary extremes—a trick that, according to bandmate Trevor Bolder, he'd mastered via a fingernail on his left hand that was so tough and hard it was "almost deformed"; nocking the string into a groove on the nail, he could bend a string almost clear across the neck of the guitar. By the end of 1968, when he picked up a Les Paul Custom from Cornell's and plugged it into his Marshall stack, he had become Hull's unchallenged guitar hero.

Good-looking, with a flint-sharp face and bony nose, Mick was friendly, a typical muso; his conversation revolved around music and women, but if he saw someone ogling his guitar he'd nod and encourage him, saying, "Go on, have a go." Then he'd shake the new acquaintance's hand enthusiastically. He was open-minded musically, as fascinated by the harmony pop of the Move as by heavy rock. And like the rest of the Rats, says bassist Keith "Ched" Cheesman, "he was a piss taker." Often, the "piss taking," or joking around, was directed at suggestions that the Rats change their "winning" formula. And by the end of 1969, Cheesman noticed that although Mick had indisputably been the best musician in Hull when Ched had first joined the band, a full year later Mick's younger rivals were gaining on him.

Mick Ronson, with the Rats, had enjoyed staying in his comfort zone. With Bowie and Tony Visconti, though, he was wrenched out of it. The process started that Saturday; he spent the day huddled with the pair hurriedly learning songs for Jeff Griffin's *BBC In Concert* episode for Sunday, February 5. It was a huge coup for Bowie to headline the new series—Marc Bolan, in contrast, was a last-minute substitution for half a show—and David's use of a guitarist he'd met two days before was a massive risk, an early example of the inspired gambles that would come to characterize his career.

The *BBC In Concert* show represented another Bowie first: his use of the BBC to prototype the next phase of his work. From the show's opening number in front of a small audience at Regent Street's Paris Cinema, a gritty, solo version of Brel's "Port of Amsterdam," there is a new toughness and sense of adrenaline. Familiar songs like "Unwashed and Somewhat Slightly Dazed" sound Dylan-esque and faintly worthy—until Ronson hooks his mutant fingernail under the guitar string and for the first time in Bowie's career, the listener is in real doubt as to where the song is heading (a feeling shared by Ronson, who gets a couple of chords wrong). Nonetheless, it's his drawn-out, exhausting guitar work that inspires announcer John Peel to pronounce the song "a bit of a treat."

"Width of a Circle," heard here for the first time, shares the sense of danger. Ronson's guitar lines seamlessly interlace with Bowie's bashed-out acoustic chords, while Visconti's bass guitar is relentlessly fluid and inventive. There are few recordings in which we get to hear a band jell in public for the very first time; this is one of them. Ronson's influences are apparent—the modal melodies evoking Hendrix, the twin-note Memphis scale taken from country licks—but are instinctively incorporated into a coherent style. In the process, David Bowie's style becomes coherent too.

After the concert, there was muttering about missed endings, wrong chords, that "it was a bit crap, really," says Cambridge. But the fact that the performance was "raw as fuck" was part of the excitement: "You could see even then that it was a lot better. Mick lifted it." "It was incredibly exciting," remembers Tony Visconti, "because we knew Mick was going to work out—he had something we needed."

Rickety and sporadic as it was, Bowie's short tour from the end of February of 1970 would be his first with a proper, consistent band since Lower Third days. Ronson had no second thoughts about joining up, but there were fleeting suggestions of augmenting the lineup with Tim Renwick, who turned up at Haddon Hall to be checked out by David and Angie. "My girlfriend came with me and Angie was checking *her* out—I remember thinking, Blimey, this is odd." Angie perhaps didn't approve, but in any case Renwick needed paying, and Ronson was happy to play for free. For days, he and David immersed themselves in practice at Haddon Hall, sitting opposite each other. John Cambridge would drop in to see how it was going: "It would be just the two of them in the bedroom with the guitar. I'd go in and they'd say, 'Hang on, John, we're just doing this.' In other words, 'piss off.'"

Ronson's arrival galvanized the Haddon Hall crew, who were fired up by his presence, and the languor that had overcome David since his father's death seemed to evaporate in the run-up to the band's debut at the Roundhouse on February 22.

While Bowie and Ronson practiced, Angie went shopping for their clothes, assisted by Mark Pritchett: "Tony was working out of Oxford Street and we all met there in the morning, but lunchtime and the whole afternoon was spent, Angie and I, scurrying around theatrical costumiers to dress them all up."

It was in this brief afternoon spent scurrying around Charing Cross Road and Fitzrovia that the foundation of David Bowie's image throughout the 1970s would be laid. In the mid-1960s, he'd become a pretty convincing mod; since that time, his attire had reverted to a vaguely posthippie style, hair curled in what Ken Pitt thought was a tribute to Bob Dylan. With his flowery shirts and afghan coats, David could have passed for Eric Clapton in his Cream heyday of 1969 or so. In his previous incarnations, David was pretty, tasteful, or cool. It was Angie—and, later, Chelita Secunda—who would push him to be outrageous.

With Pritchett in tow, Angie masterminded the band's flamboyant attire during that afternoon's shopping: a gangster outfit, with fedora, for Ronson, who was given the title Gangsterman; a leotard with an *H* sewn on the chest for Visconti, the Hypeman; a cowboy outfit for John Cambridge; and a multicolored, diaphanous concoction with many-hued scarves attached to a Lurex shirt for David: Rainbowman.

Ken Pitt claimed credit for naming the band, remembering that after Bowie told him "This is one big hype," he'd said, "Well, why not call it the Hype?" But it seems David may have gotten the idea from photographer Ray Stevenson, who'd suggested the name only to hear David respond, "We can't use it—Led Zeppelin's publishers are called SuperHype." According to Jeff Dexter, who introduced the show, the name started being bandied about after the fact: "They'd just said the name casually—it was only after certain people caught on that it crept into the vocabulary."

There was no doubt that the Roundhouse show was a major event; the *BBC In Concert* performance alerted fans that Bowie was unveiling a new work in progress, and many friends from the Three Tuns turned up for the band's support slot of Noel Redding's short-lived band Fat Mattress. Mark Pritchett was one of them and remembers the performance being "a bit of a mess." Ronson was using a 200-watt Marshall amplifier stack that totally overpowered the other musicians. "People expected quite a lot," says Pritchett, "and what they got was much of *Man Who Sold the World* at thunderous volume. A lot of that material suited thunderous volume—and a lot of it didn't. So it sounded a bit of a mess." Yet there was one thing Pritchett did notice: "At the center of all this chaos, mayhem, and noise, David was extremely relaxed."

The show would be seen as a crucial staging post on the way to glam, not least because Marc Bolan turned up and, says Visconti, watched the show in rapt attention, his chin on the stage. The band's theatrical outfits drew ridicule, according to Visconti, but David, who had seen how Lindsay Kemp could carry off the most outrageous outfits, was buoyed up by the reaction. Just as crucially, as Mark Pritchett observed: "David was moving." His body language had entirely changed: The costumes, the artifice, and the raw power of Ronson's guitar had unlocked the carefree joy of David's early R & B days.

David seemed well aware he'd turned a corner. "You could tell he knew a band was good for him," says Pritchett. During the sporadic run of dates that continued through February and March, he was relaxed, enjoying his trip to Hull for a show at the university on March 6, hanging out in the dining hall with a tiny group of fans and bemused students. Angie's presence seemed to register with them as much as the band's: "David and Angie had identical curly hair, similar skinny build; you know how people who look a little similar to each other can fall in love?" remembered one student who shared a table with them.

For David, the failure of the single celebrating his and Angie's infatuation was the only disappointment of an otherwise idyllic spring. Released the day they sat chatting in the dining hall, "The Prettiest Star" slipped into oblivion with fewer than a thousand copies sold. For Ken Pitt, the release of the single confirmed his opinion of Angie as a "predator"—and his fears that his influence over Bowie was irretrievably slipping away were confirmed in March as the two planned their marriage.

In later years, as she came to terms with their celebrated and rancorous split, Angie would publicly doubt that David had ever loved her; indeed, some of her accounts of their decision to marry quote him as asking, "Can you handle the fact that I don't love you?" On another occasion Angie described how the pair realized they were in love during their separation over Christmas 1969, which Angie spent with her parents in Cyprus, waiting eagerly for letters, and then, after a ten-day postal strike, receiving a card on which were written the words *We will marry, I promise, this year.*

Today, Angie retains much of the ebullience and enthusiasm that made her so magnetic back in 1970, but the emotional damage she's sustained since that time causes her to ascribe darker, exploitative motives to most of her ex-husband's behavior. At one point, she tells me, "I don't know *anything* that David's done that wasn't for his own benefit." Again and again we return to the topic, only to find her unable to contemplate any other interpretation.

Most of David's pronouncements over the years support this bleak picture, for when he talked about their marriage at the time, David discussed it as if it were a brand. After their notorious, catastrophically nasty split, he could hardly bear to mention Angie at all. Yet those who were emotionally close to Angie and David in their early days ascribe purer motives to their relationship. Ava Cherry, who would later become David's girlfriend even as he stayed married to Angie—a position akin to that of the king's mistress in the French court—concedes, "I do think he had love for her," before pointing out, "I'm giving her props she would never give me." Ava adds, "She was nurturing, and he needed that," but, more important, "he liked the way she thought."

Scott Richardson would later occupy a corresponding position to Ava Cherry's, as Angie's official lover and David's music buddy, and he too states, "It was genuine, a real thing. They tried to have a new kind of marriage, an open marriage, and it was absolutely brilliant what that represented."

Angie and David's relationship had been an open one from the day they met. Angie, she says, signaled the same would apply after their marriage when she arranged for them to spend the night before their wedding, on March 20, in bed with a stunning dark-haired actress they'd met through Calvin Lee. Ken Pitt had heard about the wedding from Peggy, who'd been kept in the dark by David and told Ken she intended to turn up uninvited. It was a tiny gathering; John Cambridge was one of just three men, including Roger the roadie—Mick Ronson was absent; Visconti was working. David had asked Cambridge to act as witness, but when the registrar called out, Peggy, seated a couple of rows in front, got up to sign the register. David looked around at John and shrugged his shoulders. The wedding reception was a drink in a nearby pub.

The unique nature of the Bowies' marriage was brought home to John Cambridge a couple of days later when he went to the Speakeasy with David and Angie. John and David were close friends by then, and John had often heard David frolicking with other women at Haddon Hall, but he was shocked to see David dancing with "a bloke." John said to himself, "But they only just got married!" Seeing him watching, Angie grabbed his hand and tried to pull him onto the dance floor. "I turned around; that wa'n't the way I was brought up. I'm only nineteen, still really naive." Only years later did he wonder whether shocking his drummer, and enjoying his reaction, was part of the appeal for David. And the intriguing possibility remains that David's enjoyment of the nineteen-year-old's embarrassment inspired 1972's "John, I'm Only Dancing."

The chutzpah of David's new wife would have a transformative effect on David's career in several crucial aspects. One of her first acts was to persuade Philips's Olav Wyper to advance four thousand pounds to the Hype, ostensibly to make a band album; instead, it was used to fund living expenses, an amplifier, and new tires for the van, which had arrived at Haddon Hall along with Rats' roadie Roger, aka Roger the Lodger.

With the Hype now on the way to a semiofficial status, it was time to make their studio debut, which they did on April 3, 1970—in this case with a wonderful reworking of "Memory of a Free Festival" to be issued as the U.S. follow-up to "Space Oddity." To hear each instrument warming up, and then to hear Ronson's guitar take the song by the scruff of its neck and thrust it forward, is even now a thrilling experience in which the listener can hear Bowie's career snapping into shape.

The session would also mark an ending; there had been a last-moment postponement of the session due to a double booking with a live show in Scarborough, arranged by Ken Pitt. Ken had sent a note to Haddon Hall confirming the live date, but the confusion crystallized David's dissatisfaction with the man who'd overseen his career for the past three and a half years.

Sometime in March, David called Olav Wyper's office to ask if they could meet. "He was clearly very depressed—at times very tearful," says the Philips boss. "He said he's reached this impasse with Ken, and their relationship was getting in the way of where his career should be going. And he asked what do I think, and how can I help him?" In later years, Wyper wondered whether David's tearfulness was calculated; if so, it had the desired effect, making him side with the vulnerable singer. As general manager of David's record company, he had a duty to avoid a conflict of interest, but after asking David if he had a copy of his contract with Ken—which he hadn't—he gave him the names of three firms who could advise him. The first entry on the list was a pair of people whom Wyper knew well; they had decided to go into business together just a few weeks before. Their names were Laurence Myers and Tony Defries.

In the spring of 1970, Laurence Myers was well known around the London music industry, principally as a management and accounting expert whose clients included Mickie Most. Myers was meticulous, well connected by way of his role as a show-business accountant, and was in the process of establishing his own management company, to be known as Gem, or GTO.

Tony Defries had come to Myers's and Wyper's attention as a lawyer with the legal firm of Martin Beston. Wyper had many friends who happened to be photographers, including Terence Donovan, who had called in Martin Beston to help with copyright issues; Tony Defries was the lawyer assigned to the case. Wyper attended the meeting at which Defries pitched for their business: "Tony was very bullish—he had a very firm attitude, and a belief that right was with him. I was very impressed."

Only later did Wyper meet another solicitor from Martin Beston and discover that the go-getting lawyer he had seen in action was not exactly what he seemed. "Tony was very clever. He described himself as a lawyer [and I] assumed he was a solicitor. And then I found out later that Tony was just a solicitor's clerk. He was a lawyer, which is defined as someone working in the field of law, but not what I assumed." Winning over an audience at the first impression and leaving details until later was part of Tony Defries's style.

Defries and Myers were the first names on the list provided by Olav Wyper. Fatefully, that meant they were the first to be called. There were several meetings throughout March, and Myers remembers being impressed by David Bowie: "I liked him — and I knew David was a special artist." But it turned out to be Myers's business affairs manager, Tony Defries, who realized the potential of the young singer hoping to discard his manager. For as Myers admits, it was Tony Defries who had "the vision. His great ability was, far more than I did, he knew what a star David was going to be."

The exact degree to which Defries was convinced of David's potential at their first meeting, in which David poured out his troubles, is hard to gauge. But David's dilemma appealed to Defries's problem-solving abilities. He assured David that he could extricate him from his contract with Pitt. Pitt had no concrete evidence of David's dissatisfaction until a meeting at his office on March 31, 1970, when David finally told him, "Ken, I'd like to have a go at managing myself." The news came as no surprise, says Pitt — "I'd heard of at least one other management team who'd offered David something" — but after Pitt promised to cut down on the live dates and gave David a check for two hundred pounds, it seemed the matter was settled, temporarily at least, and Pitt continued to oversee arrangements, like those for the fast-approaching sessions for the next Mercury album.

The decision to rid himself of Pitt steeled David's resolve in other respects. During a BBC radio session produced by Bernie Andrews on March 25, a dry run for the album sessions, John Cambridge found a skipping bass drum part too tricky. David and Ronson were both calm and patient: "Course you can do it, come on," Ronson kept repeating, and Cambridge managed to finish

the session. But within two weeks, John was gone. His replacement was Mick "Woody" Woodmansey, who had also taken John's
place in the Rats when Cambridge left after being asked to
rehearse during the Easter holidays. Woodmansey was a more
expansive drummer and a more serious, forceful personality, and
his complex rhythm patterns and extravagant rolls suited the
band's move to a freer, more improvisational sound. Visconti,
though, had admired Cambridge's solid, no-frills drumming, and
he was surprised to see it was Mick Ronson, rather than David,
who had instigated the sacking.

When it came to music, it seemed Ronson was every bit as
unsentimental as Bowie. And as the recording began, on April 18
at Trident, it was the guitarist who commanded the sessions, moving into the realm of recording with the same intensity with
which he'd mastered the guitar. Visconti, whose studio experience far outstripped Ronson's, fondly remembers, "It was Mick
who was our guru—anything he told us to do, we'd do." It was
Ronson who worked on arrangements, persuading Visconti to
switch to a Gibson short-scale bass for a more fluid, guitarlike
sound, wrote out synthesizer lines for Ralph Mace, and even duet-
ted on recorder with Visconti. Mick was omnipresent, dominating
the texture and the mood of *The Man Who Sold the World*—in
stark contrast to Bowie, who was at times, says Visconti, "just
plain difficult to nail down."

David had been remarkably unassertive during his first Mercury album; this time around, he seemed more confident but still
surprisingly casual, leaving huge amounts of work to Ronson and
Visconti. Visconti says, "As a novice producer I just couldn't
understand why David wouldn't want to be in the studio every
minute with us." In recent years, David has seemed nettled by
Visconti's comments, pointing out his own dominant role in the
writing: "Who else writes chord sequences like that?" But Ken
Scott, engineer on the session, also remembers Ronson and Visconti controlling every aspect of a record from which Bowie was
largely absent: "Tony and Mick did take over. How much it was
David not wanting to have anything to do with it, and how much

was Tony taking over, I don't know. But I think it was more Tony's ideas [on the album] than David's."

Visconti's frustration with Bowie derived more from "them and us" divisions than from any musical disagreements. David's infatuation with Angie was understandable, but it was galling that "David was the only one out of all of us who had money in the bank, from 'Space Oddity,' while we were living on nothing." These strange, pleasant, but almost dysfunctional circumstances were the backdrop for what would be Bowie's first great, albeit flawed, album. In his previous works, there had been little emotional commitment: "Space Oddity" encompassed simple alienation, and even in a sweet, personal song like "A Letter to Hermione" he'd sounded disappointed rather than distraught. Yet for this album he could ride on the wave of noise created by Ronson and Visconti, using them as a vehicle to intensify his own emotions.

THE recording of *The Man Who Sold the World* encapsulated an issue that would resurface throughout David Bowie's career: How much was his own work, and how much was that of his subordinates? For detractors, this reliance on his sidemen was a flaw; such arguments parallel those of the critics of contemporary artist Andy Warhol, who simply mapped out concepts and left associates like Gerard Malanga to produce the screen prints and movies.

Visconti's feelings on the subject are complex, but he summarizes his own account by stating, "With a smile on my face, I have to say that Mick and I couldn't have made such a stunning album with anyone else." The meaning seems simple: that the album is a Ronson and Visconti album with David Bowie, as opposed to a David Bowie album with Ronson and Visconti. Yet the ownership of the album is complicated, for Bowie unlocked a creativity in both Ronson and Visconti that might otherwise have remained dormant. In David's Lower Third days, his songwriting relied heavily on outright theft. The moral position here was more nuanced. Without Bowie's input, Visconti and Ronson's collaborations, as the band Ronno, were utterly forgettable. Could Bowie really have stolen something that wouldn't have existed without him?

In Bowie's frequent absences, Ronson and Visconti labored over several songs, notably "She Shook Me Cold," "Black Country Rock," and the middle section of "Width of a Circle," all of which emerged from band jams, with Ronson leading the way. Bowie took the lead for "The Man Who Sold the World," "The Saviour Machine," "The Supermen," and "After All," but even in these songs, Bowie acquired, almost by osmosis, Ronson's musical aggression, the twisted lead guitar encouraging him to explore the darkest themes he'd yet attempted.

"All the Madmen" was a touchstone of the album. Imposing and disturbing, with its theme of madness and its musical swerves from childlike whimsy to gothic heavy rock, the song was taken by many as an illustration of Bowie's alien nature. This interpretation, however, overlooks its unique genius, for in fact it is a work not of alienation but of empathy. The lyrics, delivered with a Syd Barrett childishness, address Terry's move to Cane Hill in almost literal terms. In the lyrics, the mansion that's high and on the far side of town is not an allusion to drugs or to Christ being tempted by the devil but refers simply to Cane Hill's vantage point over London. There is an almost unbearable poignancy about David's declaration that "I'd rather stay here with all the madmen," alongside Terry, than be outside Cane Hill's walls with all "the sad men." The poignancy comes from the fact that this was a wish David proclaimed in song rather than acting on in real life.

The intensity of the sessions overpowered occasional weaknesses. "She Shook Me Cold" was a straightforward knockoff of Hendrix's "Voodoo Chile." Yet the conviction with which it is delivered and the unique timbre of Bowie's voice and Ronson's guitar make the song jell in a way that David's previous homages never had. For the first time, David's material was transcending its origins.

The same applied to David's lyrics. Many of the references were conventional posthippie fare, from Nietzsche—endlessly name-dropped by Jim Morrison—to Kahlil Gibran, whose books

Bolan had posed with on *The Unicorn*. Whether David was a true adept of any of the philosophies he alluded to is doubtful. Mick Farren was, as much as anyone in 1970, in the London intellectual vanguard through his work with IT and membership in the Pink Fairies. A casual friend of Bowie, he describes him as "a bit of poser. Everyone was. Except where some people would read a book jacket and bullshit, David would bullshit, then read the book quietly one Sunday afternoon." Today, David confirms Farren's take, describing his philosophical investigations at the time as mainly consisting of "keeping a book in my pocket with the title showing."

Still, if the scholarship was sketchy, it worked emotionally. "The Man Who Sold the World" — its title, at least, surely influenced by Heinlein's celebrated *The Man Who Sold the Moon* — is the most poignant. Under- rather than overwritten, it is all the more unsettling because of its simplicity. Ronson's insistent opening riff is claustrophobic and vaguely menacing, as is the narrator's meeting with a man: "Although I wasn't there, he said I was his friend." Over two simple verses, multiple meanings emerge, all of them unsettling, speaking of death or loss of identity. Ronson's guitar line for the chorus is childishly simple, as are the lyrics. But the guitar scales that punctuate the chorus march ever upward, like a never-ending staircase, representing an eternity spent wandering. Like "All the Madmen," the song is disturbing, with an emotional intensity that is new to Bowie's work.

The complex environment that gave birth to the album *The Man Who Sold the World* became murkier still when on April 27, halfway through the sessions, David wrote to Ken informing him he no longer considered him his manager and asking him — in misphrased legal jargon — to confirm within seven days that he would cease acting as such. A week later, he and Tony Defries were at Pitt's Manchester Street office. Defries was low-key but did all of the talking. As would become his style, he confronted the problem head-on but left troublesome details until later; in this case, details about compensating Pitt for the money he'd invested in David.

For Pitt, the meeting was devastating. In hindsight, the warning signs were obvious, but David's defection had come as a cruel, unforeseen blow. Those around him then, including Wyper, remember Pitt being obviously traumatized—but also poignantly anxious to ensure David's career wouldn't suffer. Today Pitt details a host of arrangements he had planned for Bowie—including a trip to New York via a Cunard liner, using his Warhol connections—all of which might well have filled the career limbo in which the singer would soon find himself. When considering the suggestion of Olav Wyper that he was too gentlemanly, Pitt, a shadow passing over his face, responds: "Perhaps I wasn't assertive enough. But my God, I put my hand in my pocket and spent the money on David, which they weren't doing over that period."

In those early post-Pitt days, Defries played a fatherly, advisory role; in the main, he simply talked about solving problems. He was not particularly proactive at first but was an accomplished name-dropper who seemed to have a unique sympathy with the artistic temperament; he described how he would protect the precious items that they created, their intellectual copyright, as if it were a religious calling, and he explained how he was at the cutting edge of such a process, freeing artists from the whims of incompetent record companies.

The Man Who Sold the World was completed on May 22, but when the tapes were handed over to Philips, the corporation was once again embroiled in problems that seemed to justify Tony Defries's cynicism about record companies. For toward the autumn of 1970, he discovered that Olav Wyper, his champion at the label, was being ousted. David faced being an orphan artist.

The loss of Wyper was soon followed by the disappearance of Tony Visconti and Mick Ronson. Their defection would become a well-known crossroads in David Bowie's career. Another setback is, by comparison, obscure: At the end of the year, the new manager who'd promised to champion David Bowie disappeared too. Just at the point when he understood how much he needed supporters to help realize his vision, David Bowie was at his most alone.

CHAPTER 8

Kooks

It will either be a disaster, or everything will be hunky dory.

—Peter Shoot

I T'S THE MIDDLE OF 2005, and Tony Defries is holding forth. It's an impressive spectacle; the way his conversation flits from subject to subject, analyzing hidden patterns and trends, switching from science fiction to steel mills, from the Second World War to electronic substrates, is enthralling. His voice has an upper-class languor, but he's proud of his street-urchin credentials, and although his talk is grandiose, there's an engaging practicality to all of his highfalutin claims—a delight in the nuts and bolts of contracts, an innate understanding of how companies are organized, and a disdain for those who lack the command of such essentials.

This is the man whose role models, Colonel Tom Parker and Allen Klein, are two of the most controversial managers in the history of music. Fittingly, Tony Defries is the third. Like Parker, he was an integral part of his client's rise to fame. Like Allen Klein, he and his best-known client suffered the most rancorous and public of splits.

Defries is a master of the Big Lie: telling the masses his client was huge when he was as yet strictly small time, manipulating the truth on every level to advance his client, creating a fake reality that would have been envied by a Hollywood press agent of the 1930s. But then there is the little lie: the notion that Tony Defries took a chance on David Bowie when he was a washed-up one-hit wonder who no one else would touch. As those who were at the center of it all testify, the reality is rather different.

SOON after Wyper's disappearance from Philips, Tony Visconti left Haddon Hall. He and his girlfriend, Liz, moved out in July for practical reasons—Haddon Hall was getting crowded—but it marked a change in Tony's priorities, from David to Marc Bolan. That same month, Marc recorded a song named "Ride a White Swan"; by its October release he had shortened the band's name to T. Rex— famously, so that daytime DJs like Tony Blackburn could pronounce it—marking his ascension from the underground to stardom.

By September, Defries's ambitions had extended beyond being a mere legal adviser to David; he officially joined forces with Laurence Myers, using his relationship with Bowie and Bowie's social acquaintance Lionel Bart as leverage. According to Myers, Defries was employed initially as a business affairs manager, with a promise that if his signings made money, Defries would have 20 percent of Myers's new company, Gem.

With Pitt gone, it was time for Defries to eliminate another "old-school" collaborator: David's publisher, David Platz. Platz—a concentration camp survivor and a respected but not necessarily loved businessman—considered David still under contract to Essex Music, with more songs to deliver; Defries simply told Platz the contract was terminated and started looking for a new publisher. This was classic Defries grandstanding, striking an aggressive pose and leaving the details for later, and the deal caused a long-running legal dispute, with David forced to hand over several songs in later years as recompense. The legal ramifications at the time were irrelevant—if David even knew about them—for the deal represented a fresh start. Defries promised he would deliver a fresh start for David's recording contract too once his Mercury deal came up for renewal, in June of 1971.

"Our playground." Boys playing in cleared bombsites in Lambeth, ten minutes from David Jones's birthplace, 1947. Brixton was a prime target for Nazi terror weapons, thanks to British duplicity. Bombed-out buildings were omnipresent—and ideal for adventures. (Lambeth Archives)

Stansfield Road, David's street. No garden fences, no cars: kids like David's neighbors (*from left*) Graham Stevens, Leslie Burgess, and Roger Bolden could wander unhindered. (Roger Bolden)

"Always well scrubbed, with clean fingernails." The polite, neatly dressed David Jones, 1955, a year after the family's move to Bromley. (Pictorial Press)

Burnt Ash Juniors Football team with 11-year-old David (*middle row, far left*) and friends Chris Britton (*middle row, center*) and Max Batten (*bottom right*). "Bright, with oodles of personality," he was already a favorite of the school headmaster and was fast learning how to deploy his charm "as a weapon." (Max Batten)

David (*left*), 1962, in his final year at Bromley Tech, and his best friend and bandmate George Underwood (*right*), who damaged David's eye in a schoolboy fight. Both aspiring rock 'n' rollers were well known at the Tech, but the dark-haired, outgoing Underwood was more popular. "Everyone thought he was going to be big," says school friend Roger Bevan. (John Barrance)

The Kon-Rads, initially George Underwood's band, late 1962 or early 1963; David is on tenor sax. "He just wanted to be part of show business. You could feel it," says drummer David Hadfield. (Pictorial Press)

The King Bees, May 1964: David (*standing*) with (*from left*) Roger Bluck, Bob Allen, Dave Howard, and George Underwood. Their single, "Liza Jane," must count as one of the least auspicious debuts by a rock star: "I had real trouble getting it even released," says manager Les Conn. When it flopped, David abandoned George—who went on to initially greater success. (Dezo Hoffman/Rex)

The Manish Boys—tough horn-based blues, nomad lifestyle. *From left*: Woolf Byrne, John Watson, David, Paul Rodriguez, Mick Whitehead, Johnny Flux, Bob Solly. Their green van was covered with lipstick messages from girls, most of them dedicated to David. (Bob Solly)

David with the Lower Third, the Radio London Inecto show (bassist Graham Rivens is at left). "There'd be six girls at the front of The Marquee—and half a dozen of us queens at the back, watching his every move," says one regular. (Denis Taylor)

The newly christened David Bowie poses with Brian Pendleton and Phil May, guitarist and lead singer in the Pretty Things, plus Lower Third guitarist Denis Taylor ("me") and drummer Phil Lancaster. (Denis Taylor)

"He was brash, sure he was gonna make it." David's first manager, Les Conn, photographed at his home in Edgware Road, London, 2008, was crucial to his first two record deals. Conn was also an early supporter of Mark Feld — the future Marc Bolan. (Paul Trynka)

A rare photo of David's second manager, the elusive Ralph Horton (*right*). Devoted to his charge, Horton also set out to split David from his band, the Lower Third. (Denis Taylor)

Ken Pitt (in glasses), the manager who oversaw David's career from obscurity to his first hit, with the Mark Leeman Five (singer Roger Peacock is at far right), shortly before he took David on. "He had the right instincts," says one client; others considered him too "gentlemanly" for the cutthroat 1970s. (Ken Pitt)

"The most magical person," June 1967. David was capable of inspiring near obsession in experienced record company execs—but was not as inspiring when it came to delivering a hit. (Dezo Hoffman/Rex)

The Riot Squad, April 1967. *Clockwise from top left*: Del Roll, David, Butch Davis, Rod Davis, Bob Flag, and Croak Prebble. David's short, obscure tenure with the band showed, for the first time, his ability to take risks (and to copy Lou Reed). (Bob Flag)

"See my friends." By 1968, David had acquired the knack of surrounding himself with inspiring people. With (*from left*) girlfriend Hermione Farthingale, newly acquired producer Tony Visconti, and "Hutch"—the guitarist with whom he'd cut his first version of "Space Oddity." (Ray Stevenson)

Singer and songwriter Lesley Duncan, with leading mod-turned-head Jeff Dexter, in early 1968. Duncan was "like an older sister and lover" to David, turning him on to the songs of Jacques Brel—and accompanying him on UFO-hunting jaunts over Hampstead Heath. (Jeff Dexter)

"The Brits sit around whining; Americans get out there and do things." Angela Barnett, July 21, 1969; she had just stayed up with David to watch the Apollo 11 moon landings (and insisted they saw aliens in Beckenham). Starting in the summer of 1969, Angie became the dominant force in David's life. (Ray Stevenson)

David Bowie, showbiz trouper, plays his solo slot at the Beckenham Free Festival, August 16, 1969, just five days after the funeral of his father, Haywood. His ace in the hole, the single "Space Oddity," had disappeared after a brief appearance on the charts, but six weeks later would start climbing once more. (David Bebbington)

Debut of the Hype, with Tony Visconti (*left*) and new guitarist Mick Ronson (*out of view*), February 22, 1970: the antecedent of the Spiders from Mars—and glam rock. (Ray Stevenson)

"They tried to have a new kind of marriage, an open marriage, and it was absolutely brilliant what that represented." Bromley Registry Office, March 20, 1970: David with new wife Angie and mother Peggy—who told friends she had turned up uninvited. (Pictorial Press)

"Oh! You Pretty Things." David, Angie, and newborn Zowie, summer 1971, in the midst of the sessions for *Hunky Dory*. Stranded on a dysfunctional label, dismissed as a one-hit wonder, labeled "a pervert" by BBC producers, David had changed not only his look and lifestyle but the way he wrote and made music. "He cited where he was going to be. And then he did it," says one of his musicians.
(Ron Burton/Mirrorpix)

"I'm gay and I always have been." David's *Melody Maker* interview, 252 Regent Street, London, January 1972. "There was no doubt that this would work," says photographer Barrie Wentzell. Writer Michael Watts adds, "He knew exactly what he was doing." (Barrie Wentzell)

"This was serious." The Spiders make mayhem, Imperial College London, February 12, 1972. David fell into the crowd once, but would "just get up and carry on" for the tour that marked his ascent to stardom. (Ray Stevenson)

"He came not only for your daughters, but for your sons too." "Starman," *Top of the Pops*, July 6, 1972, was a moment of epiphany for a generation of teenagers. (Rex)

David and Mick Ronson share roast and two veg on the train to Aberdeen, May 15, 1973. In recent weeks, manager Tony Defries had quashed the revolt of the Spiders and arranged to groom Ronson as MainMan's next star. (©Mick Rock, 1973, 2000)

"I really did want it to come to an end." Tired and uncommunicative, David arrives for his Hammersmith "retirement," July 3, 1973. "To break up a band like that is astonishing," says one friend, Scott Richardson. "I have to credit Bowie with having a lot of courage—to say, 'I'm not coming back.'" (Mirrorpix)

"Once they could enjoy the fruits of success, the cracks started to appear." Smiles for the camera at the premiere of *Live and Let Die,* July 5, 1973, a rare photo that shows manager Tony Defries (*right*) stepping into the limelight. David and Angie's marriage was already damaged; soon his relationship with Defries would splinter too. (Harry Myers/Rex)

"Cold. Calculated." Recording "Big Brother" at Olympic Studios, with pianist Mike Garson, October 1973. Bowie now planned to outdo the Stones by adopting their loose guitar rock—and their glorification of cocaine. (Kate Simon)

Angie Bowie, on the grounds of Haddon Hall with her lover, singer Scott Richardson, 1973. "I admired her so much as a human being," says Scott. Yet he witnessed how "the things that David counted on her for got diminished, [because] there was so much sex going on." (Scott Richardson)

David with his new "official" mistress, Ava Cherry, soon after his move to New York in April 1974; wife Angie, who had in turn recruited her own official companion, Scott Richardson, would henceforth be kept at a distance. (Bob Gruen)

David dons gouster gear and declares, "I'm going to record a session." Making *Young Americans,* Sigma Sound, Philadelphia, flanked by Mike Garson, who would become Bowie's longest-serving accompanist. (Terry O'Neill/Getty)

"Cracked," July 1974. The Diamond Dogs Tour was characterized by an abundance of cocaine. "The drugs were apparent in so many ways," recalls one witness. "They actually seemed to add to the overall vibe — there was a darkness to it." (Dagmar/TopFoto)

Defries showed plenty of chutzpah with Platz, as he had with Pitt. But when it came to signing deals, as opposed to terminating them, he seemed less pushy. In those early days it was Laurence Myers, not Defries, who had good connections in the music industry. One of them was Bob Grace, who had just joined Chrysalis to set up a publishing division. In September of 1970, Myers called to ask if he'd meet one of his new clients.

Unusually, no one from David's new management company turned up for the meeting at Grace's office. Instead, David and Angie arrived unaccompanied, but if David was nervous, he didn't betray his concern for a moment. He was expansive, ravishing, charming, a natural-born salesman. Angie, too, exuded glamour. Both of them, says Grace, "really knew how to work the system," telling him about the songs David was writing, inviting him down to spend time at Haddon Hall, drawing him into their web. Before long, says Grace, Bowie was "sticking to me like a limpet."

Grace was already a fan of "Space Oddity," and he loved a new song, "Holy Holy," that David played him. Soon he had agreed to pay what was, for Chrysalis, the unprecedented sum of five thousand pounds for a five-year publishing contract with David. The deal was signed on October 23, 1970, but as the negotiations over the fine print were concluded, Grace found himself becoming "a bit suspicious" of Myers and Defries; they seemed content to let David either sink or swim on his own.

Tony Visconti, like Bob Grace, was suspicious of David's new manager. Part of this was prompted by the split with Essex, for whom Visconti still worked, and his suspicions deepened with what Visconti regarded as Defries's clumsy attempts to recruit him to Gem. Visconti's dislike of Defries was compounded by Bolan and Bowie's rivalry. Marc knew where he was heading, was more focused, seemed on the verge of a commercial breakthrough, so "David and I had a parting of the ways," says Visconti. "I felt terrible, but Marc was about to become almost a full-time job for the next two years of my life."

Visconti's departure left an opening for a producer and bassist; his immediate replacement was studio veteran Herbie Flowers, who oversaw Bowie's next single, "Holy Holy." The song was funky, its looseness and vocal sound obviously Bolan-ish, but as Flowers concedes, "Some records just don't jell." The single disappeared into oblivion on its release in January of 1971. Even David's supporters seemed to lose hope. "Maybe there's something about Bowie that doesn't run alongside the path of luck," declared Penny Valentine, a reviewer who always had a surefire feel for a hit.

By the time "Holy Holy" was released, Mick Ronson and Woody Woodmansey had disappeared too. The abiding rumor was that Defries had sent them home, but in fact the pair weren't pushed — they jumped. Mick Ronson was on his way to a Hype show in Leeds when he saw a sign on the A1 that pointed to Hull. The lure of his hometown proved too strong for the guitarist, who asked Woody, "Do we really want to do this? Or should we go back and do rock music like we've always wanted?" And Woody replied, "Yeah!" The pair would reunite with Rats singer Benny Marshall and record as Ronno with Visconti, recruiting Trevor Bolder on bass for live shows.

Before the failure of "Holy Holy," Defries had been bullish. But at the end of 1970, London's newest management guru seemed to fade away. One reason for this was that he had to wait for David's contract to expire. A second reason was that David was very needy, calling people at odd hours, turning up at their doorsteps if they didn't answer the phone, convinced that his own cause was of paramount importance. Defries could be fatherly, but as his later lieutenant Tony Zanetta points out, "He wasn't there to wipe people's ass for them."

Yet there was a more crucial reason for Defries's absence: a singer whose fame far outstripped Bowie's and who was also attempting to extricate himself from his contract. That singer was Stevie Wonder, Motown's onetime child star who would come of age in May of 1971; at that time, he would be entitled to all the royalties he'd accrued over the previous eight years, and his contract would be up for renewal. Both the size of the prize and the challenge of taking on Motown became obsessions for Defries, who spent most of the winter planning his assault on the Detroit label.

Saddled with an absentee manager, deserted by the collaborators he'd relied on so heavily, and with all the momentum of his one truly great song seemingly lost, David Bowie was finally, except for his wife, standing alone. The experience would reveal both of them at their best; however celebrated their relationship was during the media saturation of the Ziggy years, it was in the obscurity of 1971 that the pair forged a new lifestyle. Abandoned, free, the pair were reborn, reinvented.

For David, his isolation in the insulated microclimate of Haddon Hall brought out the earnest, punctual, hardworking teenager. If other people weren't going to help him complete his songs, then he'd do it himself. And all those hard-earned lessons, the songs pieced painfully together with the Lower Third, the homemade arrangements cooked up with the *Observer's Book of Music,* the chords he'd worked out alongside Mick Ronson, would finally cohere in the consciousness of David Bowie, showbiz trouper.

With the fainthearted supporters stripped away, it was Angie who formed the bounds of David's world. The hostess of Haddon Hall ministered to David's every need: brought him breakfast in bed, made him endless cups of tea, and ran out for cigarettes. She would talk to Defries to keep him interested, and then she would call Bob Grace and tell him, "Oh, you're wonderful, I don't know what we'd do without you," before confiding, "I *hate* this management." She loved being at the center of events, loved planning schemes, such as using Dana Gillespie—David's teenage girlfriend, who had reappeared on the scene—to encourage Defries to visit Haddon Hall.

The departure of the Hype brought another benefit. Tony and Liz's old room was now empty, so David moved a piano into the light and airy space, which looked out on the garden. It was a battered old upright that sounded like an ancient pub honky-tonk piano; David would sit at it for hours, obsessively working out runs. Compared with writing for the Hagstrom twelve-string that Ken Pitt had bought him, writing new songs on the piano was hard, painstaking work, but it also allowed him to fit together the harmonic elements in an entirely new way. Over days and weeks he labored obsessively, working out songs and in the process completely revamping his approach to songwriting. "The writing sessions were legendary," says Mark Pritchett, whose band Runk would test-drive David's songs. "They could be *hours* at a time. Angie might say, 'We're scheduled to do this.' He'd be, 'I'm not doing it. I'm doing this.' Just to get the runs right. And when he got it he was crazed. He was on top of the world."

David today explains, almost regretfully, how hard he had to work: "I forced myself to become a good songwriter—and I became a good songwriter. But I had no natural talents whatsoever. I made a job of work at getting good. I wasn't one of those guys who danced out of the womb like Marc." David had been raised on rock stars like Elvis, instinctive iconoclasts who could pick up microphones and transform the world. David might have been born on Elvis's birthday, but he wasn't gifted with the same instinctive talent. His regret expresses how grueling a journey it was, forcing himself to be talented.

But being made, not born, also offered boundless opportunities. Having built up a technique from scratch once, he could do it again. The piano was a new beginning, a new channel for the ideas flooding out of Bowie's consciousness. Songs came together differently on a keyboard; more fluid, based on runs rather than static chords. His writing would be dominated by the instrument for the next six years, the most creative six years of his career. Bowie's piano playing might have been "bad," in drummer Henry Spinetti's word, but his writing was sophisticated; fragments of Weimar or Sinatra songs were incorporated into the harmonic bonanza, clues that Bowie was driven more by showbiz traditions than by rock and roll. In some respects, this represented a return to the eclecticism and originality of his Deram days. But back then his ambition had far outstripped his abilities. This time around, he could realize his most audacious musical ideas with a minimum of help.

Bob Grace was staggered by Bowie's "sheer graft" throughout this new phase. "This was the most hardworking guy... talk about diligent, he redefined the word." Grace would hear the results at his office, and he found a cheap demo studio at Radio Luxembourg where they could record the songs fresh, as they came spilling out. Here David would work up songs with Runk—soon to be renamed Arnold Corns—and drummer Henry Spinetti, who still remembers David's charm in talking him into doing sessions for free.

David and Angie's world was tiny, intimate—as far as work went, they latched onto Grace, monopolizing him, jealous of others' demands on his time, traveling to and from Beckenham in cabs they sneaked onto the Chrysalis account. When David wasn't closeted at the keyboard, he'd often be found in mechanic's overalls underneath his car; over this period, thanks to his publishing income, he progressed from a 1.5-liter black 1950s Riley, to a 2.5-liter red version, and, finally, to an 1100cc Riley Gamecock, a wood-framed 1930s racer. It was probably this last machine that rolled into David and impaled his leg on the starting handle. The incident was witnessed by the Lewisham police, who found the sight of the exotic, curly-haired youth skewered by his own car hilarious—David spent a week in the hospital recovering.

As David and Angie drew Grace into their world, Grace was as taken by Bowie's wonderfully dry humor as he was by his skills as a mechanic. He was also disoriented by their obsession with taking him to celebrated gay clubs, such as Yours or Mine, usually referred to as the Sombrero, to gay movies, and to see flamboyantly gay friends, like Freddie Buretti and Mickey King, all in an attempt to get him, says Grace, to "embrace his trip."

David's "trip"—his lifestyle—had blossomed, thanks to Angie's encouragement. Although he'd been hanging out at gay clubs since his mod days, by the time he hooked up with Calvin Lee, the scene had moved upmarket to the Kensington and Notting Hill arty set. Although this time has always been painted as his "Warhol period," Bowie's circle was quintessentially English—straight out of Noël Coward or Quentin Crisp. Americans who came visiting would be confused by the bisexual vibe and by certain acquaintances, such as Ossie Clark, a man who'd briefly shared a boyfriend with Calvin Lee and was married to a woman he adored,

Celia Birtwell, whom he suspected of two-timing him with his celebrated gay friend and rival David Hockney. Lionel Bart was another paradox: Famously devoted to Alma Cogan, he would often be seen with a rent boy in tow or snuggled up to David. In fact, apart from the Brits' inferior dental work, the scene was far more glamorous than back in America. "Everyone was a dandy, so much better dressed than in New York," thought one visitor, Tony Zanetta—until he noticed that nearly every clubgoer owned just one suit, which on inspection was often slightly grubby, like the impressive facade of a country house that conceals the genteel poverty within.

Future commentators would wonder whether David's gay persona was sincere and genuine. Robert Kensell, a good-looking party animal with a passing resemblance to Terence Stamp, was part of the Sombrero scene with his friend Jonathan Barber, one of Calvin Lee's lovers. Kensell later built a thriving business as "house cocaine dealer" at Olympic Studios, but in those early days Jonathan and he would bed-hop for food and fun, sponging off hosts such as Ossie, Lionel, and Kit Lambert. "Remember, in 1970 you couldn't talk about something, unless you'd done it," he points out. "David wasn't just part of the scene. He was at the center of it."

David's flings with men were short-lived and often opportunistic; the thrill was usually in the discovery. His bisexuality was part of his appeal for many Sombrero boys—"very manly" is how one scenester describes him. And at least some of his obsession with the scene was, says Bob Grace, because of Mick Jagger: "Jagger was a role model—not an idol—and David was *convinced* he was bisexual." David was evangelistic about his lifestyle, explaining to Bob, "This is my wife, she gets boys for me, and I get girls for her—and we're all very happy!"

One of the Sombrero patrons David loved pointing to with the words "Look, isn't he gorgeous?" was Freddie Buretti. Freddie was fully six feet tall with Caravaggesque good looks, and he worked for a Kensington fashion retailer. One evening in 1971 he had a brush with the law, charged for importuning after having sex with the arresting officer. Bob Grace was called in to post bail, and despite the aggravation, he had a sneaking respect for the way that Freddie insisted on listing his occupation as "seamstress." Usually Freddie was seen hanging out with Daniella Parmar, his "girl-friend": "She was the first girl I had seen with peroxide white hair with cartoon images cut and dyed into the back," David remembers. "Blessed with absolute style, she unwittingly changed so much of how female Britain looked—after my then-wife copped her sense of style." The ambiguity of Daniella and Freddie's relationship was part of the vibe. Another of David's protégés was Mickey King—again, David loved to imply Mickey was a bedmate; it was all part of the confusion, as was the sight of Angie with scraped-back hair wearing an impeccably tailored suit chatting up women at the Sombrero. Freddie, thanks to his design skills, became a semipermanent member of the team. Mickey would drop in and out of Haddon Hall, as he did the rent-boy scene; ultimately, he would die in mysterious circumstances—stabbed by a jealous john, say his Haddon Hall friends.

The kinky, noisy buzz around Haddon Hall inspired David's buoyant mood, which was unaffected by the mess at Mercury and Philips. Although the English version of *The Man Who Sold the World* would languish in limbo until the following April, delayed by the political changes at Philips, the Americans were eager to release the album—Mercury's Robin McBride flew over that winter to collect the masters and artwork directly from Bowie. David handed him two illustrations by Arts Lab regular Mike Weller that depicted Cane Hill—they were later replaced by a photo of David reclining at Haddon Hall in his Mr. Fish dress.

Soon David's London press contacts were informed that the album was being "acclaimed in America...a sudden holocaust." The reality was rather more modest. David's American fans were mainly the Mercury staff, principally the newly appointed press officer Ron Oberman, who as "torch carrier" for David arranged a U.S. promotional tour for *The Man Who Sold the World*, starting January 27, 1971.

David arrived unaccompanied for his first trip to the United

States—Angie was five months pregnant and had decided to remain at Haddon Hall. He was in his element traveling solo, unfazed by his reception at Dulles, where Immigration detained him for a time, suspicious of his fey manner and flowing pre-Raphaelite locks.

"For some reason, they seemed to think I looked strange," he informed Ron Oberman, who'd been kept waiting in the terminal for an hour. David spent the next few days bubbling with the enthusiasm of a child, accompanied by Ron to radio and press interviews in Washington, D.C., and Chicago, partying, and going out for meals with Ron's parents, who found him every bit as charming as the Manish Boys' parents had a decade before. Oberman soon picked up on David's tastes, taking him up to Fifty-fourth Street in Manhattan to see Moondog, the poet, musician, and outsider who lived on the street clad in Viking garb; David chatted with him intently and fetched him coffee and sandwiches. When Ron was busy, David wandered around New York alone and was thrilled to see, the weekend after his arrival, that the Velvet Underground was playing the Electric Circus. He was transfixed by the group's renditions of new songs like "Sweet Jane," venturing upstairs to talk to Lou Reed after the show, telling him how he admired his songwriting and that he had covered "Waiting for the Man." Only later did he learn that Lou had left the band the previous autumn and the man he'd talked to in the legendary Dom was in fact Doug Yule. David found the notion that the Velvets could be duplicated, like a Coke can or a soup tin, enthralling—maybe the fake Lou was as authentic as the real thing? When he wasn't discussing such concepts with Ron, he picked Ron's brains on how the U.S. music industry worked, quizzing him on the company politics of Mercury and other labels.

The East Coast was graced by the earnest, purposeful David Bowie, but the West Coast was treated to a more decadent version. Writer John Mendelssohn arrived at LAX to meet the singer, who got off the plane wearing a Mr. Fish dress, looking disconcertingly like Lauren Bacall. Mick Jagger had helped publicize the kipper-tie designer's dresses for men, most famously at the Stones'

Hyde Park show in 1969. David's interpretation of the same look was radically more feminine—his dress was more ornate, and his curly hair had grown out and now cascaded in waves over his shoulders. Mendelssohn was disturbed to find his chivalrous instincts aroused by this exotic creature; soon he and his friend were struggling with David's trunk—so extraordinarily heavy they speculated he was smuggling a piano—while David sashayed along behind them, murmuring "Oh dear!" every now and then, the perfect, helpless, fluttery-lashed ingenue. Mendelssohn had agreed to write a story about the English singer for *Rolling Stone* but was so intimidated by this strange apparition that he could only think of the most inarticulate, mumbled questions, all of which David treated as if they were the most profound examples of the inquisitorial arts.

Later that evening, some of Mendelssohn's verve returned when the two arrived at the Holiday Inn and found the hotel's facilities had been augmented with a teenage girl, provided for Bowie by the future "Mayor of the Sunset Strip" Rodney Bingenheimer.

Mercury's radio promotions man on the West Coast, Bingenheimer had been abandoned by his mother in Hollywood as a teenager, but his enthusiasm for rock and roll and his frank adoration of celebrity soon helped him become sidekick to Sonny and Cher and later one of the leading scenesters. Rodney was famous as, in friend and rival Kim Fowley's words, "purveyor of a posse of pussy"—a skill he proved by sending the girl "like a welcoming present," says Mendelssohn. As Mendelssohn and Bowie reclined in the Holiday Inn lounge, listening incredulously to a hilarious duo called the Brass Doubles—an organist and drummer, each of whom played his main instrument one-handed while doubling on trumpet—they competed for Rodney's girl. David won, chatting away relentlessly in a deadpan, Jaggeresque drawl. Finally, she accepted David's offer to "come up to me room for some guitar lessons."

Like many Englishmen, David discovered the possibilities of reinventing oneself on this new continent. His skills at enchanting and confusing all onlookers blossomed; resplendent in his

dress or other exotic outfits, he perfected the knack of monopolizing people's attention. At a legendary party hosted by Tom Ayers,
one of Rodney's innumerable record-biz friends, he hovered by
the door, greeting guests, outraging the elderly ladies, enchanting
the groupies and Valley girls. In between chatting to Bingenheimer and working his wiles on a sixteen-year-old who, says
Mendelssohn with a sigh, "had certainly the most beautiful
breasts on the West Coast," Bowie had a short conversation with
Ayers, who was a house producer for RCA. David mentioned his
problems with Mercury, and Ayers told him to "look at RCA," saying, "The only thing they've got is Elvis—and Elvis can't last
forever."

It was a short but momentous exchange. The idea of supplant-
ing the king of rock and roll, whose birthday he shared and who
had inspired him as a kid, would once have seemed ridiculous.
Now an insider from Elvis's own label was suggesting the company would be lucky to have him. Riding on a wave of energy, of
excitement at the sights and sounds of California, and of the
enthusiasm of the small gaggle of Hollywood insiders, David
started contemplating the prospect of conquering America.

Even the mundane promotional visits were enjoyable. He and
John Mendelssohn spent an afternoon driving up to San Jose for a
radio interview, talking nonsense and singing their own reworking of Edwin Starr's "War," replacing the original words with
"Tits! What are they good for?" When they arrived at the station
and started chatting, they found the West Coast hippie DJ was
sneering and suspicious of the campy, obscure English singer.
Bowie was cheery, unintimidated, his deadpan humor in full flow,
and when the DJ asked him to suggest a track to play, he instantly
sealed his decadent credentials with a languid request for "anything by the Velvet Underground."

As the show ran on, Mendelssohn looked through the record
racks and spotted a copy of *The Stooges*, the debut album by Michigan's punk pioneers, notorious for having crashed and burned in
a haze of heroin that year. Intrigued, David chose "Now I Wanna
Be Your Dog" for his next selection. When the song's moronically

monumental riff and Iggy's deadpan drawl blared from the studio speakers, David's amused energy seemed to intensify. As the two drove back, Mendelssohn told him about the Stooges' lead singer, Iggy, who'd arrived on the West Coast that summer, his only clothing some ripped jeans, one change of underwear, and a pair of silver lamé gloves, and had shocked crowds, pulling a girl out of the audience by her face and dripping melted wax on his chest. David hung on his every word.

Iggy and the Stooges became a near obsession over the following months, part of a cornucopia of influences that David soaked up like a sponge, the more outré or outrageous, the better. In Chicago, Ron Oberman had played him a crazed single called "Paralyzed," by the Legendary Stardust Cowboy—David loved it and took a copy of the 45 home with him, along with a stack of albums by Kim Fowley, another West Coast eccentric.

When David returned to Britain, he was "buzzing" with the sounds and the sights he'd encountered, completely reenergized, according to his neighbor Mark Pritchett, who was given four Kim Fowley albums from the stash David brought home. The Stooges' two albums were constantly spinning on David's turntable and had an immediate effect. One of the first songs he wrote after his return was "Moonage Daydream"; stripped down and less wordy, its "put your electric eye on me, babe," hinted at the Stooges' "She got a TV eye on me." In April David worked the song up with Pritchett's band Runk (for many years, legend would have it they were the Spiders in disguise, thanks to the improbably monikered drummer Timothy James Ralph St. Laurent Thomas Moore Broadbent and bassist Peter De Somogyi, Pritchett's blue-blooded Dulwich College schoolmates). The song was written on guitar, and when the trio recorded it at the Radio Luxembourg studios with David, he was painstaking about every detail, singing out the middle instrumental section, lifted from one of Kim Fowley's Hollywood Argyles songs but used here, says guitarist Mark Pritchett, "for a Bertolt Brecht effect—like a funfair with camp overtones."

When it came to selling the song, it got campier still when

David recruited Freddie Buretti as a "lead singer," posing with him and Bob Grace for photos as Arnold Corns for a single released on the tiny B&C soul label. In an interview for *Sounds,* David touted Freddie, or Rudi, as "the new Mick Jagger," despite the fact that his voice was barely audible on the record. But that wasn't the point; the music, rushed as the recording was, signaled a new simplicity that was being sold with a new flamboyance — the serious, rather worthy David Bowie who'd extolled the virtues of the Arts Lab was being consigned to history.

"Moonage Daydream" and "Hang On to Yourself," written over the same period, were all the more impressive for being kept in reserve. It was a third song, written just a few weeks before, that signaled the beginning of the most pivotal winning streak of David's life.

The new song's origins echoed, almost spookily, those of two other songs that transformed their composers' careers. Paul McCartney's "Yesterday" arrived in a dream, marking the point at which he would assume joint leadership of the Beatles. So did Keith Richards's "Satisfaction," which he woke up humming one night in a Florida motel and which would become the Stones' first U.S. number 1. The song that was lodged in David Bowie's mind when he woke one morning early in January of 1971 would stay two places outside the Top 10. But it was just as crucial.

Bob Grace was the first person to hear the news, when his phone rang at the start of a busy day.

"I woke up at four o'clock," David told him, "had this song going in my head and I had to get out of bed, work it out on the piano and get it out of my head so I could go back to sleep."

"What's it called?" asked Grace.

" 'Oh! You Pretty Things.' "

David insisted he needed to demo the song straightaway, and Grace arranged for him to piggyback onto a session booked for a radio interview at Radio Luxembourg studios. There was no time to call in Tim Broadbent or Henry Spinetti, so David recorded the song solo, the only accompaniment the jangling of the bracelets he was wearing. Grace had become close friends with Bowie by now, drawn into his web. After pronouncing the song "stunning," he felt compelled to recruit more supporters to the Bowie cause. The best contender he could think of was Mickie Most, still the UK's best-known independent producer, who he knew would be at that year's MIDEM festival in Cannes, just a few days away.

With the rendezvous organized, Grace played the acetate for Mickie on a tiny Dansette player at a booth in the festival. He was nervous—and would have been even more nervous had he known that Most had turned down David Bowie twice over the preceding years. David had not breathed a word about these earlier failures.

Publishing lore was that if Most listened to more than ten seconds of a song, you had a chance. Grace paced around nervously as the famously opinionated producer listened to the entire song, waited until the fade-out, then announced: "Smash!" and told Grace the song would be perfect to launch the solo career of Peter Noone, from Herman's Hermits—uncool as they were, they were one of Most's biggest acts, and this was a huge coup. The fact that the song had arrived almost fully formed from David's unconscious demonstrated how, after five years of writing songs, he had bypassed the critical part of his consciousness. Before, his writing had been considered; now, it was inspired.

Plenty of other songs demoed at Radio Luxembourg showed how the short U.S. trip had provided David with a store of images to draw on. A theme was emerging. David was a pro, a man who knew how to work the system, but he had an instinctive sympathy for those who couldn't, those practitioners of what writer Irwin Chusid terms "outsider music"; erratic people like Syd Barrett, Iggy Pop, Moondog, and Stardust Cowboy Norman Carl Odam. David would follow their star-crossed careers, and their fates infuse songs like the gorgeous "Lady Stardust," demoed on March 10 along with an early version of "Moonage Daydream," and the wonderfully hokey "Right On, Mother," destined for Peter Noone.

At the same time that David was laying the bedrock of his future music, he was focusing just as diligently on reinventing his image—and, more specifically, consigning the past to oblivion.

Bill Harry, childhood friend of John Lennon and founder of *Mersey Beat* magazine, was one of London's busiest PR people; Bob Grace called him in, explaining that David's career had stalled and they were trying to generate some momentum. Harry and Bowie spent days closeted together talking about science fiction — a mutual obsession — music, and photography. Harry knew many rock and rollers, but none of them had as sophisticated a sense of visuals: Bowie brought in mood boards of photos and glossy magazine cuttings, pictures of movie stars and Egyptian pharaohs to illustrate photographic ideas, and together they plotted to airbrush David's past.

Harry helped push *The Man Who Sold the World*, which finally made it to the shelves in Britain that April, but Bowie's eyes were fixed firmly beyond that release. Armed with a stack of glossy photos by Brian Ward, Bowie and Harry went the rounds of Fleet Street and the music press. While Bill sat in the office chatting, David would go to the filing cabinet, slot in the new photo, and pull out the old shots of the curly-headed "Space Oddity" Bowie, banishing the one-shot wonder to oblivion. "He was planning ahead. He didn't seem part of the normal culture at all, sitting around in a pub or club and getting boozed up; he was collecting together images for the future," says Harry.

Their campaign reaped immediate results: a spread in the *Daily Mirror,* plus articles in the *Daily Express* and the music press. The stories paved the way for Peter Noone's single of "Oh! You Pretty Things"—with David contributing a strident, bouncing piano—that hit the Top 40 on May 22, peaking at number 12. The lumpy, pedestrian arrangement failed to hamper the song's gorgeously inventive melody, which was as fleet of foot as *White Album*–era McCartney work; Peter Noone went into print praising David Bowie as the finest songwriter since Lennon and McCartney. Suddenly, the one-hit wonder was the new kid on the block.

Bob Grace, the man who had helped engineer this career turnaround, was overjoyed: This was what he'd joined Chrysalis for, to take an artist "from demo to limo," as the saying had it. When

Terry Ellis, his boss, called him into his office, with the song still at its chart peak, Grace walked into the room expecting a promotion and a raise.

Instead, Ellis was red-faced with rage.

"This is a disaster!" Ellis yelled. "You've ruined the image of my company. The Chrysalis Music label on a pop record! How dare you? Furthermore, I have a manager outside, Tony Defries, who's absolutely furious."

Defries walked in, and the conversation turned into a heated argument, with Defries accusing Grace of trying to poach his artist and Grace responding, "If you did more for him, he'd stop hassling *me* so much!" Bill Harry had a similar encounter and was accused of interfering, and when Defries announced, "From now on, all interviews must be conducted from my office," Harry quit as David's PR man.

Today, Bill Harry insists that Defries never measured up to other managers he worked with, such as Led Zeppelin's famously aggressive Peter Grant. "I couldn't work with Defries. I found him quite unpleasant, and inflexible." But Harry and Bob Grace's accusations that Defries had left Bowie to fend for himself would not be repeated, for in the forthcoming weeks, Tony Defries would reinvent himself as completely as his client.

David Bowie had fought his way back into contention, more or less unaided. But Defries was the man who'd build an army behind him.

TONY Defries was already an expert in reinvention and repackaging. Born in 1943, reputedly near a secret airfield in North London, and just five years older than David, he claimed he'd had a similar "fractured" childhood and viewed his life in much the same mythic sense. His grandparents had fled from Russia, and young Defries had, he would tell listeners, been put into care for a year when he was just a few months old, a devastating experience during which at one point he clinically died from an asthma attack. Like David, he was conscious of growing up amid wartime ruins, in his own case as part of a Jewish family living on its wits in Shepherd's Bush, dodging gangs of Irish, Greek, and Turkish Cypriots, building a business selling factory-reject china and other oddments. He and his brother Nicholas soon discovered that an average brace of dueling pistols could be transformed into a desirable rarity once packaged in a convincingly antiqued wooden box; they were selling a fantasy, and in much the same way, Defries, who left school at fourteen, would remarket himself as a legal bigwig, and then as a manager.

Tony's unique life was carved out in a British society in a state of flux: The aristocracy was trying to pawn its possessions as European families tried to reclaim their inheritances looted by the Nazis. In this chaos, empires could be rebuilt, and Defries planned to be at the head of one. Even his many detractors concede he was shrewd; he was also fearless and would go straight to the top of whatever company he was working with to cut a deal. Just a few years older than his clients, he was nonetheless "a bigdaddy figure," as Dana Gillespie, who looked after them and shielded them from all earthly worries, puts it. Modeling himself on Colonel Parker, he told David that he would make him famous as a "one-name star," like Elvis or Dylan: a monolithically famous performer known simply as Bowie.

The nature of Defries's and Bowie's professional relationship would often be misunderstood, not least by David, despite the fact it was legally documented. Defries did not work for David; David worked for him. In David's ten-year contract, signed on March 31, 1972, with Defries's newly established MainMan empire, the singer and songwriter is referred to as Employee. The contract gives the term of Bowie's management agreement with Defries as "timeless."

Defries explains his remoteness in the spring of 1971 by saying he was simply waiting for David's Mercury contract to expire. A more pressing reason was doubtless his involvement with Stevie Wonder. By May, and the "Oh! You Pretty Things" breakthrough, Defries's Detroit mission had stalled and Wonder had agreed to renew his deal with Motown. David Bowie was therefore his best bet. But if Defries had waited until the last minute to bet on Bowie, when the time came, he would bet big. And Defries was betting with much more than money (which came, in any case, from Laurence Myers). He bet his professional life. From the moment he fully engaged himself in Bowie's career, there was never any doubt that the fate of these two men was intertwined.

Anya Wilson was the radio plugger who'd helped drive Marc Bolan's "Ride a White Swan" to number 2, and she was hired by Defries to repeat her feat for Bowie. "I had more than one knot in my stomach working for Tony, believe me," says Wilson. "He was very focused on what he wanted. I got fired several times, but he would rehire me a couple of weeks later and pay me back pay. But when he was locked in it was absolute. There was never any doubt. It was very infectious."

Defries was ready to bide his time until the end of June, when Mercury could exercise their option on David, but from May onward he worked closely, plotting with Bowie and Bob Grace. It was the publisher, with Anya Wilson, who secured another slot on *BBC In Concert*, which would be a key signpost of what was to come.

The growing sense of event was heightened with the news that Angie had given birth to Duncan Zowie Haywood Bowie at Bromley Hospital on May 30 after a drawn-out labor. David was there for the birth, which sealed Angie's position as queen to Bowie's king. But Angie, who freely admits "I was not the maternal type," would later pinpoint the aftermath of the birth as a dark portent for their relationship. Zowie—named after the Greek word meaning "life"—was a chunky eight and a half pounds, and Angie suffered a cracked pelvis, blood loss, exhaustion, and what sounds like classic postpartum depression. A few weeks after the birth, Dana Gillespie persuaded Angie to join her for a trip to her parents' summer villa in Italy. Angie recruited the redoubtable Suzi Frost, henceforth an integral part of the household, to look after Zowie during her absence and remembers David hardly raising an eyebrow at her departure. Years later, though, she'd speculate that David, for all his sexual nonconformity, retained some distinctly old-school family values and regarded the trip as an unforgivable desertion.

Yet for those around them, the birth and surrounding events seemed largely idyllic, with Angie continuing to provide a protective "cocoon" for David in which he could create. The impression of a domestic idyll was cemented with David's song "Kooks," which asked their baby, "Will you stay in our lovers' story?" Written after David had spent the day listening to Neil Young's "After the Gold Rush," its jiggling piano feel evoked Young's "Till the Morning Comes," with its central lyric quoting the Young title "I Believe in You." It was, and is, a delightful song, deft, lighthearted, totally without artifice.

The song made its public debut a couple of days after it was written, at *BBC In Concert* on June 3, 1971. Like most key events in David's life, the show was pulled together almost randomly and at the last moment. Late in May, David booked bassist Herbie Flowers and guitarist Tim Renwick for the appearance. Renwick had been an occasional visitor to Haddon Hall; David, says Junior's Eyes singer Graham Kelly, was fascinated by the guitarist— indeed, Kelly maintains that David's Lauren Bacall persona derived from the Marlene Dietrich impression that Renwick often performed as a party piece. Renwick appears on at least one long-lost song from that summer—"Hole in the Ground," with Herbie on bass and George Underwood on vocals—but his role as David's sideman evaporated at the last moment when David phoned Mick Ronson. The two had kept in touch over recent months—David took a small crew of Haddon Hall regulars down to Ronno's London showcase at Lower Temple—and Mick seized the chance, for the band's undistinguished single on Vertigo had sunk without trace. Ronson brought all his musicians down the A1; they arrived on June 1 and had one afternoon to rehearse. For Ronson, Woodmansey, and Bolder—who had joined Ronno only recently—the one afternoon was an impromptu, scary, electrifying start to a journey that would stay that way.

Their nervousness was useful, forcing them to come up with ideas, and most of the off-the-cuff riffs they pulled together would survive on David's upcoming album. David exuded happiness and positivity, overjoyed with both the arrival of Zowie and the thrill of creation. There was no overlooking his nervous energy, but he projected the conviction that this was meant to be; this was his man-child quality, that incredible sense of focus and belief that everything was simple.

THE show united Haddon Hall regulars Mark Pritchett, George Underwood, and David's schoolmate Geoff MacCormack with Ronson's band, whose singer Benny Marshall guested on a cover of Chuck Berry's "Almost Grown." The Hull musicians were "nervous as hell," yet much of the party atmosphere that is audible on the show's recording is genuine. At times, the vibe was surprisingly intimate—as in the rendition of "Kooks," dedicated to the new Bowie child, and the jokey interactions with John Peel—yet after David walked into the dressing room wearing jeans and a T-shirt and came out of it wearing his Mr. Fish dress and exuding glamour, there was no doubt that this was an accomplished coup de théâtre. At the end, David tearfully apologized to producer Jeff Griffin that he'd completely messed up the vocal on "Oh! You Pretty Things." "It hadn't even registered," says Griffin. Then once the show was over, David forgot this blip and was consumed by his next project.

In future years, people would call Bowie's mind-set for that summer "positive visualization." He announced the title of his next album, *Hunky Dory,* on the BBC at a time when the album was still a pipe dream and he was still tied to a record company he hated. The title came from a catchphrase of Peter Shoot, larger-than-life ex-RAF owner of one of Bob Grace's favorite pubs, the Bear in Esher: "It will either be a disaster, or everything will be hunky dory."

David loved the phrase. This time around, everything *would* be hunky dory. He talked about producing other acts as if he already had a star's magic touch. And he laid out the future for the band who'd been with him for just a few days, telling them about the two albums they would make in forthcoming months with a new record company, the venues they would play at the start of the coming onslaught, and where they would end up. "He had it all in his head," says bassist Trevor Bolder. "And then he cited each part of where he was going to be."

Tony Defries was the other master of positive visualization. He too would lay out the future in front of them as if it were a map. A key part of his strategy was to cut record companies out of the creative loop; Defries had the means to do that, for he would fund David's next album independently before dispensing with Mercury and approaching RCA—giving David, he explained, ownership of his own music. This was an unprecedented commitment; as his future lieutenant Tony Zanetta points out, "Tony threw the book out the window. He loved to take huge gambles. And the money it took meant nothing to him. Although of course it was Laurence's money that he was gambling with."

For David to realize his vision, he had to have the best. That included the studio, Trident, already familiar to David but then at its height of popularity after its conversion to a state-of-the-art twenty-four tracks. Grace says that Trident's main engineer, Ken Scott, was fast becoming "the hot guy at the time," thanks primarily to his work on George Harrison's *All Things Must Pass;* he got on well with David, who decided to share the production role with him. In June, David, Grace, Ken Scott, and Mick Ronson assembled at Scott's house in Catford, in southeast London, to select an album's worth of material from the Radio Luxembourg demos.

Scott had engineered David's previous two albums and agreed to the producer's role, figuring he'd gain useful experience: "I thought David was good, but he'd never be a superstar. This would be the perfect time to practice production, so if I fucked up it wouldn't really matter. But when we were sitting there listening to those demos, this lightbulb went on. I thought, Bloody hell! This is for real!"

Some kind of floodgate had been unlocked, so much so that "Star," "Moonage Daydream," and "Lady Stardust" were among the compositions saved for a later day, for there was a conscious decision to build the new album around the piano. The three standout songs—"Oh! You Pretty Things," "Changes," and "Life on Mars"—all featured broadly similar piano runs rolling forward with an irresistible momentum, but each one boasted a distinct, gorgeously memorable melody.

The contrast with "Space Oddity" could not have been more pronounced; whereas the melody on that song was constrained, claustrophobic, *Hunky Dory*'s standout melodies were fluid, swooping across an octave or more. "Life on Mars" is a typical example, cheekily based on the chord sequence of "Comme d'Habitude," also known as "My Way," a song for which David had once crafted a set of lyrics at the behest of Ken Pitt. His attempts were rejected, and if the setback had rankled, then revenge was sweet, for the new song was grandiose, its melody arguably superior to Jacques Revaux's original. The main tune arrived in Bowie's head as he was on the bus to Lewisham to buy some shoes; he hopped off the bus, "more or less loped" back to Haddon Hall, and completed the song by the late afternoon. The lyrics were enigmatic, a succession of fragmentary images witnessed by the "girl with the mousy hair," rather in the style of McCartney's "Eleanor Rigby." Only when we reach the chorus, with an octave leap up to the words "life on Mars," do we realize the song is about a yearning for escape, or transcendence. It's a thrilling trick—and a solidly traditional one, drawing on the work of songwriters like Harold Arlen.

David's three previous albums had all been complicated recordings overshadowed by politics. With *Hunky Dory,* David set out to satisfy himself, not record company executives, a freedom reflected in the album's freshness. The recording process was simple, dominated by David's childlike optimism and focus—much of which came from the reassuring presence of Mick Ronson, who as arranger carried the burden of translating the songs from piano sketches to luscious epics.

Mick didn't share David's sense of calm. He had taken some refresher piano lessons on his return to Hull; nonetheless, the assignment was far scarier than anything David had thrown at him so far. Although David did occasionally lose his composure—shouting, "Just play the song right!" when the rhythm section messed up a take of "Song for Bob Dylan"—he was masterful at motivating people, pushing Mick forward, challenging him, "Go on, do it! If it doesn't work out, it doesn't work out—but have a go!" Mick impressed both Ken Scott and Bob Grace with his quiet efficiency, but Ronson's friend Trevor Bolder noticed the guitarist was "a bag of nerves." While Bowie sat in the Trident control room looking down on the recording area, Ronson was on the studio floor, checking through manuscript pages, nervously dragging on one after another of his trademark roll-ups; close up, you could see his hands shaking. But there was little time to worry, for the sessions were rushed and David was impatient. On the songs where he played piano, there would sometimes be just a couple of run-throughs, and then the band members would have to find their own way, like session musicians, living on their wits. "It was always on the edge, wondering if they would make it through," says Scott. Occasionally they would have a rest and watch Rick Wakeman overdub piano parts at Trident's celebrated Bechstein, the one on which McCartney had pounded out "Hey Jude."

At first, the musicians wondered if David's impatience derived from a selfish desire to monopolize the studio time for his own singing—but it turned out he required only a couple of takes to nail the vocal, his microphone technique perfected by years of experience. "He was unique," says Scott, "the only singer I ever worked with where virtually every take was a master."

The truth was, he was simply burning to download his work from his mind and commit it to tape. "The Bewlay Brothers," for instance, arrived during an unsettled day and was recorded, solo, later that evening. Its title came from a cheap, old-fashioned pipe Bowie had once briefly owned, and the lyrics were inscrutable even to their creator. "Don't listen to the words, they don't mean anything," he told Scott as they prepared for a vocal take. "I've just written them for the American market, they like this kind of thing."

The album's lyrics—which were dense with allusions; both "Quicksand" and "The Bewlay Brothers" contain his most evocative images—usually came quickly ("I can't remember much redrafting at all," says Mark Pritchett). The result was a dazzling assembly of musical and lyrical imagery. The songs obviously drew from traditional English as well as cutting-edge American influences—"He stole from the best," as Trevor Bolder puts it— but the borrowed riffs and name-dropping only contributed to the simple, childlike radiance. In his days around Haddon Hall, playing with Zowie, tinkering with his Riley, or flirting with Freddie, David had forged a new manifesto; it was postmodern (you could pick and choose from the works of Warhol and Lou Reed, leaving the joins showing) and postsexual (the singer is free to play the role of man, woman, or child). *Hunky Dory* had the unspoiled, overwhelming charm of a new beginning.

IF David's new record was naive and simple, Defries's method of selling it was hard-bitten—strictly old-school. The sessions were already drawing to a close before Defries ensured he was free to sell the results to the record company of his choice. He and Laurence Myers were negotiating with people at RCA and had sent them more than half of *Hunky Dory* before Defries rid himself of Mercury.

Vice president Irwin Steinberg and A and R Robin McBride had flown over to London in the happy expectation of extending David's contract to include a fourth album for the label; as it turned out, they were like generals who had lost the battle before their troops ever took the field. "We were totally blindsided," says McBride, who had arranged what he thought would be a pleasant lunch at the Londonderry Hotel only to have Defries, soberly dressed and immaculately groomed, bypass the normal pleasantries and announce, "David will never record for you again."

Steinberg pointed out David owed them one more album under his contract.

"If you insist on a third album, you will get the biggest pile of shit ever seen on a record," Defries responded. Steinberg was a brilliant, well-read man, McBride explains, but when he was faced with an argument, his instinct was to say "Fuck you" and walk away. Which is exactly what he did. "If you want a release, you will have to pay," he informed Defries. "You will have to refund Mercury for all the recording expenses, all the art expenses, all the packaging and promotional expenses that we have undertaken on David Bowie's behalf."

This was exactly the response that Defries had hoped for; he assented to those costs, letting Steinberg believe he had won. Only later did McBride and Steinberg discover that David had already recorded an album intended for another label; only later did they realize that by buying back the two Mercury albums at cost, Defries had actually ended up making a huge amount of money. McBride and Steinberg, music fans both, had been taken in a consummate example of Defries's aggression and brinksmanship. For each, it would represent one of the most humiliating setbacks of his career.

Although he acknowledges that Defries did not utter an untruth in that fateful meeting, McBride found the encounter detestable, rivaled only by his meeting with Dylan's controversial manager Albert Grossman: "They have both helped in the success of some terribly talented people," he notes. "But both personalities belonged in the same garbage can."

As David finished *Hunky Dory* that summer, Defries was developing an almost messianic sense that he could remake the music industry, buoyed up by his coup at Mercury. He and David were hanging out together more and more, at the Sombrero or back at Haddon Hall. Defries disapproved of drug use, the mark of a loser, but rapidly bought into the Bowie lifestyle, savoring the exotic sexual frisson. David shared Tony's fascination with Americana, and together they became obsessed with the biggest coup, that of breaking America. When Andy Warhol's *Pork*, the play that so flagrantly symbolized this new world, debuted in London that summer, it was natural that David and Tony would witness the event. What few could have predicted was how they would adapt Warhol's work and use it to sell America back to itself.

Collaged from hundreds of hours of Andy's phone conversations by Tony Ingrassia—a graduate of the Theater of the Ridiculous— *Pork* was scheduled to open on August 2 and promised a healthy dose of outrage. Two gorgeous nude boys, the "Pepsodent Twins," stood impassively onstage throughout the show, while "Amanda Pork"—obviously based on Factory member Brigid Polk—talked incessantly on the phone, frolicked topless, masturbated, and engaged in hilariously deadpan conversations with the Andy Warhol character, played with a languid precision by Tony Zanetta. The play caused a predictable furor, inspiring a *Daily Mirror* exposé that ensured the Roundhouse was packed for most performances.

The Warhol troupe members were aware of David even before they arrived in London. They'd seen a "titillating" news story complete with a photo of David in his Mr. Fish dress in an issue of *Rolling Stone* that had also featured *Pork*. Within days of their arrival in town, stage manager Lee Childers and actress Kathy Dorritie, who played Pork, hit the town, looking for laughs or to get laid by posing as journalists for *Circus* magazine. It was Lee who spotted a tiny ad for Bowie in the *New Musical Express*, better known as the *NME*, and set out with Kathy and Wayne County (who played Vulva Lips) for the Country Club in Haverstock Hill in search of "the man in the dress." Instead, he complained, they found "a folkie."

After the show, Lee and Kathy were initially more taken with Angie's energy and enthusiasm than they were with the unassuming composure of the flaxen-haired "folkie," but when the *Pork* troupe actors were invited to Haddon Hall after David, Angie, and a group of Gem regulars turned up for a performance of *Pork* a couple of days later, they found the "quiet and almost drab" creature had metamorphosed. Tony Zanetta, a kind of simulacrum for Warhol, was the performer who found himself fixed in David's laser beam: "He can walk into the room and every single head would turn and it was like a light was shining. It was uncanny." They spent the evening locked in conversation, talking about artifice, makeup, glamour; Zanetta telling David about the Theater of the Ridiculous and David reciprocating with stories of Lindsay Kemp's troupe. David was warm, unaffected, with an instinctive genius at building rapport. Zanetta and the others were fascinated by the singer; after their nights at the Sombrero and the spectacle of Haddon Hall, they felt they had found kindred spirits who shared their almost childlike enthusiasms. Defries was as fascinated as David; by now he luxuriated in the atmosphere at the Sombrero and the delicious sensuality of being accompanied by Dana Gillespie, whose career he also promised to take in hand.

Despite his lofty talk, Defries was practical. At the Haverstock Hill show on July 26, David and Mick's sound was lousy, put to shame by that of the support group, Tucky Buzzard. It turned out that that group's engineer, Robin Mayhew, was working with a new kind of amplifier system that would give a singer free rein to wander around the auditorium. Mayhew was hired and told to build a new system. "Sort it out," Defries told him, "it doesn't matter what it costs." He hired Mick's old Rats roadie Peter Hunsley too, but there was a limit to his generosity with Laurence Myers's money. Whereas the road crew were kept on retainer, the musicians — Trevor Bolder and Woody Woodmansey — were sent back to Hull while David and Defries prepared for their trip to New York in September.

David was calm, self-possessed, free of self-doubt. Defries was positively messianic, eager to walk into RCA, the home of the king of rock and roll, and tell the record executives how much they needed him and his client. He wasn't afraid to set his sights high. "You've had nothing since the fifties, and you missed out on the sixties," he would tell RCA. "But you can own the seventies. Because David Bowie is going to remake the decade, just like the Beatles did in the sixties."

CHAPTER 9

Over the Rainbow

*It was, I'll do anything, play anything, say anything, wear
anything to become a star, and there's nothing wrong with that.
And there was a tremendous hunger on the part of the audience
for it too. It was that moment in time.*

— Scott Richardson

BREAKING AMERICA HAD BEEN a staple of every ambitious British rock and roller's career plan since the days of the Shadows, the early 1960s. David Bowie and Tony Defries arrived in New York convinced of their ability to conquer the new world. Given both their characters, that was no surprise. But no one could have predicted how grandiose their plans would become once they were in the country.

Defries ensured that the September 1971 trip during which he planned to close the RCA deal was heavy with symbolism by staying at the Warwick, the hotel famous for hosting the Beatles, and holding court for a cavalcade of visitors to build up a sense of event. Different people have different perceptions of that week: Lisa Robinson, who was central to the RCA signing, saw David as the star of proceedings, boyish, enthusiastic, with Defries playing the role of Colonel Parker to David's Elvis. She, her husband, Richard, and many others were caught in the spotlight of David's

176 | David Bowie: Starman

charm, which he'd learned to focus with dazzling effectiveness. He'd take words out of his companion's sentences and repeat them, as if they had crystallized thoughts in his own mind; when bumping into someone again, he'd act as if he'd been barely able to function in the intervening minutes. Sometimes, talking to him, the objects of his attention would experience that giddy, tingly feeling you get when you're in love.

Others saw Tony Defries as the star of the show. Tony Zanetta was enchanted by Bowie but found Defries had a sense of power emanating from him: "[He was] a magical person; he seemed older than he was and very wise—like a sage."

Dennis Katz, RCA's head of A and R, was eager to close the deal. As Tom Ayers had told David, the label saw Elvis Presley's sales in a seemingly irreversible decline; Katz desperately needed new talent and had been bowled over by an acetate of the earlier *Hunky Dory* tracks. But it was Richard and Lisa Robinson who would prove crucial to the signing; the couple were arbiters of cool, RCA's "company heads." Richard had joined RCA as house producer and Katz's assistant in A and R; his wife, Lisa, was New York's hippest music journalist. They would prove David's most potent champions.

History rarely records Laurence Myers's role in the RCA signing. The Gem founder opened negotiations with RCA and oversaw the contract, he says today: "I actually did the deal—I have to point that out as it's so rarely recognized!" Yet it was Defries who turned the signing into an event. Defries was adept at homing in on RCA's insecurities, commiserating with them that RCA was best known for producing washing machines. But he was "very, very charming" about it, everyone remembers. Even the money wasn't a problem; RCA agreed to a $37,500 advance on signature, which was a middling sum, "but that didn't bother Tony," says Zanetta. "He always knew he could improve on the deal later."

The RCA contract was signed on September 9—a coup for Defries, who'd promised David he would relaunch his career. But that was not enough. Between September 8 and September 9,

Defries's ambitions inflated from securing a single record contract to launching an entertainment empire.

Yet if Defries was the salesman, it was David who masterminded the product. He was a stranger in a strange land where the main participants were constantly rushing around, calling their friends on the phone, hanging out at Max's Kansas City trying to out-cool one another, but he was equally in his element, enthralling the New Yorkers just as he had the *Pork* actors. By this point, his talent for identifying people who could help him was as finely honed as his songwriting skills.

Over those two days, the entire structure of what would become MainMan was established. Zanetta was already drawn in—he represented New York cool to David, while to Defries he was both inspiration and sounding board. He would soon be given the title of MainMan president, U.S.A. (his first job would be finding and painting an office), and he became the dominant figure in the organization after Defries, with many of his instincts and off-the-cuff remarks becoming company policy.

It was Zanetta who introduced David to Andy Warhol, an event usually described as "iconic." The reality was more messy and inconclusive. David was tense, attempting to impress Warhol with a little mime based on Kemp's Pierrot shtick in which he pulled out his own intestines; the little performance went over like a lead balloon, with Warhol remaining on the edge of the conversation. David talked mainly with Allen Midgette and Glenn O'Brien, later editor of *Interview*. Warhol's only fully formed sentence was that he liked David's shoes. The meeting was filmed. In addition to David's cheesy routine, the footage is notable for another reason: With Andy Warhol; Zanetta, who played Andy in *Pork*; Midgette, who'd famously impersonated Andy on a college tour; and David, who would memorably play Andy in *Basquiat*, the sequence features four Warhols. Which is, of course, a very Warholian happening.

Having secured his meeting with Warhol, David enlisted Lisa Robinson as a coconspirator to link up with Andy's musical protégé. Once he'd learned Lisa was friends with Lou Reed, David was "absolutely intrigued," says Robinson, who arranged for them to meet over dinner at the Ginger Man, a "really straight" restaurant by Lincoln Park where Lisa often went out for steaks with her friend Fran Lebowitz. Lou and David chatted; Lou was drunk and manic, David was whispering flirtatiously, and Lou's wife, Betty, looked on adoringly.

Enthralled as Lisa was by David, she didn't quite realize the scope of his ambition. Lou was about to record his debut RCA album with Richard Robinson, who had recently produced the Flamin' Groovies' superb *Teenage Head*. Lou's meeting with David was friendly enough, an up-and-coming artist paying tribute to one whose career had apparently tanked, but there was no mention that David was thinking of working with Lou; his furtiveness would soon cause "a bit of a falling-out," says Lisa.

Later that evening, David's party, plus Richard and Lisa, moved on to Max's Kansas City. This was both viper pit and arcadia, a place where, says Lee Childers, "each night was different and each night was proclaimed the last good night of Max's for years—and of course it only got better and better." The back room had seen endless cultural and sexual unions, many of which seemed hugely significant in later years, but none of which seemed so at the time. "No one, including Andy Warhol, thought that any of this was important, much less that anyone was going to remember it," says Childers. "Everything was of itself the minute it was happening and then it was over and that's how the whole back room was. That's how I remember it—in flashes."

Although those involved could not appreciate the wider significance of the scenes played out in the back room at Max's, one unabashed fan from Beckenham could. For the fragile, thrift-store decadence and glamour of Max's would become the raw material of David Bowie's art. Just like the English bluesmen of the 1960s, Bowie would be accused of exploiting his influences; without doubt, they did bring him money and fame. Yet his encounter with a down-on-his-luck heroin addict who would one day become his closest friend—his "twin atom"—reveals him more as a fan than an exploiter.

In the seven months since David had discovered the colorful story of Iggy Stooge, the Detroit singer's life had taken successively more picaresque turns. Abandoned by his record company, he had suffered heroin overdoses and van crashes, been stranded in the Detroit projects clad in a tutu, and had recently been booted out of guitarist Rick Derringer's house after the apparent theft of Liz Derringer's jewelry by Iggy's underage girlfriend. After hearing snippets of Iggy's recent history from Lisa Robinson, David asked if they could meet. Lisa made more phone calls, and eventually Iggy was persuaded to pull himself away from the TV in his friend Danny Fields's apartment and walk up to Max's.

In future years, David would be seen as cold and manipulative, eyeing Iggy as a Victorian collector would a choice hummingbird destined for a glass cabinet in his study. The reality was almost the opposite, for it was Iggy who manipulated the event, "almost dancing" into the meeting, Zanetta noticed. Bowie and Defries were both enthralled by the cheeky raconteur. Iggy could turn on the fluttery-eyelashed flirtatiousness and build rapport just like David, but there was an idée fixe about his manner that fascinated and slightly unnerved David.

Their discussions about music and Iggy's future continued the next morning over breakfast at the Warwick, which in Defries's distinctive style could take hours, interrupted by endless phone calls and scheming. Iggy was impressed by Defries — his "big vision of what he was going to do" — and he liked David. He could see beyond the charm, and judged him "very canny, very self-possessed, and a...not *unkind* person. Which you don't usually see in people so self-aware." David played him *Hunky Dory*, and Iggy made polite noises: "It wasn't anything to do with what I was trying to do, but I realized, in terms of song-craft, he can do A, B, and C." By the end of the meeting, Iggy had agreed to go over to London and sign with Gem after he completed his methadone program.

Bowie and Defries had set out to close a recording deal — and returned with an empire. Within three days in New York, Defries had signed David's contract with RCA, discussed the rerelease of

David's old Mercury albums, recruited Zanetta to the cause, formed a relationship with Lou Reed, and brought Iggy into the Gem fold with the promise that he'd secure him a new record deal—a promise Defries fulfilled a few weeks later, signing Iggy to Columbia.

By the time David, Mick, and Angie—who had spent most of the trip visiting her parents in Connecticut—returned to London, David had become obsessed with the singer he had met at Max's. "He talked about Iggy for a full week—it was definitely all-consuming," says Bob Grace, a recollection shared by Ken Scott and Trevor Bolder. "Iggy and Lou, it was," says Bolder, "always Iggy and Lou."

DAVID was purposeful, clear-headed in the days following the New York trip, but wired too, filled with nervous energy as he prepared to unveil his new songs and his new band. The unofficial debut of the Spiders from Mars was planned for Friars Aylesbury, an assembly hall in an ancient market town an hour out of London, known for its enthusiastic audiences. In the middle of September, Ronson had called Bolder and Woodmansey back from Hull for their first show as a band. Rick Wakeman, David's top choice for pianist, had joined Yes just a few weeks before, so David phoned an old friend from Kent, Tom Parker, to play piano, jabbering in nervous gratitude when Parker said, "Of course!"

When David took the Friars stage, on September 25, he was shaking: He was dressed in baggy black culottes, red platform boots, and a women's beige jacket worn over his skinny, naked chest. "Does anyone have a heater?" was one of his asides in a set of rambling song introductions that covered Lou Reed's sense of humor and why New Yorkers felt compelled to stare into subway tunnels. "We didn't know if he was on drugs or just nervous," says Kris Needs, a Bowie fan who'd designed the flyers for the night. It was a primitive version of what would become a well-honed set, starting out with acoustic songs, including Brel's "Port of Amsterdam," the band joining in halfway through. But as Ronson cranked up his Les Paul and the energy levels increased, David's announcements grew shorter and the applause in the half-empty club grew in intensity. After closing the set with a ruthless version of "Waiting for the Man," Bowie walked into the dressing room, exultant: "That was great," he announced to Needs. "And when I come back I'm going to be completely different."

Few people outside David's immediate circle realized how soon he'd come back, or how different he'd be. But within the tiny coterie of people—David, Angie, the band, Defries, and a small crew of roadies—the activity was feverish. David and musicians spent most of October crammed in Greenwich's Underhill studio—which was, in reality, the polystyrene-lined basement of a down-at-heel Georgian building that also contained a car-parts showroom and an escort agency. *Hunky Dory* was not yet released, and David was burning to record its successor. Already, he had eight or nine songs that they'd run through every day, playing each tune just a few times before moving on to the next to keep the feel loose, unstudied. It felt democratic; "a band thing," says Bolder.

Several key songs they rehearsed—notably "Moonage Daydream" and "Lady Stardust"—dated from David's bout of songwriting in the spring, yet most of them had been assembled with astonishing speed in the previous few weeks. In the wake of *Hunky Dory*'s writing blitz, this was impressive. But that was, literally, only half the story. Bowie's onstage chatter at Aylesbury showed him struggling to articulate his obsessions with Americana, spokesmen like Dylan, Reed, and Warhol, and the "presumptuousness of the songwriter." Bowie's invention of a concept that would encompass all these diverse obsessions was, like all great concepts, simple.

In later years, David Bowie would claim the idea for the Ziggy Stardust figure came to him in a dream—gifted by the same god who had told his father to find a job at a children's charity. If so, like "Oh! You Pretty Things," it was an unconscious embodiment of all the skills that he'd mastered in the past few years.

David had experimented with a rock opera back in 1968, when he'd worked on a sequence entitled "Ernie Johnson" at Ken Pitt's apartment—a bizarre little campy cockney epic that culminated in the hero's suicide. In comparison, *Ziggy Stardust* wasn't really an opera, more a collection of snapshots thrown together and later edited into a sequence that made sense. The notion that Ziggy would be David's own alter ego emerged only at the last minute; it was a hodgepodge, later refined into a concept.

Ziggy was David's homage to the outsider; the main inspiration was undoubtedly Iggy, the singer with whom David was obsessed and whose doomed, Dionysian career path had already built its own mythology. David was well aware that Iggy, too, was a mere creation—for in their first meeting, David had learned the scary, gold-and-glitter-spattered facade hid another persona—the urbane Jim Osterberg, who was disconcertingly reminiscent of Jimmy Stewart. On his first trip to New York, he'd also discovered that a fake Lou Reed could be just as convincing as the real thing. Vince Taylor, another inspiration, was an "American" rocker who was actually born Brian Holden in Isleworth and had made it big in France. By 1966, he was washed up, and the teenage David had bumped into him in the period when Vince was hanging around La Gioconda claiming he was the messiah and pointing out UFO landing sites on a crumpled map.

Hence Ziggy was a tribute to artifice, a play on identity, alter ego placed on alter ego, a vehicle for rock and roll that allowed David if everything failed to announce that this was all ironic, just a pose.

Ziggy's surname, the reference to the Legendary Stardust Cowboy, was just as nuanced. The name encompassed David's enchantment with glamour and glitter, referenced Hoagy Carmichael's best-known song, and even touched on the relatively recent realization that, as Carl Sagan put it, we are all stardust, all of our atoms recycled through supernovae. And what was Ziggy Stardust but old, vital rock-and-roll matter, recycled, but fresh as a new world?

Ziggy wasn't born fully fledged, though. He developed bit by bit: "It was never discussed as a concept album from the start," says Ken Scott. "We were recording a bunch of songs—some of them happened to fit together, some didn't work." In October of 1971, the work in progress sounded more like 1950s rock and roll than the Stooges. A cover of Chuck Berry's "Around and Around" was in the early track listing, and the song "Hang On to Yourself" featured quotes from Eddie Cochran and Chuck Berry, as well as shades of Gene Vincent and Vince Taylor—all of them honorary Brits. David's obsession with the rapid rehearsal and recording of songs helped approximate the roughness of the Velvets and the Stooges, yet Ronson and his musicians—David too—were too competent to summon up anything like the Stooges' moronic inferno.

The straight-ahead rockers—"Hang On to Yourself" and "Suffragette City"—took Eddie Cochran's teenage rebellion as a model, using the same mix of acoustic and electric guitars as well as liberal musical quotes from "Something Else." But where Cochran's songs spoke to kids breaking the parental bonds, Ziggy Stardust's message was explicitly about sexual liberation— "Henry...I can't take you this time" and "the church of man, love." Images like "tigers on Vaseline" and the "mellow-thighed chick just put my spine out of place" made up their own manifesto: theatrical yet sleazy, delivered with an arched eyebrow.

The two songs that would open and close the album were even less reminiscent of American garage rock. Both songs were in a slow-burning 6/8 time signature—like "House of the Rising Sun" and Paul Simon's "America"—yet were starker, more stripped down. "Five Years" and "Rock 'n' Roll Suicide" are masterly, both built on minimal, almost unvarying broken chords, David's voice alone supplying the drama. Both songs illustrate how Ziggy could stage an emotional onslaught that David had never attempted— the desperation in "Five Years," the urgency in "Rock 'n' Roll Suicide" that completed Ziggy Stardust's dramatic arc. The ending "Gimme your hands...you're not alone" is pure show business, an act of audience manipulation worthy of Leni Riefenstahl, but Bowie's sympathy for Iggy, Vince, and all the other doomed rock and rollers is absolutely sincere.

Some figures, notably Angie Bowie, dispute that David Bowie

ever truly loved anyone, yet there is no doubt of his deep and enduring love for rock and roll. "Rock 'n' Roll Suicide" is all the more poignant given that just a couple of years later, Iggy Pop, abandoned by Bowie, would stab himself onstage in an event publicized as a rock-and-roll suicide that, his manager informed the press, "will only happen once."

"Rock 'n' Roll Suicide" and "Suffragette City" were among the last songs recorded in the album's main sessions, demonstrating that the album's central concept—Ziggy's rise and fall—arrived late in the day, with Chuck Berry's "Around and Around" still on the track listing. But in that whirlwind winter, events were moving fast. *Hunky Dory* was released on December 17, with the single "Changes" following it on January 7 and immediately picking up radio play. A gorgeous song, based on one of the piano runs painstakingly worked out at Haddon Hall and with a stammered chorus that echoed "My Generation" and hence emphasized its status as an anthem for a new youth movement, "Changes" didn't make the British charts this time around but "it was the breakthrough," says Anya Wilson, who had to hawk it around the radio.

In the closing weeks of 1971, as the final details of Ziggy's mythical career were penciled in, the hero was given his costume. The aesthetic was half futuristic, half thrift-shop chic, masterminded primarily by Freddie Buretti. Freddie himself cut an exotic figure, with his high-waisted pegged trousers, skinny shirts, and, occasionally, oversize shades, but when he and David cooked up their new look, they based the designs on the droogs, the futuristic teenage thugs in Stanley Kubrick's legendary, banned film *Clockwork Orange.* "But to lessen the image of violence, I decided we should go for extremely colorful and exotic material in place of the droog white cotton," says David. Freddie designed and did most of the sewing on the skinny outfits, which were copied from Britain's popular mod Lee Cooper jeans and fitted with generous, Tudor-style codpieces. To complete the look, David searched out cheap, brightly colored wrestling boots, custom-made by Russell and Bromley, whose showroom was based in North Bromley—

these kind of boots could be seen on television every Saturday afternoon in ITV's hugely popular, ludicrously choreographed wrestling shows, and they completed the aesthetic of rock-and-roll danger and vaudeville camp.

It was Angie who encouraged the next phase of David's make-over; the flowing gold locks that David had worn throughout the recording were shorn, and thus the final link with the 1960s was severed. Many of David's contemporaries — Marc Bolan and even the Nice's Keith Emerson, who wore a silver Lurex jumpsuit as he attacked his Hammond organ with a knife that October — had already glammed themselves up that year. But their flared trousers and wavy hair were in essence an evolution of the hippie look. The Ziggy persona — with its cropped hair and skinny silhouette — marked a ruthless break with the 1960s. It was finely calculated but impromptu, done in a rush.

Freddie had hardly finished sewing David's first sand-and-black quilted jumpsuit when David called Mark Pritchett late one night and asked: "Can I borrow your Les Paul? The red one?" It was raining the next day when David came to collect it; he mentioned he was off to a photo shoot with Brian Ward, the Chrysalis photographer who'd first worked with David the previous spring. This was a simple shoot, in black-and-white, David first posing with Pritchett's guitar directly outside Ward's studio on Heddon Street — the tiny U-shaped road leading off Regent Street — and then in the nearby telephone booth. The ghostly, postapocalyptic droog feel was enhanced by the cardboard boxes left out on the street, the glare of the streetlights, and the early-evening chill evident from the frost on car windshields — this would be London's coldest January for several years.

A BBC session on January 11 was booked to promote his current album, *Hunky Dory*, but the only *Hunky Dory* song played was "Queen Bitch" — its campy New York vibe especially reminiscent of the Velvets' "Sweet Jane" — the rest was dominated by "Hang On to Yourself" and the newly written "Ziggy Stardust." This was a bold, risky strategy, considering David's ever-changing musical identity, but Defries and radio plugger Anya Wilson were happy to follow David's instincts. "He was our golden boy," says Wilson. "People knew it was going to happen."

OVER that intense winter, David spent even more time thinking than he did singing. Earnest conversations at Haddon Hall ranged late into the night, freewheeling, philosophical, touching on Chuck Berry, the Velvet Underground, the postindustrial future, and Hollywood glamour. Often David would talk to Anya Wilson and her boyfriend, Dai Davies, about "the pretty things." They knew he didn't mean his old friends from the blues scene: "These are the coming generation," he told them, "a change is on its way."

As David developed his theme, they huddled around the huge corner fireplace, the air thick with the haze from his cigarettes, and listened to him develop a manifesto line by line: This was a new era, factory jobs were obsolete, and so were the Victorian values that defined their parents' lives. The coming generation would not be restricted by work or conventional sexuality. This bisexual, glittering generation was the *Homo superior*—and David would be its spokesperson.

David needed someone to carry his message. The old 1960s writers, people who'd written about David already, were out. Then Dai Davies, newly recruited as David's press mastermind, told David about the new generation of journalists, writers who were interested in theories, in manifestos, not in a pint and a chat in the pub. Together, they approached Michael Watts first; he'd read Norman Mailer and was developing a new, long-form feature style at *Melody Maker*. Next, they'd take David's new manifesto to Charles Shaar Murray at the *NME*.

In later months, Davies thought about the manifesto. There were gaps in it, bits that didn't make sense, and he wondered if David knew that and decided it didn't matter. Later still he realized what David had been doing: "He'd read about Elvis, and he'd read about Hollywood in the thirties and forties, and he was building a brand—before that language had even been invented."

Watts met Bowie upstairs in Gem's Regent Street office. The *Melody Maker* staff members were well aware of Bowie's regular presence at the Sombrero; there was a sense that David had "something to get off his chest" and a hope that Watts would get a scoop, which is exactly what happened.

Watts remembers Bowie being "slightly flirtatious" all the way through the interview, and indeed there was a delicious coyness about the whole piece, with Watts feigning a worldly, unshocked demeanor as David held forth, self-consciously messianic: "I'm going to be huge," he tells Watts, "and it's quite frightening in a way." In these words, one can sense the teenage brio that so entranced the Deram staff, but here it's augmented with a consummate display of name-dropping (Lindsay Kemp, Lou, Iggy, and the Tibet Society) and a new high-spiritedness, a feeling that he is playing a game and is a master of it. When he tells Watts, "I'm gay—and always have been, even when I was David Jones," Watts comments that there is "a sly jollity about how he says it." It was obvious that Watts was transfixed by what Bowie's next interviewer, Charles Shaar Murray, describes as "a genius for inducing a powerful, platonic man-crush in fundamentally straight guys."

For all the playfulness, this was a momentous announcement—utterly without precedent in the music business, and ravishingly brave. Gay sex was indeed nominally decriminalized in Great Britain in July of 1967, but arrests for "gross indecency" tripled in the next three years, and many of David's contemporaries would remain firmly in the closet for decades. Gem staff attempting to get airplay at the BBC had already encountered the statement that "we don't have perverts on this show." There was one precedent for David's announcement of which he was almost certainly aware: David Hockney's overt declaration of his own sexuality with his painting *We Two Boys Together Clinging* back in 1961, when gay acts could land a boy in prison. Bowie's move was safer, but more flagrant, aimed at the mass market rather than a coterie of critics. It was a thrillingly high-risk strategy—and one that David had discussed only with Dai Davies, not Defries, who anyway took the view that all publicity was good publicity.

* * *

DAVID'S sexual and image makeover had already been anticipated by Marc Bolan—who'd glammed up in the spring of 1971 and proclaimed, "I'll go up and kiss guys if I think they're nice," in *Sounds*. But Marc lacked David's chutzpah, his willingness to gamble everything—and David, of course, was in second place and needed to outdo him.

In later years, gay rights activists would criticize Bowie's coming out as mere "androgyny as chic." Some of their cynicism was probably justified, given that a few years after David outed himself, he inned himself, complaining about the commercial damage that his image had cost him in America. Rarely has such a spontaneous act of courage been followed by such a considered act of cowardice. Yet David's later retraction is irrelevant: he had let a genie out of the bottle and it would never go back in. This was a generational shift. Steve Strange, later of the Blitz Club, was twelve when Bowie made his announcement, and for him and his peers, Bowie demonstrated that they were not alone: "I grew up in Newbridge, in Wales—and as a kid I was the freak of the village. I didn't know what being gay meant, there was no sex education, but I knew it wasn't right." Bowie's appearance was a beacon that would eventually draw a generation of kids to London or a new life or both.

David was careful to have his cake and eat it too—pointing out his "good relationship" with Angie and Zowie, leaving the implication that his gay side was as camped up as the "fifty thousand" sales of *The Man Who Sold the World* in the United States. This is the interpretation David would push in the 1990s, claiming that the excitement of hanging out in the Sombrero outweighed anything physical, which was "something I wasn't comfortable with at all." This pained recollection (from a man who'd sexually exploited himself!) seems to confirm the criticisms of those who regard his gay phase as a pose, a marketing stance. Which it indeed was. Yet for David, the marketing, the pose, was part of his essence.

Witnesses like Tony Zanetta and Lee Childers were integral

members of the organization that painted David as a poster boy for bisexuality, but the pair, put on the spot, conclude that David's gay stance was primarily about culture rather than sex. "He *was* bisexual, but what he really was was a narcissist—boys or girls, it was all the same," says Zanetta. "He was attracted to the gay subculture because he loved its flamboyance. Sometimes it was just an expression of communication—sometimes it was a way of... assimilating someone. But it was never his primary thing, and once the girls came flocking it didn't matter." Michael Watts, who once commented "sometimes, honesty pays" about the revelation he extracted, today says simply, "He knew exactly what he was doing."

Within a few days of the *Melody Maker* interview, David had to contend with a much more skeptical audience: his three musicians from Hull. He had primed Mick, Woody, and Trevor by taking them to see *A Clockwork Orange* and explaining that the costumes being designed by Freddie Buretti were "futuristic" rather than something "poofs" would wear. When the three were presented with their catsuits—blue for Trevor, gold for Woody, and pink for Ronson—ready for the debut of their new set, David was faced with one of the trickiest acts of salesmanship of his career. Bolder frankly admits he was not impressed—"To be honest, it took a lot to wear that stuff"—and remembers Mick, destined for the pink jacket, as the most vociferous objector: "Mick was not up for it. Not at all." Worn down by Bowie's pure persistence, "We just sort of went along with it in the end."

When it came time to premiere the band's makeover, on January 29, the backstage area at Friars Aylesbury was closed off, possibly because of the wardrobe disputes. The crowd was double the size of September's show; kids from London—among them Freddie Mercury and drummer Roger Taylor—had taken the train up for the show, and as Walter Carlos's version of "Ode to Joy" struck up, a ripple of excitement passed through the audience. "Then there was the climax, with the strobe, and he was standing there in this blue-gray check jumpsuit and it was, Blimey! Unlike anything I'd ever seen," says Kris Needs.

The band unleashed their full *Ziggy* assault, launching into "Hang On to Yourself" and then "Ziggy Stardust"—a sonic slap in the face for the kids who expected to see and hear the David Bowie of *Hunky Dory*. Some of those already familiar anthems—"Life on Mars," "Oh! You Pretty Things"—followed, complete with a long version of "I Feel Free," Bowie disappearing to change his catsuit as Ronson let it rip on his Les Paul. "By the time they hit 'Rock 'n' Roll Suicide' the place was in total uproar," says Needs.

Dizzied by the experience, Kris made his way to the dressing room after the show. David was exultant. "Told you I'd be different," he said to him before planting a kiss firmly on the seventeen-year-old fan's lips. "It was life-changing stuff," says Needs of that evening. "That night invented the seventies, and everything that came after, glam or punk—that was the defining moment." The local newspaper's review of the show was titled "A Star Is Born."

The sense of manifest destiny and utter confidence—"I'm going to be huge, and it's quite frightening in a way"—that was surging through David would permeate the whole tiny operation over the next few weeks. That winter Tony Defries took to wearing a huge fur coat, invariably accompanied by a huge cigar; together with his prodigious nose and halo of frizzy hair, he cut "the weirdest figure," according to RCA's Barry Bethel, who remembers that the entire record company was in awe of this intimidating figure. Defries loved gathering young people around him, enthusiastic teenagers unconstrained by convention who enjoyed his mockery of record companies. Defries was a good listener, though, and took note of RCA's concerns when they heard the initial album acetates: "RCA told us *Ziggy Stardust* was great—but we needed a single," says Robin Mayhew, "something they could pull straight off the album—so David went off and wrote what he called 'Somewhere Over the Rainbow.' His 'Starman' song."

"It was at that point that the [*Ziggy*] concept finally happened," says Ken Scott. "It was the perfect single."

In stories of the songwriting of Paul McCartney and John Lennon, the rivals with whom David would soon be compared, "I Wanna Hold Your Hand" has been singled out as an early peak, a knowing song that packs in so many arresting songwriting devices, a "joyous energy and invention," as writer Ian MacDonald puts it, that its hit status was inevitable. "Starman" represents the same euphoric peak in Bowie's writing, a moment of technical supremacy.

The opening minor chords are cheekily self-referential, a quote from David's one hit, "Space Oddity," and then the story is mapped out like a novel, with supreme economy. "Didn't know what time it was," the narrator tells us to a claustrophobically tight tune. The lyrics are set against the beat, adding to the intrigue, with the last word in each line, "low-oh-oh," drawn out, pulling the listener in syllable by syllable, like a fish on a hook. Then the key changes from minor to major, Ronson's staccato guitar fires up like a searchlight in the gloom, and we hit the chorus—and as David leaps an octave, over the word "starman," we reach escape velocity and take off.

As modern as it feels, though, the song is classic, and if it seems like the music has gone from monotone to Technicolor, that's because the starman waiting in the sky matches Judy Garland's evocation of a place somewhere over the rainbow, note for note. It draws on the same emotion—a yearning for escape, from the depression and monochrome of 1939 or 1972—and the listener's response is instinctive, drawn in by the familiar, intrigued by the alien.

"Starman" was completed in the last session at Trident on February 4, and in the following weeks the band grew to share David's belief that "there was never a doubt that this wasn't going to work," says Bolder. "Everything was in place."

In typical Defries grandstanding, the manager was building his own management empire before David had even hit the charts; Dana Gillespie was already on the Gem payroll, and Iggy—now named Iggy Pop—joined her in March of 1972. Although signed as a solo artist—Defries was only interested in "stars" and considered musicians drains on his income—Iggy smuggled in guitarist James Williamson and then the remaining Stooges, who holed up in Kensington picking up schoolgirls, locating drugs suppliers, and ignoring Bowie's suggestions that he produce their album. With Defries's artists descending on London, showing up at parties and T. Rex shows, and Iggy's legend already being celebrated in papers, including *Melody Maker,* the sense that this would be David's and Defries's year was inescapable.

As David and the band prepared for a string of live shows running up to the *Ziggy* album's release date, each of them was convinced that "everything seemed right," says Bolder. "That was the weird thing, we didn't even have to think about it." Then Woody painted the front of his Ludwig drum set with the word *Spiders,* and they were a band.

The short tour opened at a tiny pub named the Toby Jug in Tolworth, Surrey. The stage was just a foot high, and the roadies crammed a full amp system and lighting rig into the room; the audience members, numbering fifty or sixty, were as transfixed as those at Aylesbury, and in the fourteen shows that followed, David recruited hard-core fans—in their dozens, not in their hundreds, but as audience member Pete Abbott, who witnessed the show at Imperial College, remembers, "It was like nothing I'd ever seen before. We knew about Bolan, but that was pop music. This was *serious.*"

At Imperial College David attempted to emulate the feat he'd seen Iggy perform in a short snippet of footage at Cincinnati, walking into the audience and being held up by them; when David tried it, he toppled to the floor, one of several tumbles he took in those weeks. "He would never let the audience know [it had happened]," says Bolder. "He would just get back up and carry on." The band roved up and down the country, David and Angie in two used Jaguars, with the crammed one-ton van bringing up the rear. In show after show, David put his moves together, developing expansive gestures that would reach the backs of the big halls when he finally played them: "He was a really good front man. He knew exactly what he was doing."

DAVID arrived at Manchester's Free Trade Hall on April 21, and when he once more attempted to crowd surf, the audience held him up. Angie's input was "vital—she drove the whole thing, made it happen," says Robin Mayhew; she operated the lights on the first shows, organized the costumes and the food. But onstage it was Mick Ronson who was king; there was no clue that this was the man who'd pored nervously over studio arrangements, for he was in total control. "If the thing was getting shaky, he would hold it together," says Mayhew. "If Bowie noticed something, say the finish of 'Ziggy Stardust' was dragging, it was Ronno would stay and direct things. No shouting or screaming, no egos."

When *The Rise and Fall of Ziggy Stardust* was released on June 6, plenty of reviewers were irritated by the audacity of the concept. *Melody Maker* described Bowie as a "superb parodist"; *Sounds*, which had applauded *Hunky Dory*, declared, "It would be a pity if this album was the one to make it…much of it sounds the work of a competent plagiarist." Those words illustrated the irrelevance of the music critic, for over the next three or four weeks it became obvious that an unstoppable juggernaut was on the move. Early in the month there was the announcement that MainMan would be presenting both Iggy Pop and Lou Reed in concert—recruiting two of America's hippest acts as supporting attractions in the Bowie circus—and just one week after its negative album review, *Sounds* decided the Bowie live show "just needs to be packed with sweating teenagers to pull it off." Over a few short weeks, a consensus emerged: If *Ziggy* was merely a joke, everybody wanted to be in on it.

There was one wobble, after the Oxford Town Hall show on June 17. This was an amazing performance, where Mick Rock—the brilliant photographer who'd joined the MainMan cavalcade at the Birmingham show on March 17—captured David kneeling in front of Mick, his arms grasping Mick's thighs as he bites at Ronson's guitar strings, with Ronson and the audience transfixed with laughter. Instant glam pornography, the "guitar fellatio" shot would be printed as a full-page ad, purchased by Defries, in the next week's *Melody Maker*. There was a flurry of concern from Ronson—not a fear of the reaction of homophobic gangs in Hull, as has been speculated, "but because the musicians, Mick and his muso mates, thought bands like Sweet were unbearably naff, manufactured. He was caught in a divide," says Dai Davies, who spent hours reassuring the guitarist that the music would be taken seriously despite such gimmickry. Bowie would later explain that he and Marc Bolan were high glam, conceptual. Blue-collar types in satin, like Sweet, were low glam.

As the band toured through the spring, there was the sense of both a groundswell of support driven by word of mouth and a potential backlash from critics who found Bowie and Defries's operation considered and manipulative. The perfect response to such cynicism came with the song that would seal the deal between David and his fans, the ultimate example of the spontaneity that coexisted with his meticulous planning.

Late in March, David had discovered that Mott the Hoople— one of his favorite bands, whom he imagined as "a heavy biker gang," says singer Ian Hunter—were splitting, and after begging them to reconsider, he invited them down to Gem's Regent Street office and played them a song that he'd just written with them in mind. "He just played it on an acoustic guitar," says Hunter. "I knew straightaway it was a hit. There were chills going down my spine. It's only happened to me a few times in my life, when you know that this is a biggie. We grabbed hold of it. I'm a peculiar singer but I knew I could handle that." "All the Young Dudes" re-imagined Mott, in reality well-behaved Hereford boys, as heavy-duty punks, *Clockwork Orange* droogs. Against a stately, descending chord sequence, the lyrics mention juvenile delinquency, acne, cockney rhyming slang, TV, and suicide at twenty-five; "All the Young Dudes" was a glorious celebration of youth in all its glamour, ephemerality, and heroism. It would be as sincere a love song as Bowie would ever write, addressed to his most enduring love: rock and roll.

Having written the definitive anthem of the 1970s, David simply gave it away. Some thought that this was a self-serving act, designed to underline his own musical omnipotence. Bob Grace, the man who'd overseen most of Bowie's recent songs, is emphatic that in giving away the song, Bowie paid a price: "I thought that was a mistake. If David had put out 'All the Young Dudes' himself that autumn, he would have been huge beyond our comprehension. It was great he gave [Mott] the song, but I'm convinced it cost him." The argument ignores the fact that Bowie remained, at heart, a fan. This was simply a spontaneous act, and in any case the music was pouring out of him.

Mott the Hoople recorded "Dudes" on May 14 at Olympic in Barnes, with David producing. Mott too had now joined the Main-Man empire, and it seemed likely the group would provide its first hit, for David's own "Starman" had now hung around for nearly two months without troubling the charts. But show by show, in little towns like Torbay and Weston Super Mare, David and the Spiders won over their audiences — a dozen here, a hundred there — before the single made a modest entry into the UK singles chart on June 24, at number 49. The following day, Dai Davies announced, with only marginal exaggeration, that "a thousand fans were turned away" from the Spiders show at Croydon Greyhound, where Roxy Music was the supporting act. But "Starman" still languished at number 41 when David and the Spiders walked into the *Top of the Pops* studio on July 5.

The song had actually made its TV debut on the celebrated kids' after-school show *Lift Off with Ayshea* on June 15 — Bowie and his Spiders followed an owl puppet named Ollie Beak — but it was the *Top of the Pops* performance, broadcast on July 6, that transfixed the nation's youth — and horrified their parents. Bowie was clear-eyed and joyous, his come-to-bed eyes inviting both girls and boys. As Ronson approached the microphone for the chorus, the sight of David languidly draping his arm around the golden-haired guitarist Ronson had a visceral impact. This was the *Melody Maker* cover made flesh.

Marc Bolan — name-dropped in the line "the DJ was playing some get-it-on rock 'n' roll" — had camped it up on *Top of the Pops* first, but he was cute, unthreatening; David and the Spiders were dangerous, a warning to lock up not only your daughters but also your sons. The moment David put his arm around Mick Ronson, teenagers across the country shared "a moment of epiphany," as ballet's enfant terrible Michael Clark puts it. "It was like 'Oh my God, maybe other people are a little bit like I feel, inside.'" In just three and a half minutes, David Bowie laid claim to the title of glam messiah and propelled his single to number 10 in what would be a twelve-week run in the charts.

DAVID may have turned up late at the glitter-rock ball—Marc Bolan had famously sprinkled glitter over his face for his "Hot Love" appearance on *Top of the Pops* back in March of 1971. Yet Bowie's intervention was definitive—it was unashamed, committed, thought through in every detail; besides, many contemporaries remembered that, with the Hype, he had helped inspire Bolan's glitter look in the first place. With their long-running mutual name-dropping, Bolan and Bowie were seen as joint creators of what was then known as glitter rock, later renamed glam—indeed, they'd both glittered up at the same time, at the hands of Chelita Secunda, fashion editor of *Nova* magazine and a much-loved (and wayward) rock-and-roll society hostess: "She always had David, Marc, and Reg—Elton John—over at her place," says Jeff Dexter. "She wore glitter herself and one day she put glitter on Marc. David was there and said, 'I want some,' and fat Reg had some too. So the birth of glam rock was definitely at Chelita's."

Just as Judy Garland's dreams of life beyond the rainbow seduced a world gripped by the Depression and threatened by war in Europe, David's blend of space-age futurism and glamour lodged in the consciousness of a generation in sore need of escape: Glitter sparkles best when set against a gray landscape. In January of 1973 a stock-market crash finally killed off the 1960s boom; the collapse in share prices was followed by an oil crisis and a full-blown recession, and the landscape became as gray as anyone could remember since the austerity of David's youth. References to the 1920s Weimar Republic, 1930s Hollywood and art deco, and even the threadbare glamour of Edwardian music halls, all images of partying amid the ruins, pervaded David's music, as it did that of emerging rivals like Roxy Music's Bryan Ferry: This was their time. Their ruthless competition added to the excitement, just as it had in 1930s Hollywood: "It was, I'll do anything, play anything, say anything, wear anything to become a star," says David's friend Scott Richardson, "and there's nothing wrong with that. And there was a tremendous hunger on the part of the audience for it too. It was that moment in time."

Other people who passed within the Bowie orbit remember that sense of mission. Cindy M was a friend of Rodney Bingenheimer; he arranged for her to meet David at Haddon Hall. She was ushered into the most bizarre of environments for an LA teenager: Gothic stained-glass windows, grandiose staircases, Persian rugs, carved elephants, shelves full of art books, and a hi-fi playing Roxy Music were some of the kaleidoscope of impressions she retains from that overwhelming afternoon, together with the luminous stars painted on the ceiling above David and Angie's bed, where she remembers spending much of her time. "Roxy Music are going to be massive too," he told her, but Cindy already had no doubt that she was in the presence of a hero in the making. When Angie arrived later, says Cindy, she got her face slapped.

EVEN as "Starman" ascended into the Top 40, David was setting out a wider agenda, one that marked him as the indisputable curator of all that was hip. As if delivering a ready-made hit to Mott the Hoople as well as producing the band's album—completed in rushed snatches over June and July—were not enough, Bowie and Defries also appointed themselves saviors of Lou Reed's career. On a New York trip in March, Defries had heard Lou's solo album was a disaster, and he arranged for David to produce its follow-up before announcing MainMan would present live shows by Iggy Pop and Lou Reed in mid-July. The two shows would form an appetizer for David and the Spiders' most crucial appearance to date, for which Defries planned to jet over a planeload of U.S. journalists ready to preview David's upcoming U.S. tour.

The venue for the July 15 show was Friars Aylesbury, the one place Defries could guarantee a packed house. By this point, *Ziggy Stardust* had hit number 5 on the UK charts (*Hunky Dory* would soon follow it, up to number 3), and it was at this show that all involved knew that David was no longer on the brink of stardom; he had made it, exactly as he and Defries had predicted. "That night, you knew this had become a movement," says Dai Davies, "when you looked into the audience and could see a hundred Ziggies." Many of the U.S. journalists, including Lisa Robinson, Lillian Roxon, Lenny Kaye, and *Creem*'s Dave Marsh, knew *Ziggy*'s primary influences firsthand. But even Marsh, a veteran of high-energy shows by the MC5 and the Stooges, thought it "a good show. The one thing you would be afraid of, that the costumes would outweigh the music, wasn't happening. This was a real songwriter, with real songs and a real band—and Ronson was fabulous."

Marsh was not alone, though, in wondering if there was something "vampiric" about Bowie's sponsorship of Iggy and Lou. At the next day's press conference at the Dorchester, Marsh walked in with his old Detroit buddy, "and it's as if somebody has taken the floor and tilted it in Iggy's direction," as all the New York journalists scurried over to see their old pal. Marsh saw David watching the melee with "eyes like darts. But how was I to know? I was just a twenty-three-year-old greeting a friend."

Work on Lou's album began at Morgan Sound in August and proceeded at a whirlwind pace, with three backup tracks recorded in a single day. Like his recruitment of Iggy, Bowie's offer to produce *Transformer* was outrageously presumptuous; it was also a tougher task than anyone could imagine, for Lou was a mess, addicted to bickering and manipulation. Many onlookers would credit arranger Mick Ronson with the bulk of the work—indeed, "he was the one on the shop floor sorting things out," says bassist Herbie Flowers, and he worked closely with David to map out the songs. David, however, had the much more difficult tasks of soothing Lou's frazzled ego, talking him out of his moods, and coping with his mind games. "Lou was extremely messed up, like a parody of a drug fiend," says Davies, who sat in on the sessions. "David was incredible, like a much older, mature producer, and would talk Lou down." Ken Scott, who on this occasion was engineering, points out, "It was a team, David, Mick, myself, everyone knew what to do. But David just understood Lou. Which no one else did, in the state he was in."

David's calm in the studio seemed almost supernatural compared to the frenzy around him, which would soon come to a peak with two elaborate shows at the Rainbow Theatre. He had planned a series of innovations: choreography by Lindsay Kemp, a multilevel set, and Warhol-style projections. All of the tiny crew were caught up in the manic preparations: Screens were improvised from paper and wood, silver paint for the scaffolding was bought cheap from a friend, choreography was worked out over a single evening at Haddon Hall. David's focus was unrelenting. He'd selected the venue, the look of the lighting, and the staging using techniques he'd seen at Cabaret and shows by the Living Theatre and filed away in his mental Rolodex for the right occasion. The look seamlessly incorporated Warhol, Jean Genet, and *Jailhouse Rock*.

At the center of it all, David planned the transformation of his own look, a further distilling of the essence of Ziggy. In his search for more outrageous clothes, he'd seen the creations of Kansai Yamamoto and had finally managed to score one leotard—red, with cutoff legs and a ludicrous bunny design that was so outré it had languished unsold. The leotard completed the classic later-period Ziggy look, joining an innovation that was just as crucial as David's musical leaps forward.

Along with Elvis's DA and the Beatles' mop tops, Ziggy's carrot-top makes up the founding triumvirate of definitive rock-and-roll dos. This creation had been sculpted earlier in July, according to David inspired by a model with a Yamamoto haircut—"It was [in] a slightly girly magazine like *Honey*, not *Vogue*." Angie called in Beckenham hairdresser Suzi Fussey, who'd long looked after Peggy's hair, to construct the elaborate concoction: razor-cut at sides and back; backcombed into a puffy fluffball, like a tropical bird's mating crest, at the front; and dyed an unforgettable flame red. "I designed the color and the haircut, but Angie had a lot to do with it—she was the one who gave David the courage to attempt the most exotic things," says Fussey, who was recruited as David's personal hairdresser and assistant shortly before the Rainbow concert.

The transformation was electrifying; just a few weeks before, David had looked cute, gamin; now he looked like an alien peacock. Yet at the center of the hubbub around his most ambitious shows to date he remained focused, relaxed, directing rehearsals with deftness and humor, taking time out to show pianist Matthew Fisher the opening chords for "Starman," delighted that someone appreciated his songwriting. Behind the alien facade, he was still reassuringly human. Early in the preparations he'd called Fisher's house; the pianist's wife, Linda, had rushed to answer the phone and got the sweetest of tellings-off: "You shouldn't be rushing in your condition," he admonished her, "when's the happy day?" Linda was shocked to realize he'd remembered Matthew's offhand remark of a few weeks back that she was pregnant; soon they were discussing breathing exercises and parenting tips. Few other musicians of that sexist time would have done the same — it was a typical example of how his charm was innate, not purely manipulative.

Those who'd known David for years, though, noticed a new "distancing" — an exclusion zone opening up around the Bowie persona. When Lindsay Kemp had first met David, the teenager had been convinced of his own talent, "but he was not starry, by God, no." But by that August, just a few months of genuine stardom, of seeing fans dressed up in his own image, had had a subtle effect. Kemp observed that David "fell for it. You know — he believed in his own iconism — it made it difficult to be close to him."

This subtle realignment, the sense that David felt himself different, special, was uncomfortable. It didn't seem to be the result of innate selfishness. It was more a reaction to the sheer intensity, a hysteria that would affect the most stable psyche. "That Rainbow show was a shock — a big shock," says Kemp. "When I saw how he captured an audience of thousands and knew exactly what to do. It was absolutely electric — I was numb from beginning to end."

The two shows were a triumph, the high point of the Spiders era; there was the sense that the ideas had been plucked out of the air, without the formulaic feel that afflicted some later performances. The audience screamed occasionally but stayed politely in their seats; for all the glitter, the attention to musical details was stunning. Matthew Fisher, the ex–Procol Harum keyboard player who had been asked to help out for the two Rainbow shows, was placed behind a screen and hence was free to walk out into the audience when he wasn't playing the piano. "His singing was simply incredible. I'd never realized how his voice is a hundred percent, spot in tune, and that if he sings out of tune on his records, it's because he wants to." The two shows, with the presence of two Bowie albums in the charts shortly afterward, sealed the deal for David. He was no longer a novelty; now he was a phenomenon—just eight weeks since that first sold-out show in Croydon.

THE sense of event was heightened two weeks later, in Manchester. Throughout the tour, both band and crew had stayed in tiny hotels and B and Bs; that evening, for the first time, they were checked into an upmarket hotel, the Manchester Excelsior, and told they could sign for whatever they wanted from room service. After a night getting wasted on the band's signature cocktail (the Spider Special, made up of brandy, advocaat, and lemonade), the assembled MainMan staff were bleary and slightly green-faced the next morning when they were greeted with a speech almost Churchillian in its scope.

"As far as RCA in America are concerned," Tony Defries informed his audience, "the young man with red hair sitting at the end of this table is the biggest thing to come out of England since the Beatles. And if we get this right there's every possibility we *will* be as big as the Beatles, if not bigger. We're relying on all of you—and you all have to learn to look and act like a million dollars!"

Like all great generals, Defries was as concerned with logistics as he was with morale, and he briskly went around the table checking on the status of instruments, amplifier back line, and the sound system. It turned out the band didn't own most of the back line. "What do you need for this, William?" Defries asked roadie Will Palin. "Er, twenty thousand pounds?" Within a couple of days, all the gear was purchased, packed up, and on its way for the Spiders' biggest adventure so far.

CHAPTER 10

Battle Cries and Champagne

David was like a lost child, looking for Angie. I'm sure he was very vulnerable and nervous. I didn't think about it at the time—what did I know?

—Tony Zanetta

T HE SEPTEMBER 22 SHOW in Cleveland launched David's assault on America, and it felt like a thrilling, surreal, high-cholesterol version of his early British dates. Local radio stations filled the airwaves with *Ziggy* songs, encouraged by Brian Sands, a friend of John Mendelssohn, who had set up a local Bowie fan club; there was a decent scattering of Ziggy clones in the six-hundred-strong audience who gave the high-powered show a riotous reception. As David and the band sat drinking during the after-show party at Hollenden House, a huge, 1960s hotel with bleached-wood interiors and space-age fiberglass furniture, the room was fizzing with excitement.

"Oh, don't worry," said Defries. "You're coming back to Cleveland at the end of the tour, and we'll be playing the big venue, with ten thousand people." The band laughed. "Yeah, yeah, yeah, Tony," they all chorused.

"But we did come back," says Trevor Bolder. "Two nights, sold out."

For David, this was the roller-coaster ride of which he'd fantasized; the people, places, and spaces in America would all make their mark on his music. Through the following months, he would be pushed through a schedule more grueling than that which had brought many tightly knit bands to grief—and he'd lap it up, devouring the experience. "He was just completely on it, the ultimate pro—a machine," says Scott Richardson, one of many who remember David's exuberance and excitement. Yet those heady months would also splinter his relationship with Angie and open up cracks in his own once-sturdy psyche.

For Tony Defries too, the challenge of conquering America was at the core of all his fantasies. He'd started with one artist and now had a stable of them. At the beginning of that year he had measured himself against Colonel Parker; now that ambition seemed too prosaic. By the end of the year, he talked of his company as the new Metro-Goldwyn-Mayer. His business was bigger than rock and roll: He traded in stars.

In order to build this lofty edifice, Defries needed a New York base, so in late 1972, Tony Zanetta found a two-bedroom apartment on the Upper East Side, bought furniture, and painted the walls. His theater background meant he was content with the occasional cash handout or gift in lieu of a salary—an important qualification for any prospective MainMan employee. Zanetta was soon joined by Lee Childers—who would become road manager and, later, advance guard, checking out venues before the band arrived—and Cyrinda Foxe, a charming Marilyn Monroe look-alike beloved of the Warhol crew. The trio were all "dreamers" with minimal business experience, but Defries loved hanging out with them, absorbing their enthusiasm. Within a few weeks, they realized Cyrinda's forte was not administration; Kathy Dorritie—Cherry Vanilla—replaced Cyrinda and proved to be the only one with any idea of how to run an office. Zanetta was handed day-to-day management of the upcoming tour, initially accompanied by the sage figure of Gustl Breuer. An elegant fifty-seven-year-old opera expert from the RCA classics department, he had been delegated by the company to oversee spending on the tour, which they had been persuaded to underwrite by the silver-tongued

Defries. Gustl joined a cavalcade of exotic characters that included hairdresser Suzi Fussey, photographer Mick Rock, the roadies Peter Hunsley and Robin Mayhew, David's friends George and Birgit Underwood, plus a team of three bodyguards led by Stuey George, an old Hull mate of Ronno's with a noticeable limp and a shady reputation.

David arrived in New York on September 17, 1972, with Angie in tow. Their weeklong cruise across the Atlantic on the QE2 was well publicized, highlighting their status as eccentric 1930s-style glamour icons. Defries considered David's stated fear of flying an affectation, inspired by one occasion when David wanted to avoid flying with Angie to Cyprus to see her parents. He naturally incorporated David's intermittent phobia into his palette of publicity gimmicks, and David became addicted to the quirky, cosmopolitan charm of traveling by boat, so the temporary fear of flying became permanent.

In their first couple of days in New York, Bowie and Ronson set out to find a replacement for the various Brit pianists who'd helped them out so far. Annette Peacock—a delightfully genre-busting artist who was briefly signed to MainMan—suggested her own pianist, Mike Garson, who was scraping together a living by giving piano lessons. It was Ronson who oversaw the auditions at RCA, sitting in with Garson in the main studio and showing him the chords to "Changes." Mick had an amazing ear for detail and fell in love with Garson's playing after just seven or eight bars. David, too, was overwhelmed—"he was simply extraordinary"—and grew to love sitting alongside the bearded, almost gentle musician on the tour bus, finding out how he ticked. Garson brought a decadent, Weimar ambience to the music, which perfectly offset the Spiders' no-nonsense R & B. He made his debut at the Cleveland show and would quickly become integral to David's music. He would also become a key player in the ultimate dismemberment of the band he augmented so perfectly.

For David, being on the road was the fulfillment of fantasies he'd treasured ever since Terry had turned him on to Jack Kerouac. He loved the long drives along the American highways in their rented bus, and as the band traveled from Cleveland to Memphis and then back to New York, he spent endless hours surveying the landscape and buildings along the roadside or chatting with George Underwood and Birgit, George's beautiful, dark-haired Danish-born wife, who'd come along for the adventure.

George was as obsessive a Yankophile as David, overjoyed to be in the land of Elvis Presley and Muddy Waters. During the drive from Cleveland to New York he was messing around on an acoustic and started to strum out the distinctive stop-start riff of Muddy's "I'm a Man." David began strumming along with him. "And then he wrote the song," says Trevor Bolder.

Other passengers claimed to have contributed to that jam, notably Will Palin, but it was Bowie who appropriated it. David had played around with some words that afternoon—at least one person remembers a variant of the song that went "We're bussing, we're all bussing"—but by the time they reached New York, ready for their prestigious slot at Carnegie Hall on September 28, David had come up with a complete lyric. He sang it in New York for Cyrinda Foxe, with whom he was canoodling—very publicly. The song was called "The Jean Genie"; everyone recognized its sensuous, reptilian hero as inspired by Iggy.

The Carnegie Hall show was, despite Bowie's bout of forty-eight-hour flu, a triumph, inspiring a deluge of press coverage. Defries particularly loved the *Rolling Stone* cover story, which applauded David's music but commented cynically on how he was invariably flanked everywhere he went by three security heavies. Defries quipped, with an all-knowing smile, "Without the security guards, he wouldn't *be* on the cover of *Rolling Stone*, would he?"

For all Defries's big talk, the initial number of confirmed shows booked for David was tiny, but the deluge of press and audience enthusiasm generated a flurry of interest from promoters, which allowed MainMan to add another eight weeks of dates. The extra shows seemed to vindicate Defries's genius in promoting David as if he were already America's biggest star, but the empty seats inside many venues would take their toll on both MainMan's finances and David's psyche. In the UK, David was not yet mainstream, but he had enough fans for the glitter kids to gather in little groups and brave the derision of rockers who hated "that poof Bowie." In an American city with a good radio station or a cool head shop, similar fans could gather and the venue would be full. But outside of that kind of enclave, few fans ventured out, and in the Midwest many of the venues' seats were conspicuously empty. Normally an English band touring the United States could rely on its record company for expertise on the ground. But this was the downside of Defries's obsession with signing with RCA, where David would be the biggest fish in a small pond. "David was stuck on the worst record label in the world," says Dai Davies, who was sent out to rustle up more shows. "And ultimately, the more money they took off RCA to try and make things happen, the longer it would take David to pay them back."

In the first few weeks, though, the feeling of infallibility was hardly punctured. When the band members convened in New York's RCA studio on October 6, most of them were surprised they were going to record their Greyhound bus jam, "The Jean Genie"—the session was so rushed that coproducer Ken Scott didn't even make it to New York. The song was like a musical collage; the title blended Jean Genet—Lindsay Kemp's idol—with Eddie Cochran's rocker "Jeanie Jeanie Jeanie." But the tune was a complete lift—how could anyone have the cheek to record it? "We all looked at each other and just thought, He's ripping off 'I'm a Man'!" says Bolder, who like Ronson knew the song via the Yardbirds' cover. It was recorded in just a couple of takes—the midsong crescendo of the Yardbirds' version was moved to the beginning, while the chorus was as simple as could be, with the band merely staying on one chord. It was a consummate example of musical thievery—in a grand tradition, for, as Underwood and Bowie both knew, Muddy Waters had borrowed the riff from Bo Diddley in the first place, and so would Mike Chapman and Nicky Chinn a few short weeks later for the Sweet's hit "Blockbuster."

Neither homage was as flagrant as Bowie's—in many ways, Bowie's lifting of the vibe and instrumentation of the Yardbirds' cover anticipated the sampling boom of the 1990s. Yet Bowie's open acknowledgment of his influences ensured that no one would ever formally charge him with plagiarism or copyright infringement.

Released on November 25, "The Jean Genie" would hit number 2 in the UK. It was a one-trick pony of a song, but that didn't matter. It kept up the momentum; Lou's "Walk on the Wild Side" shot up the chart in parallel. Lou's hit was self-consciously cool, David's childishly simple; both contributed equally to David's growing legend.

Meanwhile, the tour dates continued, moving south from Detroit and Chicago to St. Louis and Kansas City. There was gossip that David turned to drink to help cope with the stress of some of the poorly attended shows in the Midwest, notably St. Louis. Not true, according to his inner circle, but Ian Hunter, whose own tour with Mott the Hoople crisscrossed the States that autumn, bumped into his mentor several times and noted "glimpses of sadness." Some of it was sheer bewilderment; George Underwood remembers David's concerns that audiences weren't even reacting to the shows, "but they were simply open-mouthed, in amazement and shock!"

Despite the niggling worries, there were long periods when David would be "up," working on songs or enjoying the peaceful train journeys. David, accompanied by George and Birgit, or Ronson, excitedly savored the names of the huge beasts—the Texas Chief, the San Francisco Zephyr—and vied for a place in the Zephyr's magnificent Vista Dome, a Plexiglas viewing pod that gave panoramic views across the ever-changing landscape: "A couple of the band or friends, gladly one and the same most of the time, would often come and sit with me on these stretches," says David. "Ronson would love it, so too would my old chum George Underwood and his wife, Birgit. At about ten at night we'd creep up there, the air rich with the smell of grass, and laze around with guitars and a bottle of wine, watching the western moon get bigger and shinier into the early hours of the morning."

The gorgeous "Drive-in Saturday" was inspired by the succession of images he saw on the train to Phoenix and debuted in the show there on November 4—but there was a constant conflict between the buzz of ideas and the demands of his schedule, from which he was starting to shrink: "The work had to be defined by him, but that wasn't necessarily what had to be done when you're on the road. It was always a conflict," remembers Zanetta. "If left to his own devices he'd stay in a dark room in bed all day long. You had to force him to do things." The tour progressed with bursts of activity, then sudden stopovers, a disorienting existence in which many people—Angie most obviously, but David too—seemed almost manic-depressive, oscillating between energy highs, both business and sexual, and days of utter, exhausted torpor.

The nervous energy carried David through to Los Angeles for a four-day break before two shows at Santa Monica, dates full of promise thanks to the enthusiastic promotion of Rodney Bingenheimer, who by now had opened Rodney's English Disco on Sunset Strip. A mirror-walled temple to English glam, it was laid on with every staple a Brit muso could need: Watneys Bitter, sausage rolls, and teenage Valley girls. It was this period that most closely resembled Fellini's *Satyricon*. The streets were full of boys and girls, men and women offering services both sexual and pharmaceutical; Quaaludes were the drug du jour, popped like jelly beans by most of the crew, although David rarely if ever indulged. Prompted by Lisa Robinson, Lee Childers had booked band, crew, and hangers-on into the swanky Beverly Hills Hotel, where the two stars—Bowie and Defries—had their own bungalows. Elton John overlapped with Bowie on their stay; David dropped in on him and found him isolated, dwarfed by a mountain of vinyl records. Cyrinda Foxe was flown in from New York; Andy Warhol, Paul Morrissey, and Iggy Pop were on the scene; and Rodney's girls descended on the party in a frenzy of what Tony Zanetta called "kiddie decadence." "Cracked Actor," written over that week, was an almost literal depiction of the sleaze on offer; the line "since he pinned you baby" was a straight lift from the drug paranoiac argot developed by Lou Reed and John Cale in the Velvets. "Pinning someone meant they were on drugs—you'd pinned them, you'd got them," says Cale.

Rodney's regular Nancy McCrado remembers her friends Sable and Queenie, both of them in their early teens, sneaking into Mick Ronson's room, stripping off their clothes, and waiting for him naked: "Mick was really upset about it—pushed them out and locked the door." Later, Rodney's girl Lori Madox sneaked with Sable into David's room; according to Madox, David was tired but eventually proved more obliging than his lieutenant.

Roadie Robin Mayhew, like McCrado, remembers that "Ronno wasn't involved in the dubious scenes—he was more selective." Ronson's focus was legendary; the perfect example was the afternoon at the Beverly Hills Hotel when he sat and ran carefully through a preshow checklist with the roadies, asked a couple of follow-up questions, and then, the moment the business was concluded and the conversation started to wander, coolly informed them, "That's enough," and ushered them out the door so he could attend to the blonde who'd been waiting patiently on the bed. Most of the others did take advantage of Rodney's girls, many under seventeen, made up of a mix of "unsupervised rich kids or more desperate street kids," according to Rodney teen Kathy Heller. The teenagers were part of LA's rich cornucopia of pleasures, as were lobster thermidor, which everyone ordered from room service, and the Quaaludes offered by the young Hollywood boys who were desperate to get access. Even for those who'd seen some of the excesses of the 1960s, like Robin Mayhew, "it was a total eye-opener."

For the Spiders, the roadies, and the bodyguards, this was their first experience of Los Angeles; it could never be equaled. The frenetic, confused buzz surrounding them intensified from the moment Mike Garson revealed he was a member of the Church of Scientology. He talked to David first and was rebuffed ("what a ludicrous idea, expecting David to sublimate his ego to L. Ron Hubbard," quips writer Mick Farren) before approaching the rest of the organization.

Bowie, Ronson, and Bolder loved Garson's musical input, which offset his religious fervor. For David, the issue became a joke, and he labeled the pianist "Garson the Parson." But for the junior members of the crew, Scientology became a serious issue. "The other guys became obsessed, there was this righteousness about them, that they knew no wrong," remembers Mayhew. "It became bizarre, very black and dark."

Garson's evangelism for Scientology started taking effect when they arrived in LA, where he persuaded most of the entourage to visit the Scientology center—each musician was assigned his own mentor. "He tried to get me into it and failed," says Bolder, who during his visit saw "all these weird people doing weird things, tests, mind games—I didn't want to know." Bolder returned to his hotel room after a night's heavy drinking at the Whisky only to open the door and see Garson and a woman who'd been assigned to recruit him sitting on his bed. Bolder threw them out, "but Mike hounded me for years. But Woody did go back in there. And I think Scientology had a big influence on him."

Woody Woodmansey became the Spiders' best-known Scientology convert, and from his first sessions with the organization, says Bolder, he was taught to "be more positive and speak your mind. And if you're a type of person who speaks their mind anyway you're going to speak it even more. He was confident that he was a Scientologist and everything was gonna be wonderful and he couldn't fail."

Defries took little interest in the details of what was going on backstage, where the atmosphere was turning nasty, and Stuey George in particular was becoming "far too heavy," says Mayhew. "If there were fans hanging around he'd lay into them. We're saying, 'Don't be so heavy'—he'd be shouting at the kids, effing and blinding, and it was very scary for them, this heavy, colored guy with a limp who looked like he'd been through it heading for them." Tony Frost, the second of David's three bodyguards, became another Scientology convert, adding to the haze of hype and confusion emanating from the MainMan circus.

Much of the edge, intensity, and euphoria of that LA week was apparent in the Santa Monica shows on October 20 and 21. They were a triumph, the seventeen-song set offering delight after delight, running across what would be five albums. Defries had sold the tour as the biggest by an English act since the Beatles; that night's radio recording for KMET suggests that if anything, he'd undersold his charges, for this set was more adventurous, more visceral, and more proficient than anything the Fabs had delivered onstage in America. For years, the recording of the opening night's performance would be a definitive rock-and-roll bootleg; in the mid-1970s, many English punk bands would admire its high-octane assault and copy Ronson's modified chord sequence on "Waiting for the Man."

In the couple of days before David departed for San Francisco, he was required to sprinkle his magic fairy dust on yet another MainMan album, the tracks that Iggy and the Stooges had assembled at CBS studios in London. David's relationship with Iggy was complex; while Lou Reed would always pay due fealty to David, Iggy was already confiding to friends that the *Ziggy* album sounded "Mickey Mouse"; then, when the singer heard "The Jean Genie," he felt he'd been assimilated: "I just rolled my eyes and said, Oh my God—not only has he ripped the Yardbirds off but he's done me too! That was when I first realized he was taking a lot off me." The web of mutual respect and distrust was complicated by the fact that Angie had had an affair with the Stooges' Ron Asheton—celebrated for his droll humor, he resembled a young Philip Seymour Hoffman and owned a scarily comprehensive collection of Nazi uniforms—and then James Williamson, the dark, glowering lead guitarist who cordially disliked David but was, says Angie, "smart. He knew when to keep quiet."

For all the openness of the Bowies' marriage, the affair was a messy business, "a dumb thing to do," admits Williamson. When Williamson met Bowie back in Haddon Hall, David had been enthusiastic and talkative. During the mixing sessions at LA's Western Sound, he was tense, preoccupied, "this super-stilted kind of stiff guy," says Williamson. The mix was an exercise in damage control: James and Iggy had jumbled up the instruments on the multitrack, and all David could do was pull out a few instruments from the sonic holocaust and add an effect here and there. The results were, a few years later, the prime influence on

1970s punk. But at the time it was the first of many half-cocked projects. And soon, Iggy and his Stooges would be sent to Main-Man's luxurious new house in the Hollywood Hills, where they would be ignored by Defries and return to their old, druggie ways.

The last weeks of that first U.S. tour included several cancellations, poorly attended performances in San Francisco and Seattle, arguments among Defries, Davies, and the RCA staff on the ground, and friction between the Brit and American halves of the entourage. None of those problems affected David's songwriting, or his performances, which were riveting, night after night; when he was "up" he was great company, camping it up with the *Pork* crew or "taking the piss" with the Yorkshire crowd. Yet behind the scenes, the relationship that had sustained him for the past two years was splintering.

It's impossible to pinpoint the moment at which David and Angie's marriage was irrevocably doomed. By the autumn of 1972, Defries was gunning for Angie, irritated that she'd brought the Stooges over from London and charged their plane fares to MainMan. Although the amount involved was dwarfed by the huge sums MainMan was hemorrhaging on the canceled U.S. dates, it was Angie's profligacy he fixed on.

For Tony Zanetta, who occasionally found himself miserable and isolated on the bus, a defining moment came during one of the first tour stopovers, in Erie, Pennsylvania. He'd noticed that David often stepped out and became the focus of attention but at other times withdrew, lost in thought or racked by nerves. In Erie, David had retreated to his room when Angie started "fooling around" with a bodyguard, Anton Jones, the two of them skinny-dipping in the motel pool. "David was like a lost child, looking for Angie," says Zanetta. "I'm sure he was very vulnerable and nervous. I didn't think about it at the time—what did I know?"

Angie had been jealous of David's well-publicized affair with Cyrinda Foxe in New York; making loud remarks about her relationship with Anton seemed to be her way of getting back at him. "He makes me scream!" she announced to Zanetta and Davies, apparently referring to his sense of humor but with an obvious double entendre. "It was to punish David, or get more attention," says one of the tour staff, "the more male members of the entourage she was involved with, the more attention she would get. And some of them were stupid enough to go for it. It was an incredibly unhealthy situation."

Angie, maybe more than anyone, had helped David get to America. But now that they were there, her need for constant attention made for one prima donna too many. In reaction, Zanetta sacked Anton Jones, while from then on Defries would try to separate Angie from the touring party. According to Dai Davies, who witnessed Angie's and Anton's banishment, Defries's response, however cruel, was the only practical one: "It's a simple question of management, with thirty-four people and the trucks and everything else, with a tour that wasn't that successful. You can fall in behind one temperamental person. You can't fall in behind two. It becomes a nightmare."

Angie and David had exchanged wedding wristbands rather than the customary rings for their marriage in Bromley; it was during the last days of this tour that David's was snatched by a fan: "It was highly symbolic, I thought," said David recently, "our marriage was pretty much over in all but name. We were to see less and less of each other as the next year rolled around."

One can only assume that it was Scott Richardson who unwittingly contributed to the breakdown. The singer—an old friend of Iggy from the Detroit rock scene—had met Angie when she'd stopped over in Ann Arbor with the Stooges. He joined her for her reunion with David in Cleveland and soon became her official lover and—he thought—David's friend. Caught in the center of this unconventional ménage, he regards their open marriage as optimistic, naive, a loving arrangement that also represented a Faustian pact: "They had this open relationship that the fans and all the world knew about. They utilized all that to seduce the world—and it was incredibly effective. But what they were trying to do with each other ultimately backfired. And my little part, if it did end up causing distress, I apologize."

If David felt sexual jealousy of Angie, he concealed it well.

When David took up with Cyrinda Foxe, Angie indulged in a classic defense mechanism, becoming chums with Cyrinda and copying her haircut. David took on a similar role with Richardson, becoming his rock-and-roll buddy. Richardson observed that "David was pulling everybody left and right—and she was doing the same thing. And fantastic as that was for the publicity of the *Ziggy Stardust* era it was also incredibly destructive." David relied on Angie for support—she was the one who encouraged him when his nerve failed; for instance, when he worried about wearing the outrageous Kansai Yamamoto "jockstrap" outfit in Japan. Yet by the end of the U.S. trip, David seemed to have bowed to Defries's restriction and demanded Angie obey the old, sexist musicians' rule of "no wives on tour."

"David would just get in a furious mood [when Angie was around] because maybe she was too outrageous—or maybe she took over too much of the limelight," says Suzi Fussey, who worked as David's assistant. "I honestly don't know."

Watching David at close hand, working together with him later, Richardson developed bottomless respect for his abilities; as for Angie, he says, "I admired her so much as a human being." Yet he looked on as "the things that David counted on her for got diminished by the fact that there was so much sex going on. I lived in Haddon Hall and I used to wake under a pile of bodies. I thought having been on the road on America I knew what the rock-and-roll life was. I didn't have a clue until I went to England."

By the time David and the Spiders returned to New York, on December 3, Defries was already planning a Japanese tour and persuading RCA to copromote David's return to the States. During the stay, David recorded his own version of "All the Young Dudes" and a new song, "Drive-in Saturday." When he met Ian Hunter a few days later, on December 10, he played him the songs, offering the latter for release; Hunter told him it was "too complicated" for Mott. Hunter was worried about being regarded as Bowie's creature—but he listened attentively to David's advice, which was incisive and included the observation that it was impossible to run a band as a democracy. Despite his respect for David,

Hunter was growing suspicious of the MainMan cavalcade, and he kept his MainMan contract in his suitcase—he never signed it, despite several reminders.

Although he had concerns, Hunter remained full of admiration for Bowie, who was eight years younger than he but more worldly and analytical. The Mott singer concluded that David was "holding up well" under the pressure—which was about to be ratcheted up a few more notches, with an imminent brief UK tour followed by a return to the United States and then a short run of dates in Japan. A few hours after his chat with Hunter, Bowie set sail for London, the boat trip a welcome respite before the onslaught was renewed.

THE British press had closely followed and reported on the triumphs of the U.S. tour—for all the problems, it was obvious that David had made much more of an impact than Marc Bolan, who'd also toured America that autumn. Two homecoming shows at the Rainbow before Christmas had a celebratory air, with David appealing for donations and, on December 24, collecting a truckful of cuddly toys to be delivered to children in the Barnardo's homes across London to which Haywood had devoted so much of his life.

David, Angie, and Zowie spent their Christmas together at Haddon Hall, a brief break before work started again, their family gathering augmented by dozens of fans singing in the street and, according to press reports, camping in the garden. Then it was back to work on the twenty-eighth, with a string of shows starting in Manchester, interrupted by sessions back at Trident.

Completed over December and January, *Aladdin Sane*—its title announced to the campily vague interviewer Russell Harty on January 17—bore all the marks of its rushed genesis. Yet this was as much blessing as curse, for while songs were at a premium—with a rerecording of "The Prettiest Star" and a cover of the Stones' "Let's Spend the Night Together" making up the numbers—there was a freshness and grandeur to the recording, even if the internal logic was not as well developed as *Ziggy*. Mike

Garson's piano in particular added an anarchic, decadent edge, most obviously on the title track in a solo that he counts as an amazing moment in his life to this day: "I played a blues solo and David said, 'No, that's not what I'm looking for.' Then I played a little Latin solo. 'No, that's not what I'm looking for.'" David was relaxed, chatted easily to Garson, remembering their conversations on the tour bus. "Then he said to me, 'Well, you told me about playing on the avant-garde scene in New York. Why don't you try something like that?' I said, 'Are you serious?' He said, 'Absolutely.' That whole solo was one shot, one take—boom, that was it. But it came about because he got it out of me."

Garson was one of many struck by David's growing ability to inspire musicians to reach inside themselves and come up with ideas buried deep within their consciousness. Matthew Fisher, who dropped in on the Trident sessions, was also impressed by the way Bowie would communicate ideas: "He issues very strange instructions to people—not in the prosaic way I would do it. He was talking to the brass players using terms like *renaissance* and *impressionist*—it was very esoteric, but people seemed to understand."

For Garson, asked to sprinkle his piano playing like magic fairy dust over the album's best songs, David's approach was liberating; soon Mike realized he was expected to bring something new to every track, contributing, for instance, a warped-stride piano part to "Time" that was brilliantly counterpointed by Ronson's perfectly judged guitar. "That was a great piece; it was a chance for me to play in a whole other way," says Garson. "You've got to understand, if the inspiration is given to you—and it was given me—how can you go wrong?"

Garson's bravery in the studio, his willingness to take musical risks on the first or second take, was "so perfect," says Ken Scott, "you could see it was pushing the envelope." However, not every musician was proving so obliging for reasons not unconnected with Garson—or, rather, with his religion.

Drummer Woody Woodmansey had always had "strong opinions," says Trevor Bolder, but as he fell more deeply under the influence of Scientology he became even more opinionated. Woody had already clashed with Bowie over such trivial matters as the jacket he'd wear on the Russell Harty show; now his attitude affected the music too. As they were laying down the background track for "Panic in Detroit," David asked Woody to play a Bo Diddley rhythm. "No way, it's too obvious," Woodmansey retorted. Ronson had a word; Woody was immovable. "He wouldn't have any of it," according to Trevor Bolder. In the end, Woody recorded his drum part much as he wanted — David and Mick asked Geoff MacCormack to overdub congas and other percussion to get the rhythm they'd had in mind.

"Panic in Detroit" was among the last songs recorded for *Aladdin Sane*, the final overdubs laid down as Ronson and Bowie rounded up musicians for a return to America a couple of days later. John Hutchinson was sitting in his Scarborough studio apartment when he got a call from Ronson, who asked him if he was still playing guitar and then handed the phone to David. "Are you up for it?" David asked, and Hutch was in. Sax players Ken Fordham and Brian Wishaw were session regulars. Geoff Mac-Cormack, David's old Bromley schoolmate, got the call to join up for backup vocals — and to keep David company on the tour, now that Angie was banished. MacCormack duly packed in his job at *Construction News* and boarded the SS *Canberra* with David, where they settled into the routine of long dinners and nights at the bar, exchanging Oscar Wilde and Bosie witticisms.

Soon after their arrival in New York, David and Geoff went down to Max's to see Biff Rose, whose "Fill Your Heart" David had covered on *Hunky Dory;* they were more impressed by a new act who was sharing the bill — Bruce Springsteen. During rehearsals, David was revved up, almost ecstatic as he chatted with his old mate John Hutchinson. There was no hint of reproach that Hutch had left David in 1969; instead, David shared his excitement: "Who'd've thought we'd all get here?" Then back at the Gramercy Hotel, it was one of David's customary bonding sessions as he gave Hutch a run-through of his latest musical discoveries: "This is Roxy Music — the singer's a guy from Newcastle, he studied with Richard Hamilton."

After rehearsals with the new, bigger band at the RCA sound-stage (Harry Belafonte dropped by and politely asked them to turn down the volume), David took Hutch, Geoff, and Stuey to see the Rockettes at Radio City Music Hall, where they'd be playing a few days later. Absorbed by the ludicrously campy high-kicking act, David confided to Hutch that he intended to descend from the gods, just like the show they were watching, as part of their act. For a man who now refused to stay in rooms above a hotel's fourth floor, claiming vertigo, this was true devotion to his art.

On the opening night of their second U.S. tour, February 14, the show was more grandiose than ever, with five costume changes for David alone. The news that Salvador Dalí was in the house created a special buzz in a hectic night that culminated in David's succumbing to a theatrical fainting fit. Whether this was a Lindsay Kemp–style act of drama or genuine exhaustion, witnesses like MacCormack are "still not sure"—but it generated headlines worldwide.

David's recovery was evidently rapid, for by the next night he hit the town again, ending up at a reception for Steve Wonder at the club Genesis that was packed with the city's soul talent. Aretha Franklin and Gladys Knight were hanging out and broke into song, accompanied by Ava Cherry, a striking black model with bleached-blond hair. David walked straight up to Ava.

"Are you a singer?"

"Yeah," Ava assured him, stretching the truth a little before a bystander introduced them. "I've been listening to your albums for a month," she told him. "I think they're incredible." This was not a total exaggeration; Cherry's manager had helped engineer the meeting, hoping it would advance her career. But Ava was fascinated by this outlandish figure who was also a model of English charm and good manners, buzzing with energy but content to go with the flow even when she declined his invitation back to the Gramercy. Within the next couple of days, though—during which she went with David to see Charlie Mingus, spent hours with him listening to records and sharing opinions, attended rehearsals, and then had an informal audition where Defries assessed her singing—they became lovers. "Then the very next day we're up and getting breakfast," says Cherry, "and all of a sudden the door knocks and it's Angie. 'Darling! How are you?' So I'm standing there and you can picture the look on my face!"

Once she'd been briefed by David about his open marriage, Ava was shocked, simultaneously intimidated and impressed by Angie, and "really depressed. I said to David, 'Why didn't you tell me?'" Still, she found herself "a little bit in love with David," as well as entranced by the intriguing cast of characters around him. Just before David left town, he told her he'd like her to join the tour as backup singer. Cherry left her job and her apartment to wait in Chicago, where, instead of confirmation, she received a telegram saying, *Sorry, tour has been canceled.* Informed that David would catch up with her later, Ava concluded, "Thanks very much. That's completely messed up my life."

For Cherry, the realization that she could be taken up then discarded like a child's toy was an unwanted insight into the behavior of stars and their retinue. It was a lesson that many who passed through the orbit of David Bowie in the forthcoming months would share.

PART 2

Where Things Are Hollow

CHAPTER 11

Star

David acted as if everything was completely normal. I don't know if he was delusional and thought no one knew.

—Suzi Fussey

To break up a band like that is astonishing. I have to credit Bowie with having a lot of courage: to say, "I'm not coming back."

—Scott Richardson

AVID BOWIE'S THREE- or four-day idyll with Ava Cherry in New York marked a new phase his life—an era when he would be surrounded by people using him to advance their careers, when subordinates would oversee every aspect of his working day, when the world's media would pry into his life.

David's friends from 1971 and 1972 retain countless varying impressions of the man, from David the iceman to David the boyish dreamer, but Iggy Pop probably describes it best: "You're talking about a rather worldly, knowledgeable young buck who was ready to go out into the world and shoot his bolt. But who was focused on a particular target—success."

That drive for success would cause confusion or resentment from those, such as Iggy, Mick Ronson, and countless others, who had different agendas. By 1974 Iggy would be accusing David—"that fuckin' carrottop"—of "sabotaging" his work. Few of those left damaged and bitter in David's wake would realize that the newly emerged star had been as damaged by the process as they were.

In the heady opening days of 1973, though, David was "relaxed" and "sweet," according to his new lover Ava Cherry. The routine was well established—a morning call from Tony Zanetta or road manager Jaime Andrews, followed by a long bus ride, which for the Spiders was invariably set to the only two tapes they had on the eight-track player: the Stylistics and the Buddy Rich band. Check-in, sound check, a quiet moment as David did his makeup, the show, and only then was it time to relax: Geoff MacCormack hanging out with David or other band members, Ronson hanging with Hutch, Woody and Trevor with each other or occasionally their wives. Once they'd all left New York, Bowie's main social contact with the band was at the after-show parties, which were usually decorated by the best-looking local girls; they were selected from all the contenders by David's hairdresser and personal assistant Suzi Fussey. This was where Hutch learned the phrase *No head, no backstage pass*—such transactions were always more explicit and more efficient in America. With Geoff to talk to, Bowie spent less time with Mick, who would chat to Hutch over Irish coffees in the bar. Meanwhile, Garson the Parson would be preaching the benefits of Scientology to new band members like Hutch and Fordham.

For this second jaunt around the States, David took in a similar cavalcade of sights: the viewing cars in the trains; the Stetsons in Nashville; the routine at Elvis's favorite hotel, the Peabody in Memphis, where a trio of ducks waddled through the hotel lobby; each sight shared with the wide-eyed Geoff MacCormack. With a larger crew, and Geoff in tow, David spent less and less time with Trevor and Woody. Yet when they chatted, he assured them, "Don't worry, we're all going to be really, really rich." Trevor and Mick were trusting—until Woody Woodmansey heard from Mike Garson that the new pianist was on an eight-hundred-dollar-a-week salary and, stunned, shared the information with his fellow Spiders. Woody and Bolder each received fifty pounds a week. When they complained to Defries and asked when they'd get to see the riches David had promised, the MainMan boss was cold as ice: "Never mind what Bowie told you you're getting — it's what I tell you you're getting."

Mick Ronson decided he'd had enough of this runaround about pay; a few weeks into the American dates, he called Dennis Katz, who was then managing Lou Reed, to see if he could secure a record deal for the Spiders — without their singer. Katz soon called to say he'd gotten a six-figure advance from CBS. The trio were buoyed up — until a traitorous roadie informed Defries of the band's scheme. Characteristically playing hardball, Defries informed CBS that Katz had no right to negotiate for the Spiders and cut him out of the deal entirely. Then he called a meeting with the band and smoothly asked them: "Why didn't you tell me you wanted a record deal? RCA are willing to sign you — they'll pay you an advance — up front, if you want some money." According to Bolder, Defries then embarked on a textbook divide-and-conquer strategy, seeking out Ronson and offering him his own solo deal.

Meanwhile, as he plotted with Ronson, Defries lulled David's rhythm section into a false sense of security. Normally he treated Trevor and Woody with particular haughtiness, puffing on his cigar and patronizing them with highfalutin jargon if he even bothered to register their presence. Now, when Woody Woodmansey returned to the attack with his usual bluntness, demanding the sidemen receive a raise to five hundred pounds a week, Defries was uncharacteristically helpful, assuring him he'd discuss the money situation with RCA. During their last American dates in California, the manager reported back. "RCA have agreed to pay you five hundred pounds a week," he told them. "But you can't have that until we get to England — until then, you can have two hundred pounds a week, but when we get to England you'll get all the money up front [as back pay]." Delighted that Defries had finally seen sense, the Yorkshire duo chorused, "That sounds all right."

On the surface, David remained friendly. He loved Woody's

drumming, but it was probably the drummer's stubbornness during the *Aladdin Sane* sessions that marked the turning point. Once Defries had told David of Woody and Trevor's treachery, that they'd been planning behind his back to cut a record deal, David's next musical move suddenly became clear.

David's attitude to Mick Ronson was more complex; the guitarist was stubborn, but he was obliging, a problem solver, and as close a musical friend as David had. Defries wanted a Ronson solo album both to head off the Spiders' revolt and to add another act to his entertainment stable. David had recently discovered a Richard Rodgers song called "Slaughter on Fifth Avenue" and saw it as a brilliant vehicle for Ronson's solo album. He even suggested his friend—and Angie's lover—Scott Richardson as a collaborator. Buoyed up by the vision of a glittering solo career with a musical agenda provided by David, Ronson went along with the plan. The entire tour party prepared for their most exotic trip to date, a ten-show stint in Japan, still unexplored territory for most British musicians, and the members of David's rhythm section were content, unsuspecting, for what would turn out to be the Spiders' last ride.

Geoff MacCormack, who kept David company now that Angie was "encouraged" to keep her distance, had become an enthusiastic convert to the luxury of international cruising. He was disappointed to find his second trip, from Los Angeles to Yokohama, was on the SS *Oronsay*, a 1940s liner in the twilight of its career that the childhood friends nicknamed the SS *Rancid*. They spent the trip practicing phrases from Geoff's Japanese primer and treating passengers to Latin records they'd picked up in New York. Finally arriving in Yokohama on April 5 to a five-hundred-strong welcoming crowd, David was resplendent in a wide-lapelled tartan jacket and flanked by frowning matrons irritated at the intrusion, his excitement at the bizarre culture clash equaled only by his exhaustion.

It was during this leg of the tour that many of the contradictions in the MainMan empire became exposed. Endless stories of the Stooges' depredations filtered out of LA in those weeks, allegations that they'd spent company cash on smack and abortions for teenage groupies. Defries, always disapproving of drug use, ordered them thrown out of MainMan's Torrenson Drive mansion.

David was upset but didn't attempt to talk Tony out of his decision. Then, within weeks of Iggy's sacking, another of David's protégés left MainMan, a split resulting from a management meeting where a drunken, impassioned Tony Zanetta proclaimed the business was now based on "stars, not boring rock 'n' rollers." The next day, Zanetta was staggered to find his outburst had inspired the sacking of Mott the Hoople, the company's main rock and rollers (their career was unharmed, for Ian Hunter, skeptical of Defries, had never signed his management contract).

MainMan's lack of focus, the way the company was expanding in random fashion, was highlighted once the party hit Japan. David formed a mutual admiration society with Kansai Yamamoto, championing his designs, accompanying his family to the Kabuki theater, and Defries promptly announced he would now represent the designer in the West via a Japanese division, MainMan Tokyo. That spring, Defries also floated the rumor that David was to star in a movie based on Robert Heinlein's *Stranger in a Strange Land*. No names were attached to the report, which was suspiciously vague; it's likely the grandstanding was aimed as much at RCA America as at the general public, for although David's album sales were phenomenal in Britain—*Aladdin Sane* debuted at number 1 in May, bumping the Beatles' Red and Blue albums off the top—they were underwhelming in the United States.

In Japan, though, David's was the biggest debut tour of recent years; every aspect of his distinctive rock-and-roll recipe—the clothes, the makeup, all the theatrical elements—seemed to strike a chord with Japanese youth. For the band members, who were mobbed at stage doors every night and drank in the deliciously alien Japanese culture by day, the tour was an idyllic experience. Then Woody, outraged that his promised pay raise had not yet materialized, once more set out to confront Defries, this time with bassist Trevor Bolder in tow.

As ever, Woody came straight to the point. "This is a joke!

We've been promised more money, and now we find the roadies are getting more than us!"

Defries, unused to being challenged, momentarily lost his cool. "Well? I'd rather give the money to the road crew than to you."

Woody shot back, "If that's your attitude, you can stick it up your arse!" then bundled his bassist out of the room. Shortly after the meeting, Woody announced he and Trevor were going on strike. Mick Ronson eventually talked them around. "Don't make trouble," he told them, "not when it's going so well."

But it was not going well.

Even while David was being encouraged by Defries, who grandly told him how much money they'd make in Japan, his final reserves of calm, energy, and patience were being drained. On their last night in Japan, Geoff and David spent the evening in an exquisitely peaceful restaurant, dining with Geoff's newly acquired Chinese girlfriend and David's companion, a beautiful, blue-eyed French-Japanese woman. "I knew he was trying to think of some angle that would allow us to stay in Japan," says MacCormack, "but there was no way." Geoff and David had a boat to catch, the *Felix Dzerzhinsky*—named after the notorious founder of the KGB—whose crew and passengers were treated to an impromptu Bowie and MacCormack performance of "Space Oddity" and "Amsterdam." The boat journey was followed by a seven-day train trip through Siberia and on to Moscow; MacCormack's photos document the endless steppes, the stop-offs for food, and the two days spent in the rundown Intourist Hotel in Moscow. When the two finally reached East Berlin, the bombed-out hulks of buildings seemed grayer and more ominous than anything they recalled from 1950s London. The memory would stay with them both.

All the tour's members were weary on their return to London. The costumes were frayed too, held together with ad hoc repairs. There was a brief respite with a party at Haddon Hall—which Tony Visconti and new wife, Mary Hopkin, attended—but, as if to confirm the unrelenting grind of what was nearly sixteen months of repetitive, grueling touring, David's Earls Court show on May 12 was famously disastrous. Both lighting and sound were pitifully inadequate for the venue, and the familiar "jing-jing-a-jing" introduction of "Rock 'n' Roll Suicide" was transformed into "jing-jing-a—oh shit" as rhythm guitarist John Hutchinson fell off his podium in the stygian gloom. All the extra musicians, including Hutch and the sax section, were still reading music from manuscript, which they couldn't make out in the dark, and no one in the band could hear himself over the lousy monitoring system.

The show was a catastrophe, but the negative press it generated was forgotten as the tour rolled on into June. Reviewers and audiences alike were transfixed by the spectacle and the smoking music: "a total success, based on an inspired and uniquely amazing talent" was *Sounds'* verdict on the Newcastle show. David was on a high; on June 6, he partied into the night at Hallam Towers, a trendy new hotel in Sheffield. Rival singers Lulu and Labi Siffre happened to be in the city, and they played an impromptu show at the bar—but their eyes, and those of the audience, were fixed on David. Lulu's own star seemed in the descendant; it had been a decade since she'd notched up hits like "Shout," and her Eurovision song contest success of a few years earlier seemed to signal a permanent move to the lounge, chicken-in-a-basket circuit. But the tiny Scot singer was undeniably charismatic and had an infectious energy. Later that evening she disappeared—and so did David, his absence publicized by Angie, who marched up and down the hotel corridors knocking on doors in search of her missing hubby. In a strange way, Angie seemed to revel in the drama of chasing her husband around, advertising that Lulu had become another notch on the Bowie bedpost. The hilarious episode was enjoyed by all the band and crew; the next morning, David's thin-shaven eyebrow seemed to arch a little in appreciation of the hubbub of gossip over the previous night's events. But the incident also illustrated the stress and drama generated by his and Angie's supposedly open marriage.

Throughout June, David Bowie's defiantly extravagant cavalcade was a much-needed burst of color in what was otherwise a grim summer, with unemployment rising and the United Kingdom paralyzed by strikes and shadowed by an IRA bombing campaign. The success of Lou Reed's "Walk on the Wild Side," a hit in both the United States and the United Kingdom that summer, underlined Bowie's magic touch—hearing Lou drawl about how Candy Darling "never lost her head, even when she was giving head" every few hours on BBC Radio 1 represented a delicious cultural marker for a generation, and David's unstoppable momentum was illustrated by the announcement in June that he'd soon be recording a new album in France and that yet another American tour would follow in the autumn. Later in the summer, the BBC's *Story of Pop* magazine hit the streets; the "First Encyclopedia of Pop" began with Elvis—and ended with Bowie.

For a generation of kids, the Bowie tour's escapism, his visions of transcending the bonds of Earth, represented a vital beacon of hope, of glamour. But on the tour itself, what had started out as thrilling was becoming drudgery. Week by week there was less camaraderie backstage; Bolder and Woody hardly exchanged a word with David over the summer, while David's renewed friendliness with Hutch had evaporated by the time they returned to the UK. Ken Fordham's unflappability endeared him to David, who named him Ken "Funky" Fordham because he so obviously wasn't. But with shows at forty venues over fifty days, with sixteen matinee performances, everyone felt "Defries was working us to death," says Bolder, who was amazed that David survived without losing his voice. Any damage done seemed to be psychological; during a day's layoff in Torquay, Devon, the band took off to see the sights—promoter Mel Bush lent Hutch his flashy green Rover to tour the countryside—but David didn't emerge from his room. "No matter how nice the day was, you wouldn't see him. He was going very pale and thin," says Hutch. David's charisma continued to shine through, and still he seemed "excited and thrilled" in the dressing room before he went on, says Suzi Fussey, but there was a tense, almost hysterical edge to his public persona. Sometimes he seemed shaky, and his skin was stretched over his skull, pale and waxy—the contrast with the previous January's photos for *Melody Maker,* when he looked joyous and gamin, is almost painful to behold. Even Freddie Buretti's costumes were frayed and worn, obviously at the end of their life. As David recalls, it was during these dates that his enthusiasm finally gave out: "I really did want it all to come to an end. I was writing for a different kind of project and exhausted and completely bored with the whole Ziggy concept, couldn't keep my attention on the performances with much heart. Strangely enough, the rest of the tour was a success... but I was wasted and miserable."

In the run-up to the Hammersmith show, on July 3, only the roadies, MacCormack, Garson, and Ronson were informed that this endless cycle of euphoria, boredom, excitement, and exhaustion was coming to a close. It wasn't just David's stamina that was at the breaking point—MainMan's cash reserves were exhausted too.

Around mid-June, Defries realized that the upcoming U.S. dates could expose MainMan to huge losses. That same week, it became obvious that David's unparalleled, amazing streak of creativity was ending, with the announcement that the next single would be a *Hunky Dory* track, "Life on Mars."

Defries had performed an amazing feat of financial sleight of hand during the previous months by persuading RCA to underwrite his hefty financial losses on the two American tours. With the establishment of MainMan, which was more or less independent of Laurence Myers, in June of 1972, he'd lost access to his ex-partner's cash reserves. From that point the company's financial situation was always on a knife edge. When, early in 1973, RCA finally refused to underwrite the next U.S. tour, Defries decided to tackle the potential crisis head-on: He would "retire" David. David would stave off exhaustion, Defries would stave off a financial catastrophe, the Bowie enigma would be sustained, and, a crucial side benefit, the troublesome Spiders could be eliminated.

David and Defries's plans progressed, and the musicians, bar Ronson, remained oblivious. Zanetta had asked a couple whether they'd like to play with MainMan's latest act, Ava Cherry. "Why would I want to do that?" Hutch had replied, happy in the knowledge that a tour of America was imminent, with a possible jaunt to Australia thereafter. "I'm in David's band!"

As for David, his secretiveness about their disbandment did not derive from sadism—this was theater, the chance to ensure the tour's Hammersmith finale was a set piece of the most gripping drama: "Pure showbiz," remembers Suzi Fussey, "he loved that." Scott Richardson, a confidant of both Bowie and Ronson throughout the final tour, knew what was coming up, but still he reckoned, "To break up a band like that is astonishing. I have to credit Bowie with having a lot of courage: to say, 'I'm not coming back.'"

The evening of the Hammersmith show, David gave no clue as to the night's denouement. Suzi Fussey, ministering to him in the dressing room, had been tipped off by Defries but had to feign ignorance, as did the roadies and the various MainMan staff. "David acted as if everything was completely normal," she says. "I don't know if he was delusional and thought no one knew." Despite the imminent drama, he seemed rather more relaxed than normal, grateful for the coming rest. "Relieved, I think," says Fussey. "He had been frightened of becoming a parody of himself."

Bolder, Woody, and Hutch, for all their exhaustion, were fired up to be playing the Odeon, and all three of them relished the presence of Jeff Beck, guesting on guitar. Their attention was mainly on Ronson, as Bowie and the band rampaged their way through what *Sounds'* Martin Hayman called "one of the best concerts I have ever seen."

Hutch got a hint that something unusual was happening when David walked over for a word, the first time he'd spoken to him in weeks. "Don't go straight into 'Rock 'n' Roll Suicide,'" David instructed his old friend. "I'm going to say something there."

But when David announced, "Not only is it the last show of the tour, but it's the last show that we'll ever do. Thank you!" in the break, Hutch and the others were confused. Then they saw Bolder mouth the words *He's fuckin' sacked us!* The moment the closing notes of "Rock 'n' Roll Suicide" died, Bowie and Ronson disappeared. Woody and Trevor were left to find their own way home.

Presiding over the glittering gathering marking the tour's

close at the Café Royal the next night, David posed alongside Mick Jagger, the undoubted stars of a party that included Lou Reed, Keith Moon, Barbra Streisand, and Elliott Gould. It was a sweet moment, David and Mick each trying to out-camp the other, equals at last. Woody and Trevor were rock-and-roll lepers, Trevor desperately questioning Ronson—who was noncommittal, not letting on he'd known anything—while Woody's attitude was "bollocks. I want to do something else anyway." But the news of Woody's sacking was not confirmed until he received a phone call from a MainMan flunky a week later, the day of his wedding to his girlfriend, June, officiated by Mike Garson at the British Church of Scientology headquarters.

Bolder, meanwhile, had heard nothing until he was asked up to a gathering at MainMan. Walking in to see MacCormack, Zanetta and others gossiping and pouring themselves drinks, Bolder started to have a go at David—"What are you up to? How can you treat people this way?"—but he was pulled away by Mick Ronson: "Keep your mouth shut and don't say anything, other-wise you'll be gone as well. Just cool it and be quiet." When Bowie spoke to him again, telling him his next album would be a collection of covers and playing some of the songs he intended to record, Trevor did as Ronson advised. "Only then did I realize how much Mick was looking out for me. I had a wife and kids, nobody else did; Mick had been the best man at my wedding. So he protected me."

By now, Scott Richardson had been recruited by Bowie as a general rock-and-roll companion and sounding board; he accom-panied him to gigs, helped him choose songs for his covers album, and had been delegated to assist with Ronson's solo album. Richardson was one of a couple of people who were aware that, like Bowie, Roxy Music's Bryan Ferry was planning a covers album; if the knowledge hadn't inspired Bowie's own covers col-lection, it certainly put a rocket under the project. Ferry was a rival, and he'd also had the audacity to criticize Bowie in print the previous winter, pointing out how he liked to "push all [his] band back—like props in their little boxes."

The sessions at Château d'Hérouville, a glorious, slightly tatty, compact castle just outside Paris where Marc Bolan had recorded *The Slider,* were cheerful on the surface, with long lunches in the sun, but they were overshadowed by future portents, each participant conscious this was the end of an era. "It didn't feel comfortable to me," says Ken Scott. "I had other things on my mind; my wife was pregnant, and I wanted to fly back to England. My mind was elsewhere, and there were legal problems, because my royalties weren't getting paid. And that seemed to be the general thing."

The awareness that an entire era was coming to a close imbued the album with a kind of desperate nostalgia. David, Ronson, and Richardson simply picked out a bunch of 45s—the Pretty Things' "Rosalyn," the Kinks' "Where Have All the Good Times Gone," Syd and the Floyd's "See Emily Play"—and played a couple of the records to the band each morning. They learned each song in the same key, then bashed it out. David was more obviously disengaged from Angie, at ease in the studio, enjoying the carefree atmosphere of simply playing other people's songs, happy to let Mick Ronson bear most of the musical burden while he honked away on his schoolboy saxophone—but he rushed, as always, eager to lay down his vocals as quickly as possible. Ava Cherry was in Paris on a modeling job, and after she tracked David down at the Château d'Hérouville, they spent cozy afternoons together cuddled in front of the huge baroque fireplaces. David was calm but distracted, and Ava realized how he deferred his decisions to Tony Defries, relying on him—almost like a child. For her to become anything more than a temporary fixture in David's life, Tony had to give his approval. He was the gatekeeper to David's personal life, like a father or a priest, and had to be honored—and her ritual offerings took the form of demos, which David recorded with Ava in the studio.

Over those weeks, Ava also observed Bowie and Ronson's relationship up close: "Mick seemed very distraught—there was some scuttle about him doing a solo album and David wasn't totally happy about it." Mick was both a friend who David supported and a rival; just as he felt about Bolan, David wanted him to succeed but was scared of being overshadowed. Mick himself was excited by the challenge of a solo album—a "happy camper," says Ken Scott—but according to Scott Richardson, although he knew things had to change, Ronson was in mourning for his band and buried himself in work. "Really, he worked all the time," says Richardson. "Looking back on it now and listening back to it, Ronson was the force to be reckoned with musically and I think he was completely at sea about his future because that band had a real integrity. And they were gone." Bolder was later told that David had done the covers album *Pin Ups* only "to keep the band happy." Considering that Ronson knew he was leaving, that Trevor had been sacked and then recalled, and that Woody was gone, happy they weren't. "It wasn't fun," says Bolder. "It was all right. We did it, it was fun playing the songs. And Aynsley Dunbar's a great drummer, but he wasn't a Woody Woodmansey."

Throughout the *Pin Ups* sessions, David was simultaneously busy—dragging on a cigarette and drinking his usual incessant coffees while spinning plans for a new musical, *Tragic Moments*—and bored, sitting apart from the band and reading the paper while they chatted among themselves. For all the poignancy of this event, the musicians had a blast rambling around the château and catching cabs into Paris to "raid the chicks at the Crazy Horse Saloon," says Richardson. "It was great. It didn't feel like the ship was sinking from my perspective, but it obviously was."

IF, for David and Defries, *Pin Ups* derived from a simple need to deliver more product, the album nonetheless sealed Bowie's status as a phenomenon rivaled only by the Beatles or Elvis. It entered the UK charts at number 1, with its Bowie predecessors sitting nearby at 13, 19, and 26, and its standout track, "Sorrow," shipped 147,000 copies before the album's release. Although today it sounds obviously mannered, Bowie's voice a self-parody, *Pin Ups'* humor and carefree charm emphasized David's humanity, its simple odes to mod good times a welcome contrast to the intensity of *Aladdin Sane*. For all that, contemporary critics like *Rolling Stone's* Greg Shaw were quick to point out its weaknesses; Shaw cited its lack of edge and Bowie's overcooked voice and concluded: "Even in 1965, any of a thousand bands could have done better." At a time of general nostalgia, with TV-advertised 1950s and '60s compilation albums hogging the charts, *Pin Ups* was an uncharacteristically predictable move, and industry friend John Peel commented, "I'll be glad when Bryan Ferry and David Bowie get this oldies business out of their normally diverting systems."

In Bowie's string of successes that summer, there was one minor setback. After abandoning his plan for the musical *Tragic Moments*—for which he'd recorded a fifteen-minute segment at the château—David switched subjects to George Orwell's *1984*, working briefly on a script with *Pork* director Tony Ingrassia. Unfortunately, Orwell's widow, Sonia, was no rock-and-roll devotee, and when MainMan approached her for the rights to a show based on Orwell's novel, she refused, describing the notion as "bizarre." Bowie was forced to fashion his idea into a more amorphous concept. He and Defries discussed the possibility of making it into a TV show in the hope of finally achieving a mass-market breakthrough in America, and David decided to feature a couple of the songs destined for the musical in "The 1980 Floor Show," an episode of the NBC series *Midnight Special* that was to be recorded in October at his old London haunt the Marquee Club.

MOST of David's previous projects had benefited from the adrenaline rush of improvisation; it seemed natural to assume "The 1980 Floor Show" would do the same. Freddie Buretti crafted the costumes, and Bowie formed a vocal backup trio, the Astronettes, with Ava, Geoff MacCormack, and Jason Guess, whom Bowie knew through a friend who owned a soul-food restaurant. Mark Pritchett, who'd worked on the sessions that gave birth to both *Hunky Dory* and *Ziggy*, came in to augment Ronson on guitar. The new material, notably "1984/Dodo," was dense and intriguing, but the show itself was a mess—the sets looked cheesy, and the camerawork was uninspired. Even the fans who'd been invited in to make up the audience were mostly underwhelmed. "It was really disappointing," remembers writer David Thompson, "with him doing the same three songs forty times." For the musicians, the main highlight was the sight of Marianne Faithfull's backside, clearly visible in a perverted nun's costume. It was certainly more pleasing than her singing, a rather Teutonic version of Sonny and Cher's "I've Got You, Babe," during which singing partner—and, it seemed, lover—Bowie winced at her frequent bum notes. Ava Cherry remembers Defries being convinced that the production "was going to give us the juice to go into America and really be big." If he thought that, he was wrong. The show was broadcast by NBC on November 16, with its more intriguing snippets excised—Bowie's costume was declared too provocative, as was the word *suicide* in "Rock 'n' Roll Suicide"—and after its initial broadcast, the show was sent to languish in the archives, seemingly for eternity.

THE half-cocked management of "The 1980 Floor Show" was typical of MainMan's increasing disorganization. The main breadwinner, Bowie, had not as yet generated consistent profits across America, and the European market had, for some reason, been completely overlooked. Iggy had been sacked, and Mott, Lou, and Annette Peacock had fled, but the MainMan roster continued to grow amoebically, without any logic. Wayne County, later to become the celebrated punk musician Jayne County, was one of many artists who saw their projects—in her case, the *At the Trucks* film and sound track—abandoned or confined to the vaults. "To this day I hate the man," she says of Defries. "Damn his eyes, damn his soul." Simon Turner—later a cult musician who recorded for the UK's Creation and Mute labels—was another signing lost in the chaos, and guitarist Mark Pritchett remembers going to Sarm Studios in the East End to make a complete album with "some exotic South American bird, she was good" that would prove another expensive, unrealized MainMan project.

Defries always had a strangely contradictory attitude toward money: he was unconcerned about spending large sums on ambitious projects yet was penny-pinching with smaller amounts. In those autumn months, there was unrelenting office gossip about

Defries's investments in the precious-metals market to take advantage of the abolition of controls on the price of gold. According to the MainMan secretaries, Defries was speculating with MainMan's—and David's—income, although at the time the stories seemed merely to illustrate his Midas-like skills of generating even more profits. In November, Defries grandly declared that MainMan was an "international entertainment conglomerate" and put into execution his long-treasured scheme of moving his base of operations to America; before the year's end, in addition to his original Manhattan apartment, he had a loft on the Lower West Side, a penthouse on the Upper East Side, several apartments for MainMan artists, and, his pièce de résistance, a Main-Man compound of buildings in Greenwich, Connecticut. The vacuum of power this left in London, the location of MainMan's primary moneymaker, was initially filled by Hugh Attwooll, who, although he had no experience whatsoever, was hired as an agent and was then promoted to "something between office boy, chief executive, and money juggler." Most of the income came from RCA advances, publishing, and PRS royalties, all of which was generated by David and then went into "a big tub," says Attwooll. "Or, rather a small tub, actually. That was the problem." Attwooll is one of several MainMan executives who believe Tony Defries generally gets "bad press, which I'm not certain he deserves," but over the course of 1973 it became obvious that "the whole thing was completely nuts."

In the meantime, MainMan's only proven source of income, David Bowie, had his eyes on America, a destination that would shape his next musical move, says his accompanist Mark Pritchett: "He knew it was a multicultural place—black, Hispanic as much as white. And he wanted that Nile Rodgers, funky type of thing." This American vibe would inspire David's last session at Trident, on "1984/Dodo"; it was also his last session with both Ken Scott and Mick Ronson. "Within the first couple of takes, it became fundamentally clear that *all* of us—but Mick was the lead musician—weren't black funky," says Pritchett. "This was not it."

Given time, Ronson and Pritchett might possibly have mastered the stripped-down funk that David envisioned. But as far back as "Space Oddity," David had become used to having his ideas put on tape instantaneously. "David wants it *now*," says Pritchett. "He's not exactly first-take Dave, but it's 'Can't you hear what I hear?' and if it's take number four he gets frustrated: 'I'll get someone who *can* then.'"

Those Trident sessions marked the end of Mick Ronson's partnership with Bowie; Mark Pritchett, who'd worked with David since Arts Lab days, would be replaced later that year. Pritchett's departure was hardly noticed, although the events surrounding Mick's would be pored over for years by fans who knew that Ronson had been a key architect of *Ziggy Stardust*'s success. But such departures, says Pritchett—who would later be given parting gifts that included David's Jag and the Hagstrom twelve-string David had used since signing with Ken Pitt—are simply the price of progress: "Any musician that had any kind of contact with David that he enjoyed, I dare you to name one who would say that when the parting came they were any way discarded like a spent toy. Not me. And not Mick."

Mick's own feelings were mixed; he was nervous about occupying the spotlight, but his ego had been stoked by the MainMan machine. The company finally launched Mick's solo career over the subsequent months, complete with a promotional film to publicize his album, which was recorded at the Château d'Hérouville directly after *Pin Ups* with Trevor Bolder, Aynsley Dunbar, Pritchett, Scott Richardson, and others. Pritchett's last project with David was the sessions that David booked that autumn, when he used Olympic Studios in Barnes—best known for its Rolling Stones connection—almost as a demo studio.

This would be a creative period for David, although his activity was not confined to music, for Ava Cherry remembers him "staying up for forty-eight hours learning how to work a video machine, or reading fifty books at a time about one subject, stacking them up and reading them for days." The Astronettes were just one of his musical projects, inspiring new songs that included "I Am a Laser" and "I Am Divine"—later reworked as "Scream Like a

Baby" and "Somebody Up There Likes Me." Those sessions were later abandoned, for Jason Guess's bland, wavery vocals were hopelessly inadequate, but they served their purpose as David was "working out how to do a soul thing," says Cherry. They would become part of a host of sessions conducted at Olympic, as David developed new working methods. "You'd get a call, turn up, it might be just you and a drummer, it might just be you laying down something on your own, David would say, 'These are the chords, can you give it a funky feel?' He may use your part, he may decide he doesn't like it, or he might use the idea as part of something else," says Mark Pritchett.

This cut-and-paste approach — rather than the organized, succinct sessions overseen by Mick Ronson — would become a hallmark of David's post-Spiders style. He adopted a similar approach to writing lyrics, inspired by William Burroughs, whom he met on November 17 for a *Rolling Stone* feature. Writer Craig Copetas bought him all of Burroughs's books — none of which he'd properly read, despite his later claims that he'd discovered the writer "as a teenager" — and David instantly adapted Burroughs's cut-up technique to songs like "Sweet Thing/Candidate," writing a paragraph of text, cutting it up into four- and five-word sections, and then shuffling them.

Celebrity encounters that are arranged for magazines are notoriously unenlightening, but the *Rolling Stone* piece provided a perfect portrait of Bowie at his apogee in London. Copetas noted the contrast between the humble minimalism of Burroughs's Piccadilly flat and Bowie's materialism, recording the extravagance of Bowie's new rock-star house and his coterie of attendants who dispensed avocados stuffed with shrimp and Beaujolais nouveau. The contrast in their intellectual approach was stark too, with Burroughs's outlook formed by books — he was surprised to hear that Bowie had never read T. S. Eliot — and Bowie's from people, like Lindsay Kemp, Chime Rinpoche, and the cast of *Pork*. Nonetheless, there was an obvious rapport, Bowie hopping from Andy Warhol to Joe Cuba and listening intently as Burroughs rapped on orgone accumulators and infrasound.

Although David camped it up impressively for Burroughs, discoursing on tribalism and the sex life of kids, in his vitality and enthusiasm he was still recognizably the same teenager who'd talked about poetry and art when making his unsuccessful debut album. And he exhibited exactly the the same competitiveness, allying himself subtly with Mick Jagger, delighting in deconstructing him as "a white boy from Dagenham trying his damnedest to be ethnic."

Marking their ascent from being a curiosity, David and Angie had left Haddon Hall in the summer, moved briefly to Maida Vale, and then installed themselves in the customary rock-star hangout of Chelsea, at 89 Oakley Street, not far from Jagger's Cheyne Walk home. Freddie Buretti and Daniella Parmar occupied the basement of the four-story, flat-fronted, 1850s house; after a month at Oakley Street—which was long enough for her to outstay Angie's welcome—Ava Cherry moved into Daska House, an apartment building a hundred yards up the Kings Road. Various Beckenham artists reworked the house to be a model of rock-star chic: stairs painted alternately matte and glossy black, a hallway lit by car headlights, a sunken double bed. There were airbrushed murals in most of the rooms—a sunrise, based on the Sun-Pat peanut butter logo, for David; a tropical beach scene for Zowie's room, which was on the top floor, next to the office. The living room was in white shag, dominated by one of George Underwood's paintings and a larger Dalí-style work. The sunken central area was scattered with throw pillows and contained a spherical TV, a state-of-the-art video machine, and Polaroids of "exotic activities," remembers airbrush artist Mick Gillah.

Toward the end of 1973, this sleek, busy household seemed an epitome of domestic bliss, a glossier version of the Haddon Hall ethos. David was once more excited by his work, occasionally treating visitors to sights of lyrics he'd cut and pasted together from his more bizarre fan letters. Generally busy with her own projects or shopping trips, Angie still operated as a domestic goddess, treating guests to impeccably turned-out soufflés and quiches. Zowie was now an outgoing two-year-old; dressed in brightly colored dungarees, with long blond hair, he scampered around the house singing songs he made up. Only Granny was missing from this idyllic scene—although visitors to her flat on Albemarle Street remember Peggy was devoted to Zowie, she was seldom, if ever, seen at Oakley Street and never featured in David's conversation. Tony Defries was David's father figure.

Defries's absence in America was the only disquieting element in David's domestic life. Musicians, producers, girlfriends could be discarded; Defries's inspirational visions, his insights, were irreplaceable. "It could be anything: business, what people to see, girlfriends, Tony would orchestrate it all," says Ava Cherry.

At the summit of his career, released from the live-show treadmill, at last ranked alongside his teenage idols, for David the close of 1973 should have been a time to savor his success and freedom. Finally, he was given time to relax; fatefully, he was also given time to doubt. And once he'd opened himself up to them, those doubts intensified remarkably quickly. The impact on the psyche of a man who saw himself almost as Defries's son was predictable: "Devastation is the word," says Cherry, his closest companion. "They were great days, till Tony messed David's head up— really messed him up."

CHAPTER 12

The Changing Isn't Free

[Cocaine is] a cruel drug. It makes people behave like complete bastards.

—Keith Christmas

A S 1973 DREW TO A CLOSE, David Bowie in London and Tony Defries in New York both basked in their achievements. They had finally beaten the system. But neither of them could wait to join it.

Defries, the man who had derided old-school, bloated record-company management, was building an overstaffed empire that mirrored the system he despised. And David, who had constructed a manifesto that positioned him as a new species of human, couldn't wait to become chums with the previous generation of rock stars. Each of them spotted the contradictions in the other's position, but not in his own. "They were a really solid team up to that point," says Tony Zanetta, who respected—worshipped, even—both men. "But once everything stopped and they could enjoy the fruits of success, the cracks started to appear."

Those cracks would fail to damage Defries's serene sense of self-worth; David Bowie, however, could hardly bear to contemplate them, burying his worries so deep that the inevitable crisis would be utterly devastating.

In the meantime, David cast around for role models. Iggy and Lou no longer sufficed; instead, he increased his focus on their apparent antithesis, Mick Jagger. Mick was always a rival rather than an idol. Determined to topple Jagger from his pedestal, David was also fascinated by him to the point of obsession. He and Ava enjoyed several dinners with Mick and Bianca, chatting volubly, with Mick and David even noodling on a tune together one night that became the Astronettes song "Having a Good Time." But neither one could quite discard his elegant, sophisticated persona: "It was polite, intellectual—but there was a line they didn't cross," says Cherry. In later years, Angie Bowie described how she'd caught Bowie and Mick in bed; the suggestion perhaps helped sell her book but is ludicrous to anyone who saw the two together. Each man was guarded, and even twenty years later, each would be almost excessively conscious of his relative standing—the notion that one would be completely open with the other, let alone be "a bottom," was unthinkable. To Ava, the two personalities seemed similar—bright, competitive, with the same dry humor—but in reality they were very different. David was always in the grip of some obsession or enthusiasm. Not Mick. "He was never under the spell of anything," says Maggie Abbott, later the movie agent for both Mick and David. "He was always totally under control. He was a typical Leo, much more disciplined than David. He would never be taken in by anything."

Although David acted otherwise, he was intimidated by his rival, who was an old hand at managing pretenders to his throne. Jagger had led the way for so many of David's obsessions, from recruiting the coolest African American girlfriends, like Marsha Hunt, to writing lyrics in a Burroughsian cut-up style, as Mick had done for *Exile on Main Street* back in 1971. Yet at a Rolling Stones show in Newcastle that spring, it finally dawned on Bowie that he was in a position to top the Stones singer. Standing in the wings, he was telling confidant Scott Richardson about the time he'd offered to carry Brian Jones's guitar and been told to piss off. Suddenly, the pair noticed that Jagger was glaring at them from center stage. Glancing behind, they realized hundreds of fans were ignoring the band, craning their necks to see the carrot-haired presence at the side of the stage.

David and Scott accompanied Jagger and Bianca to a casino that evening, where Scott noticed that Jagger was fascinated by his rival. Thereafter Jagger would stay in regular touch, keeping tabs on David, who relished the accolade—but also found his competitive instincts reawakened. Until then, he had measured himself against Marc Bolan, who had never made an impact in the States and whose appeal in Britain would wane that autumn, prompting Marc's final split with Tony Visconti. Jagger would be an altogether more challenging friend and rival.

As was his habit, David approached the task of measuring up to Jagger by moving directly onto his turf, liberally appropriating from him. This helped inspire his choice of Olympic as his working studio, and Keith Harwood as his engineer, who was at that time the Stones' favorite. While the lyrical core of David's next album would be a reworking of his *1984* concept, its chaotic, dystopian edge intensified by his use of Burroughs's cut-up technique, the musical blueprint was unashamedly based on the work of the Rolling Stones.

The core of the album was completed within a few frenzied days at Olympic, according to bassist Herbie Flowers and guitarist Alan Parker, seasoned session men who together made up the UK soul band Blue Mink. The pair were well used to having their melodic ideas become the basis of someone else's song—for instance, they were almost totally responsible for the music on Serge Gainsbourg's superb *Melody Nelson* album but were uncredited. "That was part of what we did," says Parker, "so on high-profile sessions we would simply double the fee."

For the album that would become *Diamond Dogs*, the principal songs were well organized, with five or six background tracks laid down in roughly three or four days. Parker and Flowers both remember the development of what would become the album's best-known song, "Rebel Rebel," for David introduced it quite specifically. "I want it to sound like the Stones," he told them before showing them the song, borrowing Parker's black Les Paul to play it. Bowie's riff was up-tempo, Stonesy, but it needed honing; Parker picked the main notes out clearly, adding a particular chord shape rather than the original single note just before the chord change and a distinctive "beeeoonng" in the last line of the chorus just as David sings "I love you so."

"David played the riff to Alan, Alan made sure it was good enough to record, and then [Alan] played it," says Herbie Flowers, who remembers the electric guitar, bass, and drums laying down the background track simultaneously—which accounted for the loose feel, the song speeding up as Aynsley Dunbar launches into his stomping, on-beat drum pattern that consciously evokes the Stones' "Satisfaction."

A gloriously simple song that marked his farewell to the Ziggy era, "Rebel Rebel" would become one of Bowie's best-known singles. But Parker was shocked when he saw later that Bowie was credited in the album notes with playing the guitar on the finished version. It would be nigh impossible for even the most skilled guitarist to replace Parker's work because of the changing tempo and the sonic spill between the studio microphones. "I can tell my own playing, and my own sound," says Parker, "and I know it's me."

David's ambitions as guitarist seemed partly calculated to show Mick Ronson—whose solo career was flourishing, briefly—how well David could manage without him. "It's silly... I don't know why it would matter so much," says Parker, who'd chatted with both Ronson and Bowie at previous sessions. Such pettiness was all the more pointless considering the superb job David did of playing guitar on the remaining songs, notably the title track—which, with its cowbell and loose backup vocals, echoed "Honky Tonk Women"—and the jagged, new wave–ish guitar on "Candidate."

The pettiness, though, was easily explained, for in the closing months of 1973, David's world was falling in on him. At the beginning of the sessions, he was relatively optimistic, fired up by the challenge of learning the electric guitar, and enjoying the camaraderie of the studio; he dropped in on Mott guitarist Mick Ralph's new band, Bad Company, who were mixing at Olympic. But that camaraderie was splintered when Bowie was barred from the studio after an argument; by the end of the sessions, there was precious little goodwill remaining.

David's musical isolation, his dependence on session men—yes-men, really—had its upside, bringing a new intensity to his work. Yet outside the studio, his isolation was corrosive, worsened by the growing chaos and backbiting within MainMan. After Tony Defries's departure for New York, MainMan's cash-flow problems took a dramatic turn for the worse. One of the company's recent recruits, Corinne Schwab, did a heroic job of controlling the company's UK finances, but even she failed to talk the Château d'Hérouville out of banning all MainMan's acts in a dispute over unpaid bills. In January of 1974, Olympic followed suit. Meanwhile, tales filtered back of the profligacy of MainMan New York, where staff members had their own credit cards and limos on call. "One by one, people were telling us what was happening," says Ava Cherry. "Eventually the truth of the matter was the company was spending money like water, while David couldn't get any ready cash."

As the suspicion that Tony Defries, the father figure who controlled so much of his life, was presiding over a financial meltdown grew, David found the perfect psychological crutch, one that had contributed to the air of glamour and decadence that surrounded the Rolling Stones: cocaine.

It's fitting that this drug would reach its height as the last vestiges of the "we" decade were destroyed and the "me" decade took over. Considered at the time a safe, nonaddictive substance—"We thought it helped us be smarter and more creative," says MainMan's Tony Zanetta—cocaine would ravage the psyche of a generation of musicians. New Stones guitarist Ron Wood and Iggy were just two of its victims—Iggy would later be sent to a mental institution as a result of the drug. Guitarist Keith Christmas, who'd been part of the optimistic, cooperative Beckenham scene, saw the drug's effects on David and many others, and shudders as he recalls them. "It's a cruel drug. It makes people behave like complete bastards. Because it takes away a lot of the fearful emotional need we have not to upset other people—it allows you to feel you can upset whoever the fuck you please. I found sometimes at a party, people would be having a good time, then someone would mention coke and the whole party would change completely. 'Get some coke in, get some lines in' would be all people could talk about. The compulsive quality of it is horrifying."

Although a compulsive consumer of coffee and cigarettes, David had been almost virtuous in his avoidance of other drugs. "It was so peculiar," says Tony Zanetta, "he didn't smoke pot, he'd simply drink a couple of glasses of white wine. It was so fast—cocaine was definitely something he incorporated into what a rock star should be."

Ava Cherry remembers David's "occasional toot" overlapping with his first attacks of panic and the apparent financial crisis. "He was in a dark place, he would be crying, saying these people have taken all my money. And at the first stage [cocaine] would be a crutch: 'It calms me down.'" Angie too dates David's obsession with cocaine from these weeks: "It's what they did to him, my boy," she laments in a rare outbreak of sympathy, blaming the drug also for the breakdown of their marriage.

David's mental state would have an obvious effect on his music. Although some of *Diamond Dogs*' songs were languid and melodic—"Sweet Thing," "Candidate"—there was an obsessive quality about the recording, with jagged guitars and saxophones layered ominously on each other. The lyrical imagery too was dark—its stories of the Diamond Dogs drawn from Haywood Jones's stories of Dickensian London, when orphan kids crowded the rooftops of the London rookeries. The resulting intensity was a distinct sonic and spiritual departure from the optimism of David's three albums with the Spiders. This new territory was fertile and marked a progression in David's work, but there was a sacrifice too; in the obsessive regard to sound, texture, an almost physical heaviness, the deftness of *Hunky Dory* and *Ziggy Stardust*—with their swooping melodies and restlessly mobile chord sequences—had gone.

The break with the past was crystallized when Trevor Bolder, who'd been working with Mick Ronson on the guitarist's solo album and tour, answered the phone late one night.

"Oi, Trev!" his ex-singer greeted him. "What are you doing?"

"I'm doing nowt"—nothing—Bolder responded.

"Do you want to come and play on a song?"

Bolder agreed and turned up at Barnes to find Bowie, Mike Garson, and drummer Tony Newman working on a slow acoustic number. It was an uncomfortable experience, sitting in the studio with Bowie but no Spiders. The quartet went through the song several times before running tape. "But it was a nothing song," says Bolder, "and it obviously got dumped later."

The take complete, Bolder packed away his bass guitar while Bowie sat with his back to him.

"I'm off now, Dave, I'll see you later on," said Bolder.

Bowie didn't say a word. Bolder repeated himself.

"I'm going, then. See you! Bye."

Again, Bowie ignored him. The ex-Spider walked out of the studio in silence, taking a last look at Bowie's back, silhouetted against the control-room window. It was the last time they would share a studio.

During the same period, Wayne Bardell bumped into Bowie in Tramps Nightclub. Overjoyed to see his friend, whom he'd last talked to during the first *Ziggy* tour, he walked up to him.

"Hi, how are you?"

"Hi. Who are you?" was David's response.

"That hurt," says Bardell, who had sat in on the recording of "I Pity the Fool" and seen David regularly over the past nine years. "I was taking cocaine too...but it didn't stop me *knowing* people. This was cold. Calculated."

The freezing out of those who'd known him from his days as a struggling musician was conventional behavior for the 1970s— Marc Bolan exhibited a nastier version of the trait, again bolstered by cocaine use. David wasn't nasty; he would simply cut people off coldly. With those he still needed, he was considerate and thoughtful; after hearing from Tony Visconti that the home studio he was building was short of furniture, he sent around a Conran Shop van packed with office chairs, a dining suite, and crockery—later they'd mix the bulk of the *Diamond Dogs* tracks there.

There had always been a childlike element to David's persona— that clear-eyed earnestness was an intrinsic part of his charm. Yet that childishness was not so charming once it was distorted by the flattery of minor MainMan staff, the constant attentions of cooks and maids, and the other corrosive effects of celebrity. As Ava Cherry remembers, "Children think the whole world revolves round them. And that's the way David was encouraged to think, by everyone." Certain friends would learn to manage David's moods; notably Ron Wood, whom David knew from his Marquee days. David renewed his friendship with the guitarist once the *Diamond Dogs* sessions moved to Hilversum, where the Stones were also working. The two bonded over a mutual love of Peter Cook and Dudley Moore, memorizing and replicating their dialogues: "Ronny was very good at making you feel that you were having fun," says Ava Cherry, "and I always felt good when Ronny was coming over. Because David wasn't angry then—he'd always be laughing."

David built up a deeper, more enduring relationship over that same period. Corinne "Coco" Schwab had been hired by Hugh Attwooll in the summer of 1973. MainMan's UK office manager thought her well educated, intelligent, and capable. He soon discovered she was "smarter than me, that's for sure. I hired her and within a month I was gone—and she had my job." By the autumn of 1973, Corinne was the only person keeping the MainMan UK office afloat, for by then the financial situation was "intolerable," says Tony Zanetta; "She was abandoned in the English office, Defries refused to pay almost any bills, David was spending wildly. She certainly earned her position."

Defries liked Coco's old-school efficiency, her command of languages, and her cosmopolitan background—born, she told her friends, during her mother's shopping trip to Bloomingdale's in New York, she had been educated in America, Europe, and Kashmir. Defries initially encouraged her rise in order to diminish Angie's influence. By the autumn of 1973, Coco had become

David's personal assistant (a job Suzi Fussey turned down, eventually marrying Mick Ronson) and was installed in the top floor of Oakley Street, where she controlled access to David. Corinne would become a central character in David's life; intelligent, slim, witty, she seemed in some respects almost anonymous. This was part of her charm and her effectiveness. She was happy to devote herself utterly to David and seemed to have no agenda of her own to impose on him. Many years later David would sing of "your soothing hand that turned me round" in his song devoted to Coco, "Never Let Me Down"; the song's words speak of her as a lover, but in reality her role was more complex, like a combination mother, sister, manager, lover, and—most crucial—all-purpose intellectual confidante, rather like the paid companions once hired by refined ladies of a certain age. "David liked her because she was intellectual and they could have good conversations," says Ava Cherry, who also points out that Corinne "was in love with [David] from day one." David savored Corinne's utter devotion to his cause and would occasionally taunt Ava with the fact that he and Coco had quickly become lovers. In February, Ava was sent over to New York, ostensibly to link up with Tony Defries and prepare David's move to the city, but Cherry soon concluded that Schwab "systematically did nothing but try and get me out."

In Ava's absence, David turned to another exotic creature: Amanda Lear. The onetime muse of Bryan Ferry and acquaintance of Salvador Dalí, Lear helped celebrate David's twenty-seventh birthday by taking him to see Fritz Lang's 1927 masterpiece *Metropolis*. In the weeks before he left for America, David immersed himself in Lang's work, which, along with the staging he'd first planned for the band Arnold Corns, formed the basis of the imagery for his next American tour. From 1971 on, he'd dreamed of presenting his shows as a three-dimensional spectacle. Now he planned a new, grandiose vision, without any compromises.

DAVID arrived in New York on April 11, 1974, sailing the Atlantic with Geoff MacCormack on the SS *France*. The journey was laden with symbolism, both positive and negative; David intended to base himself in America, a country he'd long dreamed about, to soak up its vibe and conquer it. And he needed to sort out his problems, in the form of Tony Defries.

As far as soaking up the vibe, the move to New York was perfect. After moving into the Sherry-Netherland Hotel in Central Park, Bowie used Ava Cherry as his guide to the soul scene. Ava suggested they check out Harlem's Apollo Theater, where it turned out there was a show on April 26 headlined by Richard Pryor and featuring the Main Ingredient; one of RCA's few cool bands, the Harlem outfit had changed its lineup in 1972, recruiting new singer Cuba Gooding Sr. and scoring a huge soul smash with "Everybody Plays the Fool." The Apollo's audience was overwhelmingly black; the red-haired, pasty-faced Bowie stuck out like a white cat in a coal scuttle. "He loved it," says Ava. "He soaked all of it up."

There was another joyful source of Americana to be explored in 1974, in the charismatic form of Norman Fisher, a stockbroker turned art collector who was famous for the lavish parties he threw in his tiny downtown apartment. David remembers them as "the most diverse soirees in the whole of New York. People from every sector of the so and not so avant-garde would flock there—Norman was a magnet." Fisher turned David on to the most gloriously eclectic art and music: Florence Jenkins, the famously inept opera singer who attracted huge audiences in the 1920s, drawn by her ludicrous costumes and atonal performances, was a typical example. As well as providing good company, Norman also supplied cocaine for his social circle. "[But] he did not want to," says Ava. "Norman just wanted to be friends and hang with people."

Fisher remained a close friend of David's for years and epitomized the glamour of New York. But in his role as David's supplier, he unwittingly contributed to a profound transformation. "I saw David at the NBC special [in October of 1973] and didn't see any cocaine problem," says Tony Zanetta. "Then in April 1974, there it was: full-blown."

David's obviously transformed state would be yet another factor in the breakdown of his relationship with Tony Defries. David

thought that moving closer to Defries would invigorate their relationship; instead, they became more estranged. *Diamond Dogs*
gathered mixed reviews on its release in April of 1974 but was
David's best-performing album in the United States to date, peaking at number 5. Defries, however, preferred more showbizzy concepts, like *Ziggy Stardust,* and concise songs. Furthermore, he
disapproved of David's nascent plans for his next grandiose tour.

This was typical inconsistency from a man overseeing a company that now employed twenty-five full-time staff and had its
own travel agency, plus a TV, radio, and movie production company. It was all the more galling to David, considering how
Defries—who by then was a "megalomaniac," according to his
lieutenant Tony Zanetta—loved to boast of his largesse, such as
his scheme to fulfill each of his staff members' "ultimate fantasy."
(Lee Childers had his teeth done; Cherry Vanilla's bonus was
spent on a boob job.)

As ever, Defries's generosity did not stretch to David's musicians. In his first weeks in New York, David had arranged a
recording session with Lulu, calling in Main Ingredient founder
Tony Silvester to help. Silvester suggested his new guitarist Carlos
Alomar. Onetime member of the Apollo house band and a session
regular for everyone from Peter, Paul, and Mary to Roy Ayers, Carlos Alomar turned up at RCA studios and was struck by Bowie's
red hair and "mousy skin. It was so translucent. And the black
under his eyes was somewhat alarming." After the session Alomar invited David over to his house in Queens for a decent
meal—and was impressed when the singer actually turned up,
spending the evening talking about soul records and quizzing
Alomar on his work with Chuck Berry and James Brown: "He's
always surprised me like that—he's willing to go right in."

That evening David asked Carlos to join him for his forthcoming tour, and, thrilled at the prospect of leaving behind "the chitlin mentality"—represented by notoriously cheapskate employers
like James Brown and Chuck Berry—Carlos found himself a
white manager to negotiate the deal. Only then did Carlos discover that MainMan was offering just half of the eight hundred

dollars he was getting from the Main Ingredient. Regretfully, he returned to his session work and left David to find some cheaper musicians.

In his quest for a new band, David phoned Keith Christmas, who'd played acoustic guitar back on the *Space Oddity* album. A virtuoso musician with a distinctly English folk style, Christmas was out of place in Bowie's new surroundings. Arriving in New York he found David surrounded by "a bunch of pretentious fucking posers, so full of themselves with their dyed white hair and shaven heads. There was something distinctly sleazy and unpleasant about it."

The audition itself was a nonevent—Christmas was an acoustic guitarist, and his playing on the electric was barely competent—but the surroundings were bizarre, the cavernous RCA studios on the Avenue of the Americas empty but for Bowie, Christmas, and an engineer rolling tape. Whenever David wanted "a toot" he would beckon Christmas down the corridor to huddle furtively in the toilets: "So this is all strangely paranoid. I'll never forget he had this double-sided razor blade with which he's chopping out lines. When he stuck his finger on a little bindle of coke and held it up to my nose I saw how much his hand was shaking, and the meaning was, I want this stuff so much, I will risk severe personal injury for it."

The experience was disturbing. Yet, behind the paranoid, scary facade, Christmas believes, this was exactly the same person he'd known in 1969: "David actually seemed like he was completely in his element. It was a continuation of the Arts Lab days in terms of who he was as a person; the people had changed, the drugs might have changed. But the actual person might not have changed at all." In Beckenham, David had asked Christmas to embrace his hippie trip, just as he asked Bob Grace to join the sexually ambivalent Sombrero scene. The furtive ritual of sniffing cocaine in a toilet was a new trip for a new persona, but it was not a persona he would lay aside so easily.

WITHIN the first few days of arriving in New York, David contacted Michael Kamen—an old friend of Ossie Clark, another talented, transplanted Brit with a hefty coke habit with whom David hung out. Kamen ran a rock-and-roll band with sax player David Sanborn and recently recruited guitarist Earl Slick but was also a formidable classically trained musician. Kamen had written the music for a ballet based on the life of Auguste Rodin; Bowie and MacCormack attended the New York premiere and were transfixed. Kamen's cross-cultural connections echoed David's own ideas on dance and staging, and the composer was engaged as musical director.

The grandiose staging for David's new show, novel as it seemed, was in fact based on ideas he'd toyed with since May of 1971. When constructing fantasies of how to present Arnold Corns, he'd imagined the band playing in an open-sided boxing ring, surrounded by huge pillars, each of which supported a single white spot: "Remorseless, it has to be," he told a bemused Freddie Buretti. "I don't want any colors, I want it all stark." Later, his ideas for Rainbow shows were restricted by budget and time; now he raided MainMan's fast-dwindling coffers to realize his fantasies. A huge stage backdrop represented Hunger City, a decaying future metropolis, with thirty-foot-high skyscrapers augmented by a motorized bridge, a remote-control mirrored module, and a cherry picker in which David would descend from the heavens. For "Rebel Rebel," Bowie would perform in the boxing ring with oversize leather boxing gloves; even the mask he used harked back to the mime he'd filmed for Ken Pitt.

For many fans, the remodeling of David was far more dramatic than the new, mechanized backdrop. He had arrived in New York with his spiky carrottop essentially intact; now it was consigned to history in favor of a 1940s-style do with a part and floppy bangs, while the Yamamoto outfits were ditched for a double-breasted suit with high-waisted trousers, a skinny sweater, and suspenders. The style was obviously influenced by 1940s Harlem as well as by Sinatra, another hero. Yet in essence David's consciously "cool" image came from closer to home, namely, from Roxy Music's Bryan Ferry, whose stage movements he studied closely. David practiced Bryan's gestures, including a distinctive movement that the Roxy singer made with his index finger; David incorporated the wiggle into his own repertoire of stage mannerisms.

When the tour opened in Canada on June 14—less than a year after Bowie's "retirement"—the sight of goggle-eyed Ziggy clones aghast at David's new earthly manifestation and overwhelmed by the visual smorgasbord—which included loose "street" dancing, choreographed by Toni Basil—was a vindication of the weeks of preparation. Yet there was chaos with the equipment, which meant David was in constant danger of electrocution. The set blended conservatism—an emphasis on the hits, and some self-consciously bombastic arrangements—with subtlety and risk; "Jean Genie" was turned into an urban rap, like Lou's "Walk on the Wild Side," while the Ohio Players' "Here Today and Gone Tomorrow," presented at later shows, was delivered straight, showcasing the soul pipes David had been developing ever since "I Pity the Fool." Old-school session hands Herbie Flowers and Tony Newman ensured the rhythms were slick and relentless; the show "rocked real hard," as Detroiter Robert Matheu, a veteran of performances by the MC5 and the Stooges, remembered.

Yet the first run of shows, the product of such intense work and obsessiveness, would become famous as a beacon of cynicism thanks to the ill will surrounding the recording of the Philadelphia shows between July 8 and 12. Bassist Herbie Flowers was the prime mover in a threatened strike by the musicians, who arrived at the venue and noticed extra microphones; these were the first indication they'd received that MainMan intended to release an album of the night's performance without paying any extra fees. Guitarist Earl Slick recalls benefiting from Flowers's staunch performance as a shop steward in a heated dispute between MainMan and the musicians. Today, Flowers insists the argument "was blown up out of all proportion. We did ask, 'Do we get any money,' and we were told we would get the American musicians' union rate." Only a trace of disdain remains in his remark about the tour's staging: "I've always liked opera," he remarks. "But this was pantomime."

John Peel, David's old champion, was less generous in his assessment of David's prosaic cover of "Knock On Wood," which

trailed the live album in September, proclaiming it "lazy, arrogant, and impertinent." The same would apply to the *David Live*
album when it followed in October; despite many creative moments,
the performances were bombastic, sounding like the output of a
leviathan corporation rather than a singer. Still, it would be one of
David's most successful U.S. releases to date, peaking at number 8 — in the UK, it was held off the top slot by the Bay City Rollers. Many early Bowie fans, the people who'd first championed
Bowie in the press and looked for him at tiny clubs like Friars
Aylesbury, saw it as mere filler, a sign of a creative drought. Yet
within a few months, they'd be forced to rethink.

From the moment he'd seen the Main Ingredient, back in
April, David had embarked on an obsessive exploration of cutting-
edge R & B; it soon extended beyond the obligatory Aretha Franklin to boxes of soul vinyl obtained for him by LA writer Harvey
Kubernick. These included Philadelphia International singles by
Harold Melvin and the Bluenotes, Patti LaBelle, and MFSB, the
Philly soul band who recorded the theme tune to *Soul Train*. David
watched the celebrated music show every week, usually in a party
atmosphere along with fellow soul obsessives like Geoff MacCormack. Part of David's fascination with Ava Cherry was the fact
that she epitomized U.S. soul culture. As he did with so many of
his confidants, he pumped her for information, all of which fed
into his life and work. "My dad was a musician in the forties [in
Chicago] — black guys used to wear baggy pants and they called
them gousters. I told David once, 'My dad has got a couple of pairs
of ties and suits.' He was 'Really? Where? Can you bring some
over?' So I ended up bringing over a couple of my dad's silk ties
and a pair of gouster pants that had suspenders on them."

Many of David's previous stylistic swerves had taken months of
preparation; manifestos worked out at Haddon Hall, musicians
persuaded down from far-flung spots like Hull. In America, things
could move more quickly. The new lineup of musicians took a single phone call. The new look was based on a pair of pants. David
put on his gouster outfit, with silk tie and suspenders, and then
told his girlfriend, "I'm going to record a session now."

CHAPTER 13

Make Me Break Down and Cry

This was fast... When it came time to do a song we were like,
Cool, let's go! Boom, boom, boom!

—Carlos Alomar

DURING A BRIEF stopover in New York, David phoned
Carlos Alomar, the guitarist he'd met back in Queens
but had been unable to hire thanks to MainMan's stingi-
ness. "Look, Carlos," he told him, "I'm going to be coming to Philadelphia, to Sigma Sound." He employed the persuasiveness
honed over years of working with musicians: "I know you've just
finished working there and I really want you to come down." The
guitarist appreciated David's charm but needed little persuasion
to leave the chitlin circuit—once he'd established David would
match his existing salary.

Born in 1951 in Puerto Rico and brought up in New York,
Alomar had worked relentlessly—applying what he calls "due
diligence" to both his music and his schoolwork—ever since his
father, a minister on 109th Street, died when Carlos was just
fourteen. Being fined by James Brown (for missing his "hit me"
cue) and hanging out with Chuck Berry, rock-and-roll poet and
mean drunk, helped shape Alomar's Buddha-like calm but
contest-competitive persona. Alomar brought his wife, session

singer Robin Clarke, to the recordings at Sigma Sound in Philadelphia; together with their friend Luther Vandross, they were probably the key influence in the genesis of what would become *Young Americans.* "They glued it all together," as Ava Cherry remembers. "Carlos was very even-tempered, never got mad, and he made David feel he could bridge the gap between soul and where he was."

Tony Visconti, called in for a proper production job at last after a brief reunion with David to mix *Diamond Dogs* and *David Live,* was overjoyed to be back in the creative pressure cooker. But he was worried about the singer's obviously fragile state. When Tony mentioned his condition, David assured him he was fine: "And I kind of believed him, in retrospect," says Visconti. "It's hard to know exactly why, but I did. Whereas Phil Lynott told me much the same thing and I didn't." But Visconti's souvenir photo of David at the Sigma Sound desk shows him as skeletal, his skin gray and papery. As one of those in the studio with him remarks today, "David must have had an angel watching over him. He was also very fortunate this wasn't the era of AIDS—he was so promiscuous—or hepatitis. That photo says it all—but in person, it was even *more* horrible."

Inside the cocooning safety of Sigma Sound—a studio he tried out with Ava Cherry, on July 9—David was in his element. The basic pattern was established from the first day, recognizable as the same routine from his first album with Visconti: David would strum through the song on guitar or piano, the musicians would pick it up, and they'd go for a take after a few run-throughs. But this time he dictated the feel he wanted, insisting that he lay the vocals down live along with the backup track. Visconti set up a dual microphone array to cut out some of the instrumental spill onto the vocal track, and the tapes rolled. "But this was fast," says Alomar. "Remember, I brought most of the band so when it came time to do a song we were like, Cool, let's go! Boom, boom, boom! Our music was out in a week and he was like, Holy shit! These sessions were going so hard and so fast."

In a blitz of recording, the title track, "Young Americans," was first to go down, on the first day; in essence, the song was made up of a succession of TV images, from Nixon's resignation — announced just three days earlier, on August 8 — to Afro Sheen, the hair-care product whose advertisements bookended *Soul Train*. The song's story of a new-married couple echoes Bowie's own planned seduction of America — like "Oh! You Pretty Things," the song explicitly name-drops its target audience.

It's impossible to miss the musical change signaled by "Young Americans," but the song's lyrics are just as emblematic of David's magpie tendencies. A complete about-face from *Diamond Dogs'* fractured imagery, "Young Americans" is observational — musical reportage that even includes dialogue: "They pulled in just behind the bridge. He lays her down, he frowns." The music might have been funky, but the lyrical style was a straight lift from Bruce Springsteen, whom David and Geoff had seen back at Max's. To make the homage even more specific, David had laid down a cover of Bruce's "It's Hard to Be a Saint in the City," which he delivered in his new baritone croon, a kind of combination of Elvis, Sinatra, and Bryan Ferry. During the session, Tony Visconti discovered Bruce lived nearby — in a trailer, he maintains — and they invited the New Jersey singer down to the studio. Bruce was puzzled, confused that this English glam singer was covering one of his songs and praising him so extravagantly; in the end David's enthusiasm won him over, and they talked about music late into the night.

Although on many other songs the soul element was low-key, understated, the title track of *Young Americans* was self-consciously funky, a statement of intent. Exactly as he had done with *Ziggy*, David was "repositioning the brand," as Dai Davies put it. But the move was intuitive, not calculated, says Ava Cherry. "He was so happy doing this — it was simply living out what he wanted to be, living out a dream."

Several tracks from those sessions illustrated that Bowie's love for the music he was channeling was deep and heartfelt, notably the astonishing "It's Gonna Be Me." It's a gloriously stark, slow eight-bar blues, back-dropped by Mike Garson's minimal piano;

David cajoles, sketching out image after image of regret and his own sexual addiction. His voice is breathy, pitch-perfect, Aretha meets Judy Garland, one of the most accomplished vocal performances he would ever commit to tape. "Can You Hear Me," recorded in the same early sessions, is equally subtle, the final mix benefiting from a typically haunting Visconti string arrangement; "Win," started but not completed at Sigma Sound, is an almost spiritual meditation that represents a neat antithesis to the white man's conventional take on R & B. Where Surrey bluesmen like Eric Clapton expressed a faux empathy with the downtrodden, David Bowie used soul to celebrate success: "All you got to do is win—that's all ya gotta do."

In the coming months, many critics, notably *Creem*'s Lester Bangs, would tear into Bowie's appropriation of R & B; it was brazen, unashamed. Yet Bowie's unapologetic overnight makeover was a triumph compared to his friend and rival Marc Bolan's. Influenced by girlfriend Gloria Jones, Marc had dabbled with R & B for more than a year, even playing with Ike and Tina Turner on the B-side to "Nutbush City Limits." But Bolan could not bear to totally abandon his trademark style; his R & B was a compromise, buried under those familiar languid vocals. Bowie, in contrast, turned funky late but went all the way. More self-confident than Bolan, he would not hedge his bets, and his confidence in the studio was not fueled by the cocaine; it was innate. As confirmation of his imminent success, a small group of fans gathered round the studio each night. They were given the title of the "Sigma kids," regarded as a kind of lucky charm, and were finally invited in to listen to the rough mixes—perhaps predictably, they were wildly enthusiastic.

The sense of focus around the Sigma sessions provided a powerful contrast to David's chaotic private life. Ava, his new girlfriend, had helped inspire his work in the city, but during the recordings he'd frequently disappear, a cat on the prowl. "I knew the party was going on somewhere else," says Cherry of his nocturnal escapades. When Angie arrived in Philadelphia there was yet more drama; she heard Ava was on the scene and ran off toward a hotel window, threatening to throw herself out. Fortunately, Tony Zanetta had experience dealing with disturbed children: "I had learned this technique of holding them firmly so they wouldn't freak out. So I had to use it, and pin her down to the floor."

Angie's behavior was all the more extreme considering that she was one of the few at the time who didn't drink or do drugs. Her addiction was to attention, a product of a bizarre cycle in which David would decide he needed her and call her up, Angie would arrive and be ignored, and another crisis would be provoked. "It was a very odd relationship, very weird to be around," concludes Zanetta, who realized during these weeks that David was debating ridding himself of Angie. The timing was significant, for it followed, by only a few days, David's belated understanding of his relationship with MainMan.

That devastating conversation took place in a New York hotel at the end of July. Coked out of his mind, as was Zanetta, Bowie poured out his woes: "Did I work this hard, to have nothing?" The pair were discussing the money that was flooding out of Main-Man when Zanetta realized that David thought he owned half the organization. "It was odd," says Zanetta. "He didn't understand that he didn't own [half of] MainMan. We were sitting there, going over what had gone wrong and trying to keep it all together. I adored both David and Tony, so this was more than heartbreaking— it felt like the end of the world."

Traumatic as the situation was for Zanetta, for David it was far worse. He'd simply assumed he owned his own company, his own music; the situation as mapped out by Zanetta was so horrifically different, he seemed incapable of comprehending it. Zanetta tried to explain to him that he owned half his own revenue, less expenses, but had no share in the other MainMan enterprises. The obvious next step, if David wanted to find where his money was going, was to hire an accountant and go through the books, where every penny of expenditure was documented. But David had no interest in analyzing his predicament. Defries had created a magical aura, a cocoon in which David could create. Now the magic bubble had popped. Over subsequent weeks, David made no effort to investigate his contract with MainMan; he was interested only in terminating it. "It was coming to an end between them," says Zanetta, their conflicted go-between. "Part of that was money. Part of it was Defries's megalomania. In fact, they were both megalomaniacs." "Tony had been a total father figure," adds Ava Cherry; "David would do everything Tony said, would listen to his every word. When he heard about the money he was simply...afraid."

The ramifications of David's deal with MainMan were complex; there were indeed advantages to the way David's contract was set up, for it gave him control of his masters—as long as he remained with MainMan. Defries himself maintains that MainMan's unique position as owner of David's master recordings increased David's royalties from the industry standard of 10 percent to 16 percent, a cut that was, in the early 1970s, unusually generous. But one crucial aspect of their relationship is beyond debate: While David had believed he was a partner in MainMan, in reality he was an employee.

The discovery of his naïveté regarding his actual role—his employment status—was a devastating blow to David's self-esteem. His father figure had betrayed him. Ava Cherry, David's confidante, along with Coco, comforted him throughout the distraught crying jags that overcame him whenever he thought about his situation—but for most of the time, his problems were too bleak to contemplate. Instead, David fixed on Angie, deciding he could no longer cope with her outbursts. For months to come, he would continue to play his public role with his wife, maintaining the image that, as Scott Richardson puts it, "had made the world fall in love with them," but David's emotional detachment from Angie was part of his detachment from MainMan. Angie, more than David, had defined MainMan's image; it was she who had established the company's cradle at Haddon Hall, who had formed the relationship with the *Pork* crew. As Lee Childers points out, "MainMan had been created in Angie's image." For David, both were now encumbrances. But in the short term he would keep his own counsel while he worked out how to cut himself loose.

THE summer of 1974 was temperate and balmy, and when David resumed his tour—the band now augmented with Carlos Alomar, Ava Cherry, and most of the Sigma crew—his personal traumas were briefly forgotten in the excitement of creation. For the time being, David kept quiet. David informed Defries, via Tony Zanetta, that he was planning a new stripped-down production and wanted to ditch the Hunger City set and play against a white backdrop. Defries affected nonchalance at the news that the four-hundred-thousand-dollar construction was destined for the trash heap.

Over seven nights at Hollywood's Universal Amphitheater, David's claim to bona fide superstar status was laid out in the most convincing fashion. His previous "retirement" seemed only to add to his unpredictability—and glamour. The Hollywood aristocracy turned out; Diana Ross made a conspicuous appearance in a silver gown, as did her fellow Motown stars the Jackson Five.

Marc Bolan was another attendant on the triumphant hero. He had bitched about David in print earlier that year, deriding his American success as all marketing gloss. Now, pudgy and nervous, he paid due fealty to the man who had so often paid tribute to him. "David was obviously at a high point and Marc at a low point," says Zanetta, who sat with the two of them at the Beverly Wilshire. "But David did not gloat at all, he was very kind." Later that year, Marc would tell *Melody Maker* that he would be directing David in his first movie. By then, with David being courted by Hollywood's biggest stars, Marc's bravado seemed unbearably sad. Iggy Pop eventually turned up too. After his split with Main-Man and his well-publicized attacks on "that fuckin' carrottop" for sabotaging his *Raw Power* album, he had finally left the Stooges following a legendarily disastrous last tour. His last public performance had been a pathetic affair at Rodney's English Disco, which culminated in his stabbing his chest with a blunt steak knife. Now mocked around Hollywood as a trash-can drug user, Iggy missed David's show after being beaten up by a bunch of surfers in the parking lot. He turned up later to cadge food.

Burying himself in musical preparations throughout the LA shows, David seemed genuinely happy; over successive nights he coached Ava Cherry to ready her for her solo number, Luther Vandross's "Maybe It's Love." He was the perfect mentor, patient, encouraging. "He walked me through the whole thing, the movement, the way I would enter the stage. He was very nurturing; it was wonderful."

David had even seemed gracious and hospitable when a young BBC director, Alan Yentob, appeared in Hollywood, explaining that Tony Defries had, in a momentary lapse, agreed to give him access. Impressed by Yentob's explanation of the theme of the documentary—an exploration of a significant, serious artist in his new American setting—David agreed to grant him an interview.

Yentob's documentary would be unforgettable, a gripping depiction of a fractured, dislocated existence. One of the main contributors to that fractured aura was a local celebrity who introduced himself to David after one of the first Hollywood shows. Freddie Sessler, concentration camp survivor and rock-and-roll fan, was "the kind of guy who can make a party happen," says Iggy Pop. Sessler was a character whose existence was rarely acknowledged in the wider world despite the influence he had behind the scenes. For decades he acted as companion to Keith Richards and Ron Wood, loved for his Chico Marx–style gruff humor and for his ability to source the best drugs in the West. With customary ease, Freddie gained admission to the Beverly Wilshire, his pockets bulging with vials of pure Merck—pharmaceutical cocaine, far more powerful than anything available in New York. This was the mother lode, the drug lauded by Sigmund Freud as "this magical substance." From then on, Freddie would be David's companion too.

Over those weeks in Hollywood, David was also being courted by the UK's most glamorous movie icon: Liz Taylor. Their first meeting was awkward—Terry O'Neill, who photographed David for the *Diamond Dogs* sleeve, invited David to a shoot at director George Cukor's house, for which David arrived "two hours late— disheveled and out of it. Liz was pretty annoyed and on the verge of leaving, but we managed to persuade her to stay." Liz's irritation with David was outweighed by her instinct for publicity. A huge star in the 1960s, Taylor had fared less well in the 1970s and was eager to be associated with Bowie. O'Neill's photos showed the two frolicking like teenagers, Liz embracing David, holding his cigarette suggestively.

Within days she was making high-profile visits to David's rehearsals and floating the idea that David would star in *The Blue Bird*, a remake of Maurice Tourneur's 1918 movie. Her adoption of David as an up-and-coming superstar was made official during a party for Ricci Martin—Dean's son—in Beverly Hills, where they sat close to each other, chatting softly.

There was another star in the cavalcade of celebrities gathering around David and Liz that evening: John Lennon, then in the midst of his so-called lost weekend with May Pang. John was still "saucer-eyed," according to Pang, at seeing so many of his movie heroes in LA and was soaking up the vibe at the party, chatting with Elton John. Taylor called John and May over, introducing David to them in her singsong, almost childish voice. John was chummy, "but David was odd," remembers May Pang; after a few seconds he told them, "I have to go now." A few minutes later they walked into another room to see David and Liz huddled together. "It was strange—David was very thin, I remember he seemed standoffish. John didn't know what to think. Me, him, and Elton were looking at each other: What was *that* about?" Lennon was not offended, merely puzzled.

As the tour moved on to the Midwest and then the East, early in October, the soul vibe became more obvious, and Hunger City's skyscrapers finally met the wrecking ball. These shows were mocked by some observers as a patronizing wannabe-soul revue, but for band and crew these were thrilling dates, with the set evolving from one night to the next. Received wisdom has it that David's cocaine habit reduced him to such dehydration that his lips adhered to his gums; Ava Cherry, who stood close to him on the stage, remembers no such event, but there were many moments of paranoia, in particular a show in Boston that November. Before the show started, he demanded a gram of cocaine: "I'm not going on unless I get it." After scurrying around, a flunky came up with the goods. But when David walked out onstage, the first two rows stayed immobile. For some reason, most of them had dressed up in Halloween costumes for the occasion. "Skeleton masks, scary masks," says Cherry.

"Why are they doing that?" David appealed to his backup singers. "Why the masks?" He was terrified, offended that his fans saw him as a freak. As he made his way out of the music hall, he was handed a poster-sized sheet. On it were tombstones bearing his name. The poster troubled him for days. Later he mentioned it to Ava when trying to explain his own behavior: "If you don't like some of the things I do, that's why—I don't live a normal life."

Writer Mick Farren had been sent to report on the tour for the *NME,* and he found himself relishing the weird culture clash: "Like a crazed Funkadelic tour, with added cocaine, paranoia, and Scientology," he says. Farren loved the "James Brown versus Elvis vibe—obviously they'd cobbled it together on the fly, but it was kinda cool." Photographer Robert Matheu remembered the same seedy glamour in Detroit: "The drugs were apparent in so many ways—they actually seemed to add to the overall vibe, there was a darkness to it. You know, an Ike Turner thing: Ike always had that vibe, you knew he was holding." The culture clash was reflected in backstage friction among the band members: Kamen's crew seemed at odds with the Main Ingredient players; Coco Schwab was lined up against Ava Cherry, or Angie when she turned up; the Scientology vibe was still present thanks to Mike Garson; plus there were "monstrous amounts" of cocaine in evidence: "piles of the shit everywhere," says Farren. "They must have been carrying half-ounce bags. This was about as excessive as it got—in a period of excess."

When he wasn't onstage, David, whom Farren knew from his Lindsay Kemp days, looked lost, and, as in the later part of his previous American tour, "lonely." Most of the time he walked around in an overcoat with his hood up, nose dripping, twitchily rejecting any attempts at conversation. When anyone got in the elevator with him, he looked terrified. Many outsiders remember the cut-throat, paranoid atmosphere, with different cliques trying to entice outsiders back to their rooms "for some blow," each group accusing the others of being drug fiends, even of thieving money. But onstage, David was always in command; the backstage friction gave the music an edge. "David had people playing against each other onstage, to make them better," says Ava Cherry, "like the James Brown thing, always that pressure of you're in, you're out. Sometimes it was brilliant. We would fight harder to be better than each other."

The atmosphere was all the more bizarre because the darkness and paranoia were offset by the mood of "the kids," as Zanetta called them: Carlos, Robin, and Luther were wholesome and loving, relishing their big break. Although guitarist Earl Slick had his own "mindless" moments, as he remembers, he too seemed like a carefree child, in his element, while Ava Cherry, innocent and luscious, was "adored" by most of the crew. In another bizarre touch, Zowie and his nanny, Marion Skene, were around for several dates. While David was constantly distracted, when he made time for his son he was "absolutely attentive—focusing on him completely," says Zanetta. Likewise, David's boyish enthusiasm was obvious when he concentrated on the music, and at sound checks the whole crazy family would come together and unite with a wired optimism.

On the afternoons where the troupe remained in the city, at the Michigan Palace or Chicago's Crown Theater, there would be extended jam sessions at which David was filled with energy, pointing out riffs and directing arrangements, and during the October dates, new songs were added one by one: the devotional, gospely "It's Gonna Be Me" and a funked-up version of the Flares' 1963 doo-wop hit "Foot Stompin'."

That autumn and the following months up to 1975 was the period most marked by a cocaine blitz, one in which David would famously describe himself as permanently "out of my gourd." Yet even outsiders, although shocked by David's physical deterioration, were somehow convinced that this was simply another phase. "He's such a survivor," Mick Farren points out, "plus we weren't all dropping dead back then." Only in retrospect, says Mick Farren, did he reflect on the psychological burdens David had assumed: "It's like what Lennon said about Elvis: 'I don't know how he did it, 'cos there were four of us and it nearly killed us.' And of course there were only two of David."

David's performance on *The Dick Cavett Show,* taped on November 2 during the New York dates, was the high-water mark of his "out of my gourd" period, and the perfect embodiment of the tour's prickly, paranoid energy. Sniffing loudly, with his eyes flitting from side to side, David bares his teeth several times in a grimace almost like those of the skeleton masks that had freaked him out in Boston. As if in reaction, Cavett mentions black magic and how "some people said they're scared to sit and talk to you" — and David's main response is to fiddle obsessively with his cane. Cavett briefly looks truly worried, as though his guest were drawing a pentagram on the studio floor. At odd moments — a little chuckle here, his statement that when he's onstage "that's it, [I'm] complete" — he still manages to impersonate a normal human being, but mostly he revels in his fractured condition. Together with Alan Yentob's *Cracked Actor,* screened by the BBC on January 26, this would be the definitive depiction of Bowie in his most alien state; yet, in the sense that he is exploring the limits of his mental condition, he is also recognizably David Bowie in exactly the same way that the coked-out David witnessed by Keith Christmas was merely another manifestation of the person Keith had known in 1969.

As if in tribute to David's new-minted image as an icon of excess, the police raided the end-of-tour party at Atlanta's Hyatt Regency on December 1. Backup singers Geoff MacCormack and Gui Andrisano had noticed a couple of "strange guys with bad taste in clothes and suspiciously short haircuts" hanging out in the hotel suite and warned their fellow musicians. When the police broke in, none of the crew was holding, but the suite contained nine vials of cocaine, ten lumps of hashish, five bags of grass, and three roaches. Tony Zanetta, who had booked the suite, was dragged off for an overnight stay in the cells but eventually released without charges.

After an exhausting drive back to New York, David booked studio time to complete *Young Americans* at the Hit Factory, around December 3. David added more overdubs and completed "Fascination"—based on a Luther Vandross song—and "Win," and Tony Visconti flew over to London with the tapes to mix them at his home studio, happy he'd finally completed the thrilling but grueling sessions.

In his first few days back in New York, David had also called up John Lennon and May Pang; he was nervous about meeting the ex-Beatle again, and at one point called Tony Visconti over to the Sherry-Netherland Hotel to help the conversation along. Although their meeting in LA had gone nowhere, David and John had a huge amount in common. Bowie talked about John frequently; John was interested in David, friendly, but invariably puzzled. "David was still very nervous, John was happy to hang out," says May Pang. The atmosphere remained slightly awkward, all the more so when Paul and Linda McCartney—who had just bumped into John and May—entered the picture in mid-January.

The four of them went over to the Sherry to meet David, who repeatedly played the various mixes of his new album for them. "And we had heard it already. In lots of different states," says Pang. David was about to replay the acetate for John for at least the second time when John told him, "David, it's great, a great album… is there anything else we can listen to as well?" David looked devastated; John hadn't heard Paul make almost exactly the same remark a few minutes earlier, and when the John and May returned to their apartment on Fifty-second Street that night, the phone was ringing as they came through the door. "Yes, David, sorry, man, I didn't mean that," John consoled his offended, cocaine-fueled friend.

May Pang remembers that Lennon was taken aback by the size of David's coke habit, remarking to May, "I've never seen such mounds of the stuff!" But John enjoyed his company, and although he was puzzled when David told him that he was planning to add a cover version of "Across the Universe" to the album, he instantly agreed to turn up at Electric Lady Studios around January 15, for he was a studio hound. "He loved being in on the recording," says renowned engineer Eddie Kramer, who worked the session, "and just playing guitar—he was a ridiculously good rhythm player."

In the studio, the environment they both loved, John's empathy with David was obvious, Kramer observed. David too was clearly having a blast: "Whatever stimulants he was taking didn't affect his ability to be creative," says Kramer, who was present when Carlos Alomar started playing the riff adapted from the Rascals' song "Jungle Walk" that he'd added to the band's live version of "Foot Stompin'." "David said, I'll have that, or words to that effect—and he took the riff that Carlos played and made a song out of it."

Lennon was playing around on the acoustic in the lounge, singing a couple of lines from Shirley and Company's disco hit "Shame, Shame, Shame" over the top of the same one-chord vamp. "So he was working it, and David walks in and hears that," says Pang, who remembers David leaving the room and returning with a complete set of lyrics within twenty minutes.

David had misheard *shame* as *fame*—a subject he'd been discussing with John earlier, and also the title of yet another disastrous MainMan project, a Tony Ingrassia play launched just a few weeks before. The misheard word would give him his biggest hit to date. Although some key recollections vary as to whether Carlos started the vamp first and John joined in or vice versa, Bowie "was very much in charge, he knew exactly what he wanted," says Kramer, who watched David work the elements into a song once John had left the studio. Part of Lennon's guitar vamp survived in the three acoustic chords—F minor, C minor, and B-flat—that open the song and punctuate the main theme before the last verse. Carlos's riff, effective on "Foot Stompin'," was the killer element on "Fame," but it's Bowie who makes sense of it—he plays the crunchy ascending guitar riff at the end of each line.

Restricted mostly to a single chord, "Fame" is obsessive,

monotonous, and claustrophobic. On *Hunky Dory*, David had worked with piano chords; here he was playing with sound itself, using the studio as a giant cut-and-paste machine. Yet the emotional impact was just as powerful, for the song was an almost literal rendition of his life, cutting from his omnipresent worries about money ("what you need you have to borrow") to his loneliness ("takes you there where things are hollow").

"Fame," a last-minute addition to the album, which had already been trailed in the press as *Fascination* in December, would be the making of *Young Americans;* it would also arguably break it too, for David felt compelled to include his version of "Across the Universe," the song that had inspired Lennon's arrival in the studio. The cover version was a horrible mess, marred by David's warbling vocal, the most extreme example so far of his mimicking of Bryan Ferry's and Scott Walker's styles and an obvious flaw that the album's detractors would latch onto. (Lennon was just as puzzled as everyone else: "Why *that* song?" he asked May Pang.) When "Fame" became David's first U.S. number 1 the following September, John was as delighted as David. "He had that competitiveness with the others guys [e.g., Paul McCartney]—and he thought it was great," says Pang, who disappeared from John's life in February when the ex-Beatle returned to Yoko and the Dakota. May would later marry Tony Visconti, whom she'd met at the Sherry-Netherland that winter.

The excitement around the recording was one of the few high spots in a bleak winter. Much of David's Christmas was spent in a coke-fueled haze with Tony Zanetta at the Sherry-Netherland. David had lost his last vestige of faith in his father figure, and in all of MainMan, on November 18, the day that the company made its grand entrance—and its ignominious exit—on Broadway. *Fame* was a chaotic, confused comedy based on the life of Marilyn Monroe, written by Tony Ingrassia, the mastermind of *Pork*. Ingrassia's *Pork* had launched the MainMan circus; *Fame*, which closed after one performance, was its death knell, for Bowie deeply resented the reported $250,000 that had been lost on its production, money that doubtless had come from his hit records.

David's conversations with John Lennon at Electric Lady Studios confirmed his decision. John had just divested himself of Beatles manager Allen Klein and commemorated the event in one of his last great songs, "Steel and Glass," which mocked Klein's LA tan and his infamous BO ("you leave your smell like an alley cat"). Defries frequently claimed to have learned his trade from Klein; if Klein was a crook, figured David, what was Tony, Klein's student?

Over Christmas, David attempted, without success, to contact Defries, who was away in his favorite island hideaway of Mustique. The two finally met in January. The encounter accomplished nothing, as far as those close to them can tell, with neither man coming to the point. David told friends Defries had accepted his decision to leave MainMan; Defries believed he'd smoothed over David's concerns and persuaded him to stay. In later months, when their split became increasingly ugly, Defries would tell his friends how "disappointed" he was in David. He was let down by his ingratitude, his lack of understanding of commercial realities, his addiction to drugs.

When friends asked Defries, the supreme negotiator, why he had failed to negotiate a settlement at his meeting with David, he would coldly ask: "David had been working for me; why would *I* want to work for *him*?"

Defries also seemed to astutely judge Michael Lippman, the lawyer David found to represent him. Previously an agent for CMA, Lippman had pitched film work to both David and Angie; he'd been a full partner in a law firm, rather than a lowly clerk like Defries; and he was liked and trusted by those around David—but he could never match his opponent's aggression. Defries told his friends that Lippman was a very junior agent with not much to offer and that he'd advised Bowie to retain a more high-powered lawyer.

MainMan would be dismembered in David's wake, all its artists eventually dropped; Defries's subsequent management career was undistinguished. One singer did approach him for advice a few years later, Defries confided to his friends. Her name was Madonna.

In later life, Defries would be painted as cynical and manipulative, but speak to anyone who worked with him and a trace of the magic still lingers. For Defries "was never the demon figure he's made out," says Hugh Attwooll, onetime head of MainMan England. "He's a man without care. He knew he could beat the system and he did it. All he said to David was that he'd make him a star. He didn't elaborate and say I'll use a lot of your money to make it work. My view is that he gets rather a bad press. Because it *did* work—without it, David wouldn't be as famous as he is."

Over the next year, David would be dogged by disputes with Defries, who would retain a share of David's future records for the remainder of the MainMan contract term, up to 1982, with the right to reject any album he deemed uncommercial. Such onerous conditions naturally made most observers side with David. Not only was there no enduring charge of impropriety, but those who were there testify that as well as being the key figure in Bowie's rise to fame, Defries was an integral part of that period's unforgettable magic.

"What entertained him was the intellectual challenge of doing it—taking the risk and making it work," says Attwooll. "He spun a web of magic, which no one had ever done before, and persuaded RCA to spend huge amounts of money both in the UK and U.S. He was a very nice bloke, but what line he stepped over in achieving what he achieved is probably an argument that will never be satisfied."

David spent years dealing with the ramifications of the split with the figure who'd overseen his rise to fame. He'd put off his confrontation with Defries for months; David's friends, including Coco Schwab and Ava Cherry, hoped the split would finally produce some resolution. But there would be none.

David Jones had embarked on a long, grueling, ruthless journey in pursuit of fame and success; many of his peers had shown similar ambition, but few had transformed themselves so painstakingly from mediocrities to inspirational songwriters. Soon, he'd discover that the very stuff he'd created at such personal cost was lost to him. David's friends hoped that his final split with his onetime father figure would bring closure. Instead, it brought crisis.

CHAPTER 14

White Stains

He — and this is glamorizing it — did use the drugs to enlarge
his capabilities in every dimension. It really magnified his
intelligence, if you will. But it had its way with him.

—Glenn Hughes

D AVID BELIEVED THAT cutting his ties with Defries
promised mental freedom; independence in his business affairs seemed almost secondary. "Forget about the
money," David had told a couple of people, "that's all in the past."
Above all, he had confidence in his music — his new album would
finally bring him mainstream success in America and represented the ultimate bargaining chip in his relationship with RCA,
who, early in January of 1975, confirmed that they were prepared
to deal with David directly, effectively cutting Defries out of the
deal.

But by February, the awful truth dawned that the freedom
might be illusory; although David had left MainMan, MainMan —
and Defries — retained control of David's existing masters. During his conversations with John Lennon — whose business savvy
he admired — David discovered that Lennon had lost his own
publishing control and at times despaired of escaping Allen
Klein's clutches. David's contract with Defries, labeling David an

employee, was even more restrictive. "That was when David's whole mood changed," says Ava Cherry, who witnessed David's conversations with John. "He was always irritated after that, quick to get angry. David was a little bit naive—and he couldn't believe he'd really signed so much away."

While David was mired in his financial worries, the extent of his physical deterioration was revealed in gripping fashion on January 26, when Alan Yentob's *Cracked Actor* was shown on the BBC. In later years, it would be acclaimed as one of the greatest music documentaries ever made. With the minimal interview time he'd been given, Yentob lingered over every shot, capturing perfectly the emptiness and loneliness in which David was sealed. Defries's predecessor, Ken Pitt, was one of many disturbed by David's fractured, disconnected state. He concluded simply that David "was ill. That was what all the Defries big talk had done for him. This was not the David I knew. It was very disappointing."

An interview with Bruno Stein published in February's *Creem* was even more alarming, indicative of what seemed classic cocaine-induced paranoia. David was obsessed with UFO cover-ups. "And I made sightings [of UFOs] six, seven times a night for about a year when I was in the observatory," he confided to the astonished writer before pronouncing that Adolf Hitler was "a perfect figurehead." In reality, these proclamations reflected an old obsession, dating back to when he was hanging out with Lesley Duncan at Redington Road. All those who had gone UFO-spotting with him around 1967, like Jeff Dexter and Wayne Bardell, confirm, "We *did* see UFOs—absolutely." Equally, Adolf Hitler was an old favorite topic for debate, for David used to eulogize the work of Albert Speer back in Arnold Corns days. Yet what had been cheery hipsters' chat in the 1960s became ominous and disturbing in 1975.

While onlookers' reactions to David's state varied from horror to fascination to cynicism, one woman saw a solution to a movie casting problem. Maggie Abbott was an agent at CMA who'd been crucial in uniting her clients Mick Jagger and writer Donald Cammell with Nicolas Roeg for *Performance*—the definitive celluloid depiction of late-1960s decadence. She'd first heard of David through a friend who trained with him at Lindsay Kemp's studio; now David was CMA's client, and Yentob's documentary convinced her that he would be perfect for the lead role in Roeg's upcoming project *The Man Who Fell to Earth*. Abbott's tenacity played a crucial part in the genesis of the film, not least because the BBC had refused to release a video of *Cracked Actor* for Roeg and producer Si Litvinoff to watch, and she'd had to use "cunning charm" to smuggle out a copy. "Nic and Si didn't take any convincing; they knew as soon as they saw *Cracked Actor*, especially the sequence with David in the back of the limo." The pair, and Abbott, were struck by the shot of Bowie gazing out of the car window seeming totally isolated, disconnected from the world—alien.

Roeg had considered Michael Crichton, Mick Jagger, and Peter O'Toole for the role of Newton, the alien who comes to Earth in search of water and is corrupted by earthly vices. Crichton and O'Toole were unavailable; Abbott talked Roeg out of using Jagger, her other major client. Watching the documentary, Roeg noticed countless facets of Bowie that resonated with the part. But the most important one was "that curious artificial voice. It wasn't absolutely definable as a brogue or accent. Like, did it really exist?" Today, Roeg admits that although the decision to cast Bowie was obvious in retrospect, "I don't know if it was immediate." Maggie Abbott—who flew to New York in February of 1975 to show David the script—remembers David's initial response as "cautious... cool." His reserve was not as striking as his physical state, which was even worse than *Cracked Actor* had suggested; his hip bones jutted through the jumpsuit he was wearing, his skin was white, and his teeth were gray. "Ghastly" was Abbott's description. But he was astute; he understood the logic of her case, asked the correct questions, and was obviously intrigued by Abbott's connections with Roeg and Mick Jagger. She had no doubt that he could rise to the task. "He could sleepwalk through it," she told Roeg, who arranged to meet David a couple of days later.

Convinced that signing David was crucial to his movie, Roeg won him over by his gentle persistence. David forgot their meeting and was busy in a recording session, says Roeg. Roeg waited for him for most of the day, and when Bowie remembered the appointment and arrived late that evening, the pair talked for only a few minutes before David agreed to sign up.

Roeg was an undeniably impressive character, and his assiduous courting of David together with the completion of "Fame" both represented hope for Bowie. The thought of Defries's control over his work, which culminated in attempts by MainMan to injunct the release of *Young Americans,* made David feel like a helpless, naive child. David's encounters with John Lennon in January and early February brought out the best in him—his unaffected joy and enthusiasm—for he was impressed with how down-to-earth and "unstarry" Lennon was and acted the same way in his company. John too had come to genuinely like David; for all his quirks, he was a committed rock and roller, like John, and once the standoffishness faded away, David seemed simply like a younger brother who needed counseling.

But the influence of other stars was far less benign. Cherry Vanilla had left MainMan before David's split and kept in touch; she had introduced him to Norman Fisher when he'd first moved to New York, and she had brief chats with David quite regularly, the two of them gossiping away before David got to the point— which was usually a request to "borrow" her apartment for sex sessions away from the watchful eye of Ava, or Angie, who briefly lived nearby before returning to London. Then one evening Cherry saw David hurrying down the street, asked if he was okay, and he blurted out that he'd just been to see Lou Reed.

"Don't ever go near him," he warned her. "He's the devil."

Vanilla was only slightly worried: "He was on this trip, whatever Lou had done to him had freaked him out that day." By then it was well known that David was living on a diet consisting solely of "coke and milk," but like most of her circle, she was convinced that cocaine had no downside. "We didn't think of it as ill then. We thought of it as fashionable."

David's encounter with Jimmy Page in February was even more unsettling. Their acquaintance went back to Manish Boys days, but during a night Jimmy spent with Ava and Bowie at Bowie's house, the atmosphere was strained. When Page spilled wine on some silk cushions and tried to blame Ava, Bowie sent him on his way, spitting out: "Why don't you take the window."

The two glared at each other; Page seemed to be invoking dark forces against David, who in turn, says Ava Cherry, "wanted to show Jimmy that his will was stronger. Then all of a sudden, after that night, David has all these books around and is reading them."

David's battle of wills with Page helped inspire a deeper investigation of the works of "the wickedest man in the world." Jimmy Page's devotion to the work of occultist Aleister Crowley was well known—he had bought and restored Crowley's famed magical headquarters, Boleskine House, in 1971. Crowley's work was popular in hippie circles from 1969; Graham Bond, Elton John's former employer, released *Holy Magick,* an album devoted to Crowley, in 1970; Sombrero regular Robert Kensell was another follower. David himself had name-dropped Crowley in "Quicksand" and possibly "Holy Holy" too; those close to him in 1971, like Dai Davies, believe that back then Bowie had a "fashionable but fleeting interest" in mentioning Crowley's name, as he did with Nietzsche's. The meeting with Page seemed to convert what had been casual name-dropping into a full-blown obsession.

Over 1975 David embarked on a journey that would take him into the heart of psychic darkness. One key text in this journey was—according to Gary Lachman, an acquaintance of Bowie who has written on the occult—Trevor Ravenscroft's *The Spear of Destiny*. Published in 1973, the book explored Hitler's and Himmler's harnessing of occult powers, notably those of the Holy Grail and a partner artifact, the lance that pierced Christ's side. Other Bowie influences almost certainly included the hugely fashionable *The Morning of the Magicians,* by Louis Pauwels and Jacques Bergier. Together with works by Crowley and his acolytes, these formed the core of Bowie's reading list at the time. Lachman debated such subjects as the occult interests of *Outsider* author Colin Wilson with Bowie and believes "he is interested in lots of such ideas, and can speak intelligently about them. Jimmy Page went into it more deeply and was a serious devotee—Bowie picked lots of different elements and gave them a twist."

By the time Bowie met Page, the Led Zep guitarist had spent more than six years investigating Crowley's work; David's immersion was comparatively brief. Rather than harnessing dark powers, he embarked on a coke-addled quest for meaning. In 1993, Bowie would explain his fascination with Himmler's search for the Holy Grail and the Spear of Destiny as an "Arthurian need— this search for a mythological link with God. But somewhere along the line it was perverted by what I was reading and what I was drawn to."

The Rolling Stones had danced with the devil in the guise of Crowley disciple Kenneth Anger and paid a price; Bowie's new, dangerous aura would take a heavy toll on him and those around him. Obsessed and scared by the ominous forces he saw gathering, David started planning his escape from New York. It wasn't just people like Jimmy Page and Lou Reed he wanted to flee; even normally well-behaved musicians seemed to resent his presence. Aretha Franklin had mocked him at the Grammys ("I'm so happy I could kiss David Bowie"), ruining his mood for weeks, and at a party thrown by Alice Cooper's manager, Shep Gordon, Bob Dylan had delivered one of his trademark put-downs. "Glam rock isn't music," Bob had sneered, and then he'd turned his back on David while the watching industry heavyweights and their flunkies gasped.

A move to LA to get ready for the *Man Who Fell to Earth* shoot—which was delayed while Roeg and producer Si Litvinoff looked for backers—represented a clean break with such nastiness. It meant he'd be closer to his new Hollywood manager, Michael Lippman; he could also escape Ava Cherry and her complaints about his obsessive womanizing (Angie, in comparison, had given up and seemed content to pursue a mostly separate existence).

The move also meant David would be close to LA's raconteur and coke dealer par excellence Freddie Sessler. Geoff MacCormack, who flew over to join David a couple of weeks later, would characterize this period in LA as a time when "a common form of greeting was for someone simply to say hi and stick a silver spoon under your nose." Freddie would arrive with not a vial of cocaine but a plateful. The potency and quantity of Sessler's wares were unrivaled; they would contribute to David's marked mental deterioration over the summer of 1975.

Glenn Hughes, a twenty-three-year-old English bassist and singer who'd recently joined Deep Purple, had become fast friends with Bowie in LA the previous year. During their long phone conversations, Glenn—about to start on Deep Purple's last tour with Ritchie Blackmore—had offered David refuge at his house in Beverly Hills. With a sizable coke habit himself, Glenn was well aware of David's growing paranoia and was staggered to hear that David was making the train trip from New York on his own. Glenn arranged for his driver to pick up David from LA's Union Station when he arrived, around March 16, 1975. He wanted to make sure that David wasn't left alone—but it was a vain hope: "David was on his own a lot over that period," says Hughes. "He could be in a room of five or six people, with a book, and be on his own."

Over the following months, Glenn's relationship with David was deepened and tempered by their mutual obsession with cocaine: "It was a dark year—for him, and for me. I know he doesn't like to think about it now, but this is the service we have to give back to people. We have to acknowledge the dark side of what happened."

Throughout their friendship, Bowie and Hughes would have, at fleeting moments, the time of their lives—rapping wildly about music, arguing about clothes, mapping out the future. They were both still young, "invincible," and Bowie was a good friend, advising Hughes, teaching him how to use his influences but to keep moving on. He was also "a funny son of a bitch"—unusually for coke addicts, they'd spend some of their time laughing uproariously. But the enduring image of their time together is the two of them sitting alongside each other, isolated, Glenn obsessively working out riffs on the guitar, David watching the same dark, disquieting movies over and over, both of them lost in their own worlds: "It was miserable. It always is miserable."

A couple of days after his arrival in LA, David reencountered a paradigm of the West Coast lifestyle's corrosive effects in the shape of a subdued Iggy Pop. Since Iggy had last seen David, an attempted partnership with ex-Doors keyboard player Ray Manzarek had fallen apart, and Iggy had been abandoned by his self-proclaimed manager, Danny Sugerman. Late in 1974 he'd ended up at the UCLA Neuropsychiatric Institute; the police had been called to Hamburger Hamlet where Iggy was drooling and leering at the customers, and the cops had given him a choice: jail or a psych hospital. When David arrived at NPI to visit, Iggy was in a pathetic condition, withdrawing from the cocktail of drugs that had permeated his system for the last year. During his stay on the wards he had fascinated the psychiatrists, who diagnosed an excess of narcissism and, more serious, an underlying bipolar condition. Ex-Stooge James Williamson had visited, but friends like Sugerman, who had publicized his descent into oblivion, stayed away. "Nobody else came, nobody," Iggy recalled two years later. "Not even my so-called friends in LA. But David came."

Even Iggy was surprised at David's opening words: "Hey, do you want any blow?" Iggy being Iggy, he took a toot. On his first visit, David was accompanied by actor Dean Stockwell; later, Dennis Hopper tagged along, as did Ola Hudson, the clothes designer who became David's main companion over the summer. She brought her son, Saul—later known as Slash, the top-hatted, guitar-slinging founder of Guns N' Roses. The nine-year-old was still distraught at his parents' separation and understandably disoriented by his recent move from Stoke-on-Trent, the homey center of England's pottery industry, to the mental wildlands of Los Angeles; seeing his mom with Bowie was, says Slash, "like watching an alien land in your backyard."

In truth, David was equally adrift in an alien landscape. The city fascinated him—"LA is my favorite museum," he had quipped to writer Cameron Crowe while driving him on a crazy jaunt around the city in a borrowed yellow VW Bug—but between

April and June of 1975, his mental condition deteriorated from excitable but rational to near delusional. Glenn Hughes had regular phone conversations with David when he was out of LA on tour, and he checked in with his house sitter, Phil, who informed him, "There are birds of every color coming and going at all hours of the night." David's own description of what was going on was a good deal less jolly. "The conversations were scary," says Hughes. "This black magic theme crept in, and my house was near where the Sharon Tate murders were; he was convinced the whole Manson family was still around, and I found he's hid all the knives in my house. Though I didn't know it at the time, I was learning all about cocaine psychosis — which I would go through myself soon."

In May, David took Iggy into Cherokee Studios for a set of later-abandoned recordings. James Williamson, one of the few people who persevered with Iggy, accompanied him to the sessions. By now Iggy was "pretty far gone," says Williamson. Bowie, by comparison, looked together: "He always was this reserved, almost aloof kind of a guy — so he just looked like a more wasted version of that." What struck Williamson most was the "dreadful" noise on the recordings, a ground hum that would make them useless. Bowie's obliviousness to the noise was the main clue things weren't going well. "But, hey," points out Williamson, who'd narrowly evaded a smack possession charge that same year, "everybody was in trouble in LA then."

Iggy's recollections of Bowie's life at that time seem rather conventional (compared to his own existence, perhaps it was). "Sometimes I would go over to his house for a couple of days. There would be books all over the floor and Dennis Hopper stopping by — and David always had ideas. He was about to do *Man Who Fell to Earth,* and he had a great book, a slim volume about a group of people for the government who faked a Mars landing in a TV studio, a wonderful little idea for a movie, he was keen on talking about that. Then he had an idea for a rock-and-roll movie in which I would play a character called Catastrophe. I indulged him in that 'cause, well... I am open to a lot of things."

Sadly, no detailed memories of the household antics of Dennis

Hopper, Iggy Pop, and David Bowie survive; the participants' recollection of this period was patchy. Iggy by now was like a sad child, profoundly depressed at the failure of his own career; Hopper was in his own coke-fueled professional tailspin. With his nonlinear conversation, occasionally profound insights into art and movies, and his fondness for boasting about his acquaintance with Charlie Manson, the actor was another walking embodiment of Hollywood burnout.

For Ava Cherry, who felt compelled to track David down, her ex-lover looked like another burnout—the charming, driven man she'd met at a New York party in 1973 seemed to have "cracked." Ava had disappeared to Jamaica with a friend, ex–*Playboy* model Claudia Jennings, and sometime in June she managed to locate David at Michael Lippman's villa, where he'd moved from Hughes's house. Ava instantly recognized "it was over between us." Their relationship seemed a relic of the past; even David's sex drive had foundered, and on occasion she was simply scared. For a short time that summer, David came to stay at Claudia Jennings's house; Claudia was always lighthearted and positive, but Ava "felt kind of afraid. David would talk about ghosts and I didn't know how to take it. One day we were talking, he started to cry and had a glass in his hand. And it suddenly shattered. He is an intense person, there was this energy...you read about people who sit in a chair and self-combust. Claudia wasn't afraid—I was."

Bowie's fear of occult forces was equaled only by his fascination. His conflicted emotions were epitomized by his visit to Kenneth Anger, a filmmaker and friend of Church of Satan founder Anton LaVey. Bowie brought Ava Cherry along with him for the meeting, but the pair could only stomach around twenty minutes of Anger's presence. "I don't remember exactly what happened," says Cherry, "I kind of blotted it out. But then David started getting more and more manic-depressive, he would tell me stories about something that happened with Angie, that there was a ghost in the house when they lived in Beckenham." It seemed David saw ghosts wherever he looked; later he invited Ava to another house. "It's Marilyn Monroe's old house, but it's haunted," he told her. "Another haunted house. I went there, but it never was the same between us. We made love after I left there but that was it." Their relationship would peter out a few weeks later.

Around the same time—probably early June, although the dates and details vary across different accounts—David phoned Cherry Vanilla at her apartment in New York. His voice was slurred; he skipped from one thought to the next, and it was hard to know what he wanted. And then Cherry Vanilla realized that he'd "got it in his head that these girls were out to make a devil baby with him, to have him impregnate them. Nothing could convince him that this was fantasy on his part, 'cause he was coked to the gills. So he called me at my apartment and he asked me if I knew any white witches."

Fortunately, Vanilla's social circle did include one white witch—Walli Elmlark, a fellow contributor to *Circus* magazine. David took Walli's phone number, and before he put the phone down, he promised he'd produce Cherry's solo album.

Like many such yarns, the details of David's exorcism vary with the telling; years later, Angie would describe how she was called in to help perform a ceremony that took place in David's house on Doheny Drive, conducted on the phone with Walli Elmlark. He talked her through the ceremony like the control tower guiding in a novice pilot. Ava Cherry remembers David's burning a bracelet he'd been given by a singer he'd dated—another suspected witch. Other tales, including the one of David's storing body fluids in his refrigerator, look to be myths that exaggerate a situation that was already bizarre. When Cameron Crowe, *Rolling Stone*'s seventeen-year-old star writer, came to interview him at Lippman's house, Bowie lit a black candle and informed him, "Don't let me scare the pants off you...I've been getting a little trouble from the neighbors."

Paranoia, and ultimately psychosis, is a well-known side effect of frequent cocaine use, usually found in combination with sleep deprivation; users might well stay up for three days at a stretch, in which case, says Harry Shapiro of the organization DrugScope, "heaven knows what you will see." Beyond visual and auditory hallucinations, heavy users—the wealthy ones who use upwards of a gram a day—often experience "ideas of reference," that is, delusions that others are plotting against them, or narcissistic convictions that the individual is the focus of worldly and other-worldly events. This is the condition in which David spent most of the summer of 1975, a period compellingly sketched by Crowe in his article published the following February.

The ease with which Bowie flitted from one subject to another in the interview and—most striking—the moment when he pulled down a blind, convinced he'd seen a body fall from the sky, are disturbing, classic depictions of a rock-star encounter. Bowie was an old hand at overawing—or, more accurately, bullshitting—journalists, and any rational person would conclude much of his bizarre behavior was motivated by his unerring instinct for good copy. But the crayoned marks on the blinds that were meant to ward off evils spirits were genuine—Glenn Hughes found them all over his house on his return from Europe. The fractured, disconnected state that Bowie displayed to Cameron Crowe was "for real" too, according to Ava Cherry.

Crowe was late for their second interview in June; pacing around, anxiously waiting for the *Rolling Stone* reporter to turn up, David and Ava had snorted huge lines of Freddie Sessler's finest Merck, and by the time Crowe arrived "we were flying. We were fucked up, I'm not going to say we weren't." The Bowie portrayed by Crowe, Ava Cherry, and others is a classic, isolated narcissist, his mind racing from scheme to scheme. For Crowe, David dismissed, icily, the subject of MainMan; in reality, he was agonizing over the fate of his masters. "The Tony Defries thing was really affecting him," says Glenn Hughes. "Addiction is all about burying your head in the sand. But this was his period of hell." It was natural that David would construct grandiose, omnipotent fantasies in his conversations with Cameron Crowe, for this was the man who had lost his music, his birthright. He had been emasculated. Dispossessed of a huge part of what had defined his life, he really was rootless and alien.

Glenn Hughes returned to Los Angeles in May and was the

closest witness to David's desperate condition. Ava was finally out of the picture; Angie was staying, briefly, and picked Hughes up from the airport. On first impressions David seemed okay. But soon, as Bowie and Hughes stayed up for days at a stretch—four, five, or more—their existence became that of lifeless wraiths cut off from human warmth. Corinne—a source of succor, but also a gatekeeper who enforced his isolation—and driver Tony Mascia were busy with other projects, and Michael Lippman, too, had "his hands full, there was so much going on." For the weeks leading up to the filming of *The Man Who Fell to Earth*, David was lonely, and mostly alone but for occasional visitors like Hughes.

It wasn't all decadence; David could be hilariously funny. He christened Hughes "old big head," presented him with a portrait inscribed with his new title, and spent hours badgering the rock bassist to throw out his bell-bottoms and blue denim. He'd lose entire days engrossed in painting and shared his insights on various subjects freely. Hughes, a fellow soul fan, loved Stevie Wonder and wanted to record with him. "No," Bowie instructed him. "It's too obvious that you're influenced by Stevie; do something with Nina Simone instead." Only in later years did Hughes appreciate the depth of Bowie's perception.

But those moments of clarity and positivity were rare. Mostly, David would sit there, his forehead creased, "thinking, always thinking," and watching the same movies again and again. From Hughes's perspective, David's involvement with the occult was exaggerated; it was something he was frightened of, rather than drawn to. Yet Bowie's fascination with the Third Reich, often dismissed as publicity-seeking, ran disturbingly deep: "He would watch a lot of movies. Neverending Nazi stuff, which he'd watch with this constant frown on his face." Sometimes Hughes would go home to crash and return to David's house a day later to check on him, only to see him sitting in the same place, wearing the same clothes and the same frown, watching the same movies. Faced with the endless black-and-white footage, Hughes could manage little more than a coked-up "wow." David showed no evidence of racism, but his fascination with Nazi lore seemed extreme, another symptom of what Hughes saw as full-blown psychosis: "I couldn't analyze what he read or saw, I wasn't capable—his brain was simply on a tangent to everybody else's. It certainly wasn't spiritual—who is spiritual when they're on coke?"

At the time, Hughes assumed David was making some kind of sense of the images and words flooding through his consciousness. In reality, Bowie was like a babbling drunk, convinced he'd discovered the secret of the universe. Other conversations that summer made his encounters with Cameron Crowe seem a model of rationality. Talking to the *NME*'s Anthony O'Grady in August, David opined that a fascist dictatorship was on its way, explaining: "It's like a kaleidoscope—no matter how many little colors you put in it, that kaleidoscope will make those colors have a pattern...and that's what happens with TV...Who says the space people have got no eyes? You have—you've got one in every living room in the world." Then, perhaps sensing his interviewer's realization that he was talking gibberish, David added, "That's theoretical, of course."

Glenn Hughes didn't imagine that aliens were controlling his TV, but the cocaine would bring similar delusions—by the end of the year he was hiring guard dogs and security to deal with imagined intruders. Yet, in Glenn's view, David positively reveled in his paranoia: "David used to drive his Mercedes alone through Los Angeles, on blow, the most paranoid son of a bitch in the city, wearing a hat, all the way from Doheny Drive to Beverly Hills. I tried it once that year, but I was too paranoid, too loaded. He arrived at my house and I'm, How the *fuck* did you get here?"

David had undoubtedly learned to use cocaine, savoring the impact it had on his psyche. "He—and this is glamorizing it—did use the drugs to enlarge his capabilities in every dimension," says Hughes. "It really magnified his intelligence, if you will. But it had its way with him."

IRONICALLY, it was playing the part of an alien that forced this damaged creature to abandon his quest and come back to Earth. Even as he prepared for the upcoming movie shoot in New Mexico, waiting for the mostly English crew to assemble, David seemed capable of utter focus and dedication. In a strange way, David's frazzled mental state accentuated his almost childlike earnestness. He was still a showbiz pro. Given direction by Nicolas Roeg in rehearsal, he was calm, almost pliant; none of those present remember any trace of nervousness.

Shooting of *The Man Who Fell to Earth* had been delayed by problems with the intended backer, Columbia Pictures, who withdrew after realizing their choice for leading man, Robert Redford, had been supplanted. The newly formed British Lion company, led by producers Michael Deeley and Barry Spikings, stepped into the breach. There would be constant disputes over budgets and other issues, but when filming commenced late in June at Lake Fenton, New Mexico, the tight schedule and budget became an integral part of the movie's feel. When a passing tramp turned and belched in the opening shot, Roeg incorporated the scene as a motif. Bowie's limo driver, Tony Mascia, performed that job for Bowie's character in the movie, Newton. Roeg and his star shared the same instincts: "During filming, we were close and not close at the same time," says Roeg. "We didn't go out for dinner, but we were very close in understanding."

If Bowie's greatest movie was a depiction of his condition adrift in LA, the perfect example of the city's emotional blankness was the fate of Maggie Abbott. In February she'd persuaded Roeg and Bowie to work together. In March she'd made a deal with Michael Lippman, who'd demanded a large fee but was negotiated down. Around June, she gave a joint party for David and Charlotte Rampling in LA. Then in July, she heard that Lippman had barred her from the New Mexico set. The woman who'd made the movie possible didn't see Bowie for another ten years, when she bumped into him at a movie-industry party—in true Hollywood fashion, to avoid losing face, Abbott "pretended I didn't know him. He did the same."

GEOFF MacCormack accompanied Bowie and Coco to New Mexico, where he was given a sinecure as David's body double. The three spent a healthy few weeks at the Albuquerque Hilton and, later, in Santa Fe, relaxing and sightseeing in the run-up to the filming; David used the break to start painting during peaceful afternoons in the conservatory of his rented ranch-style bungalow. Over just a couple of weeks he visibly filled out, and his skin regained some of its natural glow. Roeg was worried about David's weight fluctuating if he binged on cocaine, and there seems to have been an understanding that David would not indulge during the shoot. When Bowie did succumb, Roeg decided not to react, and see where the ambiguity of the situation would take them. "I did not do or say anything. You can't reason someone out of anything. I'm not into the guilt thing or trying to cure anybody of our humanity—everybody has a sense of shame, guilt, secret happiness, accusation, or praise. There are certain things I wouldn't want to know about someone anyway, and I wouldn't want them to know certain things about me. It all goes back to this idea of exposing yourself. You have to live with yourself first."

With its echoes of Howard Hughes and David's own life, *The Man Who Fell to Earth* was, for all its art-house values and rarefied conceptualizing, simple in tone. The movie was totally reliant on Bowie's charisma—and his vulnerability. Leading woman Candy Clark was Roeg's partner; being directed in her sex scenes with Bowie by Roeg was something she says Roeg "got a kick out of. You English people can be very kinky." Clark's recollections of her leading man focus exclusively on his physicality: "He was so perfect for the role that it was very easy to imagine he was from another planet—he was beautiful, really at the height of his beauty. Really thick hair, dyed that lovely color, and his skin was just gorgeous." Her memories seem to involve scant sense of Bowie's fragility except for one instance, when "he'd drunk some milk, saw something in it—and then got sick." (His subsequent absence from the set meant that Clark had to film one key scene— where Newton reveals his alien, genital-free body, and Candy's character pisses her pants—solo.) Otherwise, Clark recalls Bowie's condition as surprisingly robust; at the end of the movie, Mary-Lou lifts Newton from the floor and places him gently on the bed, and Clark attempted to lift him only to find "he was very heavy—I couldn't budge him." The crew had to rig up a seat, mounted on a skateboard, to allow her to move the apparently emaciated entity.

On its release in May of 1976, *The Man Who Fell to Earth* would be mostly lauded by critics: "Roeg has done it again," proclaimed the *Guardian*. Bowie's crucial role won a near-unanimous warm reception; the *New Yorker's* legendary critic Pauline Kael pronounced the plot "uninvolving" but praised Bowie as "the most romantic figure in recent pictures."

Once the movie wrapped, David was confident that it would launch him as not just a movie actor but also a multimedia creative force. The formidable focus with which he approached his next project seemed to vindicate his view, as did the success of *Young Americans*—a slow burner, but a commercial breakthrough in the United States, winning gold-record RIAA status for 500,000 sales in July and the extracted "Fame" hitting number 1 on September 20. The significance was not lost on David, who was still gently reminding writers of this breakthrough five months later. For while "Fame" ascended the charts, David was already crafting a follow-up album.

Station to Station is usually regarded as the climax of David Bowie's love affair with Freud's "magical substance" as well as his definitive statement on his rootless, confused existence in Los Angeles. Yet it was more complex than that, for the album was an almost scientific experiment in risk taking; one of its key features, he told those around him, was that he'd walked into the studio with no songs prepared. *Station to Station* was also a love letter to Europe, and would be a remarkably coherent statement from a man whose grip on reality was intermittent. Just a few months later, Bowie would describe the attraction of "watching artists crack open a bit—and seeing what they're really like inside." For the first time time in years, underneath the clinical precision, a listener would find the real David Jones, devoid of masks, looking down into the abyss and upward in search of "that Godhead feeling."

There were brief rehearsals in LA before the recording of the album—not to work up material but "to get loose," says guitarist Earl Slick—and then the small crew of Bowie, Alomar, Slick, bassist George Murray, and drummer Dennis Davis convened in Cherokee Studios, a twenty-four-track facility that offered far more scope for experimentation than the sixteen-track setup at Sigma. And this, Bowie told his musicians, was the ethos of the album, "experimentation—and don't worry about how long it takes," according to Carlos Alomar. This would be a journey into sound.

The consistent reports that the album was recorded amid a blizzard of cocaine do ring true. Bowie later remarked he could remember nothing of its making. These were indeed "weird times," says Earl Slick, then just twenty-three. Slick's tough, gnarly guitar is a centerpiece of the album, winding in and out of Alomar's lithe, complementary melodies. Although most of the band remained in the studio for the early sessions, later on they would often be parachuted in and out, unsure precisely what they were contributing to: "I was at the Rainbow on Sunset—I thought I had the night off," says Slick, "and I was in a state as usual. I lived in a state. Then Tony, the maître d', said, 'Somebody is trying to find you,' so I got on the phone and they need me in the studio. It's about fucking midnight and I'm trashed and I worked until whenever we finished putting a solo down."

The state of stretching the mind till it cracked was an intrinsic part of *Station to Station;* what's surprising, in retrospect, is that this state was conscious. Bowie seemed to weave in and out of it, relishing the effect of being both trashed and in control. Blues writer and producer Neil Slaven by then had the quintessentially seventies job of star minder, traveling with Glenn Hughes, charged with the futile task of keeping him off cocaine, and he was therefore one of the few "straight" people on the scene. In the studio, despite the omnipresent huge bag of coke on the mixing desk, David was completely rational. When Slaven mentioned that the topic of their last conversation, back in 1972, was Buddhism, David became excited. "Oh, you'll like this then," he told him before handing over a sheet of yellow paper with the lyrics of a new song, "Word on a Wing." At times, Slaven looked at David, with his striking orange Weimar hair, and got the overwhelming impression of "I'm hiding behind this. But you can see me, can't you?" For all the decadent veneer, David was obviously the same singer Slaven had seen at Decca in 1967 spreading out gravel on the studio floor, reveling in the attention. If David had ever worried that his sanity could fracture forever, like Terry's, then this experiment suggested that his psyche remained intact behind the cracked facade.

Glenn Hughes, too, recalls that despite all the drugs on display David was "running the show. I was blown away by that. My mind would be all over the place when I was doing drugs, but he had total command of the sound — and this understanding of the musicians, it was like watching the greatest football manager in action."

There were other crucial, perhaps surprising, influences. Carlos Alomar had been back working in New York when he got the call. His lifestyle was essentially wholesome and straight during the recording. Told that the key word was *experimentation*, with no time limits, one of his motivations on the self-consciously epic title track was his session man's knowledge that "if a song is over three minutes you make double the royalty — glory, glory!" As he and the rhythm section experimented with the opening section of "Station to Station," messing around and adding muso tricks ("I was listening to Jethro Tull at the time," says Alomar), Bowie seized on a disquieting turnaround in the rhythm, a bar of 3/4 time followed by 5/4 time to disorient the audience, a prog-rock technique that rendered the introduction jarring and disturbing, preparing the listener for lyrics that were similarly grandiose — but sinister.

The song's mention of white stains evokes one of Crowley's most obscure works, a collection of pornographic poems he wrote under the pseudonym George Archibald Bishop. "One magical movement, from Kether to Malkuth" is a reference to the kabbalistic tree of life: Kether is the sphere of the Godhead, Malkuth the sphere of the physical world. Some commentators, notably writer Ian MacDonald, believe Bowie's understanding of the kabbalistic system drew on works like *The Tree of Life,* by Crowley's pupil Israel Regardie, and see something of the dark in Bowie's mind-set—a plausible interpretation, given Bowie's enduring interest in the Thule Society and other esoteric Nazi philosophies. Yet "Station to Station" lends itself to wonderfully diverse interpretations. It could represent absolute megalomania: that Bowie is a god who has chosen to embrace the physical world. The kabbalah reference could equally signify that Bowie has renounced the high of chemically derived nirvana in order to savor everyday existence. The song can also be read as a song of sensual love (in which case "the European canon" becomes a bad pun).

Yet despite the train sounds that open the record, "Station to Station" featured Christian imagery at its core, for its title alluded, as David would later confirm, to the Stations of the Cross. A similar yearning for salvation pervades "Word on a Wing"; almost conventionally Christian, it was written at a time when David started wearing a crucifix given to him by Michael Lippman. Later he would wear one his father had given him in his teens. They weren't just empty symbols; over time he would describe himself as "not religious—I'm a spiritual person. I believe a man develops a relationship with his own God."

Glenn Hughes, who has never previously spoken in detail of his strong but troubled friendship with Bowie, believes that David had sent himself on a journey deep into the cocaine mind-set in order to create new territory for his art. Bowie had never really suffered for his music before, not like Iggy and Vince Taylor, who were mocked and vilified by the masses. But in LA, he had staked his soul under the unrelenting California sun. "His period of hell," as Hughes puts it. "Because that stuff did have its way with him. It twisted and turned him inside out."

Some songs were cooked up in the simplest of fashions. Early in the sessions David bashed out the simplest two-chord progression on the piano and told Carlos it was a new song; then they realized the simple F-sharp-to-E riff and melody was uncomfortably close to George Benson's version of "On Broadway." Alomar transformed the rhythm with a springy, funky riff based on Cliff Nobles's classic Philly-soul instrumental "The Horse," while David's lyrics and optimistic doo-wop vibe came straight from the Diamonds' "Happy Years." Bowie's pitch-perfect, multitracked vocals were added in a quick sequence of mostly first takes, aided by Geoff MacCormack, and that, with the brief addition of a breathy melodica here and a chirruping vibra-slap there, was that. Beautifully simple, "Golden Years" transcended its influences, another perfect example that talent borrows; genius steals.

With just six songs, *Station to Station* was both sprawling and coherent; it would stand alone in David's work, the perfect gateway between American and European music. The turnaround it represented from the David Bowie of *Ziggy Stardust*—who'd arrived in the studio with a dozen songs, written and fully rehearsed—was complete. It was not an exercise in songwriting; it was a sculpture carved out of sound. In less than three years, David had not just changed genres; he had completely changed his working methods, from start to finish. This was the embodiment of the advice he'd given to Glenn Hughes earlier that year: "Do the contrary action—do something you're not used to. Let's not make it comfortable—let's make it *un*comfortable." *Station to Station*'s chart performance was perhaps the ultimate vindication of this advice; it peaked at number 3 after its release in January of 1976. The critical reception, too, was respectful, recognizing the bravery with which Bowie had staked out new territory.

Yet the fate of David's next recording showed the downside of his high-risk approach. Since signing up for *The Man Who Fell to Earth,* David had seen the challenge of composing its sound track as an intrinsic part of the project's appeal. Around November, he started work on the project, partnered by Paul Buckmaster, who'd arranged the strings on "Space Oddity." Alomar, Dennis Davis, and George Murray were called in for some of the recording, augmented by J. Peter Robinson on piano. Roughly six pieces were recorded, two of them funky-ish rock instrumentals, a ballad instrumental, later named "Subterraneans," and "Wheels"—"which had a gentle sort of melancholy mood to it," says Buckmaster. The recording, however, stretched on. Assembling a sound track required focus and discipline. Both were lacking, and, according to Buckmaster, "It just wasn't up to the standard needed."

According to Buckmaster, Bowie's sound track never approached a finished state. Yet Roeg and producer Si Litvinoff considered what they heard "brilliant," says the latter, "but [Michael] Deeley tried to get David to accept a lesser deal and was told to take a walk. To me this was a large disappointment." Litvinoff believes the movie would have been a much hotter commercial proposition with David's music and considered the replacement, by John Phillips, only "adequate." Bowie, meanwhile, was humiliated and blamed Michael Lippman for the fiasco. Lippman had made the mistake of building himself an impressive new house that autumn, partly financed by an agreed-on loan from David.

By Christmas, Lippman was out. Most of those who knew him considered him diligent and kind; he lacked the killer instinct of Tony Defries but would go on to have a more long-term career, managing both George Michael and Rob Thomas. Guitarist Earl Slick, then managed by Lippman, fell afoul of David in the messy split and was left behind when David went to Ocho Rios in Jamaica to rehearse for *Station to Station*'s upcoming tour.

The preparations provided another reminder, if one were needed, that for all his Third Reich fetishes and pharmaceutical peculiarities, David Bowie remained the consummate pro. Geoff MacCormack saw his friend in January: he'd put on weight and had a personal trainer and a suntan. He was "not perfect," but he was "better." Later that year he would meet Bob Grace, a key architect of his *Hunky Dory* breakthrough, in Paris. "I'd missed him, so we had a nice dinner and caught up," says Grace. "He told me, 'I've got over all my cocaine stuff now,' and I said, 'How's that?' and he said, 'I took that image off. I put it in a wardrobe in an LA hotel room and locked the door.'"

Grace saw a man who'd decided to abandon his wicked ways and then had simply done so. Such transformations are rare, and indeed David's second interview with Cameron Crowe, conducted in February of 1976, depicted a man still shot through with megalomania. It made for great press to launch his tour. Yet Ben Edmonds, the onetime editor of *Creem*, met the singer in the same week as Crowe and observed he was "not fucked up at all, not in the slightest—if anything, he was like a businessman in drag." The two spent much of their conversation talking about their mutual friend Iggy Pop. For a few moments, Bowie's professional veneer softened as he discussed his onetime protégé, a man who was "not so hard and all-knowing and cynical. Every artist always knows the answers of the world. It's nice to see someone who hasn't a clue—but has insights."

Bowie's comments were more perceptive than anyone could imagine, because at that precise moment Iggy indeed did not have a clue. Since walking out on Bowie, he had deteriorated from being a figure of ridicule on the Strip to living a twilight existence, sharing an abandoned garage with a male hustler called Bruce and sleeping on a stolen mattress. Thrown in jail after shoplifting some cheese and apples, Iggy found he'd run out of all his friends but one—Freddie Sessler. And the man who'd helped bring Bowie down raised Iggy up. Sessler stood bail for the singer and hired him for a telephone scam he'd cooked up. Then, when Iggy proved a lousy telemarketer, Sessler suggested a solution: "Look, you better call David. I know he likes you and wants to work with you."

"But I had too much pride," says Iggy today. "Then a few days later Freddie tells me, 'I'm going to see David, I told him I was with you—and he said, bring Iggy along.'"

The pair met up in San Diego. David was kind—genuinely so, for there was no hint of condescension in his offer to make an album with Iggy in Europe. In future months, many would comment on the amazing turnaround in Iggy's fortunes. Few people would realize that the friendship marked just as profound a change in Bowie's life. In tending to Iggy, David would heal himself too.

CHAPTER 15

Ghosts in the Echo Chambers

The guy has a lot of psychic stamina—he was perfectly able to go out and do the gigs, drive the entire continent by car, then go out to a club after almost every one until four in the morning, and do all the other things. And he never showed bad form, even once.

—Iggy Pop

FOR ALL THE ICY GRANDIOSITY of the *Station to Station* tour—undoubtedly the most intense performances David had put on since Spiders days—there was something cozy, almost domestic about the small retinue's daily routine. The tiny group revolved around David and his new best friend Jimmy, as he always called Iggy Pop. Usually, on the long drives between shows, the pair would sit in the back of David's car, the faithful Tony Mascia at the wheel. David cued up his current musical obsessions on cassette, and the two of them would exchange their reactions and insights. Often they'd talk late into the night; at other times, they'd sit silently, sipping espressos and reading without feeling obliged to chat, like old men who'd been friends for decades.

The two were heads of a cozy traveling household. Barbara Dewitt—sister of photographer Bruce Weber and onetime head of publicity at United Artists—looked after David's press, while Andrew Kent, who'd shot an amazing portfolio of Iggy during his grandiose self-immolation with the Stooges, was in-house photographer. Corinne and Pat Gibbons, previously with MainMan, looked after most of the administration. This tiny crew would ultimately form the basis of Bowie's management organization, Isolar. David's focus and attention to detail were simply phenomenal, Iggy observed: "The guy has a lot of psychic stamina—he was perfectly able to go out and do the gigs, drive the entire continent by car, then go out to a club after almost every one until four in the morning, and do all the other things. And he never showed bad form, even once."

Asked if David was psychically damaged, Iggy replies, "Of course he was—but he wasn't gonna show it. There were certain quirky, odd, theatrical, slightly megalomaniac ways of, er, relating— but I was used to that, 'cause I got some of that myself." It was not until a short break in the tour in May that David mentioned any of his troubles. In the meantime, he was relentlessly professional: always enthusiastic, efficiently checking through transparencies to be released to the press, and above all fired up by music, playing his friend pioneering records by Tom Waits, Kraftwerk, and even the Ramones—the last group, he told Iggy, was a sign that the world had not forgotten the Stooges. Carlos Alomar saw the two talking and noticed their joint explorations "somehow had a calming effect." They were similar, but different, "just like when you split an atom and it's twins."

There was something marvelously instantaneous about Iggy and David's new, deep friendship. In some respects it was completely bizarre. "I really didn't have a reference for why they were friends," says Carlos Alomar. "Nor were they musical friends." Both men were enormous narcissists and had proven irredeemably selfish over the previous year, yet each was supportive and kind to the other. Iggy didn't make special claims on David, nor did he abase himself. "There was no kowtowing, or humbling," says Alomar. If others complained about David's behavior, and Iggy could do something, he would. But when necessary, he'd be brutally honest with those who asked for his intercession: "That's how it is," he'd tell complainers, "just deal with it."

In part, each one's frank admiration for the other was driven by the fact that they were almost polar opposites. "They each want what the other one has," says a mutual friend, Eric Schermerhorn. Yet their characters were widely misunderstood. Bowie was the supposed middle-class intellectual, yet it was Iggy—in the guise of Jimmy Osterberg, school debate champion—who'd been voted Most Likely to Succeed by his junior high school classmates and who had made it to college. And Iggy was thought to be the wild man, yet it was Bowie who pushed himself and others well outside their comfort zones.

There was a simple reason, beyond the cozy family atmosphere, for the air of relative tranquillity that was evident throughout the thirty-nine arena shows of the U.S. leg of the tour, which ran through March 26, 1976. That reason was illustrated by the fourth date of the tour, in San Francisco. When David had played the city back in October of 1972, amid all of MainMan's hype and bluster, the Winterland had been embarrassingly empty. Now, the same city's Cow Palace was filled with fourteen thousand adoring fans. Speaking to *Melody Maker*'s Robert Hillburn, David described himself as "at peace," drawing a simple satisfaction from a job well done rather than looking for the "false gaiety" of *Ziggy* days. In its place was a genuine gaiety, a delight at the after-show-party presence of celebrities like David Hockney and Christopher Isherwood, who came, says Andrew Kent, "to pay homage" in LA. David's conversation with Isherwood inspired a plan for David to base himself in Berlin; he'd already thought about working in Germany, studying the recordings of engineers like Konrad "Connie" Plank as well as those of his current musical obsession, Kraftwerk. Before the tour started, he had agreed to the suggestion of Angie and his lawyer that he move to Switzerland for tax reasons. By the time the tour reached New York in March, he had confided to all his friends that he was planning to live in Germany and record there with Iggy. Only Angie was kept in the dark about the scheme.

On March 26, the U.S. leg of the *Station to Station* tour concluded with a masterly performance at Madison Square Garden followed by a star-packed party at the Penn Plaza Club. David and Iggy spent most of the evening huddled together, both of them graciously greeting old friends, like John Cale. The pair positively glowed with health; Jimmy was wearing a suit that he'd bought for a court appearance with Bowie the previous day in Rochester, New York, to answer charges following a marijuana bust at the Americana Rochester Hotel. A mug shot of Bowie survives in the Rochester Police Department files and is a classic of its genre: David impeccably suited, gazing at the camera with clear-eyed sangfroid. Perhaps his serenity reflected the irony that one of the music industry's best-known cocaine abusers had been "caught" with a soft drug that rarely figured on his esoteric menu. (The charges were later dropped.)

Both Iggy and David had decided that they'd leave their drug habits in LA; the agreement was never formal, and they'd both lapse at various times, but a measure of their success came when Iggy stayed on in New York for a couple of days after David and Coco sailed for Cannes, on March 27. For the first time, he realized the Stooges' legacy had influenced a new generation of New York bands; and also for the first time, he turned down a sniff of heroin, offered to him by ex–New York Doll Johnny Thunders.

By the time the party reunited in early April, David had come up with a rationale for his move to Berlin: a movie to be scripted by Christopher Isherwood. "I'm supposed to be living in Switzerland—but I don't know how long that will last," he told Radio One's Stuart Grundy. "I've got to come back to Berlin." Later that same evening, April 10, nightclub entertainer Romy Haag turned up for his show at Berlin's Deutschlandhalle.

Nearly six feet tall and drop-dead gorgeous, Romy's deliciously indefinable sexuality embodied the vibrant, fragile glamour of prewar Berlin that Christopher Isherwood had so compellingly recorded in the books that David had been reading in the last few weeks. Born Edouard Frans Verbaarsschott in The Hague, Romy had opened her own nightclub, Chez Romy Haag, just two years earlier and established herself as Berlin's most glamorous woman despite the historical accident of having been born a man. Romy brought a posse of her dancers and entertainers to the show; they made a dazzling spectacle and, according to Haag, "We looked at each other and that was that. The next day he had a concert in Hamburg and he was four hours late because he didn't want to leave." Thereafter, Romy became one of the many friends with whom David would spend hours chatting on the phone late into the night.

The European tour dates were a sensation; the set itself, opening with a grinding, thrilling version of "Station to Station," was sprawling but tough, seemingly anticipating the musical changes that were in the air in 1976. Yet it was David's emergence from nearly two years in limbo that was the main attraction.

His arresting, glamorous Thin White Duke persona was an intrinsic part of his appeal, especially because this was the first time he'd hit the stage in Britain since Ziggy's farewell. The contrast could not have been more pronounced: Ziggy's femininity versus the Duke's masculine 1930s neatness and fetching Weimar haircut. The hint of depravity behind the crisp white shirt and waistcoat was erotic. Perhaps his most drop-dead glamorous look to date, Bowie's European superman persona was carefully judged; it signaled his focus over the coming years, which was to build up a fan base on the Continent. David Bowie's previous tours had, incredibly, overlooked the European market; now the string of shows at huge arenas showed the pent-up demand spread by word of mouth.

The tour moved on from Germany to Bern, Switzerland, on April 17, after which there was a short layover in Zurich. Intent on building on his Ziggy-era experiences on the Trans-Siberian Railway, he announced a move into travel writing, yet another project floated and abandoned. Next David asked photographer Andy Kent to sort out the paperwork for a trip to Moscow before their next date, in Helsinki on April 24.

The journey was packed with unforgettable moments. On April 21, there was a little party to celebrate Iggy's twenty-ninth birthday; David presented him with a Polaroid camera to record their three-day trip. Once the small group—David, Iggy, Kent,

Corinne, and Pat Gibbons—reached Poland, the train clattered more slowly through an increasingly bleak landscape, and the five voyagers spent hours gazing at buildings pockmarked by machine-gun bullets and the gaunt remains of towns still shattered by bomb damage. The train stopped every now and then to pick up bottles of brown beer or the soup and peas that was the only food available. As their train pulled up alongside a goods train in Warsaw, they witnessed a gray-clad worker throwing lumps of coal up from a flatcar, piece by piece, while sleet rattled against their windows. An unforgettably dreary image, it would later be evoked in the haunting instrumental "Warszawa."

For most of the trip, the small party managed to evade official scrutiny by traveling as conventional tourists, but when the passengers transferred to a wide-gauge train at Brest, on the Russian border, they were met by the KGB and ordered to pick up two suitcases each and follow the officer to the huge interrogation room. "Then a guy who spoke English came up and said, and it was bone-chilling, 'We weren't expecting you,'" says Kent.

Kent had a copy of *Playboy* confiscated; Iggy attracted suspicion for attempted bribery because he'd impulsively given away the flowers that decorated their train compartment. David had a large trunk full of books, which the KGB rifled through, taking "one, maybe two," away, says Kent. They were on "that subject"—the Third Reich—but their removal did not cause the group any specific concern; instead, their worries centered on the travel documents that the border guards studied intently—then reluctantly conceded were in order.

The small party breathed sighs of relief as their passports and forms were handed back to them. Then, ominously, one burly, blond official, who they took to be KGB, closed their encounter with the words: "Someone will be there to meet you in Moscow."

They spent the next few hours chatting nervously, wondering what the KGB had in store for them. But, incredibly, when they pulled into Moscow's opulent, marble-lined Belorusskaya station, the platform was empty—Big Brother, as so often happened, was not as efficient as claimed, and they were free to explore. After dropping their luggage off at the Metropole—a sumptuous, historic art nouveau building that was the setting of several key Lenin speeches as well as Bulgakov's sinister novel *The Master and Margarita*—they wandered across Red Square, posing like happy schoolkids alongside Russian conscripts, then went on to a shopping trip at the huge, glass-roofed GUM department store for tourist trinkets, after which they had dinner back at the Metropole.

Their frolic in Moscow lasted just seven hours before they caught the train out, but they had not seen the end of Soviet bureaucracy, for on the way to Helsinki, the border guards chose to strip-search both David and Iggy. They were unperturbed by the experience, which was blown up by a manufactured furor about David's having disappeared: "I don't know if it was a publicity stunt or not—but it was a great one if it was," says Kent. The next publicity stunt was not so easily explained. David's quote at a press conference in Stockholm on April 24 did not appear in print until May 2, when the *Station to Station* tour, also known as the Isolar tour, hit the United Kingdom, and David greeted his fans at Victoria Station. Photographs across the media, including one by Andrew Kent, showed David's arm outstretched in what looked like a Nazi salute, and articles quoted his remarks at the Stockholm conference one week earlier: "I believe Britain could benefit from a fascist leader. After all, fascism is really nationalism." A media firestorm blew up.

Bowie qualified his Stockholm remarks to Jean Rook in the *Daily Express* a couple of days later: "If I said it—and I've a terrible feeling I did say something like it to a Stockholm journalist—I'm astounded anyone could believe it. I'm not sinister. I don't stand up in cars waving to people because I think I'm Hitler."

Rook found him sincere—there was a schoolboyish earnestness about his demeanor that enhanced his horror at being so misunderstood. Yet this was a mealymouthed politician's defense, one he would repeat in later months when he declared himself upset and hurt that anyone considered him racist. Few people did, certainly none of David's friends. "There was no trace of that," says Ava Cherry. Andrew Kent says, "I'm Jewish and I never [suspected] anti-Semitic reasons. If I'd thought that I would have quit." Movie footage of David's arrival revealed his so-called Heil Hitler salute was nothing of the kind. But there were enough quotes sitting on journalists' tape recorders to demonstrate that, while not a racist, David was happy to flirt with fascist imagery in search of a newspaper headline.

Without doubt, during that sweltering summer of 1976, Bowie's fascist chic chimed with sentiments voiced by some of his rivals. Bromley contingent head Siouxsie Sioux sneered that there were "too many Jews for my liking" in one of the Banshees' earliest songs, "Love in a Void," and in August, Eric Clapton ranted that Britain should "get the wogs out, get the coons out." Most of Britain's youth would, rightly, suspect Bowie of cheap opportunism rather than Clapton's addlepated racism, but that summer Bowie's credibility as a champion of the outsider took its first severe dent.

The tour finished in Paris on May 18, and its end was celebrated by a party at which David spent most of his time canoodling with Romy Haag. The earlier concerns were mostly forgotten as David turned his attention to working with his friend Iggy. Up to his arrival in Paris, David had intended to work in Munich with his new friend, but a change of plans was prompted by the staff at the Château d'Hérouville, the residential recording studio where David had made *Pin Ups*. Commercial manager Pierre Calamel and studio manager Laurent Thibault, the new regime there, astutely calculated that Bowie might need a refuge from the French fans crowding around the Plaza Athenée hotel and invited him back to the eighteenth-century château set in the rolling countryside of the Oise Valley, an hour's drive from Paris. Enticed by Calamel's offer of "some peace—and some French cheese," Bowie arrived that afternoon wearing a flat cap and accompanied by Iggy. Deploying his natural gentlemanly charm, he inhaled deeply to take in the distinctive smell of the grand old building and then announced to Iggy, "This is a great rock-and-roll studio."

After a long sleep—although David woke up in the night and was found wandering the grounds, confused and naked but for a

1940s-style Burberry trench coat—David called a meeting with Laurent Thibault. He brought a huge case of albums, which he played through, critiquing each of them, including a couple by Thibault's previous band, Magma, and then announced that in a couple of days he was taking a trip to his new house in Switzerland but would return in a matter of weeks to produce Iggy's solo album at the château and would use Thibault as engineer. Later, it transpired that a crucial sweetener for using the château was the prospect that David and Iggy's living costs would be picked up by a record company; David had no cash for day-to-day expenses. With the flow of MainMan-era royalties stanched and legal disputes with Michael Lippman imminent, he was forced to watch every penny. Over subsequent weeks, onlookers would be astonished to see Corinne reprimanding David for spending a hundred francs on a new jacket; when he settled the bill for Iggy's recording, David's check bounced.

In Switzerland, Angie had taken great care in selecting the first marital home the couple would actually own. The move was perhaps an act of self-deception, given that she and David had been living apart for two years, with Zowie still under the care of the redoubtable Marion Skene. Yet David had continued to maintain that deception in print, telling Cameron Crowe in February that Angie was "remarkably pleasant to keep coming back to. And, for me, she always will be." Believing that her problem-solving abilities would continue to endear her to her husband, Angie had steered her way through the Swiss bureaucracy investigating the various tax and residency issues, convinced that with this feat, as with so many others, she could prove herself indispensable. Clos des Mésanges was a luxurious house; it had seven bedrooms and a caretaker's lodge and was set on several acres of land in the village of Blonay, just above Lake Geneva. Her efforts were wasted: The first home she owned jointly with her husband would be the last. When he arrived in Switzerland, David took one look at the house, exchanged only a few vague words with Angie, and then disappeared. As she so often did, Angie swung from exhilaration to near depression, and she soon started looking for a villain in the scheme, not for the first time alighting on Corinne Schwab. Undoubtedly there was little love lost between the two women, but Corinne was in essence a convenient scapegoat, for David's dissatisfaction with his marriage predated Coco's arrival. In any case, Angie's suspicions that her marriage was doomed were correct, for it was during his brief stay in Switzerland that David, who had so far kept remarkably quiet about his problems with both Angie and Michael Lippman, first confided in Iggy, discussing the future without being too specific. "He's English," says Iggy, by way of explanation, "reserved and all that." Within a couple of days Iggy, David, and Coco set off for the château, probably stopping off in Berlin for some flat-hunting en route.

At the end of May, David was in the château for the sessions, concentrating all of his focus on Iggy. The album would be based around "Sister Midnight," a song he'd written with Carlos Alomar and played for Iggy within a couple of days of their meeting in February, telling him how he'd love to put together a solo electronic album based on a similar dark, electronic groove. It was a long way from the Stooges, but Iggy instantly responded to the challenge, realizing that in its minimal, robotic way, it boasted a unique power: "For me it was perfect! And I loved it; when I heard it I went, 'Whoa.' And there wasn't one stinker in that whole period, he only pitched me great balls — and I grabbed every one."

If there is any period in David Bowie's songwriting that is underappreciated, it is this one. The music was once again flowing out of him, and behind the twisted, distorted facade of *The Idiot*, the subtlety and deftness of David's craft was at a latter-day peak. Most songs were sketched out with David's electric piano and guitar, augmented by Laurent — Tibo — playing scratch bass. Brittany session man Michel Santangeli did the same for the drum parts; David would keep whatever bits he liked and build on them with other musicians later. Bowie had explained to Jimmy back in the spring that this would be a chance for him to explore concepts he planned to use in his own work, yet Iggy would also get the benefit of songs, such as "China Girl" and "Nightclubbing," that were more commercial than anything David had kept in stock for himself.

The pair made an engaging, odd couple: David with his severe Germanic haircut, focusing intently on the music, sitting in a lotus position on a chair by the console; Jimmy, blond, spreading out like a lizard on the floor amid sheaves of lyrics or bouncing around outside like an enthusiastic puppy when David was busy in the control room. Zowie played on the grounds, accompanied by Marion Skene or other kids from the studio household. David's old friend Daniella Parmar showed up at one point to add to the family vibe; Angie, of course, was absent. With Corinne following David around as all-purpose factotum, helper, and lover, and with Iggy sunbathing by the pool, there was an intriguing, warped domesticity about the setup. The impression was heightened by incidents like the time Iggy took a day off to see his old flame Nico in Paris. The Velvets chanteuse was known to be a diehard of the Parisian heroin scene, so Iggy or his minder had to call in regularly to reassure Coco he wasn't high, like a teenager calling home.

David was sweet with Zowie, less distracted than in the Ziggy days. For the French staff, his lack of physical affection with Zowie—he was not a tactile person—raised eyebrows, then was dismissed as typically English, which indeed it was. He didn't cuddle Zowie, but when he was with him, he gave him his full attention. One day in the dining room the staff saw David and his son chatting away; Zowie was drinking a Coke and his dad joked, "You'll get paranoid if you drink that." Instantly the five-year-old responded, "Well, no one believes what a paranoid person says anyway." Bowie laughed proudly at his son's quip; it sounded as if paranoia was a regular subject for father-son repartee.

In the opulent surroundings of the château, David took to the role of *le grand seigneur,* politely asking if he could have the main room with the fireplace, as well as a stereo—his courteous requests were invariably repeated, more forcefully, by Coco, who irritated the staff until they realized that "she had no life" and sympathized with her self-imposed "slavery." The castle's owner, composer Michel Magne, had let his musician friend Jacques Higelin take up one wing of the building, along with his girlfriend, Kuelan Nguyen, and three-year-old son, Ken. A brief affair

The Thin White Duke. In February 1976, David commenced his biggest tour to date, quoting Aleister Crowley and flirting with fascist chic. Yet despite appearances, according to new friend Iggy Pop, behind the scenes David would "never show bad form. Not even once." (Les Lambert/Rex)

The beautiful but "heavy" alien: filming *The Man Who Fell to Earth* with Nic Roeg, summer 1975. The movie shoot was a brief respite from David's consumption of Merck, potent medicinal cocaine supplied by legendary hanger-on Freddie Sessler. (Duffy/Getty)

"Der Führerling." The accusation that David had been snapped making a Nazi salute at London's Victoria Station on May 2, 1976, was unfair—but though he'd conquered cocaine by this time, his obsession with fascist imagery took longer to vanquish. (Press Association)

The Thin White Duke on furlough in Moscow: dinner at the Hotel Metropol with Corinne 'Coco' Schwab and Iggy Pop, circa April 23, 1976. The three set up home together in Berlin that summer. (Andrew Kent)

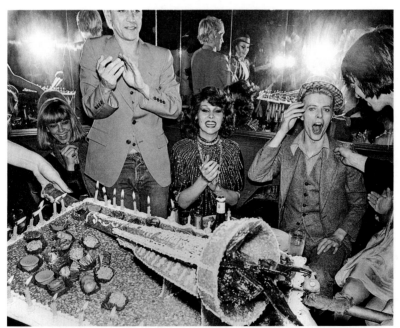

David celebrates his 30th birthday with Iggy Pop (*standing*), Romy Haag (*center*), and Coco Schwab (*out of view*), L'Ange Bleu, Paris, January 1977. "This is a guy who a year before was supposedly out of his mind on cocaine," says one friend from the time, "and here he was in sensible shoes, jacket,... flat cap, just open and chatting to everyone." (Andrew Kent)

"Everything said, 'We shouldn't be making a record here.'" Berlin's Hansa TonStudio (*left*) in 1976, among ruins that evoked Brixton in 1947. (Eduard Meyer)

David with (*from left*) Tony Visconti and Tonmeister Eduard Meyer, completing *Low* at Hansa, October 1976. (Eduard Meyer)

Filming *Marc* with old mod friend Marc Bolan, September 9, 1977 (David's old bassist, Herbie Flowers, is at left). Their last public appearance together was marred by a silly tiff that epitomized the pair's intertwined friendship and rivalry. Marc would die in a car crash on Wimbledon Common on September 16. (Rex)

"Moving On." David relaxing at London's Dorchester Hotel, September 1977, after emerging from his Berlin seclusion. Soon he would embark on a mammoth world tour, with another album, *Lodger*, recorded during a brief stop-off. (Barry Plummer)

David finally proves himself as an actor onstage, inhabiting the role of Joseph Merrick in *Elephant Man*, summer 1980. He enchanted his fellow actors — who nonetheless concluded that his was "the most horrible, horrible life." (MirrorPix)

NYC's *Daily News* shows John Lennon signing Mark Chapman's copy of *Double Fantasy*, December 8, 1980. Chapman's murder of the Beatles singer, with whom David had recently renewed a friendship, inspired his flight from New York to Switzerland. (Getty)

Hobo intellectual: David filming *Baal*, August 1981, in a rare break from his seclusion in Switzerland. The Brecht play represented a farewell to Berlin and underlined David's newly acquired intellectual credentials — but was destined to be remembered as a flop. (Rex)

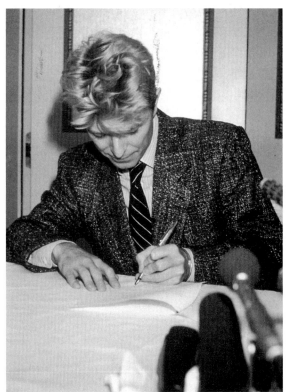

David signs on the dotted line for EMI, January 27, 1983, in a $17 million deal that today, says the A&R who signed him, would have record labels "in a line around the block." (Barry Schultz/ Sunshine/Retna)

"You have no idea…it's like they're feeding you the sun, the moon, and the stars." David Bowie, bona fide superstar, Serious Moonlight Tour. (Denis O'Regan/Starfile)

With producer Hugh Padgham (*center*) at Le Studio, Marin Heights, near Montreal, to record *Tonight*, David's move into white reggae—just as the smart money was moving out. (Yael Brandeis Perry)

"Absolute Beginners," June 1985: David at West Side Studios, making his last great single of the 1980s, written and arranged in a whirlwind with a new young band. When the session was finished, he thanked them for doing him a favor. (Kevin Armstrong)

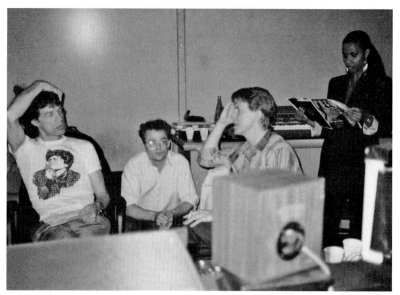

Recording "Dancing in the Street" with (*from left*) Mick Jagger, Kevin Armstrong, and singer Helena Springs. David was relaxed, Mick more "vocal and mouthy," remembers one musician. (Kevin Armstrong)

A quick cigarette with Freddie Mercury, backstage at Live Aid. David looked after his band like a mother hen during the day, devoting himself to the cause rather than his career. (Kevin Armstrong)

Famously ludicrous, *Glass Spider* marked the point at which David (here flanked by, *from left*, Erdal Kizilcay and Peter Frampton) moved from being a relaxed delegator to a nervous control freak. Still, the Berlin show on June 6, 1987, was a triumph, sparking riots in East Berlin; U2 would later lift some of Bowie's staging ideas. (Bellia/Dalle/Retna)

David visits with Hansa's Edu Meyer before the Berlin show. (Eduard Meyer)

Among friends: with girlfriend Melissa Hurley and new guitarist and confidant Reeves Gabrels, Compass Point, Nassau, late 1988, finalizing Tin Machine's debut album. (Kevin Armstrong)

"It never really gelled—it was a battle." Tin Machine, February 1989, with Reeves Gabrels (*right*) and the irrepressible Sales brothers, Tony on bass, Hunt on drums. (Ebet Roberts/Getty)

"I have never been so happy." David met Iman Abdul Majid on October 14, 1990. He later said he started thinking of baby names that first evening. (Ron Galella/WireImage)

A modest party, with only 17,000 guests, to celebrate David's 50th birthday, January 9, 1997, at Madison Square Garden. The music drew mainly on *Earthling*; the image—augmented with refurbished, all-American dental work—was state-of-the-art MTV. (Kevin Mazur/WireImage)

"He came back dressed in *Hunky Dory* mode and played a set full of hits; every one was a winner." Taking Glastonbury by storm, June 2000, with a band that included old hand Earl Slick, David finally seemed reconciled with his own past. (Melville/PA)

David, in a kimono—and "tiny Japanese slippers on his tiny feet"—greets (*from left*) Bono and Brian Eno backstage at London's Royal Festival Hall after his recreation of *Low*, June 2002. (Rex)

"A mature singer, like Tony Bennett or Frank Sinatra." A nervous David returns after his heart attack, September 8, 2005. The bandages and bruising signaled his identification with the battered state of New Orleans; his voice was now grainy and world weary too. (Rex)

"It was an unusual relationship." A rare public appearance, this time playing support— to director son Duncan Jones, for *Moon*'s appearance at the Tribeca Film Festival, NYC, April 2009. (WireImage)

"We'll see what's mean to be." David Bowie's final tour, Los Angeles, 2003. Its ultimate curtailment formed a de facto Houdini escape—a rationale for the retirement of which he'd long fantasized. (L. Cohen/WireImage)

between Kuelan and Iggy added to the edge and intensity of *The Idiot* sessions, and within its first few days it was immortalized when Iggy rewrote one of David's songs, "Borderline," to become "China Girl"—whose lyrics simultaneously implored Kuelan to come with him to Berlin and warned her away. David seemed to savor the energy and vitality that their affair represented; he, too, focused on Kuelan, rubbing her back flirtatiously or puffing on the pipe he'd lately taken to smoking, enjoying the ambiguity of the situation. "It's good for Jimmy's heart to be loved that way," he told Kuelan, almost like a father giving his consent.

Gossip from this period has David as a cocaine-raddled paranoid wreck—perhaps the best apocryphal story is of him abandoning a session after Iggy invoked occult forces by pushing him into the pool—but throughout the recording, David's main vices were beer and women. It was only when rival musicians arrived, say the staff, that the old traces of megalomania surfaced. There were rows inspired by old rivalries when Bad Company prepared to move into the studio; Edgar Froese was also frozen out after arriving at the château to add some synthesizer parts. Called up to the control room, Froese listened to a rough mix, then over dinner confided to David: "At first I didn't really like your record...but finally I know you are making very interesting things. I am very proud to be here." Casually, David told him they'd call down for him to record later. Several hours had passed when Pierre Calamel went to check on Froese, who was still sitting near the pool. "I came over and said, 'Are you okay? Do you want something more to drink?' It was a sunny, very hot day and I moved the parasol because the guy is getting very pink. And they didn't call him up. I was very sorry for him."

When the time came for Froese's flight back to Berlin, the château staff ordered him a taxi, and the Tangerine Dream founder left without a backward glance.

The surreal atmosphere of *The Idiot* sessions was even more obvious once David and Iggy left the château to make room for Bad Company. The new studio, Musicland, had been built in the basement of a Munich hotel and mall; Thin Lizzy was recording there by day; Iggy and David would piece together their gothic soundscapes by night.

Guitarist Phil Palmer was called to the phone late one night by his mum, and he spoke to a polite, charming David, who asked him to get his Telecaster and hop on a plane to Munich. Palmer found the nocturnal, subterranean sessions disconcerting— "*vampiric* would be the word." David's instructions were more psychological than musical: "Imagine you're walking down Wardour Street and as you're walking past each club you're inspired to play what's coming out of it." That would be the most specific instruction he'd get throughout the recording. The sessions were "experimental on every level," says Palmer, with the pair pushing him for more extreme guitar sounds, asking if he would like to order in any sheep brains to eat and leafing through artist monographs by Egon Schiele and Erich Heckel. "They were very supportive of each other, and just having fun. And they were... obviously experienced in some pretty weird stuff. I wasn't aware they were taking anything—but their minds were a little odd."

Engineer Thibault relished the experimentation, crafting long tape loops into electronic collages, but the nocturnal existence eventually took its toll as they concluded the mix. One night, frazzled, while David was out of the room, he made an Indian headdress out of strips of red leader tape and attached it to his head. David returned, said not a word at this ludicrous spectacle, and then disappeared to use the phone. It's likely that this was the moment David called Tony Visconti in London to ask him to assist on his own album, which he planned to start work on directly after *The Idiot*.

Around August 20, 1976, Tony Visconti arrived at 155 Hauptstrasse, a typical *altbau*, or period apartment, set on a tree-lined twin-lane avenue in Schöneberg, an anonymous district in the southwest of Berlin. Bowie had told him Iggy was living with him; Visconti knocked on the door, hugged his old friend, and said hello to Coco, whom he knew from David's "skeletoid" *Young Americans* period. "Then David said, 'This is Jimmy.' So I shake his hand and look around and say, 'Great—where's Iggy?' Everyone laughed; it kinda broke the ice."

The session had originally been booked for some preparatory work on the *Man Who Fell to Earth* tapes from Cherokee; when they were delayed, Visconti helped put the finishing touches on Iggy's album at Hansa Studio 1, on the Kurfürstendamm. Throughout the process, says Visconti, "you could see David evolving and developing his next phase from this strange record." Over the same two weeks, Visconti was plunged into another thrilling, confusing new world: "One thing about David is that he's not a workaholic. He really loves to explore his environment."

In that first stay, Visconti lodged at the Schlosshotel Gerhus, a magnificent, decayed building once owned by art collector Walter Graf von Pannwitz. They'd work at Hansa Studio 1 in the afternoons, then in the evenings go to "Romy Haag's or some dungeon club," says Visconti. Bowie was eager to share the experience of Haag's club. It was oddly wholesome; "it wasn't really a gay thing, there were kids there as well as grown-ups, it was just part of their cabaret culture. Even if you couldn't speak German you could get off on the cabaret. Romy was about six foot tall and couldn't possibly have been a woman, which added to the mystique, and we'd [always] get the best table."

Schöneberg embodied the contradictory nature of David's fascination with Berlin. Five minutes down the road was a huge Nazi bunker on Pallasstrasse, the site of Goebbels's "Total War" speech. Another five minutes away was Christopher Isherwood's old house on Nollendorfstrasse—the "deep, solemn, massive street" he'd immortalized on the opening page of *Goodbye to Berlin*, with its description of young men whistling to the women on the upper stories in hope of an assignation, a pastime in which David also indulged. It was indicative of David's mind-set that he was as interested in the iconography of Hitler's Berlin as he was in the gay communities murdered by the Nazis who were commemorated by a plaque on Nollendorferplatz, where David and Jimmy shopped for books or sipped coffee. David might visit the Brücke Museum, study works by Heckel or Ernst Ludwig Kirchner that the Nazis had declared degenerate, then wander into antique stores and examine tickets and leaflets adorned with the telltale stickers that concealed swastikas.

Jimmy was relaxed about David's Nazi fixation—hardly surprising, given that Iggy's last new work presented on the stage had involved him being whipped by his old bandmate Ron Asheton, who was wearing a Nazi uniform complete with party armband (Asheton, incidentally, claimed to have invented the "Hitler was the first pop star" line that became a virtual Bowie catchphrase). Other friends were equally nonjudgmental; one Jewish acquaintance who knew David through his time in Berlin points out, "He was always fascinated by it. But the quote David was stigmatized for, he didn't mean it in a bad way. He meant [the Nazis] knew how to work the media." Although convinced David was one of the least racist people she'd ever met, the friend does not remember his ever explaining his crass statements—only in the later Berlin days, when David had met pleasant young men whose fathers had served in the SS, did he fully realize the implications of his fixation. It wasn't until 1980 that he'd describe his flirtation with fascist chic as "ghastly stuff." At the same time, in a wide-ranging interview with Angus MacKinnon for the *NME,* he pointed out, quite reasonably, that he'd never shown racism in his personal dealings. But he didn't apologize.

TONY Visconti learned that David was starting a new album of his own when he'd been called by David and a man he introduced as his newest collaborator, Brian Eno. "They said to me, 'What are you going to bring to the table,'" says Visconti. "It was the first time I'd heard that phrase, which put me on the spot, so I had to think fast." Famously, Visconti responded that he had discovered a new digital delay unit, the Eventide Harmonizer, that could both delay a sound and change its pitch, each independently of the other. His succinct explanation of the novel unit was that "it fucks with the fabric of time"—and he was in.

One other prospective collaborator never made the session. David had wanted to recruit Michael Rother from Neu! for the new album, whose working title was "New Music Night and Day," and he asked a member of his staff to call the guitarist. Rother said yes, yet somehow German-speaking RCA staff sabotaged the collaboration, telling him Rother had declined.

When the sessions convened early in September at the Château d'Hérouville, all of the musicians were unsure as to what they'd encounter. Roy Young, Britain's best-known boogie-woogie pianist, had received a phone call from David at the Speakeasy. It was the second time David had called—Roy had been unable to make the *Station to Station* sessions—and while David was effusive, Young had no idea how his piano would fit in with Bowie's music. The same applied to guitarist Ricky Gardiner, who, like Phil Palmer, was a Tony Visconti discovery—a replacement for Michael Rother. Young and Gardiner shared a plane out to Paris, nervously picking each other's brains as to what they would face.

As it turned out, the sessions were relaxed, with David sitting on the studio floor showing Young, Gardiner, Carlos Alomar, George Murray, and Dennis Davis little riffs, getting them to add their own feel, open-minded about what they came up with. But it felt strange. Asked what his plan was, David was frank: "I'm not sure yet, till we develop it." Brian Eno, who Visconti had been told would be one of the key collaborators, did not arrive until later in the session, which increased the nervous tension, as Visconti remembers: "We had defined it as an experiment. Before we went in, we said, 'This might be a waste of a month of our lives.' And it was three weeks before we knew it was working."

All those present knew David was dealing with problems deriving from an imminent legal battle with Michael Lippman; they sensed his preoccupation, though he shared in the studio camaraderie. In the early weeks, David was more ebullient. But when Angie briefly arrived at the recording with boyfriend Roy Martin to "help the session along," as one wit puts it, there was a huge fight in one of the rooms and then the sound of glass breaking; Iggy and Visconti had to pull Martin and Bowie apart. David seemed to quite enjoy the drama, then worked up a groove with the rhythm section that became "Breaking Glass": "I've been breaking glass in your room again." The lyrics warned Angie not to look at the carpet, a reference to his drawing kabbalah symbols on the floor back in Los Angeles. "Always Crashing in the Same Car" was a reference to the time David crashed his Mercedes, depressed and drunk, in Switzerland; the accident had some comedic value because David tried to raise some much-needed cash by selling the mangled vehicle.

As the tape rolled, the musicians relaxed, gamely replaying and revising, happy to be hanging out in luxury for two weeks. Drinks and food were on call twenty-four hours a day, and Roy Young kept the staff busy replenishing the bucket of ice that he kept on top of the piano alongside a bottle of gin and a bottle of tonic. After one take, Young heard a *rat-tat-tat* in his headphones and looked up to see David at the talk-back mike, holding up a glass. "So I sent him one, mixed just how I had them," he says. "And this happened a few times."

Sometime later, Visconti announced that they had a possible take, and the band trooped in. As the tape rolled, David sat in his characteristic lotus position on a chair by the desk, hand on chin, apparently deep in thought. The tape finished, and the assembled musicians waited expectantly for several minutes to hear his verdict before they realized he was fast asleep. "And I will always remember, he scratched his head exactly like Oliver Hardy when he woke up," says Young, "and then Tony said, 'David, I think you'd better go for a lie-down.'"

David made his way to the steep stairway that led from the control room, and then there was a sudden thud followed by a series of bumps as he bounced down the wooden steps. The musicians all crowded around to check on their singer, who was sprawled in a heap on the floor below—all the musicians, that is, except for Roy Young. "I hid under my piano," he says, "petrified." The next morning David pulled up his shirt to reveal dark red welts all the way up his skinny rib cage; the spectacle was accompanied by Visconti's warning that if another gin and tonic made its way into the control room, Young would be on the next plane home.

The lack of a clear outcome of the musical experiment was confusing, but at its heart it was a simple, intuitive, brilliant leap forward. David's intentions on the album that would become *Low* was to combine the glacial electronic instrumentation that he'd heard on Kraftwerk and Tangerine Dream records with a boisterous, vibrant R & B rhythm section. In sonic terms, the result was heavily influenced by Neu!, the band founded by Kraftwerk refugee Klaus Dinger; the harmonized, resonant guitar lines of Neu! songs—like "Seeland," from their last great album, *Neu 75*—have echoes throughout *Low* and *"Heroes."* But whereas Dinger's drumming was static, a metronomic pulse, Dennis Davis's spirit and energy drive the first half of *Low* ever onward.

A restless improviser who worked in parallel with Roy Ayers throughout much of his time with Bowie, Davis was as obsessed with the recording process as Bowie and Visconti—who rigged up the Eventide Harmonizer on Davis's snare drum then fed the results through the drummer's headphones so he could interact with its superhuman clunk. The constant counterpoint of the buoyant optimism of Davis, Alomar, and Murray with the contemplative, intellectual clarity of Gardiner and Eno gives the album a delicious tension, somewhere between optimism and anomie. The music reflected exactly David's mental condition: "I was at the end of my tether physically and emotionally. But overall, I get a sense of real optimism through the veils of despair from *Low*."

Throughout the summer of 1976, while the same old financial and legal crises continued to menace him, David's main strategy—along with attempts to seek oblivion via sex or beer—was to find solace in problem solving, piecing together *The Idiot* and *Low* like giant jigsaw puzzles. Iggy was his main partner in this occupational therapy, and David's unfailing instinct for selecting collaborators had led him to Brian Eno.

David knew Eno vaguely from the very first *Ziggy* tour, when Roxy had shared the bill at the Croydon Greyhound and later at the Rainbow show. They'd not kept in touch, but when Eno turned up at the Wembley dates in May, David had exerted all his charm, telling him he'd been playing Eno's *Discreet Music* throughout the American leg of the tour. "Naturally, flattery always endears you to someone," says Eno. "I thought, God, he must be smart."

When he turned up, around ten days into the *Low* session, Eno effected a quiet revolution. Hired by Bowie because he represented a one-man entrée to ambient music, a genre he'd created pretty much single-handedly with *Discreet Music* and *Another Green World,* Eno was an inspired choice for an accomplice, for his musical twists and turns paralleled David's own journey. A grammar-school boy and art-school student, he had quit Roxy Music in July of 1973, frustrated by their abandonment of art-rock experimentation. The cultural battle that took place within Roxy— Ferry's liking for cover versions and glossy artwork versus Eno's love for the random—echoed similar conflicts being played out in Bowie's head. In broad terms, Eno was hired to play right brain to Bowie's left brain; in musical terms, he was an inspired, punctilious synthesizer craftsman. In personal terms, he and Bowie were as *sympathisch* as they come, sharing a healthy sense of humor and a healthy streak of pretension, a taste for sexual adventure, and a love of reenacting Peter Cook and Dudley Moore comedy routines.

In future years, Eno would often be credited as the producer of *Low;* this was inaccurate, but he was coconspirator as well as hired hand. Arriving late in the sessions, he sat alongside Bowie as they briefed the musicians on the next stage of the recording, like a pair of avuncular squadron commanders prepared to wave their jittery recruits into the azure. "They sat us down and played us these tapes of the [*Man Who Fell to Earth*] sound track and told us what they were planning," says Young. "It was out of our experience...and honestly, quite a few of us didn't really like the idea." Bowie was acutely conscious that RCA might have a similar reaction: "We don't know if this will ever be released," he told Young and the others, "but I have to do this."

Eno arrived when the rhythm tracks for side one of *Low* were essentially complete; Murray and Davis flew home, while Carlos, Gardiner, and Roy Young stayed on to work up the instrumental

lines. Although Eno's more unsettling managerial techniques—
like his Burroughsian use of oblique-strategy cards—were not
extensively deployed on this record, he was crucial in motivating
both the musicians and Bowie, who was distracted by legal issues.
Eno encouraged a bullish attitude in which, as Visconti puts it,
"whether the record company was behind it or not did not matter
at that point—we simply made the most far-out album we could
think of." Yet the musical discussions weren't exclusively highfalutin; the decision to augment the first batch of recordings with
an instrumental side two followed a debate about whether Bowie
fans would consider the results decent value for money. "We felt
that getting six or seven songs with David Bowie singing, with
choruses and verses, still made for a good album," says Visconti,
"then making the second side instrumental gave a perfect yin-
yang balance."

Indeed, the seven songs that made up the first side were all
intricately worked, with an impeccable internal logic; David's
singing on the main vocal lines was his most honest and unaffected in years, offset by his vibratoed Brechtian yelps for the choruses. A decade of imitators would copy the impressionistic lyrics,
the low-key narrative vocal, and the foreground snare drum, yet
none of them would share the sense of discovery of the château
sessions.

More low-key than Bowie, happy to share jokes with Iggy,
Brian Eno often took a similar tack as David, picking people's
brains for ideas, quizzing the château engineers about techniques
other studio clients had used, patiently working out how to operate the desk and tape machine before asking to be left alone so he
could painstakingly overdub harmonized parts one line at a time
using his EMS AKS suitcase synth—a glorious object that looked
like an overgrown Stylophone mated with the Tardis control
panel. Appropriately, Eno pieced together his parts to the somber
"Warszawa" on the days when David had to drive in to Paris for
soul-sapping meetings with Lippman's lawyers at the Hotel
Raphael. Once the backup tracks were finished, Visconti's wife,
singer Mary Hopkin, arrived at the château to add her "doo-doo-doo"s

to the introduction of "Sound and Vision" while Tony and Mary's son, Morgan, played with Zowie and Marion.

One day, Eno heard Morgan picking out three notes on the reception-room piano; he used the simple, somber A, B, C as the main melody of "Warszawa," later augmented with David's devotional, wordless vocals, influenced by one of Eno's favorite recordings, a Balkan boys' choir.

Although Iggy is hardly audible on the *Low* recordings—his voice appears on "What in the World," a survivor from the *Idiot* sessions—his laid-back humor was vital. He'd huddle with David after his grueling legal meetings, which went on for days in a row, and use humor to ease him out of his exhausted, sometimes tearful state.

Toward the end of the recording, Iggy's jokes developed into full-blown comedy monologues based on the endless, hilarious disasters he and his fellow Stooges had suffered. One night he described how Stooges' drummer Scotty used MainMan's cash to buy a huge drum set that got smaller and smaller at each show: "A simple beat is where it's at," Scotty assured the other Stooges, who soon realized he was selling the set off, piece by piece, to support his smack habit. Another night at the château, Iggy stripped off his shirt to show David the scars on his chest and then demonstrated how he'd been forced to roll in broken glass to end a number, the only foolproof way of making his fellow Stooges, nodding out on heroin, recognize the final bars. "We would just fall about, aching with laughter; our sides would hurt," says Visconti. David would listen to these picaresque stories for hours, shaking his head, telling Eno or Visconti, "This is unbelievable, I can't imagine any human being went through this and lived." The tales of disaster, all true and rendered without any self-pity, were somehow soothing.

There were echoes of more ancient tragedies too, according to Tony Visconti, who claims the spirits of the previous residents of the château, star-crossed lovers Frédéric Chopin and George Sand, haunted the building. Bowie, too, considered it "a spooky place—I did refuse one bedroom, as it felt impossibly cold in certain areas," he says today. Interrogated about the spectral presence, the château's staff dismiss the stories. "The ghosts were in the echo chambers," says Laurent Thibault, "that's where the odd noises came from." Yet if one delves deeper, it turns out that Visconti and Bowie were not the only ones to sense the pianist and his muse; Ritchie Blackmore had had similar experiences, and at one Ouija board session, ghostly messages were rendered in perfect Polish—Chopin's native tongue. In later years, the château staff attempted to damp down widespread gossip about spectral presences, though the stories persisted until the studio closed in the wake of owner Michel Magne's suicide.

David loved the château—"It was a joy, ramshackle and comfy"—but as his slot came to an end, his last days at the studio were marked by bickering. Visconti cordially detested rival bassist and producer Laurent Thibault, who was blamed for the presence of a reporter posing as a receptionist (she spent hours in David's room engaged in "research"). Visconti also disliked the food and the alignment of the tape machines and preferred the "Germanic efficiency" of Hansa Studios; Visconti remembers he and David suffered food poisoning from eating warm cheese. And so David, Tony, Brian, and Iggy decamped to Berlin in mid-October, shortly before the news of David's "exile" in Europe broke in the German press and then worldwide.

There were more overdubs to come at Hansa; David, Eno, and Visconti reviewed the tapes at Hansa Studio 1 on the Ku'Damm before completing "Weeping Wall" and "Subterraneans" at the newly opened studio by the Berlin wall. Their assistant and translator was Eduard Meyer, a qualified *Tonmeister*—sound master—whom the trio would soon corrupt, subverting his formal training. They went easy on him at first: When David discovered he was a skilled cellist, he asked him to add a cello line to "Art Decade." "I am sorry, Mr. Bowie," Meyer replied, "I am a score-reading musician, not an improvising one." Remembering the skills picked up from Freda Dinn's *Observer's Book of Music*, David wrote out a part in manuscript. It was among the last instrumental additions to an album that David knew represented the biggest risk of his career.

According to Visconti, when RCA heard the album, one executive told David, "If you make *Young Americans Two* instead, we'll buy you a mansion in Philadelphia!" David had been prone to occasional doubts in the past when he'd completed albums, but not this time. RCA's confusion simply hardened his resolve. If that were not enough, when Tony Defries heard an acetate of *Low*, he dismissed it as "a piece of crap that even Nic Roeg turned down" and refused to allow it to count as part of David's contractual obligation to him. What could be more perfect? *Low* would be a new beginning, and David Bowie's estranged father figure wouldn't even have a slice of it.

CHAPTER 16

Helden

*This was clearly an ex–war zone and now it was an international
boundary, which was really scary. We recorded five hundred feet
from barbed wire, and a tall tower where you could see gun
turrets, with foreign soldiers looking at us with binoculars...
Everything said we shouldn't be making a record here.*

—Tony Visconti

C HECKPOINT CHARLIE, the fabled gateway between
West and East Berlin. Tony Visconti, sitting alongside
David Bowie, Iggy Pop, and Coco Schwab, watches nervously from the car as the guard scrutinizes their passports, and
his colleagues cradle their machine guns ominously, all of them
overseen by sentries in a low, glass-fronted watchtower. Suddenly,
the guard calls for assistance: *"Friedrich, kommen sie hier!"* The
party freezes, looking on as the second guard flips through the
passports—and then both of the Prussian gray–uniformed figures, sidearms at their hips, break into laughter.

Visconti steps out of the Mercedes, and the guards point out
the passport photos. "Iggy had this platinum hair, and Bambi
eyes," says the producer. "Bowie had that dreadful curly perm
from around *Space Oddity*." The two remade, remodeled, crop-
haired stars, far from home, are forced to silently endure the

ridicule before finally driving out to the East, with its ruined buildings, derelict train tracks, women sporting fifties-style beehives, and the countryside beyond.

What might have surprised the guards even more was that, for both rock stars, abandoning the hedonism, excess, and silly haircuts of the West—exactly those values being kept out at gunpoint at Checkpoint Charlie—had brought David Bowie and Iggy Pop to a new "joy of life," as David put it. "It was an education," says Iggy Pop, "always there was the idea, we're trying to learn something here. And to be pretty disciplined about it."

In Berlin, play and so-called work were intertwined. It was a rare week that involved no recording or administration, but there were plenty of days when they could ramble however they chose. David and Iggy might spend such a day wandering around the antique markets on Winterfeldplatz or the bookshops and cafés down by St. Matthias Kirche. Iggy would often rise early and walk for five or six miles; eventually, he claimed, he explored every nook and cranny of the city. In winter, they'd sometimes take the S-Bahn to the Wannsee, a lake resort on the Havel River, for long lunches under the glass roof, not far from the villa where senior Nazis had mapped out the Final Solution. One day David showed Iggy how to prep a canvas and apply acrylic paint; both of them spent time on artwork, David in particular, at one point completing a portrait of Iggy rendered in a convincing expressionist style reminiscent of the works they'd seen at Die Brücke, a modern, tiny museum shaded by the pine trees of the Grünewald Forest. Most often, they'd simply walk, dropping in on friends without warning just to say hello, the way they used to back in the sixties, before many people owned phones.

Compared with their previous existence, this was a life of monklike restraint. But both men were realistic about the regime. Occasional excess was acceptable, but heroin, Iggy's old bête noir, was not. One evening, David took a cab back home to the Hauptstrasse, and the taxi driver mentioned he had "the dooj" ready for his friend. David warned the cabbie, coldly, that there would be dire consequences if any of the dooj—heroin—should reach his friend, but he didn't mention the incident to Iggy, careful not to appear too controlling. Both men tried every brand of German beer available, and, unlike America's omnipresent drug culture, here "there was an artsy-craftsy weekend drug culture," says Iggy. "So on the weekends we'd go meet an eccentric character who was interested in the arts, and knew other people, and maybe you'd have a little coke and get drunk and go till four in the morning to three or four clubs."

Many locals knew who Bowie and Iggy were; naturally polite, they'd pretend not to recognize Bowie when they saw him in his regular haunts, like one of the city's two Zip record stores. Instead, once David had departed with a bagful of records, fans would sneak up to the cashier and ask, *"Was hat Bowie gekauft?"*

Visitors came and went regularly over this period, most of them staying at the Schlosshotel Gerhus. Angie was among the first, arriving soon after the completion of *Low* in November of 1976. It's difficult to locate that point at which she realized her marriage was irrevocably doomed, but her disdain for her husband's and his friend's attempt to sort themselves out indicates their relationship was now poisoned by indifference and contempt: "A lot of people love the idea of going and making nice to the people you've defeated so you can treat them like slaves. That was David's going-to-Berlin story: 'Let me lie with you in case there's something we didn't take from you that I haven't learned yet' — it's pathetic." Angie's distaste extended to *Low*, and *The Idiot* too, her opinions echoing those of her old patron and nemesis Tony Defries. Unsurprisingly, that Bowie family Christmas, spent in Switzerland, would be their last together. Bowie was in Paris by January 8, 1977, for his thirtieth birthday, celebrated with Iggy and Romy Haag. *Low* was released the next week, on January 14.

Low's reception by both the press and Bowie's record company was oddly in context with the record's sleeve — the title and photo of David in profile together made up a visual pun: *Low* profile. RCA's reaction to the album was simple incomprehension; as Robin Eggar, RCA's press officer at the time, remembers, the company didn't really know what to do with *Low* or *"Heroes."* "They only put them out because they were Bowie albums—and the attitude totally was, What are we going to do with this?" Equally, David's failure to promote the album meant press coverage was modest. Yet the myth that *Low* was greeted with widespread disdain is just that, for most reviewers realized this was a major event in Bowie's career. Tim Lott, future Whitbread Prize–winning novelist, spoke for many in declaring *Low* "the most difficult piece of music Bowie has ever put his name to." The writer finished his review for *Sounds* with an appropriately fractured procession of adjectives that ended:

> So. This album might be
> Bowie's best ever.
> Eno's best ever.
> A mechanical classic.

Lott cited "Sound and Vision" as the "pinnacle" of the album; his verdict anticipated its success as a single, reaching number 3 in the UK (but stalling at 69 in the United States). Its success further confused RCA executives, who were also, Eggar points out, intimidated by Bowie, accepting his refusal to tour the album without demur and likewise caving in to his persuasion that the company should release Iggy's *The Idiot*, which came out on March 21, 1977. From RCA's point of view, David's announcement that he would tour to promote Iggy's album rather than his own was perfectly consistent in its complete flouting of commercial logic. David took over all the arrangements for the tour, calling in *Low* guitarist Ricky Gardiner as well as two brothers who had passed him a demo cassette during David's first U.S. tour, back in October of 1972.

Hunt and Tony Sales were the sons of comic Soupy Sales. They'd earned their musicians' union cards when drummer Hunt was twelve and bassist Tony was thirteen; they had hung out with Frank Sinatra, sax legend King Curtis, and other hepcats; and they'd recorded their first album with Todd Rundgren when Hunt was just sixteen. Loud, hell-raising, and formidably talented, they arrived in Berlin in February, and from the moment they got there they ensured that David and Iggy's weekend debaucheries became seven-day affairs. Their routine normally involved a late breakfast at the Schlosshotel, rehearsals from eleven until five, goulash, a quick sleep, then a trip to Romy Haag's, an old bar once frequented by the SS where patrons could use the phones on the tables to find conversational or sexual partners, or clubs in Kreuzberg, where, says Tony Sales, "I saw a real-life reenactment of that Doors LP cover, with a midget with an umbrella standing on the bar."

In the brief, intense rehearsals at the old UFA film studios—which were filled with old filing cabinets crammed with film canisters and ancient Weimar- and Nazi-era paperwork that all the band members rifled through—the brothers watched the two oddly complementary singers chat, work, and relax. "It was two schoolboys hanging out, chums," says Tony Sales. "It was a very loving relationship in a sense. David was at a place where he needed to recharge and got behind Iggy—and in return that helped him, taking the pressure off being David Bowie."

The brothers were among the first outsiders to see the singers in their new hideout. Word had leaked out in the autumn that David was holed up with the ex-leader of the Stooges, and rumors had started to spread. Back in 1976, Iggy fanzine editor Harald Inhülsen wrote letters to fellow fans speculating that David had kidnapped Iggy and was keeping him "under his thumb." The implication that Iggy was being exploited as David's sex slave was widespread, entertaining, and made its way into print. Iggy laughs and denies such hanky-panky; even Angie Bowie, always given to seeing David in the role of exploiter, doesn't believe it, asking, with her unerring eye for practical detail, "Who would be on the bottom?"

A more plausible interpretation for cynics was that Iggy's main purpose was to give David credibility; this was probably the case with Iggy's role with MainMan, but by the time of *The Idiot*, there was a selflessness to David's behavior that, says Hunt Sales, is rare in the jaded world of rock music. "David really loved him as a friend. Giving something to someone is not giving something and expecting something in return. You just give it."

It says much for the zeal with which fans followed Bowie's career that by the time the Iggy tour started, on March 1, 1977, David's absence had become a widespread obsession. For the opening date of Iggy's first-ever solo tour, David chose the town that had hosted *Ziggy*'s debut performance more than four years before, Aylesbury, affably greeting old acquaintances like promoter David Stopps and jokily inquiring, "What's a clean-cut kid like you still doing in a town like this?" and insisting the crowd not be kept outside waiting when the back-line amplifiers were delayed in customs.

Kris Needs, who'd designed the flyer for the Friars Aylesbury show in 1971, had seen Bowie in nearly all of his guises. This one was the biggest shock of all: "This is a guy who roughly a year before was supposed to be out of his mind on cocaine. And here he was in sensible shoes and a jacket, maybe a flat cap like Iggy's, just open and chatting to everyone."

When the doors opened, it took a couple of songs before the audience noticed David Bowie sitting at the side of the stage playing a Baldwin electric piano. Soon, like the Red Sea, the audience parted: Bowie fans in the Civic Hall craned their necks to look at the keyboard player, who was studiously avoiding their gaze, and hard-core Iggy fans—like Johnny Thunders, Sex Pistols bassist Glen Matlock, and Damned guitarist Brian James, all part of a London punk posse who'd traveled up for Iggy's comeback—remained at center stage. The reactions to Iggy's new guise were mixed. Johnny Thunders was dismissive: "Iggy's gone cabaret," he whined.

The punk movement had finally exploded into mainstream consciousness with the Sex Pistols' Bill Grundy's appearance the previous December. Bowie's *Station to Station* shows at Wembley in May typified the stadium rock that many punks affected to despise; even his patronage of Iggy and Lou, the twin punk figureheads, was regarded as self-serving. But few of the British punks bothered to hide the fact that they'd cut their teeth on *Ziggy*-era Bowie. Even if the Sex Pistols had stolen Bowie's microphones from the Hammersmith *Ziggy* farewell, as claimed by guitarist Steve Jones, the theft was partly an act of affection. For those attempting to break out of punk convention, especially out-side of London, Bowie would be a guiding light; Manchester's Joy Division would take *The Idiot* as a sonic and lyrical template, and Bowie's name was soon being dropped by Echo and the Bunny-men, Cabaret Voltaire, Talking Heads, and others.

In the meantime, Bowie's low-key, stage-right role alongside Iggy was another object lesson in "positioning." Soon, peers like Ray Davies and Pete Townshend would embrace the punk move-ment, donning skinny ties and losing a little bit of dignity. David's slightly aloof position located him as an insider, not a follower; he was a decent keyboard player too. But the Iggy tour was harder work than David had anticipated; he had to keep up with Iggy and the unstoppable Sales brothers. Tony and Hunt were phenomenal musicians with an almost telepathic musical bond, which meant they didn't even need to hear each other in the monitors to stay in sync, but they existed in a blaze of alcohol, native energy, and cocaine. Bassist Tony remembers "walking through the hallways of hotels naked and stoned...it was over-the-top exhaustion and then you'd do more cocaine to cover the exhaustion."

It was a mark of the new, relaxed David that his fear of flying evaporated over this tour; David boarded a 747 to New York with Andy Kent and was "perfectly fine," says the photographer. But from the moment the band hit the States, the drug use and manic behavior intensified. During a wonderfully straitlaced joint appear-ance on Dinah Shore's show, with David letting Iggy occupy the limelight, they seemed calm, as if the pair had attained a new maturity, but backstage it was another story. Tour members remember full vodka bottles hitting the rafters in Detroit, a gun pointed at the stage in California, and a walking-and-talking doll with a Nazi flag draped over it marching across a dressing room in the Midwest. Soon Iggy was overcome by a new megalomania, and things became "very dark," says bassist Tony Sales. "I was in real bad shape...but I could always stand up."

David begged off from a subsequent Iggy tour, explaining,

quite reasonably, "The drug use was unbelievable, and I knew it was killing me," but a few weeks after the first tour concluded in San Diego on April 16, he threw himself into the fray again to produce a second Iggy album, this time at Hansa in its Köthenerstrasse location, just by the Potsdamer Platz and the Berlin wall. By the time the recording started, says Iggy, "I think David was pretty sick of my rock histrionics, and I was probably pretty sick of where he was coming from, so there was a lot of friction—but on the other hand we were both really into it."

Bowie's production on what would become *Lust for Life* was, quite simply, masterful. When he heard guitarist Ricky Gardiner strumming a catchy guitar riff, he suggested Iggy use it as the basis of what became "The Passenger"; his own melodies, on "Lust for Life" and "Some Weird Sin" were powerful and muscular. Bowie showed a rare flexibility, ready to change the schedule at any moment if, for instance, Iggy had a vocal idea he wanted to nail. Iggy describes himself as "the happiest person in the world" during this period—"I was living on red wine, cocaine, and German sausage, slept in a cot, and only had a cold shower." (He adds that other musicians avoided him, as, having only a cold shower, he never used it.)

Iggy moved into his own flat in the Hinterhof—servants' quarters at the back of 155 Hauptstrasse—with girlfriend Esther Friedmann and asserted his independence. One perfect example was the song "Success": Dissatisfied with David's original melody—"a damn crooning thing," he called it—Iggy arrived at the studio early to record the song with a simpler, stripped-down tune over the Sales brothers' swinging, midtempo groove, "a controlled gallop," says Carlos Alomar. The song, as the title suggests, proclaims that success is finally on its way; Iggy's stream-of-consciousness lyrics—a car, a Chinese rug—were all the more poignant, as events would soon conspire to deny him the very luxuries he described in song.

JUST as with *The Idiot,* David's work on *Lust for Life* served as a dry run for his own project, which he started almost immediately after wrapping up Iggy's album. The centerpiece of his so-called Berlin trilogy, *"Heroes"* was the only album of the three entirely recorded in Berlin; the city permeated both the sound and the ambience of the album.

It was Hansa Studios that best embodied Berlin's grandeur and menace. The main building, on the Köthenerstrasse, had been built as the Meistersaal in 1910, a beautiful, stern clubhouse showcasing the skills of Berlin's master masons. But in 1976, it looked like a forlorn wreck in a forgotten sector of the city. Left derelict throughout most of the Second World War, the building's elegant Ionic pillars were bullet scarred, the lofty pediment blown off, the upper windows bricked up with pigeons roosting within, and a quarter of its courtyard block had simply collapsed. All around, streets retained their gap-toothed look, like Brixton in 1947, and from the second story of the building, the section of the Berlin wall leading up to Potsdamer Platz was clearly visible. "This was clearly an ex–war zone," says Visconti, "and now it was an international boundary, which was really scary. We recorded five hundred feet from barbed wire, and a tall tower where you could see gun turrets, with foreign soldiers looking at us with binoculars." Berlin, according to Visconti, was both "a dream... and [a place] where everything said we shouldn't be making a record here."

The tiny crew included Alomar, Dennis Davis, George Murray, and Visconti, all of whom would get a taxi in from the Schlosshotel Gerhus each lunchtime. According to the producer, one factor in getting the album done quickly was "David was paying my hotel bills — so he didn't want to waste time"; hence the musicians would work "an intense eight-hour day, from twelve till eight, and then hit the Berlin clubs," says Visconti. Brian Eno stayed at the Hauptstrasse, at least some of the time — Iggy often entertained listeners with descriptions of Eno's girlfriend handcuffed to a radiator, a superlative example of art-school sophistication that impressed the poster boy of rock-and-roll excess, although in reality it's doubtful Eno had the leisure for such pursuits. Eno loved the ambience; Carlos Alomar was less impressed. "The hotels were, for an American, very old European, too many back staircases. My first impression of German men was that they were pigs. They ate a lot of pork, they looked a certain way, and when it came to treating their women I was appalled…maybe it was an age thing, but the overall German experience for me was very this sucks."

The difference in atmosphere between the Château d'Hérouville and Hansa Studios had an effect from the moment the background tracks went down. On *Low*, the beats had been funky, spritely; here, four-square rhythms gave a solid, dogmatic rock feel, more evocative of Kraut rock bands like Neu! The sound was bigger, almost literally, for the musicians set up in the wood-floored main hall—Hansa Studio 2—that Visconti miked to capture an ambient zing and excitement. Working out the songs was an edgier process; the chord changes were mapped out and endlessly altered, sometimes at random.

In those first few days, Alomar's contribution was vital; mild, almost stately, he was supremely competitive but remained calm when challenged to deliver: "The mentality that I had with David was always the same: You ask me for one thing, I will supply you with a million options until you tell me to stop. And that's my claim to fame." Visconti remembers Alomar's inventiveness at crafting "subtle melodies, one after another—the ones people don't notice straightaway, but they make the song come together." "He's quite remarkable," Eno told writer Ian MacDonald later that year.

And he had to be. In 1967, David Bowie had arrived in the studio with a complete set of songs, all of them painstakingly transcribed on manuscript paper. A few years later, at the time of *Hunky Dory*, songs arrived to him seemingly by magic, in a dream or on a bus ride. Now, in the culmination of a process that had begun just two years before with *Station to Station*, David walked into the studio with not one complete song. He had completely changed the process at the heart of his music, as if he'd abandoned a conventional representational technique for a new kind of aural expressionism.

Yet buried within the abstract shards of the songs that were slowly pieced together, making sense of the random, were plenty of traces of Bowie's hard-learned traditional skills. "Sons of the Silent Age," the only song sketched out before the sessions, showed many glimpses of earlier Bowie personae: Its opening is delivered in a nasal Tony Newley croon, and the agonized swooping melody of its middle section—"baby, I'll never let you go"—is an almost exact restatement of the middle-section theme from 1971's "Width of a Circle." Then, suddenly, the melody morphs into multitracked, Lennon-esque vocals; the gloriously naive saxophone evokes a barren future world and the 1950s kitsch of the Kon-Rads or Joe Meek.

Similarly, the futuristic gleam of "V-2 Schneider"—a tribute to both the terror weapons that landscaped South London and Florian Schneider, the founder of Kraftwerk—was humanized by the glorious teenage honk of Bowie's sax; "Blackout" briefly quotes "Boney Maroney," by Little Richard acolyte Larry Williams. Like the 1930s futurism that inspired him, the music of *"Heroes"* evokes both past and future. For perhaps the first time, Bowie's long, circuitous route to his present state seemed to make sense.

For Bowie and Eno, in particular, the sessions pushed them to a new level of intensity; both hardly had any time to eat, with Bowie subsisting mainly on occasional rushed raw eggs, Eno on cereal. ("Brian would start his day with a cupful of boiling water into which he would cut huge lumps of garlic," says Bowie. "He was no fun to do backing vocals with on the same mike.") Guitarist Robert Fripp, with whom Eno had worked closely since July of 1972, was thrown into the mix for just two days, forty-eight hours, during which he fantasized fondly, in a Somerset accent, about unleashing his "sword of union" on the locals; he never got the chance.

For all of the tiny crew, their time in Berlin during *"Heroes"* would result in a series of unforgettable images: the day that Visconti cut Iggy's and David's hair and they wandered around looking like old men; visits to an antique shop whose proprietor had known Marlene Dietrich; the frenzied warehouse parties with local rebels like artist Martin Kippenberger; the day Tony Visconti saw a huge black tank rumbling down the Kurfürstendamm; the

time Edu Meyer saw a guard on a DDR machine-gun post surveying them though his binoculars and attempted to blind the man
with a lamp, causing Bowie and Visconti to duck under the control desk, terrified.

For David, these Berlin experiences had "a calming effect,"
says Alomar. But even in the act of creation, his joy was controlled.
In this, he was a complete contrast to Iggy, who would swing from
euphoria to depression—indeed, just when *"Heroes"* was being
completed, Iggy succumbed to a manic-depressive cocaine jag for
which David and Coco arranged an "intervention," asking Barbara and Tim Dewitt to whisk him away to Capri. David was "an
educated thinker—so that would rescue him from the depres-
sions," says Carlos. But David also thought "way too much." His
enjoyment of the now was always overshadowed by the thought
that it wouldn't last.

Likewise, David's trademark futurism was omnipresent in
"Heroes" but gained a new poignancy in their Potsdamer Platz
outpost. Later, describing this time in Berlin as one of the happiest periods in his life, David would pick up this poignant note: "In
some ways, sadly, [the three albums] really captured unlike anything else in that time, a sense of yearning for a future that we all
knew would never come to pass."

"Neuköln," the most desolate song of the set, epitomized the
bleakness at the center of this futuristic optimism. Haunting and
stately, it played the same role as *Low*'s "Warszawa" and was
inspired by the once grand, now grim multioccupation buildings
of the Berlin sector—actually called Neukölln—that housed the
city's Turkish *gastarbeiters*. Workers brought in to supply Berlin's
insatiable demand for labor, they were denied citizenship: state-
less, temporary residents, like David.

One song was notably simpler than the rest, based on the
same fundamental G-to-C chord change that David had used for
Iggy's song "Success" just a few weeks before and taken at a similar stately pace, Alomar's "controlled gallop." The song's melody,
when it arrived, was based on the same three notes that David
had sung on the Iggy song, and as the musicians worked on

the backup track, Alomar once again added an insistent, unforgettable guitar line that emphasized the purity of its two-chord sequence. Yet it would be Robert Fripp's majestic, yearning guitar that would underline the song's monumental quality.

In future years, rumors would persist that David had told Fripp the track was an instrumental to encourage him to play all the way through; Visconti remembers otherwise, although Eno, who left before it was complete, assumed the track would be an instrumental. He thought it sounded "heroic." Fripp recorded his guitar in the huge ballroom, stepping between two taped marks on the floor that indicated the locations at which each note would build into a feedback loop. Fripp made three passes at the song; Visconti blended all three to ensure the guitar line floated serenely overhead, without falling to earth.

When David came to add the vocals after Eno had left, he used the technique he'd seen Iggy harness on *Lust for Life*, improvising words or finalizing them at the last moment.

The improvised lyrics, simple and deep, were the making of the album's most famous song. Visconti says, "He would scribble down a few notes on the top of the piano, then say, 'Okay, drop me in after "dolphins can swim."' And that way he wrote and sang 'Heroes' simultaneously. At the end of an hour and a half we had a complete vocal."

The unique ambience of Hansa, with its view of the Berlin wall, imprinted itself on the sound as well as the imagery of "Heroes." The moment he walked onto the studio floor Visconti realized the room itself had a unique sound; when it came time to add the vocals to "Heroes," Visconti placed one Neumann mike in the normal position, close up, one fifteen feet away, and another one on the back wall. The two distant mikes were routed through a noise gate, a device to switch them on as David's voice filled the space. The effect was magnificent; Bowie's singing was the best he'd committed to tape, fresh and without artifice.

Few lyrics have been created and captured in such quick succession, and this is what gives "Heroes" much of its immediacy. The lyrics are simple but shot through with caveats. The song's lovers yearn for transcendence but will reach it only briefly. Even the moment of the lovers' bliss, as they kiss by the wall, is an act of the imagination. David claimed he had indeed seen two lovers underneath the wall; later, after Tony Visconti had divorced his wife, Mary Hopkin, David found out the lovers in question were Visconti and Antonia Maas, a nightclub singer whom he'd met and asked to sing on the album just a few days before. Yet in 2008, Maas stated that the song had been completed before their tryst— and that Bowie could not have seen them.

The six or so minutes that Bowie, Visconti, and Eno carved out were all the more precious because they were irreplaceable. To shape the song, Visconti had cut apart the master tape to edit it; to record the vocal, Visconti had mixed the three microphones onto one track on the master—all he had space for. They couldn't revise the effect or rearrange the song. This was Bowie's doing: "He quoted this Buddhist philosophy, how we live in a mire of options," says Visconti. "If you commit yourself, you're free."

Bizarrely, "Heroes," the song that would arguably become the best known of David Bowie's career, hardly set the charts on fire. In the UK, it entered the charts in October, peaking at number 24 in an eight-week run. David would come to treasure the song for the effect on his live audience: "In Europe, it is one of the ones that seemed to have special resonance." The song failed as a single in America, but according to Bowie, it would become "pivotal" in live shows: "It's a strange phenomenon...Many of the crowd favorites were never radio or chart hits; 'Heroes' tops them all."

RESISTANT as they were to *Low*, RCA summoned up enthusiasm for its successor, unleashing a memorable print campaign for its release on October 14, 1977; the press ads featured the *"Heroes"* sleeve photo—the pose based on *Roquairol*, Heckel's portrait of his friend Ernst Kirchner—accompanied by the slogan "There's New Wave, there's Old Wave, and there's David Bowie." It was a masterful piece of positioning that allowed David to remain aloof from a punk movement that, like glam before it, soon turned into a parody of itself.

The new, dressed-down David would do his own share of promotion, spending most of the autumn engaged in press and TV interviews. His first appearance, on September 9, was his most memorable; like his appearance on *Lift Off with Ayshea*, five years before, this would be in Granada Television's children's slot, designed to catch kids just back from school. Starting in late August, this half-hour slot had become the venue for the comeback campaign of David's earliest musical friend and rival, Marc Bolan, in his new TV series titled simply *Marc*.

The reunion with Marc was warm, chatty—relaxed at first, for what was their second meeting that year. In the spring, Marc had been chubby and pasty, thanks to his brandy and cocaine diet—"People used to call him the glam chipolata [sausage]," says Marc's PR man and confidant Keith Altham—but a brief reunion with David back in March had helped Marc rebuild his confidence. Marc had played Altham an acetate of "Madman," a song the pair had recorded together. "It was avant-garde, quite Eno-ish," says Altham, "and Marc said they were going to work on it together as a single. Though you never knew if there was any foundation to some of Marc's stories."

Since that first meeting, though, Marc had been through "a wonderful, hardworking summer," says his friend Jeff Dexter, who was business partners with Bolan's manager, Tony Howard. Marc cut out the cocaine and booze and instead stayed in his room writing, going out in the evening to tap into the vibe of London's punk scene, many of whose leading lights were featured on his show, which launched on August 24, 1977. Marc oversaw every aspect of each program, choosing guests that included Generation X, the Boomtown Rats, and the Jam, introducing each of them and playing three or four songs of his own with the latest lineup of T. Rex. Throughout the series "everything was on a high," according to Dexter. "And then we came to the last one in the series. The one with David."

The two men's conversation was affectionate; the only awkward moment was when it turned out David hadn't brought a guitar. Marc handed him a vintage Fender Stratocaster, insisting a little too eagerly that David keep the valuable instrument, intent on playing the role of wealthy, gracious superstar. Marc's new band was essentially David's old band—Tony Newman and Herbie Flowers—and they were greeted like long-lost friends; Jeff Dexter was also happy to see his fellow Buddhist and UFO-spotter from the Redington Road days.

Jeff left the studio to pick up Tony Howard, confident the afternoon's show would be a fitting finale to Marc's series. Things began to fall apart soon after Jeff's exit. Eager to put Bowie at ease, Bolan had asked his own guitar roadie, Cliff Wright, to attend to his guest. "They all got on okay, absolutely, it was old buddies," says Wright. "David was chatting with Herbie and Tony, they'd discussed the new song." And then it became apparent that Marc wasn't going to play on "Heroes."

This would be the song's TV debut, and David, reasonably enough, insisted on overseeing the backup track, sitting down and playing the guitar part himself. Flowers and Newman picked up the song straightaway, playing in a folksy, almost Velvets' style. "David just sat on a chair, and somehow got that feedback, it was really cool," says Wright. "Herbie and Tony were the kind of players who could pick up the song straightaway. Marc's guitar wouldn't have suited—[but] I suppose he wanted to be on TV playing it."

As the musicians swiftly assembled the background track, Marc mulled over what he considered a snub; looking "miffed," he asked Wright to fetch four bottles of wine for David, then retired to his own dressing room—with some of the bottles. "And he stayed in there," says Wright. "He felt he'd been blanked."

Sitting in his dressing room, Marc got "a little bit worse for wear," says a staff member. There was worse yet in store for his fragile ego, as Jeff Dexter discovered. On his return to the studio, accompanied by Tony Howard, Dexter found his way blocked by a burly figure who informed him, "You can't come in. This is a closed set."

After insisting, "This is our session, and no one's closed it," Dexter managed to gain entrance, only to find the union floor manager complaining he'd been banned from his own set—the entire studio had been overrun by David's security. Keith Altham, who'd brought journalist Chris Welch down to cover the show, managed to get in and found "there was some daft woman throwing her weight around, upsetting people, being really obnoxious, and this heavy-handed bunch trying to get everyone out. And it was Marc's show!"

Welch hid behind a pillar and watched as Coco Schwab, an RCA executive, and various members of Bowie's entourage argued with the crew, Tony Howard, Altham, and others. David, occupied with the music, hadn't noticed what was going on. But as the time came for the pair to record their appearances against the background tracks, the scene got ugly, says Dexter: "Right before they went on, both of them were upset. Marc particularly, he was in tears."

With the program now running late, David and Marc each taped a vocal overdub before they tackled a jam they'd worked on earlier. Marc looked slightly forlorn as he introduced "a new song" in his familiar campy murmur, and then the band launched into a chunky riff copped from Bo Diddley's "Road Runner," with David on Strat and Elvis shades. As Bowie slinks up to the mike and sings "What can I do," there's a sudden flurry in the corner of the screen, a hand grasping a microphone, a confused smile, and a streak of curly hair as Marc Bolan attempts to stand on a monitor wedge, misses, and falls off the stage and out of the picture. As the band shudders to a halt, the camera zooms to Bowie's grin, and the credits roll.

Some of the cast members of the famed Mancunian soap opera *Coronation Street* had arrived to record their own show, and they looked on as Marc laughed and picked himself up. Then the union crew, riled by the confrontation with Bowie's entourage, refused to go into overtime and reshoot. This was the last public appearance that Marc Bolan ever made. "It was a really shameful end," says Dexter. "The whole of that summer we'd been working on the shows, making sure they were as good as they could be. It was very sad. I was very affected by it."

On the train back to London, Bowie was low-key and cheery,

chatting happily to the very people his security had tried to eject from the studio, like Keith Altham: "You must read this book by Kurt Vonnegut, you won't regret it," he told him, showing him his copy of *Cat's Cradle*. "He wasn't heavy at all, once you took him away from this suffocating protection," says Altham. Back in Manchester, there was a hurried, miserable debriefing with producer Muriel Young about the fate of the program before Bolan, Howard, and Dexter returned to London. Later that night, says Tony Visconti, Marc and David went out to dinner and made up their quarrel.

The heavy-handedness that had overshadowed Bolan's show was an example of behavior that would soon become commonplace in the music industry. For writer Chris Welch, who'd championed Bowie a decade before, "It was new in pop terms—that distancing. Mick Jagger would have still been going around on the subway back then; David set this entourage to create a vibe. Really, it's just a way to draw attention to yourself." It was ironic that, having decried the hype of the MainMan years, David would unwittingly replicate the same heavy behavior.

In this respect, as in so many others, David would establish a new convention. Those who followed in his wake—Madonna, Prince—also employed a protective screen of subordinates to shield both their person and their image. To this day, packages sent to David are edited or censored; seemingly random items are removed before they reach him. Such behavior saves time for a busy man, and there would be many occasions in the future when David would venture out without his entourage. But from this period onward, much of David's reality—the sensory input of people, communications, ideas—would be filtered by other people. His life had changed, irrevocably. And at thirty, he'd grown up; that earnest, childlike quality had dissipated, and he was too savvy to attempt to prolong it. And there was a powerful reminder of his mortality to come.

THE kerfuffle around the *Marc* show would have been a passing concern but for the fact that by the time the show was broadcast, David's friend and rival was dead. Marc enjoyed a happy, quiet week after the taping of his show, but when his girlfriend, Gloria Jones, returned from America on September 15, he stayed up drinking into the small hours at the Speakeasy and then at Morton's restaurant. Marc had never learned to drive; it was Gloria who took the wheel of the purple Mini GT, which crashed into a tree on the south side of Barnes Common around five in the morning. Gloria was badly injured, her jaw broken, her foot trapped beneath the Mini's engine, but it was the left side that took the full force of the collision, and Marc's seat was crushed into the back of the vehicle. He was killed instantly.

David was devastated by Marc's death. He would be one of the highest-profile stars at Marc's funeral in Golders Green, joined by Tony Visconti and wife, Mary Hopkin, Rod Stewart, and the Damned. David would pay endless tributes to his friend and there would never be any doubt about his affection for the teenager with whom he'd fished for clothes in Carnaby Street twelve years before.

Their final appearance together had typified their relationship of interlaced respect and rivalry. It was also a stark illustration of their differences: Whereas Bolan had rested on his laurels or simply repeated himself, David had spent a dozen years relentlessly pushing himself forward. With Bolan's life over, it was more obvious than ever that David had won the race for fame they'd both embarked on. It was also more obvious than ever that, despite the companions he'd acquired in Berlin, David was now quite alone.

CHAPTER 17

I Am Not a Freak

He just had a tacky T-shirt, a pair of jeans, and a cardboard suitcase. It was the most horrible, horrible life.

—Ken Ruta

THE YEAR 1977 HAD BEEN JOYFUL—but it was a strange kind of joy, one many people wouldn't recognize. As a teenager, David had avoided doing proper schoolwork, but as an adult, he obviously enjoyed the worthiness of studying, of good old Yorkshire "graft." He'd dug deep into his reserves of psychic stamina during the Spiders era with compelling results, but this second creative streak was arguably even more impressive. There would never be another twelve months in Bowie's life as productive as those that stretched from the summer of 1976 to the summer of 1977, months in which he recorded four landmark albums: *The Idiot, Low, Lust for Life,* and *"Heroes,"* all of which would have a huge effect on the musical landscape. David knew the significance of these albums—he was filled with "a special kind of optimism" over that time, as Tony Visconti and others recall with nostalgia. Yet even as he immersed himself in work, David sensed that this special period wouldn't last.

He had always moved on briskly when he felt his musicians had nothing more to offer him. Yet he was more ruthless with himself, and even as he came to the last of his Berlin albums, he was dismantling the lifestyle that had given birth to them.

Immediately after the release of *"Heroes,"* David embarked on an old-school publicity blitz. The single was released in three languages, evoking the carefree early days of the Beatles, and David's promotion of the record took him to Rome, Amsterdam, Paris, London, and, in September, even to Elstree Studios, just north of London, where venerable crooner Bing Crosby was recording a Christmas special for ITV. Swapping scripted jokes before duetting with him on "The Little Drummer Boy," looking clean-cut and healthy, David seemed strikingly similar to the twenty-two-year-old who'd camped around on Malcolm Thomson's promotional film back in 1969; although the dialogue seemed fake, David's jokey pleasantries and engaging politeness were genuine. Many of those who encountered him over those weeks were put off their stride to find that, rather than the assertive, rather megalomaniac creature on display early in 1976, David was easygoing and pliant, even when faced with the most ludicrous questions, like that posed by radio interviewer John Tobler the following January. Tobler pointed out that with Bing Crosby's death in November and Marc Bolan's tragic accident back in September, David's most recent collaborators had both died soon after working with him. "Do you see anything sinister in that?" Tobler inquired. "No, I don't," David replied with commendable restraint before mentioning that the next act on his list—for production, not termination—was Devo. His championing of the band helped them secure a Warner Brothers deal, although time pressures meant it would be Brian Eno who produced their debut album.

In between the rounds of interviews, David spent a quiet Christmas at the Hauptstrasse—Coco cooked goose for a cozy, celebratory get-together, according to the Berlin friends who attended, including Eduard Meyer. But it would be their last Christmas break in Berlin, and it caused a public spat with Angie, an outburst that effectively announced their marriage was over. The exchange kicked off with Angie complaining to the *Sunday*

Mirror's Tony Robinson on January 8, 1978, that her husband had "without my knowledge taken our son" from the Vevey house over Christmas—in fact, she'd left Zowie with Marion Skene while she visited friends in New York. "I really want David to suffer," she told Robinson. "Perhaps the only way he'll suffer is if I do myself in." Soon after the first interview, she attempted suicide by downing sleeping pills, then smashed all the glassware in the house before throwing herself down the stairs, breaking her nose. Early in her stay at the Samaritan hospital in Vevey, Angie created so much commotion that the woman in the neighboring bed, who'd been hospitalized after a cardiac arrest, suffered a relapse.

Just six months before, David and Angie had been happily playing pool in the Tschungle, both of them with identical haircuts and trench coats, "like brother and sister," says Esther Friedmann, Iggy's girlfriend. Angie's outburst in the tabloid, attacking her husband in public for the first time, was an act of war—and desperation. It was a sign of her isolation. As one German friend put it, "She was just helpless—she had no one on her side. We'd say *Die Felle schwimmen davon*—your furs are swimming away. Everything is falling apart." Angie blamed Coco for edging her out of her husband's life, but by now her distaste for David's music and lifestyle could not be concealed: She disliked Dostoyevsky, she detested flat caps, she even hated the food he and Iggy sampled in Berlin—"They ate offal!" she exclaims today in disgusted tones, as if this alone explains her estrangement from her husband. Such distaste only sped up the inevitable, given Angie's lack of interest in sublimating her own life to David's. Now, she told Robinson, "I have to seek a divorce."

Angie's official exit made little difference to David's romantic life. Since separating from Ava Cherry in the summer of 1975, he'd relied on Coco for many of his needs—conversation, jokes, protection, and domestic necessities—although by now she'd moved into her own little apartment in the Hinterhof, like Iggy. In Berlin, both he and Iggy developed the habit of disappearing for a couple of days every now and then, "going where the drugs and girls were," says a friend. "David had his little muchachas that he would visit and Jim probably had his. Coco would wind up looking for them all over Berlin, worried something had happened."

Bowie would in future years rarely comment on his marriage to Angie; one of his most memorable observations was that the experience was "like living with a blowtorch." While his public criticisms were limited, his feelings about Angie eventually verged on hatred; he would rarely mention her by name and simply referred to her as "my ex-wife." Like Tony Defries's part in David's life, her role in David's rise to stardom, as well as her name, was airbrushed out of his personal history. The grueling intensity of life with Angie had a predictable effect on his future liaisons, which he would try to keep casual. Occasionally there'd be the odd obsession. On tour with Iggy in Vancouver, he became besotted with a boutique owner named Bessie—"beautiful, African, just as striking as Iman," according to Annie Apple, an old friend of Iggy—and he'd begged her to come back to Berlin with him. But after traveling on with him to Seattle, she'd been disturbed by the manic intensity that surrounded David; while they were eating at a Shakey's Pizza in the suburbs, Bessie noticed that fans even stole his cigarette butts. Two days of this was thrilling, but the idea of more sounded horrific. Shortly afterward, David would date another striking black woman, an ex-girlfriend of Shep Gordon, who stayed with him in Vevey for a few days before being sent back home. Toward the end of the year, David briefly dated Bianca Jagger—then still married to Mick—with the kind of exaggerated secrecy that ensured the news spread far and wide. They made an attractive couple, but the relationship didn't outlast his subsequent tour.

Instead, during his last months in the Hauptstrasse, away from his tour entourage, David reveled in dressing anonymously, spending time with Zowie, still wandering down to the Kreuzberg clubs, smoking his way through three packs of Gitanes a day, but also cycling on his Raleigh to "pretty normal places, talking about life and the books he was reading," says Tangerine Dream drummer Klaus Krüger—who David called up that spring and asked to join Iggy's band shortly after Iggy gave the Sales brothers their walking papers, directly after their last LA show, with a brutality that put David to shame.

At the end of January 1978, David started work on the movie that constituted his farewell to Berlin. *Just a Gigolo* was the brainchild of David Hemmings, the *Blow-Up* star's second movie as a director. David was at first excited by the production, which embodied many of his Berlin obsessions and was filmed around his regular haunts, including Café Wien. Hemmings had pulled off a remarkable coup, which helped draw David into the venture, by signing up Marlene Dietrich for her first film in eighteen years. David had spent hours in Berlin chatting to antique-store owners who'd known the reclusive star back in the day; the prospect of meeting her was a major part of the movie's appeal.

Hemmings was ebullient and easygoing—his catchphrase was "not too shabby, not too shabby"—and David told friends he bonded more with the old-fashioned hard-drinking actor than he had with the more intellectual Nic Roeg. But it wasn't long before the shoot started to go awry. During a celebratory dinner with Bowie, other crew members, Iggy, and Esther Friedmann, Hemmings went missing. "Something weird happened," says Friedmann. "[Hemmings] went somewhere and never came back; people were looking all over. And then David never got to meet Marlene. It turned out instead of acting with her, he was acting with a chair."

Hemmings explained later that Dietrich's brief appearance in the movie would be filmed in Paris; her half of the exchange with David was filmed on a set re-creating the Café Wien and intercut with the lines David delivered in Berlin. The scene—like the movie—was disjointed and irredeemably stilted; still, the film is a poignant last glimpse of the great German star, and David manages to look fetching while carrying a pig.

The fate of *Just a Gigolo* would typify David's cinematic career, which was more successful than those of rock-star rivals like Jagger and Sting but never came close to justifying his new job description, which he announced that year was *generalist*—a term obviously influenced by, but lacking the charm of, Eno's "nonmusician" tag. Picking out a decent script was a crapshoot in which David would never quite beat the odds—and as Hemmings's problems mounted, with finance issues and negative reactions to his first edits all publicized in the movie press, the prospect of David's biggest tour to date provided a welcome distraction.

Ranging across four continents, with seventy-eight shows, many of them in huge stadia, the Isolar II tour would put the flaky, stressful zigzagging improvisation of the *Ziggy* era to shame. The production was an ambitious, futuristic epic; it showcased the largely electronic soundscapes of *Low* and *"Heroes,"* but it also drew deep on David's musical history. Clothing designer Natasha Korniloff was a friend from the Lindsay Kemp troupe; guitarist Adrian Belew was stolen from Frank Zappa's band. Violinist Simon House had hung out with David and Hermione in 1968 and played in High Tide with Tony Hill, David's guitarist from Turquoise. Pianist Sean Mayes met David via Fumble, who'd rehearsed alongside him at Underhill and supported David for the March 1973 *Aladdin Sane* tour. Keyboardist Roger Powell came from Todd Rundgren's Utopia; the four joined Bowie stalwarts Alomar, Dennis Davis, and George Murray.

Carlos had spent six days running the band through a set based on *Low* and *"Heroes"*—brandishing a baton, like a classical conductor, for "Warszawa"—at the Showco soundstage in Dallas; David arrived on March 19, after a brief holiday in Kenya, and suggested they work up a sequence of *Ziggy* songs. The seven-piece outfit was competent, not too polished, with Mayes's stomping piano adding a vital roughness for a string of shows that were rapturously received.

Over the course of three months, the shows settled into a predictable routine. Each night after the show, there'd be the desperate race for a good restaurant or a club that was still open—Sean Mayes often acted as pathfinder, seeking out gay clubs where David and the others could arrive later. In the *Station to Station* tour the cavalcade had centered around Iggy and David, but now Carlos acted as the head of household, with David quiet, humorous, but rather distant. Meanwhile, business tensions seemed to fizz around the margins of the little crew, between Coco and Pat Gibbons, and between Pat and road manager Eric Barrett—a seasoned pro, famous for his work with Hendrix. The tensions weren't helped by what Simon House remembers as "mountains of blow." David rarely participated, although on one memorable occasion, in Paris on May 24, he stayed up for a twenty-hour coke bender after the first show; no one in the band saw him until shortly before the second night's performance. Simon House was chatting in the doorway of a dressing room when he sensed a kind of psychic vibration behind him. Turning around, he saw the singer, pale and clammy, his skin thin and papery, his whole demeanor transformed—but that night's performance was storming.

It was on the stage that the disparate English and American band members truly came together; an hour and a half of bliss, punctuated by musical communiqués and jokes—Dennis Davis was the key perpetrator, onstage and off-; often he'd attempt to render the whole band helpless by, for instance, playing a hugely extended drum fill, rolling over every drum in his set in turn in a kind of mad rhythmic monologue that would crack them all up. (Offstage, he was much the same, taking the mike whenever they were on the bus and delivering a crazy, surreal, pseudo-tour-guide commentary.) David loved it; he seemed to relish the vibrancy of his band, who would, in turn, occasionally watch him, hypnotized by the spectacle. David maintained a distance from his musicians— Sean Mayes referred to him as "His Lordship"—but even today there's a kind of loving fondness in their descriptions of sharing a stage with him. "He has some power," says House, "an aura that helps you transmit to thousands or millions of people. Freddie Mercury had it too. Maybe it's just that they wrote these colossal songs. But the music was always the one good thing on this tour."

Adrian Belew shared with House the sense that Bowie was "somewhat troubled. Maybe he was still doing some drugs, I don't know; maybe he was tired. I remember him overall as amazing to be around, but I did have a sense he was riding through it, not totally happy."

Simon House's memories of the tour are much darker, for reasons unconnected with David. The violinist's partner, Sue, was ill with Huntington's disease. Her plight was all the more sad because she wouldn't acknowledge the problem, which eventually left her hospitalized, and insisted on joining the tour. The illness manifests itself in varying guises; in her case, she'd act aggressive or drunk, causing so much racket in Tokyo that the hotel called the police. David got upset if he saw Sue standing on the side of the stage, which was understandable but made House feel like an outcast. Worse, Bowie didn't address the issue directly, so House couldn't even explain Sue's problem to him—instead, David's feelings were made known to House by David's minions. In those situations, as with most issues, it was Carlos Alomar who brought an almost spiritual, soothing attitude. "Carlos is a psychologist, a spiritualist, one of the most charming people in the world," says House. "We got on really well; I wouldn't have enjoyed the tour without him. He was the one would distract from the problems."

On the *Station to Station* tour, there had been the sense that David was the head of a family; this time around, it seemed that he was the head of a business empire. Coco and Pat Gibbons formed the nucleus of Isolar, David's management company, which changed in form over the next few years but would always have David at its apex. In those early days, the fact that David effectively managed himself marked him as a maverick; but that would change. The public's realization that he was a businessman as well as an artist came when he announced that he would release a live album, recorded primarily in Philadelphia, while the tour was still rolling across Japan. The double album was intended to both defeat the efforts of bootleggers and count toward David's RCA obligation. The album's financial motivations were undoubtedly obvious—Jon Savage of *Sounds* epitomized the reaction when he described *Stage* as "a combined summing-up, money-making and time-gaining device"—but the audacity of the live show was obvious too, even in the album's first version, released with its tracks sliced and spliced into chronological order.

By the time *Stage* was released, on September 8, 1978, David was using a short break from his tour to work on the third album in a trilogy that he'd announced back in January. Trilogies, even when rebranded triptychs, as David called this set, risk outstaying their welcome, and *Lodger*, for all the randomness involved in its recording, lacked the sense of risk and excitement that had pervaded *Low* and *"Heroes."* Some of that was due to the location: Mountain Recording Studios in Montreux was carpeted, comfortable, and bland compared to the edgy, unsettling vibe of Hansa. To the session stalwarts, like Carlos Alomar, *Lodger* was a more intellectual, less inspired affair than *"Heroes."*

For the previous album, Eno had used some of his oblique-strategy techniques on the instrumental side, notably "Sense of Doubt." On this project—working title "Planned Accidents"—they were used for the band tracks, most memorably in an exercise where Brian would point to random chords on a wall chart and ask the musicians to play them. "And then I'm like, This is not going to substitute for a group chord chart which I can write," says Alomar, "and this experiment is stupid."

"It sounded terrible," says House. "Carlos did have a problem, simply because he's very gifted and professional [and] he can't bring himself to play stuff that sounds like crap."

David encouraged the reluctant guitarist—"Come on, fellas, play along!"—although the experiment ("not Brian's finest idea," according to Tony Visconti) was ultimately abandoned. But on other occasions, Eno's oblique-strategy cards, which instructed random actions in order to bypass creative blocks, worked as theorized, Carlos admits. "One time Brian asked me something and I was blocked because I didn't understand what he wanted," says Alomar. "Then one of the cards said something like 'Remember those silent moments' and then another said 'Think like a gardener.' Some kind of eclectic weird reference. It worked—or let's say you find yourself accepting it. I would have chosen other things to play—but in hindsight it was fun."

House was one of the few musicians who had played with Eno outside of Bowie—they'd recorded together on Robert Calvert's solo album—and he loved Eno's creativity: "He's always got an idea, is always on the case." But on this project he thought the keyboardist's inspiration was ebbing away and that the prime reason for his use of oblique strategies was to cope with his own artistic block, not the musicians'.

Eno's preference seemed to be to experiment almost endlessly — hence Bowie was the one who showed decisiveness, seizing on one idea to keep things moving, impatiently overseeing the last few days when the real creativity took place. The beauty of the album came from the way that random ideas were scattered like confetti over ordinary (and, in some cases, repeated) chord structures; Adrian Belew's brilliantly warped guitar on "Boys Keep Swinging," for which the band all switched to unfamiliar instruments, a trick David and Carlos had first tried on *Lust for Life;* House's Byzantine violin, which influenced the Turkish vibe of "Yassassin," and the twisted interplay of Alomar's guitar and Visconti's swooping strings on "DJ." One night Visconti downed a bottle of tequila and wrote out an arrangement for three mandolins that became "Fantastic Voyage." "It was a beautiful moment," says House, who played the part along with Belew and Visconti.

Once the frustrations of the first few days were over, with the basic tracks montaged from tape edits, the recording sessions were blissful. The songs were sculpted into shape in the setting of an idyllic Indian summer, where the musicians basked in the gorgeous view over Lake Geneva and enjoyed chats with Eugene Chaplin, Charlie's son, who'd bring over trays of beer. "It was a perfect fortnight," says House. "Although the music didn't ever perfectly jell." The violinist had high standards, though, for he considered *Low* and *"Heroes"* perfect albums that couldn't be bettered.

Adrian Belew arrived at a later stage of the recording, once the backup tracks had been edited into shape. He was warmed up with a compliment first: "I walked in, and David, Brian, and Tony are all smiling, like they've a shared secret. Soon I ask, 'What's going on?' And they said, 'When we did all the tracks with Robert Fripp for *"Heroes"* we did them as composite tracks. We took something from each take, edited it all together to make something that was impossible to play. And you didn't know that, and you played it all live!'"

The trio were warming him up; they knew he had played the impossible, so he was expected to deliver the same at the session. Belew was sent upstairs to the recording room, where Bowie, Eno, and Visconti watched him through a closed-circuit TV camera; the guitarist's only contact with the outside world was the instructions that came over his headphones.

Belew had only just plugged in his Fender Stratocaster when he heard someone tell him, "The drummer will go one, two, three, then you come in." "What key is it?" he asked anxiously. "Don't worry about the key," he was told. "Just play!" There were maybe three passes at the music, which arrived in a torrent over his headphones, then he was told that was it. As the recording went on, that became the pattern: three goes at each song, with the resulting parts edited into one composite track. "When I heard the final versions, I had no memory of how I came up with these parts. And meanwhile they're going, 'This is the first time this guy has been in a recording studio!'" Today, Belew can't remember how any of the individual songs came about, except for "Boys Keep Swinging," where they told him that Carlos was playing drums. "It was like a freight train coming through my mind," he says of his now celebrated solo. "I just had to cling on."

Completed in March 1979 at New York's Power Plant, *Lodger* would meet with a respectful, slightly subdued reception on its release in May. Visconti blamed the lack of enthusiasm on a rushed mix. Much of the instrumentation did indeed sound thin next to the ebullient clatter of "*Heroes*"; the same applied to the emotional content, for whereas its two predecessors were deep, *Lodger* was restless and quirky. The album would attract admiration rather than visceral love or hatred, but its art-rock intellectualism sat neatly alongside emerging bands like Talking Heads—produced by Brian Eno over the same time—and New Romantic bands like Spandau Ballet, whose Germanic name, sound, and pegged pants were all based on the 1978 model David Bowie.

After the break for the main *Lodger* sessions in September, the tour continued through Australia and Japan. For Belew in particular, the experience was one of the most fulfilling in his career:

"We got to Japan and it was amazing, like the stratosphere of superfame." Seven months of touring with David "really propelled me into being the guitarist I became. He was the first person to give me the freedom to go and explore in front of twenty thousand people. When you have that scenario, you almost transcend yourself—you dig deep and find stuff you didn't know was there. I was on a permanent high."

LODGER enjoyed a decent chart run, reaching number 4 in the UK, number 20 in the United States, but for all the slackening in his chart momentum, David was positioned perfectly alongside Eno as a patron of the late 1970s New Wave. Now in his thirties, he seemed to be moving more quickly from album to album than he had in his twenties—and the impressiveness of his achievement was underlined, if it needed to be, by the fate of the two men who were his closest peers as patrons of the New Wave: Lou Reed and Iggy Pop.

After the triumph of *Transformer* and its densely wrought, emotionally grueling successor *Berlin,* Lou's music had spiraled into self-parody with *Coney Island Baby* and *Rock and Roll Heart.* Reed was short of ideas and money, and by his spring 1979 European tour he was drinking his way through two pints of scotch every three days, swigging straight from the bottle.

Lou and David had met only occasionally since MainMan days, but an air of excitement bubbled around Lou and his band in April of 1979 when they heard David would be showing up at Lou's Hammersmith Odeon date. The show was a mess. Seeing David sitting on an amplifier case at the side of the stage, Lou started screaming at his musicians and switched the set around—but once he made it through to the last number, Lou was ebullient, overjoyed to see his friend. The pair hugged each other at the side of the stage, Lou running his hands lovingly through David's hair, before they both climbed into the tour bus and set off in search of a restaurant.

The dishes were on the table at the Chelsea Rendezvous when an infamous spat broke out. Lou was sitting next to Sylvia; David sat between another woman and Lou's guitarist Chuck Hammer. Hammer heard Lou ask David if David would produce his next album.

"Yes," David agreed, "if you clean up your act."

Lou slapped David across the face, hard, once on each cheek, screaming, "Don't you *ever* say that to me! *Never* say that to me!" Lou's manager, Eric Kronfeld, wrestled him away, and for a few minutes peace reigned until suddenly Lou slapped David again. This time David's bodyguards pulled them apart, and within seconds, Lou and his party were bundled out of the restaurant.

The fracas, witnessed by an astonished Allan Jones of *Melody Maker* and Giovanni Dadamo of *Sounds,* would feature in the respective music weeklies, but neither writer saw the next act of the drama. An hour or two later, the members of Reed's band were back at the hotel, and guitarist Chuck Hammer was on the phone describing the night's events to a friend. Suddenly he heard footsteps in the corridor outside, then the sound of fists hammering on a door, and then shouts:

"Come on, Lou — I know you're in there!"

For perhaps the first time since being clocked in the eye by George Underwood, the man who had proclaimed he was "not much cop at punching" in "Kooks" was attempting to pick a fight. But if the dark prince of New York decadence was in his room (no one ever found out), he must have been cowering under his duvet, and after a few minutes of stomping up and down the hall, David left the building.

Even a month later, when David told Iggy and girlfriend, Esther Friedmann, about the fight, he was still "devastated," remembers Friedmann. The incident showed the pitfalls of helping out people you admired; relations with Iggy were strained too. The ex-Stooge had managed one fairly successful album, *New Values,* under his own steam, but since then he'd been growing increasingly depressed. David and Coco had attempted to help, taking him and Esther on holiday with them, including a trip to Kenya, "but sometimes when people are good to you it's worse," says Friedmann.

By September of 1979 Iggy was in a bad way: marooned in a residential studio in Wales, lost in a haze of dope and booze, and seemingly unable to finish the follow-up to *New Values* on his new label, Arista. David drove out with Coco to help, cheering up Iggy and the musicians with a long monologue on Johnny Binden, a gangster, hanger-on, and owner of a legendarily huge cock that he'd displayed to Dana Gillespie and Princess Margaret, among others, on Mustique. The story ended up being turned into a song, "Play It Safe." Bowie was dauntingly impressive—"like a creative playmaster," says keyboard player Barry Andrews—but his visit seemed to highlight Iggy's failure at finding his way through the corporate maze. Both men shared similar demons—narcissism, jealousy, and a tendency for a kind of musical postnatal depression once a project was completed—but David's competitive nature always inspired him to bounce back with a characteristic zest.

That competitiveness would add a satisfying edge to David's next project, for as Lou Reed hit an artistic block on his next album, *Growing Up in Public*—leaving most of the music to collaborator Michael Fonfara and writing the lyrics drunk by the studio pool—David was schmoozing Lou's guitarist Chuck Hammer. "Lou had really been an asshole [in London]," says Hammer, "and I was really impressed by David. He was just the perfect gentleman. But I always wondered, later on, if David was trying to get back at Lou, trying to break up his band a little bit."

Hammer would become a key contributor to what many Bowie fans would regard as the man's last truly great album. There's much justification for that view, for *Scary Monsters* still sparkles today. Its intense, churning grooves sound remarkably contemporary—in retrospect, it's the obvious source of Blur's angular rock attack from *Park Life* on—but despite the complexity of its arrangements, there are many moments of unaffected simplicity.

In a signal that it was a move on from his European albums, *Scary Monsters* was produced mostly at New York's Power Station, widely regarded as the best-sounding American recording studio of its time. But for the first time since *Ziggy*'s nod to 1950s rock and roll, the album also looked back, at both Bowie's career and the New Wave kids who were coming up behind him.

Popular folklore has it that Bowie was intent on scoring a hit record. Certainly that's the impression that Chuck Hammer got, for he arrived to witness a much more focused, almost conventional work ethic compared with the Eno collaboration. Although now an established artist, David was still recognizably the confident, punctual young buck remembered by teenage friends like the Manish Boys. For the recording, David, sporting a mustache and dressed in a full-length leather coat and Japanese sandals, brandished a clipboard, on which he'd tick off items on a musical to-do list. Just as in the Iggy session, he was entertaining, with that trademark flirtatious jokiness, but with a formidable sense of focus. Tony Visconti was almost scarily "on it," recording and planning ahead at the same time. "They were an absolutely unified team," says Hammer, "really impressively organized, there was no chaos — but it was very relaxed and creative too."

Hammer was called in primarily to work on a song titled "People Are Turning to Gold." He had been developing a new technique of building up synthesized layers, which he called guitarchitecture, and had sent a tape of his experiments to Bowie. As he worked on the song, which as yet had no lyrics, he quickly added distinctive "choir" parts to the chorus, then moved on to "Teenage Wildlife" and the gospelly "Up the Hill Backwards" (the latter didn't make it in, replaced by Robert Fripp's superb, frenzied electric guitar). "Chuck was very experimental for us; it was fifty-fifty whether he would make the cut," says Visconti, but as he so often did, Bowie drew an inspiring performance from the young guitarist, using it to offset the conventional electric guitar parts that Robert Fripp would record a few days later for the rest of the album. Bowie would wait another two months before writing lyrics for the song, finally naming it "Ashes to Ashes." "We did love it immensely and knew it was one of the major tracks," says Visconti.

For all the arresting sonic effects laced through "Ashes to Ashes," it was the song's melodic inventiveness that underpinned its success; it represented a return to David's old-fashioned song-writing, with a swooping melody in the verse and one of his characteristic pre-verse digressions—"the shriek of nothing is killing me"—as well as a conventional but gorgeous middle eight that seemed, with its "never done anything out of the blue," to address the age-old criticism that David was premeditated and calculating.

As a UK number 1 single, "Ashes to Ashes" seemed to signal that Bowie would dominate the eighties as convincingly as he had the seventies. For the video, an intrinsic part of the single's eventual success, he commandeered the Blitz Club—a scene that, of course, took Bowie's style as a template. In one of the first instances of his interacting with a new generation of artists that he'd influenced, he was again the epitome of charm, dropping in for an evening with the club's host Steve Strange, then inviting him to the next day's 6:00 a.m. trip to Southend for the celebrated video shoot, which reprised the Pierrot style of Lindsay Kemp, again with a costume designed by Natasha Korniloff. Now thirty-three, David was relaxed and sociable (and, says Steve Strange with pride, "when he snogged me, I got some tongue too"). If David's intent was to get back at Lou Reed, two-timing him with his guitarist and scoring a number 1 in the process had probably done it.

For all those involved, the eventual success of *Scary Monsters* was a poignant one. Even while a host of groups copied *Scary Monsters'* gritty electro-funk mélange, most of those responsible for it, including drummer Dennis Davis and bassist George Murray, were looking for new jobs. Tony Visconti, but for a brief session in Berlin, would not work with David again for another twenty-one years. "It is one of my favorite Bowie albums ever," the producer states. "I considered it going out on a high note."

For David, the album marked a happy change of setting; he had never officially left Berlin, but he was fired up by his return to New York, where he could hang with a younger generation of arty New Wavers and also resume his friendship with John and Yoko under happier, more relaxed circumstances for both of them. John's respect for David had only increased with the success of

"Fame," which put the ex-Beatle back on the charts; David still considered John, along with Mick Jagger, a role model, but his admiration for John was not intermixed with rivalry, as it was with Mick. Lennon brought out a better side of David, and he knew it. Happily, John had started writing again; David admired the unique lifestyle he'd carved out, with his and Yoko's elegant, white-carpeted, minimally furnished apartment in the Dakota, by Central Park, where John and Yoko could wander undisturbed.

As David was finishing what would become an enduring classic, he was also starting work on another, more transient triumph. The *Scary Monsters* sessions were in full flow when he took a call from Jack Hofsiss, director of *The Elephant Man*, the play based on the life of John Merrick, which David had seen in New York back in February. Hofsiss needed a replacement for Philip Anglim, who was quitting the title role. Bowie had been bowled over by the play; given just twenty-four hours to make his decision, he agreed to take on the part.

David spent time rehearsing with Hofsiss one-on-one before the cast convened for two weeks of intensive work in San Francisco. His recruitment was quintessential celebrity casting, of the kind still practiced today, so when David arrived at the Geary Theater, one might expect that his fellow actors would have been resentful about being upstaged by a rock and roller. Especially Ken Ruta; a stalwart of the American Conservatory Theater, admirer of Gielgud and Tennessee Williams, he played opposite Bowie night after night as Dr. Frederick Treves, Merrick's friend and benefactor. But Ruta is unequivocal about the new leading man: "He was incredible. Right on the money."

As one listens to the recollections of the *Elephant Man* cast, echoes of David's time on the road with the Lindsay Kemp company a dozen years before abound. Back then, Kemp points out, "He was not starry at all, my God, no." Ruta is similarly emphatic: "He was absolutely not a show-off," an opinion share by costar Jeanette Landis: "He was a very pure actor. In fact, more professional than the actor he replaced."

For just a few months, the setting mirrored that period in Bowie's late teens when he was soaking up experiences as part of Kemp's tiny crew. Given his upbringing among the imposing Victorian edifices of Brixton and the Lower Third's performances alongside the bearded lady sideshows of Margate, Bowie was well aware that the England that had feted and mocked Merrick still existed. David had visited the London Hospital and examined Merrick's bones and the poignant cardboard church he'd constructed, which—in grander form—is a centerpiece of the play, a symbol of Merrick's yearning for beauty and peace. Most of the actors in the play, including David, shared a sympathy for Merrick, heightened by the presence of the sufferers of his condition who came to see the production; the cast hadn't expected to see such startling parallels between the life of Merrick, circus freak, and that of their leading man.

Parts of David's routine were conventional. Every Sunday, he'd buy the *New York Times* and carefully read through the book reviews. Later in the week, all the books that had received raves were lying on a table in his room; soon after, he'd finished them. At the end of the week, there'd be a modest present, a token of affection, for each of his fellow actors. "It depended on your taste in diversion," says Ruta. "I usually got a nice bottle of red wine." Once the play had opened in Denver, he'd walk down to a little milk bar he'd found, just to relax or dance with some younger company.

He seemed to master the routine onstage easily too. At first, there were plenty of little lapses, none of which affected the flow. "He hadn't acted on a stage, so the acting technique wasn't completely in his control," says Ruta, "[but] thank God, he had such an imagination, so the integrity was there. There was a basic honesty. And the best gift, to me, of any great actor is that thing about listening. That doesn't happen all the time." It is an intriguing observation, for while making *Low* and *"Heroes,"* what else had Bowie been doing but listening, picking out sounds and making sense of them?

His fellow actors found Bowie's physical transformation into Merrick equally impressive: "He seemed to have captured that—better than all the other ones who wanted to be glamorous. He wasn't doing glamour. He was doing Merrick," says Jeanette Landis. When Ken Ruta later saw the movie of *The Elephant Man*, in which John Hurt, swamped under a prosthesis, plays Merrick, he found Hurt's performance far less involving than David's.

Even before David's appearance, the play had been a success; U.S. president Jimmy Carter was a fan of the book, and he and his wife had come to meet the first cast. Yet when David took over from Anglim, the upstart replacement lifted the play. "Whatever that thing is—it was nothing that is practiced or manufactured—it was there," says Ruta. *Variety*'s review of the opening night in Denver bears out Ruta's memories of the performance: "Bowie takes the stage with authority," the review commented. "Vocally, he is both quick and sensitive."

When David billed himself as "the actor" on the sleeve of *Hunky Dory*, it had seemed a pretentious claim. Now he'd earned that title. In the nomadic world of the theater, where actors develop friendships and then move on to their next productions, he was a sympathetic figure to his colleagues; unlike musicians, actors rarely expect their work relationships to last past the end of each project. As far as the Denver and Chicago cast members were concerned, Bowie was "a honey. Kind, good, bright, and he worked for his money." Jeanette Landis, his leading woman, was equally impressed: "His talent was bigger than his ego—which is rare."

Yet there was a divide between David and the other actors. It was a divide that was hardly perceptible in the week they spent in Denver, breaking the theater's box-office record. But from the time the troupe hit Chicago, on August 5, 1980, Bowie's companions were shocked by the way he was forced to live. Like Merrick, he lived the life of a freak. "It was fun in Denver, which was more or less the hinterlands. In Chicago, it was scary," says Ruta. "Mobs of people, unrelenting." Jeanette Landis too remembers, "It was out of control."

After a few days, David was forced to travel to the Blackstone Theater in a garbage truck, sneaking in and out of the building via a basement window. With fans stalking the city's main hotels, he stayed in a flat above a nearby department store. Only a couple of cast members knew its location. At one point during the run, most of his clothes were stolen. "He just had a tacky T-shirt, a pair of jeans, and a cardboard suitcase," says Ruta. "It was the most horrible, horrible life."

The incessant attention from the fans seen at close quarters was terrifying because it was relentless. Throughout the Chicago run, it didn't let up. For the first time in their careers, Ruta and Landis worked closely with security guards, hired to protect the cast. In this context, Coco, seen as intrusive by so many of David's musicians, was "a protectress," says Ruta. "Wonderful. She took care of him."

After the first few days, the cast would look over the front rows as soon as they walked onstage, wondering who would be there. One night a fan left an object on the stage. "Leave it, don't touch it," Bowie told Ruta quickly in the wings. Caught up in the feverish, intimidating atmosphere, Ruta obeyed him.

Toward the end of the Chicago run Ruta spotted one distinctive gaggle of fans in the front row: "About six girls, all weird-looking, this was before punk became crazy, all with dyed hair, all holding purses in their laps." They were there through the week, for the Saturday matinee, and again for that evening's performance. Then, as the actors took their curtain calls, all six girls rose, carrying their purses, and headed for the stage. "It was instantaneous; they were all tackled from the sides by I don't know how many plainclothesmen. And they were carrying something in their purses, metallic — they were there to do something dirty. It was just cuckoo that night." The girls were bundled out of the building by security and Ruta never found out their intentions, but he is convinced they had set out to scare David — or worse.

When the show transferred to New York on September 23, 1980 — after a two-week break for rehearsals and the installation of a higher-profile supporting cast — the media frenzy intensified. The curtain opened to a star-studded audience that included Christopher Isherwood, Andy Warhol, David Hockney, Aaron

Copland, and David's Montreux neighbor—and supposed lover—
Oona Chaplin. The New York reviews were generally either effusive or respectful, and with *Scary Monsters* nestled at number 1 on
the UK chart and number 12 in the USA, Bowie finally seemed to
have reached the status of cross-cultural icon to which, despite too
many protestations, he'd obviously aspired. John, Yoko, Iggy,
Esther, and May Pang were among the friends who pressed at the
dressing-room door after the first performances, raving about his
theatrical debut. Throughout the month, journalists from influential publications—the *New York Times,* the *London Times,* and
the *Sunday Times*—lined up for their allotted fifteen minutes,
monitored by Barbara and Tim Dewitt. In several of the interviews, David praised the anonymity of New York; like his friend
John, he loved how one could walk the city unmolested. "The
most you get is, 'Hi Dave, how's it going?'" he told the *London
Times'* Patricia Barnes.

ON December 8, 1980, exactly two weeks after the *London Times*
interview appeared, May Pang called David Bowie's Chelsea apartment to tell him she'd heard that John Lennon had been shot dead
by Mark David Chapman. Coco answered the phone. "David is out
on a date," she told May. "Get down here, now. You shouldn't be
alone."

David arrived at the apartment around the same time as May.
She remembers him screaming, *"What the hell, what the fuck is
going on with this world,"* over and over, angry, devastated. At times,
for all of them, there were flashbacks, momentary convictions that
this was a prank and hadn't really happened; again and again
they'd tell one another, "We have to be calm, we can't let our emotions take over." After he'd screamed himself to a numb acceptance, David sat in front of the TV, absorbed by the news footage of
distraught fans milling around the Dakota building and Central
Park. He was still up when May Pang left the apartment around
dawn. New York was strangely quiet as she walked home.

David played out the three remaining weeks of *Elephant Man*
but missed several nights. It was "awful, just awful," he explained

two years later. "A whole piece of my life seemed to have been taken away; a whole reason for being a singer and songwriter seemed to be removed from me. It was almost like a warning." There were rumors, never substantiated, that Mark Chapman had attended a performance of *The Elephant Man* and that he'd written down a list of targets that included David Bowie and Keith Richards. Whatever the truth, the murder in New York of the man David identified with most left him with only one option: flight.

CHAPTER 18

Snapshot of a Brain

I've never worked with an artist like that before or since. It was all beautiful images. We went to people's houses that he knew had certain things... it was like fact finders, treasure hunters, conquistadors looking for gold.

—Nile Rodgers

JUST THREE YEARS BEFORE LENNON DIED, the main fixtures in David's life had been rock-star buddies and enfant terrible artists; his main entertainment had been boozing and exploring bullet-riddled hot spots. In the summer of 1981, this was a distant memory. Now there were calm walks in the heights above Lake Geneva, and civilized drinks with Eugene Chaplin, a cheery, relaxed character who looked like a rather more rotund version of his celebrated comedian father. Most novel of all, David's house resounded with the hubbub of kids.

For several years now, Zowie's social life had been mainly confined to the children of musicians and studio staff; he played with them under the watchful eye of Marion Skene, the nanny who'd taken care of him for nearly eight years. Although Zowie had stayed with David for much of the Berlin period, David was very aware that he was often an absentee father. Now, in the tiny family's last summer in the house at Corsier-sur-Vevey, Zowie had unhindered access to his dad—and David's array of video equipment. Later, he'd vividly recall using his father's broadcast-quality U-matic videocassette player, the size of a shopping cart, for *Star Wars* parties at which he and his friends would watch George Lucas's movies, each film taking up two or three cassettes. It was the first time the ten-year-old had enjoyed a proper chance to make friends, although it turned out the idyllic sojourn would be relatively brief, because David—a conventional father—later enrolled him at the notoriously spartan boarding school Gordon-stoun, a favorite of English royalty.

Zowie's education was a typical example of the conservatism hidden behind David's unconventional exterior; in this respect, as in several others, David seemed to show the influence of his own father. Even in his Haddon Hall days, David had surprised friends with this trait; when he learned that his friend Mark Pritchett had skipped a school athletics event, David had admonished him, "You should have gone to that—it's important." As a father, he was definitely of the "you won't get your dessert till you've eaten your vegetables" school, although he wasn't bossy—he'd reason with Zowie almost as if he were a friend. As for David's real friends, they were few. Iggy would call and ask his opinion, but there were no true peers David could talk to when he needed advice. Corinne was the most zealous, but eventually David came to the conclusion that he didn't make friends that easily. Later in life, he'd realize that the only friends who'd stayed with him were those he'd known in Bromley, people like the kind, unflappable George Underwood. "There are about half a dozen [friends] that I would think of as close in the accepted sense, i.e., would I reach out to them in a time of real crisis?" he would tell his wife, Iman, many years later, reflecting how his male friends in that group "all go back to my teenage years."

ISOLATED, but for Zowie in Switzerland, David turned to professionals for help. His visceral, all-encompassing fear in the wake of Lennon's murder was "not at all an affectation—it was real," according to those who knew him. Soon after the murder, Keith

Richards started carrying a gun; David hired a new bodyguard, this time one who was literally trained to kill. His main muscleman was named Gary, an ex–Navy SEAL. (It turned out that, in his time with David, Gary never had to employ his talent for dispatching an attacker using only a spoon or some other household implement, so he occupied himself by running the flabby thirty-something rock musos in David's band through fitness routines between their overdubs in the studio.)

David started to rethink every aspect of his relationship with his fans. He took a course that taught media figures how to deal with the public; he learned how to handle casual encounters on the street and how to recognize danger signs in letters and other communications, the words to watch for that signified possible stalkers or killers. Stars were advised not to respond to some cues; in extreme cases, they were told to change their addresses.

David's fan correspondence, it turned out, was packed with danger signs. One such series of letters, from several fans writing together, opened with the typical comments about David's lyrics, makeup, and fashion. Several letters later, his correspondents had progressed to telling him of a friend's death: "We don't blame you," they informed him. When David showed the letter to his advisers, they told him to move to a new house.

David's newfound awareness of his own mortality not only inspired him to spend more time with Zowie but also led him to reestablish contact with his mother. He and Peggy stayed together over Christmas in 1980 and remained in regular contact from then on: "I've gotten closer to her," he remarked later. "I think the recognition of the frailty of age makes one more sympathetic to the earlier strains of the parent-child relationship." In contrast, Zowie's interaction with Angie was limited. David and Angie had fought a lengthy battle through the Swiss courts; Angie had been represented by celebrated palimony lawyer Marvin Mitchelson, who later claimed to have climbed a Swiss mountain in pursuit of Bowie. It was a tough case, with witnesses like Marion Skene testifying about Angie's maternal shortcomings. Faced with such opposition, Mitchelson secured a settlement of just $700,000 when the divorce was finalized in February of 1980; a derisory figure from today's perspective for a woman who was undoubtedly crucial to the creation of *Ziggy*. Once a ten-year gag order on discussing the divorce had expired, Angie blamed Corinne for most of her troubles, accusing Schwab of floating the notion of a move to Switzerland so David could take advantage of its sexist legal regime.

Angie's anger at Coco seemed to outweigh her grief at losing Zowie, for her contact with him was limited by the terms of the settlement. The years following her divorce were torrid ones. By 1983, Zowie had taken the name Joey, and in the summer of 1984, after staying with Angie and boyfriend Drew Blood at their Lower East Side tenement, he decided to break off contact with his mother. Angie blamed David—"he used his millions to poison Zowie against me"—but Tony Zanetta, who was there for Joey's and Marion Skene's visit during a sweltering New York summer, witnessed messy scenes culminating in a screaming match. "It was hard for him...maybe if Angie had devoted herself to him that summer...It was very sad." Whether or not David helped inspire Joey's estrangement from his mother, he made little effort to conceal how much he detested his ex-wife, whom he described as having "as much insight into the human condition as a walnut and a self-interest that would make Narcissus green with envy."

THROUGH the first half of 1981, David reveled in his seclusion; the focus and dedication that had usually been directed at his music was applied to "seeing [Zowie] grow...and be excited about the future." There was just one musical venture that summer, for which he only had to stroll down the road: The previous year, he'd agreed to collaborate on the theme song for Paul Schrader's remake of Val Lewton's classic movie *Cat People*. The song was Bowie's first and only collaboration with Giorgio Moroder, whose work he'd discovered back in Los Angeles. The Italian electro pioneer was best known for the chattering sequencers of songs like Donna Summer's *I Feel Love*, but for this song he constructed a bleak, minimalist soundscape based on the simplest of two chord changes. Bowie recorded his languorous, hypnotic vocal over

Moroder's background track at Mountain Recording Studios; the opening minutes would count as among the most magnificent, and restrained, of his career. A modest success on its release the next April, "Cat People (Putting Out Fire)" would become one of the most overlooked Bowie gems until Quentin Tarantino unearthed it for his Nazi splatter movie *Inglourious Basterds* in 2009.

It was during his visits to the Mountain studio—which eventually became a second home, once he'd negotiated his own, off-peak-season David Bowie discount—that David reacquainted himself with a fan turned rival who was recording in the main casino studio.

David had met Freddie Mercury back in the summer of 1970, when the Queen singer worked at a stall in Kensington Market and fitted Bowie with a pair of suede boots. Introduced to David by their mutual friend, ex-Beatstalker Alan Mair, Freddie had shyly mentioned he was rehearsing with a new band. David, then disenchanted with Ken Pitt, had replied, "Why would you want to get into *this* business?" Fortunately Freddie had ignored him, but over the next few years he would take more than a few leaves out of the Bowie book: Queen turned up regularly at Bowie shows, recorded at Trident, and hired MainMan photographer Mick Rock, while the influence of Mick Ronson's pioneering work on songs like "The Superman" was readily discernible in Brian May's trademark multilayered guitar style.

According to Mercury's personal assistant Peter Freestone, it was only by chance that Bowie learned Queen was at Mountain working on the R & B–flavored album *Hot Space*. Asked to add backup vocals on the song "Cool Cat," David stayed for a marathon session in which Queen's song "Feel Like" was transformed into "Under Pressure." David contributed the bulk of the lyrics, set over drummer Roger Taylor's descending chord sequence. By this point, Mercury had developed more of an ego than he'd had in his market-stall days, and it was the Queen drummer who was at the heart of the session, interacting with the interloper. "Roger and Bowie got on very well," according to Freestone, "although the lyrics and title idea came from Freddie and David."

David was charming, polite, sensitive in his dealings with these four relative strangers, but also remarkably confident, just as he had been in his youth when he'd shown his songs to bands like the Beatstalkers and been certain they'd accept them. "It was hard because you had four very precocious boys — and David, who was precocious enough for all of us," says Brian May. "David took over the song lyrically. It's a significant song because of David and its lyrical content — I would have found that hard to admit in the old days, but I can admit it now." David championed the song, encouraging Freddie and contributing a classic, swooping melody, as well as one of his distinctive, reflective middle-eight sections ("the terror of knowing what this world is all about").

Most of Queen were uncertain about the track, even after Bowie and Mercury reworked their vocals and mixed the recording at the Power Station in New York two weeks later — Deacon's distinctive bass line was added at the same session, hummed to him by David. Brian May was particularly unhappy, recalling the "fierce battles" around the mix and his own misgivings about the song's release as a single. It was Queen's record company, EMI, that pushed the collaboration, which finally hit the streets that September and became Queen's second number 1, reaching the top of the UK charts on November 21; it was number 29 on the U.S. charts a few weeks later.

It was a satisfying coup for David, helping to craft a hit from behind the scenes the way he had many others, and it was all the more so now given his sudden retirement from the music world. He was happy to relinquish "Under Pressure" to Queen — it would take persistent persuasion to get him to perform the song decades later — but another incentive for him to take a backseat was the fact that his contractual obligation to Tony Defries wouldn't expire until October of 1982. Queen was welcome to the the mechanical royalties for the record; better the band than David's former manager. David would lie low for a year, venturing out only to work on a project that was of interest mainly to academics and would produce one of the quirkiest, most overlooked, and — in its own way — perfect records of his career.

The project was the brainchild of Alan Clarke, a brave, gritty director best known for the controversial movie *Scum*. Early in 1981, Clarke had discussed the notion of a TV version of Bertolt Brecht's first full-length play, *Baal*, with BBC producer Louis Marks. Clarke planned a minimalist studio-based production of the 1918 play, using a pioneering split-screen effect for Brecht's trademark *Verfremdungseffekt*, in which the actor directly addresses the audience, commenting on events.

The play was "ambitious — bordering on the dangerous," says Louis Marks. "But I had great confidence in Alan Clarke; he was a great director." From the start, Clarke, Marks, and writer and translator John Willett were concerned about the casting of the central character. The three debated Steven Berkoff and Barry Humphries (Willett admired Dame Edna Everage's "demonic intensity") before the writer suggested Bowie; he knew of his work on *The Elephant Man* and guessed he "might be interested in pre-1933 Germany and even in Brecht." He'd guessed right: Clarke and Louis Marks went to see Bowie in Vevey in mid-July. "When they came back, we had our Baal," says Willett.

The casting choice was a fascinating one; the notion of an amoral hobo poet sleeping his way around the world was appropriately close to David's nomad sex-junkie existence with the Manish Boys — a life that, from his safe Swiss retreat, seemed a world away. Bowie didn't hesitate, says Marks: "The chat at his house was very brief — and then it was simply down to practicalities, him and Alan talking about how they would do it."

Marks's, Clarke's, and Willett's experiences with David closely mirrored that of *The Elephant Man*'s cast and crew. Bowie was a trouper, but the atmosphere around him was disturbing. The project was shrouded in obsessive secrecy; once rehearsals started the cast and crew were ordered not to reveal Bowie's involvement. Two security guards stood by the studio door throughout; the sign on the entrance to BBC studio 1 read simply CLASSIC PLAY.

Producer Louis Marks was a doctor of philosophy, an Oxford-educated expert on Renaissance studies; John Willett was the English-speaking world's foremost Brecht scholar and translator and had met the playwright in 1956; both of the men were bona fide intellectuals. Once David arrived in the rehearsal space in Acton, the trio sat down to discuss the play. Their conversation turned to the look of the play, and Willett explained how he saw it as reminiscent of the illustrator Masereel. "How wonderful!" David replied and mentioned he'd tracked down some of the artist's prints in Berlin, part of a growing collection of expressionist art. They discussed the Brecht *récitatif* singing style: "I think of it rather like plainsong," Bowie murmured. Willett was shocked; the comparison made complete sense but had never occurred to him. They continued talking about Brecht and the Neue Sachlichkeit art movement—the stripped-down, austere reaction to expressionism—and Bowie's understanding of that seemed just as sophisticated.

As he walked away from one discussion, Willett turned to Marks and said, "He knows more about Germany as a whole— and Brecht in particular—than anyone we know!" They didn't discuss whether David knew more than the two of them, but it was a distinct possibility.

A decade before, David had absorbed his culture from people like William Burroughs and Andy Warhol, skipping from one subject to the next like a butterfly. In his cocaine period he'd learned to focus, spending endless hours pondering alien visitations or Nazi folklore; when he later put that focus to real use, studying in Berlin galleries or poring over artist monographs, he transformed himself from a sophisticated name-dropper to a figure who could impress and even intimidate Oxford's finest intellectuals.

As discussions gave way to rehearsals, the pair were amazed by how Bowie took command of Brecht's music, imposing sense and rhythm on the words. Yet as an actor, he was totally unconventional. An actor builds up a performance from scratch, adding or modifying elements with each rehearsal. David, however, gave a completely different performance every time. Each version seemed complete, full of ideas. "Nothing he said was routine," says Willett.

There were four weeks of rehearsal in Acton before the one-week shoot, which reached a climax on the final day, August 12. Clarke had to tie up the split-screen shots and shoot the opening hymn, which was crucial both to set up the play and to establish Bowie's credibility as the central character. The pressure was on; Bowie started singing the hymn, but suddenly there was a tremendous banging heard through the studio wall. Clarke stopped the cameras and sent a messenger to studio 2 to tell them to be quiet, but the door to studio 2 was locked. With the hammering echoing around the studio, Louis Marks phoned the BBC administration; the noise stopped for a few minutes, only to start again in a slightly different location. The cycle repeated itself several times, and tempers were frayed; finally, Bowie announced, "I know how to stop this!"

He strode into the center of the studio, put his hands up to his mouth, and shouted, "Lunch!"

Suddenly, the tension evaporated. The noise did reoccur, but the filming continued, the actors and crew energized once more, and Clarke wrapped up the shoot confident he'd pulled off a difficult coup.

Bowie seemed to exert an almost superhuman influence over his distinguished colleagues, but he wasn't pompous; he was enthusiastic and sincere. When working on the songs for the TV play, he collaborated closely with Dominic Muldowney, a pioneer in interpreting Brecht's music. Toward the end, he'd confided in Muldowney that he wanted to record some of the material in Berlin; would Muldowney like to oversee the arrangements? Muldowney leaped at the chance; writer John Willett volunteered to come along too. "Really, you will?" asked David Bowie, with his dazzling charm. "You'd be doing me a terrific favor!" He went on to explain that he wanted the recordings to serve as his final album for RCA — that Muldowney would not only help bring one distinguished era of David Bowie's career to a close but also help free him for the next one.

A few weeks later, Bowie assembled with Muldowney, Willett, Tony Visconti, and Eduard Meyer for David's last recording at Hansa Studio 2. It was a relaxed session, relying heavily on the eight-strong band of Berlin musicians assembled by percussionist Sherry Bertram that included plenty of Brecht old-timers, notably a seventy-five-year-old bandoneonist who'd played in the orchestra of the first production of *The Threepenny Opera.*

Bowie arrived late for the recording, which meant Muldowney and Visconti had laid down the bulk of the backup tracks before he got there. Muldowney had an unrivaled pedigree in classical and Brecht-related music, having studied with composer Harrison Birtwistle, but was staggered at the creativity on display: Even as he arranged one string part, Visconti was already compressing and equalizing the sound, "and suddenly these four strings sounded like four tanks."

With the background tracks complete, they cleared the hall, and Visconti and Meyer set up microphones in each corner so that they could record David filling the Meistersaal with his voice, like the cabaret acts who'd performed there in the 1920s; he finished the entire set in three or four hours. It was a master class in technique, says Muldowney: "The standout was 'The Drowned Girl,' which is like an Ophelia song, where she dies in the river. He's singing about 'Her slow descent' below the water, right down in the bass baritone. Then halfway through he jumps up the octave. I play this song to composers at the Royal Opera House on courses. When he sings up to the word *smoke,* it's got smoke all around it, it's cloudy. Then we get to the *k* of *smoke* and you can see again. It's an absolute tutorial in how to paint a text. The only other person I know can do that is Frank Sinatra."

After the day's singing master class, David spent that night giving Muldowney a cultural tour. While the exhausted Visconti slept, David and Muldowney turned up first at a club in Kreuzberg where the clientele were draped over dentists' chairs and next at a New Wave club, the Tschungle. There, David danced with a beautiful, elfin, Ziggyish boy, flirtatiously sharing a cigarette with him. Later still they knocked on an imposing basement door; the peephole slid open, David was given a delighted welcome, and he and Muldowney were ushered into a transvestite bar. Chatting to the stunning creatures serving drinks,

Muldowney admired the gilt mirror that ran the length of the bar. "Thank you," one of them told him, "it was made for Hermann Göring." Around four in the morning, Muldowney returned, spent, to his hotel on the Ku'Damm, leaving David going strong in his own good-bye to Berlin.

David's anonymous exploits in Berlin were in stark contrast to the media frenzy that greeted the crew on their return to London. The news that the star, out of view for a year now, was appearing in an obscure German play inspired headlines and spreads in the *Daily Express,* the *Sun,* and most of the UK press. The *Daily Mirror* explained: "He plays a singing poet with a huge appetite for sex and wine called Baal by Germans"—a grammatically challenged précis that perhaps did not fully communicate the play's significance.

Clarke and Willett discovered that the BBC had retitled the play *Bowie in Baal* and delayed its broadcast until the spring, when they could showcase Bowie's presence via a cover story in the *Radio Times,* the BBC's glossy listings magazine. There was "a spat"; producer Louis Marks tried to fight the decision, but he failed. An obscure play, previously of interest only to academics, was now being promoted as a ratings grabber; Bowie was overshadowing both Brecht and *Baal.*

The play's transformation into a prestige production brought its own repercussions. A few weeks before the broadcast date, March 2, 1982, Louis Marks discovered that the commercial network ITV had scheduled an equally prestigious play for the same evening and it started half an hour earlier. *A Voyage Round My Father,* John Mortimer's poignant, funny memoir of the decline of his cantankerous barrister father, featured Laurence Olivier in one of his last and best-loved roles. The BBC was comprehensively upstaged; ITV trounced *Baal* in both ratings and press coverage—although the reviews of Bowie's acting were in the main complimentary. Clarke and Willett later agreed the production was hampered by its compromise between naturalism and minimalism—"It needed more edge and power," according to Willett—yet even now it remains the definitive interpretation of this fascinating, immature work. "I have no reservations about it today," says Marks, the figure who more than anyone steered the project through the BBC bureaucracy. "I was thrilled to be involved."

Baal was destined to become a lost artifact, often discussed by Brecht scholars. Today, only the CD remains to document what was not only one of Bowie's bravest artistic efforts but also his final Berlin project. The Hauptstrasse lease had expired in February of 1981, so he'd stayed in his old haunt the Schlosshotel Gerhus and went to visit Esther Friedmann, whose relationship with Iggy was splintering even as Iggy's own life was falling apart. He'd been booted out of Arista Records, was back on cocaine, and stayed drunk most of the time to swamp his awareness that his music, the one thing that had always sustained him, sounded awful. Esther had seen David help Iggy out for years; now David sat playing piano in her new apartment in Kreuzberg, counseling her. "You know a lot about art," he told her. "You should do it for a living." Friedmann followed his advice and later built up a thriving gallery business.

The Baal EP was David's final RCA release; it reached number 29 on the UK album charts in the spring of 1982. It was now an open secret that David was simply waiting out his contract with RCA. The motive was not just financial; the company's shortcomings had been obvious from David's very first U.S. tour, with their patchy efforts to arrange local airplay and promotion. The label's lack of enthusiasm for Low had not eased his disenchantment. David's solution was simply to ignore RCA while he pursued other business.

And soon the other business started to stream in, for after a year in Vevey, David was getting itchy feet. With recording on the back burner, he turned again to acting. Tony Defries had claimed he would make David into a mainstream entertainer like Liz Taylor, and with two major movie projects in 1982, David seemed to be getting close. Both were quirky concepts, although the one that looked like it would be the more popular turned out to be the bigger failure. Tony Scott, a successful director of commercials, was hoping to make a leap into cinema, like his brother Ridley; Ridley had graduated from selling Lyons Maid ice cream back in 1969, with an ad that coincidentally featured a young David, to directing *Alien* and *Blade Runner*. Tony's first shot at the mainstream was *The Hunger*, a slick, glossy vampire movie based on a novel by Whitley Strieber. With its MTV-influenced visuals, bombastic sound track, a guest appearance by goth band Bauhaus, and scenes shot in the nightclub Heaven, it was exactly the kind of film in which you'd expect to see a rock star attempting to cross over into acting, and its combination of sensationalism and dreary predictability ensured this "sensual classic of perverse fear" was a box-office flop on its release in April of 1983. Eventually, however, its goth glossiness helped the movie build a cult following, inspiring a 1990s TV series that began what was to be a long-standing relationship between Tony Scott and David's son.

Joey—who would later revert to using his first name, Duncan— was on set for some of the filming of *The Hunger;* it became a formative experience for his career. For Bowie, though, his longest stay in England since 1973 brought the family skeletons dancing out of the closet. Both his mother, Peggy, and his aunt Pat had long nursed resentments, feeling that they and David's half brother, Terry, were being neglected.

Peggy had phoned Charles Shaar Murray at the *NME* back in 1975 to share her grievances and was at the point of going public again. David's ex-manager Ken Pitt had remained in contact with her and dissuaded her from approaching the tabloids. Although admirably circumspect, Pitt saw Peggy's boredom and constant demand for attention as problems that would never be solved: "I would be on the phone to her quite often, with some issue or other. In the end I used to say to her, 'Peggy, if David were a plumber, you wouldn't even be talking about him, would you?'" Pitt's influence and David's more consistent efforts to ensure Joey remained in touch with his grandmother helped keep Peggy out of the press, but his aunt Pat was not so easily controlled; she contacted the *Sun* and the *Star* that July to tell them that David was "callous and uncaring…and needs to face up to his responsibilities."

Pat's anger was prompted by the increasingly sad condition of

Terry. David's half brother's outlook improved after his marriage to Olga in 1972 but had deteriorated in recent years. Pat would later accuse David of ignoring Terry and his wife, although her account is challenged by David's friends, including Mark Pritchett, who remembers seeing the couple at Haddon Hall. Pat's anger and bitterness derived from complex causes: She seemed to be engaged in sporadic feuds with her sister Peggy, and her relationship with her own husband, Tony, suffered under the strain of Terry's illness; there had reportedly been fistfights between Terry and his uncle. Although often accused of ignoring Terry's fate, David had wrestled with the issue of his brother, opening up to confidants and even writers, such as Timothy White, whom he told, "I've never been able to get through to [Terry] about how he really feels. I guess nobody has." David did go to see his half brother during his stay in London; his visit was followed by an unhelpful headline in the *Sun* blaring "I'm Terrified of Going Mad, Says Bowie."

Pat's attacks on Bowie over this period and thereafter ensured his reputation as a manipulative "ice man" who used and then discarded family and friends without qualms. There were indeed many instances of his unashamed devotion to "Numero uno, mate!" Yet his ruthlessness usually had an artistic motive— outside of his own career, he was genuinely kind to people, like Esther Friedmann, Iggy Pop, Tony Sales, and others. Some of David's accusers, notably his ex-wife, insist that each and every instance of David's compassion is self-serving, aimed at shoring up his own credibility. Yet there are plenty of examples of help given and not publicized; notably, David paid the school fees of Marc Bolan's son, Rolan, once he realized the Bolan estate would not do so. In other instances, Bowie helped with time, not money, searching out specialized medical treatment for the son of a writer friend. Angie's depiction of David as a flat, one-dimensional, selfish character does not ring true.

Selflessness and positivity often coexist with pettiness and grudge-bearing—David was always capable of both. An example of such duality was the way David's artistic bravery and contempt for convention was hampered by his habit of reading reviews and features about himself. He could harbor resentment at perceived slights or inaccuracies for years. In 1997, an issue of *Mojo* magazine featured Mick Ronson on its cover; two years later, David was still complaining about "the magazine that said Mick wrote all my songs!," irritated that colleagues such as Tony Visconti had highlighted Mick's influence on David's early albums.

It was such haughty pronouncements, exacerbated by the flunkies and yes-men who surround most stars, that helped inspire his nickname "the Dame," coined by *Smash Hits* writer Tom Hibbert in the early 1980s. Yet when David was liberated from his flunkies, he often confounded expectations. In March of 1982, Carol Clerk, then a news editor for *Melody Maker*, spent an afternoon drinking poteen with the Exploited and other assorted acquaintances in Matrix Studios, where they were celebrating finishing their *Troops of Tomorrow* album. Come opening time — in those days bars closed for a couple of hours in the late afternoon — the group hit a few pubs, and "late at night, really plastered," says Clerk, "we arrived at Gossips. And Bowie was in there, with some discreet security. We took a table, and to our amazement, given the terrible state of everyone, Bowie asked if he could join us."

It turned out that Bowie wanted to know all about the Exploited, thrash punk, and Mohawk fashion, and he was exactly as earnest and charming as he had been when pumping the *Pork* actors for information a decade before. He sat with the chaotic, drooling-drunk group for hours, politely buying rounds. The punks were impressed that the power of stardom ensured that the bar staff, "for the first, and only time in my life," brought drinks to the table and kept the club open beyond its 3:00 a.m. closing time. One of the few details Clerk could still recall the next morning was the way Bowie worried about Linc, the bass player from Chelsea, who'd passed out before David arrived at the table and was lying unconscious under his leather jacket. Throughout the night, like an ultracool mother hen, Bowie kept lifting up Linc's jacket, checking that Linc was still breathing, until all the parties finally staggered home.

It was in his guise as fan that David was always the most engaging; any perceived snootiness would evaporate in his boyish enthusiasm. As ever, there was no dividing line between his enthusiasms and his work; they blended into each other imperceptibly. One perfect example happened during that July, when David returned to Montreux after winding up the shoot for *The Hunger*, just in time for that year's jazz festival. This was the year that Stevie Ray Vaughan, then a struggling blues guitarist, had been championed by famed Atlantic producer Jerry Wexler, who'd persuaded Montreux mastermind Claude Nobs to present Vaughan and his band, Double Trouble.

The unsigned band played on the acoustic stage, where Vaughan's clanky, raw Texas blues brought boos and catcalls from an audience expecting cool, quiet jazz. Although their reception "did kinda hurt our feelings," says bassist Tommy Shannon, the blues trio were so fired up by their first overseas show that they later carried their amplifiers downstairs to the bar, where they jammed until dawn. As the sun came up, they noticed a figure drinking at the counter. They knew it was David Bowie; "He just had this look," says Shannon. Stevie and the band were not starstruck—they hardly knew Bowie's music—but they were impressed by his charm, the way he'd stayed up until dawn to have a word. "He was just real nice-looking, and handled himself well." He sat with them for a while, speaking mostly to Stevie, talking about guitar playing. David's enthusiasm helped banish the memory of the audience's boos, as did the response of Jackson Browne, who'd also seen the show and offered them free recording time in his home studio.

David's respite in Montreux turned out to be brief; despite the fact that he'd planned to make only a single movie in 1982, a project that he'd discussed several years before suddenly spun into action. Director Nagisa Oshima, best known for *In the Realm of the Senses*, was making a film based on the memoirs of Laurens van der Post. Oshima had approached singer Kenji Sawada to play the role of POW commander Yonoi; Sawada dropped out (he was replaced by Ryuichi Sakamoto) but only after he'd suggested

David Bowie for the part of Jack Celliers. Oshima liked casting singers or other performers—"without the peculiarities actors often acquire"—and he'd approached David during his *Elephant Man* run. David readily agreed. Producer Jeremy Thomas had already worked on two films with Nicolas Roeg; Paul Mayersberg, who wrote the script with Oshima, had done the screenplay for *The Man Who Fell to Earth*, and once Bowie joined the cast, he rewrote the part with David in mind. Thomas remembers that "Bowie knew everything about Oshima. Once he understood Oshima's interest in him, he was interested in the film. It was an ideal situation; he was immediately on board, saying, 'Tell me when and where—and I'll be there.'"

The film was intriguing, the antithesis of a conventional prisoner-of-war drama. Three key roles were played by comparative novices: Bowie as Celliers, Ryuichi Sakamoto as Captain Yonoi—the commandant who is obsessed with him—and comedian Takeshi as Sergeant Hara. At the center of this nexus is Laurens van der Post, played by Tom Conti, who attempts to bridge the huge cultural gaps among them all. Conti's humanity carries the film; Bowie's and Sakamoto's characters are stylized, almost ritualistic—both of them yearn to be archetypes.

Oshima filmed extremely fast, with no daily rushes, and Sakamoto would later comment that when he saw his own performance, "I couldn't believe how bad my acting was...I was traumatized." Bowie's portrayal of Jack Celliers—the perfect soldier who is attempting to atone for abandoning his crippled brother—is also variable, most notably in the faintly risible flashback to Celliers as a seventeen-year-old schoolboy. Nonetheless, Bowie's physical beauty, all jagged teeth and exquisite cheekbones, and ethereal air are perfect for a character who, as his initials indicate, is a Christlike figure, human but otherworldly. Flawed but meaningful, engagingly human, Bowie's performance would prove the high-water mark of his cinematic career.

In America, the movie was a box-office failure. As scriptwriter Paul Mayersberg explains, "U.S. audiences were baffled by a prison camp movie where nobody tried to escape," and roles of this caliber would ultimately dry up. But in Europe and Japan, the movie's themes of atonement, cross-cultural incomprehension, homoeroticism, and a search for meaning were more resonant, and *Merry Christmas, Mr. Lawrence* acquired the reputation of a classic. As Jeremy Thomas, who would go on to produce the films *The Last Emperor* and *Sexy Beast,* points out, "It was my first film that caught the public imagination and was shown all over the world. And it has aged well, because it was set in period — and because Bowie somehow doesn't look any older today than he did then."

The filming wrapped up with David presenting an impromptu show that was rapturously received by the crew. It marked an unexpectedly intense year, for along with filming in Rarotonga and New Zealand with Oshima and in London with Tony Scott, he'd also shuttled between Montreux and New York. Anne Wehrer and Esther Friedmann had enlisted David's help with Iggy, who had returned penniless from Haiti that summer, apparently believing he was under the influence of a voodoo curse and still in what seemed like an unstoppable downward spiral.

In the weeks when he wasn't working, David based himself in New York for much of the time. Sometimes he'd venture out of his Midtown loft with bodyguards — one musician who had a disagreement with him remembers being turfed out of the room by two attractive women, "like Bambi and Thumper, Blofeld's bodyguards in *Diamonds Are Forever*" — but by the summer David felt comfortable enough to hang out solo in musicians' haunts, like the Continental in Manhattan. Occasionally this meant chatting politely to coked-out upstarts like Billy Idol, presumably talking about the old days in Bromley, where Billy had grown up too. Idol was a regular at the club and arrived around five one morning with a friend in tow: Nile Rodgers, the founder, with Bernard Edwards, of Chic. David and Nile talked till dawn. Just a few days later, David asked Nile to produce his next album.

In hindsight, their collaboration looks like a surefire winner. At the time, it was anything but. Rodgers's hugely successful streak with Chic, Sister Sledge, and Diana Ross was a couple of years old, and since then his magic touch had deserted him; Debbie Harry's *Koo Koo* had not delivered one hit single, and his own solo album had also failed to set the charts alight. "To this day, I owe David for his commitment—because at the time I had five flops in a row," says the celebrated producer. "I mean it, five! It was really tough for me."

Rodgers was probably the most experienced producer David had ever worked with, but the way he operated with David was utterly unlike anything he'd done before or has done since. Yet if their collaboration was unique in Rodgers's experience, for David it marked the summit of a working method he'd established with Dek Fearnley and Mick Ronson many years earlier, delegating key tasks, giving his collaborators huge freedom. On the album that would become *Let's Dance*, his delegation was even more extreme, with Rodgers recruiting musicians as well as overseeing the finest details of the arrangements. It was Nile Rodgers who programmed the music. But it was David Bowie who programmed Nile Rodgers.

The process began at David's newly purchased impressive château-style house in the upper Lausanne. David and Nile spent days getting to know each other before David walked into Nile's room one morning with a twelve-string guitar. Or what had once been a twelve-string. "It had just six strings on it. Which was weird, why not use a six-string guitar in the first place?" says Rodgers. "And then he played me this song. And told me he thought it was going to be a hit."

The song was folky; David played it vaguely in the style of the Byrds, and it was called "Let's Dance." "And I was like, That's not happening, man. It totally threw me. And it was not a song you could dance to." Rodgers simply didn't understand. Was this some kind of mind game? So he called a mutual friend in New York. "Do you think David is the kind of guy who would play a trick on me?" he asked. "Is he playing me this song he says is going to be a hit to see if I'm some sort of sycophant?"

"No, he wouldn't do that," came the reply. "If he says that, he really believes it."

The information didn't help. "Oh shit! What do I do now?" Nile asked himself.

Rodgers kept mum about such worries as his discussions with David continued. For much of the time they'd talk about 1950s album sleeves as they flipped through David's collection of vinyl albums, some of them venerable originals that he'd bought twenty years before at Medhurst's in Bromley. They played records like "Twist and Shout," discussing the difference between the Beatles' sweat-drenched version and the Isley Brothers' original; they both fondled the sleeves of Henry Mancini's *Peter Gunn* and Nelson Riddle's *Route 66* sound tracks, chatted about the Chicago Art Ensemble and Lester Bowie, and they spent a lot of time listening to and looking at photos of Little Richard, the childhood hero whom David still revered. It was only later that Rodgers realized he was being programmed—brainwashed, in a musical version of *The Manchurian Candidate*. For many of Bowie's previous records, David had honed the art of briefing musicians, getting them to pull something out of their consciousness that they hadn't known existed. Now he was doing it on a bigger scale.

The simplest illustration of how this worked comes on the song "Let's Dance." Rodgers knew that if it was going to be a dance hit, it needed funking up; no problem, that was his forte. But all his previous hits had had memorable openings. The solution came from "Twist and Shout." Rodgers simply lifted the vocal stacking effect—the bit where the Beatles sent teenagers crazy—and put it at the beginning of the song: "Ah...ah...ah...ah!"

After each line of the verse there was a space, which required some kind of response. The answer was Henry Mancini's *Peter Gunn* horn riff—dropped in directly after David sings "dance the blues." "It was taken straight from that record, a thing I never did before," says Rodgers. "That [riff] seemed to me so anti-groove, but sticking it on something that was so hard groove, it was like, Shit! This is magic! And I realized that all that fifties and sixties stuff was a snapshot of Bowie's brain. Then I was like, Wow! You can do that!"

A master producer used to revving up musicians to get the

right take, Rodgers realized that he himself was being produced but was also being given absolute freedom, something no other musician had attempted. "When we did *Let's Dance* the preproduction was so clear. I've never worked with an artist like that before or since. It was all beautiful images. We went to people's houses that he knew had certain things...it was like fact finders, treasure hunters, conquistadors looking for gold and we were going and looking at everything, in museums. 'Nile, look at this picture. Look at this!' So he was like the world's greatest cook showing you, This is what we want it to be. Once I had that I was clear as a bell. I was unwavering."

The same process would apply with the other standout songs on *Let's Dance*. David played Nile Iggy's version of "China Girl," again telling him it would be a hit and that he had to work out how to make it one, which Rodgers did by adapting the opening riff from Rufus's "Sweet Thing" to give the song a Chinese feel. After their extensive discussions and the preproduction at Montreux, the sessions at New York's Power Station were brief; the studio was booked for twenty-one days, and according to Rodgers, the tracks were recorded and mixed by day seventeen. There was only one artistic disagreement: Rodgers was unimpressed by Bowie's suggestion of Stevie Ray Vaughan for most of the guitar solos, telling him the guitarist just sounded like Albert King. "This guy's different," David told him, "he's got a whole other thing going on."

Vaughan was recording his debut album at Jackson Browne's studio using downtime over the Thanksgiving holiday when he got the call. The guitarist was intrigued by the offer: "It was a challenge—and Steve was always confident about being in the studio," says Tommy Shannon. Vaughan showed up within a day or two and added his guitar parts "instantaneously," according to Nile. Vaughan played an old Fender Strat, plugged straight into an old Fender amp, all the tone coming from the player, no tricks. The same applied to the rest of the music, for *Let's Dance* was at heart a simple, minimal album. Its impact came not from electronic effects but from the intuitive musicianship of players like Vaughan and the consummately funky Tony Thompson; Tony would later be called in to play drums with Madonna, Robert Palmer, and others but would never surpass the effortless swing of *Let's Dance*.

Over the following months, David Bowie was often seen in the corridors of EMI, cutting such a refined, elegantly suited-and-booted figure that on first glance the record company execs thought he was a wealthy investor. Although he had financial advisers, he negotiated the deal himself; the story at EMI was that he persuaded the aggressive new American arm of the company to pay a huge advance purely on the basis of the backup tracks. The amount David secured for his services when he signed his contract with EMI America, on January 27, 1983, was publicized as just under seventeen million dollars.

"You know how deals are constructed," says Gary Gersh, the A and R rep who, with U.S. chairman Rupert Perry, signed Bowie to EMI. "That figure would depend on a lot of clauses. But it was a superstar deal—when maybe David's sales so far wouldn't warrant it." Many other EMI staff agreed; it was "a huge risk," in the words of David's A and R man Hugh Stanley Clarke. There was debate as to whether EMI would ever make the money back. Even at the time, Gersh agrees, all the company management had their doubts. But today, he points out, "If you were to say to *any* record company they could have that deal again—you would have a line of people around the block."

CHAPTER 19

On the Other Side

I got [the spider] built and only saw the first few shows. That was enough.

—Chip Monck

I T WAS SPRING IN THE NORTHERN HEMISPHERE, but there was a streak of autumnal gold to the light in Sydney and Carinda as David Bowie brandished a guitar in the outback or bared his backside as the surf spilled over him and his China girl. Back in Manhattan, Carlos Alomar was assembling the musicians for what would be the biggest world tour of 1983. With his typical consummate grasp of the priorities of the modern pop industry, David was filming videos on the beach.

According to Nile Rodgers, David had been happy to sit in the lounge at the Power Station while many of *Let's Dance*'s tracks were laid down, but when it came to the video art form, David kept a close eye on every aspect of David Mallett's production. "Let's Dance" was filmed in an outback village that was turned into a transplanted Mississippi Delta. David lip-synched the song in a shack, with two kids from the Aboriginal-Islanders Dance Theatre acting out a storyline based on its message, which, Bowie explained, was "It's wrong to be racist!" For "China Girl," the song inspired by Iggy's affair with Kuelan Nguyen, Bowie and Mallett cast student and model Geeling Ng; she marched around Sydney's Chinatown in a Chairman Mao outfit and reenacted the famous beach scene in *From Here to Eternity*, frolicking with David in the surf. In this idyllic interlude, the two became lovers, hanging out together in David's apartment in Elizabeth Bay.

Back in 1967, Tony Visconti had ridiculed Ken Pitt's efforts to mold David into an all-round entertainer. In 1983, the all-round potential offered by the new medium of video was an intrinsic part of his pitch to EMI. The British company's American arm was expanding fast, its success bolstered by British acts who'd been making videos to show on *Top of the Pops* for decades and who were cleaning up at the newly dominant MTV.

The few American acts who caught on — principally Michael Jackson, whose "Billie Jean" video was broadcast on the lily-white network in March of 1983 — would rule the eighties. In May, as Bowie's video drove his debut EMI single "Let's Dance" to his first simultaneous UK and U.S. number 1, the smart money was on him to dominate this decade. In the seventies he'd rebranded himself as the world's first bisexual rock star; now his niche brand was being relaunched as an international multimedia product. His star status was highlighted by a sensational appearance alongside Nagisa Oshima and Ryuichi Sakamoto at the Cannes Festival in May: Tanned, his hair a mass of blond cotton-candy floss, he joked casually with the admiring press, switching effortlessly from self-deprecation to intellectual earnestness. European critics in particular loved *Merry Christmas, Mr. Lawrence*, and it was a strong contender for the Grand Prix Spécial du Jury — although it ultimately lost to *Monty Python's The Meaning of Life*.

Far away from the glitz of Cannes, the rehearsals for David's biggest tour to date had moved to Dallas, overseen by Carlos Alomar, much like David's 1978 tour. The musicians were based around the *Let's Dance* crew, plus a three-piece horn section and Dave Lebolt (later a senior figure at Apple) on keyboards.

If there was a perfect way to do a modern tour, this was it. Spanning sixteen countries, delivering ninety-six performances, and selling more than two and a half million tickets, the Serious

Moonlight tour would become the definitive stadium event. Every decision in its progress was closely scrutinized by a triumvirate of David (or an Isolar representative), accountant Bill Zysblat, and agent Will Forte, each keeping a close eye on the logistics, the money, and one another. Its only rival in the early eighties was the Stones' 1981 Tattoo You tour, which grossed more in ticket sales but was limited to the United States and Europe. The Stones' outing was a reminder of past glories, promoting a collection of tracks dating back a decade. In contrast, Serious Moonlight captured Bowie at his peak.

Guitarist Stevie Ray Vaughan was at first thrilled about the tour and believed that he'd extracted a promise from David that his band, Double Trouble, would play support. Once rehearsals shifted from Manhattan to Dallas, Vaughan's hometown, he started hanging out with his band again. Two or three nights in, they had to sit and hear his complaints: "There was a point in the set where he was supposed to come down this ramp doing these [dance] steps," says bassist Tommy Shannon, "and that just wasn't in his nature. He'd been pushed into it anyway by management. He was having a hard time adjusting."

Vaughan was, says Shannon, focused and hardworking over this spring, but the guitarist was becoming increasingly isolated in the Bowie camp. The suggestion that Double Trouble could support was dropped. Then Vaughan saw the "Let's Dance" video, which showed David with a Fender Strat atop a mountain, appearing to play what was actually Stevie's guitar solo. Anyone used to the ways of showbiz would have accepted such a harmless deception. For a Texas bluesman, it was an outrage: "The video showed David faking it—and Stevie was *furious*," says Shannon. For Stevie, the videos, the staging, and the glitz were a distraction, a sign of fakery. Relations soured quickly. Lenny Vaughan, a pushy rock wife, says Shannon, interrupted rehearsals to brandish a newspaper that showed Stevie's photo as a full page, David's a mere single column. Bowie, who remained unruffled for most of the tour, was enraged: "Don't you ever break up my rehearsal!" backup singer Frank Simms heard him shout. "If you were a man I'd kick your ass." Lenny was barred from rehearsals, and then Vaughan, says Simms, "disappeared for five days without telling anyone" to attend the funeral of Muddy Waters. Vaughan's manager Chesley Milligan—a good ol' boy who was in over his head—demanded an extra five hundred dollars a week for Stevie and a place on the plane for himself, or his client would walk. Stevie walked.

David, who wasn't actually present at this event, would later describe Vaughan standing disconsolately by the roadside as the band boarded their bus and left town. But Stevie cheered up quickly, says Shannon: "He got in the car with us and said, 'Well, I'm not going.' And he was really relieved. When it comes down to it, Steve wanted to stay with his band." Vaughan started his own ninety-date tour that June, racking up five hundred thousand sales of his debut album by word of mouth. He and David would never meet again, according to Shannon.

As one guitarist passed out of David's orbit forever, another returned. Earl Slick had fallen out with David after *Station to Station,* thanks to disputes involving Michael Lippman, Pat Gibbons, and, says Slick, "the fact my head was up my ass." David called in Slick for the last two days of rehearsals, then did what he hadn't done the last time around and spoke to the guitarist face-to-face. "I showed up and David is going, 'Where's the Earl?'" says Slick. "I said, 'Come on!' He goes, 'All right!' Which he wouldn't have done earlier—but we were both different then. So we went out and had lunch and cleared the air because there were a lot of bad feelings. So everything was cool."

When Slick joined the *Diamond Dogs* album tour, his initiation had consisted of his having his long hair cropped, like Samson; he was livid but realized later it was part of a process of being taken out of his comfort zone. For Serious Moonlight, Slick had to endure a series of suit fittings, as clothes designed for a lanky Texas cowboy were shortened and taken in to fit his wiry Italian frame. Slick sat one-on-one with Carlos and learned the entire set during the course of forty-eight hours, drinking coffee after coffee, then headed out on a tour that made his last venture with David seem like amateur hour. "David was totally on it—the good days, the bad days, it doesn't matter. There was a lot to think about and that made it easy."

The tour opened in Brussels, and *NME* journalist Charles Shaar Murray—who'd followed Bowie since 1971—was flown over to the opening show by Bowie's management company, Isolar. In a sign of the changing times, he'd been commissioned to write the copy for the glossy tour booklet. The huge production he saw was a potent reminder of how the stakes had been raised for live shows. They continued to rise with Prince and Madonna, but in Brussels and London, says Murray, there was no hint of the flabbiness with which 1980s stadium tours have become associated: "When Tony Thompson nailed a groove down, it stayed nailed down—it was right on the money. Alomar was playing rhythm, and he'd been in the pit at the Apollo, that was all the credentials you needed."

For those earlier shows, David's voice was superb. "In a moment of euphoria I described him as the best white singer alive," says Murray. "Which I possibly overstated, but he was good enough to be rated against the best. And I'd give him the highest marks for stagecraft, charisma, and the dancing too."

All those involved in the tour felt they were breaking new ground: "There was a sense of the magnitude from literally the first day—I thought it would be enormous, and it was," says Simms. It wasn't merely the size of the venues or the luxury of the hotels. Frank Simms later played an arena tour to forty-thousand-strong crowds with Billy Joel: "They would cheer and clap—but it wasn't the same magnitude, and didn't have the same magic. With Serious Moonlight, in the larger cities, you'd have the biggest stars—in England, the royal family; in Thailand, the king, queen, and prince; in Australia, the prime minister. Then in LA you'd have movie stars, Michael Jackson—they were all there."

For a couple of weeks Geeling Ng joined the tour in France and Germany, and there was a blissful, easy happiness around the organization. The band loved her—she was unaffected, calm, "normal as apple pie," says George Simms, Frank's brother. George and his wife double-dated with David and Geeling. "It was sweet, as normal as can be, and we managed to find some places where not too many fans would bother us." George got the sense that Geeling was overwhelmed by the experience and realized "it was just a short-term thing." After accompanying David for a couple of weeks, she caught a plane back to New Zealand and a normal life, and David and band flew over to San Bernardino to play a one-time-only show at the US Festival for the widely publicized fee of one million dollars.

Headlining at an evening show that included U2, the Pretenders, and Stevie Nicks, playing to a three-hundred-thousand-strong crowd, the band walked onto the stage at eleven o'clock to a rapturous reception. "Like Jesus walking on water," says George Simms. The festival was a disaster for its sponsor, Apple's Steve Wozniak; he lost more than seven million dollars, according to the *New York Times,* with one audience member murdered in a drug deal, another dead of an overdose. But for David it was a triumph; the date raised his commercial profile enormously and helped bring more U.S. promoters on board. But with stories of the million-dollar price tag came reports that David considered the tour his "pension plan"—a sentiment guaranteed to inflame his detractors, who started to speculate that the tour was more about money than music.

David, meanwhile, dealt with the constant buzz of attention and adrenaline calmly and efficiently. He had his little strategies to retain a degree of normalcy; often, he'd hang with the Simms brothers, enjoying or sharing their humor skits. He had the gift of being able to flip instantly from lowbrow humor to regal refinement when necessary—if, say, Susan Sarandon walked in. He was a "good boy" throughout; he'd have the odd toot of cocaine socially, but he generally showed exemplary self-control. During the eight-month tour, he went on a rampage just once, in London, during a party in Frank Simms's room. There was a glint in his eye, and he gave the impression that he'd had a couple of drinks too many. He'd hit on a girl, "then he'd leave the room with her and come back fifteen or twenty minutes later—and hit on another girl. And then it would happen again. And this went on several times." Finally, one of the partygoers turned him down and complained to Frank Simms, "How dare he? Who does he think he is?" But this was an out-of-character lapse in "a very light tour, as far as drugs and other behavior. He knew his limits," says Simms. "He was under a superior degree of control."

The dizzying heights to which David's fortunes had risen were in stark contrast those of his friend Iggy, who over the same time had been touring himself into oblivion. In the spring of 1983, he had lawyers pursuing him after an incident in which he'd stamped on a girl's head at a gig in Poughkeepsie. Though this period was worse than his humiliation with the Stooges—for the music was lousy now too—he'd stayed in touch with David. On June 20, he met fan and future wife Suchi Asano, who'd gone back to retrieve her umbrella after his show in Tokyo; exactly one week later, "China Girl" hit number 2 in the UK, promising the royalties that had eluded him for so long. Iggy abandoned his tour and flew back with Suchi to LA, where they met up with David when his tour reached the LA Forum, on August 14.

It was a poignant example of how lives can turn around. Iggy—or rather Jimmy, his avuncular alter ego—was all sparkly-eyed and boyish, with his hair in a side part that made him look like Bing Crosby. Healthy and, soon, drug-free, he was teaching Suchi English, which calmed him down. They made a sweet couple. With David and George Simms, they sat around reminiscing about Berlin before David started raving about life in Lausanne; he explained the Swiss legal system, the government, the culture, and the citizen militia while Jimmy nodded attentively. Then David described the twenty-four-seat jet in which the tour members were flying, mapping out its lounge area and seating arrangements on a carpet, with the same excitement he might have had over a Heckel painting seven years before. David suggested Iggy and Suchi join the tour, which would soon be heading to the Far East. "I've got too much to sort out right now," Jimmy told him, but they agreed to meet up in December. David's other celebrity visitor at the LA Forum was Michael Jackson; the two chatted together quietly, and bystanders could not make out the conversation.

Three weeks later, on September 3, another old friend showed up. Since Mick Ronson's short, disastrous solo career under the auspices of MainMan, Mick had retreated to his comfort zone, contributing his tasteful guitar to work by Ian Hunter and Bob Dylan and building up a solid, unflashy reputation as a producer, most recently for A&M Canada. Mick arrived at David's hotel with Lisa Dalbello, whose career he was helping to relaunch; David asked him to return the next night and play. Dalbello remembers Ronson being "Okay, whatever" about the prospect, but the guitarist returned the next night and met the band. "He was kind of drunk, and I think he was intimidated," says Frank Simms. Ronson walked onstage after the encore holding Earl Slick's blue Stratocaster to a tumultuous welcome; the band launched into a rocking version of "The Jean Genie." At one point the strap slipped off Earl's blue guitar, and Ronson waved it around his head. "I thought, That's not necessary! But he was nervous," says Simms, who was standing near.

The Japanese and Australian legs of the tour, in October and November, were again huge events, unrivaled as spectacles until Michael Jackson's Bad tour in 1987 and then the Stones' Steel Wheels in 1989. But by the time the band and crew hit the Far East, a sense of being divorced from reality had overtaken all of them. The tour helped kick off the 1980s obsession with size and statistics, but the sheer size and drudgery meant that, for David more than anyone, the experience would become routine. Charles Shaar Murray notes: "I saw the footage of Bowie in Singapore. And I suddenly thought, He's turned into a rock-and-roll version of Prince Charles. In a suit, with an old-fashioned haircut like a lemon meringue on his head, talking in this posh accent, and it's very, Oh, what do you do?"

For the band the unending spectacle was numbing: "Night after night, you start to lose touch," says Frank Simms. "By the time we got to Australia we would have these tremendous parties every single night—actresses and models, buffets and drinking, then a yacht with its own caterer. I would go for two weeks without calling home. My wife said, 'I wish you'd call, you may be having fun but we miss you.' I would apologize and say, 'You have no idea...it's like they're feeding you the sun, the moon, and the stars.' I don't know how David lived with it."

The closing night of the tour, in Hong Kong, was the anniversary of John Lennon's death, December 8. At the show, David sat down at one point and began talking about John, almost as if in prayer or meditation. And then David and the band walked backstage as if in a daze and hugged one another gently before returning for the final encore. "So we ended on this very somber note," says Frank Simms. "We memorialized Lennon, and we memorialized the fact we had been together for this wonderful experience."

Most of the band went home feeling subdued. David and Coco—who, as ever, was there to keep him company once his love affairs fizzled out—stayed in the Far East, meeting up with Iggy and Suchi, after which Iggy and Suchi disappeared for an extended holiday in Bali and Java. The sights they witnessed, notably the ostentatious villas of oil magnates, each with its own open drain carrying a stream of sewage down the hill into the jungle, would be documented in Iggy's lyrics to "Tumble and Twirl," one of only two new songs to appear on David's next album, which he started recording in Morin Heights, Canada, just a few months later.

By May of 1984, David Bowie had made fifteen studio albums; each had been conceived in a burst of creativity and ideas, usually accompanied by a manifesto that was floated around the press or previewed live. Even *Let's Dance,* for which new songs had been at a premium, was born out of a love for R & B and a yearning to evoke the spirit of Little Richard. Little Richard had scored hit records without compromising himself, without losing his status as an outsider. David thought he'd finally managed the same feat.

In the old days, he had advised his friend Glenn Hughes, "When everyone turns right, turn left!" Now he himself turned right, without noticing.

A year or so later, David would compare the concept behind album sixteen, *Tonight,* to that of *Pin Ups.* He was referring to both albums' emphasis on cover versions of songs, but the comparison was also apt in that the main inspiration for *Pin Ups* was to keep a commercial enterprise moving forward. The previous time around, of course, it was Tony Defries who was intent on relieving the fans of their cash; in 1984, it was David.

This wasn't the only change in David's philosophy. Just a few years earlier, he had told pianist Sean Mayes he was "suspicious of virtuosos." Now, following the example of *Let's Dance*, he surrounded himself with them. David's key assistant for *Tonight* was Derek Bramble, previously bassist with Heatwave. Heatwave had briefly been the UK's most successful homegrown funk band and recently had gotten famous once more, thanks to keyboard player Rod Temperton, who'd crossed the Atlantic to huge success as principal songwriter on Michael Jackson's *Thriller*. Perhaps David thought Bramble would graduate to similar fame; he also valued the fact that Bramble could play "proper reggae bass lines."

David's venture into reggae would prove the most bizarre of his stylistic turnarounds. He'd fallen for the Velvets before the group had a record out, and Neu! when the band was hardly known outside Germany; now he was experimenting with white reggae just as the smart money—notably the Police—was moving out.

The location for the recording of *Tonight* was suggested by Hugh Padgham, best known as producer of the Police (and more recently McFly); he was the man who inspired the simple, yearning piano part on "Every Breath You Take," which was recorded at Le Studio in Morin Heights, a skiing resort northwest of Montreal. Padgham suggested using the same studio and volunteered to step down to an engineering role because he wanted to work with Bowie. Well aware of the restless creativity that Bowie had summoned up for a decade or more, Padgham was taken aback to find that the singer seemed simply "bored" once the sessions started. There were similar recollections from some of the studio staff, who remembered "he was obsessed with the I Ching," one of them asserting he even used it to determine if a mix was "done." The only aspect of his recording behavior that seemed to have survived from the old days was his sex addiction, and that old energy only returned when he was trailing women on the dance floor of a nearby club.

Padgham's role as engineer grew to that of producer as the sessions dragged on. He remembers some experimentation in the early stages of the album but that in general David only betrayed excitement when he talked about his friend Iggy, who was at the sessions. "David was talking about how he'd rescued Iggy. And I remember him telling lots of stories about him, like how they cut short his tour after Iggy had stamped on a girl's head and made her bite off her tongue."

Padgham was at a loss as to the intentions behind *Tonight;* the most charitable explanation is that it was designed to make some money for David's friend, for the album's nine tracks featured four Iggy credits, although the new songs, "Dancing with the Big Boys" and "Tumble and Twirl," were confused assemblages, far from the glories of *Lust for Life.* But then, "Tonight," the song Iggy and David had written for *Lust for Life,* was hardly recognizable either; cut in a sanitized reggae style, with pristine drums and a warbling competition between David and guest star Tina Turner, each of them struggling to out-emote the other. The original's thrilling, shouted intro—"I saw my baby, she was turning blue," with its reference to a heroin overdose—was bowdlerized. "I didn't want to inflict it on her," David explained to Charles Shaar Murray when it came time to promote the album. "It's not necessarily something that she would agree to be part of."

There was something sad, or deluded, about the way he sat in the Savoy with Murray attempting to justify why he had emasculated a song he'd written just six years before; suddenly he sounded as if age or mainstream success had drained his ambition—and his hearing, for at one point he claimed that the syrupy, phoned-in version of "Tonight" "still has that same barren feeling." Most strikingly, the confidence and intensity of his normal conversation had disappeared. In the old days, his music was always presented with a manifesto; now he uttered tentative generalizations such as "The interesting thing about rock is that you never think that it's going to go on for much longer. Then you find that it has."

Just two years before, when he was acting in *The Elephant Man,* he had been filled with a sense of mission; now there was a subdued, depressive undertone as he discussed his impact on society in the seventies and then told Charlie Murray, "I don't think I would ever contribute so aggressively again."

In later years David would blame the recording, pleading that the album had "great material that got simmered down to product level." Yet more fundamental was David's refusal to choose collaborators who would challenge and inspire him as well as the loss of the key motivator of his career—his appetite for risk. His next collaborator, Julien Temple, describes it as the "appreciation of the randomness of things. It's a great artistic strength, if you're bold enough to follow it."

As far as *Tonight* was concerned, that sense of risk, of the random, had ebbed away. Yet when it came to a new medium, music video, David was energized, fired up that there was still much to learn. After seeing a preview screening of *The Great Rock 'n' Roll Swindle* back in 1980, David had searched out its director, Julien Temple, and done as consummate a job of charming and interesting him in his next project as he had with Nile Rodgers for *Let's Dance.* He opened up to him, talked about his philosophy. "There is a real side of him which isn't confident. And then there is the dazzling superstar," says the director. "He can be quite a normal guy at times, with this amazing ability to transform into a glittering star. The charisma is not always there."

It was this nervous, self-critical Bowie, the "nerdy fan" persona, that Temple would immortalize in the video *Jazzin' for Blue Jean.* Temple had played with the idea of two personae on some of his previous long-form videos. But David took the self-mockery further, splitting himself into two characters: the geeky Vic, an artless cockney with an incessant, hopeless sales patter, who is attempting to impress the glacial Eve Ferret by taking her to meet Screaming Lord Byron; and Screaming Lord Byron, David's other persona, a New Romantic concoction of silk and slap, haughty and unreachable but helpless and isolated behind his painted sneer. Vic's efforts come to naught, and when Eve Ferret disappears with Screaming Lord Byron at the end of the evening, Vic shouts an accusation that rang hilariously true: "You conniving, randy, bogus, Oriental, old queen! Your record sleeves are better than your songs!"

The shoot was intense and seriously behind schedule; finally, they ran out of night for the final shots, and dawn broke. As the sun came up, David stepped out of his Vic character and complained to Julien about the ending in what Screaming Lord Bowie would describe as a Brechtian *Verfremdungseffekt* but played for laughs. "It was when he worked up a new ending that I realized how good he was at responding to crises," says Temple, "and making spur-of-the- moment decisions."

The video would be regarded as a triumph, and its energy and sense of fun helped damp down the critical backlash to *Tonight;* the album started out with promising sales, entered the UK charts at number 1, and was certified platinum by the end of November. But in the spring, when it came time to record a video for the album's only other half-decent track, "Loving the Alien," the zest he'd managed to summon up for his videos, if not his music, seemed to have dissipated.

Possessed of more self-awareness than most of his peers, Bowie was also more acutely conscious of his failures. From the 1960s on, he had made a habit of reading all his own reviews and cultivating writers and critics; from the mid-1980s, he would exist in a bizarrely bipolar world, working mostly with unfailingly approving acolytes as he made his music and then falling victim to the finely honed knives of critics once the music was unleashed. It was tough for a man who'd always been a critics' favorite to realize that, once he'd joined the mainstream with *Let's Dance* and *Tonight,* he was distinctly out of favor: the mainstream, the commercial—the Dame.

Bowie's nickname reflected some of the cynicism that had been brought on by his unashamed grab for mainstream success. Yet the attention David received from critics paled into insignificance when compared with the onslaught of the tabloid press in the wake of a family tragedy.

DAVID'S half brother, Terry, had been at Cane Hill for most of the time since David had last seen him, during filming for *The Hunger*. His isolation and depression deepened until, on December 27, 1984, he decided to end his life. He walked to the local train station, Coulsdon South, put his head down on the rails, and waited for a train to approach, then he apparently lost his resolve at the last moment. On January 16, he took advantage of Cane Hill's shortage of staff, returned to the station, and once again placed his head on the rails. This time he did not lose his nerve.

Whatever anguish David felt "we probably can't imagine," says his Beckenham friend Mark Pritchett. But the family traumas reached a new intensity when David's aunt Pat, angry at both Peggy and David for not visiting Terry often enough, shared her anger with the *Daily Mirror* and then the *Sun*. "I hope God forgives you, David, for this tragic rejection," she told the sensationalist tabloid newspaper. "David turned his back on his brother when it would have been so easy for him to do so much. David cheered him up and promised to see him again, after a time. But he never did. This has caused a big rift in our family."

Bowie decided not to attend the funeral, which became the culmination of a tabloid feeding frenzy. The note on David's bouquet, echoing Rutger Hauer's character's final soliloquy in *Blade Runner*, read: *You've seen more things than we can imagine, but all these moments will be lost—like tears washed away by the rain. God bless you—David.*

The newspapers condemned him for not attending the funeral. Later, Pat would renew her attack on David via two *Sunday Times* reporters, Peter and Leni Gillman. The couple's biography of David, published the next year, opened with a graphic account of the family mental instability, cataloged by Pat, and closed with Terry's suicide. In between, their gripping tale—which rarely mentioned David's music except where it related to schizophrenia, gay sex, or the Burns family history—presented a portrait of

an uncaring, manipulative monster. Some of David's confidants —
notably Tony Visconti, whom David had last seen during the Serious Moonlight tour—spoke to the Gillmans for the book and
were hence judged accomplices in this assault on his privacy.
Bowie would not speak to Tony for another fourteen years.

According to Ken Pitt, David's aunt Pat would come to bitterly
regret her attack on David in the wake of Terry's death. "She was
never the same. It had a big effect on the whole family. It was
very, very sad."

Numbed by this family tragedy, seeking to escape the tabloid
press, David stayed holed up in Switzerland for most of the spring
of 1985. Around May, Julien Temple had a crew ready for a video
shoot for "Loving the Alien." Bowie, the reliable showbiz trouper,
did not turn up. When they finally met, there was no haughtiness
or grand excuse; David told him he simply couldn't do it. "He was
very down. He was open about how he felt, about not feeling vibed
up to be able to do the video."

IF David was in a mental tailspin, it was fevered activity that
pulled him out of it. In June, Temple finally managed to obtain
backing for *Absolute Beginners,* his film based on Colin MacInnes's
1958 novel. Temple pursued Bowie subtly for the role, but David
proved an easy sell, excited by the role of ad exec Vendice Partners. His character's name was a reference to Vance Packard,
author of *The Hidden Persuaders,* the definitive 1950s work on
media manipulation—in fact, the movie encapsulated most of
Bowie's obsessions, including the 1950s, the birth of the youth
culture that had liberated him, the notion of being British rather
than American—and the advent of modern marketing, the
"branding" that David understood so intuitively. "David was hugely
into this, the simultaneous birth of the teenager and the creation of
a market," says Temple. "And like everything he does, there was
total commitment." Bowie learned to tap-dance for his main scene,
which involved him frolicking around a huge typewriter and climbing an adman's phony Everest, all set to his advertising anthem
"That's Motivation."

After Bowie committed the first song to tape, he told Temple he'd come up with a second. "He'd written 'That's Motivation,' which we needed. And he surprised me with 'Absolute Beginners.' He was surprised by it as well—it just kind of arrived."

"Absolute Beginners" was Bowie's last great composition of the 1980s. Like his perfect songs of the early 1970s, it arrived almost instantaneously. The song was an afterthought at an Abbey Road session arranged to demo "That's Motivation"; short of a band, David had called up an A and R man at EMI, Hugh Stanley Clarke, for suggestions. Clarke's nominations, including guitarist Kevin Armstrong, bassist Matthew Seligman, and Attractions organist Steve Naive, were instructed to turn up at Abbey Road for a session with a Mr. X.

The musicians had guessed Mr. X's identity before the session started; they were all nervous and eager to please, and the sense of unreality was intensified by David's flirtatious affability. Kevin Armstrong would go on to work with Bowie for years, but this first session nearly ended in disaster. "The only time I ever was with David Bowie that I saw him do anything with drugs was at that very first day. I don't know why he picked me, but he asked me to get him some coke halfway through the day. I rang a friend to see if he had any going—he rang me back an hour later to say he'd managed to find someone who helped him out: 'You will never guess who I've got this coke from. Angie Bowie!' And I said, 'You'll never guess who it's for—David Bowie!' "

An experienced operator might have been more circumspect, but assuming his new boss would be amused, Armstrong told him, "My mate is getting this coke from Angie!"

Bowie's affable demeanor cracked. "No, not that fucking witch! I hope she doesn't know who it's for."

"No, no, I never told my friend," lied Armstrong. "Which was not true, of course," he says today. "So I nearly had my marching orders there and then. We went on to work together for ten years so it's probably all right. And I never came across any reference to drugs from him ever again."

In fact, David Bowie after a large toot of cocaine was not

noticeably different from the Bowie who Armstrong would get to know later: "He was on sixty to eighty fags a day. He'd have a coffee machine and some Cuba Gold coffee delivered wherever he was, and it would be constantly on the brew. Seriously, he'd be chucking down the coffee and fags—and it would always be pretty neurotic and manic around him. Also, it was my first experience of being in the orbit of someone so hugely famous—there's a kind of electrical crackle around them anyway."

Fired up, Armstrong and the band laid down a demo of "That's Motivation" and were left with an hour of studio time. David played Armstrong some chords and a few lines of a new song, listened attentively as Armstrong helped sketch out the arrangement, then they explained the song to the band—eight bars at a time, recording each section piece by piece. "By not knowing the whole song, it totally forced you out of your comfort zone," says bassist Matthew Seligman. "It was an amazing technique, very art school." During the opening bars Seligman was overcome by a joyous "Velvet Underground 'Sunday Morning' kind of feeling," and he played an ebullient, melodic bass riff—"It was the sound of me being happy." He expected Bowie to comment that it was too intrusive; instead, it became an integral part of the intro. At one point in the session he arbitrarily changed key; Bowie changed key with him. It was almost telepathic: "It felt like mind control—it was very powerful, this switched-on radar."

The lyrics for "Absolute Beginners" revolved around *absolutely*— a buzzword for the movie crew. "It just seemed to be a word that everyone used a lot that year," says Temple, "maybe because Absolut vodka came out at that time and David just picked up on it." Among the simplest of Bowie lyrics ever committed to tape, the words were scribbled down and recorded in chunks. "He got an idea and followed it without thinking too much," says Armstrong. When they finished the demo, David was exuberant, thanking the musicians as if they'd done him a huge favor.

Temple was "blown away" by the demo. When the official version was recorded, only one extra touch was needed. Bowie said, "I want a duet with a girl who sounds like a shopgirl." Armstrong piped up with the news that his sister worked at the chain store Dorothy Perkins; the twenty-two-year-old Janet Armstrong duly turned up at at the studio for her first-ever professional vocal session, which also happened to become David Bowie's last Top 5 single when it was released in March of 1986. A conventional but fabulous song, it offered a tantalizing promise that *Tonight's* creative block was only temporary.

SOON after the "Absolute Beginners" demo, David called Armstrong. "I'm doing a concert for Bob Geldof for charity. It's going to be a big deal. Do you want to help me out?" Armstrong agreed, and David continued: "I've got this extra idea for a record to support it. Would you meet me at this film company in Soho at ten o'clock, and bring an acoustic?"

Armstrong arrived in Wardour Street at the appointed time. When David walked in, he was accompanied by Mick Jagger. The pair explained that they had planned a transatlantic duet for the upcoming concert but the delay caused by the satellite link made it impossible, so they'd decided to prerecord and video their number, a cover of Martha and the Vandellas' "Dancing in the Street."

When the band convened at Westside Studios, they enjoyed a fascinating glimpse of Britain's two best-known rock singers at work. Bowie arrived first; he had a copy of Springsteen's "Born in the U.S.A." and told the rhythm section to match that feel. Then Seligman and drummer Neil Conti felt a "whirling dervish" presence behind them as Jagger whizzed in, his fourteen-year-old daughter, Jade, in tow. Once the backup track was nailed, the ten or so other people present watched Mick and David camping it up and competing as they recorded their ludicrously over-the-top vocals. The two got on well, but their rivalry was obvious: "My gut reaction was to feel a bit protective of David," says Seligman. "Mick was much more vocal, mouthy—more rockist. David was the smiling, indulgent one, more good-natured about the whole thing."

The "big deal" charity show was, of course, Live Aid, an infinitely bigger deal than anyone could have imagined; the event brought out a new, noncompetitive side of David. It was the first time he'd worked with a younger band, now featuring Thomas Dolby, and before the Wembley concert he bustled around like a mother hen, despite the fact he was busy filming at Elstree for another new project, the movie *Labyrinth*. Hearing that his sax player, Clare Hirst, had confessed to her local paper that she was nervous about the show, he phoned her up and reassured her. Then he sweetly requested that the band all wear turquoise for the performance and asked Hirst if it would be okay if he grabbed her hand during " 'Heroes.' "

On the day, David was "very up—it hit home, as it did for everyone, what a great event this was," says Armstrong. David showed them the waist size of the *Young Americans* suit he was wearing, sharing his delight that, at nearly forty, he could still fit into it. The band drove by Stansfield Road on the way—a couple of them had lived in a squat there—and noticed the streets of Brixton were quiet, all the residents glued to their TVs. As David squeezed into BBC DJ Noel Edmonds's helicopter, his hands were shaking, and he kept a cigarette lit constantly—the pilots complained that the smoke was obscuring the instrument panel—but otherwise, there was no sign of nerves.

Queen, according to posterity, stole the show, but on the day no one knew or cared. David had chosen one of the youngest, most underrehearsed bands of his entire career, and he treated them as if they were doing him a favor, joshing them along, especially Seligman, whom David had nicknamed Brenda in retaliation for the bassist opining that "Blue Jean" was boring. Before they hit the stage, the band heard David shout, "Remember, no monitors for Brenda!"

There were flurries of nerves; David fluffed a line, introducing singer Tessa Niles as "Theresa"; sax player Clare Hirst stood and held out her hand at the scheduled moment, looking like an idiot while David danced on the other end of the stage; Kevin Armstrong started "Rebel Rebel" way too fast. Yet throughout, David's joy was infectious, pushing forward the band members, who were totally focused on remembering the songs they'd rehearsed exactly three times. Somehow, it was perfect, says Thomas Dolby: "To my astonishment, I felt like I was on a magic carpet ride. These songs were like our teenage anthems—my fingers just wafted along."

Of all the artists there, Bowie was the most focused on pushing the cause and not himself, cutting short his set—which up to the penultimate rehearsal had included "Fascination"—to save time for a harrowing video of starving Ethiopian children that raised donations to a new peak.

His fulsome tribute to the band—"I'll be forever in their debt"—was repeated offstage after the performance, when they all hugged, overcome with emotion. Later he dropped in on the royal box and cheekily asked Princess Di, "Will we be getting you up onstage for the grand finale?"

THE spontaneity of Live Aid would help David's reputation more or less recover the momentum it'd lost with *Tonight*, but rather than attend to his own career, he spent much of that winter working with the man who'd become his best friend. Since setting up home with Suchi in New York, Iggy had demoed his own songs with Steve Jones, eager to start his project himself. By October of 1985, the pair had made an impressive set of demos; when Iggy tracked David down to send him the tapes, he was surprised to find David was making a kids' movie, *Labyrinth*, at Elstree. (Lambasted by critics, the film would eventually win Bowie a new generation of fans, rather like Ringo's efforts on the Thomas the Tank Engine series.) Practical as ever, David told Iggy, "They're all midtempo, so you'll need some slow ones and some fast ones." He volunteered to fill in the gaps if Iggy and Suchi would join him and Coco on a working holiday in the new year.

They spent some of their three-month jaunt in Mustique, where David had bought a holiday home and installed a small recording setup. Joey came too; David was notoriously strict, demanding his son return home while the rest of the rich kids stayed out partying. "The other kids all made fun of Joey because he had to be home at ten o'clock," says one friend. "[David] was very strict—but it worked for Joey. And of course a lot of those other kids ended up as cokeheads or junkies."

After Mustique, there was skiing in Gstaad and an agreement to complete the album later in the spring. Meanwhile, David worked on promoting *Absolute Beginners,* which was released on April 4, 1986. The film had hatched a media onslaught that helped attract the backing of UK production company Goldcrest, but that ultimately brought a huge critical backlash. Temple's labor of love was vilified, becoming a celebrated box-office flop. As Temple's problems multiplied, Bowie was "genuinely supportive. A lot of the problems we had brought on ourselves, [but] I'd invested a huge amount, psychically, in that movie. And he understood."

A few weeks later, David was back, helping Iggy recover from his own legacy of failure. Aided by Erdal Kizilcay, a local multi-instrumentalist who'd worked on the *Let's Dance* preproduction, they recorded Iggy's album in two weeks, starting at ten each morning, Bowie, once more the punctual professional, schedul-ing each overdub with his clipboard. The album's standout song was "Shades"; both words and music had been written by David after he'd seen Iggy give Suchi a pair of sunglasses. "He saw that situation and turned it around...made it one of those reformed-guy songs," says Iggy. David was in the middle of a creative drought; now he gave what was, after "Absolute Beginners," his best song of the late 1980s to his friend. Kevin Armstrong arrived a few days in to add his guitar. Watching Iggy and David together, he saw Bowie's behavior as essentially selfless. "I think he was genuinely saying, Iggy needs help here, and I'm the guy that can do it; I've done it before and I'll do it again."

When the album was complete, David had his management company, Isolar, secure a deal with A&M Records. Nancy Jeffries, the A and R woman who signed the deal, remembers it had a hefty price tag so that David could recover his costs. But having worked for RCA, she knew the value of the album: "It was almost like the David Bowie record that you wished you'd had but never got." *Blah Blah Blah,* released in November of 1986, would deliver Iggy's first ever Top 50 hit and launch him on the road to some-thing resembling a conventional career.

Iggy wasn't the only one that David tried to champion during

1986. In June, he holed up in London's Edgware Road with his old manager Leslie Conn for a couple of days. They talked about Georgie Fame—whom Leslie had worked with and David had imitated in the early sixties—and they decided to resuscitate his career. David drew up an agreement offering to invest a hundred thousand pounds in Georgie Fame as part of a stable of artists to be produced by David, Bill Laswell, and Clive Langer.

The plan of building a production stable based on Bowie's hugely successful but strangely underrated role as producer was an intriguing one. He'd produced career highlights for Iggy, Lou, and Mott the Hoople, yet his production skills were rarely discussed—underappreciated, almost. Where many producers worked on developing a trademark sound, he had always used a psychological approach, energizing musicians, enabling the flow of ideas. Yet Bowie's move into mainstream production was to remain an intriguing might-have-been, for by the autumn of 1986, he'd abandoned the idea and devoted himself to his own career. Outwardly, he remained unconcerned by the state of his reputation, but in private he'd mention that he was worried about his relationship with EMI. When he started his next recording project, he told his main collaborator, Erdal Kizilcay, "Let's keep it simple," like the Iggy album. They didn't.

Recorded at Mountain and completed at New York's Record Plant Studios, Never Let Me Down was neither as good nor as bad as Tonight. In his efforts to ensure the album was a hit, David worked out each song carefully with Erdal Kizilcay beforehand, thus excising any hint of the random. It featured neither cod reggae nor any songs that were memorable (albeit derivative of his earlier work), like Tonight's "Loving the Alien." Instead, the album was filled to the brim with conventional music, lyrics, and sounds. "Never Let Me Down" was startlingly reminiscent of the opening section of John Lennon's "Starting Over"; the same breathy countertenor delivery and confessional feel, and a similar chord sequence. "Glass Spider" was preposterous, and hence at least noticeable. The utter dearth of inspiration was epitomized by the sole cover song, a retread of Iggy's "Bang Bang." The original had been an act of desperation on Iggy's part: He'd been told by Arista to deliver a hit or leave the label. David's rendition of the plodding, predictable chord sequence and coke-addled lyrics represents the very nadir. The man famous for stealing from the best was copying a dull rip-off of Billy Idol's "White Wedding."

The reviews were dreadful. That was not the biggest problem, for plenty of Bowie's contemporaries had made poor albums that had gotten bad reviews. More serious was the way that this album seemed to damn all his previous work by association. As *Rolling Stone*'s Steve Pond commented, "[Bowie] has reached a startling level of influence and status while making few genuinely groundbreaking records."

The subsequent Glass Spider tour, based on the album's silliest track, would become notorious, a celebrated disaster in David Bowie's career. Such is the disdain in which it is held that its one transcendent moment has been forgotten. It took place on the Platz Der Republik, Berlin, just north of Hansa Studio 2, on June 6, 1987.

David had dropped in to see his friend Edu Meyer, who was working on a session with David's band: "He was still the same guy I remember from *Lust for Life*, still a worker." The city was already filling with West Germans who'd made their way out to the isolated enclave of Berlin for the show. "A big event for the whole country," says Meyer, "and the [East German] government was pretty upset that it was happening so close to the wall."

That night, David launched into "Heroes" in the shade of the wall, five minutes from where the song had been conceived, and realized the song was being redefined: "As we got into it, we could hear the thousands of kids who had gathered on the other side, the East Berlin side," he says, "all joining in [the song]. It was terribly emotional." "He let them do the singing," says Edu Meyer, "and the DDR government tried to get these people away from the wall...but with no success." Fifteen years later, when David played in Berlin, he suddenly became aware that many in the audience had been part of the voices he'd heard, "the ones on the other side."

It was one of the few happy moments on the tour. Previously,

David had chosen his key collaborators, then left everything to them. Now, he was becoming a control freak, fussing over every detail, always "very, very tense," says bassist Erdal Kizilcay. After the third date, Chip Monck, stage designer for the Rolling Stones who'd been commissioned to build the huge glass spider that loomed over the stage, left the tour. "I got the thing built and only saw the first few shows. That was enough."

The contempt in which Glass Spider is now held could be the product of hindsight, part of a reaction against the obese overproduction of the late 1980s. Indeed, the tour was, according to press reports, the most successful of Bowie's career, outgrossing Serious Moonlight, with three million tickets sold for its eighty-six shows. But for the Bowie fans who'd seen his previous tours, the memory of the Glass Spider show is still traumatic. Tony Horkins, then editor of *International Musician* magazine, was one of many who walked into Wembley Stadium and was underwhelmed by the spider looming over the stage. "It wasn't just that they were obviously trying too hard; it was that they hadn't spent the money to hit what they were aiming for. The spider looked pathetic."

David was diminished by the ludicrous spectacle: "Serious Moonlight had been a big production—but it was about him, and his voice sounded great," says Horkins. "This looked like an amateur-theater production, very overblown, detached, and he was dwarfed by all these gimmicks. It didn't have any real soul." The emptiness on display was embodied by the endless guitar-masturbation contests between Carlos Alomar and David's old Bromley Tech friend Peter Frampton, both competing to see who could play more notes in a second. The juxtaposition of guitar contortions and drum-machine beats lifted from Eddie Van Halen's work on *Thriller* was five years out of date. The impression that this was an emotionally empty exercise in generating cash deepened with the announcement that Bowie's huge earnings were being further bloated by a Pepsi sponsorship deal; it was headlined by a predictably clichéd commercial in which David and Tina Turner camp around a vending machine yelping, "[It] puts my choice in my hand," to the tune of "Modern Love."

The empty virtuosity on display in London was a stark contrast to David's joyous Wembley show of just two years before. By the time the tour reached America, Erdal and Frampton were "fed up. We just wanted to go home," says Kizilcay. On several shows, David's voice gave out and Carlos had to step in. The energy with which David normally inspired his crew was gone—in fact, he started blaming them for the poor reviews. When the tour finished in New Zealand, the crew torched the glass spider: "We just put the thing in a field and set light to it. That was such a relief!" David acknowledged a couple of years later. In PR terms, the glass spider was a far bigger disaster than the apparent Nazi salute.

Some versions of history cite Glass Spider as the beginning of a high-tech touring vogue; in fact, Michael Jackson's hugely successful Bad tour of 1988 featured stripped-down staging, as did Prince's acclaimed Sign o' the Times tour of 1987. In the previous four years both young artists, as well as Madonna, had adopted David's fleet-of-foot style, and they made him look moribund and tired.

Yet, as ever, even the footnotes and failures in David Bowie's career lodged in other musicians' consciousness. Over 2009 and 2010, U2 toured their underwhelming *No Line on the Horizon* album, produced by Brian Eno. Hovering above the stage, in what was proclaimed the most lavish rock-and-roll production of all time, was a huge claw.

CHAPTER 20

It's My Life — So Fuck Off

David would ask, "Why do David Bowie and Mick Jagger both
feel compelled to keep going out touring? Why do we do this? It's
laughable."

—Adrian Belew

A T THE END of 1987, David was spending little time
mourning the fate of Glass Spider. He had something
much more threatening on his mind — a lawsuit from a
woman named Wanda Lee Nichols who accused Bowie of sexually
assaulting her in a Dallas hotel room on October 9, 1987.

As far as David's immediate social circle could tell, if he had
deep-seated worries about his career, he kept them to himself, but
he didn't conceal his worries about the Nichols lawsuit: "It was a
big deal," says one friend. "He's not invulnerable at all; it rattled
the fuck out of him." It wasn't so much the specific accusation —
which in retrospect was bizarre, the woman claiming that he'd
bitten her and then mentioned he had AIDS — as what it represented. He admitted to spending the night with Nichols but stated
the rest of her story was fantasy. From then on, whenever he was
enjoying the traditional perk of his job in a hotel room, or anywhere else, there would always be the fear of another accusation
and lengthy lawsuit.

Although a grand jury declined to indict him a month later, the accusation would hang over David for nearly three years before it was dismissed. In the first few weeks that the ramifications of Nichols's accusations started to unfold, David found a much-needed confidante in the form of Sara Terry, press agent for Glass Spider. A journalist for the *Christian Science Monitor*, Terry had joined the tour for a break soon after finishing a grueling project on child prostitutes and soldiers. She was a forthright, valued adviser, being, in the words of friend Eric Schermerhorn, "cool, aggressive, subtle, and intelligent—an alpha female just like Coco."

Sara's husband, Reeves Gabrels, also dropped in on the tour; not as outgoing as his wife, he was, says his musician friend Kevin Armstrong, "very quiet, kind, funny, shy, intellectual, one of those Americans with no mental barriers." Reeves played guitar and had studied at Berklee College of Music but had spent the previous three years at art school. He never talked about his musical ambitions with David, who assumed he was a painter, but in the tour's final days, Sara slipped David a cassette tape of Gabrels's band, The Dark. After the tour, Sara resumed her work with the *Christian Science Monitor* and moved with Reeves to London. In January of 1988, David checked out the tape and soon started recommending Gabrels for sessions. Then, in June, it turned out David needed a guitarist too. All of a sudden, David Bowie was in a hurry again. "It happened really fast," says Gabrels. "David called me, I went over to Switzerland, and we had this music to do—in a weekend."

The project was a collaboration with dance troupe La La La Human Steps; Reeves came up with an arrangement for "Look Back in Anger," with an extended, dark, clipped instrumental passage. "Because we'd only really talked about art before, when we did start working together all our reference points for sound were painterly or architectural. David was saying stuff like 'We should do something where the guitars are like flying buttresses and cathedrals.'"

The first clue that Pepsi-sponsored, preplanned Bowie had

been laid aside in favor of art-house, improvised Bowie came in what was an obscure, but for his fans legendary, performance at London's Dominion Theatre in July of 1988. The nine-minute-long performance with the Quebec dance company was part of a benefit for the London ICA arts venue; Bowie learned his dance steps for the piece, in which he acted mainly as a foil to the lithe, muscular Louise Lecavalier, in two days. On the night, there was a genuine sense of danger and eroticism that had been long missing from his music as Lecavalier leaped over him and then cradled him like a doll while Gabrels, Armstrong, and Erdal Kizilcay produced their twisted, gothic, drawn-out version of the old *Lodger* song. The show was a convincing reminder of David's talent for snatching something meaningful out of random strands.

Two weeks later, Gabrels went over to Lausanne for a weekend visit. He ended up staying a month. "Every day we'd drive down to Mountain Studios in Montreux and just work on stuff. Then go back and have a meal. Then watch *Fawlty Towers* and go to sleep."

In those two weeks during July of 1988, the pair's discussion laid the groundwork for David Bowie's next decade. The singer was open, intelligent enough to realize his predicament, and honest enough to acknowledge it. He told Gabrels that, given his huge deal with EMI, he'd felt obliged to deliver hits — "and it was kind of killing him," says Gabrels. Together, they talked and talked, searching for the inspirations that had turned David on to music in the first place. In that quest to find that old sense of excitement, there came the idea for what would become the Tin Machine band project. "If there was a plan, it was David just wanted to make the music that he wanted to make," says Gabrels. "One cool thing was that we were listening to all the same stuff: Led Zeppelin bootlegs, Cream bootlegs, Hendrix bootlegs, Miles Davis's *Bitches Brew*, Coltrane, the Pixies, Sonic Youth, Glen Branca, Stravinsky, John Lee Hooker, Buddy Guy, Junior Wells, and Muddy Waters. Put all that in a blender and you got Tin Machine."

The pair's discussions started a matter of days before a chance meeting that summer. David was launching a video of the Glass Spider tour, and Iggy's ex-bassist Tony Sales saw David, walked up, "and surprised him. And a few weeks later we were in Switzerland doing Tin Machine."

Today, Tony Sales cuts the same tall, cadaverously handsome figure that fans of *Lust for Life* and Tin Machine remember; he is calm and well-groomed and has the reasoned air of someone who has gone through hell and then recovery, which is exactly what happened after the Sales brothers split with Iggy. The way David Bowie parted from his bands seems like a master class in sensitivity compared with how Iggy sacked the brothers who had underpinned his best solo album. According to Hunt Sales, Iggy delivered their marching orders with the words "You're like heroin — and I don't need you." Soon afterward, the brothers put together a twelve-piece soul band in LA, but on his way home after yet another crazed show, Tony Sales crashed his car and ended up in the Cedars-Sinai hospital. "They found me dead, with a stick shift in my chest. I was in a coma for two and a half, three months. I almost died. And it ruined our Sales brothers thing." During Tony's months in the hospital, Iggy was conspicuous by his absence. David was the only celebrity friend who came to see him, asking, "When can we get you on the road?"

The bassist's description of David as "a friend" is at odds with the aloof, selfish figure remembered by predecessors like Trevor Bolder, yet his account is not unique. The standard history of the formation of Tin Machine is a Bowie-centered one, which involves him using the band to detonate an uncontrolled explosion in order to demolish the memory of his late-eighties hubris. Yet according to Sales, the urge to hang with his friends and help them was just as powerful a motivation for David.

Tony and his drummer brother, Hunt, arrived at Montreux Casino, hanging out and playing for a week along with David, Reeves, and producer Tim Palmer before the tiny group decided they needed a second guitarist. Kevin Armstrong—who was then, like Tony Sales, attempting to rebuild his life, having turned into a groupie-shaggin', drug-sniffin' rock monster during his last tour with Iggy Pop—answered the call and did a double take as he entered the huge room. The most significant indication of the psychological makeup of the band was laid out in front of him, in the form of a line of amplifiers—for Reeves, Tony, Armstrong, and David—all facing a huge podium in the middle of the room.

On top of the podium, which was scaled by means of a ladder, was Hunt Sales's drum set, with its monstrous twenty-four-inch bass drum. With this, the feisty, funny, crazed drummer could musically beat anyone into submission without any electronic assistance. "He is the loudest drummer I have ever worked with in my life," says Kevin Armstrong. "I almost went deaf within the first couple of days. The power and the volume was simply super-human." Producer Tim Palmer had carefully placed microphones around the studio to capture this massive sound; on Armstrong's first day, the band members wrote and recorded "Heaven's in Here."

Drummer Hunt Sales was the kind of person who, as Armstrong puts it, "consumes his own body weight in dangerous substances every day." Everyone around him "loved his freedom and his naughtiness." Tony, in contrast, was now a born-again evangelist for the cause of teetotalism; if David was standing with a glass of wine in his hand, Tony would administer a reproving lecture on the dangers of alcohol. Tony restrained himself, however, in the case of his brother, figuring such arguments would end in violence. An amazing musician like Hunt, Tony had to contend with a consequence of his car crash: memory lapses, which meant that at crucial points he sometimes forgot chord sequences, and the others had to shout them in his ear.

When they'd been in Berlin and David had recorded with the Sales brothers and Iggy, the cultural leitmotif had been expressionism—Fritz Lang and Das Neue Sachlichkeit. In Montreux eleven years later, the theme was Soupy Sales, the foul-mouthed, sexist, undoubted comedic genius who reminded the band of *The Simpsons'* Krusty the Clown, the kids' entertainer with a filthy mind. During the Mountain recording sessions, the Sales sons would call their father on an international line and route the phone call through the studio monitors; David, Hunt, Tony, Kevin, and Reeves would fall over laughing to monstrously amplified jokes like:

What do fifty thousand battered wives have in common?
They don't fuckin' listen!

Hence David Bowie's next evolution was worked out gradually, at stupendous volume, against a backdrop of filthy jokes and intellectual debates.

Bowie deferred to Reeves more than anyone else; he praised his experimentation, his "stunt" guitar, and he loved his virtuosity, encouraging him to explore more extreme effects and sounds. Yet even as Bowie's lieutenant, Gabrels could do little to pull his rhythm section into line. When the Sales brothers joined, David decided this should be a proper band, run as a democracy. Gabrels thought that, in reality, it was more like a shouting match.

The band's initial jam sessions at Montreux blended seamlessly into a recording project, with "Heaven's in Here" recorded on the first day. Then it became semiformalized with a move to Compass Point, a recording studio in the Bahamas, where David stayed in Robert Palmer's house near the beach. The sessions went on and on; not aimless or desperate, just jams with reportedly dozens of tracks recorded. Sean Lennon popped in during the school holiday with Joey, who was in the process of dropping out of Gordonstoun. Despite his schooling problems, Joey was a quiet, unspoiled kid, a fan of the Smiths — David claimed to be a fan too, but Joey seemed unconvinced. It was hilarious for the band to watch their exchanges, to see a man they thought of as the coolest dad in the world trying to impress his son. Sean, too, was earnest, thoughtful, the opposite of a showbiz brat; it was in tribute to him that the band recorded a version of John's "Working Class Hero."

The little community hanging around the beach was augmented by David's new girlfriend, Melissa Hurley, a dancer from the Glass Spider tour. The Sales brothers, rock and rollers to their core, rarely talked to Melissa. Kevin Armstrong liked her: "She was a genuinely kind, sweet person." Just twenty-two years old, with a voluptuous, almost Italian figure and a mass of wavy dark brown hair, she was caring and not at all pushy, but she had a classic 1980s fashion sense that didn't go well with David's refined cool. She bought him hats and brightly colored scarves that he would wear for a couple of days before managing to lose them. He, in turn, as a world citizen and something of an art teacher manqué, loved showing her new locations, appreciating her delight. Together, they seemed relaxed, almost childlike, and there was little surprise when in May of 1989 Melissa's parents announced that the couple had become engaged.

David's indulgence of his new girlfriend was charming, especially at the more ludicrous moments, such as when Melissa persuaded him to wear a thong (he wore it to the beach a couple of times, affecting indifference to his bandmates' sniggers). Another comic touch was the presence of hoary old British rockers Status Quo, who were working in the adjacent studio and were always ready to give lessons in pool and table football. The unspoiled, carefree air may have had something to do with the rumor that Coco, often a cause of tension between David and his musicians, had found love and was staying with a lawyer in Los Angeles.

For one band member, though, the setting was not a tropical paradise. A week or two into the recordings, David walked over to Kevin Armstrong's beach hut and told him that Tin Machine had been conceived as a four-piece; they'd like to keep Armstrong on, but as a background musician. For the guitarist, the news was "totally crushing." Yet David's management was admittedly better than in the old days; he was honest and open about Armstrong's demotion, telling him they'd work together again after Tin Machine—which they did.

Compass Point Studios was in the most perfect location, with white sand and sparkling azure sea just moments away, and beautiful spartan beach huts for the musicians. But the studio's glory days had passed with the death in a car crash of manager and engineer Alex Sadkin, in 1987, and there were frequent power cuts and technical problems. Several days in there was a tropical rainstorm; the sky went black, and huge gobbets of rain beat on the tiny gaggle of buildings. In this gothic deluge, they recorded "I Can't Read," a song of stark beauty, its throbbing bass and chaotic guitar reminiscent of UK band Joy Division—who had, of course, based their sound on Iggy's *The Idiot* and who would in turn influence emerging bands like Jane's Addiction. The song was one of several Tin Machine gems destined to be overlooked in the noise and chaos surrounding the band. Kevin Armstrong believes that that was part of the plan: "I thought some of the best work didn't make it to the first record. I think David was deliberately trying to go for a fucked-up sound; if it was too safe or polite, he'd dump it." Some of the missing songs would show up years later; for example, "Now," based on the La La La Human Steps intro, was reworked to become the title track of the *Outside* album. The exclusion of anything that sounded remotely conventional was designed to tell the public, whether they wanted to hear it or not, that the David Bowie who'd made *Never Let Me Down* was history.

The debut of Tin Machine was cooked up one night around a table at Compass Point; chatting, hanging out, the band members decided it would be good to play live. Later that night, they walked up to the band performing at a small bar in Nassau and asked if they could use their gear; forty or fifty stunned American tourists goggled at the spectacle, mouthing at each other, *Is that who I think it is?* as the band played a short set featuring "Heaven's in Here." "It was a mess, but it was a *huge* buzz," says Armstrong, "just to see the reaction of the crowd." David loved the vibe, the raw excitement of what they all called "the guerrilla gig"; together, they decided that that was how the band would proceed, a small gang, one for all, all for one.

THIS could never be a truly equal gang, of course. When the band finally started their club tour in New York, on June 14, it was David Bowie who handed each of them a thousand dollars to buy a Prada suit for the show. And when the reviews for Tin Machine had appeared, around May 22, 1989, it was naturally treated as another record by David Bowie rather than as the debut of a new outfit. The critical reaction was generally positive—Paul Du Noyer of *Q* magazine called the album "a more accessible sort of record than we're used to"—while fans were ecstatic at the prospect of seeing David Bowie play a club tour. People stood in line for days in order to get tickets for some of the European dates, small venues like Amsterdam Paradiso and Kilburn's National Ballroom. David was buoyed up, reveling in the energy of the crowd and the sheer freedom. But there was tension too; he was always nervous about fans. Kevin Armstrong had toured with Iggy in similar-size venues, and he'd noticed he had a talent for calming down fans who were deranged or high; he could simply touch their shoulders, like a Vulcan death grip, and they'd go all limp. David had never really worked in those circumstances; by the time he'd started attracting crowds in Ziggy days, he had his own security crew. Accosted by fans, he'd be polite, pleasant; if they were too persistent he'd simply ignore them, but he was always wary, never quite as relaxed amid the mayhem as Iggy.

The shows themselves were "crazed, and huge fun," says Armstrong; "a blast," according to Tony Sales. But most proper bands jell as they play shows. With Tin Machine, says Armstrong, "there was no jelling. Musically, it never really jelled because it was simply a battle. Hunt and Tony were the solidest part, then Reeves is utter chaos—although Reeves and Hunt did develop a rapport in the the the end. But you never knew what was gonna happen—it was always on the edge. Then I was shouting the chords to Tony most nights, because his short-term memory is shot. You could hardly play the same song in the same way twice. It certainly wasn't comfortable for me."

According to Iggy, David didn't get as good results out of his old rhythm section either: "I have to say, when they were with me, they swung more." And indeed, along with the band bonhomie there was a dull, dogmatic element to Tin Machine shows, demonstrated by songs like their plodding cover of "Working Class Hero." It was this worthiness and the overavoidance of the "conventional" songs lamented by Kevin Armstrong that meant the initially warm reception for *Tin Machine*—which hit number 3 in the UK, number 28 in the United States—soon petered out. The process was hastened by the release of lumpen singles, like

"Under the God," backed with a workmanlike cover of Dylan's "Maggie's Farm." Democracy has its drawbacks. As Gabrels pointedly observes, "Sometimes a benevolent dictatorship can be a good thing."

For David, there was a unique buzz about the band; he loved the Sales brothers' vibe and Hunt's special craziness. Gabrels did, too, at first: "They were like Dean Martin and Jerry Lewis," he says. "A handful. Then during Tin Machine they suddenly became like Cain and Abel. They made for a lot of extra tension and entertainment—*if* you find tension entertaining." One night in New York, Hunt had his manifesto tattooed on his back. In huge letters, the tattoo read IT'S MY LIFE. That wasn't the complete manifesto—he'd planned to have the words *so fuck off* inscribed underneath but told his fellow band members that the heavy Gothic lettering took so much work that he'd reached his pain threshold after the first three words.

The inescapable predicament of Tin Machine, of course, was that their democratic vision was a utopia. Bowie would always be blamed for Gabrels's or the Sales brothers' artistic mistakes; equally, their ideas and inventions would be credited to him. EMI had paid a huge advance for the David Bowie brand, not for Tin Machine, which would soon cause financial problems. For the time being, the man at the center of these contradictions simply enjoyed the experience for what it was. "I don't think David was frustrated at any point," says Armstrong. "Everyone was aware that he could just whip this magic carpet away, but while it was there you can't avoid letting the Sales brothers do their thing, because they are very powerful people."

David's relaxed attitude about Tin Machine's internal conflicts was understandable, given that he always had Brand Bowie to fall back on. Even as the band booked their tiny club gigs in the spring of 1989, Isolar and business manager Bill Zysblat were penciling in stadiums across the world for a full year later, and David was also preparing for the rerelease of his RCA albums.

In 1989, fans were switching from vinyl to CD, and most record companies vacuumed up maximum profits for minimal effort. The Beatles' and Stones' CD reissues were both notorious messes; in comparison, Bowie's remastering of his album catalog was expert. He selected CD specialists Rykodisc to master the albums and release them in Europe; EMI licensed them in America. The new editions were a master class in CD releases, incorporating rarities and superb packaging, while a *Sound + Vision* box set made up a kind of alternative-greatest-hits collection, including outtakes and different song versions. If there was any contradiction in the fact that one of the world's most forward-thinking artists was also one of the first to remarket his own history, it was overlooked, given that he did it so much better than his peers. The inauguration of Bill Clinton as president in January of 1993 would mark the accession to power of the baby boomers. This generation, many among them Bowie fans, had more disposable income than any of the preceding generations. Experts like David and Bill Zysblat — who would soon lead the way in promoting stadium tours with his company RZO, maximizing their financial returns — were there to help them spend it.

David had discussed the notion of a greatest-hits stadium tour with Reeves Gabrels in the first few months of Tin Machine's existence. But the guitarist believed "it didn't feel like my place to do it." If Gabrels appeared onstage with David for a greatest-hits tour, it would make Tin Machine look like a mere side project, so Gabrels suggested a musician he knew and respected and who had a link with Bowie's back catalog: *Lodger* guitarist Adrian Belew.

PERFECTLY organized, impeccably choreographed by Édouard Lock of La La La Human Steps, and presented with state-of-the-art video technology, Sound + Vision was another groundbreaking tour. An unadorned set was flanked by a huge screen showing video footage, much of it a giant moving image of David himself with which the real singer would interact. Marketed as the first and last time David would do a greatest-hits set, the tour marked a period when ten of his reissued albums were on the British charts. What would effectively be Bowie's last grandstanding stadium tour was, says musical director Adrian Belew, "sensational" for both the musicians and the crowd. "We'd walk out and start playing 'Ground Control to Major Tom,' and it would overwhelm you, this emotional feeling, then there's the video, the lights, and all these huge images floating around—it would absolutely give you the chills."

After eighteen years of touring, though, David Bowie felt anything but sensational at the live shows; this was the artist who as a teenager had told his manager he hated "ballrooms and the kids." According to Belew, several times during the Sound + Vision tour, which ran from March 4 to September 29, 1990, "David would ask, 'Why do David Bowie and Mick Jagger both feel compelled to keep going out touring? Why do we do this? It's laughable.'" The topic was raised several times, "but there was no resolving it," says Belew.

David once again deployed all his charm when he called Belew, even suggesting using Adrian's own band, Mick Hodges on drums and Rick Fox on keyboards. For Belew it was like "a dream come true, to bring my band, childhood friends, on tour. I was like a kid with a handful of candy."

For bassist Erdal Kizilcay, though, the tour was "horrible." There was a simple reason for the conflicting accounts: Your experience depended on whether you were in front of or behind the screen. For the stripped-down visuals, it turned out Belew would be Bowie's main foil; the other three would remain invisible. "It was devastating for them when they heard," says Belew, "they get to play with Bowie—and nobody can see them."

For bassist Erdal Kizilcay, a sponsorship deal arranged for the opening dates in Canada exemplified the seemingly intractable problem of David's desire for both cult status and mainstream income. David had attracted derision for accepting the Pepsi dollar in 1987; Labatt's sponsorship of the Canadian leg of the new tour was more damaging. Proclaimed an industry breakthrough by the agency that brokered it, the deal included a pause in the show for the sponsor's message, which sapped the performance's musical momentum. "It was horrible," says Erdal Kizilcay, "people left the venue—and didn't come back again. I don't know how much money he got for it but it blew up the highest point of the concert, the middle fifteen minutes. You'd come back and have to start warming up the people again, and it was, No way."

Belew doesn't remember the sponsorship slot as the main problem; for him, it was that the design of a bare metal stage with amplifiers hidden underneath, along with the limitations of the four-man lineup, meant the music would always come a distant second to the innovative visuals. "I was fairly disappointed musically throughout the tour, with myself and what we were able to do. We were under severe restraint with a small band—how do you play 'Young Americans' without a saxophone? Mike, Rick, and I had just come from a club tour where the sound is warm and everyone can hear you... Here for us it sounded metallic; the guitar sound was thin. I wish I could have done a much better job."

Despite the technical frustrations, David and Adrian were in good spirits throughout most of the tour; for the backstage boys, despite getting to use Lee Iacocca's private jet for several dates and staying in plush hotels, it was boring. During the performance, keyboardist Rick Fox was often restricted to simply pressing a button to play a sample or sequence, so in the middle of a set, he'd munch on a sandwich or a burger if he was hungry. One night, Erdal saw David make a gesture in the middle of "The Jean Genie" and thought he was being signaled to emerge from behind the curtain, which he did. Then "David shouted at me, 'Get off!' It was weird."

As the band sat on the plane at the end of the show, David "yelled and yelled" at Erdal, says Belew, "and a quiet came over everyone. We just sat there on the plane. It was horrible."

It was a one-time-only incident, but it showed how, for all the musicians, "you start with a lot of excitement and enthusiasm, then gradually you wear down," says Belew. "But that time with Erdal was the only scene—which is pretty good for a group of forty-five people traveling around the world."

David himself made a good show of enjoying the tour—he was more fun to be around than in 1978, and he took Belew out for a memorable night in Paris during which David and Mick Jagger attempted to out-camp each other on the dance floor in that distinctive blend of friendship and schoolboy rivalry. Throughout, he'd rev up Adrian, working at stretching him as a musician while trying to discuss ways he himself could tour and keep it from being routine. He didn't complain, but it was obviously hard work for him, although the band did not quite believe his widely publicized statement that this would be the last time he'd play his hits live; they thought it was just a good marketing ploy. David had introduced a telephone poll, asking fans to nominate their favorite songs for inclusion in the set, and as the tour reached Europe, the *NME* launched a campaign to lobby for the inclusion of "The Laughing Gnome." David was unfazed by their cheekiness (although, sadly, they never played the song). The tour rumbled on through Europe, heading to its conclusion in South America, and he remained much less stressed than he'd been on the 1978 tour, joking throughout, talking about Marlon Brando, singing Beatles songs.

Toward the latter half of the tour, it was obvious that David was having difficulties with Melissa. It added to his rapport with Belew, with whom he'd chat about his problems — his openness, the fact he was still having girl troubles at forty-three, was endearing. The band liked Melissa — "She was a great person, but maybe not strong enough for David," says Erdal, who'd also seen her occasionally in Switzerland — but for the later European dates she sat on the bus by herself. Then she was gone. David was gracious about the split, commenting he'd worried it was becoming "older men, younger girl situations," describing her as "such a wonderful, lovely, vibrant girl." Some years later, Melissa married Patrick Cassidy, half brother of 1970s teen heartthrob David.

For the last few dates, in South America, there was no room for the staging, so half the crew members were absent; together with an undercurrent of violence from the police, this made for an oddly anticlimactic finish for David's last huge stadium tour. After the final date, David told Adrian he'd give him a call, "and here we are nineteen years later!" says the guitarist, who hasn't gotten any calls from David. "But he's a fun person to be around. I miss him."

WHATEVER the backstage frustrations, the Sound + Vision tour, which finished up at Buenos Aires's River Plate Stadium on September 29, was followed by a life-changing encounter for David. A hairdresser friend, Teddy Antolin, had arranged a blind date for him on October 14. Later, David would comment it was love at first sight, although in fact he had been introduced to the model Iman three or four times before, at the theater and backstage at his LA show in May.

Iman Mohamed Abdulmajid was an eighteen-year-old political science major in May of 1975 when wildlife photographer Peter Beard, a friend of Baroness Karen von Blixen-Finecke (aka Isak Dinesen), spotted her at Nairobi University. She eventually agreed to her first photo shoot in return for having her tuition fees paid, and she caused a sensation on her arrival in New York when she signed with the prestigious Wilhelmina modeling agency. Iman worked closely with Thierry Mugler and became a muse for Yves Saint-Laurent. She established herself in the pre-supermodel era, a period when her fellow models, says Emma Bannister, *Marie Claire*'s fashion director at the time, were "Christie Brinkley, of 'Uptown Girl' fame, and Carol Alt—real American cheese. So Iman really stood out—she was striking, strong, and African."

Iman finally became a household face, if not a household name, by way of a Tia Maria ad in which she smoldered and smiled briefly, her cheeks striped with fluorescent green, a true world citizen selling ersatz exoticism and, by most accounts, reviving the brand. At her peak, her earnings exceeded two million a year, but by 1989 she decided she had overstayed her welcome on the modeling scene.

Nearly everyone who's met her describes her the way guitarist Eric Schermerhorn does: "She was very nice, quieter than you'd think—and also not as tall as you'd think." Iman was attracted to David straightaway but later said she truly fell in love when she found he adored reading to people, just like her father did—he was the Somali ambassador to Saudi Arabia before his country was racked by war—and was good at doing funny voices. As for David, he later said he started thinking of children's names the night they met.

The couple spent a few months together in LA, where they both owned houses, then went on an idyllic six-week trip up and down the Italian coast. If Iman had ever spent any time imagining what it would be like to be married to a rock and roller, she got a true taste of it later that summer. After rehearsals in Saint-Malo and Dublin, on August 15, Tin Machine hit the road for another tour, and they continued playing, almost nightly, all the way through to the final show at Tokyo's Budokan in February of 1992. Together with the first Tin Machine tour and his huge stadium jaunt, this was David's longest period on the road since his Spiders days. Iman would travel with David for many of the shows in America and Europe.

By the time the second Tin Machine tour came around, Kevin Armstrong was booked elsewhere; Eric Schermerhorn, a friend of Reeves Gabrels from Boston, took his place. Observing the band chemistry up close, he was amazed to see how laid-back Bowie was. But he also realized how difficult it must be for the singer to have three opinionated, boisterous musicians in constant competition. Hunt Sales was a brilliant drummer; the hedonistic swagger of his drum intro to "Lust for Life" would earn decades' worth of royalty checks for both Iggy and Bowie. Schermerhorn found Hunt the most vibrant character in the band, but also the most troublesome. It was obvious that David shared his opinion: "I think he watched Hunt self-destruct and I think it angered him, in that he was trying to help him. I think Hunt had a lot of resentment for his brother and David. Stay out of my business. It's my life, so fuck off."

Schermerhorn, as a neutral party, got to hear everybody's complaints: "I was close to Hunt because nobody else was. I was the in-between guy with everybody. Between all three of them they would come to me telling me all different things. I wanted to keep

it all running smoothly because I liked them all." Gabrels, meanwhile, had the thankless role of band manager: "The good news,
and the bad news, was I was the guy who looked at the books every
week with the tour manager and the office, keeping an eye on the
money—so I was keeping the Sales brothers from renting limou-
sines and the band from getting charged for David wanting a bigger hotel room because Iman was coming to visit, things like that.
My sideburns actually went gray in three months on that tour."

David remained generally oblivious of the band's internal disputes. Only shows in the bigger cities worried him—he was surprisingly nervous at those, and gave better performances at the smaller
venues. Even twenty-five years into his career, he still followed his
press coverage closely, but he was relaxed about the increasingly
vociferous critical drubbings the band was receiving. "He understood it happens with everyone," says Gabrels, "that it cycles."

It was not just the critics who were unimpressed. After promising early numbers for the Tin Machine debut, sales had tailed
off rapidly, with none of its singles cracking the Top 40. EMI
balked at the prospect of another Tin Machine album; the band
signed instead to the Polygram offshoot Victory, the brainchild of
Phil Carson, who'd worked with Led Zep at Atlantic. Ultimately,
the public was as unenthusiastic as EMI; *Tin Machine II* boasted
some wonderful songs, like Bowie and the Sales brothers' tran-
scendently beautiful "Goodbye, Mr. Ed" and Gabrels's "Shopping
for Girls," but, like at the live dates, the music didn't quite jell. For
Gabrels, the experience was frustrating—"I would have had one
less Hunt Sales vocal on the record"—but David seemed unconcerned. Playing and touring with Tin Machine allowed David to
act like a "normal bloke," says Eric Schermerhorn. "He'd be blown
away by the most mundane things. One time in Minneapolis
walking into a pawnshop, with loads of used radios and beat
boxes, he bought a used boom box for sixty-five dollars. He was,
'This is great!' It was like he'd never done that stuff."

Traveling with a band—as opposed to with a bunch of employ-
ees, as on the Sound + Vision tour—brought out a side of him
usually hidden under the Dame's snootiness. He was surprisingly

open, trying to round up his bandmates for trips to local junk stores or museums, mates to keep him company and share the view; he was often emotional, sometimes even tearful, especially after the occasional raid on his hotel minibar. For a man who'd been so ruthless with himself, and his musicians, there were odd, nostalgic notes. His bandmates noticed how he seemed to keep and catalog everything: drumsticks, clothing, guitar picks. The collecting demonstrated his odd relationship with his own past; often he'd be reluctant to talk about old works, yet once he started, you often couldn't stop him—then he'd reveal how many old features on himself he'd read, how many errors he wanted to correct.

Much of the apparent contradiction was explained by the fact that he was still a record nerd who treasured the albums he'd bought thirty years ago from Medhurst's and Dobell's. He didn't want to play "Space Oddity" every night until he was an old man, yet he needed his own records to slot alongside those of Little Richard and Iggy Pop in some *High Fidelity*–style ranking of the rock-and-roll greats. Later that year he'd venture to Llangynwyd in South Wales, telling locals he was researching the genealogy of the Jones family. It was not a midlife crisis, but there was an overwhelming urge to work out how he'd gotten here, and what his legacy would be.

Over the autumn of 1991, that occasional vulnerability alternated with skittish excitement, mainly because he planned to ask Iman to marry him. He put the question to her twice, both times in Paris, around October 29—the first on the Seine, to the strains of "April in Paris," the second at the Paris Olympia, where he repeated his proposal from the stage, in French, then played some saxophone as his fans cheered. It could have been hokey, "but he was pretty amazing," says Schermerhorn.

The journey with Tin Machine had been idyllic, in a fucked-up way, but it was coming to an end. "I remember once in the back of the bus, talking with the whole band and him saying, 'Listen, you guys, I'm getting older,'" says Schermerhorn. "I heard David say, 'I don't want to be doing this forever. I want to make one more record.' He didn't want to fuck around."

In public, David remained strongly committed to Tin Machine; he'd said at the beginning of the project that they'd produce three albums, and there was no sign of his reneging. But out in Japan, he gently asked Schermerhorn what he was planning to do next and offered to make a few calls for him. Soon, Schermerhorn would help Iggy Pop craft his last great record, 1994's *American Caesar*, an album partly inspired by David's suggestion that Iggy start reading history books. "They were amazing, complementary characters. They would each ask me about the other; it's amazing — each one wants what the other has got. Maybe Iggy was the better front man. But David was a better boss — he wanted people to succeed after they've worked with him. He didn't have to help me, but he did."

The tour ended at the Budokan on February 17, 1992. For the Sales brothers, there were no regrets, says Tony, who ascribes much of the reaction to the band to conservatism: "People like the excitement of something different, but if you try to change, it terrifies them and they can't accept it." Gabrels believes the project achieved David's aims, if not the band's: "Tin Machine fell on the grenade of not just Glass Spider but *Never Let Me Down* and *Tonight*. I think the intentions were good at the start and then... it got sidetracked."

Reeves Gabrels was one of many people who debated the nature of fame with David; like gold or diamonds, it was precious, but its inherent value was impossible to determine. Reeves's conclusion was that it was "a pile of shit." David, for all his contradictions, was addicted to it. Even if he abhorred the intrusions of the media, his insecurities demanded he court them, because his public persona — how he was perceived — was an intrinsic part of his own self-image. Thus the most personal, anguished emotions were things to be both concealed and displayed, most famously at the memorial concert for Freddie Mercury on April 20, 1992, a few weeks after the close of the Tin Machine tour. The show was a strange mix, reflecting Queen's quixotically diverse fan base, from heavy metalers like Guns N' Roses to Liz Taylor and Liza Minnelli. David showed an effortless understanding of the event.

Freddie may not have been a truly close friend, but their careers were closely intertwined, as two of the songs performed that night, "All the Young Dudes"—a favorite of Brian May—and "Under Pressure" illustrated. David looked composed and impossibly well groomed, with his mint green suit and GI Joe hair, next to Annie Lennox, who was seemingly made up to look like Pris, the pleasure model replicant from *Blade Runner,* and who nuzzled provocatively against his cheek on the song's climax.

The night's real resonance would come from Mick Ronson, a man who'd been as crucial an influence on the sound of Queen as David himself: David's onetime lieutenant had been diagnosed with inoperable liver cancer the previous August. Yet even the unflappable Ronson looked uncomfortable when at the close of "Heroes" David got on one knee and recited the Lord's Prayer. The press reaction ranged from support to ridicule. Few commented on what an old-fashioned figure he cut next to Annie Lennox, who could have been him twenty years earlier.

Just four days after the Wembley show, David married Iman in a civil ceremony in Montreux; once more, David's simultaneous yearning for privacy and publicity was demonstrated: The private civil service was followed by a public celebration at the St. James American Church in Florence, Italy, with the nuptials celebrated in a twenty-three-page *Hello!* magazine cover story. David wore white tie; Iman a Herve Leger oyster-colored dress with train. Joey was best man, Geoff MacCormack read Psalm 121, and Peggy had her photo taken with Bono. Yoko Ono and Brian Eno were among the guests. There were many flashes of humor in the accompanying interview, as well as instances of history being rewritten: "I don't think I ever really had what we could call a proper marriage," he said of his days with Angie. There was a conventional, happy air, as if he were grateful finally to put aside his days of androgyny and transcending moral codes and start over.

While many of the sentiments were standard *Hello!* fare— David's comments on how his friend Thierry Mugler had done "a delightful job" on designing his suit—there were moments of insight, more than in some of the more probing interviews to which David had been subjected. His open statement that while he was not formally religious, "God plays a very important part in my life" as well as his admission that he spent his first few weeks with Iman worried that his "silly sense of humor" might put her off were both illuminating demonstrations of how in his forties he was happy to admit to the strong streak of conventionality that had always run through him.

THE wedding was memorable, but the album that marked it would be generally forgotten, continuing the unhappy recent tradition of attempting commercial crossover and failing. David felt "pressured" into recruiting Nile Rodgers as producer for this next work, says Reeves Gabrels. Rodgers had gotten over his resentment that in the wake of *Let's Dance*'s huge sales, David had barely mentioned its producer, but there was a difference in intention right from the start. "I literally said, 'David, let's kick *Let's Dance* in the ass,'" says Rodgers. "He said, 'No, it's impossible. We can't do that.' 'What do you mean we can't?' 'I don't know.'"

Reeves Gabrels, meanwhile, felt "we'd put all this effort into trying to get rid of the stuff that followed *Let's Dance* to change expectations and allow David to be an artist again. So I was irritated by the notion, but, for whatever reason, they decided to do it." David, in turn, had an entirely different agenda, according to Nile Rodgers: "He made that record to mark his wedding. That's what he told me. I kept thinking, Well, 'Let's Dance' and 'China Girl' would have played fine at a wedding."

Black Tie White Noise betrayed the mix of motives behind it. Taken on its own merits, as a snapshot of influences, it made sense, was endearing, really, with its backstory of the wedding, the LA riots, even "Don't Let Me Down & Down," a song written by a Mauritanian princess and rendered in both the Indonesian language and a Brixton patois. The album was launched with the usual fanfare, heavily promoted by a new record company, Savage, which had paid David a $3.4 million advance for his services. (The deal ultimately ruined the start-up business, which declared itself bankrupt in December of 1993 amid a flurry of lawsuits.) *Black*

Tie White Noise was met by a collective sigh of relief from the critical community, who were happy that David had apparently terminated his Tin Machine experimentation. David was relaxed and playful during the sessions; there were many flashes of his old brilliance. When Nile was about to record his guitar solo for the twitchy, insistent "Miracle Goodnight," David used one of his trademark, out-of-left-field instructions: "'Imagine the fifties never existed,' he told me. I went, 'Wow, now we're in some nebulous era because if the fifties hadn't happened there would be no Jeff Beck and Hendrix.' It was a great direction." Gabrels contributed most of his guitar work when Nile was filming the *Tonight* show in California, working on several songs, including "You've Been Around" and "I Feel Free"—a song that David had lately revived with Tin Machine. Bowie covered the song, he mentioned later, in tribute to Terry and the Cream show at the Bromel Club; a second song, "Jump They Say," addressed his late brother more directly.

"I Feel Free" was shrouded in two layers of loss. There had been regular exchanges between Bowie and the ailing Mick Ronson throughout the year; David had sent several songs for the album that Ronson was struggling to complete and had publicly complimented Mick's production of Morrissey's *Your Arsenal*. The new version of "I Feel Free" was essentially finished before Ronson arrived in the studio to contribute his signature sound; Gabrels's solo was wiped to make way for his predecessor's. "It wasn't sad—it was simply great to play with him and to have him around," says Nile Rodgers. "Mick just did it and it was cool."

Ronson's presence on *Black Tie White Noise* helped generate a flurry of press on the album's release in April of 1993. Whereas David had been careful to avoid the role of elder statesman in the 1980s, he bowed to the inevitable in the early 1990s, a time when the influence of *Ziggy Stardust* was at its peak, thanks to Britpop pioneers Suede; the partnership of Bernard Butler's muscular guitar and Brett Anderson's feyness closely mirrored the Ronson/Bowie relationship.

Interviewed with Anderson for the *NME* in March, David was genial, relaxed, effortlessly taking on the mantle of founding father of Britpop—which, in most fundamental respects, he deserved, for various phases of his own career had indeed made their mark on the Smiths, Suede, and Blur. The *NME* story helped generate a sense that David was back to making personal rather than corporate albums; the intensity of "Jump They Say" powered the single to number 9 on the UK charts, while *Black Tie White Noise* debuted at number 1 in the UK.

The album's sales were a powerful vindication of Bowie's scorched-earth policy with Tin Machine and also seemed to show him fitting neatly into the 1990s while acknowledging his own past, influences like Mick and Terry, with a new honesty. Mick Ronson's death, on April 30, emphasized the passing of an era. Yet its aftermath showed that not all of David's demons had been exorcised.

Shortly after Ronson's death David paid a fulsome tribute to his best-known lieutenant: "He was really up there in the so-called hierarchy with the great guitar players ... superb, absolutely superb."

There had been no formal reconciliation after their split in the 1970s, for one was not really needed ("I've got no complaints, why would I?" Ronson told this writer in 1989), but Bowie's relationship with the guitarist who had, more than any other musician, powered him to fame remained troubled. The issue flared up at Ronson's memorial concert at Hammersmith Odeon the following April, an event at which Bowie was conspicuously absent.

Trevor Bolder, Bowie's bassist and Ronson's old friend, was told "he had a couple of issues with some people on the bill and he didn't want to get involved." Bolder also heard that David was worried about playing to a small crowd. "Fair enough. It's sad you have to worry about [such] things." But Suzi Fussey Ronson asks, "If he felt that the event wasn't big enough for him, why couldn't he have made a video, to at least say something?"

Quizzed on this subject in 1998, Bowie responded: "The truth is I was not convinced by the motivations of this event but, frankly, I prefer to stay silent." Many of David's fans questioned *his* motivations—especially considering his presence at the Freddie Mercury memorial. The reality seems to be that the rivalry between Bowie and Ronson survived the guitarist's death. For

instance, in his otherwise illuminating contributions to Mick
Rock's book *Moonage Daydream*, Bowie comments that "another
of Mick's singular abilities...was the ability to take a hook line
that I might whistle or play badly and make it sing—we worked
well together because of this talent of his as an interpreter." Suzi
Ronson was one of many who were offended by Bowie's conde-
scending attitude: "Like David had arranged all his bloody solos. I
spent five hundred dollars on that book and sent it back, saying I
was disgusted. Mick Rock and I didn't speak for a while after that."

Ken Scott, the producer who witnessed their collaboration,
agrees there were indeed instances where David was very specific
about some instrumental passages, " 'Moonage Daydream' in particular," but as for the suggestion that David's humming Mick's
solos to him was their normal practice, "I wouldn't agree. No.
That's not the way I remember it." The frostiness between the
Bowie and Ronson camps was maintained with David's reference
in the same book to Suzi Fussey, Ronson's wife and David's long-
serving personal assistant, as "a local hairdresser in Bromley or
Beckenham." There were, obviously, parts of David's past with
which he was not quite at peace.

Bowie's belated, ungracious comments on Ronson were coun-
terproductive, a case of the Dame doth protest too much, suggesting that David was more aware than he cared to admit of how
integral Ronson had been to his breakthrough. Certainly, the negligible long-term impact of *Black Tie White Noise,* a pleasant, competent album that soon vanished from human consciousness
along with the record company that released it, seemed to show
how reliant David was on a musical foil—a Ronson or a Brian Eno
whom he could feed off, someone who made his music jell. Without one, he seemed to be locked in a cycle of diminishing returns.

But that foil, that source of inspiration, didn't have to be a
musician; in the case of David Bowie's best album in nearly a
decade, a rushed commission done on a tight budget, the vital
spark came from a relatively obscure novel about a Bromley childhood that was turned into a film by the BBC.

The genesis of the project came in the closing minutes of a Q and A with one of David's favorite magazines, *Interview,* famously founded by Andy Warhol in 1969. As it so often did, the magazine sent a celebrated name to interview the month's cover star, and the choice of writer Hanif Kureishi was particularly astute, for the novelist was, like David, a Bromley boy, a fellow ex-student of Bromley Tech. In the closing moments of the encounter, Kureishi mentioned the BBC was planning a TV version of his 1990 novel *The Buddha of Suburbia,* based on Kureishi's own upbringing in southeast London. Cheekily, Kureishi asked if David would contribute the sound track. Instantly, David agreed. The pair were huddled over a mixing desk at the Mountain studios just a few days later.

The recording fell into two sections. The first was a conventional sound track, written against the video of the show. Kureishi dropped in to observe, overawed that his own work was being screened over a mixing desk, "dotted with dozens of buttons, levers, and swinging gauges," and later by the fact that David noticed a couple of pieces changed the mood of key scenes and so quickly rewrote them. Then most of the themes were extended into an album. *The Buddha of Suburbia,* like so many of Bowie's triumphs, from *The Idiot* to "Absolute Beginners," benefited from its rushed creation. "Something happened for that album," says Erdal Kizilcay. "There wasn't a big budget; David explained the story before we started. It was a challenge, it was a small budget, but David just said, 'Let's go, let's do it,' and everything worked."

Throughout the 1990s, countless music critics remember, every time a new David Bowie album was couriered to the office, it was preceded by a PR agent's guarantee that "it's his best since *Scary Monsters.*" The only album sent over without such blandishments was probably the one most worthy of them, for in its modest way, the *Buddha of Suburbia* album was a perfect evocation of not just Kureishi's youth but that of his fellow Bromley boy, now forty-six.

There were plenty of nostalgic moments in the *Buddha* album, but perhaps its most important connection with David's own life was that, like all his best works, it was made without thinking too much, moments snatched out of the ether. Bowie and Kizilcay worked alongside each other, Bowie using the instrumentalist as a kind of one-man sound library. They'd work from ten until eight, joking, eating burgers, playing records by Prince and Nine Inch Nails to get them into the mood. A fair amount of the time, they'd talk about Turkey, for Erdal was a cultural transplant to Switzerland, as Hanif Kureishi was in Bromley, as was David, the kid who'd once fondly imaged himself "the English Elvis."

A couple of songs had been sketched out on demo—notably the subtle but anthemic "Strangers When We Meet," which David had attempted with Reeves during the *Black Tie White Noise* sessions—but most of them were put together as first takes. They'd discuss an idea or chord sequence and Erdal would say, "I'll try it." Then David would laugh and say, "Don't try it—play it!" Erdal's life journey was absorbed into the work, a huge amount of which was his improvisation—for instance, the gloriously meandering "South Horizon," in which Kizilcay's simple trumpet motif, swinging drums, and busy bass duel with the piano of Mike Garson (who'd just reappeared on the scene and overdubbed his part on the other side of the Atlantic).

Yet if the musicianship was Erdal's, the driving force was David's: "He is just a master—he knows exactly what he wants. I was like his hands, his musical hands." Even the more electro tracks—heavily influenced by the newly emergent Underworld— were tougher and more South London than the glossy sheen of *White Tie*'s dance songs; "The Mysteries" was based on an Austrian classical work, sampled and reversed, rather like "Subterraneans." Fragments of the lyrics were straightforward autobiography, mostly the title track, which mentions Plaistow Grove by the railway tracks; Terry, too, is evoked with the words *ouvre le chien*, a quote from David's song dedicated to him, "All the Madmen."

The album sneaked out in Britain in November of 1993 almost unnoticed and would wait another two years for a U.S. release on BMG, although the title track reached number 35 on the UK singles chart. It was the best David Bowie album in a decade, and the first in twenty-two years to entirely miss the charts. Its creator, the man always focused on success, not only seemed unconcerned, says his collaborator Erdal Kizilcay, "he was very happy."

CHAPTER 21

The Heart's Filthy Lesson

I've got to think of myself as the luckiest guy — Robert Johnson only had one album's worth of work as his legacy.

—David Bowie

B Y 1994 DAVID SEEMED to have expended as much energy transforming himself into an underground artist as he had transforming himself into a star. Yet no one could have possibly confused his lifestyle with that of a musician struggling to make ends meet. David and Iman largely divided their time between Los Angeles, Lausanne, and Mustique, where he maintained an immaculately groomed house furnished in the airbrushed ethnic style purveyed by the most expensive international interior designers. There, he posed for *Architectural Digest* magazine atop an antique Indian mahogany lounger. "My ambition," he told conservative writer William Buckley, "is to make music so incredibly uncompromised that I will have absolutely no audience left whatsoever—and then I'll able to spend the entire year on the island."

The comments were partly a reflection of the Bowie sense of humor, but there was a serious core to the sentiment. Over the late nineties a string of worthy, arty projects—a one-man show of twenty years' worth of David's paintings at a Cork Street gallery in

1995 and a position on the editorial board of *Modern Painters* magazine a year later—gave the impression that he was simply a rich hobbyist. It wasn't true, though. In reality, his compulsion to keep busy couldn't be kept in check forever, and within months of his statement, he was planning one of the most extreme recording experiences of his career—an art project, but one he would struggle to keep uncompromised.

Mike Garson was the restlessly inventive pianist who had transformed *Aladdin Sane* and last played with David on *Young Americans*. Like many musicians decades into their career, he'd wondered if he could match the creativity of his youth. In March of 1994, as he started his first complete album with David in twenty years, those doubts were nagging at him. "Personally, I didn't think I could really meet the mark or come up to the standard that I had set on *Aladdin Sane*. I was thinking, Could I top that? I was a little doubtful. But there was this great affinity and rapport. I still remember thinking to myself, This is special. It was a gem, to me."

The inspiration for the new project came from David's chats with Brian Eno at his wedding. Eno was, of course, a hot property as a producer thanks to his work with U2's electrifying *Achtung Baby*, an album steeped in the sound of Bowie's, Eno's, and—it needs stressing—Tony Visconti's experiments in Berlin. Once Brian and David decided to work together, the collaboration started to take shape through what was in 1994 the most high-tech of methods. Reeves Gabrels first heard about the planned album just after he'd completed a tour with Paul Rodgers. He walked into a hotel room in Oklahoma City with the strains of "Alright Now" ringing in his head and saw a fax from Eno lying on the floor. Soon, fax machines around the world were spooling out apparently impossible concepts and intractable questions: "One idea that David and Brian were trying to figure out was almost like a Charles Ives thing where you have two songs playing simultaneously then have them suddenly link up where the same word, beat, everything was right on the same spot: a mathematical problem."

In essence, the work harked back to David's first trip to America, when he'd discovered the music of outsiders like Iggy Pop, the Legendary Stardust Cowboy, and the fake Lou Reed. Hoping to tap a similar source in their quest to record the most extreme music of their careers, Bowie and Eno ventured in January of 1994 to Gugging Hospital, near Vienna, where psychiatrist Leo Navratil had assembled a group of patients who would become known as outsider artists. In 1981, Navratil opened a formal *Haus der Künstler* within the hospital where these artists could live and work as a community. Bowie told *Interview* magazine later: "Some of them don't even do [their art] as an expression of themselves; they do it because their work is them. Their motivation for painting and sculpting comes from a different place than that of the average artist who's sane on society's terms."

Interviewer Ingrid Sischy was sensitive enough not to ask the obvious question, whether David Bowie's half brother might have benefited from staying in a similarly enlightened regime rather than the depressing, understaffed confines of Cane Hill. Unsurprisingly, David and Eno were "both very affected by the experience" of visiting the *Haus der Künstler.*

In some ways the album sessions, which started in March of 1994, were like a replay of the Berlin days; for Garson it was a throwback to Philadelphia and *Young Americans,* his last full album outing with Bowie. The two had been reunited after a chance remark by writer Jérome Soligny, who mentioned that the pianist had quit Scientology. Partly inspired by the news that Garson was no longer a parson, Bowie called him a few days later to overdub piano to *Buddha.* But for their first meeting in a studio in nearly twenty years, there was no nostalgia, says Garson: "He just settles into it and that's all that exists at that moment in time. If I was to meet him tomorrow I'd have to come in as a fresh artist— none of the things from the past would mean anything."

Today, Garson expresses no regret at his two-decade separation from David; rather, there is an admiration at David's immersion in the present. "We would sit down every morning when we got in the studio, push record, and just play and play and play. It was a wonderful experiment and it turned into great music. There were times when David and Brian would play us tracks through the headphones; we'd be listening to a Marvin Gaye song and improvising against it, then they'd take that away and mess around with what we got from that based on how we were influenced by that piece. I thought that was brilliant."

Reeves Gabrels arrived in Lausanne roughly a week before the album sessions, to write and to just hang out. In this new context, he realized how David might have eight hours set aside, six of which would be spent talking, "but all of that informs the two hours when the flash happens." The sessions were consciously arranged as an art happening. Each musician had his own corner in the studio; when David wasn't setting up each one's head space, talking and making suggestions, he stood at an easel, sketching the band in charcoals. He constructed his lyrics using a randomizing program on his Apple PowerBook to re-create the old cut-up technique he'd used on *Diamond Dogs*. As he had in Berlin, he was using words for their sounds and associations rather than to form linear narrative.

Eno had prepared role cards for the participants aimed at forcing them out of stock ideas and responses. At times, Garson remembers Eno holding up cards signaling chord changes and then being ignored by the Reeves-Garson-Kizilcay trio: "Erdal was incredible, like a one-man jazz-rock fusion ensemble, all filtered through his growing up in Turkey. He was like, 'I don't get this shit, what is this shit?' He would ultimately play incredibly well."

In this new atmosphere, Kizilcay, who'd worked on Bowie sessions since the preproduction for *Let's Dance*, felt uncomfortable. He missed the musical intimacy of the *Buddha* sessions and he was not a fan of Brian Eno's oblique strategies, in which each musician was assigned a character: "He wrote me something like that I was an Arabic sheikh and I wanted to marry this guy's daughter—so I needed to show him I can play psychedelic, Arabesque funk. But I don't need a letter to play Oriental stuff!"

Gabrels was more receptive: "Mine was, 'You're on the third moon of Jupiter and you're the house band.' I liked that. What was

funny was I would sometimes play that game in my head anyway." Garson's card told him "You are the morale booster of a
small ragtag terrorist operation. You must keep spirits up at all
costs." Bowie, when he wasn't sketching, was "a town crier in a
society where the media networks have tumbled down."

For Garson, this was a powerful experience: "There was a
camera too. Hours of it every day just running, fixed cameras on
each of us. So they knew it was special on some level. Then David
doing charcoals of everybody as we're improvising was almost like
another instrumentalist playing, part of the creation." All of the
musicians remember the genesis of certain key songs, including
"The Hearts Filthy Lesson" as dating from this period, with more
than thirty-five hours of songs that evolved over the sessions.
When complete, the work was edited into two CDs of material and
titled *Leon*. Brian Eno, in particular, was eager to release the
results as a black label, "with no name on it," says Gabrels, "let it
leak that it was David Bowie but put it out as a completely separate
entity, like Prince's *Black Album*. Use it as a work of art and also
something that creates interest for the next project."

As they labored in the smoke-fogged studio at Mountain, with
both Bowie and Gabrels chain-smoking one Marlboro after another,
the way ahead seemed clear. For David, there was an obvious role
model: Scott Walker, the man who had turned him on to Jacques
Brel and whose career he had followed for twenty years, ever since
hearing the singer in Lesley Duncan's room at Redington Road.
According to Gabrels, "Scott Walker was still one of David's
heroes," and the small group of musicians saw their project in a
similar uncompromising vein as Scott's more challenging works.

But near completion of the album, David encountered exactly
the same problem of finding a sympathetic record company that
had plagued Scott Walker. The best prospect was Virgin America,
now owned by EMI; according to Gabrels, it was on the company's
suggestion that David reworked the album over January of 1995,
mostly at the Hit Factory in New York. Carlos Alomar returned to
contribute sublime rhythm guitar to "I Have Not Been to Oxford
Town." Over the same period, they introduced another version of

"Strangers When We Meet," "Thru These Architect's Eyes," and "Hallo Spaceboy," which originated from a Reeves ambient tune called "Moondust."

Soon after the New York session, Kevin Armstrong got a call to turn up at Westside Studios in London; his song "Now," recorded for the first Tin Machine album but left in the vault, had become the title track of *Outside*; Armstrong also added guitar to "The Hearts Filthy Lesson" and "Thru These Architect's Eyes." The songs' dark, gothic atmosphere was offset by the breezy presence of Sabrina Guinness, heiress and ex-girlfriend of Prince Charles. Guinness had recently returned from Hollywood and was setting up a video workshop for underprivileged kids; the kids filmed the sessions. Brian Eno agreed to a taped interview with the children, the intellectual guru turned total sweetheart— "he was absolutely charming with them," says Armstrong; the kids, in turn, added their voices to "The Hearts Filthy Lesson."

That song caused one of the first artistic disagreements between Gabrels and his boss, showing how hard it could be for a musician who was simply an employee. After recording the first version, Bowie had second thoughts and rerecorded his vocals with new lyrics—based on the theme of English landscape painters. Gabrels voiced his reservations. "Maybe I was too critical, so he said, 'Why don't you go away and come back in two hours?'" says Gabrels. "I came back and heard it and said, 'David, that's nice and all—but it's kind of destroyed the essence of the song, don't you think?' And he just waved his hand. 'Fine, we'll just move on.' 'No, no, David, I don't mean to hurt you.' 'No, forget it, we'll just go to another track. We'll come back to that next month.'"

The pair never discussed the subject again, but when it came to the mix David had reverted back to the original. The final version eventually ended up in a celebrated slot over the end titles to David Fincher's twisted serial-killer movie *Seven*—perhaps a treatise on English landscape artists would not have done the trick.

It was, of course, typical of the entertainment industry that David and Brian had started the project inspired by an artistic community who were blissfully heedless of commercial pressures and then had to rework their initial concept to get a record deal. Yet the album would soon undergo a second reworking at David's hands, intended to restore the art-house element he thought had been lost. Over 1995, he added spoken-word recordings, reshaping the album into a concept piece based on a surreal murder story he'd written for Q magazine in late 1994 titled "The Diary of Nathan Adler," what Bowie called a "non-linear gothic drama hyper-cycle." The plot revolved around the murder and dismemberment of fourteen-year-old runaway Baby Grace Blue, her body parts destined for a Damien Hirst–style artwork, with Bowie's Nathan Adler providing a Philip Marlowe–type voiceover in a dodgy Brooklyn accent.

Challenging, complex, often thrilling, overlong, and—in the spoken segues—undoubtedly self-indulgent, 1. Outside finally made it to the record shops on September 25, eighteen months after the first Montreux sessions. Its release met with a deluge of media attention, most of it effusive—"bold and fascinating," said Tom Doyle of Q—although there were dissenters; the San Francisco Examiner proclaimed it "pretentious and nearly tuneless."

In what would soon prove a habit, Bowie chose to lead with an uncompromising single—"The Hearts Filthy Lesson"—accompanied by a deliberately provocative video directed by Sam Bayer, also responsible for Nirvana's "Smells Like Teen Spirit." The video was a magnificently squelchy snuff-movie assemblage, whose cabinet-of-freaks sepia styling echoed the video for Nine Inch Nails' "Closer"—which was famously broadcast on MTV with "Scene Removed" captions to denote the cuts. As was surely intended, MTV duly refused to show Bowie's promo, which was later broadcast in edited form, and the single limped to 92 in the United States, 35 in the UK.

Bayer's video, the MTV kids with body piercings and tattoos assembling a Minotaur from spare body parts, perfectly embodied the mid-1990s aesthetic—so perfectly as to suggest that Bowie was merely jumping on a fashionable bandwagon. If anyone had the form for that crime, it was he. Yet, in fairness, bands like Smashing Pumpkins, Marilyn Manson, Nine Inch Nails, and, of course, Nirvana, who had recorded a limpid version of "Man Who Sold the World" back in November of 1993, all took elements of their dense, claustrophobic sound from Bowie. In any case, Bowie's incursion into the MTV alternative scene was aimed more at getting his groove back than at pursuing commercial success.

EVEN as Bowie's music started to pass out of youth culture, as a father and forty-something he seemed to have a more profound understanding of it. In 1971, he'd predicted a postsexual society, throwing together a youth manifesto that was, in retrospect, half-baked. In the 1990s, many of his pronouncements about art provoked sniffiness, with adjectives like *portentous* being directed at him by interviewers such as British writer Chris Roberts. Yet in retrospect, Roberts realized the insight behind some apparently throwaway comments. When the two met in 1995, Bowie predicted a "non-linear" society, telling him, "I think that we as a culture embrace confusion. We're happy to recombine information, we take event horizons incredibly fast. The generations— and I *can* use that plurally now—underneath me have an ability to scan information much quicker than my lot, and don't necessarily look for the depth that maybe we would."

In a couple of sentences, he'd summed up how the information society was starting to change, anticipating how people would consume media over the forthcoming decades. Within that interpretation, though, there was the unmistakable implication that in the coming years, the cultural impact of a single pop star, however famous, would be limited. The manifesto was becoming more modest.

The impact of 1. *Outside* too was limited, and not just for reasons of cultural change; the narrative segments, in particular, would become unbearably irritating on repeated listening, and in subsequent years the album would fall out of favor. Yet two decades later, when albums are indeed being consumed in non-linear fashion, shuffled on iTunes with the irritating portions removed, *Outside* is being seen in a different light, according to pianist Mike Garson, who has lately become convinced that the album is a career highlight: "I remember thinking, This is quite a special album—because it was a little far out. Maybe people wouldn't get it for a long time but recently I've had a lot of calls and e-mails—I have a feeling that people are starting to get it."

When *Outside* was being recorded, Bowie had played down his affinity with younger bands like Nine Inch Nails, saying that his major influence was the Swiss industrialists the Young Gods. But when it came time to promote *Outside* on the road, Bowie chose to explicitly link himself with Trent Reznor, touring on a joint bill with NIN in a deliberately challenging move that left him open to trend-hopping jibes and even hostile reactions.

Bowie's band now sported a new rhythm section with drummer Zachary Alford and bassist Gail Ann Dorsey; George Simms, last seen on the Serious Moonlight tour, was on backup vocals, and Peter Schwartz was selected as musical director so David wouldn't have a "favorite child" among Carlos, Reeves, and Garson, all previous incumbents. The tour opened on September 14 in Hartford, Connecticut, and finished in LA in late October. Nine Inch Nails' set included Bowie's "Scary Monsters" and "Subterraneans"; Bowie joined them for "Reptile" and "Hurt."

Mike Garson says, "I thought that was a brilliant move. We were standing on the side of the stage every night and watched them play their set. I was intrigued. In the middle of the show, when Nine Inch Nails were going off, our band would come on, David would sing 'Hurt' and Trent Reznor would sing the David Bowie song, and it was amazing."

For Reznor, the experience was thrilling but intimidating. Sometimes he'd find himself hoping that Bowie wouldn't be there when he walked into the dressing room so he wouldn't have to talk to him. "Not that I didn't like him. But I felt like I had to impress him. I had to impress his band. I couldn't just let my hair down."

Reeves: "It was a cool idea but also hard work because we would have to front-load our set with the up stuff because we'd be coming off the Nine Inch Nails encore. Also we did a meld where Carlos and I would join Nine Inch Nails. I remember playing

'Hurt' with them, then I did a little solo guitar intro in a little narrow spotlight so they could move gear on and off the stage without anybody seeing. Then we would begin our set with 'Hallo Spaceboy' with Trent still onstage and go into 'The Motel' from there. It was a tough one; some of the Nails crowd would leave when we came on, then our crowd would come in from the lobby. It made us work really hard—in a good way."

IN November, the band hit the UK, with Morrissey replacing NIN. The UK leg started with a four-night run at Wembley. The tour was a prime example of an older artist refusing to play his greatest hits—although "Look Back in Anger," "Scary Monsters," and "Teenage Wildlife" were all delivered in ruthlessly efficient versions— and it met with the predictable response. If there were any Phil Collins fans in the audience, taking the stage to Philip Glass's "Some Air" and opening with "The Motel" was an admirably effective method of dispersing them. Morrissey left the UK tour after the first ten dates, taking offense at Bowie's suggestion their sets should overlap as they had done on his American tour. Morrissey was not as accommodating as Trent Reznor of a move "which deprives people of saying good-bye to me," he asserted later, adding for good measure, "He's a business, you know. He's not really a person."

On February 19, 1996, as the European leg of the tour came to a close, there was a rather more fulsome tribute from Tony Blair, Labour Party leader, who hailed David as "an innovator" as he presented him with a Brit Award for Lifetime Achievement. The future world statesman was six years younger than David, who later commented he'd only turned up at the awards ceremony to perform his current single, "Hallo Spaceboy"—if so, the publicity tactic worked, for the Pet Shop Boys' remix of the song entered the UK charts two weeks later at number 12.

The success of "Hallo Spaceboy" was a welcome vindication in a year during which David's public and the critics gave his new material a generally grudging reception. His own enthusiasm, though, was fired up to a new peak. After a short break in the spring, the band—stripped down to Gabrels, Garson, Alford, and

Gail Ann Dorsey (whose vocals on a superb version of "Under Pressure" were now a staple of the set)—returned to Europe for festival dates in June and July; just a couple of days after the band returned home David called Gabrels to tell him he'd booked Philip Glass's studio in New York and they'd start recording in two weeks' time.

"That summer was the end of *Outside* and beginning of *Earthling*," says Gabrels. "I had written about six tracks, more like electronic stuff, on my laptop. I was trying to write without guitar at that point because we'd been crossing paths with bands like Underworld and Prodigy." The sessions would be the most intense and untroubled of David's 1990s work—the band called the studio the Clubhouse, and visitors included David Lynch and Lou Reed, with whom David had now made his peace. Inspired by the sounds they'd heard over the summer—Bowie was an Underworld fan, Gabrels favored the Prodigy—the team made a conscious decision to abandon tradition, says the guitarist: "I felt everybody was looking around them, musically, and thought, Fuck, it's the end of the millennium and we're still playing like we're in the Rolling Stones. We've got to get on this otherwise people are gonna look back at us and say we were lame."

Rather than playing conventional electric guitar, Gabrels used a Roland processor, which digitally modeled different guitar sounds; the entire album was recorded on hard disk, rather than on tape, allowing vocals and instrumental parts to be cut and pasted within a song. As they excitedly explored this new world, their guide was Mark Plati, who'd been working at Looking Glass since 1991. Tutored in the bass guitar at Indiana University by Duke Ellington's nephew William, Plati moved to New York in 1987 and engineered, programmed, and played at Arthur Baker's Shakedown studios while also filling the same role for superstar DJ Junior Vasquez. Plati had helped Gabrels craft the samples used for the summer dates, and over the three weeks in which they made the album, he became its coproducer, making music out of bits of sonic "junk"—old tracks and samples that he and Reeves found around the studio.

Working with Brian Eno, David had gone through complex psychological techniques to bypass writers' block; for *Earthling*, his simply using a computer did much the same thing. The songs arrived quickly, lyrics assembled on Post-it notes, decisions made on the fly, vocals recorded first or second take, notably "Little Wonder," where they ended up using the original guide vocal. David was approaching his fifties, but his voice and writing sounded fresh, revitalized—there were many echoes of his youth, a Tony Newley inflection in "Little Wonder," a trace of "Letter to Hermione" in "Dead Man Walking," which also featured the simple two-note guitar riff Jimmy Page had shown him at IBC studios with the Manish Boys three decades earlier.

If it came easy, though, *Earthling* didn't stay the course. By its release in January of 1997, drum and bass and Bowie's main obsession, Underworld, were both mainstream phenomena; although many reviews of the time praised the rejuvenated songwriting, the album was doomed to be consigned to history as seemingly another exercise in bandwagon-jumping. Even the title, *Earthling*, seemed crassly self-referential, while the Alexander McQueen Union Jack frock coat looked like an attempt to cash in on Britpop, which was the talk of the spring. Yet despite the air of dad at the disco, the passion was real, and it inspired Bowie and Gabrels to sneak to that summer's Phoenix Festival and play as the Tao Jones Index before their main set.

WHEN David celebrated his fiftieth birthday at a packed Madison Square Garden on January 8, 1997, the lineup seemed carefully chosen to emphasize the birthday boy's cutting-edge credentials. Fans like the Smashing Pumpkins, Robert Cure, Frank Black, and Dave Grohl were there to duet on better-known songs, but his own set was dominated by material from his last two albums; Lou Reed—"the king of New York," as David fulsomely introduced him—was the only contemporary, joining him for "Queen Bitch" and "Waiting for the Man." It wasn't until the end, after crowd and band had sung him "Happy Birthday," that he ran through

"Under Pressure" and "Heroes" and then closed the evening with a beautifully simple "Space Oddity."

It was a powerful ceremony, a convincing testament to his musical impact, but over the same period that the exacting preparation had been going on for the show, a more intimate package was being assembled. For months, Iman had been calling up friends, some of whom hadn't seen David for years, asking them to contribute an artwork to be bound into a book, each piece marking a moment of their life with this supposedly cold, calculating individual. The work, a collection of drawings and writing, was supremely moving, according to those who have seen it, an unaffected tribute to a man who is simply, as boyhood friend Geoff MacCormack puts it, "very funny—a good mate." Friends from Bromley, Berlin, and New York contributed—Iman charmed each of them, discovering new stories about her husband. Only Iggy, according to friends, didn't contribute.

For many of David's peers, hitting the age of fifty was a dark moment; a few, such as Keith Richards, relished emulating heroes like John Lee Hooker and playing long into the good night. For Iggy, just three months younger than David, his fiftieth year on the planet was a time to split with his wife, Suchi, and embark on a crazed affair with an Argentinean girl who inspired his crisis-ridden *Avenue B* album. David, though, seemed idyllically happy with Iman, telling friends and even people he bumped into casually on planes and in airports that getting married was the best thing that had ever happened to him; the part of him that was utterly conventional seemed to have gained dominance.

One gleaming signpost of this conventionality was the perfect white teeth he now sported. The disappearance of his slightly crooked, overlapping fangs in favor of even, Hollywood-style crowns would later become the subject of a hilariously sleazy British TV show, *Celebrity Surgery*, featuring several Bowie acolytes, all of whom thought they were contributing to a conventional documentary. The snippet is now a YouTube classic, studded with poignant comments from fans mourning the departure of his iconic English gnashers. The teeth completed a style makeover that also included a small alternative-rock goatee, and the body art applied by a tattooist, popular with the Yakuza, in Kyoto in 1992 — a figure riding a dolphin, overlaid with a Japanese serenity prayer and Iman's name in Kanji on his left calf. (Iman reciprocated with a Bowie knife above her right ankle.)

There was something about David's well-groomed, alternative appearance that looked distinctly airbrushed and American, the product of spending more time with New York's fashion and music crowd (Iman disliked the Lausanne house, which the couple put up for sale the following year). They both loved the city, and in the following years could often be seen huddled deep in conversation in cafés near their condo at 708 Broadway. Still, he remained distinctly British, for Iman brought out his playful, funny side and loved the ever-present dry humor. Many a New York waiter would be caught out by his little jokes, handing him a hot rolled towel only for Bowie to look at it quizzically and ask, "Is it dead?" Even the occasional toot of cocaine was consigned to the past; now he rarely drank to excess, and while he cut a cool rug in his frock coat for that summer's tour, he was content to leave Reeves Gabrels to check out the dance culture with which he'd aligned himself: "He couldn't really go to raves — nor was he inclined to, being, at that point, sober for a long time."

Gabrels and Bowie developed as close a musical relationship as any Bowie had had, all the more complex because the guitarist was from a younger generation, someone who'd grown up on Bowie's music. Gabrels would teeter between waves of euphoria at working with a childhood hero and frustration at dealing with Bowie's organization and niggles about percentage breakdowns on songwriting credits, which seemed to crop up around that time. Many of Bowie's musicians cite him as among their best employers — "I'm his biggest fan, in that respect," says Carlos Alomar — but others found dealing with Isolar consistently unpleasant. Bowie's management gave some collaborators, like Erdal Kizilcay, the impression they should take the percentage offered and count themselves lucky. The Bowie camp had a point — after all, any musician working with David was practically guaranteed an overnight transformation of his financial fortunes—but such arguments were especially hard to stomach in the late nineties at a time when David was gaining new fame, not for music but for the money he was fast accumulating.

Bowie bonds, the controversial means by which David raised fifty-five million dollars against revenues from his back catalog, would cause a sensation within the music industry. The bonds, securities issued against Bowie's future royalties for the next ten years, would also make a star of David Pullman. The man most associated with the Bowie bond, Pullman would, at age thirty-nine, be named one of *Time* magazine's top one hundred innovators and would go on to package similar deals for other musicians. Soon he was being celebrated in profiles across the world's press. The most convincing testament to the fame of the bond phenomenon arrived in 2001 in the shape of a thriller, *Something Wild,* in which novelist Linda Davies wove a complex plot around the issue of Bowie bonds: "Linda's book gives readers a look at how exciting this industry can be," gushed Pullman in a press release around its launch.

Bowie banked fifty-five million dollars from the deal, some of which was reportedly used to pay British taxes. However, David wanted the money for quite another reason: to buy back his own music.

When David had negotiated his split from Tony Defries in March of 1975, his ex-manager retained a percentage of all the music David recorded right through to 1982. This percentage was on a sliding scale, reportedly a full 50 percent of Bowie's share on the pre-1975 releases and less thereafter, but the money was due in perpetuity. Defries retained co-ownership of the masters—and even retained the right, he claimed, to issue further Bowie recordings, a right he exploited from the early 1990s with the release of the Santa Monica '72 live album in 1994, plus other albums based on BBC and Astronettes sessions. In the mid-1990s, Isolar opened negotiations with their predecessor for Bowie to finally buy out his rights. The talks, according to Defries's friends, were amicable: David's people told Defries's people he wanted the assets "to pass on to his children." None of the parties involved has ever confirmed how much of David's fifty-five million went to Defries, but some of those peripherally involved suggest it was at least half. If so, Tony Defries made over twenty-seven million dollars, an impressive return for the five hundred thousand pounds it had cost him to buy Bowie's masters from Laurence Myers back in the summer of 1972.

Over subsequent years, the notion of Bowie bonds would be raised again and again, often with the implication that David, like Mick Jagger, was obsessed with money, a lower-middle-class boy wanting to make up for childhood austerity. Few commented on the fact that, at the age of fifty, he was paying tens of millions to reclaim his own life's work. Following the transaction, Tony Defries bought an impressive estate in Virginia, and on top of his considerable existing assets, he now had millions to invest—a practice in which he'd always been an expert. David had purchased his own past.

IF the motivations for Bowie seeking another fifty-five million dollars were misunderstood, the furor signaled a period when his name was invariably connected with commerce. The implications of Bowie bonds were closely followed within the financial industry, although the gloss was taken off them by a series of lawsuits between Pullman and various other parties over who had invented the bonds. The final verdict indicated that the inspiration for the bonds came not from financial whiz kid David Pullman but from David's own business manager Bill Zysblat. The controversy around the issue would never subside. Lamont Dozier, the acclaimed Motown songwriter, would later sue the advisers who worked on his own bond issue; in 2004, in the wake of EMI's financial problems, Bowie bonds were downgraded by Moody's, the leading credit ratings agency, to one notch above junk grade.

Since the days when he had kept a close eye on finances on the Serious Moonlight tour, Bill Zysblat—who also worked for the Stones—had become David's key adviser. Following the excitement generated by the Bowie bonds, Zysblat also planned a Bowie bank—an idea that was eventually dropped after irregularities were found at the bank chosen to operate the scheme—and, in the summer of 1998, he announced that he was going to create an Internet provider called BowieNet.

Over the past few years, David had become as fired up by the Internet as he was by art and music: "He was right at the forefront, and it made sense he would be," says Thomas Dolby, Bowie's Live Aid keyboard player. Dolby had moved to the West Coast to launch an Internet start-up company, and Bowie had shared his excitement. "It was a hedonistic thing—of being in the moment, of getting a thrill, a rush out of what he was experiencing." Dolby had lived through a similar arc, seeing contemporaries like David Byrne progress from hanging out at the Mudd Club to exploring the medium of video. "These were the lightning rods for creativity. And he was very fired up—what he was seeing was a return to a grassroots movement. He could have a ringside seat and be in control, do spontaneous things and get instant feedback."

Bowie's life would be mapped out online for at least the next decade, yet his influence went beyond his own site, or his own music. According to some industry insiders, he was mapping the very future of the World Wide Web. Technology writer John Naughton later cited Bowie as a "leading futurologist," the originator of some of the "most perceptive observations anyone's ever made about our networked world." In the late 1990s, Bowie saw the Web's potential for building new communities, yet he also spotted the long-term implications for copyright, predicting how authorship and intellectual property would become endangered. Most presciently, in 2002 he suggested that music "is going to become like running water or electricity," anticipating the rise of streaming services. Bowie would always stop short of describing himself as any kind of visionary—his opinions on the evolution of modern culture were usually confined to promotional interviews. But his perceptiveness inspired Naughton to comment in 2010, "If you want to know the future, ask a musician."

In January of 1998, David was promoting the launch of his

own Web sites, davidbowie.com and bowieart.com, and on September 1 he launched an Internet provider, BowieNet (subscription fee $19.95 per month). One of the staff at Outside, his PR company, recalls that the launch was "one of the most stressful things I can remember; there would be webcasts with him, Boy George, Visconti—and he absolutely loved it." The obsession— David would also drop in on his own chat rooms, his handle "Sailor"—was also recreational; he'd spend hours trawling the World Wide Web or looking for bargains on eBay.

Over the same year that the Bowie brand was launched online, the man himself was launched as an independent, digital entity. Toward the end of 1998, David called Reeves Gabrels over to London to join him and Iman at a meeting with a computer game company, Eidos. The developer needed not only a sound track; "they wanted David, Iman, and me to be a character in a game," says Gabrels. "So we started talking about how to do it, set up in a hotel room, and started writing." The resultant game, Omikron, was a cult classic, albeit no mainstream success, but "Survive," the main song Bowie and Gabrels crafted for the game, was a gem, simple and unaffected, almost *Scary Monsters* in vibe without any of the overcomplexity and overthinking that seemed synonymous with 1990s Bowie.

During that most multimedia of years, it was perhaps fitting that a meeting that would have a profound effect on his future work was hatched as a result of a kids' cartoon. David had been asked to contribute a song to *The Rugrats Movie* (also featuring Iggy) and he called Tony Visconti to produce the vaguely retro song, "Safe." Visconti took the call, and his eyes "welled up. I hadn't realized how much I missed him." Sadly, the song wouldn't make the film, for the scene featuring it was cut. But their relationship had been rekindled.

As one friendship was being patched up, another was coming to its end. The Omikron project expanded into a full-blown album, first called *The Dreamer,* later renamed *Hours;* it was started in Bermuda, where David and Iman now had a holiday home. In search of a low-key, emotional feel, Bowie and Reeves reverted to conventional one-on-one songwriting methods. According to Reeves, he'd originally intended two of the songs, "The Pretty Things Are Going to Hell" and "Survive," for his own solo album. Throughout, his guitar work was tasteful, less exhibitionist than before—"I'm not sort of Jackson Pollocking my way through it, it's more Norman Rockwell."

After the aggression and exuberance of its predecessors, *Hours* was widely interpreted as a reflection on mortality. There is a distinct world-weariness about songs such as "Thursday's Child," exacerbated by David's Nick Cave–influenced vocal—at other points, particularly in "The Dreamers," Scott Walker comes to the fore in what is one of David's more vocally self-effacing albums. The instrumentation too was conventional, predictable at times, in what seemed to be a "genre-free" album, as if in conscious overreaction to its predecessor. The best songs, notably "Seven" and "Thursday's Child," were potential masterpieces, but their predictable, occasionally plodding arrangements suggested that David's assured instinct for picking the right setting had deserted him. As if to confirm this, the sleeve, always an intrinsic part of the appeal of Bowie albums, was a mess; despite being crafted by noted San Francisco collagist Rex Ray, it was a hammy mix of designer clutter and mawkishness with its photo of the long-haired Bowie cradling his short-haired alter ego.

Most listeners took the autumnal mood as Bowie reflecting on his life. In his talks with Reeves, David had said that "it was autobiographical but it wasn't his biography, it was someone close to him. There was some discussion about whether he was writing from my point of view. I don't know. The end was nigh. I knew I needed to go, it just took a long time to figure out how."

Gabrels had helped lead Bowie out of the creative cul-de-sac of the late 1980s, but both parties sensed it was time to move on. Mark Plati, the computer wizard behind *Earthling*, had now moved into a more conventional role as bassist, a change essentially initiated by Reeves. Gabrels had thus prepared his own replacement. There was no falling-out, says the guitarist: "I was basically burning out. A lot of it didn't have to do with David as much as with time away from home, time on the road, and just dealing with some of the people around him. I thought it was amicable."

In his later years, David was sometimes remarkably gracious about his previous collaborators; this was certainly the case with Reeves, to whom David would often publicly express his gratitude. Still, the pair soon fell out of touch. "I think it got misinterpreted over time—Coco got in there after I left," says Reeves. "I was no saint either at the end, but my crimes were entirely personal. I was trying to make my way home at that point—literally! I felt like if I had stayed I was going to become everything I disliked in musicians I had known—bitter and twisted—or I was gonna die because I would be so miserable I would just drug myself to death. I just knew I was done with that. There were also personal complications because I was having a child with David's wardrobe mistress. That played into their hands as a source of shit-stirring." Gabrels's last appearance with Bowie would be at the VH1 *Story-tellers* performance, filmed in August of 1999. (It was a good, slightly nostalgic show, with some hilarious anecdotes, such as the time when, in Ziggy guise, David discovered he was expected to use the dressing-room sink as a urinal. "My dear man, I can't piss in the sink!" he protested. "Son," the promoter replied, "if it's good enough for Shirley Bassey, it's good enough for you.")

While *Hours* was undistinguished, its marketing was world-class. The buildup to its October 4 release featured a "cyber song contest," offering fans the chance to contribute four lines of lyric to one song, "What's Really Happening." Alex Grant, from Ohio, won out over eighty thousand entrants to sign a fifteen-thousand-dollar publishing contract and attend the recording session. Bowie's Web site unveiled the album cover one section at a time, striptease style, while announcing the album would be available as a download before its CD release—another first for an established artist. And if this weren't sufficient media saturation, in the run-up to release, "Heroes" blared out regularly from British TV screens in an eight-and-a-half-million-pound campaign for CGU Insurance, which, the ad agency announced, "focuses on the consumer as 'hero' for taking responsibility for the financial future." The promotion, and the fans' genuine affections for the more traditional, unvarnished Bowie, helped the album to number 5 in the UK—although American sales were disappointing, and at number 47 it was his worst solo chart performance since *Ziggy Stardust*.

But as the century drew to its close, there was welcome vindication from the *Sun*, whose readers voted him the biggest star of the twentieth century, beating Michael Jackson and Liam Gallagher; in a *Q* magazine poll on the greatest star of the century, he beat Madonna to come sixth after Lennon, McCartney, Cobain, Dylan, and Elvis. On Christmas Eve that year, he spent two and a half hours chatting with nineteen thousand fans on an intermittent Internet feed, thanking the kids who mentioned that their parents thought him a bad influence, promising new sessions with Tony Visconti, throwing in a good joke every line or two, mentioning his son was standing by with a saucepan, and then explaining that the Christmas tree had been decorated, "but our balls keep tending to fall off." It had been a good half a century.

THE fresh new decade was a good one too. David and Iman had been trying for a child since the late 1990s, resorting to IVF, Iman said later, and she'd undergone two unsuccessful bouts before conceiving naturally. The pair announced Iman's pregnancy on February 13, monopolizing headlines worldwide (the competition for cheesiest headline was won by music365.com, whose story was entitled "Nappy Ch-ch-changes..."). Iman later told *Jet* magazine she'd used an old African technique to get pregnant: holding a borrowed baby, kindly supplied by Christie Brinkley during a *Vogue* shoot the previous September.

Of all the regrets David voiced in public, the fact that his son had gone through such an irregular upbringing was the one he mentioned most often. After leaving Gordonstoun, Joey had worked briefly with handicapped kids in Switzerland, and then at the Jim Henson workshop, a connection he'd made during his dad's work on *Labyrinth*, before winning a scholarship to the College of Wooster in Ohio to study philosophy. Once there, he started using his given first name, Duncan. In 1999, David had suggested Duncan accompany him to the shoot for Tony Scott's TV series of *The Hunger;* Scott became a mentor to Duncan, inspiring a love affair with cinema. In February of 2000, the *Daily Mail* trumpeted the news that the "quiet and polite" Duncan had enrolled at the London Film School.

RIGHT at the beginning of 2000, David knew there would be parallels with the summer that Duncan was born, for Glastonbury organizer Michael Eavis had called before Christmas and asked him to return to the festival, twenty-nine years after his first appearance there. The spring was dominated by the preparations, with Earl Slick returning to the fold, joining Plati, Gail Ann Dorsey, drummer Sterling Campbell, and backup singers Holly Palmer and Emm Grynner. There were three warm-up shows in New York, one of which was canceled when David's voice gave out. Perhaps for that reason, David was conspicuously nervous before his Sunday-night slot at the festival on June 25.

BBC executive producer Mark Cooper oversaw the live coverage and remembers, "He took the place by storm. He came back dressed in *Hunky Dory* mode and played a set full of hits; every one was a winner." The performance was fabulous; only one factor stopped the set from being the live broadcast of the year. "[Bowie's organization] told us they would only let us broadcast six songs. I wept. It was such a stonking set, he had the whole crowd eating out of his hand. And it was painful to come off it." The BBC executives were struck by the contrast between David's cheery demeanor and the difficult, almost miserly attitude of his organization when it came to broadcasting the show: "I always thought of Bowie as someone good at hoarding his past," says one of them, "paying it out a bit at a time. Like Scrooge." Cooper, meanwhile, saw the performance as a life-changing event that should have been shared more widely: "An artist can be reborn with a performance like that, get another ten years in their career. He's earned the right to deliver things on his terms, but I think it was a mistake. Because this was the moment."

There was another nod to 1971 two days later with a show at the BBC Radio Theatre, which echoed the show at which he'd premiered the newly written "Kooks." Then, back in New York, he started sessions on the 1960s-themed album that he'd trailed in the December webcast. Named *Toy*, the proposed album was inspired by one of his first great songs, "Let Me Sleep Beside You"—"place your ragged doll with all your toys and things and deeds." With Mark Plati overseeing, they cut a terrific version, imbued with the spirit of Mick Wayne, who'd played on the BBC version—the Hull guitarist, Ronson's predecessor, had died in a house fire in June 1994, his work forgotten. Tony Visconti, whose inspirational arrangement for the song had marked his debut collaboration with Bowie, was called in for some of the sessions, in which David delved deeply into his own back pages. He rerecorded *Ziggy*-era numbers, such as the jewel-like "Shadow Man"; a near masterpiece, this obscure, forgotten work illustrated the quality and breadth of the song catalog he'd built up over thirty-five years.

Though they'd been working hard, there was a most welcome interruption to the sessions on August 15 with the birth of Alexandria Zahra Jones at Mount Sinai Hospital in New York. The pair celebrated the event in the now obligatory cover feature in *Hello!*, sharing with the public their bliss, their fantasies of later having a boy they could name Stenton, after David's father, and the universal frustration with builders, whose delays prevented their move to their new, bigger apartment in Chelsea in time for the birth. In the early days, Iman mentioned that David was doing his share of diaper changes for Alexandria—her name inspired by the ancient Greco-Egyptian seat of culture. The notion of a multimedia superstar dealing with such down-to-earth routines was heartwarming, but apparently the novelty wore off, for three years later, in blokeish mode, he announced, "I don't do nappies."

A year after Alexandria's birth, David was still describing his main job as "daddyfying," his excitement at the new experience just as all-consuming as the obsessions of his youth. His work schedule was light; there was a short break filming a hilarious, self-parodic cameo for Ben Stiller's *Zoolander*, plus more frustrating weeks spent wrestling with problems over the completed *Toy* album—in June, David mentioned "scheduling conflicts" with EMI/Virgin. In reality, this was a terminal falling-out triggered by managerial conflicts within the company. He was unconcerned by the hassles, as far as anyone could tell; instead, he seemed to have settled in to life in New York. The public perception was of him as a culture buff, always visiting the ballet or a new exhibition, hanging out with local musos like Moby and Lou Reed, all of which he did. But he was just as happy Googling randomly in "the bunker," his computer and work room; waking up at six in the morning and dealing with e-mails before taking Lexi in her buggy for a walk around SoHo or Greenwich Village; or sitting chatting to Iman over a bowl of pasta by a restaurant window, the two of them smiling graciously if they happened to be interrupted.

In his first few years as a New Yorker, he still considered moving back to London; it was a part of who he was. But over the next couple of years he came to detest British celebrity culture, the prospect of enduring "having a camera lens stuck in either my face or my wife and child's face every morning." He had reverted to much the same sentiments he'd expressed in 1980, the feeling that New York was the perfect place to wander, seek out interesting book or antique shops, pick up the urban buzz without being hassled. Only once did he venture out to perform that spring, to Carnegie Hall for the Tibet House Benefit on February 26, 2001. Together onstage for the first time since the Hype, he and Tony Visconti played an extraordinary version of "Silly Boy Blue." After they'd recorded it together in December of 1966, it had disappeared without trace, prompting David's thoughts of giving up music; now the pair were backed by Philip Glass on piano and Moby on guitar, and they led the enraptured crowd in a chant of "Chime chime chime" in tribute to the monk David had gone to see at the Tibet Center when he was contemplating a new career.

The sense that, as a new father, David was becoming reconciled to his own past deepened in the aftermath of his mother's death. Margaret Mary Jones's passing was announced on April 2, and for David had come "out of the blue." Several faces from his youth were at the funeral, including Ken Pitt and Pat Antoniou, the aunt who had so publicly accused David of callousness to his half brother and prolonged the feuds that had blighted the Burns family for half a century. When David saw her, he "walked straight over, threw his arms around her," says Ken Pitt, the one man who had stayed in touch with all the various disconnected branches of the family. "He was absolutely wonderful."

A ghost had been laid to rest, but others would remain. On May 11, Freddie Buretti died of cancer in Paris. David had kept nearly all the costumes Freddie had made for him. And the problems with *Toy* deepened during the summer; the record would be a casualty of Mariah Carey's legendarily disastrous album *Glitter,* which sold so badly that Virgin was forced to pay a reported nineteen million dollars to terminate her contract early; Nancy Berry, who had signed Bowie as well as Carey, was fired. But even before *Toy*'s fate was sealed, David was planning its replacement. In June, he came to stay with Tony and his new girlfriend at their "humble," drafty, wooden three-story home in suburban West Nyack, New York. The pair worked on songs together in Tony's loft, just as they had in the Haddon Hall basement, only this time they would cut and paste ideas in Pro Tools rather than Mark Pritchett's Revox. On their second day, Tony took David to see Allaire, a beautiful wood-lined recording studio set in the Catskills. It felt like a finely crafted Edwardian yacht and had panoramic views over the reservoir that quenches the thirst of New York City. The moment David stepped in the room, he said later, "I knew exactly what lyrics I was to write—although I didn't yet know what the words themselves were."

When they started recording, David brought his "little family," who stayed in a tiny house on the grounds some of the time; there he remained until the album was essentially finished. One morning, he got up around five, as was his habit, looked out of the windows, and saw two deer grazing below in the field, in the fresh light of the rising sun. In the distance a car was driving slowly past the reservoir, and then words started streaming out of him and tears ran down his face. The song was "Heathen": "I didn't like writing it. There was something so ominous and final about it." The lyrics read as if he is taking leave of a lover, but the object he addresses is life.

The song was indeed bleak, but throughout *Heathen*, there is a visceral connection with the world David saw around him, and an almost loving engagement with his craft (later he'd enumerate all the instruments he played in the sessions, which included his Stylophone and Brian Eno's old EMS synth).

For the past two decades, Bowie had wrestled with the worry about whether, in his later years, he could ever "contribute so aggressively" again. In the relaxed, almost spiritual atmosphere of Allaire, he had found his answer, for a renewed confidence and passion pervades each of the songs. There was a luminous simplicity about most of the material that evoked *Hunky Dory*, but where *Hunky Dory* speaks of rebirth, of the shiny and new, *Heathen* displays a hard-won confidence in a life that's been well lived, like beautifully worn leather: quirky, almost baby voices on "A Better Future," drifting, dark drum loops on "The Angels Have Gone," impassioned singing, reminiscent of "Heroes," on "Slow Burn." Perhaps there wasn't the visceral thrill of the twenty- and thirty-something Bowie, but there was nonetheless the sense that this was a classic album that didn't suffer by comparison with *Scary Monsters*.

Many of the reviews of the album were colored by the knowledge that Bowie and Visconti were still out in the Catskills on 9/11; Iman was back in the New York apartment, and David was on the phone with her as she saw the second plane hit. When David returned to Manhattan, there was an ominous gap in the familiar view from the kitchen window; Iman realized that many of the men who used to greet her and Lexi as she wheeled the buggy by the local FDNY station a couple of blocks away were probably dead. It would cement the family's relationship with the city; David headlined October's Concert for New York City and would talk no more of moving back to London. But for all the fear and anxiety David sensed in the air, people convinced there would be a further attack, he was infectiously optimistic, recounting

Lexi's baby words verbatim to friends, reading her books, telling those around him how lucky he was.

The sense of event around the release of *Heathen* in June of 2002 was palpable—the presence of Tony Visconti seemed to fire up fans far more than an Internet marketing campaign. The excitement was stoked up by a show at New York's Roseland Ballroom and then his appearance at the culmination of his own Meltdown festival at London's Festival Hall. The series had been controversial—or rather "disappointingly unadventurous," according to the *London Evening Standard*—for his involvement as curator was patchy, with his attention diverted by negotiations with new record company Sony. Yet the closing night was a sensation, mostly for the performance of *Low*, in its entirety, followed by *Heathen*. Mark Plati had prepared by listening through the original Hansa and Château d'Hérouville multitracks; massive, long-obsolete reels of two-inch tape that had to be baked in an oven to stop them crumbling into dust; he crafted individual mixes that he gave to each band member, a kind of karaoke version of the album. The show was "genuinely overwhelming; people did recognize the magnitude of the event," says Glenn Max, who had struggled to put the festival together; as the band launched into "Always Crashing in the Same Car," the audience came to its feet, and pretty much stayed there. The only problem with the show was that by the close of *Low*, the audience was drained. "It had been so dazzling, you almost needed a two-hour run around the block to recover," says Max, but then the band came out again, David now changed from his Thin White Duke shirt and waistcoat into a white silk suit for a gripping rendition of *Heathen*.

When the applause died down, Bono and Brian Eno were among those lining up for admission to the tiny dressing room; this event alone was great theater, David looking spent but cool as a cucumber, dressed in a kimono "with little Japanese slippers on his tiny Japanese feet," remembers Glenn Max. When David introduced Brian Eno to Mark Plati, he told him, "This is the man responsible for all of this." Thinking Bowie meant he was the architect of the Queen Elizabeth Hall, Plati pointed at the ceiling and murmured, "Nice job!"

For both the album and the tour that promoted it, there was a consensus in the coverage: This was an artist who, if not at the peak of his giddy career, was nonetheless still producing work that towered over that of most of his younger rivals. And with the fevered activity, he said, "I'm very confident and trusting in my abilities right now." The old sense of having to rush that had driven him through the 1970s was renewed. Back then, the impetus came from youthful ambition; now it came from what seemed an excessive sense of his own mortality. "I've got to think of myself as the luckiest guy," he said that summer, "Robert Johnson only had one album's worth of work as his legacy." After smoking obsessively, trying brand after brand for forty years, he'd managed to cut down to a minimum now that he was a father.

The *Heathen* tour concluded in late October of 2002, marked by shows at each of New York's five boroughs, but David was thinking of songs even as he settled back into his daily routine of walks and reading sessions with Lexi, visits to Iman at the Seventh Avenue office of her cosmetics company, and his three-times-a-week boxing sessions at a nearby gym.

After a couple of days of preproduction in November, he and Visconti were ready to start work again in January. This time they recorded in New York, at Looking Glass, but in their smaller studio, which gave a more constrained, urban feel "to capture the angst of NYC," says Visconti. He and David worked closely together, making decisions quickly; there was a matter-of-factness about the recording, much of it using David's touring band. Mike Garson, like Chuck Hammer and Dominic Muldowney before him, was struck by how intuitive their musical relationship was: "I worked with perfect love with Tony Visconti. He's an incredible guy."

Throughout his life, David had developed his unrivaled genius for getting the best out of musicians; in just two songs, "The Loneliest Guy" and "Bring Me the Disco King," he seemed to reach into Garson to inspire something new. The latter track, with

Garson's minimal, milky chords underpinned by a drum loop saved from *Heathen,* was as fine as anything they'd recorded together in the last thirty years. "You promised me the ending would be clear," David sang, in a voice rendered cloudy by four decades of Gitanes and Marlboros; after twenty-eight albums, he was still constructing songs that were fiercely understated yet would yield up new secrets with repeated listens.

From the Spiders onward, one of the most frequently voiced accusations about David's work was that he exploited his musicians and influences—that he was really a curator, not a creator. But as Garson attests, he had a practiced, effective, and indeed almost mystical ability to inspire them to create something entirely new: "Somehow his being-ness and his essence pulls out the best," says the pianist. "He might give you little guidances but never says do this or do that. Just by his space I always tend to play my best stuff, to contribute every aspect of my playing. I don't think I would have come up with those solos had he not been there."

Garson, in his own way, summarizes all the issues of how David conjured up music from his musicians. In his early days, the word *vampiric* was used more than once to describe how he benefited from other musicians' creativity. Yet in reality, he rarely took from them—he inspired them, as Garson points out, to summon up ideas that would never have existed without him. In these years, David Bowie was always modest about the achievements to which he laid claim, but he was demonstrably correct when he told Livewire.com: "To not be modest about it, you'll find that with only a couple of exceptions, most of the musicians that I've worked with have done their best work by far with me. I can shine a light on their own strengths. Get them to a place they would never have gotten to on their own." This was a bold claim, but as Garson and others attest, it was true. He didn't take. He gave.

TONY Visconti thought that David looked tired when he next saw him. *Reality* was released, to a warm response, on September 15, 2003, and in October David embarked on his biggest tour of the past five years. In retrospect, the portents had been stacking up for months; at the time, the tour was thrilling. "We didn't sit on our laurels—at one point we had sixty or seventy songs in our repertoire," says Garson. "He would call things out from nowhere sometimes and we would just play them in front of three thousand people. It was pretty brave." Yet on November 12, the Toulouse show was canceled after David developed laryngitis; two days later, he resumed the shows, only for the first leg of the U.S. tour to be delayed for a week when he came down with influenza. Come January he was back on the road again, but tragedy struck on May 6 in Miami; the night's performance was canceled after a lighting engineer fell to his death. Then on June 18, his outdoor show in Oslo was interrupted when a female fan threw a lollipop that hit his left eye. For a few moments his composure deserted him as he demanded to know who had thrown the object—then, relaxing, he warned them, "I've only got one good eye, you know," before telling them he planned to retaliate by making the concert extra long. Five nights later, in Prague, David cut short his set after fifteen songs, complaining of what felt like a trapped nerve in his shoulder. He played one more show, at the Hurricane Festival in Scheesel on Saturday, June 25, before collapsing backstage in agony.

For the next nine days, BowieNet would trail the message that the tour had been canceled "due to continuing pain and discomfort from a trapped/pinched nerve." Only when David was back in New York on July 8 did his U.S. publicist announce that he had undergone emergency angioplasty for a blocked artery. Two days later, press reports quoted a tour insider who asserted that David had suffered a heart attack backstage and had undergone surgery the night of his collapse: "The heart surgery wasn't routine. It was a lot more serious than anyone is letting on." David's friends would later be told that the procedure involved stents—springlike mesh tubes that are fitted inside an artery to keep it open—a less-invasive alternative to coronary bypass surgery and that happened to be a specialty of the Klinik St. Georg in Hamburg, where he'd been rushed after the Scheesel show.

On July 28, David was photographed walking around the

streets of New York City's Chinatown. Wearing a Stetson and a green T-shirt, he shook hands with well-wishers, then stepped into a health-food shop to stock up on tea and a variety of ancient Chinese remedies. One year later, Iman told friends that David was still busy with writing and recording: "We're not retiring people," she said.

EPILOGUE

The Houdini Mechanism

*The thing I remember was a sense of wanting to escape: to
parachute out, to find a strategy that would give a glorious exit.
That was what he was looking for. A stunning escape
mechanism—a Houdini escape from pop stardom.*

—Julien Temple

Wasn't he brave? To do what he did?

—George Underwood

Aliens are immortal; that was what fans continued to
believe in the months that followed David's heart attack,
months punctuated by tantalizing glimpses of the man
in the audience for shows by Gail Ann Dorsey and Arcade Fire
and at the occasional red-carpet event. It was more than a year
later, September 8, 2005, before David stepped once more into the
limelight, an event fraught with nerves, emotion, and warmth.

The rehearsal for the Condé Nast Fashion Rocks show, organized in aid of the Hurricane Katrina victims, was nerve-racking.
Bowie had not met up with Mike Garson, his sole accompanist,
until their rehearsal the afternoon of the show. Various performers and crew were busy around Radio City Music Hall; then, as

Garson rippled into the opening chords at the rehearsal, he noticed, "Everybody who was performing that night was listening—you could hear a pin drop." "Life on Mars," the song that had been gifted to the twenty-three-year-old Bowie on the bus to Lewisham, sounded radically different from any previous version.

Garson had first played the song with David at his New York debut thirty-two years earlier, but at the Fashion Rocks performance that evening, he was more nervous than he could ever remember being, his feet and knees shaking as he sat down at the grand piano and Alicia Keys announced, "My good friend David Bowie." The key of the song had been shifted all the way down from F to B; the new key was tricky, unfamiliar, "and if I screwed up, it would almost inevitably make him screw up. There was no one else to cover up. No safety net."

David was even more tentative; he was out of practice, almost a little scared. "You have a heart problem, you've got to be wondering to yourself, Am I gonna drop dead onstage?" says Garson. "Anything could go through the mind—you've had a rough period, you don't know if that's gonna happen again." Yet as Bowie settled slowly into the song in front of an enthralled audience, there was something magical about the moment for Garson: The fact that their rendition was on the edge and vulnerable gave it a new depth. "It was poignant and nostalgic. It was magical—one of the deepest things we've done, with factors that go beyond the laws of music, rhythm, harmony, melody, and intonation and all that. It was a deeper thing. Almost more of a spiritual experience."

The sight of David walking up to the mike stand and then nervously clutching it, almost as if for comfort, was affecting and—as the camera panned to show him wearing high-water pants, with a bandaged wrist and what looked like a black eye—faintly ludicrous. With the key at which David sang lowered by half an octave, there was a sense of the changing of the seasons from spring to fall. The song had originally been delivered by a young buck, a snotty challenge to Sinatra. Tonight, even in the lower key, that glorious octave leap up to "Mars" that had launched a career was no longer effortless and transcendent; it spoke of pain. David

Bowie was not facing down the Chairman of the Board; he was following in his footsteps. "He came out as a mature singer that night, like Tony Bennett or Frank Sinatra, someone with presence. A gentleman in his fifties who was not about to try and do something that a twenty-year-old would. It was phenomenal," says Garson.

There were countless resonances in those moments. The high-water pants, the bandage, and the black-eye makeup reflected many ludicrous outfits of the past. Yet its reference to Louisiana's flooded, battered state also reached back to the aura around New Orleans, where Little Richard had recorded those first songs that electrified the boy from Bromley. In the flicker of doubt so plainly evident as he hit the high note on "Mars"—or what was once a high note—it became obvious this was a great, profound Bowie performance. It was the first in years that boasted the on-the-edge danger—the omnipresent fear that "it could have fallen apart," as Garson puts it—that had characterized his career.

Yet it was also the first David Bowie performance in which the boyish radiance, the charisma that had so entranced Ken Pitt during Bowie's rendition of a Judy Garland song in 1965, had plainly faded away. That radiance had become a platform on which a mediocre musician had built his acknowledged genius. Now, as he sang the haunting melody that marked his debut as a great songwriter, all most people noticed was the fragility of his voice and the solidity of his frame.

The spectacle of David Bowie, older gentleman, was one that his fans found hard to contemplate. Over subsequent days and months, as still photos and then videos—the kind of view behind the gilded curtain that would have been unthinkable in the Main-Man era—spread around the World Wide Web, the fans' reaction ranged from affection and sympathy to horror and ridicule. "He's a mess" was one of the kinder opinions. "He looks a bit...dead," stated YouTube commenter Lindadox before adding insult to injury: "[And] the hair isn't quite working for him."

OVER the course of the next year, occasional flurries of activity encouraged some observers to liken this quiet period to the pregnant pause that followed *Scary Monsters*. There were more guest appearances; "(She Can) Do That," cowritten with trance pioneer Brian Transeau for the abysmal *Top Gun*–wannabe movie *Stealth;* a guest vocal on Kashmir's "The Cynic"; plus backup vocals for TV on the Radio, the Brooklyn band that over 2005 and 2006 would notice his appreciative, expensively suited presence at the side of the stage for every show in New York City. Then in September, David guested on Courtney Pine's BBC Radio 2 show, and when the saxophonist asked David if he was working on a project, he told him, "Yeah, I've started writing already and...er...it looks pretty weird, so I'm happy." A few weeks later he signed up to play Nikola Tesla, his finest movie role in years, for Christopher Nolan's *The Prestige*, which depicted two rival magicians, each obsessed with staging the most glamorous, shocking disappearing act.

Still, the next major outing was not until 2006, in a tribute to Britain's most celebrated, most reclusive rock casualty, Syd Barrett. David Gilmour was playing London's Albert Hall on May 29 and had just sailed through a complete performance of his recent soft-rock solo album *On an Island* when the audience members were jarred out of their slumbers with the words "I'd like to announce Mr. David Bowie!" Syd's famous fan—elegantly dressed, spookily reminiscent of actor John Hurt—paused momentarily at the rapturous applause and almost shyly murmured the words, "I hope I warrant that." For the crowd, it was an "extraordinary, unexpected, real pinch-yourself moment," according to audience member Ian Gittins. There were nostalgic flashes of that London voice—"almost East End"—whose whimsy, style, and above all Englishness had been inspired by the Pink Floyd singer. At the end of the year, their version of "Arnold Layne" was released on single and download and would crack the UK Top 20.

Yet during the weeks that the news and photos of David's appearance at Albert Hall spread, so did quotes from an off-the-cuff exchange at a *Vanity Fair* party that same month: "I'm fed up with the industry," he told Jada Yuan. "And I've been fed up for quite some time...Just don't participate. I'm taking a year off— no touring, no albums. I go for a walk every morning, and I watch a ton of movies. One day, I watched three Woody Allen movies in a row." On June 5 came the news that Bowie would guest on what turned out to be a hilarious episode of comedian Ricky Gervais's *Extras*. Gervais's humor had always traded on embarrassment, the agonizing silence that follows an attempted joke or insight; here, Bowie brilliantly parodies his own image as a stony-faced manipulator, mercilessly mocking the "little fat man" who attempts to bond with him, recruiting the crowd around him for a sing-along. "Little Fat Man (with the Pug-Nosed Face)" would be the most significant new Bowie song of an entire half a decade. Distressingly, fans noted, David seemed to confine himself to walk-on roles, with the occasional appearance at a fashion-related event, and another tantalizing guest spot at New York City's Black Ball benefit that November, again backed by Mike Garson and duetting with Alicia Keys on "Changes."

Even David's virtual appearances were becoming infrequent. Since 2005, the updates in his BowieNet journal had become more desultory; on October 5, 2006, David Bowie penned the most enthusiastic entry in years: "Yesterday I got to be a character on—tan-tara—*SpongeBob SquarePants*. We, the family, are thrilled. Nothing else need happen this year, well, this week anyway." And nothing else did. For in January of 2007 came the news that a live date that was to close a Bowie-curated High Line Festival the following May had been quietly canceled. In place of the Bowie show was a live rendition of "Little Fat Man" with Ricky Gervais and then...nothing.

As David Bowie disappeared from the music scene, the interpretation that this was the calm before a new burst of activity was natural, given what had been a prodigious work rate in the previous forty years. The off-the-cuff remark—"Just don't participate"—surely represented a passing disenchantment. The prospect of a permanent retirement seemed unthinkable—except that retirement was an option for which David had been longing for at least twenty years.

It was in the lull after *Tonight* that Bowie had first shared a yearning for escape with director Julien Temple, who points out: "He does always appear very vibed up. But maybe he's not underneath."

Over that period Temple had accompanied the singer to Brixton Carnival, watching his minders clearing a path ahead of him, witnessing the problems of "that bubble life." Having seen David work over three separate phases of his career, the director understood that the biggest problem David had to contend with was the "grueling nature of reinvention. The huge creative surge required to do that again and again. It takes its toll, psychically—and that's beyond the normal clichés of fame. The pressures of stardom do take their toll—even on David, who may not appear as overwhelmed by them as others."

About their conversations over 1987 and 1989, Temple said, "The thing I remember was a sense of wanting to escape: to parachute out, to find a strategy that would give a glorious exit. That was what he was looking for. A stunning escape mechanism—a Houdini escape from pop stardom."

Over those years, of course, Bowie's career was sliding in a downward creative spiral. The reception of *Never Let Me Down* and the debacle of the Glass Spider tour had delayed Bowie's fantasy Houdini escape.

For well over a decade, at least part of David Bowie had been seeking to make that glorious exit; that one grandiose explosion behind which he could disappear. Ultimately, mortality provided its own, less glamorous escape mechanism. And as one of David's friends points out, "If you were in hospital after a heart scare, would you be wishing you'd spent more time flogging yourself on tour? Or would you be wishing you could spend more time with your five-year-old?"

IN the meantime, those around David moved on. Today, Coco is back from California, and she works with David fairly closely once more. Having devoted decades of her life to caring for him, her duties are now less stressful. She has time to walk around Manhattan, with a dog to keep her company.

Iggy Pop reunited with his Stooges to be feted at festivals around the world, but by the late 1990s David had lost touch with the man who, more than anyone, had benefited from his help. Asked about their friendship by writer Robert Phoenix, David acknowledged, "I probably shouldn't talk about it," while admitting that "we have drifted away from each other." The problem was a simple clash of egos: "Jimmy," he said, had come to resent the fact that "he couldn't do a fucking article without my name being mentioned." Over recent years, Iggy repaired his relationships with Stooges' guitarists Ron Asheton and James Williamson, with whom he had fallen out spectacularly. Yet there is still a certain reserve when he discusses David, a man with whom he was indisputably closer. According to one mutual friend of the two, "I think in any close friendship you can use the word *love*— and in many friendships you'll see that one person loves the other more than the other loves him or her. I believe David loved Jim more than Jim loved David. And in the end, I think Jim found he could manage without him." Three months younger than David, Iggy continues to tour with the reformed Stooges. He looks frail in person, with a noticeable limp, but still hits the stage with the joyous energy of a spring lamb.

The career of Tony Defries, the man who benefited the most from Bowie's success, was as eventful as that of his onetime employee. After falling out with his next management charge, John "Cougar" Mellencamp, Defries steered the troubled early career of Sandy Dillon, was involved in inconclusive negotiations to manage Madonna, invested in a steel plant, and recently claimed to have patented a new means of converting solar energy into electricity. In August of 2007, he announced the imminent publication of an autobiography, but six months later the book was abandoned as news leaked out that Defries had lost twenty-two million dollars in a Cayman Islands tax shelter set up by the Swiss bank Julius Baer. That spring, the IRS started tracing Defries's contacts, investigating whether he'd paid taxes on the huge sum; over the same period, lawyers working for Griffin, to whom he'd sold the rights for several Bowie rarity and live albums in the early

1990s, were in pursuit, as rumors spread that the Svengali had abandoned his estate in Virginia and disappeared to Europe. In 2009, he appeared to have resolved any disputes with the tax authorities and returned to the United States, but the twenty-two million dollars, a huge proportion of the money David Bowie had paid to reclaim the most fertile period of his creativity, had disappeared forever.

More repercussions of the troubled relationship between Bowie and MainMan rumbled on. In 2009, five years after Bowie bonds were downgraded by credit rating agency Moody's, headlines around the world read "Is Bowie to Blame for the Credit Crunch?" BBC journalist Evan Davis claimed the global financial meltdown was caused by bankers who took their cues from David Bowie; seeing him securitize his future income, they followed his lead with their mortgage business, with disastrous results (subsequently, other financial experts surfaced to ridicule the charge). Bowie's own financial fortunes are thought to have declined gently in the recession. In 1997, *Business Age* magazine estimated his wealth at $917 million; this is regarded by most financial experts as an exaggeration. A recent report by the *Sunday Times* puts his wealth at £100 million (approximately $165 million). In 2012, his back catalog will be available for license once more, and many fans hope to see what is thought to be the most intriguing set of unreleased recordings of audio and video outtakes of any major recording artist.

Yet in the early years of the twenty-first century, there was one person in David Bowie's life whose career was taking shape even as David Bowie let his own lie fallow. In November of 2004, Duncan Jones painstakingly re-created the England of 1979 — a world he had known only briefly — for a commercial celebrating the twenty-fifth anniversary of McCain's oven chips. His first press interview didn't even mention his father's identity. After he was recruited by ad guru Trevor Beattie and attracted the gimlet-eye glare of the *Daily Mail* for the "lesbian kiss outrage" of his 2006 TV commercial for the fashion brand FCUK, a few reports mentioned his parentage. Then in 2009, Duncan Jones elegantly stepped out into the world's media to publicize his thoughtful, lovingly crafted debut movie, *Moon*.

Duncan's interviews provided a revealing insight into the life of David Bowie, father. There were stories of how they'd worked on stop-frame animation together, and of David's bringing home bootleg videos of *Star Wars*. There was also evidence of how David had kept a tasteful distance to avoid overshadowing his son (Bill Zysblat, David's business manager, was credited as executive producer on the film, but there was no mention of Mr. Jones Senior). It is probably unfair to note the presence of the words *I think* in Duncan's description of his upbringing: "I think we always loved each other, but he was travelling and working a lot, and I was in his custody, so it was...tricky, because obviously there were people who would look after me, but a lot of the time he might not be around. So it was an unusual relationship."

David had often voiced his guilt over his son's unsettled childhood, but there was some vindication of the way he'd nudged his son toward the cinema in the overwhelming positive reaction to *Moon*, which was made with the unthinkably tiny budget of five million dollars, grossed six million in the first nine weeks of release, and picked up two international awards before clinching Duncan a BAFTA for most promising newcomer in February of 2010. Jones politely dismissed suggestions that his modest science fiction gem had been influenced by his dad's "Space Oddity" (or, indeed, Kubrick's *2001*), citing instead later influences such as *Silent Running* and *Blade Runner*. But there was plenty of resonance with his father's work. The isolation and loneliness of *Moon*'s sole protagonist, Sam Bell, evokes the lonely childhood of Duncan Jones and the isolation of his father. More profoundly, Bell takes solace in creating a church out of balsa, an image that echoed Merrick's cardboard church and the "cathedral made of matchsticks" that David had extolled in one of his *Heathen* interviews as a symbol of the British amateur tradition — that compulsion to perfect a job whether or not anyone will see it. Lastly, Bell is imprisoned in a cycle of rebirth, wearing out each new manifestation of himself until finally he manages to achieve, as Bowie never did, his "Houdini escape."

David's appearance with Duncan at the Sundance Film Festival on January 23, 2009, was a surprise event, fleeting but perfectly timed; remaining in front of the camera long enough to ensure a flurry of press for the movie, David dressed in gray and let his son do the talking. At a Q & A after the screening, Duncan thanked his father for giving him "the time to work out what I wanted to do — because it's taken me a while."

Other than an appearance alongside Iman for *Moon*'s debut at the Tribeca Film Festival in April, this was Bowie's only media outing of the year. In 2010, Iman generally appeared on red carpets solo, although David turned up in a tux and black scarf for his wife's acceptance of her Council of Fashion Designers of America Fashion Icon award. And every few months there would be a new reissue: the DVD based on his VH1 *Storytellers* appearance, ten years after it was recorded; a fortieth-anniversary edition of the *Space Oddity* album, complete with an iPhone app that allowed fans to mix their own versions of David's debut hit.

For the fans, Bowie's continuing absence seemed an almost unforgivable desertion. Day by day, fewer of them pay the sixty-dollar-a-year subscription fee for BowieNet, while the bowieart .com Web site closed down entirely in 2008. The faithful huddle together on the Net, their numbers diminishing. Despite the continuing reissues of his classic works, there was a growing consensus among fans and business figures that this man was not maintaining his work; that it was like a grand estate with weeds sprouting in the garden and paint flaking from the window frames. What could he possibly be doing that was more important than attending to them?

"IT is the wrong way round," says George Underwood as he pours coffee into a china mug decorated with one of his serene, slightly disturbing paintings and places a couple of lemon curd biscuits on a plate. Yesterday George celebrated his sixty-first birthday with the aid of a giant basket of Fortnum and Mason delicacies sent by his school friend and ex-bandmate. Today, we sip coffee and sample some of the goodies as George describes his 1958 trip to the Isle of Wight with a ukulele and a washboard bass in the back of the van. He talks about the cocky letters sent to millionaires and the times his best mates shot him looks "like daggers" because he'd scored his own record deal with Mickie Most, who groomed him for success, advising him on the music business and driving him around the West End in his Roller.

For many fellow pupils from Bromley and kids who'd hung around the King Bees, George—good-looking, outgoing—was the boy most likely to. Yet his career in music was impressive but short. After one single with Mickie Most, something happened: "I will never know what caused it, but the men in white coats came to take me away." Confined to Cane Hill for three months, he would never know if someone had slipped a tab of acid in his drink or if some other random stimulus triggered his breakdown. A promising career was over. It was, he says, "a blessing in disguise. Because I don't think I'd be sitting here talking to you. I would have said yes to everything—and ended up dead somewhere."

David, his friend once more, would eventually secure the success he craved. George, over the same period, established himself as an artist and illustrator, crafting dozens of record and book covers for David, Marc Bolan, Gentle Giant, and countless others. Today, sitting in his elegant, airy North London house, his artworks studded throughout like jewels, there is still a kind of wonder for what his friend achieved. Not for the money or the fame but simply: "Wasn't he brave? To do what he did?"

Yet with the admiration, there's a sense of what David missed out on: family, all the little tokens of which surround us, the photos, the well-worn objects that signal a well-worn life. For a moment, I feel pity for Underwood's friend. And then George mentions how David has lived his life "the wrong way round." How the twenty-year-old who loved kids is finally getting the chance to spend time with his own, as a sixty-one-year-old.

A few weeks later I find other old friends whom David has started calling again, telling them of his nine-year-old daughter, as if what she's up to is more interesting than his current business. Often he'll open a phone call by putting Lexi on the phone for a chat. As if there just might be a legacy more important than the hundreds of songs known to remain in the Bowie vault.

IN the meantime, the music is not static. Every new generation of musicians, whether aiming at the stadium or the college circuit, takes some part of Bowie's legacy as a template. As Ian McCulloch, a leader of the generation of musicians that followed Bowie in the 1970s, puts it, "He changed the face of music. And the world. Everybody's got mad hair or mad clothes now—when he kicked off in 1973 it was rare. I was twelve when 'Starman' came out, and it connected with me in a way that no other record ever had. I was still impressionable and naive—and at that moment I knew exactly what I wanted to do."

Generations since have experienced similar epiphanies. Bowie has been derided for billing himself as a cult artist, a seemingly ludicrous claim for someone who has scored so many Top 10 singles, yet there is a truth in this, for his music continues to speak to outsiders, to those who are either on the edge or wish to go there. For Charles Francis of Pixies, whose music would define the 1990s so-called alternative rock scene, it was the Bowie of *Low*, *"Heroes,"* and *The Idiot* that called to him: "It was so brave." That sentiment occurs again and again: "He showed no fear," says Nicolas Godin of Air, who discovered the same trio of albums while training as an architect in Versailles; the French band's "humble" career was inspired by the example of how Bowie mixed electronics and rock, but Godin stresses that Bowie's influence goes far beyond this: "He's the total artist—the look, the voice, the talent to compose, the stage presence. The beauty. Nobody is like that anymore. Everybody is reachable; he was unreachable."

So many other artists have picked up on aspects of Bowie's work, from Madonna to Lady Gaga, Radiohead to Momus, the enigmatic Scots musician who laments that "I was lucky, as a teenager, to have someone like that to latch onto. Bowie wasn't just a rock star in the seventies—he was an exemplary creative animal. He took influences from so many sources: from Kabuki, from Jean Genet and William Burroughs, from the New York downtown art scene, from Die Brücke, and so on. Because of his influence, musicians could take their cue from other art forms. I saw an interview with him where he said he thought he might have been a good teacher if he hadn't been a rock star because he loves introducing people to cultural things and seeing their excitement. And I thought, Well, you've been both!"

Philip Glass, a composer, friend, and interpreter of Bowie, also laments what now seems like an all-too-brief period when popular music and experimentation coexisted. "What Bowie and Eno were trying to do was to redefine certain parameters in pop music. To work less in terms of formula and to work in a more experimental fashion. The idea was that pop music had an art form to it; it wasn't always commercial music, it didn't always have to be entertainment music, those people could work in another mode. It was this funny world of art-rock, which has since disappeared. But it was a beautiful moment for a while."

John Lennon, the man who acted almost as an elder brother to David Bowie, occasionally complained how the world always wanted more from his band. The Beatles made eleven albums together, he'd tell people: "What more could you want?" As David Bowie wanders around New York watching his daughter grow up, he's entitled to share Lennon's sentiment. Yet even those who worked with David in the past can't help joining in the fans' longing that once again this man will free the music that will otherwise stay locked within. "I'm waiting," says Mike Garson. "The magic is not in the air right now. We're in a little bit of a slump so maybe in a couple of years he'll start hearing the next thing."

Still, there remains the uncertainty of that elusive alchemy. Can the man who transformed himself perform that magic again?

"If he's not feeling it, who knows?" says Garson. "Sometimes an artist knows when to cool it. Why do something if you're not feeling it or hearing it? We'll see what's meant to be."

Discography

DAVID BOWIE

**

Recorded: November 1966–February 1967; Decca Studios, West Hampstead, London. Released: Deram, June 1, 1967. Chart Peak: Not on UK or US charts. Key Personnel: Derek "Dek" Fearnley (bs, arrangements); John Eager (dms); Derek Boyes (kbds, early songs only); plus session musicians unknown. Producer: Mike Vernon.

Nineteen-year-old David Bowie had bowled over Decca executives, who were convinced of his genius. This first studio album provides convincing evidence of the fact—in everything but the songs. The sheer breadth and ambition of the material—from the kooky sci-fi epic "We Are Hungry Men" to the earnest, Lionel Bart–ish "When I Live My Dream"; the playfully sinister "Uncle Arthur" to the disturbingly psychotic "Please Mr. Gravedigger" (which references the Myra Hindley murders)—is staggering, even today. His confidence in the studio was, in retrospect, astounding, but the young Bowie lacked the skills to realize his lofty ambitions and it's only the more conventional material, such as "When I Live My Dream" and the "The Laughing Gnome" single, that succeeds on its own terms. Although later derided, this quirky album established Bowie's reputation amid a small crowd of London faces. More crucially still, it gave him his first experience of using the studio like a giant sketch pad, a technique that would become fundamental to his career.

DAVID BOWIE

***

Also called *Space Oddity* (UK 1972 re-release); *Man of Words/Man of Music* (US). Recorded: June–September 1969; Trident Studios, London. Released: Philips/Mercury, November 1969. Chart Peak: 17 (UK), didn't make US charts. Key Personnel: Mick Wayne, Tim Renwick (gtr); John "Honk" Lodge (bs); John Cambridge (dms); Keith Christmas (acoustic gtr). Producer: Tony Visconti.

A failure of an album that betrayed its creator's lack of confidence, Bowie's second release was almost an afterthought to his breakthrough song, "Space Oddity," its style and song selections arranged by committee. Predictably, perhaps, it therefore never quite transcends its obvious influences and limitations to become a coherent statement in its own right. Yet in the larger context of David's career, it has many moments of charm, for the very reason that it is unconsidered and confused. "Letter to Hermione" is gorgeously gauche, while "Cygnet Committee" is a grandiose construction that shows David attempting to piece together a philosophy and style—and failing. Only "Space Oddity" truly transcends its intentions.

THE MAN WHO SOLD THE WORLD

****

Recorded: April–May 1970; Trident and Advision Studios, London. Released: Mercury, November 1970 (US); Philips, April 1971 (UK). Chart Peak: 26 (UK); 105 (US). Both on RCA re-release. Key Personnel: Mick Ronson (gtr); Tony Visconti (bs); Mick "Woody" Woodmansey (dms); Ralph Mace (Moog synthesizer). Producer: Tony Visconti.

Bowie's first truly gripping work, *The Man Who Sold the World* is dark in sound and tone. Crucially it took collaborators—fellow artists, even—to fashion David Bowie's sound for him, and engineer Ken Scott confirms that Tony Visconti and Mick Ronson labored on their own for much of the album. Yet, for all that, the spark that fires up this album was Bowie's: In framing the concept and delegating crucial tasks, he inspired his collaborators to surpass anything they achieved on their own (the work of Ronson, Visconti, and Woodmansey as Ronno would be famously dull). However erratic David's involvement, the album's sense of unease—the disturbing unreality of the title track, the twisting visions of "Width of a Circle," the childlike empathy of "All the Madmen"—derives entirely from Bowie, who seems most himself when he relies most on others.

HUNKY DORY

*****

Recorded: July 1971; Trident Studios, London. Released: RCA, December 1971. Chart Peak: 3 (UK); 93 (US). Key Personnel: Mick Ronson (gtr); Trevor Bolder (bs); Mick "Woody" Woodmansey (dms); Rick Wakeman (pno). Producers: Ken Scott and David Bowie.

The opening salvo of the majestic trio of albums that launched the Bowie legend was understated compared to its successors. While there were plenty of out-there moments—the campiness of "Queen Bitch," the louche tribute to Andy Warhol, and the enigmatic "The Bewlay Brothers"—overall, *Hunky Dory*'s appeal was subtle, deriving mainly from the faultless effervescence of the writing. Above all, there is an infectious love of life and a sure-footed sense of destiny: "Oh! You

Pretty Things" slogan—"make way for the *Homo superior*"—is self-aggrandizing, a campy joke and a manifesto for a kooky philosophy. *Hunky Dory* is as crucial a part of Bowie's cultural legacy as its better-known successor, for where *Ziggy* essentially involved donning a quilted catsuit, *Hunky Dory* was based on self-transformation and positive visualization. *Ziggy*'s songs are skilled and knowing, *Hunky Dory*'s are translucently innocent and effortless: "Oh! You Pretty Things" was inspired by a dream; "Life on Mars" arrived on a bus trip to Lewisham; "Kooks" was arranged and recorded within days of Duncan's birth. The arrangement and playing, too, is instinctive but faultless, the product both of Mick Ronson's unrivaled musicality and of Bowie's motivational skills. The tributes to Warhol, Dylan, and Lou Reed are both naive and cynical; by paying them fealty, Bowie also gives himself license to assimilate them. Lastly, "Changes" would be the manifesto that energized Bowie and all around him; matching a luscious McCartney-style melody with a powerful Lennon-style message, it would only graze the charts but, crucially, would energize a tiny group of believers, who helped their golden boy ascend to fame over the months that followed.

THE RISE AND FALL OF ZIGGY STARDUST AND THE SPIDERS FROM MARS

*****

Recorded: November 1971–January 1972; Trident Studios, London. Released: RCA, June 1972. Chart Peak: 5 (UK); 75 (US). Key Personnel: Mick Ronson (gtr); Tony Visconti (bs); Trevor Bolder (bs); Mick "Woody" Woodmansey (dms). Producers: Ken Scott and David Bowie.

If *Hunky Dory* came from the heart, *Ziggy* came from the head. The constituent elements were being assembled as early as January 1971, when David wrote the magnificent, pile-driving "Moonage Daydream" a few days after hearing his first Iggy record. Other crucial blocks were hoisted into place right up to the final days of recording, with the breakthrough single "Starman" written well into the sessions. Inspired by Iggy and fifties rocker Vince Taylor, *Ziggy* was rather polite in comparison; its songs more precise and both delivery and production arguably overrefined. (Only the Santa Monica bootleg, an underrated influence on seventies punk that was officially released in 2008, demonstrates the power of the Spiders in their prime.) Instead, it's the drama of the ideas that give the album its power, opening and closing with two magnificent ballads, "Five Years" and "Rock 'n' Roll Suicide," and taking the listener on an exhausting emotional roller coaster in between. The songs function perfectly as rock and roll, with Mick Ronson's guitar the electricity that brings each finely crafted chord sequence to life, so perfectly that they'd inspire a generation of rock bands—even Iggy and his Stooges, who lifted the "Suffragette City" central chord change for their punk anthem "Search and Destroy." Yet they also stand apart from rock and roll, which gives them a wider power, for *Ziggy* works overall as a drama that demands suspension of disbelief from each of us and hence makes us all participants. Even today, it's a thrill to be part of the action.

ALADDIN SANE

*****

Recorded: October 1972; RCA, NYC, December 1972 and January 1973; Trident, London. Released: RCA, April 1973. Chart Peak: 1 (UK), 17 (US). Key Personnel: Mick Ronson (gtr); Trevor Bolder (bs); Mick "Woody" Woodmansey (dms); Mike Garson (pno); Ken Fordham, Brian Wilshaw (sax). Producers: Ken Scott and David Bowie.

Both slicker and sketchier than its predecessor, *Aladdin Sane* is in some ways a more convincing document on the nature of fame and show business than *Ziggy*—its flakiness adds authenticity. The strained, edgy cover of "Let's Spend the Night Together" is shallow, yet glamorous; "The Jean Genie," too, is outrageously slick, a magnificently flagrant rip-off of the Yardbirds. Yet the album's great songs are cavernous in their depth, with Mike Garson's rippling piano evoking decadence or oblivion in haunting songs like "Aladdin Sane" and "Time," while Ronson and Bolder's musicianship is devastatingly sophisticated, most notably on "Lady Grinning Soul." The personal dramas being played out add to the edginess: "The Prettiest Star" is a restatement of David's paean to Angie, recorded just as he decided his marriage was doomed, while arguments over Woody's drumming on "Panic in Detroit" helped inspire the termination of the Spiders just as they were at their peak.

PIN UPS

**

Recorded: July–August 1973; Château d'Hérouville, Paris. Released: RCA, October 1973. Chart Peak: 1 (UK); 23 (US). Key Personnel: Mick Ronson (gtr, etc.); Trevor Bolder (bs); Aynsley Dunbar (dms); Mike Garson (pno); Ken Fordham (sax); Geoff MacCormack (perc, backup vox). Producers: Ken Scott and David Bowie.

Recorded in a race to beat Bryan Ferry's covers album, *Pin Ups* was an odd blend of nostalgia and cynicism. Mick Ronson had mixed feelings about his imminent solo career, Trevor Bolder and Ken Scott were completely estranged, while David affected indifference to the power struggles around him. *Pin Ups* was therefore nostalgic not only for the good times of sixties London (some of it seen through the eyes of the Yank—Scott Richardson—who helped choose the tracks), but for the Spiders themselves. The album is both a Warholian display of appropriation—featuring songs like the Who's "Anyway, Anyhow, Anywhere," which Bowie had already used once with the Lower Third—and a demonstration of Bowie the unabashed fan. For Americans, the album represented a brilliantly decadent collection of garage-band nuggets; for many Brits, the covers were predictable, insipid, and watered down, with the frenzied teenage angst of songs like the Easybeats' "Friday on My Mind" reworked into turgid, platform-booted camp. Unashamedly exploitative, intermittently vital, the album fell well short of brilliance except in one respect: It was a devastating "so what?" riposte to those who claimed that Bowie's music was merely a cynical reworking of the music of the Who, the Kinks, and the Yardbirds.

DIAMOND DOGS

****

Recorded: December 1973–January 1974; Olympic Studios, London and Studio L, Hilversum, the Netherlands. Released: RCA, April 1974. Chart Peak: 1 (UK); 5 (US). Key Personnel: Herbie Flowers (bs); David Bowie, Alan Parker (gtr); Aynsley Dunbar, Tony Newman (dms); Producer: David Bowie (Tony Visconti oversaw mix).

Bowie's depiction of a future dystopia was messy and sprawling, inspired by George Orwell's *1984*, but also permeated with the paranoia now besetting his friends and colleagues. Previous sessions had been focused and compact; *Diamond Dogs*—once the nucleus had been assembled around Blue Mink musicians Flowers, Parker, and Newman—was confused, with overdubs layered on messily and Spiders' bassist Trevor Bolder called in (perhaps out of desperation) to help salvage one song. Bowie's songwriting changed too; the melodic inventiveness and rolling chord sequences he'd first harnessed on *Hunky Dory* disappeared, and instead there was a new concentration on texture, simple rock chord sequences, and swaggering rhythms heavily influenced by the Rolling Stones, whom Bowie aimed to knock off their pedestal. Adding to the mess, there was confusion about the credits, and the catchy "Rebel Rebel" stands out like a sore thumb alongside the resonant "Sweet Thing" and the bizarre, hellish funk of "1984." Overall, the album is a beautiful mess, its confused melee every bit as appropriate as *Ziggy*'s finely honed choreography.

DAVID LIVE

*

Recorded: July 8–12, 1974; Tower Theatre, Philadelphia, PA. Released: RCA, October 1974. Chart Peak: 2 (UK); 8 (US). Key Personnel: Earl Slick (gtr); Mike Garson (pno); Herbie Flowers (bs); Tony Newman (dms); David Sanborn (sax); Richard Grando (baritone sax); Pablo Rosario (perc); Geoff MacCormack, Gui Andrisano (backup vox). Producer: Tony Visconti.

The old-school showbiz element of Bowie's career was never more evident than in MainMan's revival of the neglected tradition of covers and live albums, designed primarily to keep the corporate presses rolling. Widely lambasted on release, *David Live* does indeed show his music coarsened, with overcooked backing and over-emoted singing replacing the electrifying joy of, say, the Spiders' Santa Monica bootleg. The album is not totally devoid of charm—Sanborn's sax interlacing with the "All the Young Dudes" chorus; the shuffling undercurrent of drums and bass on "Rebel Rebel"—but the album highlight, "Here Today, Gone Tomorrow," is perhaps the ultimate indictment. In this setting, it sounds stripped down and affecting, but one listen to the Ohio Players' jewel-like original reminds us how lumpen the Bowie machine has become.

YOUNG AMERICANS

****

Recorded: August 1974; Sigma Sound, Philadelphia, PA, and January 1975; Electric Lady, NYC. Released: RCA, March 1975. Chart Peak: 2 (UK); 9 (US). Key Personnel: Carlos Alomar (gtr); Willie Weeks (bs); Andy Newmark (dms); Mike Garson (pno); David Sanborn (sax); Larry Washington (conga); Pablo Rosario (perc); Ava Cherry, Luther Vandross, Robin Clark, Anthony Hinton, Diane Sumler, Geoff MacCormack (backing vox). "Fame" and "Across the Universe" musicians include Earl Slick, John Lennon (gtr); Emir Kassan (bs); Dennis Davis (dms). Producer: Tony Visconti.

The commercial success of *Young Americans* was so overwhelming, the stylistic makeover so complete, that it has become a set piece, an exemplar of an artist often viewed as manipulative or cold-blooded. Yet the opposite is the case: The genesis of *Young Americans* was instinctive, born of a fan's enthusiasm, and the album was recorded on the hoof, like the material that inspired it. The rushed recording adds an edge and adrenaline readily audible on the title track, a splicing of brittle funk with Springsteen-style lyrical imagery that given more gloss would have sounded trite. "Can You Hear Me?" and "Fascination," too, are entrancing, sketched out quickly. The album's high and low points were similarly rushed. "Fame," recorded in New York, is an impressionistic assemblage that, with its unvarying central chord sequence and riff adapted from the Rascals' "Jungle Walk," anticipated the sampling culture of the eighties and nineties; "Across the Universe," the other last-minute addition, is a cloying example of Bowie's new, over-emoted yodeling singing style, partly inspired by Bryan Ferry; worse, it bumped off "It's Gonna Be Me"—a superb showpiece for Bowie's voice. Sketchy and inconsistent from today's perspective, the album in 1975 restored the momentum lost by the unconvincing *David Live*, while the impressionistic working methods pioneered here would underpin Bowie's career through the rest of the decade—and more.

STATION TO STATION

*****

Recorded: November 1975; Cherokee and Record Plant Studios, Los Angeles, CA. Released: RCA, January 1976. Chart Peak: 5 (UK); 3 (US). Key Personnel: Carlos Alomar, Earl Slick (gtr); Dennis Davis (dms); George Murray (bs); Roy Bittan (pno); Geoff MacCormack (backup vox). Producers: David Bowie and Harry Maslin.

The key turning point in Bowie's recording career, *Station to Station* marked the transition from conventional songs written on the piano or guitar and recorded at breakneck speed to slabs of sound constructed entirely in the studio. Even those songs sketched out before Bowie arrived at Cherokee, such as "Golden Years," were transformed within it—all of its key elements worked up while the studio clock was running. Most accounts depict Bowie undergoing some kind of cocaine-induced breakdown at the end of 1975; his psychological trauma was indeed extreme, but during the sessions even drug buddies like Glenn Hughes noted he was in full command of the studio. Given that Bowie himself has little memory of this time, we will never get a more coherent picture of his mental state than in the contents of this album. The title track is obsessive, megalomaniacal, yearning for spiritual clarity yet oddly muso (the churning rhythms and heavy textures were inspired by Jethro Tull); the catchy, mildly deranged "TVC 15"—its vocal interjections obviously influenced by the Yardbirds' "Good Morning Little Schoolgirl"—was a comic take on Bowie's recent months spent watching grainy World War II footage over and over; while the magnificent, sensitive "Golden Years" also reflects Bowie's ability to surface from a cocaine jag and dispense insightful career advice or relate a hilariously deadpan joke. Although the melodicism of *Hunky Dory* was a thing of the past, *Station to Station* is packed with invention—a bizarre blend of spritely and monumental themes—and marks the point at which David Bowie moved from pop musician to phenomenon.

Low

*****

Recorded: September–early October 1976; Château d'Hérouville, Paris. Overdubbed and mixed Hansa Studio 2, Berlin. Released: RCA, January 1977. Chart Peak: 2 (UK); 11 (US). Key Personnel: Brian Eno (vocals, kbds, and treatments); Carlos Alomar, Ricky Gardiner (gtr); Dennis Davis (dms); George Murray (bs); Roy Young (pno, organ). Producers: David Bowie and Tony Visconti.

Its title was a reference to both being low profile and David's mental state— he was beset by marital and management problems. Yet those troubles were offset by the thrill of a new beginning, and an album that was dismissed by many on release as inaccessible stands today as joyous, uplifting, and optimistic. The glacial beauty of Brian Eno's EMS synthesizer, which dominates side two, is balanced by the zest and humanity of side one. Bowie's voice is rendered naked and unaffected, with many songs enlivened by distinct soul references—for instance, the melody from "Stand By Me" that echoes "Always Crashing in the Same Car." As if to help orient the listener, the album follows an impeccable internal logic: Concise, up-tempo instrumentals bookend side one, which is chock-full of catchy melodies and rhythms, to contrast with the icy languor of side two. As Bowie intended, this is great art, but it's great pop music too.

"Heroes"

*****

Recorded: May 1977; Hansa Studio 2, Berlin. Released: RCA, October 1977. Chart Peak: 3 (UK); 35 (US). Key Personnel: Carlos Alomar, Robert Fripp (gtr); Dennis Davis (dms); George Murray (bs); Brian Eno (synths, etc.). Producers: David Bowie and Tony Visconti.

The only album of Bowie's "Berlin trilogy" to be recorded entirely in the city—at Hansa's capacious Studio 2—"Heroes" was a tougher, heavier album than its predecessor, with chunkier rhythms overlaid by Robert Fripp's audacious guitar work, all recorded in two days flat. Bowie's lyrics and singing were freer, the most intuitive, improvised, and simple of his career. The songs were assembled in almost random fashion from odd snippets, then lovingly overlaid, with odd little melodies—a marimba here, a koto there—emerging on every new listen. Although the album is less funky and more Germanic than *Low*, the key figure alongside Bowie and Eno is Carlos Alomar, whose inventive, infectious guitar melodies underpin most of the songs—most notably the title track, where he powers the music on even as Robert Fripp's guitar soars above and Bowie's voice, totally without artifice, cranks up the emotional temperature. His simplest, most affecting, and most memorable song, the title track sounds timeless today but was out of time in 1977, only reaching number 24 on the UK singles charts.

STAGE

**

Recorded: April–May 1978; the Spectrum, Philadelphia, PA, Providence Civic Center, Providence, RI, and Boston Garden, Boston, MA. Released: RCA, September 1978. Chart Peak: 5 (UK); 44 (US). Key Personnel: Carlos Alomar, Adrian Belew (gtr); Dennis Davis (dms and perc); George Murray (bs); Simon House (vln); Sean Mayes (pno); Roger Powell (kbds and synth).

An impressive memento of a challenging, innovative tour, *Stage* still sounds bravely unconventional today; its finest moments are, rather than the expected crowd-pleasers, the glacial and uncompromising "Warszawa" and the spiky, off-kilter "Breaking Glass." In isolation, the Ziggy-era tracks falter, sorely lacking the muscularity of the original versions, but Bowie's voice, at least, is mostly flawless, undiminished.

LODGER

****

Recorded: September 1978 and March 1979; Mountain Recording Studios, Montreux, Switzerland, and Record Plant, NYC. Released: RCA, May 1979. Chart Peak: 4 (UK); 20 (US). Key Personnel: Carlos Alomar, Adrian Belew (gtr); Dennis Davis (dms); George Murray (bs); Brian Eno (synths, etc.);

Simon House (vln); Sean Mayes (pno); Roger Powell (synth). Producers: David Bowie and Tony Visconti.

Both more conventional and more intellectual than its predecessors, *Lodger* was the last of Bowie's Berlin trilogy (or triptych, as he termed it) but is distinct in both mood and method—and disappointing in comparison. The singing is mannered—self-conscious yelps on "Red Money," Bowie channeling David Byrne channeling Bowie on "DJ," and an alarmingly literal Scott Walker imitation on "Look Back in Anger"—the songs more conventional, and the recording process dryer, in every sense of the term. Still, once preconceptions are abandoned, the album is studded with delights. It's quirky rather than emotional, with delicious detailing: the fairground Arabic lilt of "Yassassin," the unassumingly romantic theme of "Fantastic Voyage," the constant tension between the plain, almost predictable chord sequences and the random guitar and vocal explosions scattered throughout. Although *Lodger* would never equal the emotional impact of *Low* or *"Heroes,"* it nonetheless defined the sound of eighties art rock, and echoes of its spiky, New Wave quirkiness can still be heard today.

Scary Monsters (and Super Creeps)

*****

Recorded: February 1980; Record Plant, NYC. April 1980; Good Earth, London. Released: RCA, September 1980. Chart Peak: 3 (UK); 12 (US). Key Personnel: Carlos Alomar, Robert Fripp (gtr); Chuck Hammer (synth gtr); Dennis Davis (dms); George Murray (bs); Roy Bittan (pno); plus Pete Townshend (gtr); Andy Clarke (synth). Producers: David Bowie and Tony Visconti.

Recorded during yet another frenzy of activity as Bowie re-explored New York and prepared for *The Elephant Man*, *Scary Monsters* was a kind of organized pop version of *Lodger*. The endless experimentation favored by Brian Eno was abandoned; instead, Bowie stalked the sessions with a clipboard, ticking off items on a to-do list for songs that were mostly sketched out in advance. The material was almost old-fashioned in Bowie terms: "Up the Hill Backwards" evokes both Bill Withers's "Lean on Me" and *Young Americans;* "Ashes to Ashes" features the old-school musical bridge ("the shriek of nothing is killing me") used in classic Bowie songs from the Lower Third's "Can't Help Thinking about Me" to "China Girl." Self-references abound; "Teenage Wildlife" addresses Bowie's influence on the world over the classic two-chord change of "'Heroes,'" while, of course, Major Tom pops up once more on "Ashes to Ashes"—an impossibly sophisticated assemblage adorned by the guitar synth of Chuck Hammer, who noted the almost telepathic bond between Bowie and Tony Visconti as they seized on musical ideas and honed the sound intuitively. The dense, tough, rock-meets-funk backup was hugely influential—listen to Blur, the Strokes, and dozens of art-rock bands for evidence—and represents Bowie's most versatile band ever at their very peak. A few months later, they'd all be looking for new jobs.

BAAL

****

Recorded: September 1981; Hansa Studio 2, Berlin. Released: RCA, February 1982. Chart Peak: 29 (UK); not on charts in US. Key Personnel: Dominic Muldowney (gtr, arrangements). Main backup comes from Berlin session musicians headed by percussionist Sherry Bertram. Producer: Tony Visconti.

The blinkered view of Bowie's career is that his last great album was *Scary Monsters*, yet this contract-filler—recorded in two rushed days in Berlin—is, in its own way, a masterpiece. The setting of Brecht's songs is small scale, almost domestic, with most of David's vocals dropped in during a single afternoon. The result is a master class in singing and an album that is always intriguing. One's first impression is that it's polite and formal, but on better acquaintance, the album is as great an evocation of Bowie's Berlin years as *"Heroes,"* for it preserves magnificently the last echoes of Brecht's adopted city.

LET'S DANCE

****

Recorded: December 1982; Power Station, NYC. Released: EMI, April 1983. Chart Peak: 1 (UK); 4 (US). Key Personnel: Stevie Ray Vaughan, Nile Rodgers (gtr); Carmine Rojas, Bernard Edwards (bs); Rob Sabino (kbds); Tony Thompson, Omar Hakim (dms). Producers: David Bowie and Nile Rodgers.

Vilified in the decades after its release, partly because it signaled the rise of mainstream Bowie, it is arguable that *Let's Dance* is one of his most underrated albums. It was certainly one of his most influential, for its luxurious, minimal sound, dominated by Tony Thompson's swinging drums, stripped-down R & B horns, and tough but exhibitionist guitar, would become a template for the late eighties. It's fair, too, to comment that it launched the era of form over function for Bowie, as well as his followers; with just eight tracks, including old collaborations with Iggy Pop and Giorgio Moroder and a cover of "Criminal World," written by arty New Wavers Metro, he was plainly short of good songs. But not of great ones, for the title track—which, according to producer Nile Rodgers, started life as a folksy Byrds-style ditty—and the impeccably infectious "Modern Love" were pinnacles of eighties pop. "China Girl," too, is a sumptuously pimped-out version of the dark, gothic original, completing the irresistible opening trio of songs that announced Bowie's ascension to the mainstream. Other songs—"Without You," "Ricochet," "Criminal World"—are assemblages of pleasant noises and pass the time nicely. "Shake It" is dull, and "Cat People" desecrates the memory of a Bowie classic—it was lost until exhumed by Tarantino for *Inglourious Basterds*. While not a Great Album, *Let's Dance* is at least a Great Eighties Album.

TONIGHT

*

Recorded: May–June 1984; Le Studio, Morin Heights, Canada. Released: EMI,
September 1984. Chart Peak: 1 (UK); 11 (US). Key Personnel: Carlos Alo-
mar (gtr); Derek Bramble (bs); Carmine Rojas (bs); Omar Hakim (dms).
Producers: David Bowie, Derek Bramble, and Hugh Padgham.

In retrospect, every failing of *Tonight* had been evident in Bowie's career to
date: a rushed recording, shameless lifting of ideas, overwrought vocals, undistinguished songs, and excessive reliance on sidemen. But on *Tonight,* they all
came together at once, a perfect storm of mediocrity. The prime example of
Tonight's failure is its best song, "Loving the Alien"; a decent, subtle tune, it also
represented a crucial loss of confidence, for whereas previously Bowie had
taken his stylistic cues from the underground, here he sources from the
mainstream—the chorused guitar sounds from the Police, the vocal "ah ah"s
from Laurie Anderson, and the marimbas from the Thompson Twins. The
Iggy songs were originally decent enough but were mostly reworked into leaden
white reggae. Worse still, the warbling vocal style, apparently influenced by
Bryan Ferry, plumbs new depths on "Tonight" and "God Only Knows," which,
with its clumsy, predictable arrangement, sounds like a pub singer hoping for
wedding and bar mitzvah jobs—two decades on, David had reinvented the
Kon-Rads. As one of his musicians once commented, David Bowie was known
for "stealing from the best." Now the self-proclaimed tasteful thief was pilloried
for taking something worthless.

NEVER LET ME DOWN

*

Recorded: Circa December 1986; Mountain Recording Studios, Montreux,
Switzerland, and Power Station, NYC. Released: EMI, April 1987. Chart
Peak: 6 (UK); 34 (US). Key Personnel: Carlos Alomar, Peter Frampton (gtr);
Erdal Kizilcay (bs, dms, kbds, etc.); Carmine Roja (bs); Philippe Saisse
(pno, kbds). Producers: David Bowie and David Richards.

For Bowie's career, preconceptions and received wisdom are often wrong;
however, the 1980s consensus that *Never Let Me Down* stinks still holds true
today. Bereft of inspiration, fantasizing of one last hit to provide a glorious exit,
Bowie abandoned the intuitive, impressionistic approach to recording he'd used
for a decade and prepared meticulously. Perhaps it was lack of confidence that
inspired his bizarre vocal mimicry—on the title song he copies John Lennon;
on "Day-In Day-Out" it's Prince; "Bang Bang" is a cover of Iggy Pop copying
Billy Idol, while the laughably slushy "Zeroes" sounds like a Michael Jackson
reject. Bowie had gone from "'Heroes'" to "Zeroes" in just a decade. More confused even than his Deram debut, the album was a strange throwback to David
Jones, the teenager who'd mimicked his idols for Shel Talmy. As with those

earliest efforts, the results were not so much awful as forgettable. The album seemed to indicate a man in the grip of a midlife crisis, adrift without talented sidemen—but for the fact that, over the same period, he'd bashed out superb songs for director Julien Temple and friend Iggy Pop.

Tin Machine

**

Recorded: August 1988–spring 1989; Mountain Recording Studios, Montreux, Switzerland, and Compass Point, Nassau, Bahamas. Released: EMI, May 1989. Chart Peak: 3 (UK); 28 (US).

Key Personnel: Reeves Gabrels (gtr); Tony Sales (bs); Hunt Sales (dms); Kevin Armstrong (gtr, kbds). Producers: Tin Machine and Tim Palmer.

Tin Machine's debut was greeted mostly with relief and enthusiasm by fans and critics, who were grateful for another album that, like *Low* and *Station to Station*, offered elements of challenge and mystery. The feelings of gratitude eventually evaporated, with the very same material criticized as pompous, dogmatic, and dull. The worst Tin Machine songs did indeed deserve that description—many were assemblages of blues clichés, while the cover of "Working Class Hero" is turgid and monotonous. All the same, some of the material was Bowie's best in years: "Prisoner of Love," obviously Pixies influenced, still sounds fresh today; "Run" is haunting despite its resemblance to "Don't Fear the Reaper"; and "I Can't Read" is simply spellbinding, Bowie's most emotionally affecting song of the decade. Outside of those gems, though, the album is hard to love—which was quite possibly Bowie's intention, for the band apparently worked on more commercial, memorable songs that never made the final edit, presumably because Tin Machine was designed primarily to implement a scorched-earth policy and wipe out everyone's memory of 1980s Bowie.

Tin Machine II

*

Recorded: October 1989 and March 1991; Studio 301, Sydney, and A&M, Los Angeles, CA. Released: Victory, September 1991. Chart Peak: 23 (UK); 126 (US). Key Personnel: Reeves Gabrels (gtr); Tony Sales (bs); Hunt Sales (dms). Producers: Tin Machine, Tim Palmer, and Hugh Padgham.

Released as the enthusiasm for the album *Tin Machine* was already fading outside of diehard fans, *Tin Machine II* exhibited exactly the same virtues and drawbacks as its predecessor's, each of them magnified. Most of the album was prosaic, predictable rock 'n' roll, and if people were bored by the bluesy jams of the first album, they could hardly be excited about hearing Hunt Sales, an excellent drummer, display his mediocre abilities as a singer—twice! "Goodbye Mr. Ed," however, was a beautiful song, destined to become a lost classic.

Black Tie White Noise

**

Recorded: 1992; Mountain Recording Studios, Montreux, Switzerland, and 38Fresh and Hit Factory, NYC. Released: Savage Records, April 1993. Chart Peak: 1 (UK); 39 (US). Key Personnel: Pugi Bell, Sterling Campbell (dms); Barry Campbell, John Regan (bs); Nile Rodgers (gtr); Richard Hilton, Philippe Saisse, Richard Tee (kbds); plus guests including Lester Bowie (tpt), Mick Ronson (gtr, "I Feel Free"), Mike Garson (pno, "Looking for Lester"). Producers: David Bowie and Nile Rodgers.

Bowie's most commercially successful album for years saw him being feted by a new generation of fans and featured on the cover of youth-oriented magazines alongside young guns like Britpop pioneers Suede. Songs like the tough, edgy "Jump They Say," devoted to his half brother, Terry, and the stripped-down, taut "Miracle Goodnight"—which featured the welcome return of Bowie on sax—further heightened the sense of renaissance. But there were plenty of cloying moments too, such as the cutesy "Don't Let Me Down & Down," featuring David singing in a kind of Brixton Caribbean patois, and the general overpolite, airbrushed sheen of the album meant that when it disappeared from the shelves following the bankruptcy of record label Savage, few bemoaned its passing.

The Buddha of Suburbia

****

Recorded: circa September 1993; Mountain Recording Studios, Montreux, Switzerland. Released: Universal, December 1993. Chart Peak: 87 (UK); didn't make US charts. Key Personnel: Erdal Kizilcay (gtr, bs, kbds, tpt, etc.); David Richards (programming, etc.); Mike Garson (pno); Lenny Kravitz (gtr). Producers: David Bowie and David Richards.

A rushed recording, assembled as an expanded version of the themes Bowie and multi-instrumentalist Erdal Kizilcay had conjured up for Hanif Kureishi's BBC film, *The Buddha of Suburbia* featured much the same collection of dance beats and melodies as *Black Tie White Noise*. It demonstrated what could be achieved by lack of time and lack of expectations, for it is throughout a far more gripping album than its predecessor. The title song is conventional—shimmering guitars and midpaced drum machine—but displays a beguiling simplicity long absent from Bowie's work; it's shot through with the loneliness of suburbia and kicks into action with a vintage, impassioned middle eight. Other songs—notably "Strangers When We Meet"—are his catchiest material in years, but never overblown, while there is experimentation aplenty in the form of grandiose and disturbing tracks such as "Sex and the Church" and "South Horizon," as well as the welcome return of pianist Mike Garson. Undoubtedly Bowie's best album in nearly a decade, it was given a low-key, belated release by Universal, limped out on to the schedules, and disappeared without trace.

1. Outside

***

Recorded: March–November 1994; Mountain Recording Studios, Montreux, Switzerland, and Westside Studios, London. January 1995; Hit Factory, NYC. Released: ISO/Virgin, September 1995. Chart Peak: 8 (UK); 21 (US). Key Personnel: Reeves Gabrels (gtr); Brian Eno (synths, treatments); Erdal Kizilcay (bs); Mike Garson (pno); Sterling Campbell (dms); plus Carlos Alomar, Kevin Armstrong (gtr), and Joey Barron (dms). Producers: David Bowie, Brian Eno, and David Richards.

Bowie's long-awaited reunion with Eno is a fascinating curator's egg, developed over drawn-out sessions that featured Bowie painting and the musicians each allotted bizarre roles, with much of the action filmed by underprivileged kids. It features the best of Bowie (the courage, the ability to spur musicians on to new creative heights) and the worst (overthinking, weighing his material down with too many ideas). The album is packed with significant songs—the hard-bitten, ominous "The Hearts Filthy Lesson," "Thru These Architect's Eyes," and "I Have Not Been to Oxford Town"—but as a musical experience it's hampered by a ludicrous voiceover and the sense that its maker was simply trying too hard.

Earthling

**

Recorded: 1996; Looking Glass Studios, NYC. Released: BMG, February 1997. Chart Peak: 6 (UK); 39 (US). Key Personnel: Reeves Gabrels (gtr, synth, programming); Mark Plati (programming, etc.); Mike Garson (pno); Gail Ann Dorsey (bs); Zachary Alford (dms, perc). Producers: David Bowie, Reeves Gabrels, and Mark Plati.

Bowie would be mocked as a "dad at the disco" for this collection of mostly drum and bass tracks, but there is a rush of excitement in the opening moments that banishes cynicism: "Little Wonder" features the return of cheeky, cockney Bowie, its agile, sweet melody perfectly offset by crunchy guitar and clattering drum machine; like *Outside*'s "Hallo Spaceboy," it's a classic that stands outside of style. But the trick soon wears thin. Despite some innovative structures, like the slightly loopy "Looking for Satellites," and ruthlessly efficient rock songs, like "Dead Man Walking," the album soon develops into a drearily repetitive loop, each chorus followed by two bars of chattering drums and then a heavy guitar riff. As a whole, the album is conservative and formulaic—even the self-referential title and Union Jack cover seem to indicate a jaded palate. Those faults would have been forgivable had the album been released two years earlier; its appearance just as the nineties drum and bass craze was subsiding suggested Bowie was content to surf on someone else's wave rather than make his own.

HOURS

**

Recorded: April 1999; Seaview Studios, Bermuda, and Looking Glass, NYC. Released: ISO/Virgin International, October 1999. Chart Peak: 5 (UK); 47 (US). Key Personnel: Reeves Gabrels (gtr); Mark Plati (bs); Mike Levesque and Sterling Campbell (dms); Holly Palmer (backup vox, "Thursday's Child"). Producers: David Bowie and Reeves Gabrels.

Refreshingly unadorned, sometimes hauntingly intimate, *Hours* abandoned the high-tech cut-and-paste of its predecessor for a production that was distinctly down-home—indeed, too much so, for the real David Bowie is surely to be found more in gloss and artifice than in dressed-down introspection. Although some material was thin—"What's Really Happening?," for instance, a collaboration with fan Alex Grant and featuring a melody lifted from "You Keep Me Hanging On"—songs like "Seven" and "Thursday's Child" were finely crafted; beautiful even. But the distinctive Bowie voice that he'd rediscovered on *Earthling* was gone, replaced mainly with a Nick Cave–ish throaty baritone. The third in a string of stylistic turnarounds, the album once again suggested a return to the teenage Bowie struggling to find a unique voice— and rather like *Space Oddity, Hours,* for all its finely crafted moments, ended up being less than the sum of its parts.

HEATHEN

****

Recorded: Mostly August–September 2001; Allaire Studios, NY, and Looking Glass Studios, NYC. Released: ISO/Columbia, June 2002. Chart Peak: 5 (UK); 14 (US). Key Personnel: Tony Visconti (bs); Matt Chamberlain (dms); David Torn (gtr); plus guests including Pete Townshend and Dave Grohl. Producers: David Bowie and Tony Visconti.

Bowie's long-awaited reunion with Tony Visconti was almost unassuming; gone were the intense sonic textures, overlayered production, and the sense that Bowie was trying too hard. In their place was simple, unassuming songwriting, clarity, and, above all, that wonderful voice, a glory pretty much absent since *Baal,* Bowie's last work with Tony Visconti. At the first listening, songs like "Slip Away" and "Everyone Says Hi" perhaps sound unadventurous, too tasteful and luxurious, with their smooth fretless bass and luscious strings—but they have that niggling sense of unease that draws the listener back in. "Sunday" and "Heathen," with their spiraling, disturbing instrumentation, are enchanting, intriguing dramas, showcasing the immense potential of Bowie's reunion with his best-known producer.

REALITY

***

Recorded: January 2003, Looking Glass Studios, NYC. Released: ISO/Columbia, September 2003. Chart Peak: 3 (UK); 29 (US). Key Personnel: Gerry Leonard, Earl Slick, David Torn (gtr); Mark Plati (bs); Sterling Campbell (dms); Mike Garson (pno). Producers: David Bowie and Tony Visconti.

Thirty years on from the albums that made his name, *Reality* shows Bowie as the consummate professional. The angst and paranoia is seemingly consigned to the past, in favor of a reassuringly familiar edginess: "Pablo Picasso" is, as one would guess, quintessential art rock, "The Modern Lovers" meets Bob Dylan; the throbbing "She'll Drive the Big Car" is vaguely reminiscent of "Ashes to Ashes"; "Days" is a conventional, confessional love song ("all you gave, you gave for free"). It's all intriguing but faintly familiar—the outsider has finally come in from the cold. Yet there is still darkness in this heart, above all on the magnificent "Bring Me the Disco King": Mike Garson's majestic piano echoes into the distance, Bowie's voice is foregrounded, more prominent than on any previous recordings, revealing new depths of experience and musicality. It holds out the intriguing prospect that, rather than simply revisiting his past, like so many of his peers, David Bowie has the potential to conjure up pleasures as yet unknown.

Notes and Sources

Unless specifically noted otherwise, all sources refer to the author's own interviews. A full list of interviewees follows at the end of this section. I've endeavored to acknowledge every significant quote and fact presented in this book; in time I will post more background information—deleted scenes, alternate takes, but hopefully no corrections—at www.trynka.com.

CHAPTER 1: When I'm Five

Opening paragraph is based on interview with Eric Schermerhorn. Description of Brixton draws on recollections from Roger Bolden, who lived at 7 Stansfield Road; David West; Linda Stagg; Sue Larner; Linda McCartney; Barbara Gray; Suzanne Goldschmitt; and Val Wilmer (who lived nearby in Streatham and would later become a key expert on Caribbean culture in Brixton). The problems for mothers attempting to buy nappies and candles around December 1947 were recorded by Florence Speed, Grace Golden, and Judy Haines for their Mass Observation diaries, and were quoted in David Kynaston's *Austerity Britain* (Bloomsbury, 2007), a superb depiction of this largely forgotten era, which was complemented by Dominic Sandbrook's *Never Had It So Good* (Abacus, 2006) and Peter Hennessy's *Having It So Good* (Allen Lane, 2006).

Information on the Jones family's tenure in Brixton comes from electoral records in Lambeth Archives. Background information on David's family comes from Ken Pitt's *Bowie: The Pitt Report*, and Peter and Leni Gillman's *Alias David Bowie*, both of which drew on interviews with Pat Antoniou; information on Haywood Jones's Barnardo's career was supplied by Dorothy Howes at the charity; helpful recollections of Peggy were provided by her friend Aubrey Goodchild.

Early Bromley and Burnt Ash memories: Max Batten, John Barrance, Richard Comben, Susan Hill, Gill Hymas, Jan Powling, Peter Prickett; ex–Bromley Tech pupils and friends who offered helpful insights include Mike Bassett, Chris Britton, Nick Brooks, Peter Davidson, Greg D'Souza, John Edmonds,

Pete Goodchild, Cary Granger, John Kendall, Len Outridge, Colin Ovenden, Brian Payne, Howard Phillips, Alan Reader, Andy Twiner, Adrian White, and Keith Wilkinson. David's *Quatermass* recollections and later quotes on his early record-buying habits come from his 2006 Nokia Recommenders "Sounds of My Universe" Web site interview. "Everyone finds empathy in a nutty family" is from David's 1976 *Playboy* interview with Cameron Crowe. The conclusion in the final paragraph that George Underwood, rather than David, was considered "the boy most likely to" comes from many Bromley kids who remember his presence on the stage rather than David's; as another contemporary, Roger Bevan, puts it, "It was George was the singer, who did a great Elvis impression. Everyone reckoned he was going to be big."

CHAPTER 2: "Numero Uno, Mate!"

Main sources include George Underwood, who was interviewed for a *Mojo* feature on the recording of "Liza Jane," Geoff MacCormack, Dorothy Bass, Les Conn, David Hadfield, and Dick Taylor. Quotes on David's job at Nevin D. Hirst from Mat Snow's 1995 interview for *Q*. David's recollections of hanging out with Marc Bolan are from Paul Du Noyer's *Mojo* interview in July of 2002. This interview, and Du Noyer's later thoughts and insightful comments, can be found at his Web site, www.pauldunoyer.com. The date of the King Bees' debut and other details come from John Bloom's *It's No Sin to Make a Profit* (W. H. Allen, 1970). Special thanks to Dorothy Bass, whose diary of those early days was hugely helpful in pinning down the King Bees' live dates and who has recorded a typical week in a Bromley teen's life as follows:

Monday: R & B at the Bromley Court Hotel or the Marquee; Tuesday: R & B at the 100 Club; Wednesday: R & B/jazz at the Court or folk at the Star & Garter (Bromley High Street); Thursday: R & B at the Marquee or trad at the Court; Friday: R & B at the Bell or the Court or folk at Catford Bridge (presumably a pub in Catford); Saturday: modern jazz at the Marquee.

CHAPTER 3: Thinking about Me

The Manish Boys section relies on recollections from band members Bob Solly, Paul Rodriguez, Woolf Byrne, Johnny Flux, and Mick Whitehead; special thanks to Bob and Woolf for the access to their diaries and cuttings. Lower Third interviewees were Denis Taylor and Graham Rivens. Special thanks to Kenny Bell, who invited me to a pinot grigio–fueled Denmark Street reunion that featured many key figures of that era, including Mike Berry, Terry King, and Simon White.

Terry King and John Singer provided invaluable insights into the background of Ralph Horton; other key interviewees were Shel Talmy, Wayne Bardell, Kenney Jones, Jeff Dexter, and Tony Hatch. Information on Marc Bolan's early career is from Mark Paytress's wonderful book *Bolan: The Rise and Fall of a 20th Century Superstar* (Omnibus, 2006).

CHAPTER 4: Laughing Gnome

Principal sources, in addition to those detailed for the previous chapter, are Ken Pitt, Hugh Mendl, Mike Vernon, Tony Hall, Derek "Dek" Fearnley, John "Hutch" Hutchinson, Alan Mair, Tom Parker, and Neil Slaven. Most dates quoted come from Ken Pitt's paperwork and Decca records. Special thanks to the Riot Squad, one of the most mysterious bands ever to play behind David; I was treated to an impromptu Squad reunion with Bob Flag, George Butcher, and Del Roll in an Essex pub, which gave me a wonderful insight into those carefree, zany days. Thanks to Paolo Hewitt, Jeff Dexter, and Graham Marsh for sharing their thoughts on mod, and Marcus Gray for sharing his insights into the Deram/Essex connection and also pointing out the Ian Brady and Myra Hindley references in "Please Mr. Gravedigger."

CHAPTER 5: I Wish Something Would Happen

Principal interviewees: Chris Welch, Ken Pitt, Hugh Mendl, Tony Visconti, Steve Chapman, Lindsay Kemp, Mick Farren, Gordon Rose, Michael Garrett, Jeff Dexter, Vernon Dewhurst, Ray Stevenson, John Hutchinson. The story of how David discovered Jacques Brel via Lesley Duncan comes from David's Nokia Recommenders "Sounds of My Universe" Web site interview (although David doesn't mention Lesley by name). David's "he got all sniffy" quote about Marc Bolan is from Paul Du Noyer's Bowie interview in *Mojo* in July of 2002; David's description of Terry's schizophrenic fit during the Cream show at the Bromel Club comes from his *NME* interview in March of 1993.

CHAPTER 6: Check Ignition

Main sources: Ray Stevenson, Keith Christmas, Alan Mair, Tony Visconti, Calvin Mark Lee, Simon Hayes, Mark Pritchett, Angie Bowie, Terry Cox, John Cambridge, Tim Renwick, Gron Kelly, Olav Wyper, David Bebbington, Jeff Griffin. The account of how the Philips album was recorded cross-references the memories of Cambridge, Renwick, Christmas, and Tony Visconti. The author's own interview with Gus Dudgeon has been greatly improved with a transcript of a longer, more detailed interview conducted by Fred Dellar in March of 1978.

Bowie fans will notice I don't mention Tony Visconti's anecdote about how Mick Ronson attended the final overdubs for the Philips album, principally because Visconti believed Cambridge had brought Mick to the session, and John is adamant that he did not.

CHAPTER 7: All the Madmen

Opening description is based mainly on interviews with Mark Pritchett, whose mother, Donna, was housekeeper at Haddon Hall. The description of Pitt's visit to the session for "The Prettiest Star" derives from my interview with David Bebbington, cross-referenced with Tony Visconti; Bebbington also attended the Arts Lab session at which David first mentioned his half brother, Terry. Early history of Mick Ronson is based on accounts by Keith Herd—who recorded the Rats' first sessions—Rats bassist Keith Cheesman, Rats drummer John Cambridge, and Ronno bassist Trevor Bolder. Other sources for the chapter include Jeff Griffin, Ray Stevenson, Laurence Myers, Olav Wyper, and Ken Scott, whose account is crucial because it confirms Visconti's suggestions that he and Ronson were solely responsible for major sections of *The Man Who Sold the World*. Lastly, Mick Farren's contention that David quoted Kahlil Gibran and Nietzsche on the basis of reading book jackets is confirmed by Dai Davies, who spent many late nights discussing philosophy with David the following year.

CHAPTER 8: Kooks

Main interviews for this chapter: Bob Grace, Bill Harry, Anya Wilson, Herbie Flowers, Henry Spinetti, Robin McBride, Ron Oberman, John Mendelssohn, Ken Scott, Trevor Bolder, Lee Childers, Tony Zanetta and Robin Mayhew. Much of the information on Tony Defries comes from David Thompson, who collaborated with Tony on an abandoned autobiography; his information was augmented by interviews with Laurence Myers—who is often written out of the story—and Olav Wyper. Tony Visconti's account of his dealings with Tony Defries comes from his book *Bowie, Bolan, and the Brooklyn Boy* (HarperCollins, 2007); Angie Bowie's description of Zowie's birth is based on her account in *Backstage Passes*. Details of how David's new deal left him with an obligation to Essex Music—ultimately settled with several *Scary Monsters* songs, including "Up the Hill Backwards"—were provided by Simon Platz. The story of David meeting Doug Yule and thinking he was Lou Reed was described in *Record Collector* magazine, September 2001. Robert Kensell, a Sombrero regular, gave a great account of the club. Special thanks to Mark Pritchett, who provided unique insights into Bowie's songwriting during the most crucial period of his career. Evidence that David initially intended to book Herbie Flowers and Tim Renwick for his "Kooks" BBC session came from Jeff Griffin, who has a booking sheet dated just one week earlier that names them in the band lineup, replaced by the future Spiders at the last moment.

CHAPTER 9: Over the Rainbow

Main sources for David and Defries's trip to RCA are Danny Fields, Iggy Pop, Lisa Robinson, and Tony Zanetta. Throughout this period, Tony Zanetta is an excellent objective source, and I'm grateful to him for subjecting himself to perhaps a dozen interviews. Zanetta and Henry Edwards's book *Stardust* (Michael Joseph, 1986) has been widely criticized—by Nicholas Pegg, among others—but while its coverage of the other eras is flaky, it gives a brilliant overview of the MainMan years. For the run-up to the "I'm gay and I always have been" *Melody Maker* interview, Dai Davies—perhaps David's closest and most objective confidant of the period—was an inexhaustible definitive source of insights. It was also Dai Davies, as one of those dealing closely with Ronson, who points out that his misgivings about the Spiders' makeover were more about muso credibility than homophobia in Hull (which of course did, and does, exist). The fact that "Somewhere Over the Rainbow" was also plagiarized for "The White Cliffs of Dover" was first pointed out by musicologists interviewed for a Radio 4 documentary in October of 2009 that was dedicated to the wartime anthem (incidentally, there are no bluebirds over Dover). Barry Bethel quote courtesy of Mike Berry. Other interviews: Lee Childers, Tom Parker, Kris Needs, Will Palin, Trevor Bolder, Ken Scott, Mark Pritchett, Robin Mayhew, Jeff Dexter, Dave Marsh, Herbie Flowers, Suzi Fussey, Matthew Fisher, Lindsay Kemp. Spider Special recipe is courtesy of Will Palin. Ian Hunter interview is courtesy of Kris Needs. David Bowie wrote about the Legendary Stardust Cowboy and Vince Taylor, one inspiration for Ziggy, in the edition of *Mojo* that he guest-edited in July of 2002; David's account of the creation of the Ziggy jumpsuits comes from *Moonage Daydream: The Life and Times of Ziggy Stardust* by Bowie and Mick Rock (Palazzo, 2005).

Chapter 10: Battle Cries and Champagne

The accounts of the Cleveland after-show episode, the writing of "The Jean Genie," and the problems recording "Panic in Detroit" come from Trevor Bolder. Main sources are as for the previous chapter, with the addition of Scott Richardson, James Williamson, John "Hutch" Hutchinson, and Ava Cherry. Descriptions of David's boat trip and attendance at the Bruce Springsteen show are described by Geoff MacCormack in his book *From Station to Station* (Genesis, 2007). Special thanks to Rodney Bingenheimer for putting me in touch with six of the Rodney's English Disco regulars, including Kathy Heller, Nancy McCrado, and Lori Madox. The effects of Scientology on the MainMan organization were described primarily by Trevor Bolder and Robin Mayhew. The Iggy quote "I just rolled my eyes" comes from Cliff Jones's interview with Iggy in 1996. (Iggy was much more polite about his ex-buddy during my interviews with him.) David's "highly symbolic" quote, illustrating just how early his marriage seemed doomed, comes from Mick Rock's *Moonage Daydream*. Ian Hunter's "holding up well" observations about Bowie and some other dates come from his excellent *Diary of a Rock and Roll Star*.

Additional research on this chapter, specifically the Mike Garson interview, is by onetime Mott the Hoople fan-club organizer Kris Needs.

Chapter 11: Star

Descriptions of the US routine are based on interviews with Bolder, Zanetta, Mayhew, Fussey, Davies, and Hutchinson, augmented with dates and references from Zanetta's *Stardust*, MacCormack's *From Station to Station*, and Mick Rock's *Moonage Daydream*. Details of the Spiders' attempts to sign with Columbia are based on Trevor Bolder's account; David's seduction of Lulu, with Angie Bowie in pursuit, was witnessed by John Hutchinson and recently confirmed by Lulu in her autobiography *I Don't Want to Fight* (Time Warner, 2003). Other sources include interviewees from the previous chapter, plus Ken Scott, Scott Richardson, Jayne County, Mark Pritchett, Hugh Attwooll, and Ava Cherry. Descriptions of the interior of Oakley Street come from its decorators, Mick Gillah, Chris Goodchild, and Aubrey Goodchild.

CHAPTER 12: The Changing Isn't Free

David's relationship with Mick Jagger was sketched out primarily by Ava Cherry, Scott Richardson, and the pair's agent, Maggie Abbott. *Diamond Dogs* description, and especially the genesis of "Rebel Rebel," comes from Alan Parker and Herbie Flowers. Special thanks to the ever-diplomatic Herbie for an objective view of a controversy that has fascinated musicians for years, including Nile Rodgers, who points out, "I could never believe it was David played that guitar." Other sources are as for the previous chapter, plus Wayne Bardell, Keith Christmas, and Carlos Alomar. The Apollo dates were supplied by the Frank Schiffman Apollo Theatre Collection—thanks to Christine S. Windheuser of the NMAH Archives Center. David went to at least two Apollo shows, one around September 18 with comic Franklyn Ajaye, the Spinners, and the Temptations. Richard Pryor and the Main Ingredient shared a bill on April 26 with Inner Voices, who were out on prison leave. The archives contain brief assessments of each performance: Richard Pryor, who had yet to achieve widespread fame on *Saturday Night Live,* is pronounced: "Dirty, dirty! But funny, funny! Absolute control of audience...Excellent!"

Descriptions of Norman Fisher come from Ava Cherry, Cherry Vanilla, and David's recollections on Nokia Recommenders. David's Nuremberg-influenced lighting scheme was recalled by Mark Pritchett. Other details of New York in 1974 come from *The Ossie Clark Diaries* (Bloomsbury, 1998). David's soul-record collection was detailed by Geoff MacCormack, Ava Cherry, and Harvey Kubernick.

CHAPTER 13: Make Me Break Down and Cry

Key sources include Ava Cherry, Tony Zanetta, Carlos Alomar, Tony Visconti, Iggy Pop, and May Pang. Details of Bowie's position as "employee" of MainMan come from his contract dated March 31, 1972. Terry O'Neill's account of David's meeting with Liz Taylor conflicts with Zanetta's version, which is that Liz Taylor first met David when she arrived at a rehearsal. Zanetta's version is in *Stardust,* page 276.

Description of the Hyatt Regency bust relies on MacCormack's account in *From Station to Station.* Reports of Iggy's reunion with David come from Ron

Asheton and others interviewed for the author's biography of Iggy, *Open Up and Bleed* (Sphere, 2008). Sources for the recording of "Fame" are Carlos Alomar (who mentions here, for the first time to my knowledge, how David played a key guitar riff on the song), Eddie Kramer, and May Pang. Carlos Alomar does not remember Lennon singing "Shame, Shame, Shame"; however, May Pang contends that "I was the only one not on drugs and that's what happened." Her version is supported by the fact that the song's descending melody, first heard at 3:01, is essentially identical to the chorus of "Shame, Shame, Shame." The simplest explanation is that David heard John singing the line but Carlos didn't. Thanks to Keith Badman, author of *The Beatles: After the Break-Up* (Omnibus, 1999), who pinned down Paul's arrival in New York as January 10 and places the "Fame" session as circa January 15 to January 20. Defries's share of Bowie's work up to 1982 was first uncovered by the Gillmans, who had access to Main-Man paperwork and put the relevant date as September 30, 1982. However, David's original contract, as mentioned above, dates from March 31, 1972.

CHAPTER 14: White Stains

Main sources: Ava Cherry, Maggie Abbott, Cherry Vanilla, Geoff MacCormack, Glenn Hughes, Earl Slick, Iggy Pop, James Williamson, Carlos Alomar, Ben Edmonds. For this chapter, I owe a huge debt to writer Rob Hughes, who shared all the interview transcripts for his excellent *Uncut* article on *The Man Who Fell to Earth*. This helped give me a vital sense of the wider context behind the movie; it was vital, too, for Roeg's and Litvinoff's accounts of what happened to Bowie's sound track for the movie. All the quotes from Candy Clark, Nicolas Roeg, and Si Litvinoff come from Rob's transcripts. Thanks also to Joel McIver, Glenn Hughes's biographer, for sharing information and putting me in touch with Glenn. Slash quote is from *Slash: The Autobiography* (Harper, 2008). Paul Buckmaster quotes come from his interview with David Buckley in the *Mojo* Bowie birthday special, January 2007.

Thanks to Gary Lachman for providing extensive background information on Bowie and the occult. The obvious influence of Trevor Ravenscroft's *The Spear of Destiny* and other texts and Bowie's avowed interest in gnosticism has inspired a huge amount of sometimes hilarious background reading. The Net is a good place to investigate these theories. One amusing fantasist, contacted by this author and quoted widely elsewhere, claimed to have intimate knowledge of Bowie's early involvement with characters like Stephen Ward and other members of the Profumo circle. Disappointingly, such conspiracy theorists omit any details that might shore up their batty fantasies. Some of Bowie's key works are in fact intimately connected with an alleged line of occult power running across London—mapped by Nazi theorists—which supposedly leads to Omphalos, the spiritual center of the British Empire, according to the London Psychogeographical Society. *Space Oddity* was recorded in Deptford Creek on this line of power—where Christopher Marlowe was allegedly sacrificed by dark forces involving the magician John Dee—and *Ziggy Stardust* was rehearsed nearby in Greenwich, which is Omphalos itself. The line of power also bisects Bromley Road. I hope an expert will investigate this subject more deeply.

More seriously, there is a brilliant analysis of the concepts invoked in *Station to Station* by the late Ian MacDonald, reprinted in *The People's Music* (Pimlico, 2003). Gary Lachman explores the 1960s history of the occult in *Turn Off Your Mind: The Mystic Sixties and the Dark Side of the Age of Aquarius* (Sidgwick and Jackson, 2002).

Information on David's involvement with Walli Elmlark comes from Cherry Vanilla, who goes on to say that after writing down the telephone number, David promised he'd produce Cherry's next album. "Bowie said, 'I'll be in New York in a week, I'll see you then.' I was floating around on cloud nine—Bowie's going to produce my record! The next week I'm at Norman Fisher's and Norman gave this party for Bowie...the top of the fireplace was all white with coke. I walked up to David and said, 'When are we going to talk about the record?' He said something to me in German, turned away, and I didn't see him again for years."

Deep Purple live dates come from http://www.deeppurpleliveindex.com/.

CHAPTER 15: Ghosts in the Echo Chambers

Main interviews: Andrew Kent, Iggy Pop, Carlos Alomar, Laurent Thibault, Pierre Calamel, Marc Zermati, Philippe Auliac, Roy Young, Tony Visconti, Angie Bowie, Kuelan Nguyen, Phil Palmer, Eduard Meyer. David's intention to record with Iggy at Musicland was first mentioned in Iggy's interview with *Punk* magazine in March of 1976. My thanks to Christophe Geudin, who interviewed Laurent Thibault for *Recording Musicien* magazine, exchanged ideas with me, and helped me make several breakthroughs in understanding *The Idiot*. Bowie's confused communications with Michael Rother were first revealed in Tobias Rüther's *Helden: David Bowie und Berlin* (Rogner und Bernhard, 2008). Brian Eno quotes are from Stephen Dalton's *Uncut* interview; more background on Eno comes from *On Some Faraway Beach: The Life and Times of Brian Eno*, by David Sheppard, and Eno's insightful interview with Ian MacDonald in *NME*, November 1977.

CHAPTER 16: Helden

Opening section is based on an interview with Tony Visconti; the description of a typical day in Berlin comes from Iggy Pop, augmented by the recollections of Edu Meyer, one of the recipients of Bowie and Iggy's surprise visits. Main interviews: Angie Bowie, Edu Meyer, Hunt Sales, Tony Sales, Esther Friedmann, Ricky Gardiner, Kris Needs, Carlos Alomar. David's quote on "a sense of yearning for a future that we all knew would never come to pass" is from *Uncut*.

Thanks to David Sheppard for sharing his thoughts on this period in Eno's artistic life; Eno's quotes are from Ian MacDonald's *NME* interview. The section covering Bowie's appearance on *Marc* derives from interviews with Keith Altham, Jeff Dexter, Chris Welch, and Cliff Wright. Information on Marc's fatal car crash comes from Mark Paytress's research.

CHAPTER 17: I Am Not a Freak

Main sources for David's later days in Berlin are Edu Meyer, Esther Friedmann, and Klaus Krüger. *Stage* and *Lodger* sources: Adrian Belew, Carlos Alomar, Simon House, and Tony Visconti, augmented by Sean Mayes's *Life on Tour with David Bowie: We Can Be Heroes*. "Just a Gigolo" background was aided by Michael Watts's feature for *Melody Maker* in February of 1978. The Lou Reed encounter is based primarily on Chuck Hammer's recollections. Other interviewees: Barry Andrews, Steve Strange. Primary *Elephant Man* interviews: Ken Ruta, Jeanette Landis. The description of David's reaction to John Lennon's murder comes primarily from May Pang.

CHAPTER 18: Snapshot of a Brain

Duncan Jones talked about his viewing sessions of *Star Wars* in the *New York Times*, June 3, 2009. David's bodyguard and stalker-avoiding routine were described by Kevin Armstrong and others. David's "I've gotten closer to her" quote about Peggy comes from his interview with Timothy White, *Musician*, May 1983. Figures for Mitchelson's divorce settlement for Angie come from *Ladies' Man: The Life and Trials of Marvin Mitchelson*, by John A. Jenkins (St. Martin's, 1992); Angie's comment that David "used his millions to poison Zowie against me" comes from the *Daily Mail*, which has featured Angie many times over the years; David's "As much insight into the human condition as a walnut" quote comes from the same source. Brian May's "It was hard because you had four very precocious boys" quote comes from Mark Blake's interview for the *Mojo* special edition of 2008. The *Baal* section derives from interviews with Louis Marks and Dominic Muldowney, plus John Willett's fascinating essay "Brecht for the Media," 1982.

Jeremy Thomas and Ryuichi Sakamoto quotes come from the short documentary film "The Making of *Merry Christmas, Mr. Lawrence*" on the special edition of *Merry Christmas, Mr. Lawrence*. Other interviews: Esther Friedmann, Carol Clerk, Tommy Shannon, Gary Lachman, Nile Rodgers, Gary Gersh, Hugh Stanley-Clarke.

CHAPTER 19: On the Other Side

Principal interviews: Tommy Shannon, Frank Simms, Earl Slick, Charles Shaar Murray, Hugh Padgham, Julien Temple, Kevin Armstrong, Matthew

Seligman, Clare Hirst, Thomas Dolby, Iggy Pop, Nancy Jeffries, Erdal Kizilcay, Edu Meyer, Tony Horkins. Bowiedownunder.com had a fascinating, useful account of the filming of the "Let's Dance" and "China Girl" videos. Thanks to David Buckley, who put me in touch with Hugh Padgham and whose Bowie biography *Strange Fascination* (Virgin, 1999) gives a superb account of the making of *Tonight*. For *Open Up and Bleed*, I believed the assurances of Iggy's management that David's tale of Iggy stamping on a fan's head was apocryphal; now, thanks to Ed Hunter and Noel Tepper, we know the fan was Lucille Reed of Poughkeepsie, who won a settlement from Iggy's lawyers. Most of the quotes from Pat Antoniou come from pieces in the *Sun* and the *Daily Mirror* throughout the spring of 1985, accessed via the British Library at Colindale. Records of David's plans to set up his own production stable with Bill Laswell came from paperwork in the possession of Les Conn.

CHAPTER 20: It's My Life—So Fuck Off

Principal interviews: Kevin Armstrong, Reeves Gabrels, Tony Sales, Hunt Sales, Eric Schermerhorn, Adrian Belew, Erdal Kizilcay, Emma Bannister, Nile Rodgers. Much of the information on David and Iman's first meeting comes from (where else?) *Hello!* magazine. The story of David's trip to Wales first appeared in the *South Wales Echo*, September 1992. David's quote "The truth is I was not convinced by the motivations of this event" comes from *Rock et Folk* magazine, December 1998. Interviews around the Mick Ronson tribute include Suzi Ronson, Trevor Bolder, and Ken Scott. Ronson's quote comes from an interview I did with him for *International Musician* magazine in February of 1989, in which it was obvious he was a little sniffy about Bowie—but had no complaints. In the same interview, Ronson and I discussed whether David's switch to a deeper, more baritone voice was influenced by his wanting to sound like Iggy. Ronson's conclusion was "Sound like Iggy? He wanted to be Iggy!" Hanif Kureishi tells his own story of *The Buddha of Suburbia* at hanifkureishi .com. His site also contains his 1999 story "Strangers When We Meet."

CHAPTER 21: The Heart's Filthy Lesson

This chapter would not have been possible without the inspiration, help, and persistence of Kris Needs, who did the bulk of the research on the *Outside* sessions and conducted the detailed, insightful interviews with Reeves Gabrels, Mike Garson, and Mark Plati. Other sources for this chapter: Kevin Armstrong, Erdal Kizilcay, Tony Visconti (augmented with material from *The Brooklyn Boy*), Carlos Alomar, Thomas Dolby, Mark Cooper, Glenn Max. The background on Bowie bonds is sourced primarily from court records and judgments in the *Pullman v. Prudential and Zysblat* case, decided in favor of the latter by Supreme Court judge Ira Gammerman in judgment 600772/01, July 2003. Duncan Jones's career was summarized in, among others, the *New York Times*, June 2009.

Over the period in question, David's Web chats at www.davidbowie.com provide consistent, often hilarious insights into his family life and music. Bowie's account of the making of *Heathen* comes from his excellent interview for *Livewire*, June 16, 2002.

Epilogue: The Houdini Mechanism

The title of this chapter, and much of the reasoning, derives from Julien Temple's conversations with David early in 1985. Bowie fans will also recognize a resonance with his intriguing performance as Nikola Tesla in Christopher Nolan's *The Prestige*—a movie whose title and plot revolve around the notion of making a magnificent exit. Fan quotes are posted on the YouTube video of the Fashion Rocks show of September 8, 2005. The "pregnant pause" theory was advanced by, among others, Nicholas Pegg in the *Mojo* special of 2007; the announcement of Bowie's appearance at High Line and its cancellation both appeared on www.davidbowie.com. David confided his estrangement from Iggy to Robert Phoenix on gettingit.com, October 1999. Details of Defries's disastrous investment in the Cayman Islands was reported on Wikileaks, March 3, 2008. Information on Defries's planned autobiography *Gods and Gangsters* comes from his press release of 2008. Duncan Jones's quote about his relationship with his father comes from the *Daily Telegraph*, July 14, 2009. Ian McCulloch quote is from *Mojo*, issue 100.

Other interviews: Julien Temple, Mike Garson, Ian Gittins, George Underwood, Momus, Charles Francis, Nicolas Godin.

General Sources

UK chart positions are sourced throughout from *The Q Encyclopedia of Rock Stars;* US positions from *Billboard.* I also used the index of UK chart runs at polyhex.com.

My invaluable source for the various brands of cigarettes favored by Bowie over the years was Jarvis Cocker's interview with David for *The Big Issue,* December 1997. BowieNet.com, bowiewonderworld.com, 5years.com, bowiegoldenyears.com, teenagewildlife.com, and www.illustrated-db-discography.nl were also invaluable throughout.

Background Reading

All written sources used in the book are cited within the notes. The following books made for invaluable Bowie background reading and reference.

Alias David Bowie, Peter and Leni Gillman (Hodder and Stoughton, 1986)
Backstage Passes: Life on the Wild Side with David Bowie, Angie Bowie with Patrick Carr (Orion, 1993)

Bowie, Jerry Hopkins (Macmillan, 1985)

Bowie: The Pitt Report, Ken Pitt (Omnibus, 1985)

The Complete David Bowie, Nicholas Pegg (Reynolds and Hearn, 2000)

The Dark Stuff: Selected Writings on Rock Music 1972–1993, Nick Kent (Penguin, 1994)

David Bowie: A Chronology, Kevin Cann (Vermilion, 1983)

David Bowie: Moonage Daydream, David Thompson (Plexus, 1989)

Diary of a Rock and Roll Star, Ian Hunter (IMP, 1996)

Free Spirit, Angie Bowie (Mushroom, 1981)

Johnny Thunders: In Cold Blood, Nina Antonia (Jungle, 1997)

The Life and Death of Andy Warhol, Victor Bockris (Bantam, 1989)

Life on Tour with David Bowie: We Can Be Heroes, Sean Mayes (IMP, 1999)

Lou Reed: The Biography, Victor Bockris (Hutchinson, 1994)

Low, Hugo Wilcken (Continuum, 2005)

Mick Ronson: The Spider with the Platinum Hair, Weird and Gilly (IMP, 2003)

New York Rocker, Gary Valentine (Sidgwick and Jackson, 2002)

On Some Faraway Beach: The Life and Times of Brian Eno, David Sheppard (Orion, 2008)

The Q Encyclopedia of Rock Stars (Dorling Kindersley, 1996)

Rebel Heart, Bebe Buell (St. Martin's, 2001)

Strange Fascination: David Bowie—the Definitive Story, David Buckley (Virgin, 1999)

Wonderland Avenue: Tales of Glamour and Excess, Danny Sugerman (William Morrow, 1989)

All magazines and periodicals quoted within the text are detailed in the notes. The principal magazines used for background reading include *Billboard, Circus, Creem, Disc, East Village Other, Denim Delinquent, End Times, Entertainment World, Evo, Fifth Estate, Fusion, Gay Power, Goldmine, GQ, Guitar, Guitarist, International Musician, Jazz & Pop, Melody Maker, Mojo, Motorbooty, Motor City Rock and Roll News, NME, Pavilion, Phonograph Record, Q, Record Mirror, Record World, Rock Scene, Rolling Stone, Sounds, Stereo Review, Strange Things, Trouser Press, Variety, Village Voice, Wire, Zig Zag.*

Copies of the *Times,* the *Sunday Times,* the *Sun,* and the *Daily Mirror* were all accessed courtesy of the British Library reading rooms. Thanks to Q, Mojo, Johnny Black, Fred Dellar, and Richard Morton Jack for use of their archives.

Acknowledgments

As ever, my deepest thanks go to Julian Alexander, an oasis of calm and good sense in a changing world, as well as a rigorous commentator in the earliest days of this project. Thanks also to my US agent, Sarah Lazin, for her acumen and encouragement.

I also count myself very lucky to work with Antonia Hodgson and John Parsley, of Little, Brown UK and US, respectively. Both of them shared complementary, multiple, sustained insights, without which this would not have been the same book. They were also good company, and I look forward to another Bowie tour into the nether regions of Soho (and his personal life) soon.

Others deserving of thanks are probably too many to mention, but a brief list would include Martin Aston, Louis Barfe, Mark Blake, Tony Beasty, Kenny Bell, Johnny Black, Romain Blondel, Billy Bragg, Anne Bourgeois-Vignon, Dave Burrluck, Chris Charlesworth, Fred Dellar, Peter Doggett, Roger Dopson, Richard England, Miles Evans, Eve Fegyveres, Carl Ferris, Marcus Fuhrmann, Ken Garner, Debra Geddes, Pat Gilbert, Marcus Gray, Paul Guimaraes, Sue Harris, Paulo Hewitt, Martin Hopewell, Laurie Hornsby, Dorothy Howes, Jim Irvin, Leonora Jackaman, Graham Johnson, Kieron Jones, Ashley Kahn, Terry King, Spencer Leigh, Colin MacKenzie, Graham Marsh, Ian Muir, John Myer, Kris Needs, Mark Paytress, Christopher Porter, John Reed, Carlton Sandercock, Josh Saunders, Mat Snow, Bob Solly, Michael Stimson, Dave Thompson, Geoff Travis, Gerald Wallis, Dorian Wathen, Cliff Watkins, David Wells, Marc Zermati.

Thanks also to all the staff at *Mojo* magazine, especially Mark Blake, Jenny Bulley, Danny Eccleston, Phil Alexander, Ian Harrison, and Andrew Male. Not to forget Chris Ingham—*Mojo*'s "Doctor Rock"—for sharing thoughts on Bowie's songwriting, and Dave Brolan for photoresearch.

People who offered help with the Iggy book, which proved pivotal in this book, include Christophe Geudin, who helped me locate Laurent Thibault, and Tony Zanetta, whose patience seemed inexhaustible. Thanks, once more, to my schoolmate Nick Hunter, the only fifteen-year-old kid I knew who had a copy of Bowie's Santa Monica bootleg, from which we worked out our own (dreadful) version of "Waiting for the Man." David Buckley was a confidant on my Iggy book who should have been a rival on this book but was as helpful and generous with his insights as ever. Kat Johnson, both on this book and *Open Up and Bleed*, did a heroic job of helping with transcription. Most profoundly, my everlasting thanks and appreciation to Lucy and Curtis; as mentioned at the Trafalgar Tavern, in the last ditch I will always think of you.

Thanks to all my interviewees for sharing their time and insights. They are: Maggie Abbott, Carlos Alomar, Keith Altham, Keith Andrew, Barry Andrews, Bernie Andrews, Annie Apple, Kevin Armstrong, Ron Asheton, Hugh Attwooll, Philippe Auliac, Jim Avery, Emma Bannister, Wayne Bardell, John Barrance, Mike Bassett, Max Batten, David Bebbington, Kenny Bell, Adrian Belew, Mike Berry, Rodney Bingenheimer, Roger Bolden, Trevor Bolder, Angie Bowie, Stephen Braine, Chris Britton, Nick Brooks, Bebe Buell, Rodney Burbeck, George Butcher, Woolf Byrne, Pierre Calamel, John Cale, John Cambridge, Steve Chapman, Keith Cheesman, Ava Cherry, Lee Childers, Keith Christmas, Carol Clerk, Richard Comben, Les Conn, Mark Cooper, Jayne County, Terry Cox, Sydney Curtis, Peter Davidson, Dai Davies, Vernon Dewhurst, Jeff Dexter, Wolfgang Diebeling, Thomas Dolby, Bryan Drew, Greg D'Souza, Gus Dudgeon, Ben Edmonds, John Edmonds, John Edward (Johnny Flux), Robin Eggar, Mick Farren, Derek "Dek" Fearnley, Danny Fields, Matthew Fisher, Bob Flag, Herbie Flowers, Kim Fowley, Charles Francis, Esther Friedmann, Reeves Gabrels, Michael Garrett, Mike Garson, Gary Gersh, Mick Gillah, Dana Gillespie, Ian Gittins, Max Glenn, Nicolas Godin, Suzanne Goldschmitt, Aubrey and Chris Goodchild, Bob Grace, Cary Granger, Shaun Greenfield, Barbara Gray, Jeff Griffin, Tony Hall, David Hadfield, Bill Harry, Tony Hatch, Simon Hayes, Kathy Heller, Keith Herd, Susan Hill, Clare Hirst, Gill Hymas, Chuck Hammer, Tony Horkins, Simon House, Glenn Hughes, John "Hutch" Hutchinson, Norman Ingram, Nancy Jeffries, Kenney Jones, Graham Kelly, Lindsay Kemp, John Kendall, Robert Kensell, Andrew Kent, Terry King, Erdal Kizilcay, Eddie Kramer, Klaus Krüger, Harvey Kubernick, Gary Lachman, Jeanette Landis, Sue Larner, Calvin Mark Lee, Suzanne Liritis, Dorothy Bass Macedo, Lori Madox, Alan Mair, Louis Marks, Dave Marsh, Linda McCartney, Nancy McCrado, Geoff MacCormack, Robin McBride, Robin Mayhew, John Mendelssohn, Hugh Mendl, Eduard Meyer, Momus, Dominic Muldowney, Charles Shaar Murray, Laurence Myers, Kuelan Nguyen, Kris Needs, Ron Oberman, Len Outridge, Colin Ovenden, Hugh Padgham, Will Palin, Phil Palmer, May Pang, Alan Parker, Tom Parker, Brian Payne, Les Payne, Howard Phillips, Ken Pitt, Mark Plati, Simon Platz, Iggy Pop, Jan Powling, Peter Prickett, Mark Pritchett, Alan Reader, Tim Renwick, Scott Richardson, Graham Rivens, Lisa Robinson, Nile Rodgers, Paul Rodriguez, Derek "Del" Roll, Suzi Ronson, Gordon Rose, Ken Ruta, Hunt Sales, Tony Sales, Carlton Sandercock, Eric Schermerhorn, Ken Scott, Matthew Seligman, Tommy Shannon, Harry Shapiro, Frank Simms, John Singer, Neil Slaven, Earl Slick, Bob Solly, Henry Spinetti, Linda Stagg, Hugh Stanley-Clarke, Ray Stevenson, David Stopps, Steve Strange, Shel Talmy, Denis Taylor, Dick Taylor, Julien Temple, Laurent Thibault, Dave Thompson, Andy Twiner, Diana Udall, George Underwood,

Mike Vernon, Tony Visconti, Chris Welch, David West, Adrian White, Simon White, Mick Whitehead, Keith Wilkinson, James Williamson, Val Wilmer, Anya Wilson, Jonathan Wingate, Cliff Wright, Olav Wyper, Roy Young, Tony Zanetta, Marc Zermati.

Sadly, since I started work on this book and its predecessor, *Open Up and Bleed*, the following interviewees have passed away: Ron Asheton, Les Conn, Hugh Attwooll, Carol Clerk, and Derek "Dek" Fearnley. All of them were enthralling raconteurs; I will miss speaking to them again, as I will Ian MacDonald, always one of the most thought-provoking writers on *Mojo*, and Mick Ronson, who was unfailingly tolerant with me as a starstruck novice writer.

Index

Note: The abbreviation DB refers to David Bowie

About the Author

Paul Trynka was formerly the editor of *Mojo* magazine (1996–2003). He has also been the editorial director of *Q* magazine, launch editor of *The Guitar Magazine*, and editor in chief of New Projects at Emap. He is the author of *Iggy Pop* (Broadway 2007), *Portrait of the Blues*, and *Denim*, a history of the fabric. He lives in London. www.trynka.net